ROTHMANS RUGBY LEAGUE YEARBOOK 1995-96

Raymond Fletcher and David Howes

ROTHMANS

HEADLINE

D0272957

© Rothmans Publications Ltd 1995

First published in 1995
by HEADLINE BOOK PUBLISHING

10 9 8 7 6 5 4 3 2 1

COVER PHOTOGRAPHS

Front Cover: (Left) Former New Zealand Rugby Union All Black Va'aiga Tuigamala, who crowned his first full season in Rugby League by making 39 1994-95 appearances for Wigan, finishing third top tryscorer with 25 touchdowns. (Right) A rare painting of action from the 1903 Rugby League Challenge Cup final at Leeds. Halifax, in blue, defeated Salford 7-0 in front of a crowd of 32,507. Acknowledgement is paid to Andrew Hardcastle for the loan of the print.

Back Cover: Great Britain full back Jonathan Davies scoring the only try in the Lions' 8-4 victory over Australia in the first John Smith's Test at Wembley in October 1994. The shot was one of a portfolio of three which earned Gerald Webster, of the *Rugby Leaguer*, the title of John Smith's International Photographer of the Year 1994.

ACKNOWLEDGMENTS

The compilers would like to acknowledge the assistance of the Rugby League Record Keepers' Club, club secretaries and individuals in providing material as a further source of reference for accuracy.

PHOTOGRAPHERS

Modern day domestic photographs in this *Rothmans Rugby League Yearbook* are mainly from the files of the *Rugby Leaguer*. The compilers acknowledge the co-operation of Chief Photographer Gerald Webster and his staff.
The colour photograph on the front cover, plus a significant number of black-and-white contributions, are by freelance photographer Andrew Varley.

British Library Cataloguing in Publication Data
Rothmans Rugby League Yearbook – 1995-96
1. Rugby football – Great Britain –
Periodicals
793.33.3.0941 GV945.9.G7

ISBN 0 7472 7817 2

Photoset by Dalmax Origination, London

Reproduced, printed and bound in Great Britain by
The Bath Press, Avon

HEADLINE BOOK PUBLISHING
A division of Hodder Headline PLC
338 Euston Road
London NW1 3BH

Rothmans Rugby League Yearbook 1995-96

CONTENTS

1. Editorial Preface   5

2. Coaches Select XIII   6

3. Super League   9

4. Memories   15
1994-95 Headlines   16
June 1994 to May 1995   20

5. Clubs   31
Honours, records, coaching registers, Great Britain registers, 1994-95 signings registers, players' summaries and match analyses

6. Records   149
Leading scorers 1994-95   150
Outstanding scoring feats 1994-95   150
Record-breaking feats 1994-95   151
Milestones 1994-95   158
Leading scorers 1895-1994   164
All-time records   171
All-time record scoring and appearance charts   176

7. Cups   183
Challenge Cup   184
Regal Trophy   207
Premiership Trophies   223
Charity Shield   241
World Club Challenge   243

8. League   245
1994-95 Championship   246
Divisional review   249
Divisional records   252
Championship play-off finals   255

9. Tables   257
Final league tables
1895-96 to 1994-95   257

10. Coaches   305
Index of coaches 1974-95   306
Dossier of coaches 1994-95   310

11. World Cup   315
Squads, teams, results, scorers and final tables 1954-92   316

12. 1994 Kangaroos   337
Tour review   338
Tour data   340
Match by match   343

13. Down Under   361
1994 Sydney Grand Final   361
British players in Grand Finals   363
1994 State of Origin series   364
France tour of Papua New Guinea, Australia and Fiji 1994   368
New Zealand tour of Papua New Guinea 1994   370

14. Great Britain 373
    1994-95 Test review 374
    Test results and records 375
    Teams 1977-94 381
    Register 391
    Tour summaries 401
    Tour squads 403
    World Cup data 410
    All-time scoring charts 414

15. England and Wales 417
    1994-95 review 418
    European Championship 424
    1975 World Championship 425
    England results and records 426
    Wales results and records 428
    England teams 429
    England register 432
    Wales teams 434
    Wales register 438
    England and Wales results
    synopsis 440

16. Under-21s 441
    1994-95 review 442
    Under-21 results 443
    Under-21 register 444
    Under-21 records 446
    Under-24 results 446
    Under-24 register 446

17. Transfers 447
    Review 1994-95 448
    Overseas register 1994-95 449
    Record transfers 451

18. Awards 453
    Man of Steel 1995 454
    Teams of the Month 1994-95 458
    Entertainer of the Month
    1994-95 458

19. Referees 459
    Honours 1994-95 459
    Senior Referees 1995-96 459

20. Alliance 461
    Final tables and cup results
    1994-95 461

21. Pot Pourri 463
    Diary of landmarks 1895-1995 463
    Disciplinary review 1994-95 465
    Sponsorship review 1994-95 468
    Queen's honours 468

22. Attendances 469
    Club review 469
    Competition review 471
    20,000-plus crowds
    since 1985 471
    Analysis 1994-95 473

23. Fixtures 475
    Stones Bitter Championship
    1995-96 476
    First Division 1995-96 477
    Second Division 1995-96 478
    Principal dates 1995-96 480

SUPER LEAGUE . . . HOW THE EVENTS UNFOLDED

4 April

League Chief Executive Maurice Lindsay makes an urgent, unreported trip to London for talks with BSkyB TV after Murdoch's News Ltd make first confirmed approach about a European Super League.

Wigan's World Club Challenge match against Canberra cancelled as a direct result of the revolutionary changes in Australia. The match was due to be played in June.

5 April

The RL Council has a scheduled meeting at Headingley, Leeds. Summer rugby is to be debated but Super League is not on the agenda. During the meeting Lindsay takes telephone calls and tells the Council of News Ltd's approach.

Talks are arranged between the Board of Directors and News Ltd with the outcome to be put to a special meeting of club chairmen three days later.

There is no official statement from the League but news begins to filter through that the European Super League is on its way. First reports are of Murdoch putting up £50m for a Super League to be played during summer.

6 April

Reports from Australia that Murdoch's number two, Ken Cowley, has said a Super League deal has already been struck with the British League.

7 April

A meeting of First Division club chairmen, plus one from the Second Division, Hull Kingston Rovers, meet with Lindsay and League Chairman Rodney Walker at Huddersfield. The Super League details are outlined for the first time.

8 April

The revolutionary decision is made at Central Park, Wigan . . . a Super League of 14 clubs will start in the summer of 1996. The five-year deal is reported to be worth £77m, but the shock proposal that 15 clubs should be involved in mergers starts a major controversy.

Two new clubs from France would be included in the Super League, while a Welsh side based in Cardiff is planned for the new First Division.

The Super League clubs will each receive over the five years a total of £5m with the First Division clubs each getting a one-off payment of £100,000.

The Super League is to be as follows:

Existing clubs: Bradford Northern, Halifax, Leeds, St. Helens, Wigan.

News clubs, including proposed mergers: Calder (Castleford, Featherstone Rovers, Wakefield Trinity), Cheshire (Warrington, Widnes), Cumbria (Barrow, Carlisle, Whitehaven, Workington Town), Humberside (Hull, Hull Kingston Rovers), Manchester (Oldham, Salford), South Yorkshire (Doncaster, Sheffield Eagles), London, Paris, Toulouse.

The First Division will be:

Batley, Bramley, Dewsbury, Highfield, Huddersfield, Hunslet, Keighley Cougars, Leigh, Rochdale Hornets, Ryedale-York, Swinton, Welsh XIII.

The top four Super League clubs will take part in a World Club Championship with leading Australian and New Zealand clubs.

There will be no promotion or relegation for the first two seasons.

An interim competition will be played during the 1995-96 winter with a Premier Division of Super League clubs and a new First Division. Clubs will play each other only once.

The whole package was voted in unanimously by the 32 senior clubs. Non-league members Blackpool Gladiators and Nottingham City also voted in favour with Chorley abstaining.

Despite the unanimous decision there were misgivings immediately the meeting was over with Keighley already considering legal action at being left out of the Super League despite looking certain to be promoted as Division Two champions.

9 April

There is an air of unreality at the Sunday afternoon matches as the shock of mergers sinks in. The first protests take place at grounds where supporters fear the end of their club.

Leeds chief executive Alf Davies accuses the League of "holding a gun to the heads of clubs" to force through the changes. He claims chairmen were told "vote in favour or you are out".

10 April

Australian Rugby League Chairman Ken Arthurson says he feels betrayed by Lindsay and claims it will be the end of British Lions and Kangaroos tours.

An all-party Parliamentary Rugby League group of MPs and peers call for a meeting with the League after expressing alarm at prospect of the game being sold "lock, stock and barrel to a private media interest".

10 April

The Rugby League Players' Association secretary Nick Grimoldby seeks meeting with Lindsay to discuss how players' contracts will be affected by the Super League. There is also concern over many players becoming redundant as mergers reduce the number of clubs.

11 April

Leeds announce they will now give full support to summer rugby after failing to win their battle to keep to winter.

Keighley's hopes of a Super League place are raised after Lindsay says the League will reconsider their case if they can raise £1.5m to improve their ground.

12 April

Halifax board make surprise decision to seek merger with Bradford Northern. There is also talk of Ryedale-York moving to Gateshead.

Salford and Oldham fail to agree on a merger to form new Manchester club.

Australian League chief Ken Arthurson writes an open letter to British supporters accusing "Murdoch empire of attempting to destroy a great English tradition".

The British Amateur Rugby League Association say they will continue to play in winter.

13 April

Keighley intend to sue the League after a meeting of Super League club chairmen reject their claim to join the elite.

South Pacific countries indicate they will support the official Australian Rugby League and reject Murdoch's money.

14 April

Widnes and Warrington merger called off as each club is allocated a Super League place after France decide to enter only one club.

More demonstrations at the traditional Good Friday derby matches which will be the last if mergers go ahead.

18 April

Centenary World Cup is saved following a weekend trip to Australia by Lindsay. The League Chief Executive met top Australian officials to discuss international affairs but was unable to guarantee the future of the Ashes Test series or official tours.

20 April

National Conference League club Chorley to sue the League for compensation after being excluded from the Super League format.

Lord Rees to chair specially appointed four-man committee which will adjudicate on mergers of clubs.

Labour Party moves to refer Super League

to the Office of Fair Trading and the Monopolies and Merger Commission.

21 April
Great Britain to make a shortened tour of Australia and New Zealand in October 1996. But the Australian Rugby League says it will be unofficial and the Ashes will not be at stake.

Halifax chairman Tony Gartland resigns following strong criticism and fans' hostile reaction to his proposed plan to merge with Bradford Northern.

23 April
Top British players are targeted by the Kerry Packer-backed Australian Rugby League as they step up the battle against Murdoch's Super League. Ellery Hanley, the Leeds captain and Great Britain coach, is believed to have already agreed a deal.

The British League's response is to declare that they will use Murdoch money to pay top players "loyalty bonuses" to keep them in this country.

Castleford pull out of proposed merger with Featherstone and Wakefield as they aim for Super League status on their own.

24 April
Keighley hold meeting in Leeds to announce the serving of a writ on the League for being omitted from the Super League. They seek damages after claiming their omission has cost them £300,000 in lost sponsorship.

25 April
Wigan Test winger Martin Offiah rejects £1m Packer offer to play in the Australian League and pledges his allegiance to Britain after accepting a massive "loyalty bonus" deal.

The League issued a "loyalty" list of players who would be staying in Britain. They include Nigel Wright, Andrew Farrell and Martin Dermott (Wigan), Bobby Goulding, Alan Hunte, Sonny Nickle, Chris Joynt, Steve Prescott (St. Helens).

But others who are destined for Australia include Gary Connolly, Jason Robinson, Martin Hall (Wigan) plus Jonathan Davies (Warrington) and John Devereux (Widnes).

Featherstone members vote against a merger with Wakefield.

There are growing threats from top clubs that they will go it alone if present Second Division clubs continue to block the Super League plans. Eight clubs are seeking legal advice over "an unconstitutional lack of consultation".

26 April
More players sign British "loyalty" contracts. They include Wigan contingent Va'aiga Tuigamala, Henry Paul, Scott Quinnell, Mick Cassidy, Terry O'Connor, Simon Haughton and Craig Murdock, plus Scott Gibbs (St. Helens).

Super League debate in the House of Commons lasts 90 minutes. Sports Minister Iain Sproat appeals to a Commons committee to launch an investigation into Murdoch's plans.

27 April
Board of Directors call a special general meeting in four days' time, increasing speculation that more clubs will be included in the Super League.

28 April
Leeds stand off Garry Schofield and Wigan captain Shaun Edwards join forces in attacking the way the League has handed out "loyalty bonuses". The Cup final rivals made their surprise attack during the traditional Wembley walkabout the day before the big game. Both felt bitter at not receiving "loyalty bonuses" despite their long Great Britain service.

29 April
Schofield continues his "loyalty" attack in the Wembley dressing room immediately after the final, being prepared to lead a players' revolt.

30 April

All change – the Super League plans are restructured after a near six-hour meeting of clubs at the Hilton Hotel, near Huddersfield. The surprise decisions resulted in a return to three divisions and a withdrawal of merger proposals.

Widnes were the only club to vote against the proposals, while Keighley were absent as they consulted their lawyers.

The clubs were allocated places on the basis of where they finished in the 1994-95 season, except for London, Paris and National Conference club Chorley.

The 12-club Super League will be:
Bradford Northern, Castleford, Halifax, Leeds, London B., Oldham, Paris, St. Helens, Sheffield, Warrington, Wigan, Workington T.

First Division (11): Batley, Dewsbury, Featherstone R., Huddersfield, Hull, Keighley C., Rochdale H., Salford, Wakefield T., Whitehaven, Widnes.

Second Division (10): Barrow, Bramley, Carlisle, Chorley, Highfield, Hull K.R., Hunslet, Leigh, Ryedale-York, Swinton.

National Conference club Chorley were a surprise entry in the Second Division, but there was no place for Doncaster, who were in the hands of a receiver. And the idea of a Welsh club has been dropped at least for the time being.

Promotion and relegation is likely to be on a one up/one down basis. The new season will kick off on 28 March 1996 after an interim season based on the new format.

Murdoch raised his cash injection from £77m to £87m to be shared as follows: Super League clubs each to receive £900,000 per season for five years; First Division clubs to get between £200,000 and £700,000 on a merit scale each term with £150,000 per season for Second Division clubs.

It was also revealed that soccer giants Newcastle United had inquired about entering a club.

1 May

Keighley say they are continuing their legal action against the League and will seek £500,000 compensation for being left out of the Super League.

2 May

Widnes start legal proceedings against the League after losing their Super League place when it was reduced to 12 clubs.

The League hit back at Schofield's claim that Leeds players had not been offered "loyalty" bonuses. They said Ellery Hanley, Craig Innes and Alan Tait had been offered money after an application from Leeds for financial assistance. Leeds had not put Schofield's name forward and therefore he was not on the League's "loyalty" list.

17 May

Tom Smith resigns as a Widnes director because of a conflict of interest in the Super League dispute with his role as a member of the League's Board of Directors.

26 May

Widnes lose legal battle against the League and face costs of about £50,000. A High Court judge in Manchester, Mr. Justice Jonathan Parker, said there was no serious issue to be tried and accepted that the 30 April vote of 32-1 in favour of the Super League proposals represented the overwhelming wish of the game.

Two-year drug ban for Bloem

MEMORIES

Britain's hopes burnt to Ashes

Wales slog it out to be champions

League go for Super set-up

Reilly attracted away on eve of Australia series

MEMORIES

1994-95 HEADLINES

Behind the scoring feats and records of the 1994-95 season were a number of stories which made the headlines (also see the chapter SUPER LEAGUE):

HANLEY REPLACES REILLY

Great Britain's preparations for the John Smith's Test series against Australia were thrown into disarray when Malcolm Reilly resigned as coach only a month before the Kangaroos arrived.

Amid growing rumours, Reilly confirmed on 22 August that he would be joining Australian club Newcastle Knights as coach in the November.

It was hotly debated whether Reilly would remain as Britain's coach for the Tests, but he ended the speculation by resigning on 26 August. A little later he stepped down as Halifax's coach to be succeeded by Steve Simms on 12 September.

The speculation now centred on who would succeed Reilly as Britain's coach with Keighley Cougars' Phil Larder emerging as favourite. But with his expected appointment imminent, Reilly's former assistant withdrew from contention because he objected to an overseas advisor — New Zealander Graham Lowe — being given a major role in Britain's preparations. Ironically, Lowe's ill health prevented him playing any part.

Ellery Hanley was appointed Britain's coach on 29 August, initially for one year starting with the Test series against Australia.

Although Hanley (33) had been Leeds' coach for three years he remained second in command to team manager Doug Laughton and the Britain job was his first in which he would be in full control.

Hanley named Sheffield Eagles team manager Gary Hetherington as his assistant on 2 September. The pair would also be in charge of England for the John Smith's European Championship with Hetherington taking over as coach for Great Britain Under-21s.

Hetherington's appointment was over-shadowed by the confusion over Steve Watson's re-appointment as Britain's manager. The Hull director accepted, resigned and then agreed to remain as manager — all on the same day.

At the end of May 1995, Hanley agreed a two-year £650,000 deal with the Australian Rugby League, thus quitting his coaching roles with England, for the Halifax Centenary World Cup, and Leeds.

FRAMING THE FUTURE

Several months before the Rupert Murdoch-backed Super League produced the biggest revolution in the game's 100-year history, an official *Framing The Future* report also provoked heated debate and controversy.

Produced on 30 August, it called for a soccer-style Premier League and the merger of some clubs.

The hard-hitting report by sports marketing firm GSM was commissioned by the Rugby Football League and followed a 12-month survey.

Gary Hulme of GSM said that although Rugby League was an excellent product there were too many clubs in too small an area for the game to be marketed properly. The report said many clubs were in serious financial trouble with only four in Division One making a profit.

After studying the report, the League's Board of Directors put forward several revolutionary proposals for the clubs to consider. They included a 15-club Premier League with stringent minimum facilities standards, two lower divisions of eight and the eventual abolition of the levy paid by Division One clubs.

Amid growing threats of a breakaway by Division One clubs if the proposals were not carried out, the momentous meeting took place at League headquarters on 5 October.

The 35 clubs, including three now in the National Conference League, voted for a 16-club Premier League but decided against splitting the Second Division into two.

Many other suggestions in the *Framing The Future* were also accepted with the prospect of voting powers being changed to three votes for Premier clubs, two for Second Division clubs and one each for the Conference clubs.

The 3-2-1 voting change was made following another major meeting of clubs on 15 February when it was also decided to introduce a salary cap and a transfer ban to and from Australia, while reducing the overseas quota from three to two players per club.

The salary cap, based on a percentage of income, meant that from 1995-96 no club would be allowed to spend more than 50 per cent of its income on players' salaries. That would be reduced to 45 per cent the second year and then 40 per cent.

DRUG SHOCKS

There was a series of drugs-related stories that hit the headlines with the banning of Jamie Bloem and David Stephenson the most serious.

● Bloem, Doncaster's South African full back, became the first British-based player to test positive for taking a performance-enhancing drug and was banned for two years on 29 November.

Bloem (23) was given a random test after Doncaster's home league match against St. Helens on 8 November and found to have the anabolic steroid Nandrolone in his system and evidence of testosterone.

Bloem's appeal against the two-year ban, the maximum permitted for a first offence, was rejected.

A former Western Province Rugby Union player, Bloem switched to Rugby League with Capetown Coasters before coming to England in 1992.

He had brief spells with Castleford and Oldham before joining Doncaster in September 1993.

Bloem later claimed in a *Mail on Sunday* article that drug-taking was rife in Rugby League and was backed up by Doncaster forward Sonny Whakarau. But both withdrew their claims and apologised.

Bloem's allegations brought a disrepute charge and he was reprimanded. But his ban was extended six months by the Yorkshire Amateur League because he played for Doncaster-based Woodlands 'A' against Garforth in a Division Seven match on 21 January.

● Stephenson (22), Oldham's promising hooker, was banned for two years on 31 May after testing positive for steroids. His test after the Silk Cut Challenge Cup semi-final against Wigan on 25 March showed traces of Nandrolone.

● Barrie Ledger (32), the Swinton and former Great Britain winger, was also suspended after testing positive for the use of cannabis following a match at Ryedale-York on 6 November.

Ledger's ban was announced on the same day that Bloem was suspended but details were delayed until after a second sample was tested. He was then banned for six months.

● Bradford Northern full back Dave Watson (28) and winger David Myers (23) were both fined £2,000 and suspended for four months by the League after failing to supply urine samples for drug testing following the 42-24 home league defeat of Hull on 19 February. The bans began from the day of the match.

Watson had also been drugs tested a week earlier after the Silk Cut Challenge Cup tie at Leeds when the sampling officers said there had been some irregularity.

When Watson failed to attend a Bradford board meeting to discuss the whole situation he was transfer listed at £150,000.

In addition to his fine and suspension, Watson was warned that he faced a life ban if he breached the drugs control regulations again.

Three years earlier, while with Halifax, the New Zealander had been banned for three months after testing positive for cannabis. He signed for Bradford soon after.

17

Myers claimed his failure to give a sample was due to a misunderstanding. He thought the time for the test, 1700 hours, meant 7.00pm and had turned up 10 minutes before then.

Nearly three weeks earlier, the winger had been banned until the end of the season for deliberately bumping into referee John Connolly during a Cup tie at Leeds, as detailed later in this section.

The League took no action against Bradford coach Peter Fox for allegedly obstructing drugs officials after the Leeds and Hull matches. They said that the League's Board of Directors had "been faced with incomplete and confusing evidence".

● Dennis Smith of Whitehaven was suspended for three months on 15 February after the forward tested positive for the stimulant Ephedrine following the match at Dewsbury on 15 January. He said it was to cure a cold.

● Dean Pay of Australia hit the headlines on 11 November when it was revealed he had tested positive for taking pseudo-ephedrine after the first John Smith's Test against Great Britain at Wembley on 22 October when he played as a substitute forward.

The substance was contained in the medicine Sudafed, which Pay said he was taking to cure a cold and the Australian Rugby League took no action because it is not banned in their country.

They also took no action against scrum half Ricky Stuart who, it was learned much later, had tested positive for the same substance after the second Test on 5 November.

The Australians' lack of action did not please League officials who pointed out that they had fined Great Britain full back Graham Steadman £1,000 after he was found to have taken a banned substance in a cough medicine before a Test match in New Zealand in 1992.

● The League confirmed their determination to prevent drug-taking becoming a major problem and said they would increase and improve their testing procedure.

They decided to test players at training during and out of season in addition to continuing to test two players from each side from one game each weekend.

MYERS CLASHES WITH REFEREE

David Myers of Bradford Northern was banned for the rest of the season and fined £250 after being found guilty of deliberately colliding with referee John Connolly during the Silk Cut Challenge Cup tie at Leeds on 12 February.

The winger had been referred to the League's Disciplinary Committee by referee executive Greg McCallum, who had spotted the incident while studying a video of the match which included three flare-ups.

McCallum also reported Myers for deliberately kicking at a group of players, but he did not suffer a separate penalty for that offence.

Myers had twice been sent to the sin bin during the match, first for holding down a player after a tackle and then for his part in a brief melee. The ban ended on 30 May.

GRATION QUITS

Harry Gration (44) resigned as the League's public affairs executive on 9 February — after only a year in the job. The former BBC television and radio personality said he wished to return to broadcasting.

Gration was succeeded by the *Sun*'s Rugby League correspondent Paul Harrison (52), who was given the new title of media manager when he began on 3 April.

McCALLUM RULES

Top Australian referee Greg McCallum was appointed the League's Referees' Coaching Director, starting his two-year contract in October.

Fred Lindop became the first Controller of Referees in November 1988 but he was laid off during League financial cutbacks four years later.

McCallum made an early impact as he

insisted on a speeding up of the play-the-ball with referees told to penalise players for holding down opponents after a tackle. This led to many players being sent to the sin bin for the offence in the early weeks of the clampdown.

McCallum also introduced "on-field reporting". This enabled a referee who was uncertain about possible foul play to report the player involved to the League, who would then study a video of the incident and decide whether to refer the player to the disciplinary committee.

The system — which had been used in Australia for several seasons — was introduced on 1 March, initially for Division One matches only.

Oldham's Wilson Marsh was the first player to be referred to the League, by referee Stuart Cummings following an incident in a Division One home match against Wakefield Trinity on 5 March. It was decided Marsh had no case to answer.

There were three more similar cases before Gary Mercer (Leeds), Paul Broadbent (Sheffield Eagles) and Gordon Lynch (Doncaster) became the first reported players to be referred to the Disciplinary Committee following incidents in matches on 19 March.

All three were found guilty. Mercer and Broadbent, who were reported for spear tackles in the same match by Russell Smith, were each suspended for one match. Lynch was fined £50 for tripping a Featherstone Rovers player and being reported by Alan Bates.

In-goal judges were also introduced by McCallum with the first in place for the Division Two match between Huddersfield and Bramley on 26 March.

DONCASTER FOLD

Doncaster appeared to have lost their fight to continue as a troubled season ended with the club's financial problems ruling them out of the game's immediate restructuring under the new Super League format.

Ironically, it came at the end of Doncaster's first season in Division One. And after struggling financially since being founded in 1951 they were going at a time when other clubs were sharing the millions media tycoon Rupert Murdoch was pouring into the game.

On 15 December, Doncaster were reported to have debts of £1.4m when former coach Tony Fisher, who had been sacked a week earlier after a clash with chairman John Desmond, sought a winding-up order to recover money he claimed he was owed.

The club received a three-month stay of execution at the Doncaster County Court when they were placed under an administrator in the hope that a rescue package could be put together.

But the result was an announcement by the administrator on 7 March that the club was to merge with Sheffield Eagles. It brought an angry reaction from Doncaster fans, who claimed it was a takeover.

Doncaster's hopes of surviving on their own were raised dramatically 10 days later by a surprise decision by the League that a number of Doncaster players could become free agents.

Sheffield's merger offer, which ensured Doncaster completed their fixtures for the season, was dependent on none of those players becoming free agents. They, therefore, withdrew from the deal.

The League then said they would take over the cost of running the club until the end of the season.

Meanwhile, Fisher had been active with a consortium that was planning to rescue the club with a £250,000 package and a move from Tattersfield to the Stainforth greyhound stadium.

Although the administrators put Doncaster into liquidation on 23 March the battle to save the club continued although Fisher joined Dewsbury as coach and the consortium decided not to continue with their bid.

Property firm Kingstock Holdings then emerged as the new owners and Doncaster completed their fixtures, finishing at the bottom. But their demise appeared to be accepted when they were not included in the new Super League structure although efforts were still being made to revive the club during the close season.

WORLD SEVENS

The Coca-Cola World Sevens in Australia caused another controversy over the non-availability of players for club and country at a crucial part of the season.

It reached a peak when Wigan winger Martin Offiah was withdrawn from Great Britain's sevens squad because of injury but played for his club and scored a hat-trick against Castleford.

The League explained Offiah could play for Wigan because he had been declared unfit by Britain's doctor, Ansar Zaman. But the row continued as Dr. Zaman was also Wigan's club doctor.

The Sevens on the weekend of 4 February also weakened England's team for their John Smith's European Championship match against Wales. Denis Betts, Lee Jackson and Chris Joynt, plus Offiah, who would all have been automatic England choices, were allowed to play in the Sevens.

Bradford Northern utility back Neil Summers replaced Offiah and the 10-man squad was:

John Bentley (Halifax), Steve Prescott (St. Helens), Francis Cummins (Leeds), Tony Smith (Castleford), Steve Blakeley (Salford), Paul Sterling (Hull), Denis Betts (Wigan, Capt), Lee Jackson (Sheffield E.), Chris Joynt (St. Helens), Neil Summers (Bradford N.). Sheffield's Gary Hetherington was team manager.

Britain's elimination from the event after only two matches brought a protest from League Chief Executive Maurice Lindsay, who said it was ridiculous that they should be involved in only 28 minutes play after travelling 12,000 miles.

Britain beat Penrith 28-16 but lost 30-10 to St. George and were eliminated because they did not finish in the top two of their group.

Manly beat Fiji 36-12 in the final at Sydney. The first day's games were played in Brisbane and the three-day event attracted a total of 75,000 spectators.

JUNE

Garry Schofield awarded the OBE . . . Wigan crowned World Club Champions with a 20-14 victory over Brisbane Broncos in Brisbane .... Castleford's record tryscorer St. John Ellis signs for Australian club South Queensland Crushers .... Leeds recruit Esene Faimalo from Widnes .... Want-away Paul Moriarty priced at £190,000 by Widnes .... Centenary World Cup draw seeds England and Australia for the final, Wales receiving a tough grouping with France and Western Samoa .... Australia agree to add St. Helens to their John Smith's Tour itinerary .... Castleford prop Dean Sampson suspended for four matches after trial by video for Stones Bitter Premiership foul on Wigan's Kelvin Skerrett .... The League decide to appoint a development officer in Ireland .... Wakefield Trinity offer loose forward Richard Slater at £80,000 .... Wigan's Frano Botica agrees to join Auckland Warriors after the 1994-95 British season .... Oldham agree to sell their 110-year-old Watersheddings ground for £1.25m to pay off debts and move to a new stadium .... Salford sign Australian full back Scott Mahon from Parramatta on a winter contract .... Graeme West confirmed as coach of Wigan on a two-year contract .... Halifax forward Gary Lord moves to Oldham .... Huddersfield appoint George Fairbairn as coach .... Wakefield Trinity sign New Zealand Test half back Aaron Whittaker .... Roger Millward appointed coach of Ryedale-York .... Bramley decide to stay at McLaren Field for another season .... Widnes consider proposal from the local council for the sale of Naughton Park and development of a new stadium .... Leigh skipper John Pendlebury joins Wigan's coaching staff .... Wigan Test forward Denis Betts signs a five-year contract with Auckland Warriors to start after the 1994-95 season .... Wales coach Clive Griffiths takes on his role as assistant coach of Warrington in a full-time capacity .... Castleford scrum half Mike Ford joins new Australian club South Queensland Crushers .... Leeds sign St. Helens packman George Mann .... Hunslet to play most 1994-95 fixtures away from Elland Road, at Bramley's McLaren Field, before moving to a new home in South Leeds .... Dewsbury list New Zealander Glen Bell at £25,000 and Marquis Charles at £20,000 .... Hunslet skipper Paul Harkin joins Wakefield Trinity's coaching staff .... Bradford Northern fail in a bid to sign Australian Test forward Paul Sironen .... Warrington put six players on offer headed by prop Gary Tees at £35,000, centre Tony Thorniley at £30,000 and former Test winger Mark Forster at £20,000 .... Widnes anger at new League advisory panel pricing Paul Moriarty at £50,000, plus a further £15,000 after 20 games, and Esene Faimalo at £80,000 .... Salford prop Terry O'Connor moves to Wigan .... Keighley Cougars recruit scrum half Chris Robinson from Halifax .... US cable company Prime Television pay £1.3m for the rights to the Centenary World Cup .... Wakefield Trinity recruit New Zealand tourist Robert Piva .... League agree to allow London Broncos to play up to 10 overseas imports .... Bramley director Ronnie Teeman elected as League President for season 1994-95 .... Northampton Knights one of four new clubs admitted to the National Conference League .... Workington Town Chairman Kevan Gorge and Tom Smith, of Widnes, elected to the League's Board of Directors, taking the places of Stephen Ball and Chris Caisley ....

JULY

Widnes winger David Myers moves to Bradford Northern, who take Frenchman Serge Laugier on an extended trial .... A further major operation ends Kevin Ward's hopes of playing for St. Helens again .... Ryedale-York sign Doncaster utility player Andy Gascoigne .... Oldham recruit Widnes forward Paul Davidson and Rochdale Hornets stand off Steve Gartland .... Huddersfield sign Salford centre Greg Austin .... Ellery Hanley sues prop Andy Dannatt three years after suffering a broken jaw .... Widnes scrum half Bobby Goulding joins St. Helens .... Wigan recruit utility back Henry Paul from Auckland Warriors, waiving a transfer fee for Test prop Andy Platt .... Castleford centre Grant Anderson moves to Halifax .... Proposed Government legislation on tobacco advertising threatens future sponsorship of Rugby League by Silk Cut and Regal .... Former St. Helens prop Stuart Evans launches a campaign to be able to return to Rugby Union .... Castleford sign centre Richard Goddard from Wakefield Trinity and scrum half Gareth Stephens from Leeds .... Vince Fawcett moves from Leeds to Workington Town .... Bradford Northern recruit New Zealander Robbie Paul, brother of Wigan's Henry .... Hull list full back Richard Gay at £97,500 .... Sheffield Eagles sign South Sydney full back Darrell Trindall on a winter contact .... St. Helens winger Les Quirk transferred to Whitehaven .... International Board Tribunal orders Auckland Warriors to pay £23,000 to St. Helens for Tea Ropati and £7,500 each to Oldham and Warrington for Se'e Solomona and Duane Mann respectively .... League Tribunal prices Esene Faimalo's move from Widnes to Leeds at £80,000 .... Featherstone Rovers sign Sheffield Eagles scrum half Mark Aston .... Junior Kiwi Tevita Vaikona joins Hull .... Widnes in double swoop for Warrington centre Tony Thorniley and Rochdale Hornets winger Jason Green .... Hull recruit New Zealander Shane Endacott .... Leeds offer centre Simon Irving at £65,000 .... Rochdale Hornet's Cavill Heugh moves to London Broncos in exchange for fellow prop Chris Whiteley and cash .... Widnes sign Barrow's Australian utility man Anthony

Singleton .... League Tribunal price Bobby Goulding's move from Widnes to St. Helens at £135,000 plus £25,000 on fourth appearance for Britain and/or England during his three-year contract .... Paul Moriarty's transfer from Widnes to Halifax given a Tribunal rating of £50,000, plus £15,000 after 20 games and £15,000 after 40 games .... Richard Gay makes his peace at Hull .... Leigh grant Jason Donohue a free transfer .... International Board scrap policy of neutral referees .... Widnes sign Andy Collier from Leigh .... Castleford forward Andy Fisher joins Dewsbury .... Keighley Cougars sign Dewsbury packman Darren Fleary .... Oldham recruit Joe Faimalo, brother of Esene .... Leigh put in the hands of an administrator .... The League appoint top Australian referee Greg McCallum as Referees' Coaching Director .... Batley sign Hull centre Paul Harrison .... League Tribunal orders Halifax to pay £85,000 for Castleford centre Grant Anderson, plus £15,000 after four international appearances .... Also Castleford to fork out £75,000 to Wakefield Trinity for Richard Goddard, plus £25,000 after four international caps .... Plus Widnes to receive £17,000 from Oldham for Paul Davidson .... Australians allocated a 14th John Smith's Tour fixture, against Cumbria at Workington .... Huddersfield hand over £16,000 for Bradford Northern winger Brimah Kebbie .... League Chief Executive Maurice Lindsay lashes clubs for abusing the Transfer Tribunal by asking and offering unrealistic fees .... League Tribunal orders Keighley Cougars to pay £15,000 to Halifax for Chris Robinson, plus £5,000 after 30 first team games .... London Broncos decide to stay at Barnet Copthall for another season .... Bradford Northern capture Jason Donohue on a free transfer from Leigh .... Leeds ask £15,000 for veteran prop Mike O'Neill ....

AUGUST

Salford sign Warrington's Mike Gregory for £35,000 .... New Zealander Darrall Shelford moves from Bradford Northern to Huddersfield on a free transfer .... Wigan's Ian Gildart joins Wakefield Trinity .... Bramley offer winger Vince Nickle at £20,000 and hooker Gary Barnett at £5,000 .... Hunslet recruit winger Scott Limb from Featherstone Rovers .... Ryedale-York's Paul White, David Close and Steve Pryce move to Hunslet with Andy Precious and Richard Francis in exchange .... League Tribunal order Wigan to pay Oldham £40,000 for prop Barrie McDermott, plus three instalments of £30,000 after 30 games, 60 games and an international debut .... Mark Aston's move from Sheffield Eagles to Featherstone Rovers given a League Tribunal rating of £100,000 .... Hull sign New Zealander Maea David from the Canterbury club .... League Tribunal price Gary Lord's transfer from Halifax to Oldham at £35,000 .... Halifax sign Hull K.R. skipper and scrum half Wayne Parker .... Widnes recruit Leigh's Tongan prop Lee Hansen .... Warrington winger Neil Kenyon joins Keighley Cougars .... Hull K.R. winger Bright Sodje moves to Sheffield Eagles in exchange for David Plange .... Ryedale-York transfer utility back Iain Wigglesworth to Bramley .... Hull K.R. and Workington Town stage an exhibition match in Scotland's Galashiels .... Wakefield Trinity clinch capture of New Zealand stand off David Bailey .... Whitehaven offer full back David Lightfoot at £10,000 .... Huddersfield's Australian duo Brad Davis and Jason Laurence join Ryedale-York .... Paul Hutchinson valued at £30,000 by Ryedale-York .... Prop John Glancy returns to Sheffield Eagles after a six-year break .... Oldham sign New Zealand stand off Wilson Marsh .... Wigan and Salford agree a fee for Terry O'Connor of £75,000, plus £10,000 for an international debut .... The League announce a £500,000 international kit deal with Puma .... Rochdale Hornets scrum half Ian Bates moves to Dewsbury for £9,000 .... Doncaster recruit South African trio Pierre Grobellaar, John Assor and Pierre Assor .... Salford list John Gilfillan (£15,000), Tex

Evans (£25,000), Paul O'Neill (£7,000), Andy Fairclough (£5,000) and Austin Donegan (£5,000) .... Huddersfield sign Australian centre Dean Hanger from Leigh .... Hull's Gareth Cochrane moves to Keighley Cougars .... Bradford Northern offer Paul Grayshon at £25,000 .... Keighley Cougars complete a deal with Wigan for South African full back Andre Stoop .... Hull sign winger Leroy McKenzie from Moseley RU .... Salford seal short-term contract with New Zealand Test winger Jason Williams from Canterbury-Bankstown .... New Zealander Jason Temu joins Oldham .... Veteran prop forward Mike O'Neill leaves Leeds to rejoin Widnes .... Great Britain and Halifax coach Malcolm Reilly accepts a two-year contract with Australian club Newcastle Knights .... Hunslet pay £3,000 to Keighley Cougars for Carlton Farrell .... Hull recruit Ryedale-York prop forward Steve Craven .... Halifax decide to retain the services of Malcolm Reilly until a successor is appointed .... Wigan sign Carcassonne second row forward Cael Tirac .... Widnes agree to pay £15,000 to Rochdale Hornets for winger Jason Green and £10,000 to Warrington for Paul Myler .... Malcolm Reilly resigns as Great Britain coach .... Prop forward Wayne Jackson signs for Doncaster in £40,000 move from Hull K.R. .... Leeds loose forward and assistant coach Ellery Hanley is appointed coach of Great Britain for the John Smith's Test series with Australia .... Bramley offer prop forward Andy Marson at £15,000 .... Hull K.R. sign utility back Gary Atkins from Ryedale-York .... Keighley Cougars recruit Austalian forward Grant Doorey, formerly with Easts and Manly .... The League presents a crisis document entitled *Framing the Future* which promotes a Premier League and the possible merging of clubs .... Clubs give the League the go-ahead to formulate plans for a Premier Division .... Ryedale-York sign veteran Keith Mumby from Bradford Northern .... Huddersfield celebrate the opening of their new Alfred McAlpine

Stadium with victory over Barrow.

SEPTEMBER

Barrow sign centre Steve Ashcroft from Chorley .... Uncapped trio Martin Pearson, Harvey Howard and Mick Cassidy named in Great Britain's 25-man training squad .... Denis Ramsdale resigns as coach of Barrow .... Salford offer hooker Mark Lee at £60,000 and threequarter Jason Critchley at £125,000 .... Sheffield Eagles' goal-kicking full back Darrell Trindall returns home to Australia after only one match because of domestic problems .... Halifax list full back Steve Lay at £40,000 and forward Lee Harland at £45,000 .... Keighley Cougars complete the signing of centre Simon Irving from Leeds .... Widnes recruit Junior Kiwi Willie Crowley .... Steve Simms leaves Leigh to take over as coach of Halifax .... Dewsbury mark the opening of their new Crown Flatt ground in Owl Lane with a 76-8 hammering of Barrow .... Leigh appoint Denis Ramsdale as coach, having formerly served as assistant coach .... Former Halifax and Keighley Cougars coach Peter Roe given the role at Barrow .... The League's Board of Directors propose a Premier League of 16 .... The League orders a new clampdown on high tackles .... Doncaster sign centre Terry Manning from Featherstone Rovers .... Four British-based New Zealanders selected for an October tour of Papua New Guinea — Kevin Iro (Leeds), Brendon Tuuta (Featherstone Rovers), Aaron Whittaker (Wakefield Trinity) and Tawera Nikau (Castleford) .... All four clubs raise objections with the New Zealand Rugby League .... Broken arm rules New Zealander Willie Crowley out of Widnes contract .... The League launch Little League, a junior mini-rugby programme, with the support of Puma and the Government's Sportsmatch .... Featherstone Rovers move quickly to sign New Zealand tourist Mark Nixon to replace Great Britain squad member Martin Pearson, ruled out for the season with a knee injury ....

Carlisle's Welsh international hooker Barry Williams listed at £18,000 after missing training .... Mike Peers quits as coach of Highfield .... Hunslet sign Castleford hooker Chris Watson for £8,000 .... Rochdale Hornets sign prop forward Paul Grayshon from Bradford Northern .... Prop forward Cliff Eccles moves from Rochdale Hornets to Salford .... Huddersfield ask £50,000 for Fijian forward Joe Naidole .... Hull move to sign French Test forward Ezzedine Attia .... Hull's Andy Dearlove and Paddy Khan move to Hull K.R. in exchange for hooker Lee Richardson .... Centre Mal Meninga named as skipper of the Australian tourists for a record second time on his record fourth Kangaroo tour .... London Broncos sign teenager Sid Domic from parent club Brisbane Broncos .... Mal Meninga turns down a contract with London Broncos . . . Kevin Iro ruled out of New Zealand's Papua tour with a hamstring injury .... Great Britain add Wigan's Barrie McDermott and Sheffield Eagles' Daryl Powell to the training squad .... Doncaster sign prop forward Chris Whiteley from London Broncos.

OCTOBER
Workington Town sign French scrum half Vincent Banet .... Featherstone Rovers ordered to pay £12,000 to Carcassonne for second row man Daniel Divet .... Three-match ban rules Sonny Nickle out of the first John Smith's Test at Wembley .... The new Alfred McAlpine Stadium at Huddersfield chosen to stage the 1994-95 Regal Trophy final in January .... Australia cite Wigan prop forward Barrie McDermott for use of the elbow on tourist Paul Sironen in the club match at Central Park .... Barrie McDermott suspended for two matches and fined £1,000, but cleared to play in the first John Smith's Test at Wembley .... Wigan stand off Nigel Wright returns on loan to Wakefield Trinity for the rest of the season .... Bradford Northern offer winger Daio Powell at £60,000 .... Centre Phil

Eden returns to Wakefield Trinity after a loan spell at Halifax and immediately signs for Castleford in exchange for winger David Nelson .... Warrington give trials to Junior Kiwi hooker Tukere Barlow .... Featherstone Rovers release Australian coach Steve Martin .... Workington Town sign half back Gus O'Donnell on loan from St. Helens .... Former St. Helens assistant coach Frank Barrow appointed to the Tonga coaching staff for the Centenary World Cup .... David Ward leaves Batley to take the coaching reins at Featherstone Rovers .... Scrum half Andy Gregory appointed to the coaching staff at Salford .... Rugby League's oldest professional player, Jeff Grayshon, appointed caretaker player-coach of Batley .... Hull sign forward Gary Rose from Leeds .... Great Britain pull off shock 8-4 victory over Australia in the first John Smith's Test at Wembley despite having skipper Shaun Edwards sent off .... Huddersfield and Whitehaven each fined £1,250 for brawling .... Leigh loan teenage forwards Simon Baldwin to Halifax and Scott Martin to Sheffield Eagles .... Widnes further discuss the sale of Naughton Park to the local council for development of a 12,000-seater municipal stadium .... London Broncos sign Kangaroo tourists Michael Hancock and Kevin Walters on short-term contracts .... Shaun Edwards banned for three matches for Wembley dismissal.

NOVEMBER
Great Britain call up Graham Steadman and Bobby Goulding in place of injured Jonathan Davies and suspended Shaun Edwards .... Workington Town take Warrington duo Kevin Ellis and Rowland Phillips, plus Carlisle hooker Barry Williams, on loan for the rest of the season .... Australia win the second John Smith's Test 38-8 at Old Trafford .... Swinton and Dewsbury fined £1,500 each, with £500 suspended, for brawling, six players — three from each side — receiving suspensions .... Hunslet list seven players headed by Jason

Wright, Ian Rose and David Croft at £8,000 each .... Doncaster sign hooker Colin Maskill from Leeds in £10,000 deal .... Halifax pull off double signing of young Leigh forwards Simon Baldwin and Paul Rowley .... St. Helens threequarters Alan Hunte and Scott Gibbs sign summer contracts with Manly .... Swinton sign ex-professional half back Brett Clark from amateurs Mayfield .... Former French RU President Jacques Fouroux proposes a new French Rugby League set-up and a new international competition involving France, England, Wales and Australia .... Jeff Grayshon confirmed as coach of Batley .... Denis Ramsdale resigns as coach of Leigh .... Featherstone Rovers' New Zealand Test centre Iva Ropati returns home after serving only eight months of a two-year contract .... Australia retain the Ashes with a 23-4 victory at Elland Road .... Warren Wilson joins Featherstone Rovers from Halifax .... Leeds refuse to release French scrum half Patrick Entat to play for a President's XIII against the touring Australians .... New Australian club North Queensland Cowboys announce the capture of Warrington's Jonathan Davies on a two-year £185,000 contract .... Bradford Northern sign Wakefield Trinity's centre Gary Christie in exchange for threequarters Daio Powell and Steve McGowan .... Doncaster's South African full back Jamie Bloem banned for two years for taking steroids.

DECEMBER
Sheffield Eagles hooker Lee Jackson named as the first-ever John Smith's International Player of the Year .... Warrington offer prop forward Phil Sumner at £125,000 .... Former Test full back Paul Charlton succeeds Hugh Waddell as coach of Carlisle .... Jonathan Davies agrees a new two-year deal with Warrington, featuring a summer spell Down Under .... Leigh appoint ex-Wigan prop forward Ian Lucas as their 19th coach in 20 years .... Clubs give the League the go-ahead to introduce a salary cap .... Australian Test duo Michael Hancock and

Kevin Walters pull out of London Broncos contracts because of injury .... Doncaster sack Tony Fisher as coach and promote assistant Ian Brooke to the role .... Tony Gordon axed as coach of Hull, assistant coach Phil Windley and prop forward Russ Walker taking over as joint caretaker coaches .... Hull K.R. winger Julian Barkworth moves to Hull in exchange for Welsh winger Marcus Bernard .... Featherstone Rovers announce the capture of Batley scrum half Glen Tomlinson for season 1995-96 .... Workington Town sign centre Kevin Pape from Carlisle .... Keighley Cougars recruit Morley RU winger Simon Wray, brother of Castleford's Jon .... The Rugby Football Union ban varsity RU centre Adrian Spencer for 12 months after learning that he played a handful of matches as an amateur with London Crusaders .... Carlisle sign Barrow scrum half Mike Kavanagh .... Batley sign Salford centre John Gilfillan for £7,500 .... Batley skipper Jimmy Irvine joins Huddersfield .... Doncaster, facing debts of £1.4m, go into administration .... Rochdale Hornets pay Castleford £5,000 for prop forward Keith England after an extended loan period .... The League launches "Project 2000" in a bid to increase the skill levels of young players .... New Director of Referees, Australian Greg McCallum, launches a clean-up at the play-the-ball .... Rocky Turner quits Doncaster at 25 for business reasons .... Widnes confirm offer of £35,000 for Batley scrum half Glen Tomlinson despite his alleged signing for Featherstone Rovers .... St. Helens sign centre Andy Northey from Waterloo RU .... Huddersfield loan out French utility back Laurent Lucchese to Sheffield Eagles, and forward Joe Naidole to Featherstone Rovers .... St. Helens forced to abandon plans to sign Tongan centre Peaufai Leuila after losing an appeal to the Department of Employment for a work permit .... Castleford coach John Joyner agrees a new two-year contract .... Salford sign controversial Australian full back Scott Wilson from Canterbury Bankstown .... Want away prop forward Mark Sheals priced at £50,000 by Wakefield Trinity .... Widnes sign Australian centre Sean Alvarez, of Spanish parentage.

JANUARY
Great Britain and Wales star Jonathan Davies of Warrington awarded the MBE .... Swinton winger Barrie Ledger banned by the League for six months for smoking cannabis .... The League recognises the formation of the Welsh Rugby League to steer a development programme .... Hull and Halifax announce plans for ground redevelopment .... Great Britain assistant coach Gary Hetherington put in charge of their World Sevens squad .... Leigh sign Warrington scrum half Steve Griffiths on loan .... St. Helens re-sign veteran New Zealander Mark Elia .... David Hobbs steps down as coach of Wakefield Trinity .... Bradford Northern sign back row forward Paul Round from Halifax .... Barrow part company with skipper Bob Eccles and hooker Chris Honey .... Swinton recruit Oldham's David Chrimes on loan .... The League discipline Wigan referee Ian Ollerton and two touch judges after television video evidence proves that a try was wrongly awarded .... Wales extend qualification to include players of Welsh grandparentage .... Wigan's Barrie-Jon Mather signs a summer contract for new Australian club Western Reds .... Ryedale-York dismiss coach Roger Millward .... Wakefield MP David Hinchliffe calls for Rugby Union to be barred from National Lottery grant aid while exercising discrimination against Rugby League .... Wigan's Denis Betts chosen as captain of the British sevens squad .... Jamie Bloem fails in appeal to have drug sentence reduced .... Leeds packman Richie Eyres opts to play for Wales, having already played for England, after the League rule that Welsh grandparentage qualifiers can have the choice .... Wales also select newly qualified Anglos Paul Atcheson, Martin Hall, Kelvin Skerrett and Neil Cowie for the John

Smith's European Championship tie with England .... Wigan offer Barrie-Jon Mather at £150,000 .... St. Helens forward Ian Connor returns to Swinton on loan .... Swinton sign Leigh full back David Tanner .... League chiefs Rodney Walker and Maurice Lindsay meet Rugby Union International Board officials Vernon Pugh and Keith Rowlands for informal talks in London .... Beverley amateur club beat professionals Highfield in the third round of the Silk Cut Challenge Cup .... Leigh appoint Willie Johnston as assistant coach .... Allan Bateman signs a summer contract with Australian club Cronulla .... Oldham's Charlie McAlister moves to Rochdale Hornets.

FEBRUARY
Wales beat England 18-16 at Cardiff in the John Smith's European Championship .... Ryedale-York take Hull duo Terry Smirk and Ian Stevens on loan .... The League and their Australian counterparts call for a two-year ban on international transfers .... Great Britain knocked out of the World Sevens at the first hurdle, with protests lodged when they do not even qualify for the consolation plate competition .... Warrington offer Chris Rudd and Rob Myler at £80,000 each .... Castleford win appeal to the League that Dean Sampson's absence from the England international with Wales should count towards his four-match suspension .... Doncaster's Jamie Bloem reprimanded for newspaper allegations following his two-year ban for drug offences and banned further six months for playing in an amateur match ... Second Division centre Nick Pinkney, of Keighley Cougars, called up for an England debut versus France .... Harry Gration quits as Rugby League Public Affairs Executive after less than a year in the post .... A Wigan-St. Helens Silk Cut Challenge Cup replay forces the withdrawal of nine players from the England squad to meet France at Gateshead .... Reshaped England beat France 19-16 in the John Smith's European

Championship .... The League to step up drug testing procedure after Whitehaven's Denis Smith suspended for three months for taking a banned substance contained in a cold cure .... Rugby League Council adopt a new system of three votes for the First Division clubs, two for the Second Division and one for the National Conference League members .... Salary cap introduced by the Council starting with 50 per cent of income being allocated for spending on players, being reduced to 40 per cent within two years .... The Council also agree two-year ban on long term Anglo-Aussie transfers, plus reduction of overseas quota players per club from three to two .... Bradford Northern duo Dave Watson and David Myers refuse to provide a urine sample for Sports Council drugs testers .... Castleford prop Martin Ketteridge joins Halifax in exchange for Lee Harland .... Featherstone Rovers' Brendon Tuuta interviewed by police after allegedly striking a young girl spectator at Workington .... Sheffield Eagles announce signing of Workington Town's Australian prop Kyle White for season 1995-96 .... St. Helens forward Chris Joynt joins Australian club Newcastle Knights on a summer contract .... Rugby League Chief Executive Maurice Lindsay appointed chairman of the Major Sports Committee of the CCPR .... Welsh international Adrian Hadley asks for a move at Widnes .... Bradford Northern list Dave Watson at £150,000 after failing to attend a board meeting and training session .... Bradford Northern's David Myers suspended for the rest of the season after being found guilty of deliberately running into referee John Connolly.

MARCH

Halifax Building Society announces sponsorship of the Centenary World Cup .... Ground safety and stadium redevelopment crisis forces Halifax to consider ground sharing with Huddersfield or Bradford Northern .... Leigh secure their future at Hilton Park with a ground-sharing deal with non-League soccer club Horwich RMI .... Leigh strip the players of their club blazers after post-match "celebrations" following a 94-4 Silk Cut Challenge Cup defeat at Workington .... Leigh also put on offer stand off John Gunning and forward Mark Meadows .... Oldham sign Wigan centre Mike Neal on loan following his temporary service with Doncaster .... Swinton edge out Leigh to sign St. Helens prop forward Ian Connor .... Sheffield Eagles withdraw Doncaster merger offer following a "breach of confidentiality" .... St. Helens half back Gus O'Donnell joins Keighley Cougars on loan .... Late drop goal gives France a 17-16 victory over Great Britain in the John Smith's Under-21 international at Albi ... Wales beat France 22-10 at Carcassonne to lift the John Smith's European Championship title for the first time in 57 years .... Oldham's Wilson Marsh becomes the first player to be referred to the League under the new on-report system, although no further action is taken .... Wigan anger Auckland Warriors by announcing a new joint deal with stand off Frano Botica .... Sheffield Eagles take over the Doncaster club in a rescue package agreed with the Tattersfield club's administrators .... Auckland-bound Denis Betts agrees to return to Wigan for part of the 1995-96 season .... Oldham confirm a move from Watersheddings after 100 years' occupancy to a £6 million 10,000-capacity stadium near Oldham Athletic FC .... Barrow's John McKelleher returns to Sydney for a shoulder operation .... Bradford Northern winger David Myers loses his appeal against a ban to the end of the season for pushing referee John Connolly .... Wakefield Trinity offer New Zealand prop Robert Piva at £35,000 .... A six-man group launches a takeover bid at Bradford Northern .... Leigh buy back the club from the administrator .... Barrie-Jon Mather withdraws his transfer request at Wigan .... Batley recruit on-loan winger Stuart Cocker from Workington Town .... Bradford Northern winger David Myers given concurrent ban of four months, plus a fine of £2,000, for failing to take a drug test .... Bradford Northern coach Peter Fox fined £500, half suspended for 12 months, for making a rude gesture to the Odsal crowd .... Garry Jack resigns as coach of Salford, scrum half Andy Gregory taking over as caretaker coach .... Swinton list utility player Paul Gartland at £50,000 .... Rugby Union International Board agrees to allow Rugby League converts back into Union after a three-year break ... Castleford loose forward Tawera Nikau agrees a summer contract with Sydney club Cronulla ... Swinton ask for bids for want-away prop forward Tony Barrow .... Australian Scott Wilson walks out on Salford .... Ryedale-York price Tim Sharp at £6,000 .... St. Helens offer forward John Harrison at £25,000 .... Sheffield Eagles call off their merger with Doncaster after the League declare that a group of the Tattersfield players are free agents .... Bradford Northern utility back Dave Watson banned for four months and fined £2,000 for failing to take a drug test .... Bramley and Highfield each fined £750, with £500 suspended for 12 months, for brawling .... Salford confirm Andy Gregory's appointment as coach .... St. Helens sign Doncaster centre Vila Matautia .... Gary Mercer (Leeds), Paul Broadbent (Sheffield Eagles) and Denis Gordon (Doncaster) become the first on-report players to be referred to the Disciplinary Committee .... Wigan's Test winger Jason Robinson signs a summer contract with South Sydney .... Leigh sign Wigan prop Dave Riley and Keighley Cougars utility back Phil Ball on loan .... Doncaster bought out of administration by the owners of the Tattersfield ground .... Salford release Australian forward Wayne Marshall .... Salford recruit on-loan Warrington duo Rob Myler and Phil Sumner .... Rochdale Hornets fine Australian David Anderson £100 after being sin-binned seven times and sent off once .... Wakefield Trinity offer New Zealand stand off David Bailey at £18,000 .... Wigan

threaten to withdraw from the 1995 World Club Challenge unless outstanding monies are paid by Brisbane Broncos for the 1994 showpiece .... St. Helens halve the asking price for prop Andy Dannatt to £30,000 .... St. Helens offer Tommy Hodgkinson, Sean Casey, Peter Cannon, Jason Roach and Peter Atherton for a combined total of £110,000 .... Whitehaven sign St. Helens winger Anthony Fenlon on loan until the end of the season .... Australian Rugby League supremo Ken Arthurson asks British counterparts to reconsider summer rugby proposals because of the threat to the international tour cycle .... Leigh exchange loose forward Scott Martin for Salford duo Steve Wynn and Ged Stazicker.

APRIL

England skipper Daryl Powell moves from Sheffield Eagles to Keighley Cougars for £135,000, a transfer record for both clubs ... Hull K.R. pay Sheffield Eagles £10,000 for scrum half Tim Lumb ... Dewsbury sign Eric Kibe from Hunslet ... Media magnate Rupert Murdoch launches a rebel Star League in Australia — part of his power battle with Australia Rugby League television promoter Kerry Packer — putting the Anglo-Aussie transfer ban on players and the World Club Challenge under threat ... Batley open a new stand and launch a £2.8m ground improvement scheme ... Rugby League Council give agreement in principle to summer rugby ... Rugby League's Board of Directors given permission by the Council to talk to Rupert Murdoch about the setting up of a European Super League ... Workington Town prop James Pickering flies back Down Under for personal reasons ... Halifax offer threequarter Richard Smith for £25,000 ... Club chairmen unanimously vote in favour of accepting a £77 million package from Rupert Murdoch featuring the formation of 14-club Super League, wholesale mergers of clubs, the inclusion of teams from Paris and Toulouse and the playing of international football only against other Murdoch-allied countries ... Swinton transfer list Paul Lord at £10,000 ... England forward Anthony Farrell asks for a move from Sheffield Eagles ... Fans and MPs mount anti-merger campaigns ... Second Division promotion favourites Keighley Cougars protest to the League regarding lack of Super League status and are told to raise £1.5m for ground improvements before any reconsideration ... Halifax open merger talks with neighbours Bradford Northern despite both being given Super League entry ... Proposed merger partners Salford and Oldham fail to find any common ground at feasibiity meeting ... Ryedale-York conceive plans of a Super League partnership with Gateshead Council ... The French League decide to enter only Paris in the Super League ... Widnes chosen to take the Super League place reserved for non-participating French entrant Toulouse ... Keighley Cougars decide to sue the League for loss of status following promotion from the Second Division ... Oldham and Salford agree not to merge but to fight for independent membership of the Super League ... The Pacific Island countries pledge allegiance to the Australian Rugby League ... Wigan lift the Stones Bitter Championship for the sixth successive season ... Rochdale Hornets propose that Super League clubs be excluded from the Silk Cut Challenge Cup ... The Australian Rugby League scrap the two-month-old Anglo-Aussie ban on transfers ... The League decide to use in-goal judges at Wembley for the first time ... Peaceful anti-merger pitch protests staged by fans at several Easter Holiday matches ... League Chief Executive Maurice Lindsay visits Australia for talks with the Australian Rugby League and secures the staging of the Halifax Centenary World Cup ... But the Sydney meeting confirms the cancellation of the planned Great Britain tour Down Under in the summer of 1996 ... Whitehaven, Barrow and Carlisle reject merger plans to join Workington Town to enter the Super League as Cumbria, leaving

Town as the nominees ... A National Heritage Committee report recommends that Government grant aid be cut off while Rugby Union practises discrimination against Rugby League ... Canberra rekindle plans for the staging of the 1995 World Club Challenge against Wigan ... Keighley Cougars clinch the Second Division Championship with a club record 104-4 win over Highfield, Batley also being promoted ... Leeds line up Wakefield Trinity loose forward Mike Forshaw ... Castleford shareholders decide to consult a QC after voting not to merge with Wakefield Trinity and Featherstone Rovers ... Australian Rugby League representatives backed by Kerry Packer announce the signing of a group of top British players to be valid once they become out-of-contract, including Wigan's international trio Gary Connolly, Jason Robinson and Martin Hall ... While Rupert Murdoch's News Ltd helps finance "loyalty bonuses" for bonuses" for players to stay in Britain, including Martin Offiah, Bobby Goulding, Va'aiga Tuigamala and Chris Joynt ... Keighley Cougars issue a writ against the League regarding the Super League structure ... Oldham fine second row forward David Bradbury £500 after being sent off for punching Castleford forward Lee Harland, who suffered a broken jaw ... Halifax decide not to merge with Bradford Northern following the resignation of their chairman Tony Gartland ... Featherstone Rovers members vote against any merger ... Great Britain to stage a 1996 autumn tour involving Rupert Murdoch's Australian and New Zealand XIIIs and club sides ... MPs speak out against Rupert Murdoch's Super League deal in a special House of Commons debate ... Oldham's David Bradbury suspended for seven months by the League's Disciplinary Committee for breaking Lee Harland's jaw ... Wigan lift the Silk Cut Challenge Cup for the eighth successive season by beating Leeds 30-10 at Wembley ... Newcastle United soccer club declare an interest in forming a Rugby

League team to join the Super League ... Club chairmen decide to revise Super League plans and bring in three divisions of 12-11-10, the Super League itself to contain the top ten clubs from the 1994-95 season plus London and Paris ... A revised financial package is boosted by a further £10m investment by Rupert Murdoch ... The third tier includes the re-introduction of Chorley ... Leeds stand off Garry Schofield warns of the possibility of strike action as discontent grows over allocation of "loyalty bonuses".

MAY

Widnes launch a High Court action after being omitted from the new Super League format ... Featherstone Rovers, 11th in the completed First Division table, stake a claim to be first reserve for the Super League ... Whitehaven reveal plan for a £2.5m redevelopment including a 3,000-capacity stand ... Halifax sign ex-Doncaster prop Wayne Jackson ... Centre John Schuster decides to stay at Halifax ... Warrington's Allan Bateman joins Cronulla on a three-year contract ... Keighley Cougars adjourn their High Court action for a second time ... Wigan and Wales hooker Martin Hall opts to sign for the Australian Rugby League ... Ryedale-York revert to the title of York ... Caretaker coach Stewart Horton confirmed as coach of York ... St. Helens duo Scott Gibbs and Alan Hunte pull out of Australian summer contracts because of injury and family reasons respectively ... Warrington's Jonathan Davies signs a two-year deal with the Australian Rugby League ... Warrington recruit Featherstone Rovers centre Andy Currier for £80,000 ... Bradford Northern pay £30,000 to St. Helens for hooker Tommy Hodgkinson ... Oldham hand over £50,000 for Warrington stand off Francis Maloney ... On-loan stand off Nigel Wright ends on-loan stay with Wakefield Trinity to return to Wigan ... Kiwi stand off Tony Kemp leaves Castleford to join Leeds ... Newcastle United FC invited League Chief Executive Maurice Lindsay for

formation talks ... The League to receive £2m grant aid from the Football Trust ... England RU full back Paul Hull offered £200,000-plus to join Warrington ... Wigan pull out of the World Club Challenge because of the Rugby League political uncertainty ... Widnes sign Whitehaven's Australian centre Mick Pechey . . . South Africa express interest in joining the Super League ... On the eve of departure to join the Auckland Warriors, Wigan's Denis Betts is voted Stones Bitter Man of Steel ... Widnes threequarter John Devereux fined £300, with £100 costs and £100 compensation after pleading guilty to criminal damage to a collecting box after the BBC's Sports Review of the Year ... Wigan full back Paul Atcheson joins Oldham for £50,000 ... Stephen Ball resigns as chairman of Batley ... St. Helens appoint former League Public Affairs Executive David Howes as their first-ever Chief Executive ... Oldham recruit winger Rob Myler from Warrington for £50,000 ... London Broncos sign full back Paul Hauff from sister club Brisbane Broncos . . . Featherstone Rovers' winger Ikram Butt moves to London Broncos ... Australian coach Brian Smith, formerly with Hull, turns down the Bradford Northern role ... Ellery Hanley confirms his leaving of the England and Leeds coaching job for a two-year £650,000 contract with the Australian Rugby League ... Widnes recruit Swinton's goalkicking hooker Paul Gartland ... Former Australian Test hooker Benny Elias rejects Warrington ... Widnes lose a High Court application for an injunction to stop the Super League going ahead, at a cost of £50,000 ... Teenage utility back Iestyn Harris puts in a transfer request at Warrington ... Newcastle United FC put back entry plans to 1997 ... Ex-Doncaster forward Sonny Whakarau joins Sheffield Eagles ... Warrington sign Huddersfield prop Dave King for £15,000 ... Leeds new recruit Tony Kemp signs a summer contract with South Queensland Crushers.

St. Helens hooker Keiron Cunningham, scorer of four tries in 19 appearances in his 1994-95 debut season.

BARROW 1994-95 MATCH ANALYSIS

Date	Com-petition	H/A	Opponent	Rlt	Score	Tries	Goals	Atten-dance	Referee
21.8.94	SD	H	Rochdale H.	L	22-48	Everett (2), Atkinson, Robinson	Kavanagh (3)	870	Burke
28.8.94	SD	A	Huddersfield	L	12-50	Atkinson, Everett	Kavanagh (2)	—	—
4.9.94	SD	H	London B.	L	10-16	Kerr, Trainor	Kavanagh	782	Galtress
11.9.94	SD	A	Dewsbury	L	8-76	Everett	Atkinson (2)	—	—
18.9.94	SD	H	Ryedale-York	L	14-45	Crarey, Shaw	Atkinson (3)	807	Oddy
25.9.94	SD	A	Whitehaven	L	18-26	Atkinson, Honey, Rhodes	Atkinson (2), Kavanagh	—	—
2.10.94	SD	H	Keighley C.	L	10-24	Westwood	Atkinson (3)	1648	Lee
9.10.94	SD	H	Leigh	L	30-32	Ashcroft, Atkinson, Rhodes, Robinson, Trainor	Atkinson (5)	1048	Kirkpatrick
16.10.94	SD	A	Hull K.R.	W	1-0		Kavanagh (dg)	—	—
30.10.94	SD	H	Hunslet	L	8-21	Robinson	Atkinson (2)	1086	Oddy
6.11.94	SD	A	Rochdale H.	L	6-32	McKelleher	Carter	—	—
13.11.94	SD	H	Huddersfield	L	6-22	Crarey	Shaw	1014	Kirkpatrick
24.11.94	RT(1)	H	Nottingham C.	W	138-0	Ashcroft (5), Everett (3), Robinson (3), Shaw (3), Slater (3), Carter (2), Quayle (2), Westwood (2), Kerr, McKelleher, Jamie Smith	Carter (17)	500	Lee
4.12.94	RT(2)	A	Hull	L	16-26	Eccles, Quayle	Carter (4)	—	—
11.12.94	SD	A	London B.	L	6-30	Eccles	Carter	—	—
26.12.94	SD	A	Carlisle	L	20-22	Atkinson, Eccles, Everett, McKelleher	Carter (2)	—	—
1.1.95	SD	H	Highfield	L	12-14	Jamie Smith, Shaw	Carter, Shaw	676	Oddy
4.1.95	SD	H	Dewsbury	L	14-24	Robinson, Westwood, Whalley	Atkinson	638	McGregor
8.1.95	SD	A	Batley	L	6-36	Quayle	Atkinson	—	—
15.1.95	SD	H	Bramley	W	34-20	Ashcroft, Atkinson, Jamie Smith, Trainor, Whalley	Atkinson (7)	638	Presley
22.1.95	CC(3)	H	East Leeds	W	56-0	Ashcroft (2), McKelleher (2), Whalley (2), Everett, Shaw, Jeff Smith, Jamie Smith, Trainor	Atkinson (6)	708	Carter
29.1.95	SD	A	Ryedale-York	L	11-20	Everett, Trainor	Atkinson, Ruane (dg)	—	—
5.2.95	SD	A	Whitehaven	L	8-31	Walker	Atkinson (2)	1330	Carter
12.2.95	CC(4)	A	Featherstone R.	L	22-50	Atkinson, Hannah, Robinson, Jamie Smith	Atkinson (3)	—	—
19.2.95	SD	A	Keighley C.	L	6-28	White	Atkinson	—	—
6.3.95	SD	A	Leigh	W	14-12	Robinson, Ruane	Atkinson (3)	—	—
12.3.95	SD	H	Swinton	W	37-14	Everett (2), Jeff Smith (2), Clayton, Creary	Atkinson (6), Ruane (dg)	768	McGregor
19.3.95	SD	H	Hull K.R.	L	18-50	Everett, Robinson, Trainor	Atkinson (3)	915	Ollerton
26.3.95	SD	A	Hunslet	L	24-26	Clayton (2), Ashcroft, Trainor	Ruane (3), Atkinson	—	—
2.4.95	SD	H	Batley	L	25-32	Atkinson, Everett, Robinson, Ruane	Ruane (4, 1dg)	1059	R. Connolly
9.4.95	SD	A	Bramley	L	8-18	Ashcroft	Ruane (2)	—	—
14.4.95	SD	H	Carlisle	W	14-6	Wilson	Ruane (4, 2dg)	1045	Burke
17.4.95	SD	A	Highfield	W	34-8	Trainor (3), Clayton, Ruane, Wilson	Atkinson (4), Ruane	—	—
23.4.95	SD	A	Swinton	L	13-28	Creary	Atkinson (4, 1dg)	—	—

BATLEY

Ground: Mount Pleasant (01924-470062)
First Season: 1895-96
Nickname: Gallant Youths
Chairman: Ron Earnshaw
Secretary: Richard Illingworth
Honours: **Championship** Winners, 1923-24
Challenge Cup Winners, 1896-97, 1897-98, 1900-01
Yorkshire Cup Winners, 1912-13
Beaten finalists, 1909-10, 1922-23, 1924-25, 1952-53
Yorkshire League Winners, 1898-99, 1923-24

RECORDS
Match
Goals: 13 by Simon Wilson v. Leigh
26 Mar 1995
Tries: 5 by Joe Oakland v. Bramley,
19 Dec 1908
Tommy Brannan v. Swinton,
17 Jan 1920
Jim Wale v. Bramley, 4 Dec 1926
Jim Wale v. Cottingham,
12 Feb 1927
Tommy Oldroyd at Highfield,
6 Mar 1994
Points: 30 by Simon Wilson v. Leigh
26 Mar 1995
Season
Goals: 127 by Simon Wilson, 1994-95
Tries: 29 by Jack Tindall, 1912-13
Points: 300 by Simon Wilson, 1994-93
Career
Goals: 463 by Wharton "Wattie" Davies,
1897-1912
Tries: 123 by Wharton "Wattie" Davies,
1897-1912
Points: 1,297 by Wharton "Wattie" Davies,
1897-1912
Appearances: 421 by Wharton "Wattie" Davies,
1897-1912

Highest score: 78-22 v. Leigh
26 Mar 1995
Highest against: 78-9 at Wakefield T.,
26 Aug 1967
Attendance: 23,989 v. Leeds (RL Cup),
14 Mar 1925

COACHING REGISTER
● **Since 1974-75**

Don Fox	Nov 72 - Oct 74
Alan Hepworth	Nov 74 - Apr 75
Dave Cox	May 75 - June 75
Trevor Walker	June 75 - June 77
Albert Fearnley	June 77 - Oct 77
Dave Stockwell	Oct 77 - June 79
*Tommy Smales	June 79 - Oct 81
Trevor Lowe	Oct 81 - May 82
Terry Crook	June 82 - Nov 84
George Pieniazek	Nov 84 - Nov 85
Brian Lockwood	Nov 85 - May 87
Paul Daley	July 87 - Apr 90
Keith Rayne	May 90 - Apr 91
David Ward	May 91 - Oct 94
Jeff Grayshon	Oct 94 -

Ex-forward

GREAT BRITAIN REGISTER
(4 players)

Norman Field	(1)	1963
Frank Gallagher	(8)	1924-26
Carl Gibson	(+1)	1985
Joe Oliver	(4)	1928

1994-95 SIGNINGS REGISTER

Signed	Player	Club From
19.7.94	Harrison, Paul	Hull
1.8.94	McWilliams, Chris	Ovenden ARL
21.8.94	Moverley, Robert	Stanningley ARL
22.9.94	Walton, Gary	Ossett T. ARL
1.10.94	*Wilson, Warren	Halifax
16.12.94	Gilfillan, John	Salford
11.3.95	Cocker, Stuart	Workington T.
12.4.95	Bailey, Mark	Ovenden ARL

BATLEY 1994-95 PLAYERS' SUMMARY

	Date of Birth	App	T	G	D	Pts	Previous club	Signed
Bailey, Mark		0+1	—	—	—	—	Ovenden ARL	12.4.95
Bargate, Lee	12.9.71	3	2	—	—	8	Middleton ARL	27.6.90
Bownass, Mark	1.6.66	1	—	—	—	—	Dewsbury Colts	2.8.90
Brook, Richard	18.2.70	2+1	—	—	—	—	Hunslet	7.9.93
Cameron, Mick	19.12.67	25	1	—	—	4	Australia	8.9.92
Cass, Mark	17.11.71	29+5	14	—	—	56	Hull	29.2.92
Child, Darren	30.10.66	34	1	—	—	4	Morley RU	13.9.90
Cocker, Stuart	8.5.66	10	8	—	—	32	Workington T.	11.3.95
Craven, Nigel	24.11.70	4	1	—	—	4	Batley Boys ARL	15.8.90
Dyson, Jeremy	15.2.72	5	—	13	—	26	Thornhill ARL	29.8.91
Ellison, Paul		1	—	—	—	—		
Gilfillan, John	11.3.65	17	5	—	—	20	Salford	16.12.94
Grayshon, Jeff	4.3.49	1+15	—	—	—	—	Featherstone R.	11.8.91
Green, Mark		0+1	—	—	—	—		
Harrison, Paul	24.9.70	28+1	14	—	—	56	Hull	19.7.94
Heron, Wayne	5.5.61	9+13	2	—	—	8	Bradford N.	22.2.90
Irvine, Jimmy	28.4.60	24+2	7	—	—	28	Halifax	2.10.92
McWilliams, Chris	1.6.69	35	7	—	1	29	Ovenden ARL	1.8.94
Middleton, Graham	2.11.70	6+13	3	—	—	12	Leeds	1.7.93
Mirfin, Phil	20.11.68	27+5	9	1	—	38	Castleford	
Moverley, Robert	18.1.69	0+1	1	—	—	4	Stanningley ARL	21.8.94
Moxon, Darren	17.9.70	35	11	—	—	44	Bradford N.	11.12.92
Parkinson, Andrew	8.7.65	34+1	2	1	—	10	Dewsbury	2.1.90
Pastre, Regis	23.3.70	2+1	1	—	—	4	France	16.8.93
Scott, Mark	30.1.65	9+4	1	—	—	4	Batley Boys ARL	9.5.84
Thornton, Gary	9.3.63	35+1	20	—	—	80	Wakefield T.	24.8.90
Tomlinson, Glen	18.3.70	35	26	—	1	105	Australia	29.8.91
Walker, Steve	8.11.69	33+1	20	—	—	80	Dudley Hill ARL	17.12.92
Walton, Tony	20.12.63	21+3	2	—	—	8	Doncaster	1.10.93
Whitchurch, Gary		0+1	—	—	—	—		
Wilson, Simon	22.10.67	39	12	125	2	300	Batley Boys ARL	16.11.84
Wilson, Warren	3.5.63	3	—	—	—	—	Halifax	1.10.94
TOTALS								
32 players			170	140	4	964		

BATLEY 1994-95 MATCH ANALYSIS

Date	Com-petition	H/A	Opponent	Rlt	Score	Tries	Goals	Atten-dance	Referee
21.8.94	SD	H	Huddersfield	W	13-0	Harrison	Wilson (4), Tomlinson (dg)	2079	Asquith
28.8.94	SD	H	Carlisle	W	44-16	McWilliams (2), Irvine (2), Moxon, Thornton, Scott Tomlinson	Wilson (6)	829	Redfearn
4.9.94	SD	H	Highfield	W	66-0	Bargate 2), Cass (2), Middleton (2), Walker (2) Harrison, McWilliams Thornton, Tomlinson Wilson	Wilson (7)	1007	Nicholson
11.9.94	SD	A	Ryedale-York	L	8-35	Thornton, Tomlinson			

(Continued)

Date	Com-petition	H/A	Opponent	Rlt	Score	Tries	Goals	Atten-dance	Referee
18.9.94	SD	H	Whitehaven	W	22-6	Harrison (2), Tomlinson Walker	Dyson (3)	1021	Atkin
25.9.94	SD	A	London B.	L	2-30	—	Dyson	—	—
2.10.94	SD	H	Rochdale H.	W	22-12	Tomlinson (2), Walker	Dyson (5)	1113	Nicholson
9.10.94	SD	A	Keighley C.	W	26-22	Thornton (2), Moxon Wilson	Wilson (4, 2dg)	—	—
16.10.94	SD	H	Swinton	W	10-6	Harrison, Walker	Wilson	1272	Galtress
30.10.94	SD	A	Leigh	W	32-8	Walker (2), Cass, Harrison Tomlinson, Wilson	Dyson (4)	—	—
6.11.94	SD	A	Huddersfield	L	14-15	Cass, Harrison	Wilson (3)	—	—
13.11.94	SD	A	Carlisle	W	26-12	Wilson (2), Harrison, Mirfin Parkinson	Wilson (3)	—	—
22.11.94	SD	H	Ryedale-York	W	4-2	Mirfin		1256	Galtress
27.11.94	RT(1)	H	Queens	W	38-8	Moxon (2), Cass, Craven, Irvine, Moverley, Pastre	Wilson (5)	607	Holdsworth
7.12.94	RT(2)	H	Ryedale-York	W	36-8	Tomlinson (3), Heron, McWilliams, Walker	Wilson (6)	719	Gilmour
11.12.94	SD	A	Highfield	W	50-0	Tomlinson (4), Walker (2) Harrison, Moxon Thornton, Wilson	Wilson (5)	—	—
18.12.94	RT(3)	H	St. Helens	D	22-22	Harrison (2), McWilliams, Thornton	Wilson (2), Parkinson	3017	Cross
20.12.94	RT(3) Replay	A	St. Helens	L	22-50	Parkinson, Tomlinson, Wilson	Wilson (5)	—	—
26.12.94	SD	A	Dewsbury	L	0-16			—	—
2.1.95	SD	H	Bramley	W	18-16	Thornton, Tomlinson, Walker	Wilson (3)	907	Carter
8.1.95	SD	H	Barrow	W	36-6	Cass (2), Thornton (2), Cameron, McWilliams, Tomlinson	Wilson (4)	935	Atkin
15.1.95	SD	H	Hull K.R.	W	22-6	Cass (2), Mirfin	Wilson (5)	1502	Galtress
22.1.95	CC (3)	H	Shaw Cross	W	32-4	Thornton (4), Cass, Gilfillan, Walker	Wilson (2)	1126	Atkin
29.1.95	SD	A	Whitehaven	L	8-30	Mirfin	Mirfin, Wilson	—	—
5.2.95	SD	H	London B.	L	10-22	Irvine	Wilson (3)	1106	McGregor
12.2.95	CC(4)	A	Beverley	W	30-20	Gilfillan, McWilliams, Moxon, Tomlinson, Walker Wilson	Wilson (3)	—	—
19.2.95	SD	A	Rochdale H.	W	22-18	Walton (2), Moxon, Walker	Wilson (3)	—	—
26.2.95	CC(5)	H	Wigan	L	4-70	Thornton		3800	Morris
6.3.95	SD	H	Keighley C.	W	8-6	Middleton	Wilson (2)	2852	Smith
12.3.95	SD	A	Hunslet	W	34-22	Cocker (2), Mirfin, Moxon, Thornton, Tomlinson	Wilson (5)	—	—
19.3.95	SD	A	Swinton	W	24-16	Walker (2), Cocker, Tomlinson	Wilson (4)	—	—
26.3.95	SD	H	Leigh	W	78-22	Walker (3), Mirfin (2), Thornton (2), Child, Cocker, Heron, Moxon,, Tomlinson, Wilson	Wilson (13)	1182	Redfearn
2.4.95	SD	A	Barrow	W	32-25	Cass, Cocker, Mirfin, Thornton, Tomlinson, Wilson	Wilson (4)	—	—
9.4.95	SD	A	Hull K.R.	W	33-10	Tomlinson (2), Harrison, Cass, Mirfin	Wilson (6), McWilliams (dg)	—	—
14.4.95	SD	H	Dewsbury	W	46-6	Cocker (2), Cass, Harrison, Irvine, Moxon, Walker, Wilson	Wilson (4)	3372	Cross
17.4.95	SD	A	Bramley	W	18-10	Tomlinson (2), Gilfillan, Irvine	Wilson	—	—
23.4.95	SD	H	Hunslet	L	26-28	Cocker, Gilfillan, Irvine, Moxon, Wilson	Wilson (3)	2211	Bates
7.5.95	SDP(1)	H	Dewsbury	W	20-16	Cass, Gilfillan, Thornton	Wilson (4)	2034	Kirkpatrick
14.5.95	SDP(SF)	H	Huddersfield	L	6-13	Harrison	Wilson	2582	Smith

BRADFORD NORTHERN

Ground: Odsal Stadium (01274-733899)
First Season: 1895-96 as "Bradford". Disbanded and became Bradford Northern in 1907-08. Disbanded during 1963-64 and re-formed for start of 1964-65. Re-titled Bradford Bulls from the start of 1995-96
Nickname: Bulls
Chairman: Chris Caisley
Secretary: Gary Tasker
Honours: **Championship** Beaten finalists, 1947-48, 1951-52
War Emergency League Championship winners, 1939-40, 1940-41, 1944-45
Beaten finalists, 1941-42
Division One Champions, 1903-04, 1979-80, 1980-81
Division Two Champions, 1973-74
Challenge Cup Winners, 1905-06, 1943-44, 1946-47, 1948-49
Beaten finalists, 1897-98, 1944-45, 1947-48, 1972-73
Regal Trophy Winners, 1974-75, 1979-80
Beaten finalists, 1990-91, 1992-93
Premiership Winners, 1977-78
Beaten finalists, 1978-79, 1979-80, 1989-90
Yorkshire Cup Winners, 1906-07, 1940-41, 1941-42, 1943-44, 1945-46, 1948-49, 1949-50, 1953-54, 1965-66, 1978-79, 1987-88, 1989-90
Beaten finalists, 1913-14, 1981-82, 1982-83, 1991-92
Yorkshire League Winners, 1899-1900, 1900-01, 1939-40, 1940-41, 1947-48

RECORDS

Match
Goals: 14 by Joe Phillips v. Batley, 6 Sep 1952
Tries: 7 by Jim Dechan v. Bramley, 13 Oct 1906
Points: 36 by John Woods v. Swinton, 13 Oct 1985
Season
Goals: 173 by Eddie Tees, 1971-72
Tries: 63 by Jack McLean, 1951-52
Points: 364 by Eddie Tees, 1971-72
Career
Goals: 779 by Keith Mumby, 1973-90 & 1992-93
Tries: 261 by Jack McLean, 1950-56
Points: 1,828 by Keith Mumby, 1973-90 & 1992-93
Appearances: 580+8 by Keith Mumby, 1973-90 & 1992-93
Highest score: 76-0 v. Leigh East, 17 Nov 1991
Highest against: 75-18 at Leeds, 14 Sep 1931
Attendance: 102,569 Warrington v. Halifax (RL Cup final replay), 5 May 1954
Home match: 69,429 v. Huddersfield (RL Cup), 14 Mar 1953

COACHING REGISTER
● **Since 1974-75**

Ian Brooke	Jan 73 - Sep 75
Roy Francis	Oct 75 - Apr 77
Peter Fox	Apr 77 - May 85
Barry Seabourne	May 85 - Sep 89
Ron Willey	Oct 89 - Mar 90
David Hobbs	Mar 90 - Oct 91
Peter Fox	Oct 91 -

Veteran loose forward Dave Heron, who made 26 appearances in 1994-95, his farewell campaign at Odsal.

39

GREAT BRITAIN REGISTER
(33 players)

David Barends	(2)	1979
Eric Batten	(4)	1946-47
Ian Brooke	(5)	1966
Len Casey	(5)	1979
Gerald Cordle	(1)	1990
Willie Davies	(3)	1946-47
Karl Fairbank	(10+6)	1987-94
Tony Fisher	(8)	1970-78
Phil Ford	(7)	1987-88
Trevor Foster	(3)	1946-48
Deryck Fox	(1)	1992
Jeff Grayshon	(11)	1979-82
Ellery Hanley	(10+1)	1984-85
David Hobbs	(1+1)	1989
Dick Jasiewicz	(1)	1984
Jack Kitching	(1)	1946
Arthur Mann	(2)	1908
Keith Mumby	(11)	1982-84
Brian Noble	(11)	1982-84
Paul Newlove	(5+1)	1993-94
Terry Price	(1)	1970
Johnny Rae	(1)	1965
Bill Ramsey	(+1)	1974
Alan Rathbone	(4+1)	1982-85
Alan Redfearn	(1)	1979
David Redfearn	(6+1)	1972-74
Kelvin Skerrett	(8)	1989-90
Tommy Smales	(3)	1965
Bert Smith	(2)	1926
Jimmy Thompson	(1)	1978
Ken Traill	(8)	1950-54
Ernest Ward	(20)	1946-52
Frank Whitcombe	(2)	1946

1994-95 SIGNINGS REGISTER

Signed	Player	Club From
29.6.94	Gande, Allan	Oulton ARL
29.6.94	Horton, Neil	Oulton ARL
29.6.94	Maskill, Steven	Oulton ARL
29.6.94	Mulligan, James	Oulton ARL
29.6.94	Roughton, Dave	Redhill ARL
29.6.94	Scanlon, Noel	Dewsbury Moor ARL
29.6.94	Shaw, Graeme	Moldgreen ARL
29.6.94	Waters, David	Moldgreen ARL
4.7.94	Myers, David	Widnes
8.7.94	Paul, Robbie	Waitakere, NZ
11.7.94	Bourneville, Eugene	Auckland Vulcans, NZ
13.7.94	Varley, Nathan	Queensbury ARL
18.8.94	Donohoe, Jason	Leigh
8.9.94	Clegg, Jason	Littleborough ARL
17.10.94	Heffrey, Gavin	—
24.11.94	Christie, Gary	Wakefield T.
22.12.94	Round, Paul	Halifax
11.1.95	Simpson, Joe	West Bowling ARL

Northern utility back Roger Simpson, scorer of 11 tries in 1994-95.

BRADFORD NORTHERN 1994-95 PLAYERS' SUMMARY

	Date of Birth	App	T	G	D	Pts	Previous club	Signed
Austerfield, Shaun	11.9.75	2	1	—	—	4	Oulton ARL	23.11.92
Bourneville, Eugene	19.6.72	24+4	1	—	—	4	New Zealand	15.4.94
Christie, Gary	23.1.72	17	11	—	—	44	Wakefield T.	24.11.94
Clark, Trevor	28.5.62	15	4	—	—	16	Featherstone R.	13.8.92
Clegg, Jason	24.3.71	3+3	—	—	—	—	Littleborough ARL	8.9.94
Cordle, Gerald	29.9.60	5	2	—	—	8	Cardiff RU	12.7.89
Dixon, Paul	28.10.62	30+2	14	—	—	56	Leeds	1.8.93
Donohue, Jason	18.4.72	2+6	—	—	—	—	Leigh	18.8.94
Fairbank, Karl	1.6.63	18+1	6	—	—	24	Elland ARL	24.7.86
Fox, Deryck	17.9.64	34	3	123	3	261	Featherstone R.	9.9.92
Fraisse, David	20.12.68	20+1	8	1	—	34	Sheffield E.	20.5.94
Greenwood, Adam	26.5.67	5+4	—	—	—	—	Calder V. ARL	27.1.92
Hall, Carl	10.8.69	23+1	11	1	—	46	Doncaster	4.5.94
Hamer, Jon	23.2.66	20+8	2	—	—	8	Elland ARL	29.8.84
Hepworth, Phil	6.10.73	6+1	1	—	—	4	Dudley Hill ARL	10.8.93
Heron, David	1.3.58	13+13	—	—	—	—	Leeds	27.7.92
Holding, Neil	15.12.60	2+1	1	1	—	6	St. Helens	1.7.93
McDermott, Brian	16.3.70	23+3	3	—	—	12	Eastmoor ARL	22.9.92
Medley, Paul	21.9.66	21+13	13	—	—	52	Halifax	31.8.89
Myers, David	31.7.71	28	12	—	—	48	Widnes	4.7.94
Newlove, Paul	10.8.71	27+1	25	—	—	100	Featherstone R.	13.7.93
Paul, Robbie	3.2.76	10+3	4	—	—	16	New Zealand	8.7.94
Powell, Roy	30.4.65	33+2	3	—	—	12	Leeds	28.2.92
Round, Paul	24.9.63	0+2	1	—	—	4	Halifax	22.12.94
Russell, Phil	4.4.75	3	1	—	—	4	Waterhead ARL	30.6.92
Simpson, Roger	27.8.67	21+1	11	—	—	44	Moldgreen ARL	17.1.85
Summers, Neil	10.10.68	31+1	14	2	—	60	Headingley RU	4.6.90
Turpin, David	21.1.73	6+1	3	—	—	12	Dudley Hill ARL	13.8.91
Watson, Dave	24.5.66	26+1	13	—	—	52	Halifax	19.8.92
Winterburn, Carl	8.9.70	0+1	—	—	—	—	Birkenshaw ARL	9.9.93
TOTALS								
30 players			168	128	3	931		

Representative appearances 1994-95

Fox — England (2,1t,5g); Fraisse — France (1); Newlove — Britain (1+1,1t); England (1);
Simpson — England (+1); Cordle — Wales (+1); D. Powell — Wales (+1,1t).

BRADFORD NORTHERN 1994-95 MATCH ANALYSIS

Date	Competition	H/A	Opponent	Rlt	Score	Tries	Goals	Attendance	Referee
23.8.94	SBC	A	Sheffield E.	W	26-8	Newlove (2), Summers, Watson	Fox (5)	—	—
28.8.94	SBC	H	Oldham	W	36-14	Newlove (3), Watson, Fairbank, Medley	Fox (6)	6160	Presley
2.9.94	SBC	A	Wakefield T.	W	44-12	Fraisse (2), Dixon, Fox, Fairbank, Hepworth Myers, Summers	Fox (6)	—	—
7.9.94	SBC	H	Warrington	W	16-10	Fairbank, Newlove, Watson	Fox, Summers	7110	Campbell
11.9.94	SBC	H	Widnes	W	48-4	Myers (3), Hall (2), Summers (2), Fox, Watson	Fox (6)	5975	R. Connolly
16.9.94	SBC	A	Featherstone R.	W	42-16	Watson (2), Fraisse, Medley Myers, Newlove, Summers	Fox (7)	—	—
25.9.94	SBC	H	Workington T.	W	30-2	Cordle (2), Dixon, Fraisse, Newlove, Watson	Fox (3)	6314	Smith
2.10.94	SBC	A	Hull	W	12-6	Summers, Watson	Fox (2)	—	—
7.10.94	SBC	A	Warrington	L	2-25		Fox	—	—
16.10.94	SBC	H	St. Helens	L	12-51	Dixon, Turpin	Fox (2)	7352	Campbell
30.10.94	SBC	A	Castleford	L	18-39	Fraisse, Medley, Myers, Watson	Fox	—	—
6.11.94	SBC	H	Sheffield E.	W	40-4	Dixon, Fraisse, Hall, Medley Myers, Newlove, Russell	Fox (6)	4794	Morris
13.11.94	Tour	H	Australia	L	0-40			9021	Cummings
22.11.94	SBC	A	Oldham	L	12-32	Fox, Simpson	Fox (2)	—	—
27.11.94	SBC	H	Wakefield T.	W	34-0	Paul (2), Christie, Dixon, Medley, Newlove	Fox (5)	5339	Ollerton
7.12.94	RT(2)	H	St. Esteve (Fr)	W	32-6	Austerfield, Holding, Medley Myers, Simpson, Summers Turpin	Fraisse, Holding	2250	Holdsworth
11.12.94	SBC	A	Widnes	W	34-15	Newlove (2), Hamer, Medley, Simpson, Watson	Fox (5)	—	—
18.12.94	RT(3)	A	Whitehaven	W	34-14	Dixon (2), Fraisse (2), Medley Newlove, Watson	Fox (3)	—	—
26.12.94	SBC	A	Halifax	D	16-16	Newlove (2), Dixon	Fox (2)	—	—
1.1.95	SBC	H	Salford	W	24-18	McDermott (2), Summers, Newlove, Round	Fox (2)	5056	Presley
8.1.95	RT(4)	A	Widnes	L	10-23	Simpson (2)	Fox	—	—
11.1.95	SBC	A	Doncaster	W	36-18	Clark, Dixon, Medley, Powell Newlove, Summers, Watson	Fox (5)	—	—
15.1.95	SBC	A	Leeds	L	30-46	Myers (3), Dixon, Watson	Fox (5)	—	—
20.1.95	SBC	H	Wigan	L	10-14	Dixon	Fox (3)	6425	Morris
5.2.95	SBC	A	Workington T.	L	14-32	Hall, McDermott	Fox (3)	—	—
12.2.95	CC(4)	A	Leeds	L	14-31	Clark, Medley	Fox (2, 2dg)	—	—
15.2.95	SBC	H	Featherstone R.	L	16-24	Christie, Dixon, Hall, Turpin	—	3016	R. Connolly
19.2.95	SBC	H	Hull	W	42-24	Hall (3), Christie (2), Hamer, Myers, Simpson	Fox (5)	3561	Bates
17.3.95	SBC	A	St. Helens	L	27-36	Newlove (2), Clark, Dixon	Fox (5, 1dg)	—	—
26.3.95	SBC	H	Leeds	L	10-30	Christie, Hall	Fox	6980	Morris
2.4.95	SBC	H	Doncaster	W	74-18	Newlove (3), Christie (2), Simpson (2), Summers (2), Bourneville, Clark, Dixon, Paul	Fox (9), Hall, Summers	3681	Tennant
9.4.95	SBC	A	Wigan	L	34-60	Christie (3), Medley, Powell, Simpson	Fox (5)	—	—
14.4.95	SBC	H	Halifax	W	30-22	Fairbank (2), Newlove (2), Simpson	Fox (5)	6886	Tennant
17.4.95	SBC	A	Salford	W	16-14	Fairbank, Hall, Paul	Fox (2)	—	—
23.4.95	SBC	H	Castleford	L	26-40	Medley (2), Summers (2), Simpson	Fox (3)	6163	Campbell
5.5.95	PT(1)	A	Leeds	L	30-50	Christie, Hall, Newlove, Powell, Summers	Fox (5)	—	—

BRAMLEY

Ground: McLaren Field (until end of 1994-95, Leeds RU, Kirkstall from 1995-96)
First Season: 1896-97
Nickname: Villagers
Chairman: Jeff Wine
Secretary: Anthony Sugare
Honours: **BBC2 Floodlit Trophy** Winners, 1973-74

RECORDS
Match
Goals: 11 by Bernard Ward v. Doncaster, 1 Sep 1974
Tries: 7 by Joe Sedgewick v. Normanton, 16 Apr 1906
Points: 28 by Bernard Ward v. Doncaster, 1 Sep 1974
Season
Goals: 138 by Steve Carroll, 1991-92
Tries: 34 by Peter Lister, 1985-86
Points: 288 by Steve Carroll, 1991-92
Career
Goals: 926 by John Wilson, 1953-64
Tries: 140 by Peter Lister, 1982-91
Points: 1,903 by John Wilson, 1953-64
Appearances: 406+4 by John Wolford, 1962-76
Highest score: 62-14 v. Dewsbury, 30 Oct 1988
Highest against: 92-7 v. Australia, 9 Nov 1921
Attendance: 12,600 v. Leeds (League), 7 May 1947 — at Barley Mow
7,500 v. Bradford N. (RL Cup), 17 Feb 1972 — at McLaren Field

COACHING REGISTER
● **Since 1974-75**

Arthur Keegan	May 73 - Sep 76
Peter Fox	Sep 76 - Apr 77
*Tommy Smales	May 77 - Dec 77
Les Pearce	Jan 78 - Oct 78
Don Robinson	Oct 78 - May 79
Dave Stockwell	June 79 - June 80
Keith Hepworth	June 80 - May 82
Maurice Bamford	May 82 - Oct 83
Peter Jarvis	Oct 83 - Apr 85
Ken Loxton	Apr 85 - Dec 85
Allan Agar	Dec 85 - Apr 87
Chris Forster	June 87 - Nov 87
Tony Fisher	Nov 87 - Feb 89
Barry Johnson	Mar 89 - Dec 90
John Kear	Dec 90 - Jan 91
Roy Dickinson	Jan 91 - Apr 92
Maurice Bamford	Apr 92 - Sep 93
Ray Ashton	Sep 93 -

Ex-forward

1994-95 SIGNINGS REGISTER

Signed	Player	Club From
22.7.94	Quinlan, Brian	Old'm St. Annes ARL
28.7.94	Perks, Jonathan	Waterhead ARL
8.8.94	Garrett, Paul	Saddleworth ARL
8.8.94	Greenwood, Barry	Saddleworth ARL
21.9.94	Riddlesden, Eddie	Halifax
23.9.94	Lister, Peter	Doncaster
22.9.94	Kerr, Ken	Prosperpine, Aus
16.2.95	*Bailey, Dennis	Dewsbury
24.3.95	Thornton, Michael	Higginshaw ARL
16.4.95	Agar, John	—
16.4.95	Morse, Ian	—
18.4.95	Finnan, Andy	Brookhouse ARL
20.4.95	Wine, Jeff	—

Peter Fox, coach at Bramley in 1976-77, gaining promotion from the Second Division.

BRAMLEY 1994-95 PLAYERS' SUMMARY

	Date of Birth	App	T	G	D	Pts	Previous club	Signed
Agar, Andy	27.5.73	14+4	—	—	—	—	Pudsey ARL	4.6.91
Ashton, Ray	26.10.60	19+8	4	1	1	19	Workington T.	6.10.93
Bailey, Dennis	15.2.66	4	4	—	—	16	Dewsbury	16.2.95
Bell, Kevin	13.10.64	21+1	6	—	—	24	Wakefield R. ARL	2.7.91
Blankley, Dean	28.10.68	25	12	—	2	50	Castleford	2.11.90
Clark, Nathan	26.12.72	6+2	3	—	—	12	Oldham	18.3.94
Coen, Darren	28.9.60	1+1	—	—	—	—	Dewsbury	9.8.91
Creasser, Dean	18.8.70	15	2	36	—	80	Bison S. ARL	17.12.91
Finnan, Andy	31.7.65	1+1	1	—	—	4	Brookhouse ARL	18.4.95
Fisher, Julian	4.10.70	13+3	3	—	—	12	Normanton ARL	15.12.92
Francis, Norman	2.10.64	12+1	5	—	—	20	Oldham	11.10.91
Fraser, Paul	19.6.70	1+7	—	—	—	—		22.5.89
Freeman, Glen	9.4.72	29+4	4	—	—	16	Pudsey ARL	4.6.91
Freeman, Wayne	30.4.74	27+5	11	—	—	44	Pudsey ARL	27.8.91
Garrett, Paul	29.9.72	33	8	—	—	32	Saddleworth ARL	8.8.94
Greenwood, Barry	16.1.69	25+1	8	—	—	32	Saddleworth ARL	8.8.94
Hall, Dean	5.9.69	17+3	3	—	—	12	Dewsbury	15.8.93
Harker, Keith	27.9.72	5	1	—	—	4	Ryedale-York	4.3.91
Jackman, Emmerson		0+1	—	—	—	—		
Jewitt, Roy	26.2.72	25+1	2	—	—	8	Waterhead ARL	18.5.93
Kerr, Ken	18.10.69	12	9	—	—	36	Australia	22.9.94
Laws, Mark	26.4.71	5+6	1	10	—	24	Ryedale-York	3.3.94
Long, Gordon	5.1.70	31	8	6	1	45	Westgate ARL	17.6.93
Lister, Peter	16.11.59	1	—	—	—	—	Doncaster	23.9.94
Maltby, Mark	17.9.73	1	—	—	—	—		
Marson, Andy	19.5.65	24	6	—	—	24	Hunslet	12.8.91
Middleton, Roger	18.12.70	0+2	—	—	—	—	Nottingham C.	29.12.93
Morse, Ian	19.4.69	2	1	—	—	4	Normanton ARL	27.9.92
Perks, Jonathan	4.1.72	10+1	5	26	—	72	Waterhead ARL	28.7.94
Quinlan, Brian	9.4.70	21+8	4	1	—	18	Oldham St. Annes ARL	22.7.94
Riddlesden, Eddie	26.9.67	2	—	—	—	—	Halifax	29.7.92
Sharp, Ron	6.10.64	18	2	—	—	8		16.3.88
Stead, Richard	22.3.70	2	—	3	—	6	Normanton ARL	15.12.92
Thornton, Michael	22.8.74	5+2	2	—	—	8	Higginshaw ARL	24.3.95
Treyhurn, Rod		0+1	—	—	—	—		
Wigglesworth, Iain	25.4.67	15+2	5	—	—	20	Ryedale-York	16.11.93
TOTALS								
36 players			120	83	4	650		

BRAMLEY 1994-95 MATCH ANALYSIS

Date	Com-petition	H/A	Opponent	Rlt	Score	Tries	Goals	Atten-dance	Referee
21.8.94	SD	H	Dewsbury	L	15-22	Ashton, W. Freeman Garrett	Perks, Blankley (dg)	828	Oddy
28.8.94	SD	A	Hull K.R.	L	10-34	Quinlan, Blankley	Quinlan	—	—
4.9.94	SD	A	Carlisle	L	12-15	W. Freeman, Perks	Perks (2)	—	—
11.9.94	SD	H	Whitehaven	W	30-14	Bell, Blankley, W. Freeman, Greenwood, Long, Marson	Laws (2), Long	501	McGregor
18.9.94	SD	A	Swinton	L	22-24	Bell, W. Freeman, G. Freeman Greenwood	Perks (3)	—	—
25.9.94	SD	H	Keighley C.	L	2-18	—	Laws	2225	Redfearn
2.10.94	SD	A	Leigh	L	12-22	Bell, D. Hall	Laws (2)	—	—
9.10.94	SD	H	Highfield	W	46-0	Blankley (2), Francis (2), D. Hall, Harker, Laws, Long, Marson, Wigglesworth	Laws (3)	487	Cross
16.10.94	SD	A	London B.	L	12-40	Kerr, Wigglesworth	Ashton, Long	—	—
30.10.94	SD	H	Huddersfield	L	16-24	Kerr (2), Perks	Perks (2)	1287	Bates
6.11.94	SD	A	Dewsbury	W	20-18	Kerr, Perks, Wigglesworth	Perks (3), Blankley (dg), Long (dg)	—	—
13.11.94	SD	H	Hull K.R.	L	24-26	Blankley, Jewitt, Perks,	Perks (4)	531	Asquith
27.11.94	RT(1)	H	Mysons	W	40-14	Garrett (2), Blankley, Kerr, Long, Quinlan, Wigglesworth	Perks (6)	302	Tennant
4.12.94	RT(2)	A	Keighley C.	L	4-28	Long	—	—	—
11.12.94	SD	H	Carlisle	W	34-0	Blankley (2), Kerr (2), Ashton, Bell, Francis	Perks (3)	238	Ollerton
26.12.94	SD	H	Hunslet	L	8-16	Marson	Perks (2)	1200	Burke
2.1.95	SD	A	Batley	L	16-18	Blankley, G. Freeman, Long	Creasser (2)	—	—
8.1.95	SD	H	Ryedale-York	W	27-12	Ashton, Bell, Francis,	Creasser (3), Ashton (dg)	720	Redfearn
15.1.95	SD	A	Barrow	L	20-34	W. Freeman, Greenwood, Kerr	Creasser (4)	—	—
22.1.95	CC(3)	H	Woolston R.	W	42-2	Greenwood (2), Bell, Jewitt, G. Freeman, Quinlan, Sharp	Creasser (7)	238	Steele
29.1.95	SD	H	Swinton	W	30-10	W. Freeman (2), Creasser, Greenwood, Long	Creasser (5)	647	Gilmour
5.2.95	SD	A	Keighley C.	L	8-24	D. Hall, Long	—	—	—
12.2.95	CC(4)	A	Oldham	L	10-70	Greenwood, Perks	Creasser	—	—
6.3.95	SD	A	Highfield	W	30-6	Bailey (3), Craesser, Fisher, Marson	Creasser (3)	—	—
12.3.95	SD	A	Rochdale H.	W	14-8	Blankley (2), Bailey	Creasser	—	—
19.3.95	SD	H	London B.	L	6-38	Fisher	Creasser	550	Redfearn
26.3.95	SD	A	Huddersfield	L	26-42	Thornton (2), Ashton, Freeman, Marson	Creasser (3)	—	—
2.4.95	SD	A	Ryedale-York	L	12-28	Freeman, Garrett	Creasser (2)	—	—
6.4.95	SD	H	Leigh	W	28-24	Blankley, Clarke, Garrett, Marson, Sharp	Creasser (4)	250	Burke
9.4.95	SD	H	Barrow	W	18-8	Fisher, Garrett, Greenwood	Long (3)	250	Nicholson
14.4.95	SD	A	Hunslet	L	20-22	Garrettt (2), Clark, Freeman	Laws (2)	—	—
17.4.95	SD	H	Batley	L	10-18	Francis, Morse	Long	1125	Holdsworth
19.4.95	SD	A	Whitehaven	L	6-50	Finnan	Stead	—	—
23.4.95	SD	H	Rochdale H.	L	20-40	Clarke, Freeman, Long, Quinlan	Stead (2)	538	Galtress

CARLISLE

Ground: Gillford Park (01228-401212)
First Season: 1981-82. Carlisle City entered the League in 1928-29 but withdrew after 10 matches
Chairman: Alan Tucker
Secretary: Doug Fisher

RECORDS
Match
Goals: 10 by Barry Vickers at Nottingham C., 11 Mar 1990
Tries: 4 by Gary Peacham v. Workington T., 25 Jan 1987
Kevin Pape v. Rochdale H., 11 Feb 1987
Points: 24 by Barry Vickers at Nottingham C., 11 Mar 1990
Season
Goals: 113 by Steve Ferres, 1981-82
Tries: 25 by Mick Morgan, 1981-82
Gary Peacham, 1984-85
Points: 242 by Steve Ferres, 1981-82
Career
Goals: 352 by Barry Vickers, 1988-92
Tries: 192 by Kevin Pape, 1984-94
Points: 768 by Kevin Pape, 1984-94
Appearances: 324 by Kevin Pape, 1984-94
Highest score: 60-0 v. Nottingham C., 11 Mar 1990
Highest against: 112-0 at St. Helens, 14 Sep 1986
Attendance: 5,903 v. Workington T. (League), 6 Sep 1981 — at Brunton Park
2,042 v. Workington T. (RL Cup), 30 Jan 1994 — at Gillford Park

COACHING REGISTER
● **Since formation in 1981**

Allan Agar	May 81 - June 82
Mick Morgan	July 82 - Feb 83
John Atkinson	Feb 83 - Feb 86
Alan Kellett	Feb 86 - May 86
Roy Lester	June 86 - Nov 88
Tommy Dawes	Dec 88 - Jan 90
Cameron Bell	Feb 90 - Apr 94
Hugh Waddell	Apr 94 - Dec 94
Paul Charlton	Dec 94 -

1994-95 SIGNINGS REGISTER

Signed	Player	Club From
16.8.94	Farrimond, Jonathan	St. Nicholas Arms ARL
16.8.94	Gardner, Marc	Linton Holme ARL
16.8.94	Knubley, Stuart	Penrith, Aus
16.8.94	Lynch, Matthew	Wigton RU
16.8.94	Pears, Gary	Linton Holme ARL
16.8.94	Quayle, Barry	Frizington ARL
26.8.94	Johnson, Willie	Highfield
3.9.94	*Robinson, Jeff	Chorley
3.11.94	Armstrong, Ian	—
3.11.94	Bitcon, Stephen	—
3.11.94	Brookes, Mark	—
3.11.94	*Newell, John	Workington T.
28.12.94	Dinsdale, Edwin	Whitehaven
6.1.95	Meteer, Paul	Egremont ARL
26.1.95	Ruddy, Gary	Askam ARL
1.2.95	Haile, Gary	Lowca ARL
1.2.95	Thurlow, Jason	Barrow

Tommy Dawes, who experienced a 13-month stint as coach of Carlisle.

CARLISLE 1994-95 PLAYERS' SUMMARY

	Date of Birth	App	T	G	D	Pts	Previous club	Signed
Armstrong, Derek	2.11.66	10+8	3	—	—	12	Hawick RU	20.4.92
Blake, Paul	17.11.70	3	—	—	—	—	Wigton RU	19.8.93
Brierley, Steve	30.3.61	32	1	—	—	4	Platform One ARL	22.8.83
Brookes, Mark	11.3.69	0+1	—	—	—	—		3.11.94
Charlton, Gary	5.3.67	32	6	—	1	25	Whitehaven	27.11.90
Charlton, Jason	29.1.71	17+11	—	—	—	—		
Chorley, Mark	31.8.70	6+3	—	—	—	—	Egremont ARL	27.7.93
Day, Glen		13+2	2	—	—	8		
Dinsdale, Edwin	3.12.67	11+1	1	—	—	4	Whitehaven	28.12.94
Gardner, Marc	2.6.74	6+1	3	—	—	12	Linton Holme ARL	16.8.94
Graham, George	19.1.66	29	7	—	—	28	Stirling County RU	22.10.91
Haile, Gary	30.8.68	4+2	3	—	—	12	Lowca ARL	1.2.95
Holtz, Darren		2+2	—	—	—	—		
Johnson, Willie	26.10.60	10	1	—	—	4	Highfield	26.8.94
Kavanagh, Mike	5.2.71	13	2	2	—	12	Barrow	
Knox, Simon	14.10.72	32	12	—	—	48	Hensingham ARL	1.12.91
Knubley, Stuart	8.9.68	15+4	6	—	—	24	Penrith	16.8.94
Lynch, Matthew	6.12.69	9	—	—	—	—	Wigton RU	16.8.94
McMullen, Alan	1.8.62	1	—	—	—	—	Workington T.	3.10.93
Manning, Phil	23.2.62	14+2	4	—	—	16	Ayr RU	13.8.90
Meteer, Paul	11.2.70	6+3	—	—	—	—	Egremont ARL	6.1.95
Newell, John	10.1.67	6+4	2	—	—	8	Workington T.	3.11.94
Pape, Kevin	17.12.61	7	8	—	—	32	Glasson R. ARL	29.7.84
Paxton, Colin	19.6.71	22	3	—	—	12	Hawick RU	3.1.92
Quayle, Barry	13.1.73	20+3	6	—	—	24	Frizington ARL	16.8.94
Richardson, Willie	6.10.60	34	4	96	—	208	Whitehaven	11.12.92
Robinson, Jeff	9.9.71	10+1	—	—	1	1	Chorley	3.9.94
Ruddy, Gary	9.12.73	3	—	—	—	12	Barrow	26.1.95
Russell, Danny	24.12.69	34	14	—	—	56	Australia	23.8.93
Scott, Tony	17.5.62	7+6	—	—	—	—	Horse & Farrier ARL	9.4.84
Tait, Alan	20.9.67	0+2	—	—	—	—	Carlisle RU	9.1.93
Thurlow, Jason	18.12.69	11	7	—	—	28	Barrow	1.2.95
Underwood, Brian		0+1	—	—	—	—		
Waddell, Hugh	1.9.59	24	8	—	—	32	Sheffield E.	9.1.94
Wikinson, Les	9.4.70	0+2	—	—	—	—	Aspatria H. ARL	9.1.93
Williams, Barry	15.5.71	0+3	—	—	1	1	Broughton Red R. ARL	6.9.89
TOTALS								
36 players			106	98	3	623		

Representative appearances 1994-95
Pape — Cumbria (1); Knox — Cumbria (1).

CARLISLE 1994-95 MATCH ANALYSIS

Date	Competition	H/A	Opponent	Rlt	Score	Tries	Goals	Attendance	Referee
21.8.94	SD	H	London B.	L	16-38	Pape, Graham, Knox	Richardson (2)	408	Cross
28.8.94	SD	A	Batley	L	16-44	G. Charlton, Knox, Russell	Richardson (2)	—	—
4.9.94	SD	H	Bramley	W	15-12	Pape, Waddell	Richardson (3), Williams (dg)	328	Kirkpatrick
11.9.94	SD	A	Rochdale H.	L	32-42	Pape (3), Brierley, Russell	Richardson (6)	—	—
18.9.94	SD	A	Hunslet	W	26-22	Russell (2), G. Charlton, Pape	Richardson (5)	—	—
25.9.94	SD	H	Swinton	L	16-36	G. Charlton, Johnson, Pape	Richardson (2)	410	Ollerton
5.10.94	SD	A	Dewsbury.	L	20-38	Graham (2), Richardson (2)	Richardson (2)	—	—
9.10.94	SD	A	Hull K.R.	L	0-52			—	—
16.10.94	SD	H	Highfield	W	28-8	Waddell (2), D. Armstrong, Pape	Richardson (6)	324	Lee
30.10.94	SD	A	Keighley C.	L	14-46	Knox, Waddell	Richardson (3)	—	—
6.11.94	SD	A	London B.	L	16-23	Quayle, Russell	Richardson (4)	—	—
13.11.94	SD	H	Batley	L	12-26	Knox, Russell	Richardson (2)	370	Redfearn
27.11.94	RT(1)	H	Dudley Hill	W	25-12	Newall (2), D. Armstrong Knox	Richardson (4) Robinson (dg)	206	McGregor
3.12.94	RT(2)	H	Dewsbury	L	16-30	D. Armstrong, Knox, Quayle	Richardson (2)	287	Redfearn
11.12.94	SD	A	Bramley	L	0-34	—	—	—	—
18.12.94	SD	H	Rochdale H.	L	16-18	Kavanagh, Knox	Richardson (4)	205	Gilmour
26.12.94	SD	H	Barrow	W	22-20	Graham, Knox, Knubley, Waddell	Richardson (3)	294	Burke
31.12.94	SD	A	Whitehaven	L	4-36	Waddell	—	—	—
8.1.95	SD	H	Huddersfield	L	20-26	Russell, Thurlow, Waddell	Richardson (4)	416	Kirkpatrick
15.1.95	SD	A	Leigh	L	20-32	Graham, Knox, Russell Waddell	Richardson (2)	—	—
22.1.95	CC(3)	H	Dudley Hill	W	34-4	Knubley (2), G. Charlton Kavanagh, Quayle, Richardson	Richardson (5)	204	Tennant
29.1.95	SD	H	Hunslet	L	12-32	Ruddy (3)	—	260	Steele
5.2.95	SD	A	Swinton	L	18-40	Dinsdale, Knox, Quayle	Richardson (3)	—	—
12.2.95	CC(4)	H	Widnes	L	2-40		Richardson	615	R. Connolly
19.2.95	SD	H	Dewsbury	L	10-36	Russell, Thurlow	Richardson	287	Atkin
6.3.95	SD	H	Hull K.R.	L	32-40	Quayle (2), G. Charlton,, Graham, Thurlow	Richardson (6)	255	Presley
12.3.95	SD	A	Ryedale-York	L	22-49	Gardner (2), Knubley, Thurlow	Richardson (3)	—	—
19.3.95	SD	A	Highfield	W	56-14	Knubley (2), Thurlow (2), Day, Graham, Haile, Knox, Paxton, Russell	Richardson (6), Kavanagh (2)	—	—
26.3.95	SD	H	Keighley C.	W	12-2	Manning, Russell	Richardson (2)	989	Cross
2.4.95	SD	A	Huddersfield	L	24-36	Manning (2), Paxton, Russell	Richardson (4)	—	—
9.4.95	SD	H	Leigh	W	22-20	G. Charlton, Haile, Paxton, Thurlow	Richardson (3)	219	Carter
14.4.95	SD	A	Barrow	L	6-14	Russell	Richardson	—	—
17.4.95	SD	H	Whitehaven	W	16-13	Gardner, Haile, Knox	Richardson (2)	624	Galtress
23.4.95	SD	H[1]	Ryedale-York	L	23-28	Day, Manning, Richardson Russell	Richardson (3), Charlton (dg)	246	McGregor

H[1] at Gateshead

CASTLEFORD

Ground: Wheldon Road (01977-552674)
First Season: 1926-27. There was also a
Castleford team from 1896-97 to
1905-06 inclusive
Nickname: Tigers
Secretary: Denise Cackett
Honours: **Championship** Beaten finalists,
1938-39, 1968-69
Challenge Cup Winners, 1934-35,
1968-69, 1969-70, 1985-86
Beaten finalists, 1991-92
Regal Trophy Winners, 1976-77,
1993-94
Premiership Beaten finalists,
1983-84, 1993-94
Yorkshire Cup Winners, 1977-78,
1981-82, 1986-87, 1990-91, 1991-92
Beaten finalists, 1948-49, 1950-51,
1968-69, 1971-72, 1983-84,
1985-86, 1987-88, 1988-89
Yorkshire League Winners,
1932-33, 1938-39, 1964-65
Eastern Division Championship
Beaten finalists, 1963-64
Charity Shield Beaten finalists,
1986-87
BBC2 Floodlit Trophy Winners,
1965-66, 1966-67, 1967-68, 1976-77

RECORDS
Match
Goals: 17 by Geoff "Sammy" Lloyd v. Millom,
16 Sep 1973
Tries: 5 by Derek Foster v. Hunslet,
10 Nov 1972
John Joyner v. Millom, 16 Sep 1973
Steve Fenton v. Dewsbury,
27 Jan 1978
Ian French v. Hunslet, 9 Feb 1986
St. John Ellis at Whitehaven,
10 Dec 1989
Points: 43 by Geoff "Sammy" Lloyd v. Millom,
16 Sep 1973

Season
Goals: 158 by Geoff "Sammy" Lloyd, 1976-77
Tries: 40 by St. John Ellis, 1993-94
Points: 334 by Bob Beardmore, 1983-84
Career
Goals: 875 by Albert Lunn, 1951-63
Tries: 206 by Alan Hardisty, 1958-71
Points: 1,870 by Albert Lunn, 1951-63
Appearances: 585+28 by John Joyner, 1973-92
Highest score: 94-12 v. Huddersfield,
18 Sep 1988
Highest against: 62-12 at St. Helens,
16 Apr 1986
Attendance: 25,449 v. Hunslet (RL Cup),
9 Mar 1935

COACHING REGISTER
● **Since 1974-75**
Dave Cox   Apr 74 - Nov 74
*Malcolm Reilly   Dec 74 - May 87
Dave Sampson   May 87 - Apr 88
Darryl Van de Velde   July 88 - May 93
John Joyner   May 93 -
*Shortly after his appointment Reilly returned
to Australia to fulfil his contract before
resuming at Castleford early the next season.*

*A 1994-95 tally of 22 tries in 36 games for Castleford
scrum half Tony Smith.*

GREAT BRITAIN REGISTER
(28 players)

Arthur Atkinson	(11)	1929-36
Kevin Beardmore	(13+1)	1984-90
Bill Bryant	(4+1)	1964-67
Lee Crooks	(5)	1992-94
Jim Croston	(1)	1937
Bernard Cunniffe	(1)	1937
Billy Davies	(1)	1933
Derek Edwards	(3+2)	1968-71
St. John Ellis	(+3)	1991-94
Keith England	(6+5)	1987-91
Mike Ford	(+2)	1993
Alan Hardisty	(12)	1964-70
Dennis Hartley	(9)	1968-70
Keith Hepworth	(11)	1967-70
Shaun Irwin	(+4)	1990
John Joyner	(14+2)	1978-84
Brian Lockwood	(7)	1972-74
Tony Marchant	(3)	1986
Roger Millward	(1)	1966
Steve Norton	(2+1)	1974
David Plange	(1)	1988
Malcolm Reilly	(9)	1970
Peter Small	(1)	1962
Graham Steadman	(9+1)	1990-94
Gary Stephens	(5)	1979
Doug Walton	(1)	1965
Johnny Ward	(3)	1963-64
Kevin Ward	(14)	1984-89

1994-95 SIGNINGS REGISTER

Signed	Player	Club From
23.6.94	Ellerker, Martin	Redhill ARL
1.7.94	Hill, Andrew	Kippax ARL
11.7.94	Stephens, Gareth	Leeds
17.7.94	Goddard, Richard	Wakefield T.
13.9.94	*Morris, Lynton	Wakefield T.
28.9.94	Strong, David	Kippax ARL
12.10.94	Eden, Phil	Wakefield T.
19.1.95	*Sampson, Lee	Hunslet
20.1.95	Palmer, Craig	Featherstone R.
17.2.95	Harland, Lee	Halifax
22.3.95	Oldfield, David	Redhill ARL
28.3.95	*Sharp, Tim	Ryedale-York
10.4.95	Skidmore, Andrew	—

Castleford loose forward Tawera Nikau, scorer of eight tries in 1994-95.

CASTLEFORD 1994-95 PLAYERS' SUMMARY

	Date of Birth	App	T	G	D	Pts	Previous club	Signed
Blackmore, Richard	2.7.69	37	24	—	—	96	New Zealand	17.7.91
Coventry, James	9.2.77	2+6	—	—	—	—	Castleford Academy	9.2.94
Crooks, Lee	18.9.63	30+1	2	111	—	230	Leeds	8.1.90
Darley, Paul	26.1.74	5+1	—	—	—	—	Kippax Welfare ARL	18.9.92
Eden, Phil	13.12.63	1+4	3	—	—	12	Wakefield T.	12.10.94
Flowers, Jason	30.1.75	14+6	2	—	—	8	Redhill ARL	12.5.93
Flowers, Stuart	18.4.71	0+2	1	—	—	4	Fryston ARL	17.1.94
Goddard, Richard	28.4.74	25+5	10	—	—	40	Wakefield T.	17.7.94
Harland, Lee	4.9.73	3+3	2	—	—	8	Halifax	17.2.95
Hay, Andy	5.11.73	31+3	10	—	—	40	Redhill ARL	12.11.90
Kemp, Tony	18.1.68	36	18	4	2	82	Australia	25.7.93
Ketteridge, Martin	2.10.64	16+4	—	25	—	50	Moorends ARL	22.6.83
McAllister, Terry	29.9.71	0+1	—	—	—	—	Redhill ARL	10.3.89
Middleton, Simon	2.2.66	30+2	17	1	—	70	Knottingley RU	20.4.91
Morris, Lynton	18.5.72	0+1	—	—	—	—	Wakefield T.	13.9.94
Morrison, Tony	17.12.65	21+5	5	—	—	20	Swinton	27.5.92
Nikau, Tawera	1.1.67	32	8	—	—	32	Ryedale-York	19.8.91
Palmer, Craig	3.1.71	0+1	—	—	—	—	Featherstone ARL	20.1.95
Price, Simon	15.11.73	1	—	—	—	—	East Leeds ARL	14.9.91
Russell, Richard	24.11.69	31	2	—	—	8	Oldham	13.8.93
Sampson, Dean	27.6.67	30	11	—	—	44	Stanley R. ARL	1.9.86
Smales, Ian	26.9.68	15+2	—	—	—	—	Featherstone R.	21.8.93
Smith, Chris	31.10.75	36	17	—	—	68	Redhill ARL	28.1.92
Smith, Tony	16.7.70	36	22	—	—	88	Wheldale ARL	25.1.88
Steadman, Graham	8.12.61	23+3	14	16	2	90	Featherstone R.	23.8.89
Stephens, Gareth	15.4.74	5+2	1	—	—	4	Leeds	11.7.94
Sykes, Nathan	8.9.74	6+19	—	—	—	—	Moldgreen ARL	14.9.91
Tonks, Ian	13.2.76	0+1	—	—	—	—	Redhill ARL	13.2.93
Wray, Jon	19.5.70	15+1	4	—	—	16	Morley RU	24.10.90
TOTALS								
29 players			173	157	4	1,010		

Representative appearances 1994-95
Steadman — Britain (1); Russell — England (1); Goddard — England (1), GB Under-21s (2); Hay — GB Under-21s (1); T. Smith — England (+1); C. Smith — GB Under-21s (2).

CASTLEFORD 1994-95 MATCH ANALYSIS

Date	Competition	H/A	Opponent	Rlt	Score	Tries	Goals	Attendance	Referee
21.8.94	SBC	A	Widnes	W	30-16	Blackmore, Kemp, Middleton, T. Smith, Steadman	Crooks (5)	—	—
28.8.94	SBC	H	Workington T.	W	26-14	C. Smith (2), Middleton (2), Kemp	Crooks (3)	4951	Ollerton
4.9.94	SBC	A	Hull	W	48-18	Kemp (3), Hay, Middleton, Nikau, T. Smith, Steadman	Ketteridge (6), Crooks (2)	—	—
11.9.94	SBC	H	Sheffield E.	W	28-9	Steadman (2), Blackmore, Nikau, C. Smith	Ketteridge (2), Steadman (2)	4231	Campbell

(Continued)

Date	Competition	H/A	Opponent	Rlt	Score	Tries	Goals	Attendance	Referee
18.9.94	SBC	A	St. Helens	L	14-47	Hay, Stephens	Crooks (2), Ketteridge	—	—
23.9.94	SBC	H	Wigan	L	28-31	Goddard (2), Nikau, Sampson T. Smith	Ketteridge (3), Steadman	6665	Campbell
30.9.94	SBC	A	Leeds	D	14-14	Goddard, Sampson	Crooks (3)	—	—
9.10.94	SBC	H	Salford	W	34-6	Blackmore, Crooks, Russell, Sampson, T. Smith, Steadman	Crooks (4), Steadman	4036	R. Connolly
12.10.94	Tour	H	Australia	L	12-38	Blackmore, Eden, C. Smith		11,091	J. Connolly
16.10.94	SBC	A	Doncaster	L	28-35	Wray (2), Russell, Sampson Steadman	Ketteridge (4)	—	—
30.10.94	SBC	H	Bradford N.	W	39-18	Blackmore, Hay, Kemp, Sampson, C. Smith, T. Smith Steadman	Ketteridge (3), Steadman (2, 1dg)	6319	R. Connolly
6.11.94	SBC	H	Widnes	W	26-6	Eden (2), Blackmore	Crooks (7)	4196	Ollerton
13.11.94	SBC	A	Workington T.	D	4-4		Crooks (2)	—	—
27.11.94	SBC	H	Hull	W	52-10	T. Smith (2), Steadman (2), Kemp, Sampson, C. Smith, Wray	Crooks (10)	4726	Cummings
3.12.94	RT(2)	H	Halifax	W	32-26	Blackmore (2), C. Smith (2), Kemp, Sampson	Crooks (4)	4740	Campbell
9.12.94	SBC	A	Sheffield E.	W	27-16	T. Smith, Middleton, Blackmore (2), Goddard	Crooks (3), Steadman (dg)	—	—
20.12.94	RT(3)	A	Dewsbury	W	30-2	Blackmore, Goddard, Kemp, Middleton, T. Smith	Crooks (3), Steadman (2)	—	—
26.12.94	SBC	H	Featherstone R.	W	32-16	Middleton (2), J. Flowers, Kemp, Steadman, Wray	Crooks (4)	8807	Cummings
7.1.95	RT(4)	A	Leeds	W	34-14	T. Smith (2), Middleton, Morrison, Sampson	Crooks (5), Ketteridge (2)	—	—
15.1.95	RT(SF)	A	Wigan	L	6-34	Kemp	Crooks	—	—
18.1.95	SBC	A	Warrington	L	24-25	C. Smith (2), Middleton, Nikau	Ketteridge (4)	—	—
22.1.95	SBC	A	Halifax	L	24-30	Blackmore, Kemp, Sampson, C. Smith	Crooks (4)	—	—
29.1.95	SBC	H	St. Helens	W	18-16	Middleton, C. Smith	Crooks (5)	5345	Bates
5.2.95	SBC	A	Wigan	L	6-46	Hay	Crooks	—	—
12.2.95	CC(4)	A	Warrington	L	2-17	—	Crooks	—	—
17.2.95	SBC	H	Leeds	L	16-22	Hay, T. Smith	Crooks (4)	6426	Morris
26.2.95	SBC	A	Wakefield T.	W	36-25	Blackmore (2), S. Flowers, Goddard, Kemp, Middleton, Nikau	Crooks (3), Steadman	—	—
12.3.95	SBC	A	Salford	W	48-16	Blackmore (2), Hay (2), C. Smith (2), Middleton, Steadman	Crooks (7), Kemp	—	—
15.3.95	SBC	H	Oldham	W	34-14	Blackmore, Kemp, Morrison, Sampson, Steadman	Crooks (6), Steadman	3422	Asquith
19.3.95	SBC	H	Halifax	W	16-13	Kemp, Morrison, Sampson	Crooks (2)	5716	Morris
31.3.95	SBC	H	Warrington	L	24-37	S. Flowers, Middleton, Morrison, T. Smith	Crooks (4)	3563	Morris
9.4.95	SBC	H	Doncaster	W	25-18	T. Smith (4)	Crooks (4), Kemp (dg)	3515	Lee
14.4.95	SBC	A	Featherstone R.	W	27-6	Crooks, Goddard, Harland, Kemp	Crooks (4), Middleton, Kemp (dg)	—	—
17.4.95	SBC	H	Wakefield T.	W	86-0	Blackmore (3), Hay (2), Kemp (2), Middleton (2), C. Smith (2), T. Smith (2), Goddard, Harland, Nikau, Steadman	Steadman (6), Kemp (3)	4443	R. Connolly
20.4.95	SBC	A	Oldham	W	18-10	Hay, Morrison, C. Smith	Crooks (3)	—	—
23.4.95	SBC	A	Bradford N.	W	40-26	Blackmore (2), Nikau (2), T. Smith (2), Goddard, Steadman	Crooks (4)	—	—
7.5.95	PT(1)	H	Warrington	L	22-30	Blackmore (2), Goddard, Middleton, T. Smith	Crooks	5462	Morris

DEWSBURY

Ground: Crown Flatt, Owl Lane
(01924-465489)
First Season: 1901-02
Chairman: Ken Davies
Honours: **Championship** Winners, 1972-73
Beaten finalists, 1946-47
War Emergency League
Winners, 1941-42 (1942-43 won
final but championship declared
null and void because Dewsbury
played an ineligible player.)
Beaten finalists, 1943-44
Division Two Champions, 1904-05
Challenge Cup Winners, 1911-12,
1942-43
Beaten finalists, 1928-29
Yorkshire Cup Winners, 1925-26,
1927-28, 1942-43
Beaten finalists, 1918-19, 1921-22,
1940-41, 1972-73
Yorkshire League Winners, 1946-47
BBC2 Floodlit Trophy Beaten
finalists, 1975-76

RECORDS
Match
Goals: 13 by Greg Pearce at Blackpool G.,
4 Apr 1993
Tries: 8 by Dai Thomas v. Liverpool C.,
13 Apr 1907
Points: 32 by Les Holliday v. Barrow,
11 Sep 1994
Season
Goals: 145 by Nigel Stephenson, 1972-73
Tries: 40 by Dai Thomas, 1906-07
Points: 368 by Nigel Stephenson, 1972-73
Career
Goals: 863 by Nigel Stephenson, 1967-78 &
1984-86
Tries: 144 by Joe Lyman, 1913-31
Points: 2,082 by Nigel Stephenson, 1967-78 &
1984-86
Appearances: 454 by Joe Lyman, 1913-31

Highest score: 90-5 at Blackpool G., 4 Apr 1993
Highest against: 82-0 at Widnes, 30 Nov 1986
Attendance: 26,584 v. Halifax (Yorks Cup),
30 Oct 1920 — at Crown Flatt

COACHING REGISTER
● **Since 1974-75**

Maurice Bamford	June 74 - Oct 74
Alan Hardisty	Oct 74 - June 75
Dave Cox	June 75 - July 77
Ron Hill	July 77 - Dec 77
Lewis Jones	Dec 77 - Apr 78
Jeff Grayshon	May 78 - Oct 78
Alan Lockwood	Oct 78 - Oct 80
Bernard Watson	Oct 80 - Oct 82
Ray Abbey	Nov 82 - Apr 83
*Tommy Smales	May 83 - Feb 84
Jack Addy	Feb 84 - Jan 87
Dave Busfield	Jan 87 - Apr 87
Terry Crook	Apr 87 - Dec 88
Maurice Bamford	Dec 88 - Dec 90
Jack Addy	Dec 90 - Aug 93
Norman Smith	Aug 93 - Apr 95
Tony Fisher	Apr 95 -

Ex-forward

GREAT BRITAIN REGISTER
(**6 players**)

Alan Bates	(2+2)	1974
Frank Gallagher	(4)	1920-21
Jim Ledgard	(2)	1947
Roy Pollard	(1)	1950
Mick Stephenson	(5+1)	1971-72
Harry Street	(4)	1950

1994-95 SIGNINGS REGISTER

Signed	Player	Club From
21.7.94	Fisher, Andy	Castleford
25.7.94	Crouthers, Kevin	Stanley R. ARL
5.8.94	Bonson, Paul	Hunslet
8.8.94	Bates, Ian	Rochdale H.
29.10.94	McKelvie, Danny	Ryedale-York
18.11.94	Palmer, Glen	North Harbour, NZ
1.12.94	Wood, Daniel	Hunslet Boys ARL
3.1.95	Johnston, Lyndon	Ossett T. ARL
18.3.95	Firth, Jason	Thornhill ARL
2.4.95	*Kibe, Eric	Hunslet
3.4.95	Turner, Robert	Doncaster

DEWSBURY 1994-95 PLAYERS' SUMMARY

	Date of Birth	App	T	G	D	Pts	Previous club	Signed
Agar, Richard	20.1.72	26+4	4	102	—	220	Travellers Sts.	26.8.93
Bates, Ian	2.3.68	29+1	5	—	—	20	Rochdale H.	8.8.94
Bell, Glen	26.3.65	4+3	1	—	—	4	New Zealand	10.8.91
Bonson, Paul	18.10.71	17+4	—	—	—	—	Hunslet	5.8.94
Charles, Marquis	5.12.66	2+1	2	8	—	24	Bramley	24.12.91
Cocks, Mark	12.5.74	4	—	—	—	—	Redhill ARL	17.6.91
Collins, Darren	7.3.73	4+1	1	—	—	4	Clayton ARL	26.5.92
Conway, Mark	31.1.64	2+1	—	2	—	4	Wakefield T.	22.6.93
Cornforth, Phil	16.11.69	20+2	5	—	—	20	Bradford N.	1.6.92
Crouthers, Kevin	3.1.76	9+2	4	—	—	16	Stanley R. ARL	25.7.94
Delaney, Paul	18.10.68	26	4	—	—	16	Leeds	21.5.91
Dickinson, Andy	26.8.61	9+6	—	—	—	—	Huddersfield	1.7.90
Ellis, John	12.11.66	2	—	—	—	—	York	15.9.89
Fisher, Andy	17.11.67	33	15	—	—	60	Castleford	21.7.94
Graham, Nathan	23.11.71	34	12	5	—	58	Dewsbury Colts	23.11.89
Haigh, Mark	24.1.70	4+2	—	—	—	—	Hanging Heaton ARL	26.7.89
Holliday, Les	8.8.62	26+1	9	21	1	79	Widnes	14.6.93
Johnston, Lyndon	24.1.68	2	—	—	—	—	Ossett Trinity ARL	3.1.95
Jordan, Trent	31.7.69	9+5	2	—	—	8	Highfield	2.3.94
Kelly, Neil	10.5.62	9+10	2	—	—	8	Wakefield T.	31.10.88
Kibe, Eric	23.3.71	4	1	—	—	4	Hunslet	2.4.95
Longo, Davide	9.12.75	31	20	—	2	82	Stanley R. ARL	1.7.93
McCrae, Ian	13.12.71	5+3	1	—	—	4	Wigan	11.2.93
McKelvie, Danny	10.10.69	20+3	3	—	—	12	Ryedale-York	29.10.94
Marchant, Tony	22.12.62	21+2	13	—	—	52	Bradford N.	13.1.94
North, Chris	6.1.76	5	3	—	—	12	Stanley ARL	27.4.94
Palmer, Glen	2.4.70	2+4	—	—	—	—	New Zealand	18.11.94
Parker, Russell	2.7.71	9+1	3	—	—	12	Redhill ARL	19.8.92
Rogers, Darren	6.5.74	16	6	—	—	24	Stanley R. ARL	31.5.91
Rombo, Eddie	19.3.67	32	21	—	—	84	Leeds	28.11.91
Shuttleworth, Paul	18.3.64	1	—	—	—	—	Salford	14.6.85
Turner, Robert	14.3.69	5	1	1	1	7	Doncaster	3.4.95
Williams, Shane	20.10.71	23+10	11	—	—	44	Dewsbury C. ARL	1.6.92
Worthy, Paul	14.5.68	23+6	5	—	—	20	Leeds	21.5.91
TOTALS								
34 players			154	139	4	898		

DEWSBURY 1994-95 MATCH ANALYSIS

Date	Competition	H/A	Opponent	Rlt	Score	Tries	Goals	Attendance	Referee
21.8.94	SD	A	Bramley	W	22-15	Longo (2), Marchant, Williams	Holliday (3)	—	—
4.9.94	SD	A	Leigh	L	12-22	Fisher, Graham	Holliday (2)	—	—
11.9.94	SD	H	Barrow	W	76-8	Holliday (3), Longo (2), Marchant (2), Williams (2), Bates, Cornforth, McRae, Rogers, Rombo	Holliday (10)	3427	Atkin
18.9.94	SD	A	Keighley C.	L	8-46	Rombo	Holliday (2)	—	—
25.9.94	SD	H	Highfield	W	60-0	Marchant (3), Fisher (2), Graham (2), Rombo (2), Bates Longo, Rogers	Holliday (4), Graham (2)	1259	Galtress
5.10.94	SD	H	Carlisle	W	38-20	Agar, Bates, Delaney, Fisher Longo, Marchant, Williams	Agar (5)	1014	McGregor
9.10.94	SD	H	London B.	W	23-8	Graham, Holliday, Longo, Williams	Agar (3), Holliday (dg)	1543	Gilmour
16.10.94	SD	A	Ryedale-York	W	30-22	Collins, Fisher, Graham, Longo, Parker	Agar (5)	—	—
25.10.94	SD	H	Swinton	W	30-4	Delaney, Fisher, Graham, Parker, Rombo	Agar (5)	2022	Galtress
30.10.94	SD	H	Hull K.R.	W	20-6	Bell, Rombo, Worthy	Agar (3), Graham	2429	Burke
6.11.94	SD	H	Bramley	L	18-20	Cornforth, Fisher, Marchant	Agar (3)	1889	Kirkpatrick
13.11.94	SD	A	Swinton	W	24-12	Graham, Longo, Marchant	Agar (6)	—	—
20.11.94	RT(1)	H	XIII Catalan (Fr)	W	22-4	Rombo (3)	Agar (5)	1196	Asquith
3.12.94	RT(2)	A	Carlisle	W	30-16	Fisher, Graham, Holliday, McKelvie, Parker, Rombo	Agar (3)	—	—
11.12.94	SD	H	Leigh	L	6-16		Agar (3)	1444	Burke
20.12.94	RT(3)	H	Castleford	L	2-30		Agar	3325	Ollerton
26.12.94	SD	H	Batley	W	16-0	Bates, Longo, Williams	Agar (2)	3995	Bates
1.1.95	SD	A[1]	Hunslet	W	18-16	Longo, Rombo	Agar (5)	—	—
4.1.95	SD	A	Barrow	W	24-14	Agar, Longo, Crouthers, Marchant	Agar (4)	—	—
8.1.95	SD	A	Rochdale H.	L	20-21	Agar, Graham, Longo, Rombo	Agar (2)	—	—
15.1.95	SD	H	Whitehaven	L	8-18	Rombo	Agar (2)	1197	Atkin
3.2.95	CC(3)	H	Kells	W	72-12	Longo (2), Marchant (2), Cornforth, Crouthers, Delaney, Fisher, Graham, Holliday, McKelvie, Rombo, Worthy	Agar (10)	439	Cross
5.2.95	SD	A	Highfield	W	68-12	Longo (2), Williams (2), Cornforth, Crouthers, Delaney, Graham, Marchant, McKelvie, Rombo, Worthy	Agar (10)	—	—
12.2.95	CC(4)	A	Keighley C.	L	12-24	Rombo	Agar (4)	—	—
19.2.95	SD	A	Carlisle	W	36-10	Longo (2), Agar, Cornforth, Holliday, Jordan, Kelly	Agar (4)	—	—
6.3.95	SD	A	London B.	L	16-22	Rombo (2), Crouthers, Jordan		—	—
22.3.95	SD	H	Keighley C.	W	20-2	Graham, Kelly, Rombo	Agar (4)	2424	Lee
26.3.95	SD	A	Hull K.R.	L	4-20	Holliday		—	—
29.3.95	SD	H	Huddersfield	L	12-40	Holliday, Rogers	Agar (2)	2047	Oddy
2.4.95	SD	H	Rochdale H.	L	10-30	Fisher	Agar (3)	1169	Oddy
4.4.95	SD	H	Ryedale-York	D	9-9	Rombo	Conway (2), Turner (dg)	926	Gilmour
9.4.95	SD	A	Whitehaven	L	12-37	Fisher, Williams	Graham (2)	—	—
14.4.95	SD	A	Batley	L	6-46	Fisher	Agar	—	—
17.4.95	SD	H	Hunslet	W	46-16	Williams (2), Charles, Fisher, Rogers, Rombo, Turner, Worthy	Agar (7)	1105	Nicholson
23.4.95	SD	A	Huddersfield	W	52-26	North (2), Fisher, Rogers (2), Bates, Kibe, Longo, Worthy	Charles (6), Turner, Longo (2dg)	—	—
7.5.95	SDP(1)	A	Batley	L	16-20	Charles, Fisher, North	Charles (2)	—	—

A[1] at Elland Road, Leeds

DONCASTER

Ground: Tattersfield (as at end of 1994-95)
First Season: 1951-52
Nickname: Dons

RECORDS
Match
Goals: 12 by Tony Zelei v. Nottingham C.,
   1 Sep 1991
   Robert Turner v. Highfield,
   20 Mar 1994
Tries: 5 by Carl Hall v. Mysons
   31 Oct 1993
Points: 32 by Tony Zelei v. Nottingham C.,
   1 Sep 1991
Season
Goals: 123 by Robert Turner, 1993-94
Tries: 21 by Mark Roache, 1989-90
Points: 272 by Robert Turner, 1993-94
Career
Goals: 850 by David Noble, 1976-77, 1980-89
   & 1992
Tries: 104 by Mark Roache, 1985-
Points: 1,751 by David Noble, 1976-77, 1980-89
   & 1992
Appearances: 305+15 by David Noble, 1976-77,
   1980-89 & 1992
Highest score: 96-0 v. Highfield, 20 Mar 1994
Highest against: 75-3 v. Leigh, 28 Mar 1976
Attendance: 6,440 v. Leeds (League),
   4 Sep 1994 — at Tattersfield
   10,000 v. Bradford N. (RL Cup),
   16 Feb 1952 - at York Road Stadium

COACHING REGISTER
● **Since 1974-75**

Ted Strawbridge	Feb 73 - Apr 75
Derek Edwards	July 75 - Nov 76
Don Robson	Nov 76 - Sep 77
Trevor Lowe	Sep 77 - Apr 79
*Tommy Smales	Feb 78 - Apr 79
Billy Yates	Apr 79 - May 79
Don Vines	Sep 79 - Jan 80
Bill Kenny	June 80 - May 81
Alan Rhodes	Aug 81 - Mar 83
Clive Sullivan	Mar 83 - May 84
John Sheridan	June 84 - Nov 87
Graham Heptinstall	Nov 87 - Jan 88
John Sheridan	Jan 88 - Apr 89
Dave Sampson	May 89 - Jan 92
Geoff Morris	Jan 92 - Nov 92
Tony Fisher	Nov 92 - Dec 94
Ian Brooke	Dec 94 -

*Ex-forward, who shared the coaching post
with Trevor Lowe for just over a year.*

1994-95 SIGNINGS REGISTER

Signed	Player	Club From
13.6.94	Foster, Matthew	Featherstone Academy
14.6.94	Gay, Mark	Queensbury ARL
16.6.94	Barrens, Neil	ARL
17.6.94	Williamson, Leon	Eastmoor ARL
1.7.94	Lynch, Gordon	Wakefield Academy
24.8.94	Jackson, Wayne	Hull K.R.
11.8.94	Grobellaar, Pierre	South Africa
6.9.94	Farrar, Mark	Otley RU
7.9.94	Okiwe, Anderson	Nottingham C.
14.9.94	Manning, Terry	Featherstone R.
23.9.94	Osborne, Jason	NZ
30.9.94	Elridge, Jon	ARL
30.9.94	*Neal, Mike	Wigan
30.9.94	Whiteley, Chris	London B.
14.10.94	Frankland, Nick	ARL
8.11.94	Maskill, Colin	Leeds
22.12.94	Marsh, Anthony	Stanley R. ARL
23.12.94	*Hayes, Bradley	Sheffield E.

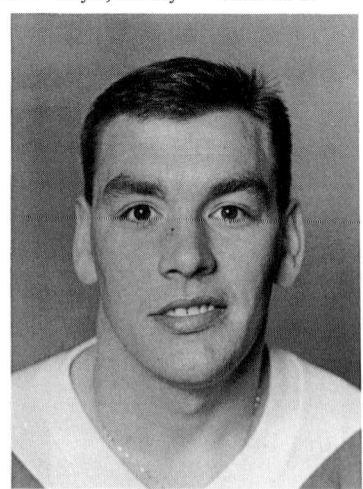

*Hooker Colin Maskill, a November 1994 recruit by
Doncaster from Leeds.*

DONCASTER 1994-95 PLAYERS' SUMMARY

	Date of Birth	App	T	G	D	Pts	Previous club	Signed
Barron, Neil		1+1	—	—	—	—		
Beardmore, Paul	5.5.70	0+1	—	—	—	—		8.7.87
Bloem, Jamie	26.5.71	10	9	—	—	36	Oldham	1.9.93
Bowes, Tony	14.6.70	5	1	—	—	4	Walnut Warriors ARL	4.1.92
Bramley, Darren		1+2	1	—	—	4		
Carlyle, Brendan	25.12.68	18+6	4	—	—	16	Hull	25.11.93
Eaton, Barry	30.9.73	13	3	3	—	18	ARL	13.8.93
Ellis, John	12.11.66	0+9	2	—	—	8	ARL	1.9.93
Elridge, John	21.1.73	2	—	—	—	—	ARL	30.9.94
Evans, David	17.6.69	22+1	5	—	—	20	Staffs. Poly ARL	3.1.92
Evans, John	22.7.62	0+2	—	—	—	—	Bentley ARL	25.8.87
Farrar, Mark	27.7.68	10	2	—	—	8	Otley RU	6.9.94
Fletcher, Ian	4.3.65	0+3	—	—	—	—	York	28.3.89
Foster, Mathew	10.6.76	6+1	1	—	—	4	Featherstone R. Academy	13.6.94
Frankland, Nick	11.8.70	0+1	—	—	—	—	Featherstone M. ARL	14.10.94
Green, Alex	9.2.71	29+1	5	74	3	171	Bradford N.	10.2.93
Grobellaar, Pierre		2+1	—	—	—	—	South Africa	11.8.94
Hayes, Brad	22.4.67	16	2	—	—	8	Sheffield E.	23.12.94
Jackson, Wayne	19.9.67	17+1	1	—	—	4	Hull K.R.	24.5.94
Lingard, Glynn	1.1.69	29+1	2	—	—	8	Scarborough P.	15.9.92
Lynch, Gordon	8.4.75	2+4	—	—	—	—	Wakefield Academy	1.7.94
Manning, Terry	4.12.65	22+1	4	—	—	16	Featherstone R.	14.9.94
Maskill, Colin	15.3.64	19	—	—	—	—	Leeds	8.11.94
Matautia, Vila	31.8.69	22	4	—	1	17	New Zealand	1.12.93
Miller, Tony	30.3.68	27+1	3	—	—	12	Oldham	14.2.91
Neal, Mike	4.9.73	13+1	8	—	—	32	Wigan	30.9.94
Okiwe, Anderson	4.5.64	2	—	—	—	—	Nottingham C.	7.9.94
Osborne, Jason		2	—	—	—	—	New Zealand	23.9.94
Pell, Richard	17.10.66	1+1	—	—	—	—	Cutsyke ARL	3.1.92
Pennant, Audley	26.2.63	23+6	7	—	—	28	Bradford N.	24.9.85
Roache, Mark	24.10.62	5	—	—	—	—	Castleford	2.9.85
Rothwell, Andy	5.9.67	16	3	—	—	12	Moorends ARL	4.1.94
Rowse, Martin	8.3.69	1	—	—	—	—	Leeds	3.1.92
Stimpson, Mark	7.5.72	2	—	—	—	—		
Thornton, Wayne	31.8.66	3+4	—	—	—	—	Castleford	13.8.92
Tomlinson, Maxwell	12.4.70	9+2	1	—	—	4	Moortown RU	1.10.93
Tuffs, Simon	3.2.65	7+1	—	—	—	—		
Turner, Robert	14.3.69	11+3	1	—	1	5	Warrington	8.8.93
Whakarau, Sonny	13.1.66	29+1	8	—	—	32	Bramley	14.7.93
Whiteley, Chris	31.1.67	2	—	—	—	—	London B.	30.9.94
Williamson, Leon	22.8.74	8	3	—	—	12	Eastmoor ARL	17.6.94
Zelei, Tony	5.1.68	9+7	4	—	—	16	Wakefield T.	23.3.90
TOTALS								
42 players			84	77	5	495		

DONCASTER 1994-95 MATCH ANALYSIS

Date	Com-petition	H/A	Opponent	Rlt	Score	Tries	Goals	Atten-dance	Referee
21.8.94	SBC	A	St. Helens	W	29-30	Bloem (2), Matautia, Pennant Whakarau	Green (4, 1dg)	—	—
26.8.94	SBC	H	Widnes	W	21-6	Evans, Bloem (2), Green	Green (2, 1dg)	3221	Holdsworth
4.9.94	SBC	H	Leeds	L	6-16	Pennant	Green	6440	Ollerton
11.9.94	SBC	H	Wakefield T.	W	22-10	Ellis (2), Pennant, Whakarau	Green (3)	3977	Tennant
18.9.94	SBC	A	Oldham	L	8-44	Lingard	Green (2)	—	—
25.9.94	SBC	H	Warrington	L	8-30	Pennant	Green (2)	3299	Morris
2.10.94	SBC	A	Salford	L	12-22	Farrar, Turner	Green (2)	—	—
9.10.94	SBC	H	Halifax	L	0-72			4384	Atkin
16.10.94	SBC	H	Castleford	W	35-28	Bloem (3), Carlyle, Matautia, Neal	Green (5), Turner (dg)	3767	Cross
30.10.94	SBC	A	Workington T.	L	16-19	Matautia, Neal	Green (4)	—	—
8.11.94	SBC	H	St. Helens	L	5-24	Green	Matautia (dg)	3931	Presley
13.11.94	SBC	A	Widnes	D	12-12	Green (2)	Green (2)	—	—
27.11.94	SBC	A	Leeds	L	18-38	Bloem (2), Matautia	Green (3)	—	—
4.12.94	RT(2)	A	Warrington	L	14-44	Neal, Whakarau	Green (3)	—	—
11.12.94	SBC	A	Wakefield T.	L	14-28	Bowles, Neal, Pennant	Green	—	—
26.12.94	SBC	A	Sheffield E.	L	22-30	Eaton, Foster, Lingard, Neal	Green (3)	—	—
11.1.95	SBC	H	Bradford N.	L	18-36	Rothwell (2), Eaton	Green (3)	3750	J. Connolly
15.1.95	SBC	H	Hull	W	42-38	D. Evans (2), Hayes, Jackson, Manning, Whakarau, Zelei	Green (7)	3482	Morris
22.1.95	SBC	A	Featherstone R.	L	16-34	D. Evans, Miller, Rothwell	Green (2)	—	—
24.1.95	SBC	H	Wigan	L	10-28	Zelei, Whakarau	Green	4506	Tennant
5.2.95	SBC	A	Warrington	L	20-68	Neal (2), Miller	Green (4)	—	—
12.2.95	CC(4)	H	Sheffield E.	L	12-22	Neal, Williamson	Green (2)	2585	Bates
15.2.95	SBC	H	Oldham	L	14-22	Carlyle, D. Evans	Green (3)	1803	Kirkpatrick
19.2.95	SBC	H	Salford	L	12-19	Miller, Williamson	Green (2)	2030	Campbell
12.3.95	SBC	A	Halifax	L	6-50	Farrar	Green	—	—
19.3.95	SBC	H	Featherstone R.	L	19-22	Carlyle, Eaton, Pennant	Green (3, 1dg)	2825	Bates
2.4.95	SBC	A	Bradford N.	L	18-74	Carlyle, Green, Manning	Green (3)	—	—
5.4.95	SBC	A	Wigan	L	4-44	Whakarau		—	—
9.4.95	SBC	A	Castleford	L	18-25	Hayes, Manning, Pennant	Eaton (3)	—	—
14.4.95	SBC	H	Sheffield E.	L	16-56	Zelei (2), Whakarau	Green (2)	2950	Lee
17.4.95	SBC	A	Hull	L	12-42	Bramley, Whakarau	Green (2)	—	—
23.4.95	SBC	H	Workington T.	L	16-50	Manning, Tomlinson, Williamson	Green (2)	2975	Kirkpatrick

Doncaster full back Jamie Bloem, scorer of nine tries in 10 games in 1994-95 before being banned for a drugs offence.

FEATHERSTONE ROVERS

Ground: Post Office Road (01977-702386)
First Season: 1921-22
Nickname: Colliers
Chairman: Steve Wagner
Secretary: Robin Hays
Honours: **Championship** Beaten finalists, 1927-28
Division One Champions, 1976-77
Division Two Champions, 1979-80, 1992-93
Challenge Cup Winners, 1966-67, 1972-73, 1982-83
Beaten finalists, 1951-52, 1973-74
Second Division/Divisional Premiership Winners, 1992-93
Beaten finalists, 1987-88
Yorkshire Cup Winners, 1939-40, 1959-60
Beaten finalists, 1928-29, 1963-64, 1966-67, 1969-70, 1970-71, 1976-77, 1977-78, 1989-90
Captain Morgan Trophy Beaten finalists, 1973-74

RECORDS
Match
Goals: 13 by Mark Knapper v. Keighley, 17 Sep 1989
Tries: 6 by Mike Smith v. Doncaster, 13 Apr 1968
Chris Bibb v. Keighley, 17 Sep 1989
Points: 30 by Mark Knapper v. Keighley, 17 Sep 1989
Season
Goals: 163 by Steve Quinn, 1979-80
Tries: 48 by Paul Newlove, 1992-93
Points: 391 by Martin Pearson, 1992-93
Career
Goals: 1,210 by Steve Quinn, 1975-88
Tries: 162 by Don Fox, 1953-66
Points: 2,654 by Steve Quinn, 1975-88
Appearances: 440 by Jim Denton, 1921-34

Highest score: 86-18 v. Keighley, 17 Sep 1989
Highest against: 70-2 at Halifax, 14 Apr 1941
Attendance: 17,531 v. St. Helens (RL Cup), 21 Mar 1959

COACHING REGISTER
● **Since 1974-75**

*Tommy Smales	July 74 - Sep 74
Keith Goulding	Sep 74 - Jan 76
†Tommy Smales	Feb 76 - May 76
Keith Cotton	June 76 - Dec 77
Keith Goulding	Dec 77 - May 78
Terry Clawson	July 78 - Nov 78
†Tommy Smales	Nov 78 - Apr 79
Paul Daley	May 79 - Jan 81
Vince Farrar	Feb 81 - Nov 82
Allan Agar	Dec 82 - Oct 85
George Pieniazek	Nov 85 - Nov 86
Paul Daley	Nov 86 - Apr 87
Peter Fox	May 87 - Oct 91
Allan Agar	Oct 91 - Aug 92
Steve Martin	Sep 92 - Oct 94
David Ward	Oct 94 -

*Ex-forward
†Ex-scrum half

GREAT BRITAIN REGISTER
(16 players)

Tommy Askin	(6)	1928
Chris Bibb	(1)	1990
John "Keith" Bridges	(3)	1974
Terry Clawson	(2)	1962
Malcolm Dixon	(2)	1962-64
Steve Evans	(5+3)	1979-80
Deryck Fox	(9+4)	1985-92
Don Fox	(1)	1963
David Hobbs	(7+1)	1984
Gary Jordan	(2)	1964-67
Steve Molloy	(1)	1994
Arnold Morgan	(4)	1968
Steve Nash	(16)	1971-74
Paul Newlove	(7+3)	1989-93
Peter Smith	(1+5)	1977-84
Jimmy Thompson	(19+1)	1970-77

Featherstone Rovers winger Ikram Butt, the first Asian to gain international representation, making his debut for England against Wales at Cardiff in the 1995 John Smith's European Championship.

1994-95 SIGNINGS REGISTER

Signed	Player	Club From
20.6.94	Baines, Mark	West Hull ARL
20.6.94	Horsfield, Lee	West Hull ARL
23.6.94	Morgan, Dave	Travellers ARL
1.7.94	Aston, Mark	Sheffield E.
18.7.94	Ellis, Mark	Hunslet
1.8.94	Divet, Daniel	Carcassonne, Fr.
19.8.94	Banquet, Frederic	France
19.8.94	*Webster, Mark	Wakefield T.
2.9.94	*Arundel, Stuart	Halifax
22.9.94	*Nixon, Mark	NZ
28.10.94	*Lyman, Paul	Hull K.R.
8.11.94	Sims, Jason	Redhill ARL
17.11.94	Wilson, Warren	Halifax
29.12.94	Naidole, Joseph	Huddersfield
12.1.95	Wyvill, Shaun	—
31.1.95	Rodger, Brett	NZ
1.2.95	Frankland, Nick	Featherstone M.W. ARL
21.3.95	Swinson, Gavin	—
27.3.95	*Morris, Lynton	Wakefield T.

FEATHERSTONE ROVERS 1994-95 PLAYERS' SUMMARY

	Date of Birth	App	T	G	D	Pts	Previous club	Signed
Aston, Mark	27.9.67	28+1	5	85	2	192	Sheffield E.	1.7.94
Banquet, Frederic		20	15	17	—	94	France	19.8.94
Battye, Neil	11.8.63	0+1	—	—	—	—	Oldham	
Butt, Ikram	25.10.68	31	6	—	—	24	Leeds	9.8.90
Calland, Matt	20.8.71	25+1	16	—	—	64	Rochdale H.	8.9.93
Casey, Leo	17.9.65	22+5	—	—	—	—	Oldham	26.7.90
Currier, Andy	8.4.66	11	3	1	—	14	Widnes	11.8.93
Divet, Daniel	11.12.66	27+1	8	—	—	32	Hull	1.8.94
Ellis, Mark	23.5.67	2+2	—	—	—	—	Hunslet	26.3.94
Frankland, Nick	11.8.70	0+1	—	—	—	—	Featherstone M.W. ARL	1.2.95
Gibson, Carl	23.4.63	35	10	1	—	42	Leeds	25.8.93
Gunn, Richard	25.2.67	9+9	—	—	—	—	Leeds	24.9.92
Hughes, Darren	19.6.74	14+3	4	—	—	16	Leeds	2.9.93
Molloy, Steve	11.3.69	34	6	—	—	24	Leeds	3.11.93
Morris, Lynton	18.5.72	1	—	—	—	—	Wakefield T.	7.3.95
Naidole, Joe	23.12.72	7+4	1	—	—	4	Huddersfield	29.12.94
Nixon, Mark	5.2.68	18+6	6	—	—	24	New Zealand	22.9.94
O'Brien, Richard	25.10.71	0+2	—	—	—	—	West Hull ARL	27.4.93
Pearson, Martin	24.10.71	5	1	20	—	44	Travellers ARL	16.11.88
Price, Gary	9.3.61	3+17	3	—	—	12	Leeds	4.8.89
Price, Gary H.	28.10.69	31	6	—	—	24	Wakefield T.	28.8.93
Rodger, Brett		15+1	8	—	—	32	New Zealand	3.1.95
Roebuck, Neil	4.10.69	23+8	2	—	—	8	Castleford	13.1.93
Ropati, Iva	18.7.68	9	2	—	—	8	New Zealand	4.11.93
Senior, Lee	27.8.74	3	1	1	—	6	Sharlston ARL	1.10.92
Simpson, Owen	12.9.65	5	2	—	—	8	Keighley	9.11.90
Sims, Jason	15.7.70	13+3	—	—	—	—	Redhill ARL	8.11.94
Southernwood, Graham	5.11.71	26+3	8	—	—	32	Castleford	17.2.94
Thompson, Alex	16.11.74	2+1	—	—	—	—	Travellers ARL	21.10.92
Tuuta, Brendon	29.4.65	31	8	—	—	32	Australia	14.9.90
Wilson, Warren	3.5.63	5+1	—	1	—	2	Halifax	17.11.94

TOTALS

31 players			121	126	2	738		

Representative appearances 1994-95

Banquet — France (2+1, 2t); Butt — England (1); Divet — France (3).

FEATHERSTONE ROVERS 1994-95 MATCH ANALYSIS

Date	Com-petition	H/A	Opponent	Rlt	Score	Tries	Goals	Atten-dance	Referee
21.8.94	SBC	H	Wigan	L	24-36	Currier (2), Butt, Calland	Pearson (4)	5504	Campbell
28.8.94	SBC	A	Leeds	L	14-36	Calland (2)	Pearson (3)	—	—
4.9.94	SBC	H	Warrington	W	26-10	Divet (2), G. H. Price	Pearson (7)	3892	R. Connolly
11.9.94	SBC	A	Salford	D	24-24	Aston, Gibson, Pearson, Southernwood	Pearson (4)	—	—
16.9.94	SBC	H	Bradford N.	L	16-42	G. H. Price (2), Molloy	Pearson (2)	4039	Cummings
25.9.94	SBC	A	Wakefield T.	L	0-15	—	—	—	—
4.10.94	SBC	H	Workington T.	W	46-0	Banquet (2), Divet (2), Currier, Molloy, Ropati, Southernwood	Aston (7)	2862	Campbell
9.10.94	SBC	A	Widnes	L	18-28	Banquet, Divet, Ropati	Aston (3)	—	—
25.10.94	SBC	H	Halifax	L	14-22	Gibson, Southernwood	Aston (3)	4689	Annersley (Aus)
30.10.94	SBC	A	Oldham	W	20-10	Banquet, G. Price, Senior	Aston (4)	—	—
13.11.94	SBC	H	Leeds	L	28-30	Banquet, Butt, Calland, Gibson, Tuuta	Banquet (3), Aston	5615	Harrigan
21.11.94	SBC	A	Wigan	L	6-30	Tuuta	Senior	—	—
27.11.94	SBC	A	Warrington	L	14-18	Banquet, Butt, Nixon	Banquet	—	—
4.12.94	RT(2)	A	Whitehaven	L	12-18	Calland, Gibson	Currier, Wilson	—	—
11.12.94	SBC	H	Salford	L	12-20	G.H. Price (2)	Aston (2)	2707	R. Connolly
26.12.94	SBC	A	Castleford	L	16-32	G. Price (2), Molloy	Aston (2)	—	—
6.1.95	SBC	H	Hull	L	26-29	Tuuta, Butt, Calland, Naidole, Gibson	Aston (3)	2628	J. Connolly
11.1.95	SBC	H	Sheffield E.	L	14-24	Gibson, Nixon, Tuuta	Aston	2309	Bates
15.1.95	SBC	A	St. Helens	L	20-26	Calland, Gibson, Southernwood	Aston (4)	—	—
22.1.95	SBC	H	Doncaster	W	34-16	Rodger (2), Butt, Calland, Gibson, Hughes	Aston (5)	3631	Cummings
5.2.95	SBC	H	Wakefield T.	W	22-15	Hughes, Southernwood, Tuuta	Aston (5)	4097	J. Connolly
12.2.95	CC(4)	H	Barrow	W	50-22	Rodger (3), Calland (2), Gibson, G.H. Price, Southernwood	Aston (9)	1973	Cross
15.2.95	SBC	A	Bradford N.	W	24-16	Hughes (2), Molloy, Nixon	Aston (4)	—	—
19.2.95	SBC	A	Workington T.	L	2-13	—	Aston	—	—
26.2.95	CC(5)	A	Salford	W	30-10	Aston, Divet, Rodger, Tuuta	Aston (6, 2dg)	—	—
12.3.95	CC(QF)	A	Whitehaven	W	42-14	Banquet (4), Nixon, Rodger, Roebuck	Aston (7)	—	—
19.3.95	SBC	A	Doncaster	W	22-19	Aston (2), Rodger	Aston (5)	—	—
26.3.95	SBC	H	St. Helens	W	34-27	Aston, Divet, Gibson, Nixon, Roebuck, Tuuta	Aston (5)	3621	Campbell
1.4.95	CC(SF)	N[1]	Leeds	L	22-39	Butt, Calland, Divet, Southernwood	Aston (3)	—	—
5.4.95	SBC	A	Hull	L	8-28	Calland	Aston (2)	—	—
9.4.95	SBC	A	Halifax	L	8-34	Southernwood	Aston (2)	—	—
14.4.95	SBC	H	Castleford	L	6-27	Calland	Aston	4563	Bates
17.4.95	SBC	A	Sheffield E.	L	16-26	Banquet, Simpson, Tuuta	Banquet (2)	—	—
20.4.95	SBC	H	Widnes	W	32-20	Banquet (2), Calland (2), Molloy, Simpson	Banquet (4)	2017	Morris
23.4.95	SBC	H	Oldham	W	36-14	Banquet (2), Calland, Molloy, Nixon	Banquet (7), Gibson	3284	R. Connolly

N[1] at Elland Road, Leeds

HALIFAX

Ground: Thrum Hall (01422-361026)
First Season: 1895-96
Nickname: Thrum Hallers
Secretary: David Fleming
Honours: **Championship** Winners, 1906-07, 1964-65
Beaten finalists, 1952-53, 1953-54, 1955-56, 1965-66
War Emergency League Beaten finalists, 1942-43, 1944-45
Division One Champions, 1902-03, 1985-86
Challenge Cup Winners, 1902-03, 1903-04, 1930-31, 1938-39, 1986-87
Beaten finalists, 1920-21, 1940-41, 1941-42, 1948-49, 1953-54, 1955-56, 1987-88
Regal Trophy Winners, 1971-72
Beaten finalists, 1989-90
Premiership Trophy Beaten finalists, 1985-86
Second Division Premiership Beaten finalists, 1990-91
Yorkshire Cup Winners, 1908-09, 1944-45, 1954-55, 1955-56, 1963-64
Beaten finalists, 1905-06, 1907-08, 1941-42, 1979-80
Yorkshire League Winners, 1908-09, 1920-21, 1952-53, 1953-54, 1955-56, 1957-58
Eastern Division Championship Winners, 1963-64
Charity Shield Winners, 1986-87
Beaten finalists, 1987-88

RECORDS
Match
Goals: 14 by Bruce Burton at Hunslet, 27 Aug 1972
Tries: 8 by Keith Williams v. Dewsbury, 9 Nov 1957
Points: 32 by John Schuster at Doncaster, 9 Oct 1994
Season
Goals: 147 by Tysul Griffiths, 1955-56
Tries: 48 by Johnny Freeman, 1956-57
Points: 362 by John Schuster, 1994-95

Career
Goals: 1,028 by Ron James, 1960-72
Tries: 290 by Johnny Freeman, 1954-67
Points: 2,191 by Ron James, 1960-72
Appearances: 481 by Stan Kielty, 1946-58
Highest score: 82-8 v. Runcorn H., 14 Oct 1990
Highest against: 64-0 at Wigan, 7 Mar 1923
Attendance: 29,153 v. Wigan (RL Cup), 21 Mar 1959

COACHING REGISTER
● **Since 1974-75**

Derek Hallas	Aug 74 - Oct 74
Les Pearce	Oct 74 - Apr 76
Alan Kellett	May 76 - Apr 77
Jim Crellin	June 77 - Oct 77
Harry Fox	Oct 77 - Feb 78
Maurice Bamford	Feb 78 - May 80
Mick Blacker	June 80 - June 82
Ken Roberts	June 82 - Sep 82
Colin Dixon	Sep 82 - Nov 84
Chris Anderson	Nov 84 - May 88
Graham Eadie	May 88 - Aug 88
Ross Strudwick	Aug 88 - Feb 89
Alan Hardisty	Feb 89 - Apr 89
John Dorahy	June 89 - Aug 90
Peter Roe	Aug 90 - May 91
Roger Millward	May 91 - Dec 92
Malcolm Reilly	Jan 93 - Sep 94
Steve Simms	Sep 94 -

Malcolm Reilly, who resigned as coach of Halifax in September 1994.

GREAT BRITAIN REGISTER

(32 players)

Alvin Ackerley	(2)	1952-58
Arthur Bassett	(2)	1946
Jack Beames	(2)	1921
Nat Bentham	(2)	1929
John Bentley	(1)	1994
Harry Beverley	(2)	1937
Oliver Burgham	(1)	1911
Arthur Daniels	(3)	1952-55
Will Davies	(1)	1911
Colin Dixon	(1)	1968
Paul Dixon	(3+3)	1987-88
Percy Eccles	(1)	1907
Terry Fogerty	(+1)	1966
Tony Halmshaw	(1)	1971
Karl Harrison	(8+3)	1991-94
Michael Jackson	(+2)	1993
Neil James	(1)	1986
Robbie Lloyd	(1)	1920
Alf Milnes	(2)	1920
Stuart Prosser	(1)	1914
Dai Rees	(1)	1926
Charlie Renilson	(7+1)	1965-68
Joe Riley	(1)	1910
Ken Roberts	(10)	1963-66
Asa Robinson	(3)	1907-08
Derrick Schofield	(1)	1955
John Shaw	(5)	1960-62
Cyril Stacey	(1)	1920
John Thorley	(4)	1954
Jack Wilkinson	(6)	1954-55
Frank Williams	(2)	1914
David Willicombe	(1)	1974

1994-95 SIGNINGS REGISTER

Signed	Player	Club From
1.7.94	Anderson, Grant	Castleford
7.7.94	Moriarty, Paul	Widnes
15.7.94	Slicker, George	Waterhead ARL
4.8.94	Parker, Wayne	Hull K.R.
10.8.94	Jackson, Darryl	Ryedale-York
25.8.94	Greenwood, Stephen	Park Amateurs ARL
2.9.94	*Eden, Phil	Wakefield T.
2.9.94	*Richardson, Sean	Featherstone R.
5.10.94	Slicker, Michael	Leigh East ARL
21.10.94	*Edwards, Michael	Oldham
24.10.94	Baldwin, Simon	Leigh
4.11.94	*Connor, Ian	St. Helens
4.11.94	*Marriott, Karl	Rochdale H.
8.11.94	Rowley, Paul	Leigh
22.11.94	Charnock, Ben	Ovenden ARL
20.12.94	Munro, Damian	Waterhead ARL
22.12.94	Gillespie, Carl	Old Crossleyans RU
2.1.95	Sewell, Andrew	Huddersfield
26.1.95	*Hope, Martin	Wigan
16.2.95	Ketteridge, Martin	Castleford

England debutant Simon Baldwin, an October 1994 signing from Leigh.

HALIFAX 1994-95 PLAYERS' SUMMARY

	Date of Birth	App	T	G	D	Pts	Previous club	Signed
Anderson, Grant	21.2.69	1+1	—	—	—	—	Castleford	1.7.94
Anderson, Paul	25.10.71	0+1	—	—	—	—	Leeds	16.9.93
Bailey, Mark	5.5.68	3+1	—	—	—	—	St. Helens	4.3.92
Baldwin, Simon	31.3.75	23+1	5	—	—	20	Leigh	24.10.94
Bentley, John	5.9.66	33	29	—	—	116	Leeds	21.8.92
Burton, Danny	17.5.75	0+2	—	—	—	—	Oulton ARL	5.8.93
Connor, Ian	21.3.70	0+1	—	—	—	—	St. Helens	4.11.94
Dean, Craig	20.10.76	11	2	—	—	8	Leigh East ARL	1.7.93
Divorty, Gary	28.1.66	31+3	6	—	3	27	Leeds	21.8.92
Eden, Phil	13.12.63	3+1	3	—	—	12	Wakefield T.	2.9.94
Fieldhouse, John	28.6.62	31+1	3	—	—	12	Oldham	17.10.91
Gillespie, Carl	25.7.70	6+5	2	—	—	8	Old Crossleyans RU	22.12.94
Greenwood, Steve	13.10.75	0+2	—	—	—	—	Park ARL	25.8.94
Hagan, Michael	12.8.64	34	7	—	1	29	Australia	2.9.93
Hallas, Graeme	27.2.71	11+3	4	—	—	16	Hull K.R.	29.10.92
Hampson, Steve	14.8.62	10	3	—	—	12	Wigan	2.7.93
Harland, Lee	4.9.73	2+4	1	—	—	4	Leeds	20.8.93
Harrison, Karl	20.2.64	21	2	—	—	8	Hull	8.8.91
Highton, Paul	10.11.76	0+1	1	—	—	4	Waterhead ARL	2.8.93
Jackson, Michael	11.10.69	12+8	2	—	—	8	Wakefield T.	13.7.93
Ketteridge, Martin	2.10.64	6+5	1	—	—	4	Castleford	16.2.95
Lawless, Johnny	3.11.74	4+1	—	—	—	—	Siddal ARL	1.6.92
Lay, Steve	28.3.68	5	—	—	—	—	Hunslet	5.11.93
Marshall, Richard	9.10.75	1+1	—	—	—	—	St. Helens Academy	14.6.93
Martindale, Michael	13.9.74	2+1	—	—	—	—	Saddleworth ARL	5.8.93
Moriarty, Paul	16.7.64	30	8	—	—	32	Widnes	7.7.94
Munro, Damian	6.10.76	1	1	—	—	4	Waterhead ARL	20.12.94
Parker, Wayne	2.4.67	24	3	—	—	12	Hull K.R.	4.8.94
Perrett, Mark	18.7.73	16+4	4	—	—	16	Ovenden ARL	18.9.91
Preston, Mark	3.4.67	30+1	21	—	—	84	Wigan	11.6.91
Round, Paul	24.9.63	4+3	3	—	—	12	Wakefield T.	10.1.94
Rowley, Paul	12.3.75	19+4	5	—	—	20	Leigh	8.11.94
Schuster, John	17.1.64	34	19	142	2	362	Australia	22.8.93
Sewell, Andy	5.4.69	0+1	—	—	—	—	Huddersfield	2.1.95
Smith, Richard	18.6.73	14+6	5	—	—	20	Siddal ARL	18.5.92
Southernwood, Roy	23.6.68	15+5	1	—	—	4	Castleford	24.8.90
Tiffany, Richard	25.5.73	0+1	—	—	—	—	Dudley Hill ARL	25.3.92
Turner, Craig	10.3.73	5+2	3	—	—	12	Siddal ARL	17.1.92

TOTALS

38 players			144	142	6	866		

Representative appearances 1994-95

Baldwin — England (1+1), GB Under-21s (1); Bentley — England (1); Harland — GB Under-21s (1); Harrison — Britain (3), England (1); Moriarty — Wales (3); Perrett — Wales (3), GB Under-21s (1); Rowley — GB Under-21s (1).

HALIFAX 1994-95 MATCH ANALYSIS

Date	Competition	H/A	Opponent	Rlt	Score	Tries	Goals	Attendance	Referee
21.8.94	SBC	A	Oldham	W	40-20	Round (2), Bentley, Hagan, Fieldhouse, Moriarty, Preston	Schuster (6)	—	—
28.8.94	SBC	H	St. Helens	L	22-30	Preston (2), Perrett, Schuster	Schuster (3)	6197	Cummings
4.9.94	SBC	A	Widnes	L	10-17	Bentley, Hampson	Schuster	—	—
11.9.94	SBC	H	Hull	W	46-12	Divorty (2), Preston (2), Bentley, Hampson, Perrett, Schuster	Schuster (7)	4161	Smith
18.9.94	SBC	H	Wakefield T.	W	40-10	Bentley (2), Eden (2), Harrison, Moriarty, Schuster	Schuster (6)	5388	Smith
25.9.94	SBC	A	Salford	W	24-12	Eden, Perrett, Preston, Schuster	Schuster (4)	—	—
9.10.94	SBC	A	Doncaster	W	72-0	Bentley (3), Schuster (3), Divorty, Hagan, Hallas, Hampson, Parker, Preston, Southernwood	Schuster (10)	—	—
16.10.94	Tour	H	Australia	L	12-26	Bentley, Smith	Schuster (2)	8352	Holdsworth
25.10.94	SBC	A	Featherstone R.	W	22-14	Hallas, Parker, Preston, Schuster	Schuster (3)	—	—
30.10.94	SBC	H	Sheffield E.	W	24-20	Bentley, Fieldhouse, Harland, Round, Schuster	Schuster (2)	5732	Holdsworth
6.11.94	SBC	H	Oldham	W	34-8	Schuster (2), Bentley, Preston, Smith	Schuster (7)	5604	J. Connolly
13.11.94	SBC	A	St. Helens	L	14-18	Hagan, Rowley	Schuster (3)	—	—
25.11.94	SBC	H	Widnes	W	27-10	Bentley (2), Preston, Schuster	Schuster (5), Divorty (dg)	4219	R. Connolly
3.12.94	RT(2)	A	Castleford	L	26-32	Bentley (2), Moriarty (2)	Schuster (5)	—	—
7.12.94	SBC	H	Warrington	W	19-6	Dean, Rowley, Schuster	Schuster (3), Divorty (dg)	4559	Tennant
11.12.94	SBC	A	Hull	W	21-16	Moriarty, Rowley, Schuster	Schuster (4), Hagan (dg)	—	—
26.12.94	SBC	H	Bradford N.	D	16-16	Baldwin, Bentley	Schuster (4)	9801	J. Connolly
1.1.95	SBC	A	Leeds	L	14-42	Divorty, Harrison	Schuster (3)	—	—
13.1.95	SBC	A	Workington T.	L	10-36	Parker, Preston	Schuster	—	—
22.1.95	SBC	H	Castleford	W	30-24	Preston (2), Divorty, Gillespie, Moriarty, Schuster	Schuster (3)	6018	Campbell
29.1.95	SBC	A	Wakefield T.	W	30-8	Bentley (2), Baldwin, Dean, Divorty	Schuster (5)	—	—
5.2.95	SBC	H	Salford	L	24-27	Smith (3), Munro, Schuster	Schuster (2)	5292	Morris
12.2.95	CC(4)	A	Huddersfield	L	30-36	Hagan (2), Fieldhouse, Turner	Schuster (7)	—	—
19.2.95	SBC	A	Warrington	D	14-14	Baldwin, Bentley	Schuster (3)	—	—
12.3.95	SBC	H	Doncaster	W	50-6	Bentley (3), Preston (2), Ketteridge, Perrett, Rowley, Schuster	Schuster (7)	4301	Holdsworth
19.3.95	SBC	A	Castleford	L	13-16	Bentley, Jackson	Schuster (2, 1dg)	—	—
26.3.95	SBC	H	Workington T.	W	39-20	Bentley (2), Hagan, Jackson, Moriarty, Preston	Schuster (7, 1dg)	3808	Lee
29.3.95	SBC	H	Wigan	W	18-16	Bentley, Preston	Schuster (5)	7383	Lee
2.4.95	SBC	A	Wigan	L	6-62	Rowley	Schuster	—	—
9.4.95	SBC	H	Featherstone R.	W	34-8	Baldwin, Bentley, Gillespie, Hallas, Schuster	Schuster (7)	4590	Kirkpatrick
14.4.95	SBC	A	Bradford N.	L	22-30	Preston (2), Hallas, Moriarty	Schuster (3)	—	—
17.4.95	SBC	H	Leeds	W	23-16	Bentley (2), Turner	Schuster (5), Divorty (dg)	6951	Kirkpatrick
23.4.95	SBC	A	Sheffield E.	L	24-32	Preston (2), Highton, Turner	Schuster (4)	—	—
7.5.95	PT(1)	A	St. Helens	L	16-32	Baldwin, Hagan, Schuster	Schuster (2)	—	—

HIGHFIELD

Ground: Hoghton Road, Prescot
First Season: 1922-23 as Wigan Highfield.
Became London Highfield in
1933-34. Became Liverpool Stanley
in 1934-35 and changed to
Liverpool City in 1951-52. Became
Huyton in 1968-69 and changed to
Runcorn Highfield in 1984-85.
Became Highfield in 1991-92.
Chairman: Geoff Fletcher
Secretary: Brian Morris
Honours: **Lancashire League** Winners,
1935-36

RECORDS
Match
Goals: 11 by Peter Wood v. Batley, 21 Oct 1984
Tries: 5 by John Maloney v. Bramley,
25 Apr 1931
Points: 30 by Norman Barrow v. Keighley,
31 Mar 1991
Season
Goals: 126 by Peter Wood, 1984-85
Tries: 28 by John Maloney, 1930-31
Points: 240 by Peter Wood, 1984-85
Career
Goals: 304 by Wilf Hunt, 1955-66
Tries: 204 by John Maloney, 1926-45
Points: 731 by Wilf Hunt, 1955-66
Appearances: 413 by John Maloney, 1926-45
Highest score: 59-11 v. Bramley, 4 May 1934
Highest against: 104-4 v. Keighley C,
23 Apr 1995
(home game at Rochdale)
Attendance: 18,000 v. Wigan (League),
2 Sep 1922 — at Tunstall Lane,
Pemberton
1,600 v. Halifax (League),
6 Jan 1991 — at Hoghton Road

COACHING REGISTER
● **Since 1974-75**

Terry Gorman	Aug 74 - May 77
Geoff Fletcher	Aug 77 - June 86
Frank Wilson	July 86 - Nov 86
Arthur Daley ⎫	Nov 86 - Apr 87
Paul Woods ⎭	
Bill Ashurst	Apr 87 - Jan 89
John Cogger	Jan 89 - Feb 89
Geoff Fletcher	Feb 89 - Apr 89
Dave Chisnall	June 89 - Oct 90
Alan Bishop	Oct 90 - Apr 91
Chris Arkwright	Apr 91 - Aug 91
Willie Johnson	Aug 91 - Apr 93
Mike Peers	Apr 93 - Sep 94
Chris Arkwright	Sep 94 -

GREAT BRITAIN REGISTER
(4 players)

Ray Ashby	(1)	1964
Billy Belshaw	(6)	1936-37
Nat Bentham	(6)	1928
Harry Woods	(5)	1936

1994-95 SIGNINGS REGISTER

Signed	Player	Club From
4.8.94	*Hudson, Julian	Blackpool G.
14.8.94	Goulding, Michael	Wigan St. Pats. ARL
14.8.94	Hester, Terence	Bramley
14.8.95	Swift, Mark	Wigan St. Pats. ARL
16.8.94	Clansey, John	Kirby Rangers ARL
16.8.94	Owen, Glyn	Boilermakers ARL
21.8.94	*Crehan, Craig	Boilermakers ARL
25.8.94	Del Ferro, Giasone	Thatto Heath ARL
2.9.94	*Bannon, John	Rochdale H
8.9.94	Measures, Damien	Blackbrook ARL
16.12.94	Briggs, Jack	RU
19.12.94	Jackson, Mark	Pilkington Recs. ARL
5.2.95	Smith, Sebastian	RU
8.2.95	Crehan, Craig	Boilermakers ARL
9.2.95	Parkman, Russell	Crosfields ARL
10.3.95	Pittman, David	Crosfields ARL

HIGHFIELD 1994-95 PLAYERS' SUMMARY

	Date of Birth	App	T	G	D	Pts	Previous club	Signed
Ashurst, Paul		5+1	—	—	—	—		
Bamber, Simon	3.6.63	8+1	—	—	—	—		
Bannon, John	4.4.75	26	4	—	—	16	Rochdale H.	2.9.94
Barnes, Dave	21.10.73	17+3	—	—	—	—	Wigan St. Judes ARL	7.11.92
Barrow, Norman	5.8.65	12	1	—	—	4	Thatto Heath ARL	29.1.91
Barrow, Shaun	8.11.67	16	—	—	—	—	St. Helens	24.8.89
Bridge, Russell	8.10.64	7	—	—	—	—	Leigh	
Briggs, Jack	1.8.68	13+3	2	—	—	8	RU	16.12.94
Brown, Dave	17.2.65	4+2	—	—	—	—	Whitehaven	24.8.93
Carr, Mike	14.11.64	6	—	—	—	—	Pilkington Rec. ARL	11.8.92
Clansey, John	25.8.66	9	1	—	—	4	Kirkby R. ARL	16.8.94
Crehan, Andy	27.11.67	22+1	1	—	—	4	Swinton	3.2.94
Crehan, Craig	18.5.75	9+1	—	—	—	—	Boilermakers ARL	21.8.94
Denning, Mike	11.1.65	3+3	—	—	—	—	Pilkington Rec.ARL	22.9.92
Dolan, Shaun	1.1.70	25+1	3	—	—	12	Blackbrook ARL	24.8.89
Drinkwater, Matt	18.4.75	24+6	5	—	—	20	Woolston ARL	16.8.93
Ferro, Giasone Del	16.12.70	30	6	—	—	24	Thatto Heath ARL	25.8.94
Finney, Ian	2.9.72	11+5	—	—	—	—		
Forber, Gary	22.1.68	7	1	—	—	4	Swinton	28.2.91
Goulding, Mike	29.7.73	6+2	1	—	—	4	Wigan St. Patricks ARL	14.8.94
Griffiths, David	9.4.69	1	—	—	—	—	Blackpool G.	21.1.94
Haggerty, Gary	9.4.61	0+1	—	—	—	—	Wakefield T.	10.11.92
Hester, Terry	21.1.65	1	—	—	—	—	Bramley	12.3.93
Hudson, Julian	14.6.67	20	5	—	—	20	Blackpool G.	14.3.93
Jackson, Mark	13.7.68	1	—	—	—	—	Pilkington Rec. ARL	19.12.94
Johnson, Chris	29.5.60	22+6	1	20	—	44	Blackpool G.	16.3.93
Johnson, Kevin	4.4.72	1	—	—	—	—		
Littler, Paul	25.8.66	22+6	—	—	—	—	Thatto Heath ARL	3.2.91
Meadows, Kevin	27.2.61	4+5	1	—	—	4	Chorley B.	4.9.92
Measures, Damien	2.6.73	7+5	—	—	—	—	Blackbrook ARL	8.9.94
Ogburn, John	30.10.64	2	2	—	—	8	Simms Cross ARL	25.3.94
Owen, Glyn	4.3.71	26+1	5	1	—	22	Sutton Blrmakers ARL	16.8.94
Parkman, Russ	31.5.75	2	—	—	—	—	Crosfields ARL	9.2.95
Partington, Carl		8	—	—	—	—	Rochdale H.	
Pemberton, Tony	26.5.64	0+1	—	—	—	—	Blackpool G.	12.3.92
Pilat, Stewart	25.10.73	1	—	—	—	—	Woolston ARL	24.8.93
Pitman, Gary		4+2	—	—	—	—		
Potter, Ian	6.8.58	1	—	—	—	—	Bramley	13.11.92
Rippon, Andy	10.2.65	26+2	2	16	—	40	Swinton	
Smith, Seb	26.5.72	6+2	—	—	—	—	RU	5.2.95
Swift, Mark	2.12.71	11	1	—	—	4	Wigan St. Patricks ARL	14.8.94
Worthington, Peter	9.12.64	2	—	—	—	—	Simms Cross ARL	25.3.94
Trialist		1	—	—	—	—		
TOTALS								
43 players			42	37	—	242		

68

HIGHFIELD 1994-95 MATCH ANALYSIS

Date	Competition	H/A	Opponent	Rlt	Score	Tries	Goals	Attendance	Referee
21.8.94	SD	H	Hull K.R.	L	10-68	Ogburn (2)	C. Johnson	319	Kirkpatrick
28.8.94	SD	A	Ryedale-York	L	6-66	C. Johnson	C. Johnson	—	—
4.9.94	SD	A	Batley	L	0-66	—	—	—	—
11.9.94	SD	H	Leigh	L	8-80	Hudson	C. Johnson (2)	672	Redfearn
18.9.94	SD	H	London B.	L	8-30	Drinkwater, Meadows	—	146	Burke
25.9.94	SD	A	Dewsbury	L	0-60	—	—	—	—
2.10.94	SD	H	Huddersfield	L	6-30	—	C. Johnson (3)	1071	Kirkpatrick
9.10.94	SD	A	Bramley	L	0-46	—	—	—	—
16.10.94	SD	A	Carlisle	L	8-28	Bannon	C. Johnson (2)	—	—
30.10.94	SD	H	Rochdale H.	L	8-28	Rippon, Swift	—	500	Lee
6.11.94	SD	A	Hull K.R.	L	4-78	Bannon	—	—	—
13.11.94	SD	H	Ryedale-York	L	20-24	Clancy, Dolan, Hudson	C. Johnson (4)	320	Atkin
27.11.94	RT(1)	H	Ovenden	W	12-6	Forber, Owen	C. Johnson (2)	285	Carter
4.12.94	RT(2)	H[1]	Widnes	L	2-50	—	C. Johnson	1199	Lee
11.12.94	SD	H	Batley	L	0-50	—	—	385	Gilmour
18.12.94	SD	A	Leigh	L	14-50	Del Farro, Drinkwater	C. Johnson (3)	—	—
1.1.95	SD	A	Barrow	W	14-12	Del Farro, Hudson	Rippon (3)	398	Steele
8.1.95	SD	H	Swinton	L	14-44	Del Farro (2), Hudson	Rippon	398	Steele
15.1.95	SD	A	Hunslet	L	0-56	—	—	—	—
22.1.95	CC(3)	H	Beverley	L	4-27	N. Barrow	—	226	Gilmour
25.1.95	SD	H	Whitehaven	L	6-86*	Goulding	Rippon	150	Galtress
29.1.95	SD	A	London B.	L	4-42	Crehan	—	—	—
5.2.95	SD	H	Dewsbury	L	12-68	Drinkwater, Owen	Rippon (2)	431	Burke
19.2.95	SD	A	Huddersfield	L	16-74	Briggs (2), Dolan	Rippon (2)	—	—
6.3.95	SD	H	Bramley	L	6-30	Drinkwater	C. Johnson	274	Atkin
12.3.95	SD	A	Keighley C.	L	0-68	—	—	—	—
19.3.95	SD	H	Carlisle	L	14-56	Drinkwater, Hudson, Rippon	Owen	195	Steele
26.3.95	SD	A	Rochdale H.	L	6-78	Bannon	Rippon	—	—
2.4.95	SD	A	Swinton	L	14-44	Owen (2), Del Farro	Rippon	—	—
9.4.95	SD	H	Hunslet	L	14-44	Bannon, Del Farro	Rippon (3)	280	Burke
14.4.95	SD	A	Whitehaven	L	0-60	—	—	—	—
17.4.95	SD	H	Barrow	L	8-34	Owen	Rippon (2)	195	Redfearn
23.4.95	SD	H[2]	Keighley C.	L	4-104	Dolan	—	2928	Steele

H[1] at St Helens
* Abandoned after 63 min. because of waterlogged pitch. Result stands
H[2] at Rochdale H.

HUDDERSFIELD

Ground: Alfred McAlpine Stadium
(01484-530710)
First Season: 1895-96; added Barracudas to title
from 1984-85 to 1987-88 inclusive
Nickname: Fartowners
Chairman: Bob Scott
General
Manager: Les Coulter
Honours: **Championship** Winners, 1911-12,
1912-13, 1914-15, 1928-29,
1929-30, 1948-49, 1961-62
Beaten finalists, 1913-14, 1919-20,
1922-23, 1931-32, 1945-46, 1949-50
Division Two Champions, 1974-75
Division Three Champions, 1991-92
Challenge Cup Winners, 1912-13,
1914-15, 1919-20, 1932-33, 1944-45,
1952-53
Beaten finalists, 1934-35, 1961-62
Second Division Premiership
Beaten finalists, 1994-95
Yorkshire Cup Winners, 1909-10,
1911-12, 1913-14, 1914-15, 1918-19,
1919-20, 1926-27, 1931-32, 1938-39,
1950-51, 1952-53, 1957-58
Beaten finalists, 1910-11, 1923-24,
1925-26, 1930-31, 1937-38, 1942-43,
1949-50, 1960-61
Yorkshire League Winners,
1911-12, 1912-13, 1913-14, 1914-15,
1919-20, 1921-22, 1928-29, 1929-30,
1948-49, 1949-50, 1951-52
Eastern Division Beaten finalists,
1962-63

RECORDS
Match
Goals: 18 by Major Holland v. Swinton Park,
28 Feb 1914
Tries: 10 by Lionel Cooper v. Keighley,
17 Nov 1951
Points: 39 by Major Holland v. Swinton Park,
28 Feb 1914

Season
Goals: 147 by Ben Gronow, 1919-20
Tries: 80 by Albert Rosenfeld, 1913-14
Points: 332 by Pat Devery, 1952-53

Career
Goals: 958 by Frank Dyson, 1950-63
Tries: 420 by Lionel Cooper, 1947-55
Points: 2,072 by Frank Dyson, 1950-63
Appearances: 485 by Doug Clark, 1909-29
Highest score: 142-4 v. Blackpool G.
26 Nov 1994
Highest against: 94-12 at Castleford, 18 Sep 1988
Attendance: 32,912 v. Wigan (League), 4 Mar
1950 (at Fartown), 9,348 v. Halifax
(RL Cup), 12 Feb 1995 (at Alfred
McAlpine Stadium)

COACHING REGISTER
● **Since 1974-75**

Brian Smith	Jan 73 - Mar 76
Keith Goulding	Mar 76 - Dec 76
Bob Tomlinson	Jan 77 - May 77
Neil Fox	June 77 - Feb 78
*Roy Francis	-
Keith Goulding	May 78 - July 79
Ian Brooke	July 79 - Mar 80
Maurice Bamford	May 80 - May 81
Les Sheard	June 81 - Nov 82
Dave Mortimer	Nov 82 - Aug 83
Mel Bedford	Aug 83 - Nov 83
Brian Lockwood	Nov 83 - Feb 85
Chris Forster	Feb 85 - Dec 86
Jack Addy	Jan 87 - Mar 88
Allen Jones Neil Whittaker }	Mar 88 - Nov 88
Nigel Stephenson	Nov 88 - Mar 90
Barry Seabourne	Mar 90 - Feb 91
Mick Blacker Francis Jarvis }	Feb 91 - Sep 91
Alex Murphy	Sep 91 - Apr 94
George Fairbairn	June 94 -

*Although Roy Francis was appointed he was
unable to take over and Dave Heppleston
stood in until the next appointment.*

GREAT BRITAIN REGISTER
(24 players)

Jim Bowden	(3)	1954
Ken Bowman	(3)	1962-63
Brian Briggs	(1)	1954
Stan Brogden	(9)	1929-33
Jack Chilcott	(3)	1914
Doug Clark	(11)	1911-20
Don Close	(1)	1967
Dick Cracknell	(2)	1951
Jim Davies	(2)	1911
Frank Dyson	(1)	1959
Ben Gronow	(7)	1911-20
Fred Longstaff	(2)	1914
Ken Loxton	(1)	1971
Stan Moorhouse	(2)	1914
Bob Nicholson	(3)	1946-48
Johnny Rogers	(7)	1914-21
Ken Senior	(2)	1965-67
Tommy Smales	(5)	1962-64
Mick Sullivan	(16)	1954-57
Gwyn Thomas	(8)	1920-21
Dave Valentine	(15)	1948-54
Rob Valentine	(1)	1967
Harold Wagstaff	(12)	1911-21
Harold Young	(1)	1929

1994-95 SIGNINGS REGISTER

Signed	Player	Club From
19.7.94	Bruce, Jonathan	Dudley Hill ARL
19.7.94	Maddison, David	Huddersfield Academy
29.7.94	Kebbie, Brimah	Bradford N.
31.7.94	St. Hilaire, Marcus	Moldgreen ARL
1.8.94	Marchant, Adam	Huddersfield Academy
8.8.94	Milner, Lee	Huddersfield Academy
11.8.94	Shelford, Darrall	Bradford N.
17.8.94	Simpson, Ian	ARL
18.8.94	Austin, Greg	Salford
18.8.94	Bastow, Wayne	Shaw Cross ARL
19.8.94	Hanger, Dean	Leigh
7.9.94	Taylor, Mick	Bradford N.
7.10.94	Kerry, Steve	Oldham
16.12.94	*Irvine, Jimmy	Batley
16.2.95	Smith, Gary	Normanton ARL
17.2.95	*Stead, Richard	Bramley

Huddersfield centre Darrall Shelford, who made 32 appearances in his first campaign in 1994-95.

HUDDERSFIELD 1994-95 PLAYERS' SUMMARY

	Date of Birth	App	T	G	D	Pts	Previous club	Signed
Austin, Greg	14.6.63	39	52	—	1	209	Salford	18.8.94
Barnett, Steve	8.10.68	16+1	—	—	—	—	Bradford N.	22.9.92
Barton, Ben	4.12.74	11+6	6	—	—	24		1.7.93
Bruce, Jonathan	30.10.71	3+3	1	—	—	4	Dudley Hill ARL	19.7.94
Coulter, Gary	12.7.69	14+7	5	—	—	20	Doncaster	17.1.92
Flanagan, Neil	11.6.70	11	4	—	1	17	Oldham	21.8.92
Hanger, Dean	24.2.70	35+4	22	—	—	88	Leigh	19.8.94
Hellewell, Phil	23.4.67	34+1	7	18	—	64	Bradford N.	22.9.92
Irvine, Jimmy	28.4.60	4	—	—	—	—	Batley	16.12.94
Kebbie, Brimah	21.9.65	10	2	—	—	8	Bradford N.	29.7.94
Kerry, Steve	10.3.66	30	9	50	4	140	Oldham	7.10.94
King, David	6.9.67	34+1	12	—	—	48	London C.	25.8.93
Lucchese, Laurent	4.4.73	2	—	7	—	14	France	24.8.93
Maders, Martin	29.6.73	9+10	1	—	—	4	Saddleworth ARL	30.1.92
Meillam, Paul	30.8.70	0+3	—	—	—	—	York All Blacks ARL	24.8.90
Moore, Johnny	8.7.74	1	—	—	—	—	Park Amateurs ARL	15.8.92
Naidole, Joe	23.12.67	2+5	2	—	—	8	Deighton W. ARL	8.1.90
Needham, David	25.10.64	3	—	—	—	—	Workington T.	27.11.92
Pearce, Greg	2.9.67	26	6	97	2	220	Halifax	15.9.93
Pearson, Richard	9.10.74	15+7	11	—	—	44	Ovenden ARL	31.10.91
Pickles, Damien	2.12.70	1	—	—	—	—	Halifax	11.8.93
Pucill, Andy	19.11.67	29	1	—	—	4	Swinton	21.8.92
Reynolds, Simon	10.3.73	34	23	—	—	92	Moldgreen ARL	27.8.93
Richards, Basil	9.7.65	37+1	9	—	—	36	Warrington	27.8.93
St. Hilaire, Lee	15.2.67	23+2	5	—	—	20	Huddersfield Academy	30.12.92
St. Hilaire, Marcus	26.1.77	1	—	—	—	—	Moldgreen ARL	31.7.94
Senior, Gary	11.9.62	7+16	3	—	—	12	Hunslet	21.8.89
Shelford, Darrall	29.7.62	30+2	7	—	—	28	Bradford N.	11.8.94
Taylor, Mick	11.9.61	20+6	3	—	—	12	Bradford N.	7.9.94
Thomas, Ian	6.11.64	26	21	—	—	84	Huddersfield Sups. ARL	3.6.83
TOTALS								
30 players			212	172	8	1,200		

Representative appearances 1994-95
Reynolds — GB Under-21s (+1).

HUDDERSFIELD 1994-95 MATCH ANALYSIS

Date	Competition	H/A	Opponent	Rlt	Score	Tries	Goals	Attendance	Referee
21.8.94	SD	A	Batley	L	0-13	—	—	—	—
28.8.94	SD	H	Barrow	W	50-12	Flanagan, Kebbie, Austin (2), King, Thomas (2), Richards, Naidole, Shelford	Pearce (5)	4300	Lee
4.9.94	SD	A	Swinton	L	18-20	Austin, Shelford, Thomas	Pearce (3)	—	—
11.9.94	SD	H	Hunslet	W	42-18	Reynolds (3), Austin (2), Hanger, Richards, Thomas	Pearce (5)	2549	Ollerton
18.9.94	SD	A	Leigh	L	18-20	Austin, King, Reynolds	Pearce (3)	—	—
25.9.94	SD	H	Hull K.R.	W	23-10	Coulter, Flanagan, King, Richards	Pearce (3), Flanagan (dg)	3410	Bates
2.10.94	SD	A	Highfield	W	30-6	Austin (3), Flanagan, Pearce	Pearce (5)	—	—
9.10.94	SD	H	Rochdale H.	W	46-12	Kerry (2), Austin, Hanger, Kebbie, Naidole, Pearce, Reynolds	Pearce (7)	3023	Lee

(Continued)

72

Date	Com-petition	H/A	Opponent	Rlt	Score	Tries	Goals	Atten-dance	Referee
16.10.94	SD	A	Whitehaven	L	18-24	Austin (2), Senior	Pearce (3)	—	—
30.10.94	SD	A	Bramley	W	24-16	Austin (2),Kerry, Richards	Pearce (4)	—	—
6.11.94	SD	H	Batley	W	15-14	Reynolds	Pearce (5, 1dg)	4301	Lee
13.11.94	SD	A	Barrow	W	22-6	Austin (2), Kerry, Reynolds	Pearce (3)	—	—
26.11.94	RT(1)	H	Blackpool G.	W	142-4	Austin (9), Hanger (5), Reynolds (3), Thomas (3), Hellewell, Barton, Coulter, Pearson, Richards, Flanagan	Hellewell (12), Lucchese (7)	1111	Asquith
4.12.94	RT(2)	H	St Helens	L	11-52	Hellewell	Pearce (3, 1dg)	5534	Bates
11.12.94	SD	H	Swinton	W	32-20	Thomas (2), Coulter, Hanger, Shelford, Reynolds	Pearce (4)	2342	Cross
18.12.94	SD	A[1]	Hunslet	L	26-28	Pearson (2), Hanger, Pucill, Reynolds	Hellewell (3)	—	—
26.12.94	SD	A	Ryedale-York	L	12-42	Austin, Reynolds	Hellewell (2)	—	—
31.12.94	SD	H	Keighley C.	L	10-15	Hanger, Thomas	Hellewell	5365	J. Connolly
8.1.95	SD	A	Carlisle	W	26-20	Austin (2), Richards	Kerry (7)	—	—
15.1.95	SD	H	London B.	W	20-8	Austin, Hellewell, Richards, Taylor	Kerry (2)	2350	Ollerton
22.1.95	CC(3)	H	Wigan St. Judes	W	44-10	Austin (3), Hanger, Kerry, King, Reynolds	Kerry (8)	1308	Oddy
29.1.95	SD	H	Leigh	W	50-6	King (2), Austin, Barton, Hanger, Hellewell, Kerry, Pearson, Shelford, Thomas	Kerry (5)	—	—
5.2.95	SD	A	Hull K.R.	D	22-22	St Hilaire (2), Thomas	Kerry (5)	—	—
12.2.95	CC(4)	H	Halifax	W	36-30	Austin (2), Hanger (2), Taylor, Thomas	Kerry (6)	9348	Campbell
19.2.95	SD	H	Highfield	W	74-16	Reynolds (3), Austin (2), King (2), Pearson (2), Barton, Bruce, Hanger, Senior, St Hilaire	Kerry (9)	1609	Carter
26.2.95	CC(5)	A	Keighley C.	W	30-0	Austin, Hanger, King, Reynolds, Taylor, Thomas	Kerry (3)	—	—
12.3.95	CC(QF)	A	Oldham	L	12-23	Hanger, Reynolds	Kerry (2)	—	—
19.3.95	SD	H	Whitehaven	W	42-4	Austin (2), Reynolds (2), Kerry, St Hilaire, Thomas	Pearce (7)	2660	Lee
22.3.95	SD	A	Rochdale H.	W	26-20	Barton, Hanger, King, Thomas	Pearce (4), Kerry (2dg)	—	—
26.3.95	SD	H	Bramley	W	42-26	Thomas (2), Austin, Hanger, Hellewell, Pearce, Reynolds, St. Hilaire	Pearce (5)	2166	Cummings
29.3.95	SD	A	Dewsbury	W	40-12	Austin (4), Hanger, Pearson, Richards, Thomas	Pearce (4)	—	—
2.4.95	SD	H	Carlisle	W	36-24	Pearson (3), Austin (2), Thomas (2), Hanger	Pearce (2)	2300	Atkin
9.4.95	SD	A	London B.	D	24-24	Austin, Hellewell, King, Pearce	Pearce (4)	—	—
14.4.95	SD	H	Ryedale-York	W	34-7	Shelford (2), Austin, Kerry, King, Maders	Kerry (3), Pearce (2)	2213	Ollerton
17.4.95	SD	A	Keighley C.	D	22-22	Austin, Barton, Hanger, Shelford	Pearce (3)	—	—
23.4.95	SD	H	Dewsbury	L	26-52	Coulter (2), Austin, Pearson, Reynolds	Pearce (3)	2756	Smith
7.5.95	SDP(1)	H	Rochdale H.	W	36-10	Austin, Barton, Hellewell, Kerry, Pearce, Senior	Pearce (6)	2412	Bates
14.5.95	SDP(SF)	A	Batley	W	13-6	Pearce, Richards	Pearce (2), Kerry (dg)	—	—
21.5.95	SDP(F)	N[1]	Keighley C.	L	6-26		Pearce (2), Austin (dg), Kerry (dg)	—	Smith

A[1] at Elland Road, Leeds
N[1] at Manchester U.F.C.

HULL

Ground: The Boulevard (01482-329040)
First Season: 1895-96
Nickname: Airlie Birds
Chairman: David Latham
Chief Exec: Stephen Ball
Honours: **Championship** Winners, 1919-20,
1920-21, 1935-36, 1955-56, 1957-58
Beaten finalists, 1956-57
Division One Champions, 1982-83
Division Two Champions, 1976-77,
1978-79
Challenge Cup Winners, 1913-14,
1981-82
Beaten finalists, 1907-08, 1908-09,
1909-10, 1921-22, 1922-23, 1958-59,
1959-60, 1979-80, 1982-83, 1984-85
Regal Trophy Winners, 1981-82
Beaten finalists, 1975-76, 1984-85
Premiership Winners, 1990-91
Beaten finalists, 1980-81, 1981-82,
1982-83, 1988-89
Yorkshire Cup Winners, 1923-24,
1969-70, 1982-83, 1983-84, 1984-85
Beaten finalists, 1912-13, 1914-15,
1920-21, 1927-28, 1938-39, 1946-47,
1953-54, 1954-55, 1955-56, 1959-60,
1967-68, 1986-87
Yorkshire League Winners,
1918-19, 1922-23, 1926-27, 1935-36
Charity Shield Beaten finalists,
1991-92
BBC2 Floodlit Trophy Winners,
1979-80

RECORDS
Match
Goals: 14 by Jim Kennedy v. Rochdale H.,
7 Apr 1921
Geoff "Sammy" Lloyd v. Oldham,
10 Sep 1978
Tries: 7 by Clive Sullivan at Doncaster,
15 Apr 1968
Points: 36 by Jim Kennedy v. Keighley,
29 Jan 1921

Season
Goals: 170 by Geoff "Sammy" Lloyd, 1978-79
Tries: 52 by Jack Harrison, 1914-15
Points: 369 by Geoff "Sammy" Lloyd, 1978-79
Career
Goals: 687 by Joe Oliver, 1928-37 & 1943-45
Tries: 250 by Clive Sullivan, 1961-74 &
1981-85
Points: 1,842 by Joe Oliver, 1928-37 & 1943-45
Appearances: 501 by Edward Rogers, 1906-25
Highest score: 86-0 v. Elland, 1 Apr 1899
Highest against: 66-16 at Wigan, 23 Apr 1995
Attendance: 28,798 v. Leeds (RL Cup),
7 Mar 1936

COACHING REGISTER
● **Since 1974-75**

David Doyle-Davidson	May 74 - Dec 77
Arthur Bunting	Jan 78 - Dec 85
Kenny Foulkes	Dec 85 - May 86
Len Casey	June 86 - Mar 88
Tony Dean Keith Hepworth	} Mar 88 - Apr 88
*Brian Smith	July 88 - Jan 91
*Noel Cleal	Sep 90 - Apr 92
Royce Simmons	May 92 - Apr 94
Tony Gordon	May 94 - Dec 94
Russ Walker/Phil Windley	Dec 94 - May 95
Phil Windley	May 95 -

Joint coaches Sep 90 - Jan 91.

Former New Zealand national coach Tony Gordon, who undertook an eight-month stint at the Boulevard in 1994.

GREAT BRITAIN REGISTER
(35 players)

Billy Batten	(1)	1921
Harold Bowman	(8)	1924-29
Frank Boylen	(1)	1908
Robin Coverdale	(4)	1954
Mick Crane	(1)	1982
Lee Crooks	(11+2)	1982-87
Andy Dannatt	(3)	1985-91
Gary Divorty	(2)	1985
Jim Drake	(1)	1960
Bill Drake	(1)	1962
Paul Eastwood	(13)	1990-92
Steve Evans	(2)	1982
Vince Farrar	(1)	1978
Dick Gemmell	(2)	1968-69
Emlyn Gwynne	(3)	1928-29
Tommy Harris	(25)	1954-60
Karl Harrison	(3)	1990
Mick Harrison	(7)	1967-73
Billy Holder	(1)	1907
Lee Jackson	(11)	1990-92
Mark Jones	(+1)	1992
Arthur Keegan	(9)	1966-69
Steve McNamara	(+2)	1992-93
Edgar Morgan	(2)	1921
Steve Norton	(9)	1978-82
Wayne Proctor	(+1)	1984
Paul Rose	(1)	1982
Garry Schofield	(15)	1984-87
Trevor Skerrett	(6)	1980-82
Billy Stone	(8)	1920-21
Clive Sullivan	(17)	1967-73
Harry Taylor	(3)	1907
Bob Taylor	(2)	1921-26
David Topliss	(1)	1982
Johnny Whiteley	(15)	1957-62

1994-95 SIGNINGS REGISTER

Signed	Player	Club From
1.7.94	Vaikona, Tevita	Canterbury Card'ls, NZ
4.7.94	Fairburn, Jason	Isberg Celtic ARL
20.7.94	Donkin, Matthew	Beverley ARL
1.8.94	Kitching, Chris	Hull Academy
7.8.94	Smith, Andy	Hull Academy
14.8.94	McKenzie, Leroy	Moseley RU
22.8.94	Craven, Steve	Ryedale-York
21.9.94	Clark, Garry	—
22.9.94	Buttle, Shane	Hull Dockers ARL
22.9.94	David, Maea	Canterbury Card'ls, NZ
22.9.94	Endacott, Shane	Canterbury Card'ls, NZ
22.9.94	Richardson, Lee	Hull K.R.
19.10.94	Rose, Gary	Leeds
2.11.94	Stockdale, Ian	Sheffield E.
7.12.94	*Barkworth, Julian	Hull K.R.
6.2.95	McCracken, John	Mysons ARL
24.2.95	Pearson, Carl	Leeds
10.3.95	*Hutchinson, Rob	Hull K.R.

Hull full back Richard Gay, an England debutant in 1995 and the scorer of four tries in 19 games for Hull.

75

HULL 1994-95 PLAYERS' SUMMARY

	Date of Birth	App	T	G	D	Pts	Previous club	Signed
Aston, Jon	5.6.76	1+2	—	—	—	—	Hull K.R.	16.6.93
Busby, Dean	1.12.73	23+5	7	—	—	28	Bransholme ARL	1.2.90
Cassidy, Jez	30.3.74	11	4	—	—	16	Hull Academy	31.10.92
Craven, Steve	9.4.72	4+2	2	—	—	8	Ryedale-York	22.8.94
Danby, Rob	30.8.74	15+4	3	—	—	12	Hull Boys ARL	30.8.91
David, Maea		17	4	—	—	16	New Zealand	22.9.94
Dixon, Mike	6.4.71	22+1	3	—	—	12	East Park ARL	29.8.89
Donkin, Matt	23.11.71	0+1	—	—	—	—	Beverley ARL	20.7.94
Endacott, Shane	3.9.71	17	5	—	—	20	New Zealand	22.9.94
Gay, Richard	9.3.69	19	4	—	—	16	Hull Boys ARL	13.9.89
Gray, Kevin	10.12.75	7+1	5	—	—	20	Minehead ARL	1.7.92
Greenwood, Brandon	28.4.72	5	1	—	—	4	Ovenden ARL	16.3.93
Hewitt, Mark	17.3.74	21+3	8	77	2	188	Hull Academy	9.3.93
Jackson, Anthony	20.11.69	20+7	9	—	—	36	Greatfield ARL	8.7.88
Jones, Mark	22.6.65	2+2	—	—	—	—	Neath RU	12.10.90
Kitching, Chris	1.8.77	3	1	—	—	4	Hull Academy	1.8.94
McKenzie, Leroy	2.9.69	20	1	—	—	4	Moseley RU	14.8.94
McNamara, Steve	18.9.71	32	2	12	—	32	Skirlaugh ARL	15.6.89
Nolan, Gary	31.5.66	31	13	—	—	52	Hull Dockers ARL	2.4.91
Nolan, Rob	2.10.68	13+2	3	1	—	14	Hull Colts	1.1.88
O'Donnell, Craig	2.10.73	2	2	—	—	8	Hull Boys Club ARL	23.7.91
Richardson, Lee	29.10.68	9	—	—	—	—	Hull K.R.	22.9.94
Rose, Gary	25.7.65	16+5	1	—	—	4	Leeds	19.10.94
Sharp, Jon	8.3.67	18+5	1	—	—	4	Travellers ARL	12.3.84
Smirk, Terry	5.8.66	9+5	2	22	5	57	Hull Dockers ARL	23.10.91
Sterling, Paul	2.8.64	16	9	—	—	36	Brad & Bingley RU	19.8.93
Stevens, Ian	18.2.67	2	—	—	—	—	Swansea RU	11.12.91
Street, Tim	29.6.68	27+2	3	—	—	12	Leigh	29.11.93
Vaikona, Tevita	18.8.74	27	8	—	—	32	New Zealand	1.7.94
Walker, Russ	1.9.62	9+6	—	—	—	—	Barrow	8.1.90
Wilson, Richard	5.2.75	1+1	—	—	—	—		
Wilson, Rob	31.8.72	6+6	1	—	—	4	West Hull ARL	13.8.91
Windley, Johan	20.8.75	4+4	—	—	1	1	Isberg ARL	19.8.93
TOTALS								
33 players			102	112	8	640		

Representative appearances 1994-95
Cassidy — GB Under-21s (+1); Gay — England (2,1t); Hewitt — GB Under-21s (1+1,4g):
McNamara — England (1+1); Walker — Cumbria (1).

HULL 1994-95 MATCH ANALYSIS

Date	Com-petition	H/A	Opponent	Rlt	Score	Tries	Goals	Atten-dance	Referee
21.8.94	SBC	H	Warrington	D	16-16	Gay, Hewitt	Hewitt (4)	5180	J. Connolly
28.8.94	SBC	A	Salford	L	28-33	R. Nolan, O'Donnell (2), Greenwood, Dixon	Smirk (4)	—	—
4.9.94	SBC	H	Castleford	L	18-48	Craven (2), G. Nolan	Hewitt (3)	5371	Morris
11.9.94	SBC	A	Halifax	L	12-46	Jackson, Smirk, R. Wilson	—	—	—
18.9.94	SBC	A	Workington T.	L	8-18	Street	Smirk (2)	—	—
25.9.94	SBC	H	Oldham	L	17-21	G. Nolan, Smirk	Smirk (4, 1dg)	4411	Presley
2.10.94	SBC	H	Bradford N.	L	6-12	Sterling	Smirk (2dg)	5375	Cummings
9.10.94	SBC	A	Sheffield E.	L	14-38	G. Nolan, Sterling, Vaikona	Smirk	—	—
16.10.94	SBC	A	Wakefield T.	W	29-22	Cassidy, Endacott, Jackson, Vaikona	Smirk (6, 1dg)	—	—
28.10.94	SBC	H	Wigan	L	12-19	Cassidy, Sterling	Smirk)(2)	5406	Annersley (Aus)
6.11.94	SBC	A	Warrington	L	8-22	—	Smirk (3), Hewitt	—	—
13.11.94	SBC	H	Salford	W	29-16	Hewitt (2), Sterling (2), Vaikona	Hewitt (4), Smirk (dg)	4042	Morris
27.10.94	SBC	A	Castleford	L	10-52	Endacott, Hewitt	Hewitt	—	—
4.12.94	RT(2)	H	Barrow	W	26-16	Endacott, Hewitt, G. Nolan, Sterling	Hewitt (5)	2325	Burke
11.12.94	SBC	H	Halifax	L	16-21	Danby, G. Nolan	Hewitt (4)	4838	Presley
18.12.94	RT(3)	H	Wigan	L	14-38	Endacott, R. Nolan	Hewitt (3)	6203	Smith
26.12.94	SBC	H	Leeds	L	20-24	Busby, Jackson, G. Nolan	Hewitt (4)	6925	R. Connolly
6.1.95	SBC	A	Featherstone R.	W	29-26	Vaikona (2), Gay, Cassidy, Sterling	Hewitt (4,1dg)	—	—
15.1.95	SBC	A	Doncaster	L	38-42	Sterling (2), Cassidy, Endacott, G. Nolan, Hewitt	Hewitt (7)	—	—
22.1.95	SBC	A	St Helens	L	18-54	Busby (2), Gay	Hewitt (3)	—	—
29.1.95	SBC	H	Workington T.	L	22-26	Street (2), Dixon, Vaikona	Hewitt (3)	3948	Campbell
5.2.95	SBC	A	Oldham	L	14-19	Busby, Hewitt, Jackson	Hewitt	—	—
12.2.95	CC(4)	A	Workington T.	L	6-30	Danby	Hewitt	—	—
19.2.95	SBC	A	Bradford N.	L	24-42	Jackson (2), Kitching, Rose	Hewitt (4)	—	—
3.3.95	SBC	H	Sheffield E.	L	16-20	Danby, David, G. Nolan	McNamara (2)	2710	Morris
12.3.95	SBC	H	St. Helens	L	32-43	Gray (2), G. Nolan (2), Busby, Vaikona	McNamara (4)	3572	Cummings
19.3.95	SBC	H	Wakefield T.	W	11-10	G. Nolan	McNamara (3), Windley (dg)	3460	Holdsworth
24.3.95	SBC	A	Widnes	L	18-42	Busby, Sharp, Vaikona	McNamara (3)	—	—
29.3.95	SBC	H	Widnes	W	24-18	Busby, Jackson	Hewitt (8)	2421	Bates
5.4.95	SBC	H	Featherstone R.	W	28-8	David , Gay, Jackson, G. Nolan	Hewitt (6)	3219	Morris
14.4.95	SBC	A	Leeds	L	19-44	Hewitt, McKenzic, G. Nolan	Hewitt (3, 1dg)	—	—
17.4.95	SBC	H	Doncaster	W	42-12	Gray (2), McNamara (2), David, Dixon, R. Nolan	Hewitt (7)	3441	Bates
23.4.95	SBC	A	Wigan	L	16-66	David, Gray, Jackson	Hewitt, R. Nolan	—	—

HULL KINGSTON ROVERS

Ground: Craven Park (01482-74648)
First Season: 1899-1900
Nickname: Robins
Chairman: Barry Lilley
Secretary: Ron Turner
Honours: **Championship** Winners, 1922-23,
1924-25
Beaten finalists, 1920-21, 1967-68
Division One Champions,
1978-79, 1983-84, 1984-85
Division Two Champions,
1989-90
Challenge Cup Winners, 1979-80
Beaten finalists, 1904-05, 1924-25,
1963-64, 1980-81, 1985-86
Regal Trophy Winners, 1984-85
Beaten finalists, 1981-82, 1985-86
Premiership Winners, 1980-81,
1983-84
Beaten finalists, 1984-85
Second Division Premiership
Beaten finalists, 1989-90
Yorkshire Cup Winners, 1920-21,
1929-30, 1966-67, 1967-68, 1971-72,
1974-75, 1985-86
Beaten finalists, 1906-07, 1911-12,
1933-34, 1962-63, 1975-76, 1980-81,
1984-85
Yorkshire League Winners,
1924-25, 1925-26
Eastern Division Championship
Winners, 1962-63
Charity Shield Beaten finalists,
1985-86
BBC2 Floodlit Trophy Winners,
1977-78
Beaten finalists, 1979-80

Winger David Plange, scorer of 35 tries in 34 games in his debut season at Hull K.R.

RECORDS

Match

Goals: 14 by Alf Carmichael v. Merthyr Tydfil,
8 Oct 1910
Mike Fletcher v. Whitehaven,
18 Mar 1990
Colin Armstrong v. Nottingham C.
(at Doncaster), 19 Aug 1990
Tries: 11 by George West v. Brookland R.,
4 Mar 1905
Points: 53 by George West v. Brookland R.,
4 Mar 1905

Season

Goals: 199 by Mike Fletcher, 1989-90
Tries: 45 by Gary Prohm, 1984-85
Points: 450 by Mike Fletcher, 1989-90

Career

Goals: 1,192 by Cyril Kellett, 1956-67
Tries: 207 by Roger Millward, 1966-80
Points: 2,489 by Cyril Kellett, 1956-67
Appearances: 481+8 by Mike Smith, 1974-91
Highest score: 100-6 v. Nottingham C. (at
Doncaster), 19 Aug 1990
Highest against: 76-8 at Halifax, 20 Oct 1991

Attendance: 27,670 v. Hull (League),
3 Apr 1953 — at Boothferry Park,
Hull C. AFC
8,557 v. Hull (League), 1 Jan 1991
— at new Craven Park

COACHING REGISTER
● **Since 1974-75**

Arthur Bunting	Feb 72 - Nov 75
Harry Poole	Dec 75 - Mar 77
Roger Millward	Mar 77 - May 91
George Fairbairn	May 91 - May 94
Steve Crooks	May 94 -

GREAT BRITAIN REGISTER
(26 players)

David Bishop	(+1)	1990
Chris Burton	(8+1)	1982-87
Alan Burwell	(7+1)	1967-69
Len Casey	(7+2)	1977-83
Garry Clark	(3)	1984-85
Alec Dockar	(1)	1947
George Fairbairn	(3)	1981-82
Jack Feetham	(1)	1929
Peter Flanagan	(14)	1962-70
Frank Foster	(1)	1967
David Hall	(2)	1984
Paul Harkin	(+1)	1985
Steve Hartley	(3)	1980-81
Phil Hogan	(2+2)	1979
Roy Holdstock	(2)	1980
Bill Holliday	(8+1)	1964-67
David Laws	(1)	1986
Brian Lockwood	(1+1)	1978-79
Phil Lowe	(12)	1970-78
Roger Millward	(27+1)	1967-78
Harry Poole	(1)	1964
Paul Rose	(1+3)	1974-78
Mike Smith	(10+1)	1979-84
Brian Tyson	(3)	1963-67
David Watkinson	(12+1)	1979-86
Chris Young	(5)	1967-68

1994-95 SIGNINGS REGISTER

Signed	Player	Club From
8.8.94	Plange, David	Sheffield E.
28.8.94	Hill, Kenny	Travellers Saints ARL
1.9.94	Atkins, Gary	Ryedale-York
22.9.94	Dearlove, Andy	Hull
8.12.94	*Barnard, Marcus	Hull
7.3.95	*Marsden, Lee	Ryedale-York
10.3.95	Lumb, Tim	Sheffield E.

Seven tries in 22 games in 1994-95 for Hull K.R.
hooker Richard Chamberlain.

HULL KINGSTON ROVERS 1994-95 PLAYERS' SUMMARY

	Date of Birth	App	T	G	D	Pts	Previous club	Signed
Adams, Jonathan	20.4.76	9+7	6	—	—	24	Minehead ARL	8.2.93
Atkins, Gary	12.10.66	23	13	—	—	52	Ryedale-York	1.9.94
Bibby, Mike	23.10.70	16+5	7	—	—	28	East Park ARL	21.6.89
Brown, Gary	5.9.74	27	22	—	—	88	Embassy ARL	16.9.92
Chamberlain, Richard	1.4.73	22	7	—	—	28	Greatfield ARL	1.6.91
Charles, Chris	7.3.76	10+8	2	—	—	8	Hull Boys ARL	2.2.94
Charlesworth, Adam	8.6.73	18+2	3	—	—	12	Hull University ARL	8.6.93
Chatfield, Gary	26.7.67	14	4	7	1	31	Eureka ARL	24.8.90
Cook, Graham	3.10.70	1+1	—	—	—	—	Greatfield Jnr ARL	14.7.90
Coult, Mick	14.10.69	19+1	7	—	—	28	Scunthorpe RU	13.10.93
Crane, Mike	11.2.71	23+4	15	—	—	60	Greatfield ARL	14.7.90
Dearlove, Andy	19.9.72	11+5	3	—	—	12	Hull	22.9.94
Everitt, Bob	15.4.75	1	—	—	—	—	Hull K.R. Academy	9.8.93
Farr, Stuart	10.9.66	1	—	—	—	—		
Fletcher, Mike	14.4.67	31+1	9	142	—	320	Hull K.R. Colts	28.9.85
Fletcher, Paul	17.3.70	36	11	—	—	44	Eureka ARL	1.9.87
Halafihi, Nick	23.12.67	5+2	2	—	—	8	London C.	22.12.93
Harrison, Chris	28.9.67	36	1	—	—	4	Eureka ARL	23.9.91
Harrison, Des	10.10.64	10+3	—	—	—	—	Hull K.R. Colts	16.4.85
Hill, Kenny	20.9.68	4+3	1	—	—	4	Travellers Saints ARL	28.8.94
Hoe, Sean	3.12.70	15+3	2	—	—	8	ARL	14.7.90
Khan, Paddy	28.2.69	6+2	1	—	—	4	Hull	22.11.86
Leighton, Jamie	5.9.73	8+9	2	—	—	8	Crown Malet ARL	22.7.91
Lumb, Tim	19.2.70	8+1	2	1	1	11	Sheffield E.	10.3.95
Marsden, Lee	28.1.68	0+1	—	—	—	—	Ryedale-York	7.3.95
O'Brien, Craig	4.4.69	5+2	—	—	—	—	West Hull ARL	28.9.88
Oliver, Richard	15.1.72	5	3	—	—	12	Hull RU	26.11.93
Plange, David	24.7.65	34	35	—	—	140	Sheffield E.	8.8.94
Richardson, Steve	5.10.68	2+2	1	—	—	4	Greatfield ARL	9.8.91
Sage, Tim	6.4.70	5+1	—	—	—	—	Eureka ARL	16.9.92
Scott, Paul	7.10.74	3+1	—	—	—	—	Hull Academy	23.7.93
Speckman, Paul	17.10.66	21+3	2	—	—	8		21.1.85
Thompson, Andy	29.6.68	17+4	8	—	—	32	Hull K.R. Colts	24.8.87
Vannet, Paul	19.10.62	8+1	—	—	—	—	Workington T.	7.9.89
Wardrobe, Neil	12.9.72	14	2	—	—	8	Beverley RU	30.9.92
TOTALS								
35 players			171	150	2	986		

HULL K.R. 1994-95 MATCH ANALYSIS

Date	Com-petition	H/A	Opponent	Rlt	Score	Tries	Goals	Atten-dance	Referee
21.8.94	SD	A	Highfield	W	68-10	Coult (3), Crane (3), P. Fletcher, Hoe, Plange, Richardson, M. Fletcher	M. Fletcher (12)	—	—
28.8.94	SD	H	Bramley	W	34-10	C. Harrison, Plange (3), Leighton, M. Fletcher, Hill	M. Fletcher (3)	1687	Kirkpatrick
4.9.94	SD	A	Hunslet	W	60-20	Crane (3), Brown (2), Adams, Atkins, Chamberlain, Chatfield, Coult, Plange	M. Fletcher (8)	—	—
11.9.94	SD	H	Swinton	W	50-0	Crane (3), Plange (2), Chatfield, P. Fletcher, Leighton, Speckman	M. Fletcher (7)	1998	Redfearn
18.9.94	SD	H	Rochdale H.	W	19-2	Crane, Plange	M. Fletcher (5), Chatfield (dg)	2158	Redfearn
25.9.94	SD	A	Huddersfield	L	10-23	Bibby, Crane	M. Fletcher	—	—
4.10.94	SD	A	Whitehaven	L	14-28	Plange (2), P. Fletcher	Chatfield	—	—
9.10.94	SD	H	Carlisle	W	52-0	Brown (3), Atkins (2), Plange (2), Crane, Hoe, Oliver	Chatfield (6)	1657	Galtress
16.10.94	SD	H	Barrow	L	0-1	—	—	1792	Redfearn
30.10.94	SD	A	Dewsbury	L	6-20	Plange	M. Fletcher	—	—
6.11.94	SD	H	Highfield	W	78-4	Plange (5), Adams (3), Oliver (2), Thompson (2), P. Fletcher, Khan, Wardrobe	M. Fletcher (9)	1460	Burke
13.11.94	SD	A	Bramley	W	26-24	Plange, Speckman, Thompson, Wardrobe	M. Fletcher (5)	—	—
27.11.94	RT(1)	H	Hensingham	W	48-8	M. Fletcher (3), Coult Thompson (3), P. Fletcher, Plange	M. Fletcher (6)	1158	Kirkpatrick
4.12.94	RT(2)	A	Oldham	L	0-28	—	—	—	—
11.12.94	SD	H	Hunslet	W	24-12	Atkins (2), Adams, Bibby	M. Fletcher (4)	—	—
18.12.94	SD	A	Swinton	W	38-22	Crane (2), Brown, Coult Charlesworth, Halafihi	M. Fletcher (7)	—	—
26.12.94	SD	A	Keighley C.	L	12-24	Atkins, Charles	M. Fletcher (2)	—	—
8.1.95	SD	H	London B.	W	38-4	Atkins (2), Plange (2), Brown, P. Fletcher, Thompson	M. Fletcher (5)	1860	Burke
15.1.95	SD	A	Batley	L	6-22	Plange	M. Fletcher	—	—
18.1.95	SD	H	Ryedale-York	W	22-14	Brown (2), Plange (2)	M. Fletcher (3)	1470	Redfearn
24.1.95	CC(3)	H	Thornhill	W	58-6	Brown (4), P. Fletcher (2), M. Fletcher, Plange, Coult, Charlesworth	M. Fletcher (9)	1143	McGregor
29.1.95	SD	A	Rochdale H.	L	10-28	M. Fletcher, Plange	M. Fletcher	—	—
5.2.95	SD	H	Huddersfield	D	22-22	Brown, P. Fletcher, M. Fletcher, Plange	M. Fletcher (3)	2220	Kirkpatrick
12.2.95	CC(4)	A	London B.	W	26-20	Brown (2), Chamberlain, Crane, Plange	M. Fletcher (3)	—	—
19.2.95	SD	H	Whitehaven	L	6-12	Brown	M. Fletcher	1628	Redfearn
26.2.95	CC(5)	H	Whitehaven	L	14-18	Halafihi	M. Fletcher (5)	2511	Kirkpatrick
6.3.95	SD	A	Carlisle	W	40-32	Brown (3), Bibby (2), Chatfield (2)	M. Fletcher (6)	—	—
12.3.95	SD	H	Leigh	W	35-8	Brown (2), Chamberlain, Charles, Plange	M. Fletcher (7), Lumb (dg)	1379	Carter
19.3.95	SD	A	Barrow	W	50-18	Atkins (3), Bibby (2), Lumb, Plange, Thompson	M. Fletcher (9)	—	—
26.3.95	SD	H	Dewsbury	W	20-4	Atkins, M. Fletcher, P. Fletcher	M. Fletcher (4)	1904	Parker
2.4.95	SD	A	London B.	L	22-34	Chamberlain (2), Atkins	M. Fletcher (5)	—	—
9.4.95	SD	H	Batley	L	10-33	Bibby, Dearlove	Lumb	2302	McGregor
14.4.95	SD	H	Keighley C.	L	6-14	Lumb	M. Fletcher	3626	J. Connolly
17.4.95	SD	A	Ryedale-York	L	22-37	Chamberlain, Charlesworth, Dearlove, Plange	M. Fletcher (3)	—	—
23.4.95	SD	A	Leigh	L	24-34	Adams, Chamberlain, P. Fletcher, Plange	M. Fletcher (4)	—	—
7.5.95	SDP(1)	A	Keighley C.	L	16-42	Plange (2), Dearlove	M. Fletcher (2)	—	—

81

HUNSLET

Ground: McLaren Field, Bramley (1994-95);
South Leeds Stadium from 1995-96
First Season: 1895-96. Disbanded at end of
1972-73. Re-formed as New
Hunslet in 1973-74. Retitled
Hunslet from start of 1979-80
Chairman: Graham Liles
Secretary: Derek Blackman
Honours: **Championship** Winners, 1907-08,
1937-38
Beaten finalists, 1958-59
Division Two Champions, 1962-63,
1986-87
Challenge Cup Winners, 1907-08,
1933-34
Beaten finalists, 1898-99, 1964-65
Second Division Premiership
Beaten finalists, 1986-87
Yorkshire Cup Winners, 1905-06,
1907-08, 1962-63
Beaten finalists, 1908-09, 1929-30,
1931-32, 1944-45, 1956-57, 1965-66
Yorkshire League Winners,
1897-98, 1907-08, 1931-32

RECORDS

Match
Goals: 12 by Billy Langton v. Keighley,
18 Aug 1959
Tries: 7 by George Dennis v. Bradford N.,
20 Jan 1934
Points: 28 by Tim Lumb v. Runcorn H.,
7 Oct 1990
Richard Pell v. Wigan St. Patricks,
22 Jan 1995

Season
Goals: 181 by Billy Langton, 1958-59
Tries: 34 by Alan Snowden, 1956-57
Points: 380 by Billy Langton, 1958-59

Career
Goals: 1,044 by Billy Langton, 1955-66
Tries: 154 by Fred Williamson, 1943-55
Points: 2,202 by Billy Langton, 1955-66
Appearances: 569+10 by Geoff Gunney, 1951-73
572 by Jack Walkington, 1927-48

Highest score: 76-4 at Nottingham C.,
21 Feb 1993
Highest against: 76-8 v. Halifax, 27 Aug 1972
Attendance: 24,700 v. Wigan (RL Cup),
15 Mar 1924 (at Parkside)

COACHING REGISTER
● **Since 1974-75**

Paul Daley	Apr 74 - Aug 78
Bill Ramsey	Aug 78 - Dec 79
Drew Broatch	Dec 79 - Apr 81
Paul Daley	Apr 81 - Nov 85
*Peter Jarvis	Nov 85 - Apr 88
*David Ward	July 86 - Apr 88
Nigel Stephenson	June 88 - Oct 88
Jack Austin	
John Wolford	}Oct 88 - Jan 89
David Ward	Jan 89 - May 89
Graeme Jennings	Sep 89 - Apr 90
Paul Daley	May 90 - Dec 93
Steve Ferres	Jan 94 -

Joint coaches from July 1986.

*Former Great Britain hooker David Ward, coach at
Hunslet for two spells in the 1980s.*

GREAT BRITAIN REGISTER
(23 players)

Billy Batten	(9)	1907-11
Harry Beverley	(4)	1936-37
Alf Burnell	(3)	1951-54
Hector Crowther	(1)	1929
Jack Evans	(4)	1951-52
Ken Eyre	(1)	1965
Brian Gabbitas	(1)	1959
Geoff Gunney	(11)	1954-65
Dennis Hartley	(2)	1964
John Higson	(2)	1908
Dai Jenkins	(1)	1929
Albert Jenkinson	(2)	1911
Bill Jukes	(6)	1908-10
Bernard Prior	(1)	1966
Bill Ramsey	(7)	1965-66
Brian Shaw	(5)	1956-60
Geoff Shelton	(7)	1964-66
Fred Smith	(9)	1910-14
Sam Smith	(4)	1954
Cecil Thompson	(2)	1951
Les White	(7)	1932-33
Dicky Williams	(3)	1954
Harry Wilson	(3)	1907

1994-95 SIGNINGS REGISTER

Signed	Player	Club From
18.7.94	Bonson, Paul	Featherstone R.
29.7.94	Limb, Scott	Featherstone R.
1.8.94	Close, David	Ryedale-York
2.8.94	Pryce, Steve	Ryedale-York
16.8.94	Lundy, Danny	Hunslet Academy
18.8.94	Brannan, Shaun	ARL
18.8.94	Farrell, Carlton	Keighley C.
18.8.94	Kennedy, Matthew	ARL
18.8.94	Peach, Chris	Hunslet Parkside ARL
25.8.94	Darkes, Richard	Bradford N.
25.8.94	*Watson, Chris	Castleford
2.9.94	Holroyd, Robert	Bradford N.
10.9.94	Field, Michael	Oulton ARL
10.9.94	Steele, Matthew	Ryde Eastwood ARL
12.9.94	*Barrett, Anthony	Leeds
15.9.94	*Boyer, Alan	Sheffield E.
23.9.94	Peach, Simon	Garden Gate ARL
23.9.94	Warden, Lee	Nottingham C.
7.10.94	Pell, Richard	Doncaster
14.10.94	Punchard, Richard	Lock Lane ARL
25.10.94	Hannon, Martin	Wingham ARL
25.10.94	O'Donnell, Wayne	Wingham ARL
28.10.94	Crossland, Richard	Firths ARL
26.11.94	Hewitt, Richard	Keighley C.
2.12.94	*Rowse, Martin	Doncaster
29.12.94	Assame, Martin	—
29.12.94	Brown, Richard	Panthers ARL
29.12.94	Newell, Paul	Hunslet Academy
29.12.94	Perkins, Ian	Hunslet Academy
29.12.94	Richardson, Antonio	A&W College ARL
6.1.95	Francis, David	East Leeds ARL
12.1.95	*Stott, Darren	Dewsbury
26.1.95	*Whitehead, Paul	Castleford
3.2.95	*Pickles, Damien	Huddersfield
7.2.95	Handley, Geoff	Queens ARL
10.2.95	Prigmore, Dean	Castleford
25.2.95	Burns, Paul	Eastmoor ARL
28.2.95	*Minter, Steven	Featherstone R.
24.3.95	*Miller, Vincent	Rochdale H.
24.3.95	*Viller, Jason	Rochdale H.

HUNSLET 1994-95 PLAYERS' SUMMARY

	Date of Birth	App	T	G	D	Pts	Previous club	Signed
Barrett, Tony	26.10.73	1	—	—	—	—	Leeds	12.9.94
Boothroyd, Giles	17.3.69	22	10	—	1	40	Castleford	17.8.93
Brannan, Shaun	2.12.74	0+1	—	—	—	—	ARL	18.8.94
Brook, David	4.2.71	29+3	13	2	4	60	Middleton ARL	4.6.90
Brown, Wayne	28.4.67	4	—	—	—	—		
Burrow, Paul	8.5.64	10	3	—	—	12		18.4.89
Close, David	7.5.66	28+1	7	47	3	125	Ryedale-York	5.4.94
Coyle, Michael	5.3.71	30+2	16	—	—	64	Middleton ARL	18.7.90
Currie, Eugene	25.2.65	5+2	—	—	—	—		16.9.92
Daniel, Alan	1.2.69	1+1	—	—	—	—	Queens ARL	6.1.91
Darkes, Richard	5.10.68	4	1	—	—	4	Bradford N.	25.8.94
Farrell, Carlton	23.6.66	32+1	3	—	—	12	Keighley C.	18.8.94
Grant, Robert		19	3	—	—	12		
Holroyd, Bob	24.11.71	7+2	1	—	—	4	Bradford N.	2.9.94
Jowitt, Warren	9.9.74	18+7	2	—	—	8	Stanley R. ARL	6.9.93
Kerona, Jonas		4	—	—	—	—	Western Samoa	
Kibe, Eric	23.3.71	17+1	4	—	—	16	Kenya RU	23.4.93
Lambert, Matt		21	3	—	—	12		
Lee, Neil	23.8.75	4+10	4	—	—	16	Middleton ARL	1.2.94
Limb, Scott	15.6.73	33	29	3	—	122	Featherstone R.	25.3.94
Longstaff, Jason	8.2.71	0+3	—	—	—	—	Oulton ARL	26.1.94
McElhatton, Craig	24.2.70	0+1	—	—	—	—	Wakefield T.	18.12.92
McKelvie, John	19.5.67	1	—	—	—	—	Toronto Workers	2.9.92
Minter, Steve	17.3.73	0+1	—	—	—	—	Featherstone R.	28.2.95
Peach, Chris	13.3.77	0+1	—	—	—	—	Hunslet P. ARL	18.8.94
Pell, Richard	17.10.66	22+2	5	54	—	128	Doncaster	18.2.94
Pickles, Damien	2.12.70	0+5	—	—	—	—	Huddersfield	3.2.95
Pryce, Steve	12.5.69	34	5	—	—	20	Ryedale-York	2.8.94
Punchard, Richard	10.5.68	0+2	1	—	—	4	Lock Lane ARL	14.10.94
Rose, Ian	24.10.66	1	—	—	—	—	Ossett T. ARL	14.7.92
Rowse, Martin	8.3.69	5+1	—	—	—	—	Doncaster	18.2.94
Sampson, Roy	28.11.61	0+1	—	—	—	—	Dewsbury	17.2.87
Simpson, Ian	21.11.70	1+2	—	—	—	—		
Sowery, Gary	5.5.69	5+2	—	—	—	—		16.9.92
Steele, Matthew	10.1.70	9+1	—	—	—	—	Ryde Eastwood ARL	10.9.94
Stott, Darren	8.12.72	0+2	—	—	—	—	Dewsbury	12.1.95
Viller, Jason	29.10.71	2+3	1	—	—	4	Rochdale H.	24.3.95
Watson, Chris	9.9.67	29	7	—	—	28	Castleford	25.8.94
White, Paul	5.11.64	32	8	—	—	32	Ryedale-York	5.3.91
Whitehead, Paul	9.3.72	3+3	1	—	—	4	Castleford	26.1.95
Wilson, Sean	13.3.72	3+4	1	—	—	4	Hunslet P. ARL	28.3.91
Wright, Jason	14.3.73	6	—	—	—	—		6.12.90
TOTALS								
42 players			128	106	7	731		

HUNSLET 1994-95 MATCH ANALYSIS

Date	Com-petition	H/A	Opponent	Rlt	Score	Tries	Goals	Atten-dance	Referee
21.8.94	SD	A	Leigh	L	0-49	—	—	—	—
28.8.94	SD	H	London B.	W	25-14	Coyle (2), Watson (2)	Close (4, 1dg)	520	Bates
4.9.94	SD	H	Hull K.R.	L	20-60	Brook, Coyle, Darkes	Close (4)	792	Oddy
11.9.94	SD	A	Huddersfield	L	18-42	Holroyd, Limb, Pryce	Close (3)	—	—
18.9.94	SD	H	Carlisle	L	22-26	Coyle (2), Burrow, Watson	Close (3)	502	Lee
25.9.94	SD	A	Rochdale H.	L	12-46	Burrow, White	Close (2)	—	—
2.10.94	SD	H	Ryedale-York	W	26-10	Brook, Burrow, Coyle, Limb	Close (5)	582	Ollerton
9.10.94	SD	A	Swinton	L	20-46	Jowitt, Pell, Watson, Wilson	Pell (2)	—	—
16.10.94	SD	A	Keighley C.	L	10-66	Lee, Limb	Limb	—	—
30.10.94	SD	A	Barrow	W	21-8	Coyle (2), Farrell, Limb	Limb (2), Brook (dg)	—	—
6.11.94	SD	H	Leigh	W	13-4	Brook (2)	Brook (2,1dg)	505	Atkin
13.11.94	SD	A	London B.	L	2-40	—	Pell	—	—
19.11.94	RT(1)	H	St Esteve (Fr)	L	14-18	Kibe, Punchard	Pell (3)	521	Lee
11.12.94	SD	A	Hull K.R.	L	12-24	Limb, White	Pell (2)	—	—
18.12.94	SD	H[1]	Huddersfield	W	28-26	Limb (2), Boothroyd, Pryce	Pell (5), Close	1326	Kirkpatrick
26.12.94	SD	A	Bramley	W	16-8	Pryce (2), Lee	Pell (2)	—	—
1.1.95	SD	H[1]	Dewsbury	L	16-18	Boothroyd, Pryce, Brook	Close, Pell	1594	Cummings
8.1.95	SD	A	Whitehaven	L	14-27	Boothroyd, Limb (2)	Pell	—	—
15.1.95	SD	H	Highfield	W	56-0	Limb (5), Boothroyd (2), Close, Lambert, Pell	Pell (8)	262	McGregor
22.1.95	CC(3)	H	Wigan St Patricks	W	64-4	Coyle (2), Kibe (2), Pell (2), Boothroyd, Close, Farrell, Limb, White	Pell (10)	342	Presley
29.1.95	SD	A	Carlisle	W	32-12	Coyle (2), Boothroyd, Grant, Jowitt, Limb	Pell (4)	—	—
5.2.95	SD	H	Rochdale H.	W	25-18	Boothroyd, Brook, Coyle, Kibe	Pell (4), Close (dg)	731	Galtress
12.2.95	CC(4)	H	Salford	D	32-32	Close (2), Boothroyd, Coyle, Lee, Pell	Pell (4)	1112	Ollerton
15.2.95	CC(4) Replay	A	Salford	L	10-52	Brook (2)	Close	—	—
19.2.95	SD	A	Ryedale-York	W	19-18	Limb (2), Farrell, Lambert	Pell, Brook (dg)	—	—
6.3.95	SD	H	Swinton	W	6-4	Lee	Close	533	Redfearn
12.3.95	SD	H	Batley	L	22-34	Limb (2), Brook, Watson	Close (3)	1054	R. Connolly
19.3.95	SD	H[1]	Keighley C.	L	18-33	Close, Lambert, Watson	Close (2), Pell	2823	Kirkpatrick
26.3.95	SD	H	Barrow	W	26-24	White (2), Close, Grant, Whitehead	Close (3)	383	Golden
2.4.95	SD	H	Whitehaven	W	22-20	Grant, Limb, White	Close (4, 1dg), Brook (1dg)	506	Galtress
9.4.95	SD	A	Highfield	W	44-14	Limb (3), Brook (2), Coyle, Viller, Watson	Pell (5), Close	—	—
14.4.95	SD	H	Bramley	W	22-20	Limb (2), Brook, Coyle	Close (3)	616	McGregor
17.4.95	SD	A	Dewsbury	L	16-46	Limb (2), White	Close	—	—
23.4.95	SD	A	Batley	W	28-26	Boothroyd, Brook, Close, Limb, White	Close (4)	—	—

[1] at Elland Road, Leeds

KEIGHLEY COUGARS

Ground: Cougar Park (01535-602602), previously titled Lawkholme Park until the 1992-93 season.
First Season: 1901-02. Added Cougars to title at start of 1991-92.
Nickname: Cougars
Chairman: Mike O'Neill
Secretary: Jack Wainwright
Honours: **Division Two** Champions, 1902-03, 1994-95
Division Three Champions, 1992-93
Challenge Cup Beaten finalists, 1936-37
Second Division Premiership Winners, 1994-95
Yorkshire Cup Beaten finalists, 1943-44, 1951-52

RECORDS

Match
Goals: 15 by John Wasyliw v. Nottingham C., 1 Nov 1992
Tries: 5 by Ike Jagger v. Castleford, 13 Jan 1906
Sam Stacey v. Liverpool C., 9 Mar 1907
Nick Pinkney v. Hunslet, 16 Oct 94
Nick Pinkney v. Highfield (away game at Rochdale), 23 Apr 1995
Points: 36 by John Wasyliw v. Nottingham C., 31 Oct 1993

Season
Goals: 187 by John Wasyliw, 1992-93
Tries: 45 by Nick Pinkney, 1994-95
Points: 490 by John Wasyliw, 1992-93

Career
Goals: 967 by Brian Jefferson, 1965-77
Tries: 155 by Sam Stacey, 1904-20
Points: 2,116 by Brian Jefferson, 1965-77
Appearances: 372 by Hartley Tempest, 1902-15
David McGoun, 1925-38
Highest score: 104-4 v. Highfield (away game at Rochdale), 23 Apr 1995
Highest against: 92-2 at Leigh, 30 Apr 1986
Attendance: 14,500 v. Halifax (RL Cup), 3 Mar 1951

COACHING REGISTER
● **Since 1974-75**

Alan Kellett	Jan 73 - May 75
Roy Sabine	Aug 75 - Oct 77
Barry Seabourne	Nov 77 - Mar 79
Albert Fearnley (Mgr)	Apr 79 - Aug 79
Alan Kellett	Apr 79 - Apr 80
Albert Fearnley	May 80 - Feb 81
Bakary Diabira	Feb 81 - Sep 82
Lee Greenwood	Sep 82 - Oct 83
Geoff Peggs	Nov 83 - Sep 85
Peter Roe	Sep 85 - July 86
Colin Dixon	July 86 - June 89
Les Coulter	July 89 - Apr 90
Tony Fisher	June 90 - Sep 91
Peter Roe	Sep 91 - Apr 94
Phil Larder	May 94 -

GREAT BRITAIN REGISTER
(1 player)

Terry Hollindrake	(1)	1955

1994-95 SIGNINGS REGISTER

Signed	Player	Club From
1.7.94	Robinson, Chris	Halifax
6.7.94	Fleary, Darren	Dewsbury
10.7.94	Harrison, Michael	Dewsbury Moor ARL
4.8.94	Cochrane, Gareth	Hull
11.8.94	Kenyon, Neil	Warrington
16.8.94	Stoop, Andre	Wigan
17.8.94	Tupaea, Shane	Oldham
8.9.94	Irving, Simon	Leeds
27.10.94	Wray, Simon	Morley RU
17.11.94	Roberts, Robert	East Leeds ARL
27.11.94	Larder, David	Sheffield E.
3.3.95	*O'Donnell, Gus	St. Helens
4.4.95	Powell, Daryl	Sheffield E.

KEIGHLEY COUGARS 1994-95 PLAYERS' SUMMARY

	Date of Birth	App	T	G	D	Pts	Previous club	Signed
Appleby, Darren	14.6.67	12+16	6	—	—	24	Featherstone R.	18.9.92
Ball, Phil	20.6.69	1	—	—	—	—	Wigan	5.6.92
Berry, Joe	7.5.74	0+11	1	—	—	4		2.9.93
Butterfield, Jeff	13.8.64	3	—	—	—	—		10.8.91
Cochrane, Gareth	18.9.74	30+1	6	-	—	24	Hull	4.8.94
Creasser, David	18.6.65	11+1	1	4	—	12	Leeds	4.2.94
Delaney, Andy	11.9.74	0+1	1	-	—	4	Dewsbury Moor ARL	22.7.93
Dixon, Keith	16.9.66	22+6	19	5	—	86	Keighley Academy ARL	28.8.84
Doorey, Grant	3.2.68	22	5	—	—	20	Australia	
Eyres, Andy	1.10.68	39	25	-	—	100	Widnes	24.3.91
Fleary, Darren	2.12.72	37	3	-	—	12	Dewsbury	6.7.94
Gately, Ian	21.3.66	34+2	5	—	—	20	Australia	14.6.93
Gibson, Chris	9.10.75	0+1	1	—	—	4	Featherstone Academy	15.3.94
Hall, Steve	7.9.67	19	4	—	—	16	Dudley Hill ARL	13.7.91
Hill, Brendan	15.9.64	17+12	7	-	—	28	Halifax	22.10.93
Hinchliffe, Andy	26.10.69	1	—	—	—	—	RU	21.11.91
Irving, Simon	22.3.67	34	22	152	—	392	Leeds	8.9.94
Kenyon, Neil	26.10.67	14+2	9	-	—	36	Warrington	11.8.94
Larder, David	5.6.76	9+10	3	—	—	12	Sheffield E.	27.11.94
O'Donnell, Gus	11.12.70	2	—	—	—	—	St. Helens	3.3.95
Pinkney, Nick	6.12.70	37	45	—	—	180	Ryedale-York	13.5.93
Powell, Daryl	21.7.65	7	4	—	—	16	Sheffield E.	4.4.95
Race, Wayne	17.4.66	5	1	—	—	4	Doncaster	13.8.91
Ramshaw, Jason	23.7.69	39	11	—	4	48	Halifax	27.7.92
Robinson, Chris	2.9.70	33	7	—	—	28	Halifax	1.7.94
Senior, Andy	31.8.75	0+1	—	—	—	—	Keighley Academy	11.1.94
Stephenson, Phil	17.6.72	10+10	3	—	—	12	Clayton ARL	19.3.91
Stoop, Andre	8.10.66	32	14	—	—	56	Wigan	16.8.94
Tupaea, Shane	24.12.63	6+2	—	—	—	—	Oldham	17.8.94
Walker, John	27.12.68	8	8	8	—	48	Otley RU	29.10.91
Wood, Martin	24.6.70	33+3	20	15	—	110	Scarborough P.	17.1.92
Wray, Simon	19.5.70	3	1	—	—	4	Morley RU	27.10.94
TOTALS								
32 players			232	184	4	1,300		

Representative appearances 1994-95

Cochrane — GB Under-21s (+1); Pinkney — England (1,1t).

KEIGHLEY COUGARS 1994-95 MATCH ANALYSIS

Date	Competition	H/A	Opponent	Rlt	Score	Tries	Goals	Attendance	Referee
21.8.94	SD	H	Whitehaven	W	38-8	Pinkney (3), Walker (2), Appleby, Eyres	Walker (4), Wood	3051	Tennant
28.8.94	SD	A	Rochdale H.	W	30-16	Pinkney (2), Stoop, Creasser, Walker, Stephenson	Creasser (3)	—	—
4.9.94	SD	H	Ryedale-York	D	18-18	Hill (2), Dixon, Stoop	Creasser	3536	Gilmour
11.9.94	SD	A	London B.	W	30-10	Wood (2), Irving, Ramshaw, Stoop	Irving (5)	—	—
18.9.94	SD	H	Dewsbury	W	46-8	Wood (2), Eyres, Gateley, Irving, Pinkney, Stoop	Irving (9)	3918	Asquith
25.9.94	SD	A	Bramley	W	18-2	Eyres, Kenyon, Stoop	Irving (3)	—	—
2.10.94	SD	A	Barrow	W	24-10	Cochrane, Dixon, Hall	Irving (6)	—	—
9.10.94	SD	H	Batley	L	22-26	Eyres, Irving, Pinkney	Irving (5)	4198	Tennant
16.10.94	SD	H	Hunslet	W	66-10	Pinkney (5), Stoop, Dixon, Eyres, Fleary, Irving, Kenyon, Wood	Irving (7)	3016	Asquith
								3016	Asquith

(Continued)

Date	Competition	H/A	Opponent	Rlt	Score	Tries	Goals	Attendance	Referee
30.10.94	SD	H	Carlisle	W	46-14	Pinkney (4), Eyres, Fleary, Hill, Irving, Walker	Irving (5)	3667	Atkin
6.11.94	SD	A	Whitehaven	W	38-8	Irving (2), Pinkney (2), Doorey, Eyres	Irving (7)	—	—
13.11.94	SD	H	Rochdale H.	W	28-13	Dixon, Irving, Pinkney, Walker	Irving (6)	3887	Oddy
27.11.94	RT(1)	H	Chorley	W	56-0	Pinkney (3), Walker (3), Doorey, Gibson, Hall, Larder, Ramshaw, Wood	Walker (4)	2370	Gilmour
4.12.94	RT(2)	H	Bramley	W	28-4	Hall (2), Pinkney (2), Robinson, Stoop	Irving (2)	2515	Atkin
11.12.94	SD	A	Ryedale-York	W	52-12	Dixon (3), Ramshaw (2), Gately, Hill, Irving, Pinkney, Wood	Irving (6)	—	—
18.12.94	RT(3)	H	Sheffield E.	W	26-10	Cochrane, Dixon, Robinson, Stoop	Irving (5)	3914	R. Connolly
26.12.94	SD	H	Hull K.R.	W	24-12	Eyres, Pinknew, Robinson, Stephenson	Irving (4)	4922	Presley
31.12.94	SD	A	Huddersfield	W	15-10	Irving, Ramshaw	Irving (3), Ramshaw (dg)	—	—
8.1.95	RT(QF)	H	Warrington	L	18-20	Eyres, Pinkney, Stoop	Irving (3)	5685	Holdsworth
11.1.95	SD	H	London B.	L	14-25	Dixon (2)	Irving (3)	3894	Presley
15.1.95	SD	A	Swinton	W	48-6	Wood (2), Cochrane, Eyres, Irving, Pinkney, P. Stephenson, Stoop	Irving (8)	—	—
24.1.95	CC(3)	H	Chorley	W	68-0	Dixon (2), Irving (2), Larder (2,) Appleby, Berry, Delaney, Eyres, Hill, Kenyon, Pinkney, Ramshaw	Irving (6)	1849	Lee
1.2.95	SD	H	Leigh	W	38-6	Eyres (2), Dixon, Doorey, Pinkney, Stoop, Wood	Irving (5)	2931	Oddy
5.2.95	SD	W	Bramley	H	24-8	Eyres (3), Pinkney, Stoop	Irving (2)	3515	Asquith
12.2.95	CC(4)	H	Dewsbury	W	24-12	Pinkney (2), Cochrane, Irving, Robinson	Irving (2)	3815	Cummings
19.2.95	SD	H	Barrow	W	28-6	Appleby, Dixon, Doorey, Pinkney, Wray	Dixon (4)	2866	McGregor
26.2.95	CC(5)	H	Huddersfield	L	0-30	—	—	5700	Bates
6.3.95	SD	A	Batley	L	6-8	Pinkney	Irving	—	—
12.3.95	SD	H	Highfield	W	68-0	Eyres (3), Irving (3), Appleby (2), Dixon (2), Doorey, Gately	Irving (9), Dixon	3005	Nicholson
19.3.95	SD	A	Hunslet	W	33-18	Gately (2), Appleby, Fleary, Wood	Irving (6), Ramshaw (dg)	—	—
22.3.95	SD	A	Dewsbury	L	2-20	—	Irving	—	—
26 3.95	SD	A	Carlisle	L	2-12	—	Irving	—	—
2.4.95	SD	A	Leigh	W	34-13	Kenyon (2), Pinkney (2), Eyres, Ramshaw	Wood (5)	—	—
9.4.95	SD	H	Swinton	W	42-6	Kenyon (3), Wood (3), Race, Robinson	Wood (5)	4221	Ollerton
14.4.95	SD	A	Hull K.R.	W	14-6	Ramshaw, Wood	Wood (3)	—	—
17.4.95	SD	H	Huddersfield	D	22-22	Cochrane, Eyres, Irving, Pinkney	Irving (2), Wood	5224	Campbell
23.4.95	SD	A[1]	Highfield	W	104-4	Pinkney (5), Eyres (3), Earnshaw (3), Wood (2), Cochrane, Dixon, Hill, Irving, Kenyon, Powell, Robinson	Irving (12)	—	—
7.5.95	SDP(1)	H	Hull K.R.	W	42-16	Dixon (2), Irving (2), Powell (2), Hill	Irving (7)	3346	J. Connolly
14.5.95	SDP(SF)	H	London B.	W	38-4	Wood (2), Irving, Pinkney, Robinson, Stoop	Irving (7)	3627	Morris
21.5.95	SDP(F)	N[1]	Huddersfield	W	26-6	Eyres, Pinkney, Powell, Wood	Irving (4), Ramshaw (2 dg)	—	Smith

A[1] at Rochdale H. N[1] at Manchester U.F.C.

LEEDS

Ground: Headingley (0113-278-6181)
First Season: 1895-96
Nickname: Loiners
Chairman: Dennis Greenwood
Chief Exec: Alf Davies
Honours: **Championship** Winners, 1960-61,
1968-69, 1971-72
Beaten finalists, 1914-15, 1928-29,
1929-30, 1930-31, 1937-38, 1969-70,
1972-73
League Leaders Trophy Winners,
1966-67, 1967-68, 1968-69, 1969-70,
1971-72
Challenge Cup Winners, 1909-10,
1922-23, 1931-32, 1935-36, 1940-41,
1941-42, 1956-57, 1967-68, 1976-77,
1977-78
Beaten finalists, 1942-43, 1946-47,
1970-71, 1971-72, 1993-94, 1994-95
Regal Trophy Winners, 1972-73,
1983-84
Beaten finalists, 1982-83, 1987-88,
1991-92
Premiership Winners, 1974-75,
1978-79
Beaten finalists, 1994-95
Yorkshire Cup Winners, 1921-22,
1928-29, 1930-31, 1932-33, 1934-35,
1935-36, 1937-38, 1958-59, 1968-69,
1970-71, 1972-73, 1973-74, 1975-76,
1976-77, 1979-80, 1980-81, 1988-89
Beaten finalists, 1919-20, 1947-48,
1961-62, 1964-65
Yorkshire League Winners,
1901-02, 1927-28, 1930-31, 1933-34,
1934-35, 1936-37, 1937-38, 1950-51,
1954-55, 1956-57, 1960-61, 1966-67,
1967-68, 1968-69, 1969-70
BBC2 Floodlit Trophy Winners,
1970-71

RECORDS
Match
Goals: 13 by Lewis Jones v. Blackpool B.,
19 Aug 1957

Tries: 8 by Fred Webster v. Coventry,
12 Apr 1913
Eric Harris v. Bradford N.,
14 Sep 1931
Points: 31 by Lewis Jones v. Bradford N.,
22 Aug 1956

Season
Goals: 166 by Lewis Jones, 1956-57
Tries: 63 by Eric Harris, 1935-36
Points: 431 by Lewis Jones, 1956-57

Career
Goals: 1,244 by Lewis Jones, 1952-64
Tries: 391 by Eric Harris, 1930-39
Points: 2,920 by Lewis Jones, 1952-64
Appearances: 608+18 by John Holmes, 1968-89
Highest score: 102-0 v. Coventry, 12 Apr 1913
Highest against: 74-6 at Wigan, 10 May 1992
Attendance: 40,175 v. Bradford N. (League),
21 May 1947

COACHING REGISTER
● **Since 1974-75**

Roy Francis	June 74 - May 75
Syd Hynes	June 75 - Apr 81
Robin Dewhurst	June 81 - Oct 83
Maurice Bamford	Nov 83 - Feb 85
Malcolm Clift	Feb 85 - May 85
Peter Fox	May 85 - Dec 86
Maurice Bamford	Dec 86 - Apr 88
Malcolm Reilly	Aug 88 - Sep 89
David Ward	Sep 89 - May 91
Doug Laughton	May 91 -

*Doug Laughton, who took over as coach of Leeds
in May 1991.*

GREAT BRITAIN REGISTER
(74 players)

Les Adams	(1)	1932
John Atkinson	(26)	1968-80
Jim Bacon	(11)	1920-26
Ray Batten	(3)	1969-73
John Bentley	(1)	1992
Jim Birch	(1)	1907
Stan Brogden	(7)	1936-37
Jim Brough	(5)	1928-36
Gordon Brown	(6)	1954-55
Mick Clark	(5)	1968
Terry Clawson	(3)	1972
David Creasser	(2+2)	1985-88
Lee Crooks	(1)	1989
Willie Davies	(2)	1914
Kevin Dick	(2)	1980
Roy Dickinson	(2)	1985
Paul Dixon	(8+1)	1990-92
Les Dyl	(11)	1974-82
Richard Eyres	(+2)	1993
Tony Fisher	(3)	1970-71
Phil Ford	(5)	1989
Dick Gemmell	(1)	1964
Carl Gibson	(10)	1990-91
Bobby Goulding	(1)	1992
Jeff Grayshon	(2)	1985
Bob Haigh	(3+1)	1970-71
Derek Hallas	(2)	1961
Ellery Hanley	(2)	1992-93
Fred Harrison	(3)	1911
David Heron	(1+1)	1982
John Holmes	(14+6)	1971-82
Syd Hynes	(12+1)	1970-73
Billy Jarman	(2)	1914
David Jeanes	(3)	1972
Dai Jenkins	(1)	1947
Lewis Jones	(15)	1954-57
Ken Jubb	(2)	1937
John Lowe	(1)	1932
Paul Medley	(3+1)	1987-88
Steve Molloy	(1)	1993
Ike Owens	(4)	1946
Steve Pitchford	(4)	1977
Harry Poole	(2)	1966
Roy Powell	(13+6)	1985-91

Dai Prosser	(1)	1937
Keith Rayne	(4)	1984
Kevin Rayne	(1)	1986
Bev Risman	(5)	1968
Don Robinson	(5)	1956-60
David Rose	(4)	1954
Garry Schofield	(29+2)	1988-94
Barry Seabourne	(1)	1970
Brian Shaw	(1)	1961
Mick Shoebottom	(10+2)	1968-71
Barry Simms	(1)	1962
Alan Smith	(10)	1970-73
Stanley Smith	(10)	1929-33
David Stephenson	(4+1)	1988
Jeff Stevenson	(15)	1955-58
Squire Stockwell	(3)	1920-21
Alan Tait	(1+4)	1992-93
Abe Terry	(1)	1962
Arthur "Ginger" Thomas	(4)	1926-29
Phil Thomas	(1)	1907
Joe Thompson	(12)	1924-32
Andrew Turnbull	(1)	1951
Hugh Waddell	(1)	1989
Billy Ward	(1)	1910
David Ward	(12)	1977-82
Fred Webster	(3)	1910
Dicky Williams	(9)	1948-51
Harry Woods	(1)	1937
Geoff Wriglesworth	(5)	1965-66
Frank Young	(1)	1908

1994-95 SIGNINGS REGISTER

Signed	Player	Club From
1.7.94	Brown, Gavin	Milford ARL
1.7.94	Faimalo, Esene	Widnes
1.7.94	Haines, Ronnie	Gloucester RU
6.7.94	Windas, Chris	Minehead
15.7.94	Mann, George	St. Helens
25.8.94	Smith, Kris	Eccles ARL
1.10.94	Hughes, Adam	Milford ARL
24.11.94	Tait, Steve	—
29.11.94	Julian, Allan	ARL
16.12.94	Hudson, Lee	Eccles ARL
20.2.95	Riley, Carl	Dewsbury Moor ARL
3.3.95	Crooks, Ian	Myson Juniors ARL
23.3.95	Oatridge, Paul	Queens ARL
7.4.95	Robinson, Craig	ARL

LEEDS 1994-95 PLAYERS' SUMMARY

	Date of Birth	App	T	G	D	Pts	Previous club	Signed
Cook, Paul	23.7.76	8+1	4	16	—	48		1.12.92
Cummins, Francis	12.10.76	41	21	29	—	142	St. John Fisher ARL	12.10.93
Entat, Patrick	18.9.64	19+1	2	—	—	8	France	23.5.94
Eyres, Richard	7.12.64	33+2	8	—	—	32	Widnes	16.9.93
Faimalo, Esene	11.10.66	40+2	6	—	—	24	Widnes	1.7.94
Fallon, Jim	27.3.65	39	24	—	—	96	Bath RU	6.7.92
Fozzard, Nick	22.7.77	0+3	—	—	—	—	Shaw Cross ARL	27.7.93
Gibbons, David	18.1.76	1	—	—	—	—	East Leeds ARL	10.8.93
Golden, Marvin	21.12.76	0+1	1	—	—	4	Hunslet Parkside ARL	22.12.93
Hanley, Ellery	27.3.61	34	41	1	—	166	Wigan	6.9.91
Harmon, Neil	9.1.69	17+19	2	—	—	8	Warrington	24.8.93
Hassan, Phil	18.8.74	4+2	1	—	—	4	St. Pauls ARL	10.8.93
Holroyd, Graham	25.10.75	31+3	12	134	1	317	Siddal ARL	24.9.92
Howard, Harvey	29.8.68	26+6	1	—	—	4	Widnes	4.1.94
Innes, Craig	10.9.69	38	13	—	—	52	New Zealand RU	4.1.92
Iro, Kevin	25.5.68	39	19	—	—	76	Australia	29.10.92
Julian, Alan	23.2.70	0+1	—	—	—	—	Milford ARL	24.11.94
Leatham, Jim	10.10.74	2+6	—	—	—	—	Leeds Academy	7.9.93
Lowes, James	11.10.69	36	6	—	—	24	Hunslet	30.9.92
Mann, George	31.7.65	20+15	6	—	—	24	St. Helens	15.7.94
Mercer, Gary	22.6.66	37+1	14	—	—	56	Warrington	5.8.92
Morley, Adrian	10.5.77	1+2	1	—	—	4	Eccles ARL	10.5.94
Rose, Gary	25.7.65	0+1	—	—	—	—	Featherstone R.	2.9.93
Scales, Jonathan	28.7.74	1	—	—	—	—	Gosforth RU	28.3.93
Schofield, Garry	1.7.65	33+3	19	—	4	80	Hull	23.10.87
Schultz, Matthew	9.8.75	0+4	—	—	—	—	Hull ARL	9.8.92
Shaw, Michael	16.7.75	0+1	—	—	—	—	Elland ARL	3.3.93
Tait, Alan	2.7.64	37	13	—	—	52	Widnes	14.8.92
Vassilakopoulos, Marcus	19.9.76	9+9	—	—	—	—	Hull ARL	20.9.93
TOTALS								
29 players			214	180	5	1,221		

Representative appearances 1994-95
Cummins — England (1,1t), GB Under-21s (2); Eyres — Wales (2); Howard — England (1);
Leatham — GB Under-21s (+1); Schofield — Britain (+2), England (1).

LEEDS 1994-95 MATCH ANALYSIS

Date	Competition	H/A	Opponent	Rlt	Score	Tries	Goals	Attendance	Referee
19.8.94	SBC	A	Workington T.	W	22-16	Iro (2), Mercer, Schofield	Holroyd (3)	—	—
28.8.94	SBC	H	Featherstone R.	W	36-14	Iro, Schofield, Mercer, Innes, Hanley, Cook	Holroyd (6)	12,305	J. Connolly
4.9.94	SBC	A	Doncaster	W	16-6	Cummins, Entat, Tait	Holroyd (2)	—	—
9.9.94	SBC	A	Wigan	L	6-38	Mercer	Holroyd	—	—
18.9.94	SBC	H	Salford	W	26-20	Tait (2), Fallon, Hanley, Holroyd	Holroyd (3)	11,598	Morris
25.9.94	SBC	A	Widnes	W	48-10	Faimalo (2), Cummins, Eyres, Hanley, Holroyd, Iro, Schofield, Tait	Holroyd (6)	—	—
30-.9.94	SBC	H	Castleford	D	14-14	Cummins, Hanley	Holroyd (3)	12,837	J. Connolly
5.10.94	Tour	H	Australia	L	6-48	Tait	Cummins	18,581	Smith
9.10.94	SBC	A	St. Helens	L	18-25	Fallon (2), Entat, Iro	Cummins	—	—
16.10.94	SBC	H	Sheffield E.	W	30-18	Fallon (3), Hassan, Mercer, Schofield	Holroyd (3)	10,014	Annersley (Aus)
30.10.94	SBC	H	Wakefield T.	W	38-10	Hanley (3), Fallon (2), Iro, Schofield	Cummins (5)	11,616	Presley
6.11.94	SBC	H	Workington T.	W	42-16	Schofield (2), Tait (2), Eyres, Fallon, Lowes, Mercer	Cook (5)	10,044	Tennant
13.11.94	SBC	A	Featherstone R.	W	30-28	Hanley (2), Eyres, Faimalo, Tait	Cummins (5)	—	—
27.11.94	SBC	H	Doncaster	W	38-18	Hanley (3), Schofield (2), Mercer	Cummins (7)	10,653	Campbell
4.12.94	RT(2)	H	Swinton	W	54-24	Hanley (2), Holroyd (2), Schofield (2), Faimalo, Golden, Iro	Holroyd (9)	4867	Smith
11.12.94	SBC	H	Wigan	W	33-28	Cummins (2), Fallon (2), Hanley	Holroyd (5), Cummins, Schofield (dg)	20,053	Cummings
18.12.94	RT(3)	A	Workington T.	W	18-14	Cummins, Hanley, Schofield	Holroyd (3)	—	—
26.12.94	SBC	A	Hull	W	24-20	Hanley (2), Cummins, Holroyd	Holroyd (4)	—	—
1.1.95	SBC	H	Halifax	W	42-14	Cummins (3), Fallon, Tait, Hanley, Schofield	Holroyd (7)	19,218	Campbell
7.1.95	RT(4)	H	Castleford	L	14-34	Hanley (2)	Holroyd (3)	10,650	Cummings
11.1.95	SBC	A	Oldham	W	21-14	Fallon, Hanley, Holroyd	Holroyd (4), Schofield (dg)	—	—
15.1.905	SBC	H	Bradford N.	W	46-30	Hanley (3), Schofield (2), Eyres, Innes, Mercer	Holroyd (6)	14,058	Campbell
22.1.95	SBC	H	Warrington	W	30-0	Innes (4), Fallon, Howard	Holroyd (3)	12,360	Bates
3.2.95	SBC	H	Widnes	W	36-4	Hanley (4), Iro, Mercer	Holroyd (6)	10,080	Holdsworth
12.2.95	CC(4)	H	Bradford N.	W	31-14	Hanley (2), Mercer (2), Holroyd	Holroyd (5), Schofield (dg)	16,095	J. Connolly
17.2.95	SBC	A	Castleford	W	22-16	Cummins, Hanley, Mann, Tait	Holroyd (3)	—	—
26.2.95	CC(5)	H	Ryedale-York	W	44-14	Fallon (4), Innes, Iro, Mann	Holroyd (5), Cummins (3)	9473	Smith
1.3.95	SBC	A	Salford	W	26-8	Hanley (2), Innes, Lowes, Mann	Cummins (3)	—	—
12.3.95	CC(QF)	H	Workington T.	W	50-16	Hanley (3), Cummins, Eyres, Iro, Mann, Schofield	Holroyd (9)	15,452	Tennant
19.3.95	SBC	A	Sheffield E.	L	22-31	Cummins, Lowes, Mann, Mercer	Holroyd (3)	—	—
22.3.95	SBC	H	St. Helens	L	20-31	Cummins (2), Holroyd, Lowes	Holroyd (2)	11,668	Holdsworth
26.3.95	SBC	A	Bradford N.	W	30-10	Cummins, Eyres, Faimalo, Hanley, Tait	Cook (5)	—	—
1.4.95	CC(SF)	N[1]	Featherstone R.	W	39-22	Fallon (2), Hanley (2), Schofield, Tait	Holroyd (5), Schofield (dg)	(21,485)	Campbell
4.4.95	SBC	H	Oldham	W	40-20	Cook (2), Cummins (2), Holroyd, Innes, Iro	Holroyd (6)	10,032	Cummings
7.4.95	SBC	A	Warrington	W	17-11	Hanley, Holroyd, Iro	Holroyd (2, 1dg)	—	—
14.4.95	SBC	H	Hull	W	44-19	Fallon (3), Cummins (2), Harmon, Innes, Iro, Schofield	Cook (4)	11,204	Campbell

(Continued)

92

Date	Competition	H/A	Opponent	Rlt	Score	Tries	Goals	Attendance	Referee
17.4.95	SBC	A	Halifax	L	16-23	Cook, Innes, Morley	Cook (2)	—	—
23.4.95	SBC	A	Wakefield T.	W	30-14	Iro (2), Eyres, Harmon, Mercer, Tait	Cummins (3)	—	—
29.4.95	CC(F)	N2	Wigan	L	10-30	Lowes	Holroyd (3)	(78,550)	Smith
5.5.95	PT(1)	H	Bradford N.	W	50-30	Iro (3), Faimalo, Fallon, Holroyd, Lowes, Mercer, Schofield	Holroyd (7)	7373	Cummings
14.5.95	PT(SF)	H	St. Helens	W	30-26	Cummins, Innes, Iro, Mann, Mercer	Holroyd (5)	11,879	Cummings
21.5.95	PT(F)	N3	Wigan	L	12-69	Eyres, Innes	Holroyd (2)	(30,160)	Cummings

N1 at Elland Road, Leeds
N2 at Wembley
N3 at Manchester U.F.C.

Leeds half back Graham Holroyd, scorer of 317 points in 1994-95, fends off Workington Town's Billy McGinty in the Silk Cut Challenge Cup quarter-final at Headingley.

LEIGH

Ground: Hilton Park (01942-674437)
First Season: 1895-96
Chairman: Mick Higgins
General
 Manager: Wendy Stott
Honours: **Championship** Winners, 1905-06
Division One Champions, 1981-82
Division Two Champions, 1977-78,
1985-86, 1988-89
Challenge Cup Winners, 1920-21,
1970-71
Lancashire Cup Winners, 1952-53,
1955-56, 1970-71, 1981-82
Beaten finalists, 1905-06, 1909-10,
1920-21, 1922-23, 1949-50, 1951-52,
1963-64, 1969-70
BBC2 Floodlit Trophy Winners,
1969-70, 1972-73
Beaten finalists, 1967-68, 1976-77

RECORDS

Match
Goals: 15 by Mick Stacey v. Doncaster,
28 Mar 1976
Tries: 6 by Jack Wood v. York, 4 Oct 1947
Points: 38 by John Woods v. Blackpool B.,
11 Sep 1977
John Woods v. Ryedale-York,
12 Jan 1992

Season
Goals: 173 by Chris Johnson, 1985-86
Tries: 49 by Steve Halliwell, 1985-86
Points: 400 by Chris Johnson, 1985-86

Career
Goals: 1,043 by Jim Ledgard, 1948-58
Tries: 189 by Mick Martyn, 1954-67
Points: 2,492 by John Woods, 1976-85 & 1990-92
Appearances: 503 by Albert Worrall, 1921-35 &
1936-38
Highest score: 92-2 v. Keighley, 30 Apr 1986
Highest against: 94-4 at Workington T.,
26 Feb1995
Attendance: 31,324 v. St. Helens (RL Cup),
14 Mar 1953

COACHING REGISTER
● Since 1974-75

Eddie Cheetham	May 74 - Mar 75
Kevin Ashcroft	June 75 - Jan 77
Bill Kindon	Jan 77 - Apr 77
John Mantle	Apr 77 - Nov 78
Tom Grainey	Nov 78 - Dec 80
*Alex Murphy	Nov 80 - June 82
*Colin Clarke	June 82 - Dec 82
Peter Smethurst	Dec 82 - Apr 83
Tommy Bishop	June 83 - June 84
John Woods	June 84 - May 85
Alex Murphy	Feb 85 - Nov 85
Tommy Dickens	Nov 85 - Dec 86
Billy Benyon	Dec 86 - Mar 90
Alex Murphy	Mar 90 - Aug 91
Kevin Ashcroft	Sep 91 - June 92
Jim Crellin	June 92 - Sep 92
Steve Simms	Nov 92 - Sep 94
Denis Ramsdale	Sep 94 - Nov 94
Ian Lucas	Dec 94 -

*From Dec 80 to June 82 Clarke was
officially appointed coach and Murphy
manager.

GREAT BRITAIN REGISTER
(19 players)

Kevin Ashcroft	(5)	1968-70
Joe Cartwright	(7)	1920-21
Dave Chisnall	(2)	1970
Joe Darwell	(5)	1924
Steve Donlan	(+2)	1984
Des Drummond	(22)	1980-86
Peter Foster	(3)	1955
Chris Johnson	(1)	1985
Frank Kitchen	(2)	1954
Jim Ledgard	(9)	1948-54
Gordon Lewis	(1)	1965
Mick Martyn	(2)	1958-59
Walter Mooney	(2)	1924
Stan Owen	(1)	1958
Charlie Pawsey	(7)	1952-54
Bill Robinson	(2)	1963
Joe Walsh	(1)	1971
Billy Winstanley	(2)	1910
John Woods	(7+3)	1979-83

1994-95 SIGNINGS REGISTER

Signed	Player	Club From
14.7.94	McCulley, Steve	Leigh East
29.7.94	Shepherd, Paul	Leigh Miners ARL
29.7.94	Weall, Jerome	Wigan St. Pats. ARL
5.8.94	McCloughlin, Paul	Warrington Academy
12.8.94	Jones, Ken	Leigh Miners ARL
12.8.94	Measures, Neil	St. Helens
12.8.94	O'Loughlin, Jason	St. Helens
24.8.94	Liku, Tau	Mu'a Saints, NZ
24.8.94	Marsh, Paul	St. Helens
2.9.94	*Tyrer, Sean	Whitehaven
3.9.94	*Fletcher, Darren	Chorley
13.11.94	Bannon, John	Rochdale H.
22.11.94	*Booth, John	Highfield
24.11.94	Cotton, Lee	Spring View ARL
26.11.94	Ball, Robert	Leigh Academy
6.12.94	Hannan, Sheldon	Leigh East ARL
29.12.94	Bannister, Shaun	Wigan St. Pats. ARL
29.12.94	Ingram, David	Leigh Academy
3.1.95	*Griffiths, Steve	Warrington
10.1.95	Hall, Darren	Leigh East ARL
23.1.95	Wilson, Christian	Wigan St. Pats. ARL
15.2.95	Wynne, Stephen	Salford
19.2.95	Halsall, Ian	Rochdale H.
10.3.95	*Honey, Chris	Barrow
16.3.95	*Reeves, Robert	Keighley C.
21.3.95	*Riley, David	Wigan
30.3.95	Stazicker, Ged	Salford
30.3.95	Tuavao, Harmon	Widnes St. Maries ARL
31.3.95	Wilkinson, Chris	Swinton

Former Great Britain hooker Colin Clarke, coach of Leigh for seven months from June to December 1982.

Leigh centre Steve Donlan, capped twice for Great Britain in 1984, while touring Down Under.

95

LEIGH 1994-95 PLAYERS' SUMMARY

	Date of Birth	App	T	G	D	Pts	Previous club	Signed
Baldwin, Simon	31.3.75	8	4	—	—	16	Leigh E. ARL	31.3.92
Ball, Rob	22.3.76	9+1	1	—	—	4	Leigh Academy	26.11.94
Bannister, Shaun	23.9.69	20	5	—	—	20	Wigan St. Patricks ARL	29.12.94
Bannon, John	4.4.75	1	—	—	—	—	Rochdale H.	13.11.94
Blakeley, Mike	22.11.70	13	5	50	1	121	Leigh M. ARL	16.7.90
Booth, John	14.9.66	9	—	—	—	—	Highfield	22.11.94
Bridge, Russ	8.10.64	11+4	4	—	—	16	Fulham	12.10.90
Cawley, Steve	10.6.71	17	4	—	—	16	Leigh M. ARL	4.10.93
Cheetham, Andrew	25.1.75	3	1	—	—	4	Orrell St. James ARL	9.12.93
Costello, John	10.3.70	18+4	4	—	—	16	Leigh M. ARL	6.9.91
Cottom, Lee	16.11.71	3+2	2	—	—	8	Spring View ARL	24.11.94
Daniel, Paul	16.3.74	15+2	3	—	—	12	Leigh M. ARL	18.8.93
Davies, Glyn	3.12.74	15+2	3	4	—	20	St. Helens	11.11.93
Fanning, Sean	16.6.69	13+3	8	35	—	102	Hare & Hounds ARL	5.4.92
Griffiths, Steve	15.12.64	4	—	—	—	—	Warrington	3.1.95
Gunning, John	30.3.69	6+5	1	1	—	6	Leigh E. ARL	10.1.93
Halsall, Ian	25.1.73	4	—	—	—	—	Rochdale H.	19.2.95
Hill, David	4.9.68	25+1	4	—	—	16	Blackbrook ARL	5.10.88
Ingram, David	4.1.75	14+2	7	—	—	28	Leigh Academy	29.12.94
Jones, Ken	21.2.62	5+4	—	—	—	—	Leigh Miners ARL	12.8.94
Jukes, Neil	23.5.76	0+2	—	—	—	—	Rosebridge ARL	31.3.94
Lever, Dave	2.2.70	4+4	—	—	—	—	St. Helens	
Liku, Tau	21.2.71	14+1	9	—	—	36	Tonga	22.4.94
McCulley, Steve	14.7.77	2+1	—	—	—	—	Leigh East ARL	14.7.94
McLoughlin, Paul	27.3.75	18+4	6	—	—	24	Warrington Academy	5.8.94
Maloney, Sean	15.11.73	10+1	4	—	—	16	Leigh East ARL	16.6.93
Marsh, Paul	18.6.74	12+1	—	—	—	—	St. Helens	24.1.94
Martin, Scott	29.12.74	22	11	—	—	44	Leigh East ARL	29.12.91
Meadows, Mark	9.5.65	17+4	2	—	—	8	Oldham	21.12.93
Measures, Neil	11.1.71	17+4	1	—	—	4	St. Helens	12.8.94
O'Loughlin, Jason	29.11.70	18+3	4	—	—	16	St. Helens	12.8.94
Pratt, Gareth	23.8.69	9+1	1	—	—	4	Mayfield ARL	5.9.92
Reeves, Bob	16.5.70	3	1	—	—	4	Keighley C.	16.3.95
Riley, David	20.11.74	0+1	—	—	—	—	Wigan	21.3.95
Rowley, Paul	12.3.75	10	6	—	—	24	Leigh M. ARL	29.3.92
Sarsfield, Mark	22.3.71	21	13	—	—	52	Widnes	24.9.93
Stazicker, Ged	2.1.68	6	—	—	—	—	Salford	30.3.95
Tanner, David	29.9.65	6	2	4	—	16	St. Helens	5.1.92
Tuavao, Hamoni	26.9.68	2+5	1	—	—	4	Widnes St. Maries ARL	30.3.95
Weall, Jerome	27.8.75	1	—	—	—	—	Wigan St. Patricks ARL	29.7.94
Webster, David	20.10.68	5+3	—	—	—	—	Rochdale H.	3.4.94
Wilkinson, Chris	2.3.65	5	2	17	1	43	Swinton	31.3.95
Wilson, Christian	13.8.75	11+2	2	—	—	8	Wigan St. Patricks ARL	23.1.95
Winstanley, Paul	9.5.74	3+2	—	—	—	—	Wigan St. Patricks ARL	24.6.93
Wright, David	13.10.74	19	2	—	—	8	Wigan	26.3.94
Wynne, Steve	9.12.71	7	3	—	—	12	Salford	15.2.95

TOTALS

			T	G	D	Pts		
46 players			126	111	2	728		

Representative appearances 1994-95
Martin — GB Under-21s (1,1t)

LEIGH 1994-95 MATCH ANALYSIS

Date	Competition	H/A	Opponent	Rlt	Score	Tries	Goals	Attendance	Referee
21.8.94	SD	H	Hunslet	W	49-0	Sarsfield (2), Baldwin, Davies, Martin, O'Loughlin, Pratt, Rowley, Wright	Blakeley (6, 1dg)	1828	Gilmour
28.8.94	SD	A	Whitehaven	L	8-16	Cawley	Blakeley (2)	—	—
4.9.94	SD	H	Dewsbury	W	22-12	Blakeley (2), Cheetham	Blakeley (5)	1529	Cross
11.9.94	SD	A	Highfield	W	80-8	Rowley (3), Baldwin (2), Sarsfield (2), Tanner (2), Blakeley, Costello, Cawley, Davies, Martin, O'Loughlin	Blakeley (10)	—	—
18.9.94	SD	H	Huddersfield	W	20-18	Cawley, Daniel, Meadows	Blakeley (4)	2486	Tennant
25.9.94	SD	A	Ryedale-York	L	14-15	Bridge, McLoughlin	Blakeley (3)	—	—
2.10.94	SD	H	Bramley	W	22-12	O'Loughlin, Rowley, Sarsfield Martin	Blakeley (3)	1464	Burke
9.10.94	SD	A	Barrow	W	32-30	Sarsfield (2), Baldwin, Cawley, Martin, Rowley	Blakeley (4)	—	—
16.10.94	SD	A	Rochdale H.	L	16-52	Blakeley (2), Martin	Blakeley (2)	—	—
30.10.94	SD	H	Batley	L	8-32	Meadows	Blakeley (2)	2130	Gilmour
6.11.94	SD	A	Hunslet	L	4-13	—	Tanner (2)	—	—
13.11.94	SD	H	Whitehaven	L	10-30	Bridge, Costello	Tanner	1339	McGregor
27.11.94	RT(1)	H	Leigh M.W.	W	18-12	Daniel, Measures	Blakeley (4), Tanner	2561	Galtress
4.12.94	RT(2)	A	Sheffield E.	L	10-46	Bridge, Sarsfield	Blakeley	—	—
11.12.94	SD	A	Dewsbury	W	16-6	Costello, Martin	Blakeley (4)	—	—
18.12.94	SD	H	Highfield	W	50-14	Cottom (2), Fanning (2), Martin (2), Bannister, Bridge, Costello	Fanning (4), Davies (3)	1147	Redfearn
26.12.94	SD	H	London B.	W	24-10	Hill (2), Bannister, Fanning	Fanning (4)	1764	Holdsworth
15.1.95	SD	H	Carlisle	W	32-20	Bannister, Fanning, Gunning, Ingram, McLoughlin	Fanning (6)	1329	Carter
22.1.95	CC(3)	H	Heworth	W	40-28	Ingram (4), Fanning, Wright, McLoughlin	Fanning (6)	1094	R. Connolly
25.1.95	SD	A	Swinton	L	4-28	Daniel	—	—	—
29.1.95	SD	A	Hudersfield	L	6-50	Martin	Gunning	—	—
1.2.95	SD	A	Keighley C.	L	6-38	Fanning	Fanning	—	—
5.2.95	SD	H	Ryedale-York	L	16-42	Fanning, Maloney, Martin	Fanning (2)	1183	Oddy
19.2.95	CC(4)	A	Swinton	W	34-22	Martin, Bannister, Fanning, Maloney, Sarsfield, Wilson	Fanning (5)	—	—
26.2.95	CC(5)	A	Workington T.	L	4-94	Sarsfield	—	—	—
6.3.95	SD	H	Barrow	L	12-14	Hill, Wynne	Fanning (2)	1226	Gilmour
12.3.95	SD	A	Hull K.R.	L	8-35	Ball, Wynne	—	—	—
19.3.95	SD	H	Rochdale H.	L	20-36	McLoughlin (2), Maloney, Reeves	Fanning (2)	1052	Burke
26.3.95	SD	A	Batley	L	22-78	Davies, Ingram, Liku, Maloney	Fanning (3)	—	—
2.4.95	SD	H	Keighley C.	L	13-34	Liku, Wilkinson	Wilkinson (2, 1dg)	2364	Gilmour
6.4.95	SD	A	Bramley	L	24-28	Hill, McCloughlin, Wilkinson, Wilson	Wilkinson (4)	—	—
9.4.95	SD	A	Carlisle	L	20-22	Liku (2), Ingram, O'Loughlin	Wilkinson (2)	—	—
14.4.95	SD	A	London B.	L	6-60	Liku	Davies	—	—
17.4.95	SD	H	Swinton	W	24-10	Liku (2), Bannister, Wynne	Wilkinson (4)	1077	Gilmour
23.4.95	SD	H	Hull K.R.	W	34-24	Sarsfield (3), Liku (2), Tuavao	Wilkinson (5)	1341	Nicholson

LONDON BRONCOS

Ground: Barnet Copthall (0181-203 4211)
First Season: 1980-81. Began as Fulham.
Became London Crusaders at start
of 1991-92 and changed to London
Broncos in 1994-95
Chairman: Barry Maranta
General
Manager: Robbie Moore
Honours: **Division Two** Champions, 1982-83
Second Division Premiership Beaten
Finalists, 1993-94

RECORDS

Match
Goals: 11 by Steve Guyett v. Huddersfield,
23 Oct 1988
Greg Pearce v. Runcorn H.,
26 Aug 1990
Tries: 4 by Mark Riley v. Highfield, 17 Oct 1993
Mark Johnson at Highfield, 1 Apr 1994
Scott Roskell at Bramley, 19 Mar 1995
Points: 24 by John Gallagher v. Bramley,
27 Mar 1994

Season
Goals: 159 by John Gallagher, 1993-94
Tries: 4 by Mark Johnson, 1993-94
Points: 384 by John Gallagher, 1993-94

Career
Goals: 309 by Steve Diamond, 1981-84
Tries: 74 by Hussein M'Barki, 1981-84 &
1988-91
Points: 691 by Steve Diamond, 1981-84
Appearances: 148+14 by Hussein M'Barki,
1981-84 & 1988-91
Highest score: 66-12 v. Keighley C., 8 May 1994
Highest against: 72-6 v. Whitehaven, 14 Sep 1986
Attendance: 15,013 v. Wakefield T. (RL Cup),
15 Feb 1981 — at Craven Cottage
1,878 v. Bradford N. (Regal Trophy),
19 Dec 1993 — at Barnet Copthall

COACHING REGISTER
● **Since formation in 1980**

Reg Bowden	July 80 - June 84
Roy Lester	June 84 - Apr 86
Bill Goodwin	Apr 86 - May 88
*Bev Risman	May 88 - Feb 89
Phil Sullivan	Feb 89 - Mar 89
Bill Goodwin	Mar 89 - Apr 89
Ross Strudwick	June 89 - Feb 93
Tony Gordon	Feb 93 - May 94
Gary Grienke	May 94 -

Team manager

GREAT BRITAIN REGISTER
(1 player)

John Dalgreen	(1)	1982

1994-95 SIGNINGS REGISTER

Signed	Player	Club From
18.7.94	Heugh, Cavill	Rochdale H.
15.8.94	Shaw, Darren	Brisbane B., Aus
18.8.94	Croston, Mark	Blackpool G.
18.8.94	Liddel, Peter	Wests, Aus
24.8.94	Massey, Luke	Moorebank ARL
30.9.94	Domic, Sidney	Brisbane B., Aus
4.11.94	Scourfield, Jon	—
2.12.94	Langer, Kevin	Ipswich Jets, Aus
7.2.95	Wilkinson, Richard	Surrey Heath RU
11.2.95	Braddock, Steven	Surrey Heath ARL
22.2.95	Harvey, David	—
1.3.95	*Roach, Jason	St. Helens
10.3.95	*Evans, David	Doncaster
15.3.95	*Stevens, Paul	Wigan
31.3.95	*Booth, Craig	Oldham

John Gallagher, scorer of 86 points for the Broncos in 1994-95.

LONDON BRONCOS 1994-95 PLAYERS' SUMMARY

	Date of Birth	App	T	G	D	Pts	Previous club	Signed
Booth, Craig	28.10.70	7	1	28	—	60	Oldham	31.3.95
Bryant, Justin		28+4	6	—	—	24		
Campbell, Logan	23.5.71	13	10	—	—	40	Australia	10.1.94
Carroll, Bernard	3.3.69	0+8	—	—	—	—	South London ARL	14.1.94
Chambers, Paul	21.6.68	1+1	—	—	—	—	Rosslyn Park RU	17.8.93
Croston, Mark	14.1.70	2	—	—	—	—	Blackpool G.	18.8.94
Domic, Sidney	8.2.75	18+1	8	—	—	32	Australia	30.9.94
Ekoku, Abi	13.4.66	11	7	—	—	28	St. Marys ARL	29.7.93
Evans, Dave	17.6.69	4+1	3	—	—	12	Doncaster	10.3.95
Gallagher, John	29.1.64	12	2	39	—	86	Leeds	1.7.93
Green, Craig		35	11	9	2	64		
Harvey, David	26.1.71	0+1	—	—	—	—		22.2.95
Heugh, Cavill	31.8.62	29+5	4	23	—	62	Rochdale Hornets	21.7.93
Johnson, Mark	28.2.69	31	19	—	—	76	South Africa	18.3.93
Langer, Kevin	8.6.63	21+1	6	—	—	24	Australia	2.12.94
Liddell, Peter	6.2.72	25+5	2	—	—	8	Australia	18.8.94
Luxon, Geoff	2.6.71	0+2	—	—	—	—	Crystal Palace ARL	19.8.93
McCarthy, Ray		1+1	—	—	—	—		
McIvor, Dixon	30.1.68	1+2	—	—	—	—	South London ARL	18.8.93
Massey, Luke	7.7.70	20+6	2	—	—	8	Australia	24.8.94
Pitt, Darryl	31.5.66	12+15	14	1	—	58	Australia	7.12.89
Rae, Tony		12	2	—	—	8	Australia	
Riley, Mark	16.6.67	20	12	—	—	48	Peckham ARL	6.10.92
Roach, Jason	2.5.71	11	5	—	—	20	St. Helens	1.3.95
Roskell, Scott	25.4.69	31	23	—	—	92	Australia	27.8.92
Rosolen, Steve	16.11.68	14+1	2	—	—	8	Australia	2.1.92
Rotheram, Dave	16.8.68	15+10	10	—	—	40	W. London Inst. ARL	28.8.90
Scourfield, Jon	20.5.69	7	5	—	—	20		4.11.94
Shaw, Darren	5.10.71	33+2	—	—	—	—	Australia	15.8.94
Smith, Chris	8.8.66	9+2	1	7	—	18	Twickenham RU	30.8.91
Stevens, Paul	7.10.74	9+1	1	—	—	4	Wigan	15.3.95
Stewart, Sam	5.12.62	33+2	4	—	—	16	Australia	17.8.93
Why, Adrian	14.6.67	0+1	—	—	—	—	Fulham ARL	3.9.91
Trialists		3	—	3	—	6		

TOTALS

			T	G	D	Pts		
34 players			160	110	2	862		

LONDON BRONCOS 1994-95 MATCH ANALYSIS

Date	Competition	H/A	Opponent	Rlt	Score	Tries	Goals	Attendance	Referee
21.8.94	SD	A	Carlisle	W	38-16	Campbell (3), Pitt (2), Riley, Roskell, Stewart	Gallagher (3)	—	—
28.8.94	SD	A	Hunslet	L	14-25	Gallagher, Pitt, Campbell	Gallagher	—	—
4.9.94	SD	A	Barrow	W	16-10	Campbell, Johnson, Rotheram	Gallagher (2)	—	—
11.9.94	SD	H[1]	Keighley C.	L	10-30	Ekoku, Riley	Pitt	1302	Presley
18.9.94	SD	A	Highfield	W	30-8	Ekoku (2), Riley (2), Green, Smith	Green (3)	—	—
25-9-94	SD	H[1]	Batley	H	30-2	Campbell (2), Riley (2), Massey, Rotheram	Green (2), Trialist	793	Cross
2.10.94	SD	H[1]	Swinton	W	40-29	Green (2), Johnson (2), Campbell, Riley, Rotheram	Smith (4), Green (2)	735	Asquith
9.10.94	SD	A	Dewsbury	L	8-23	Johnson	Trialist (2)	—	—
16.10.94	SD	H[1]	Bramley	W	40-12	Ekoku (2), Johnson (2), Campbell, Domic, Riley, Stewart	Smith (3), Heugh	625	McGregor
21.10.94	SD	H	Rochdale H.	W	12-3	Pitt, Ekoku	Heugh (2)	1202	Asquith
30.10.94	SD	H	Ryedale-York	L	10-13	Roskell	Heugh (3)	687	McGregor
6.11.94	SD	H[1]	Carlisle	W	23-16	Scourfield (3), Domic, Johnson	Heugh, Green (1dg)	580	Galtress
13.11.94	SD	H	Hunslet	W	40-2	Roskell (2), Pitt (2), Riley (2), Green, Liddell	Heugh (4)	674	Bates
27.11.94	RT(1)	H	Hemel Hempstead	W	34-16	Rotheram (2), Campbell, Johnson, Riley, Roskell	Heugh (5)	668	Atkin
4.12.94	RT(2)	A	Salford	L	14-16	Riley, Rotheram	Heugh (3)	—	—
11.12.94	SD	H	Barrow	W	30-6	Roskell (2), Domic, Johnson, Scourfield, Stewart	Heugh (3)	575	Tennant
26.12.94	SD	A	Leigh	L	10-24	Pitt, Roskell	Heugh	—	—
8.1.95	SD	A	Hull K. R.	L	4-38	Scourfield	—	—	—
11.1.95	SD	A	Keighley C.	W	25-14	Roskell (2), Langer, Pitt, Rotheram	Green (2,1dg)	—	—
15.1.95	SD	A	Huddersfield	L	8-20	Langer	Gallagher (2)	—	—
22.1.95	CC(3)	H	Ellenborough R.	W	30-10	Roskell (3), Pitt (2), Bryant	Gallagher (3)	363	Kirkpatrick
29.1.95	SD	H	Highfield	W	42-4	Johnson (2), Rotheram (2), Bryant, Domic, Heugh, Rosolen	Gallagher (5)	501	Lee
5.2.95	SD	A	Batley	W	22-10	Green (2), Pitt, Rae	Gallagher (3)	—	—
12.2.95	CC(4)	H	Hull K.R.	L	20-26	Johnson, Pitt, Stewart	Gallagher (4)	908	Asquith
26.2.95	SD	A	Swinton	W	38-26	Heugh (2), Roskell (2), Liddell, Rosolen	Gallagher (7)	—	—
6.3.95	SD	H	Dewsbury	W	22-16	Bryant, Green, Johnson, Rotheram	Gallagher (3)	870	Oddy
15.3.95	SD	H	Whitehaven	W	18-16	Bryant (2), Green, Gallagher	Gallagher	603	Presley
19.3.95	SD	A	Bramley	W	38-6	Roskell (4), Johnson, Langer, Roach	Gallagher (5)	—	—
26.3.95	SD	A	Ryedale-York	L	12-25	Johnson (2), Roskell	—	—	—
2.4.95	SD	H	Hull K.R.	W	34-22	Evans (2), Booth, Heugh, Langer, Rae, Roach	Booth (3)	807	Smith
9.4.95	SD	H	Huddersfield	D	24-24	Domic (2), Evans, Roskell	Booth (4)	501	Cross
14.4.95	SD	H	Leigh	W	60-6	Green (3), Domic (2), Johnson (2), Roach (2), Langer, Massey	Booth (8)	902	Morris
18.4.95	SD	A	Rochdale H.	L	4-22		Booth (2)	—	—
23.4.95	SD	A	Whitehaven	W	30-12	Pitt (2), Ekoku, Johnson, Stevens	Booth (5)	—	—
8.5.95	SDP(1)	H	Whitehaven	W	28-1	Bryant, Langer, Roach, Roskell	Booth (6)	837	R. Connolly
14.5.95	SDP(SF)	A	Keighley C.	L	4-38	Roskell	—	—	—

H[1] at Hendon FC

OLDHAM

Ground: Watersheddings (0161-624-4865)
First Season: 1895-96
Nickname: Roughyeds
Chairman: Jim Quinn
Secretary: Karen Scott
Honours: **Championship** Winners, 1909-10,
1910-11, 1956-57
Beaten finalists, 1906-07, 1907-08,
1908-09, 1921-22, 1954-55
Division One Champions, 1904-05
Division Two Champions, 1963-64,
1981-82, 1987-88
Challenge Cup Winners, 1898-99,
1924-25, 1926-27
Beaten finalists, 1906-07, 1911-12,
1923-24, 1925-26
**Second Division/Divisional
Premiership** Winners, 1987-88,
1989-90
Beaten finalists, 1991-92
Lancashire Cup Winners, 1907-08,
1910-11, 1913-14, 1919-20, 1924-25,
1933-34, 1956-57, 1957-58, 1958-59
Beaten finalists, 1908-09, 1911-12,
1918-19, 1921-22, 1954-55, 1966-67,
1968-69, 1986-87, 1989-90
Lancashire League Winners,
1897-98, 1900-01, 1907-08, 1909-10,
1921-22, 1956-57, 1957-58

RECORDS

Match
Goals: 14 by Bernard Ganley v. Liverpool C.,
4 Apr 1959
Tries: 7 by James Miller v. Barry, 31 Oct 1908
Points: 30 by Abe Johnson v. Widnes, 9 Apr 1928

Season
Goals: 200 by Bernard Ganley, 1957-58
Tries: 49 by R. Farrar, 1921-22
Points: 412 by Bernard Ganley, 1957-58

Career
Goals: 1,365 by Bernard Ganley, 1951-61
Tries: 173 by Alan Davies, 1950-61
Points: 2,775 by Bernard Ganley, 1951-61
Appearances: 626 by Joe Ferguson, 1899-1923

Highest score: 70-10 v. Bramley, 12 Feb 1995
Highest against: 67-11 at Hull K.R., 24 Sep 1978
Attendance: 28,000 v. Huddersfield (League),
24 Feb 1912

COACHING REGISTER
● **Since 1974-75**

Jim Challinor	Aug 74 - Dec 76
Terry Ramshaw	Jan 77 - Feb 77
Dave Cox	July 77 - Dec 78
Graham Starkey (Mgr)	Jan 79 - May 81
Bill Francis	June 79 - Dec 80
Frank Myler	May 81 - Apr 83
Peter Smethurst	Apr 83 - Feb 84
Frank Barrow	Feb 84 - Feb 84
Brian Gartland	Mar 84 - June 84
Frank Myler	June 84 - Apr 87
*Eric Fitzsimons	June 87 - Nov 88
*Mal Graham	June 87 - Apr 88
Tony Barrow	Nov 88 - Jan 91
John Fieldhouse	Jan 91 - Apr 91
Peter Tunks	Apr 91 - Feb 94
Bob Lindner	Feb 94 - Apr 94
Andy Goodway	May 94 -

Joint coaches June 87 - Apr 88

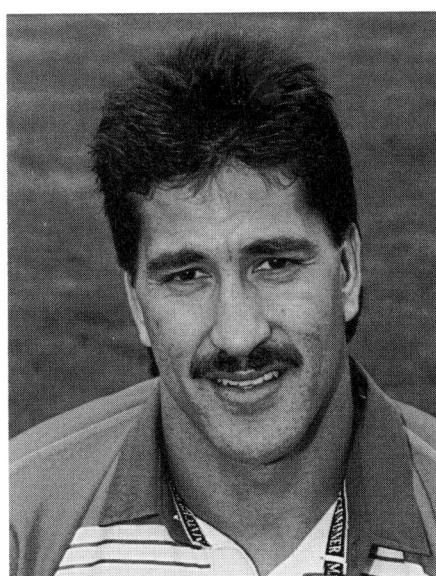

*Oldham loose forward Mike Kuiti, who made 36 appearances
in 1994-95.*

GREAT BRITAIN REGISTER
(40 players)

Albert Avery	(4)	1910-11
Charlie Bott	(1)	1966
Albert Brough	(2)	1924
Terry Clawson	(9)	1973-74
Alan Davies	(20)	1955-60
Evan Davies	(3)	1920
Terry Flanagan	(4)	1983-84
Des Foy	(3)	1984-85
Bernard Ganley	(3)	1957-58
Andy Goodway	(11)	1983-85
Billy Hall	(4)	1914
Herman Hilton	(7)	1920-21
David Hobbs	(2)	1987
Dave Holland	(4)	1914
Bob Irving	(8+3)	1967-72
Ken Jackson	(2)	1957
Ernest Knapman	(1)	1924
Syd Little	(10)	1956-58
Tom Llewellyn	(2)	1907
Jim Lomas	(2)	1911
Bill Longworth	(3)	1908
Les McIntyre	(1)	1963
Terry O'Grady	(5)	1954
Jack Oster	(1)	1929
Dave Parker	(2)	1964
Doug Phillips	(3)	1946
Frank Pitchford	(2)	1958-62
Tom Rees	(1)	1929
Sid Rix	(9)	1924-26
Bob Sloman	(5)	1928
Arthur Smith	(6)	1907-08
Ike Southward	(7)	1959-62
Les Thomas	(1)	1947
Derek Turner	(11)	1956-58
George Tyson	(4)	1907-08
Hugh Waddell	(4)	1988
Tommy White	(1)	1907
Charlie Winslade	(1)	1959
Alf Wood	(4)	1911-14
Mick Worrall	(3)	1984

1994-95 SIGNINGS REGISTER

Signed	Player	Club From
1.7.94	Lord, Gary	Halifax
18.7.94	Hill, Howard	Hensingham, ARL
20.7.94	Gartland, Stephen	Rochdale H.
20.7.94	Hayes, Darren	Waterhead ARL
29.7.94	Davidson, Paul	Widnes
10.8.94	McKinney, Chris	Hensingham ARL
12.8.94	Battye, Neil	Leeds
17.8.94	Twist, Michael	Oldham Academy
2.9.94	Faimalo, Joe	Hawkes Bay, NZ
22.9.94	Marsh, Wilson	Manukau C., NZ
30.9.94	Temu, Jason	Manakau, NZ
6.3.95	*Neal, Mike	Wigan

A tally of 152 points in 1994-95 for Oldham utility back Paul Topping.

OLDHAM 1994-95 PLAYERS' SUMMARY

	Date of Birth	App	T	G	D	Pts	Previous club	Signed
Abram, Darren	27.9.67	32+1	15	—	—	60	Rochdale H.	19.2.93
Belle, Adrian	23.11.70	18	5	—	—	20	Rochdale H.	22.10.93
Bradbury, David	16.3.72	3+8	3	—	—	12	Leigh M. ARL	15.8.91
Burns, Gary	10.2.72	1+1	—	—	—	—		20.12.93
Clarke, John	3.3.74	20	1	—	—	4	East Leeds ARL	1.5.93
Crompton, Martin	29.9.69	32+1	13	—	5	57	Wigan	7.9.93
Davidson, Paul	1.8.69	7+9	1	—	—	4	Widnes	29.7.94
Faimalo, Joe	28.7.70	32+1	5	—	—	20	New Zealand	2.9.94
Gartland, Steve	3.10.70	13+5	3	11	1	35	Rochdale H.	20.7.94
Gibson, Wally	5.4.67	29+2	8	—	1	33	Huddersfield	25.9.92
Goulbourne, Alfie	23.6.75	1	—	—	—	—	Isberg C. ARL	10.6.93
Green, Iyan	21.4.72	3+8	2	—	—	8		25.8.93
Heslop, Nigel	4.12.63	7+4	1	—	—	4	Orrell RU	18.2.93
Hill, Howard	16.1.75	0+1	—	—	—	—	Hensingham ARL	18.7.94
Irwin, Shaun	8.12.68	20+2	6	—	—	24	Castleford	11.8.93
Jones, David	7.12.67	21+1	5	—	—	20	Wakefield T.	13.8.93
Kuiti, Mike	18.3.63	33+3	6	—	—	24	Rochdale H.	11.8.93
Lord, Gary	6.7.66	33+2	5	—	—	20	Halifax	1.7.94
Marsh, Wilson	28.4.69	10+4	3	44	1	101	New Zealand	22.9.94
Neal, Mike	4.9.73	5+3	3	—	—	12	Wigan	6.3.95
Norman, Paul	25.3.74	4+2	—	—	—	—	Parkside ARL	25.9.92
Parr, Chris	31.5.71	10+3	—	—	—	—	Swinton	19.10.93
Ranson, Scott	20.9.67	30	14	—	—	56	Swinton	6.2.92
Richards, Craig	27.1.70	4+6	3	—	—	12	Bradford N.	
Sherratt, Ian	9.8.65	27	2	—	—	8	Salford	8.11.91
Stephenson, David	6.10.72	16	1	—	—	4	Queens Park ARL	3.2.92
Temu, Jason	17.4.72	26+2	2	—	—	8	New Zealand	30.9.94
Topping, Paul	18.9.65	31+1	7	62	—	152	Leigh	27.9.93
TOTALS								
28 players			114	117	8	698		

Representative appearances 1994-95
Clarke — GB Under-21s (1).

OLDHAM 1994-95 MATCH ANALYSIS

Date	Com-petition	H/A	Opponent	Rlt	Score	Tries	Goals	Atten-dance	Referee
21.8.94	SBC	H	Halifax	L	20-40	Abram, Richards	Gartland (6)	5412	Smith
28.8.94	SBC	A	Bradford N.	L	14-36	Gibson, Richards (2)	Gartland	—	—
4.9.94	SBC	H	Wigan	L	10-58	Irwin, Ranson	Gartland	6222	Campbell
11.9.94	SBC	A	Warrington	L	6-55	Crompton	Gartland	—	—
18.9.94	SBC	H	Doncaster	W	44-8	Crompton (2), Abram, Faimalo, Heslop, Irwin, Lord, Topping	Topping (6)	3861	Cross
25.9.94	SBC	A	Hull	W	21-17	Abram (2), Jones	Topping (4), Crompton (dg)	—	—
2.10.94	SBC	H	St Helens	D	18-18	Jones, Lord	Topping (5)	4278	Smith
9.10.94	SBC	A	Wakefield T.	L	16-21	Kuiti (2), Crompton	Topping (2)	—	—
14.10.94	SBC	H	Widnes	W	29-0	Abram, Crompton, Irwin, Lord, Ranson	Topping (4), Crompton (dg)	2774	Presley
30.10.94	SBC	H	Featherstone R.	L	10-20	Abram	Topping (3)	3763	Campbell
6.11.94	SBC	A	Halifax	L	8-34	Abram, Temu		—	—
22.11.94	SBC	H	Bradford N.	W	32-12	Abram (2), Gibson (2), Clarke, Lord	Topping (3), Compton (2dg)	4063	Holdsworth
27.11.94	SBC	A	Wigan	L	0-46			—	—
4.12.94	RT(2)	H	Hull K.R.	W	28-0	Abram, Faimalo, Irwin, Jones, Ranson	Topping (4)	2277	Carter
11.12.94	SBC	H	Warrington	W	52-22	Green (2), Topping (2), Abram, Crompton, Kuiti, Ranson, Marsh	Topping (8)	3527	Campbell
18.1.2.94	RT(3)	A	Widnes	L	6-20	Irwin	Topping	—	—
26.12.94	SBC	A	Salford	W	16-12	Belle, Crompton	Topping (4)	—	—
1.1.95	SBC	H	Workington T.	W	20-10	Ranson (3), Kuiti	Topping (2)	3880	Morris
11.1.95	SBC	H	Leeds	L	14-21	Irwin, Topping	Topping (3)	4080	Holdsworth
22.1.95	SBC	H	Sheffield E.	L	12-14	Crompton, Ranson	Topping (2)	3101	J. Connolly
5.2.95	SBC	H	Hull	W	19-14	Abram, Crompton	Marsh (4, 1dg), Topping	3226	R. Connolly
12.2.95	CC(4)	H	Bramley	W	70-10	Abram (2), Gartland (2), Gibson (2), Ranson (2), Belle, Davidson, Marsh, Topping	Marsh (11)	2788	McGregor
15.2.95	SBC	A	Doncaster	W	22-14	Gibson, Kuiti	Marsh (7)	—	—
19.2.95	SBC	A	St Helens	L	22-32	Ranson (2), Gartland, Kuiti	Marsh (3)	—	—
25.2.95	CC(5)	A	Warrington	W	17-6	Faimalo, Ranson	Marsh (4), Gartland (dg)	—	—
6.3.95	SBC	H	Wakefield T.	L	10-12	Ranson	Marsh (3)	3352	Cummings
12.3.95	CC(QF)	H	Huddersfield	W	23-12	Crompton (2), Topping	Marsh (5), Gibson (dg)	8182	Bates
15.3.95	SBC	A	Castleford	L	14-34	Gibson, Marsh	Marsh (3)	—	—
19.3.95	SBC	A	Widnes	L	4-40		Marsh (2)	—	—
25.3.95	CC(SF)	N[1]	Wigan	L	20-48	Belle (2), Bradbury, Sherratt	Marsh (2)	(12,749)	Smith
4.4.95	SBC	A	Leeds	L	20-40	Bradbury, Faimalo, Neal, Sherratt	Gartland (2)	—	—
9.4.95	SBC	A	Sheffield E.	W	17-12	Belle, Jones, Lord, Topping	Crompton (dg)	—	—
14.4.95	SBC	H	Salford	W	28-16	Neal (2), Gibson, Lord, Stephenson	Topping (4)	3965	R. Connolly
17.4.95	SBC	A	Workington T.	L	12-34	Crompton (2), Jones		—	—
20.4.95	SBC	H	Castleford	L	10-18	Temu	Topping (3)	2840	Campbell
23.4.95	SBC	A	Featherstone R.	L	14-36	Abram, Faimalo	Topping (3)	—	—

N[1] at Huddersfield

ROCHDALE HORNETS

Ground: Spotland (01706-48004)
First Season: 1895-96
Nickname: Hornets
Chairman: Peter Rush
Secretary: Paul Reynolds
Honours: **Challenge Cup** Winners, 1921-22
Regal Trophy Beaten finalists, 1973-74
Lancashire Cup Winners, 1911-12, 1914-15, 1918-19
Beaten finalists, 1912-13, 1919-20, 1965-66, 1991-92
Lancashire League Winners, 1918-19
BBC2 Floodlit Trophy Beaten finalists, 1971-72

RECORDS

Match
Goals: 14 by Steve Turner v. Runcorn H., 5 Nov 1989
Tries: 5 by Jack Corsi v. Barrow, 31 Dec 1921
Jack Corsi v. Broughton Moor, 25 Feb 1922
Jack Williams v. St. Helens, 4 Apr 1933
Norman Brelsford v. Whitehaven, 3 Sep 1972
Points: 32 by Steve Turner v. Runcorn H., 5 Nov 1989
Steve Turner v. Blackpool G., 31 Oct 1993

Season
Goals: 150 by Martin Strett, 1994-95
Tries: 30 by Jack Williams, 1934-35
Points: 346 by Martin Strett, 1994-95
Career
Goals: 741 by Walter Gowers, 1922-46
Tries: 103 by Jack Williams, 1931-37
Points: 1,497 by Walter Gowers, 1922-46
Appearances: 456 by Walter Gowers, 1922-46

Highest score: 92-0 v. Runcorn H., 5 Nov 1989
Highest against: 79-2 at Hull, 7 Apr 1921
Attendance: 8,150 v. Oldham (Div. 2), 26 Dec 1989 — at Spotland
26,664 v. Oldham (RL Cup), 25 Mar 1922 — at Athletic Grounds

COACHING REGISTER
● **Since 1974-75**

Frank Myler	May 71 - Oct 74
Graham Starkey	Oct 74 - Nov 75
Henry Delooze	Nov 75 - Nov 76
Kel Coslett	Nov 76 - Aug 79
Paul Longstaff	Sep 79 - May 81
Terry Fogerty	May 81 - Jan 82
Dick Bonser	Jan 82 - May 82
Bill Kirkbride	June 82 - Sep 84
Charlie Birdsall	Sep 84 - Apr 86
Eric Fitzsimons	June 86 - June 87
Eric Hughes	June 87 - June 88
Jim Crellin	June 88 - June 89
Allan Agar	July 89 - Jan 91
Neil Holding	Jan 91 - Apr 91
Stan Gittins	Apr 91 - Jan 93
Peter Regan	Jan 93 - Oct 93
Steve Gibson	Oct 93 -

GREAT BRITAIN REGISTER
(8 players)

Johnie Baxter	(1)	1907
Jack Bennett	(6)	1924
Joe Bowers	(1)	1920
Terry Fogerty	(1)	1974
Ernest Jones	(4)	1920
Malcolm Price	(2)	1967
Jack Robinson	(2)	1914
Tommy Woods	(2)	1911

1994-95 SIGNINGS REGISTER

Signed	Player	Club From
2.6.94	Hilton, Patrick	Mayfield ARL
21.6.94	Whitehead, Sean	Saddleworth ARL
1.7.94	Bunce, Martin	Waterhead ARL
21.7.94	Maudsley, Steven	Saddleworth ARL
30.7.94	Melling, Alex	Swinton
7.8.94	Robey, Nicholas	Orrell St. James ARL
11.8.94	Swan, Martin	Old'm St. Annes ARL
14.8.94	Bradbury, Justin	Seddon Atkinson ARL
14.8.94	Laugier, Serge	Avignon, Fr.
18.8.94	England, Keith	Castleford
18.8.94	Reid, Wayne	Salford

1.9.94	Coop, Chris	—		4.11.94	*Litherland, Roy	Halifax	
1.9.94	McCarthy, Brian	Western Reds, Aust.		21.11.94	Farrell, Michael	Waterhead ARL	
9.9.94	*Gilfillan, John	Salford		9.12.94	*Sharp, Henry	Halifax	
21.9.94	Grayshon, Paul	Bradford N.		7.2.95	Cameron, Steven	—	
4.10.94	Mannion, Kevin	Orrell St. James ARL		7.2.95	Crowther, Steve	Waterhead ARL	
7.10.94	Mort, Craig	Saddleworth R. ARL		31.3.95	*Meadows, Mark	Leigh	
21.10.94	*Griffiths, Mark	Wigan		1.4.95	Bailey, David	Wakefield T.	

ROCHDALE HORNETS 1994-95 PLAYERS' SUMMARY

	Date of Birth	App	T	G	D	Pts	Previous club	Signed
Anderson, David		25	14	—	—	56	Australia	
Atherton, Lee	1.11.74	10+1	1	—	—	4	Orrell St. James ARL	31.5.94
Bailey, David		6	6	—	—	24	Wakefield Trinity	1.4.95
Bunce, Martin	9.2.75	3	—	—	—	—	Waterhead ARL	1.7.94
Churm, Chris	20.9.66	28	24	—	—	96	Oldham St. Annes ARL	1.4.94
Coop, Chris	25.1.69	1+1	—	—	—	—		1.9.94
Diggle, Craig	2.4.75	2+1	3	—	—	12	Mayfield ARL	13.8.93
England, Keith	27.2.64	32+1	4	—	—	16	Castleford	18.8.94
Fell, David	25.4.66	29+5	12	—	—	48	Salford	28.1.94
Gibson, Steve	23.11.62	29	23	—	—	92	Salford	5.10.93
Gilfillan, John	11.3.65	9	4	—	—	16	Salford	9.9.94
Grayshon, Paul	11.7.67	16+4	2	—	—	8	Bradford N.	21.9.94
Griffiths, Mark	12.11.74	2	—	—	—	—	Wigan	21.10.94
Hall, Robert	13.5.71	6+1	—	—	—	—	Rochdale H.	12.8.93
Higginson, Paul		2	—	—	—	—		
Hilton, Pat	11.7.71	4+7	2	—	—	8	Mayfield ARL	2.6.94
Kay, Martin	16.2.71	21+3	1	—	—	4	Oldham St. Annes ARL	20.8.90
Laugier, Serge	16.8.68	0+1	—	—	—	—	France	14.8.94
McAlister, Charlie	17.3.63	0+2	—	—	—	—	Oldham	
McCarthy, Brian	20.3.74	11+6	4	—	—	16	Australia	1.9.94
Mannion, Kevin	31.8.78	1	—	—	—	—	Orrell St. James ARL	4.10.94
Marriott, Karl	21.11.69	8	4	—	—	16	Mayfield ARL	17.8.89
Maudsley, Steve	7.10.67	24+1	3	—	—	12	Saddleworth ARL	21.7.94
Meadows, Mark	9.5.65	4+2	—	—	—	—	Leigh	7.2.95
Miller, Vinny	1.3.64	4	3	—	—	12	Fitton Hill ARL	7.1.94
Mort, Craig	21.9.72	0+2	—	—	—	—	Saddleworth ARL	7.10.94
O'Keefe, Paul	28.6.71	2	—	—	—	—		15.12.91
Pachniuk, Richard	24.3.71	10	6	—	—	24	Oldham	19.2.93
Pitt, Darren	14.5.71	8	—	—	—	—		12.8.93
Pratt, Gareth		2+6	—	—	—	—		
Ratu, Emon	30.10.65	23+11	5	—	—	20	Swinton	12.8.93
Reid, Wayne	15.12.69	31	1	—	—	4	Salford	18.8.94
Robey, Nick	6.9.77	0+2	—	—	—	—	Orrell St. James ARL	1.4.94
Ryan, Matt		16+1	1	—	—	4	Australia	
Sharp, Henry	17.9.66	17	9	—	—	36	Halifax	9.12.94
Stewart, Mike	16.1.66	20+7	7	—	—	28	Blackpool G.	29.7.92
Strett, Martin	4.4.68	33	12	148	2	346	Oldham	17.12.93
Turner, Steve	5.12.61	12+4	1	6	3	19	Swinton	22.2.88
Whitehead, Sean	16.1.66	4	—	—	—	—	Saddleworth ARL	21.6.94
TOTALS								
39 players			152	154	5	921		

ROCHDALE HORNETS 1994-95 MATCH ANALYSIS

Date	Com- petition	H/A	Opponent	Rlt	Score	Tries	Goals	Atten- dance	Referee
21.8.94	SD	A	Barrow	W	48-22	Churm (2), England (2), Stewart (2), Gibson, Hilton	Strett (8)	—	—
28.8.94	SD	H	Keighley C.	L	16-30	Churm (2), Fell	Strett (2)	2304	Nicholson
4.9.94	SD	A	Whitehaven	L	10-24	Churm	Strett (3)	—	—
11.9.94	SD	H	Carlisle	W	42-32	Gilfillan (2), Gibson, Kay, Maudsley, Ryan, Stewart, Strett	Strett (5)	711	Galtress
18.9.94	SD	A	Hull K.R.	L	2-19	—	Strett	—	—
25.9.94	SD	H	Hunslet	W	46-12	Gibson (4), Churm (2), Strett, Maudsley	Strett (7)	816	Kirkpatrick
2.10.94	SD	A	Batley	L	12-22	Atherton, Ratu	Strett (2)	—	—
9.10.94	SD	A	Huddersfield	L	12-46	Fell, Gibson	Strett (2)	—	—
16.10.94	SD	H	Leigh	W	52-16	Fell (2), Gibson (2), McCarthy (2), Gilfillan, Stewart, Strett	Strett (8)	1210	Bates
21.10.94	SD	A	London B.	L	3-12	—	Strett (1, 1dg)	—	—
30.10.94	SD	A	Highfield	W	28-8	Miller (2), Anderson, Churm, McCarthy	Strett (4)	—	—
6.11.94	SD	H	Barrow	W	32-6	Churm, Gibson, Gilfillan, Maudsley	Strett (6)	817	Gilmour
13.11.94	SD	A	Keighley C.	L	13-28	Churm, Ratu	Strett (2, 1dg)	—	—
27.11.94	RT(1)	H	Woolston R.	W	34-10	Anderson (2), Fell, Gibson, McCarthy, Stewart	Strett (5)	576	Bates
4.12.94	RT(2)	A	Wigan	L	12-34	Hilton	Strett (4)	—	—
11.12.94	SD	H	Whitehaven	W	48-14	Gibson (3), Anderson (2), Sharp (2), Churm, Fell	Strett (6)	916	McGregor
18.12.94	SD	A	Carlisle	W	18-16	Sharp, Stewart, Strett	Strett (3)	—	—
26.12.94	SD	H	Swinton	W	24-18	Churm, Grayshon, Turner	Strett (6)	1384	Oddy
8.1.95	SD	H	Dewsbury	W	21-20	Churm (2), Gibson	Strett (4), Turner (dg)	1317	Gilmour
15.1.95	SD	A	Ryedale-York	W	36-10	Churm (2), Anderson, Fell, Gibson, Ratu	Strett (6)	—	—
22.1.95	CC(3)	H	Lock Lane	W	48-16	Gibson (3), Strett (3), Anderson (2), Churm	Strett (6)	616	Asquith
29.1.95	SD	H	Hull K.R.	W	28-10	Sharp (2), Gibson, Strett	Strett (5), Turner (2dg)	1027	Redfearn
5.2.95	SD	A	Hunslet	L	18-25	Churm (2), Strett	Strett (3)	—	—
12.2.95	CC(4)	A	Ryedale-York	L	12-18	Churm	Strett (4)	—	—
19.2.95	SD	H	Batley	L	18-22	Churm, Strett	Strett (5)	1123	Oddy
12.3.95	SD	H	Bramley	L	8-14	Pachniuk	Strett (2)	811	Galtress
19.3.95	SD	A	Leigh	W	36-20	Ratu (2), Churm, Grayshon, Pachniuk, Stewart	Strett (6)	—	—
22.3.95	SD	H	Huddersfield	L	20-26	Marriott (2), Churm, Diggle	Strett (2)	1423	Asquith
26.3.95	SD	H	Highfield	W	78-0	Anderson (2), Diggle (2), Gibson (2), Pachniuk (2), Sharp (2), England, Fell, Marriott, Strett	Strett (11)	726	McGregor
2.4.95	SD	A	Dewsbury	W	30-10	Fell (3), Anderson, Pachniuk	Strett (5)	—	—
9.4.95	SD	H	Ryedale-York	W	30-16	Anderson, England, Gibson, Reid, Sharp	Strett (5)	926	Steele
14.4.95	SD	A	Swinton	L	14-16	Bailey, Strett	Strett (3)	—	—
17.4.95	SD	H	London B.	W	22-4	Bailey, Pachniuk, Sharp	Turner (5)	824	Atkin
23.4.95	SD	A	Bramley	W	40-20	Bailey (4), Anderson (2), Fell	Strett (6)	—	—
7.5.95	SDP(1)	A	Huddersfield	L	10-36	Churm, Marriott	Turner	—	—

107

RYEDALE-YORK

Ground: Ryedale Stadium (01904-634636)
First Season: 1901-02 as York. Became Ryedale-York at start of 1989-90. Reverted to York at the start of 1995-96.
Nickname: Wasps
Chairman: John Stabler
Secretary: Ian Clough
Honours: **Division Two** Champions, 1980-81
Challenge Cup Beaten finalists, 1930-31
Yorkshire Cup Winners, 1922-23, 1933-34, 1936-37
Beaten finalists, 1935-36, 1957-58, 1978-79

RECORDS
Match
Goals: 12 by Gary Pearce at Nottingham C., 4 Oct 1992
Tries: 6 by Roy Hardgrave v. Bramley, 5 Jan 1935
David Kettlestring at Keighley, 11 Mar 1990
Points: 28 by Gary Pearce at Nottingham C., 4 Oct 1992
Season
Goals: 146 by Vic Yorke, 1957-58
Tries: 35 by John Crossley, 1980-81
Points: 318 by Graham Steadman, 1984-85
Career
Goals: 1,060 by Vic Yorke, 1954-67
Tries: 167 by Peter Foster, 1955-67
Points: 2,159 by Vic Yorke, 1954-67
Appearances: 449 by Willie Hargreaves, 1952-65
Highest score: 84-0 at Nottingham C., 4 Oct 1992
Highest against: 75-3 at Warrington, 23 Sep 1950
Attendance: 14,689 v. Swinton (RL Cup), 10 Feb 1934 — at Clarence Street
4,977 v. Halifax (Div. 2), 5 Jan 1990 — at Ryedale Stadium

COACHING REGISTER
● **Since 1974-75**

Keith Goulding	Nov 73 - Sep 74
Gary Cooper	Dec 74 - Sep 76
Mal Dixon	Sep 76 - Dec 78
Paul Daley	Jan 79 - May 79
David Doyle-Davidson	July 79 - July 80
Bill Kirkbride	Aug 80 - Apr 82
Alan Hardisty	May 82 - Jan 83
Phil Lowe	Mar 83 - Mar 87
Danny Sheehan	Mar 87 - Apr 88
Gary Stephens	Apr 88 - June 91
Derek Foster	July 91 - Nov 92
Steve Crooks	Nov 92 - May 94
Roger Millward	June 94 - Dec 94
Stewart Horton	Jan 95 -

GREAT BRITAIN REGISTER
(7 players)

Edgar Dawson	(1)	1956
Harry Field	(3)	1936
Geoff Smith	(3)	1963-64
Jeff Stevenson	(4)	1959-60
Mick Sullivan	(1)	1963
Basil Watts	(5)	1954-55
Les White	(4)	1946

1994-95 SIGNINGS REGISTER

Signed	Player	Club From
30.6.94	Gascoigne, Andy	Doncaster
1.7.94	Jackson, Darryl	Nottingham C.
1.8.94	Francis, Richard	Hunslet
9.8.94	Davis, Bradley	Huddersfield
9.8.94	Laurence, Jason	Huddersfield
10.8.94	*Litherland, Roy	Halifax
11.8.94	Ramsey, Neville	London B.
25.8.94	Heptinstall, Jason	Roundhill ARL
25.8.94	Mumby, Keith	Bradford N.
28.8.94	Luxon, Geoff	London
21.9.94	*Clarke, Andrew	Doncaster
14.10.94	*Fletcher, Ian	Doncaster
14.10.94	*McGowan, Andrew	Doncaster
26.12.94	Ramsey, Chris	Brotherton ARL
13.1.95	Preston, Stephen	—
13.1.95	Smith, David	—
3.2.95	*Smirk, Terry	Hull
19.2.95	Nicholson, Gavin	Oulton ARL
1.4.95	Mountain, Gary	—
17.4.95	Cain, Mark	New Earswick ARL

RYEDALE-YORK 1994-95 PLAYERS' SUMMARY

	Date of Birth	App	T	G	D	Pts	Previous club	Signed
Adie, Charlie	8.3.73	2+3	—	—	—	—	Heworth ARL	13.8.92
Atkins, Garry	12.10.66	1	1	—	—	4	Castleford	31.7.92
Cain, Mark		0+1	—	—	—	—	New Earswick ARL	17.4.95
Connell, Phil	14.11.69	13	3	—	—	12	Bramley	28.7.92
Craven, Steve	9.4.72	1	—	—	—	—	York All Blacks ARL	28.2.90
Davies, Brian		8	3	—	—	12		
Davis, Brad	13.3.68	31	15	2	1	65	Huddersfield	9.8.94
Deakin, Leigh	27.12.72	32	25	—	—	100	Leeds	9.8.93
Dobson, Steve	27.4.63	20+4	7	1	9	39	Sheffield E.	23.7.90
Fletcher, Ian	4.3.65	19+4	2	—	—	8	Doncaster	14.10.94
Francis, Richard	10.9.64	2	1	—	—	4	Hunslet	1.8.94
Gascoigne, Andy	2.4.62	33+1	12	—	—	48	Doncaster	30.6.94
Hayes, Richard	21.2.70	30+1	2	—	—	8	York All Blacks ARL	13.1.89
Heptinstall, Jason	3.12.69	2	—	—	—	—	Roundhill ARL	25.8.94
Hopcutt, Chris	6.12.69	28	14	21	—	98	Scarborough P.	12.11.91
Horton, Stewart	10.9.63	32	4	—	—	16	Castleford	27.8.87
Jackson, Darryl	6.2.71	15+11	2	—	—	8	Nottingham C.	8.12.93
Johnson, Mick		2+1	—	—	—	—		
Judge, Chris	7.11.72	17+1	7	—	—	28	Heworth	11.9.92
Kettlestring, David	18.11.67	0+4	2	—	—	8	York All Blacks ARL	8.1.90
Laurence, Jason	23.1.70	32	12	—	—	48	Huddersfield	9.8.94
Litherland, Roy	1.11.70	7	4	3	—	22	Halifax	10.8.94
Luxon, Geoff	2.6.71	1	—	—	—	—	London B.	28.8.94
Mawer, Keith	14.10.74	1	—	—	—	—	Acorn ARL	12.5.94
Mountain, Gary		1+2	2	—	—	8		1.4.95
Mumby, Keith	21.2.57	3+4	2	1	—	10	Bradford N.	25.8.94
Pallister, Alan	4.12.70	3+1	—	—	—	—	York All Blacks ARL	1.11.90
Precious, Andrew	10.10.70	21+1	2	49	6	112		
Ramsden, Mick	13.11.71	20+6	8	—	—	32	York Civil Serv. ARL	1.6.91
Ramsey, Chris	8.9.71	1+1	—	—	—	—	Brotherton	26.12.94
Ramsey, Neville	7.4.63	30+4	4	—	—	16	London B.	11.8.94
Sharp, Tim	20.2.70	14+2	2	—	—	8	Featherstone R.	30.6.93
Smirk, Terry	5.8.66	0+2	—	—	—	—	Hull	13.1.95
Smith, Dave	13.9.72	3+5	2	—	—	8		13.1.95
Spears, Mark		1	—	—	—	—		
Sullivan, Graham	27.1.67	10+2	1	34	—	72	Punch Bowl ARL	27.7.87
Thomas, Dean	10.5.66	15	7	—	—	28	L'pool St. Helens RU	26.8.93
Tichener, Lee	5.8.71	0+3	—	—	—	—	Bramley	1.7.93
Trialist		4+1	1	5	—	14		
TOTALS								
39 players			147	116	16	836		

RYEDALE-YORK 1994-95 MATCH ANALYSIS

Date	Competition	H/A	Opponent	Rlt	Score	Tries	Goals	Attendance	Referee
21.8.94	SD	A	Swinton	L	18-19	Atkins, Hopcutt, Litherland	Sullivan (3)	—	—
28.8.94	SD	H	Highfield	W	66-6	Sullivan, Deakin (3), Litherland (2), Dobson, Connell (2), Hayes, Sharp (2), Kettlestring (2)	Sullivan (2), Litherland (3)	881	McGregor
4.9.94	SD	A	Keighley C.	D	18-18	Dobson (2), Deakin	Sullivan (3)	—	—
11.9.94	SD	H	Batley	W	35-8	Davis (2), Deakin, Dobson, Ramsden	Sullivan (7), Dobson (dg)	1426	Bates
18.9.94	SD	A	Barrow	W	45-14	Deakin (3), Laurence (2), Davis, Gascoigne, Litherland	Sullivan (6), Dobson (dg)	—	—
25-9-94	SD	H	Leigh	W	15-14	Deakin, Mumby	Sullivan (3), Dobson (dg)	1541	McGregor
2.10.94	SD	A	Hunslet	L	10-26	Deakin, Gascoigne	Sullivan	—	—
9.10.94	SD	H	Whitehaven	L	18-48	Davis, Deakin, Francis	Sullivan (3)	1065	Redfearn
16.10.94	SD	H	Dewsbury	L	22-30	Davis (2), Connell, Mumby	Hopcutt (2), Mumby	1189	Nicholson
30.10.94	SD	A	London B.	W	13-10	Deakin, Ramsey	Hopcutt (2), Precious (dg)	—	—
6.11.94	SD	H	Swinton	W	52-6	Ramsden (3), Gascoigne (2), Hopcutt (2), Judge (2), Horton	Hopcutt (6)	1015	Bates
13.11.94	SD	A	Highfield	W	24-20	Davis, Gascoigne, Hopcutt, Ramsey	Hopcutt (4)	—	—
22.11.94	SD	A	Batley	L	2-4	—	Hopcutt	—	—
27.11.94	RT(1)	H	West Hull	W	26-9	Hopcutt (2), Davis, Deakin, Ramsey	Sullivan (2), Hopcutt	668	Oddy
7.12.94	RT(2)	A	Batley	L	8-36	Laurence	Sullivan (2)	—	—
11.12.94	SD	H	Keighley C.	L	12-52	Horton, Jackson	Sullivan (2)	2277	Kirkpatrick
26.12.94	SD	H	Huddersfield	W	42-12	Davis (2), Deakin, Hayes, Hopcutt, Horton, Judge, Laurence	Hopcutt (5)	1455	Campbell
8.1.95	SD	A	Bramley	L	12-27	Hopcutt (2), Laurence	—	—	—
15.1.95	SD	H	Rochdale H.	L	10-36	Fletcher, Ramsden	Precious	954	Burke
18.1.95	SD	A	Hull K.R.	L	14-22	Horton, Ramsden	Precious (3)	—	—
22.1.95	CC(3)	H	Barrow Island	W	50-20	Gascoigne (3), Thomas (3), Judge (2), Deakin, Jackson	Precious (5)	521	Burke
29.1.95	SD	H	Barrow	W	20-11	Ramsden, Smith	Precious (6)	681	Ollerton
5.2.95	SD	A	Leigh	W	42-16	Hopcutt (2), Davis, Deakin, Judge, Laurence, Thomas	Precious (7)	—	—
12.2.95	CC(4)	H	Rochdale H.	W	18-12	Deakin, Thomas	Precious (4, 1dg), Dobson 1dg	1005	Lee
19.2.95	SD	H	Hunslet	L	18-19	Hopcutt, Judge, Thomas	Precious (2, 2dg)	943	Galtress
26.2.95	CC(5)	A	Leeds	L	14-44	Davis, Gascoigne	Precious (2), Dobson	—	—
6.3.95	SD	A	Whitehaven	L	13-20	Davies, Smith	Davis (2), Precious (dg)	—	—
12.3.95	SD	H	Carlisle	W	49-22	Deakin (3), Dobson (2), Davies, Fletcher, Gascoigne, Laurence	Precious (6), Dobson (dg)	709	Cross
26.3.95	SD	H	London B.	W	25-12	Davis, Deakin, Ramsden, Thomas	Precious (3, 1dg) Dobson (2dg)	737	Nicholson
2.4.95	SD	H	Bramley	W	28-12	Laurence (2), Dobson, Hopcutt	Precious (6)	742	Lee
4.4.95	SD	A	Dewsbury	D	9-9	Deakin, Precious	Dobson (dg)	—	—
9.4.95	SD	A	Rochdale H.	L	16-30	Deakin, Gascoigne, Laurence	Precious (2)	—	—
14.4.95	SD	A	Huddersfield	L	7-34	Deakin	Precious, Dobson (dg)	—	—
17.4.95	SD	H	Hull K.R.	W	37-22	Davis (2), Mountain (2), Hopcutt, Laurence, Precious, Trialist	Precious, Trialist, Davis (dg)	1190	Carter
23.4.95	SD	A[1]	Carlisle	W	28-23	Davies, Deakin, Gascoigne, Laurence, Ramsey	Trialist (4)	—	—

A[1] at Gateshead

ST. HELENS

Ground: Knowsley Road (01744-23697)
First Season: 1895-96
Nickname: Saints
Chairman: Eric Ashton
Chief Exec: David Howes
Honours: **Championship** Winners, 1931-32, 1952-53, 1958-59, 1965-66, 1969-70, 1970-71
Beaten finalists, 1964-65, 1966-67, 1971-72
League Leaders Trophy Winners, 1964-65, 1965-66
Club Championship (Merit Table) Beaten finalists, 1973-74
Division One Champions, 1974-75
Challenge Cup Winners, 1955-56, 1960-61, 1965-66, 1971-72, 1975-76
Beaten finalists, 1896-97, 1914-15, 1929-30, 1952-53, 1977-78, 1986-87, 1988-89, 1990-91
Regal Trophy Winners, 1987-88
Premiership Winners, 1975-76, 1976-77, 1984-85, 1992-93
Beaten finalists, 1974-75, 1987-88, 1991-92
Lancashire Cup Winners, 1926-27, 1953-54, 1960-61, 1961-62, 1962-63, 1963-64, 1964-65, 1967-68, 1968-69, 1984-85, 1991-92
Beaten finalists, 1932-33, 1952-53, 1956-57, 1958-59, 1959-60, 1970-71, 1982-83, 1992-93
Lancashire League Winners, 1929-30, 1931-32, 1952-53, 1959-60, 1964-65, 1965-66, 1966-67, 1968-69
Western Division Championship Winners, 1963-64
Charity Shield Winners, 1992-93
BBC2 Floodlit Trophy Winners, 1971-72, 1975-76
Beaten finalists, 1965-66, 1968-69, 1970-71, 1977-78, 1978-79

RECORDS

Match
Goals: 16 by Paul Loughlin v. Carlisle, 14 Sep 1986
Tries: 6 by Alf Ellaby v. Barrow, 5 Mar 1932
Steve Llewellyn v. Castleford, 3 Mar 1956
Steve Llewellyn v. Liverpool C., 20 Aug 1956
Tom Van Vollenhoven v. Wakefield T., 21 Dec 1957
Tom Van Vollenhoven v. Blackpool B., 23 Apr 1962
Frank Myler v. Maryport, 1 Sep 1969
Shane Cooper v. Hull, 17 Feb 1988
Points: 40 by Paul Loughlin v. Carlisle, 14 Sep 1986

Season
Goals: 214 by Kel Coslett, 1971-72
Tries: 62 by Tom Van Vollenhoven, 1958-59
Points: 452 by Kel Coslett, 1971-72

Career
Goals: 1,639 by Kel Coslett, 1961-76
Tries: 392 by Tom Van Vollenhoven, 1957-68
Points: 3,413 by Kel Coslett, 1961-76
Appearances: 519+12 by Kel Coslett, 1961-76
Highest score: 112-0 v. Carlisle, 14 Sep 1986
Highest against: 78-6 at Warrington, 12 Apr 1909
Attendance: 35,695 v. Wigan (League), 26 Dec 1949

COACHING REGISTER
● Since 1974-75

Eric Ashton	May 74 - May 80
Kel Coslett	June 80 - May 82
Billy Benyon	May 82 - Nov 85
Alex Murphy	Nov 85 - Jan 90
Mike McClennan	Feb 90 - Dec 93
Eric Hughes	Jan 94 -

GREAT BRITAIN REGISTER
(54 players)

Chris Arkwright	(+2)	1985
Len Aston	(3)	1947
Billy Benyon	(5+1)	1971-72
Tommy Bishop	(15)	1966-69
Frank Carlton	(1)	1958
Eric Chisnall	(4)	1974
Gary Connolly	(7+3)	1991-93
Eddie Cunningham	(1)	1978
Rob Dagnall	(4)	1961-65
David Eckersley	(2+2)	1973-74
Alf Ellaby	(13)	1928-33
Les Fairclough	(6)	1926-29
John Fieldhouse	(1)	1986
Alec Fildes	(4)	1932
Alf Frodsham	(3)	1928-29
Peter Gorley	(2+1)	1980-81
Bobby Goulding	(1+2)	1994
Doug Greenall	(6)	1951-54
Jonathan Griffiths	(1)	1992
Paul Groves	(1)	1987
Roy Haggerty	(2)	1987
Mervyn Hicks	(1)	1965
Neil Holding	(4)	1984
Dick Huddart	(12)	1959-63
Alan Hunte	(7)	1992-94
Les Jones	(1)	1971
Chris Joynt	(7+1)	1993-94
Tony Karalius	(4+1)	1971-72
Vince Karalius	(10)	1958-61
Ken Kelly	(2)	1972
Barry Ledger	(2)	1985-86
Paul Loughlin	(14+1)	1988-92
Stan McCormick	(1)	1948
Tom McKinney	(1)	1957
John Mantle	(13)	1966-73
Roy Mathias	(1)	1979
Glyn Moses	(9)	1955-57
Alex Murphy	(26)	1958-66
Frank Myler	(9)	1970
George Nicholls	(22)	1973-79
Sonny Nickle	(1+5)	1992-94
Harry Pinner	(5+1)	1980-86
Andy Platt	(4+3)	1985-88
Alan Prescott	(28)	1951-58
Austin Rhodes	(4)	1957-61
Jim Stott	(1)	1947
Anthony Sullivan	(1)	1991
Mick Sullivan	(10)	1961-62
Jim Tembey	(2)	1963-64
Abe Terry	(10)	1958-61
John Walsh	(4+1)	1972
Kevin Ward	(1+2)	1990-92
John Warlow	(3+1)	1964-68
Cliff Watson	(29+1)	1963-71

1994-94 SIGNINGS REGISTER

Signed	Player	Club From
3.6.94	Perelini, Apollo	Norths, Aus.
5.7.94	Booth, Simon	Leigh
27.7.94	Goulding, Bobby	Widnes
16.8.94	Hayes, Joey	—
19.12.94	Northey, Andy	Waterloo RU
26.12.94	Walsh, Philip	—
28.12.94	Capewell, Brian	—
28.12.94	Waterworth, John	—
3.1.95	Elia, Mark	Widnes
31.3.95	Matautia, Villa	Doncaster

Ian Pickavance, scorer of seven tries and a drop goal in 33 games in 1994-95.

ST. HELENS 1994-95 PLAYERS' SUMMARY

	Date of Birth	App	T	G	D	Pts	Previous club	Signed
Booth, Simon	9.12.71	10+2	1	—	—	4	Leigh	5.7.94
Casey, Sean	9.12.71	6+1	1	—	—	4	Blackbrook ARL	16.12.91
Cooper, Shane	26.5.60	33	5	—	—	20	New Zealand	13.10.87
Cunningham, Keiron	28.10.76	19	4	—	—	16		28.10.93
Dannatt, Andy	20.11.65	4+7	—	—	—	—	Hull	23.9.93
Dywer, Bernard	20.4.67	13+1	2	—	—	8	Hare & Hounds ARL	22.5.84
Elia, Mark	25.12.62	12+4	8	1	—	34	Widnes	3.1.95
Fogerty, Adam	6.3.69	24+3	6	—	—	24	Halifax	29.7.93
Gibbs, Scott	23.1.71	19	6	—	—	24	Swansea RU	18.4.94
Goulding, Bobby	4.2.72	36	11	148	7	347	Widnes	27.7.94
Griffiths, Jonathan	23.8.64	10+6	2	—	—	8	Llanelli RU	22.5.89
Haigh, Andy	3.9.75	9+1	6	—	—	24	Crosfields ARL	10.8.93
Harrison, John	10.3.65	0+2	—	—	—	—	Parkside ARL	30.12.87
Hodgkinson, Tommy	15.4.70	1	—	—	—	—	Blackbrook ARL	1.2.89
Hunte, Alan	11.7.70	29	29	—	—	116	Wakefield T.	3.3.89
Joynt, Chris	7.12.71	31	14	—	—	56	Oldham	2.9.92
Leatham, Andy	30.3.77	0+1	—	—	—	—	Crosfields ARL	30.3.94
Loughlin, Paul	28.7.66	19+2	10	2	—	44	St. Helens Colts	8.8.83
Lyon, David	3.9.65	17+1	8	—	—	32	Warrington	23.9.92
Martyn, Tommy	4.6.71	20+2	12	5	2	60	Oldham	2.8.93
Matautia, Vila	31.8.69	2+3	2	—	—	8	Doncaster	31.3.95
Morley, Chris	22.9.73	2+4	1	—	—	4	Woolston R. ARL	16.12.91
Neill, Jonathan	19.12.68	23	1	—	—	4	Kells ARL	27.7.87
Nickle, Sonny	4.5.69	35	10	—	—	40	Sheffield E.	3.7.91
Northey, Andy	17.2.72	11+2	5	—	—	20	Waterloo RU	19.12.94
Perelini, Apollo	16.7.69	20+7	4	—	—	16	Western Samoa RU	3.6.94
Pickavance, Ian	20.9.68	21+12	7	—	1	29	Swinton	10.9.93
Prescott, Steve	26.12.73	34	20	5	—	90	Nutgrove ARL	3.11.92
Sullivan, Anthony	23.11.68	31	22	5	—	98	Hull K.R.	29.4.91
Veivers, Phil	25.5.64	14+14	5	—	1	21	Australia	18.9.84
Waring, Phil	5.3.75	2	—	—	—	—	Eccles ARL	7.12.93
TOTALS								
31 players			202	166	11	1,151		

Representative appearances 1994-95

Gibbs — Wales (1); Goulding — Britain (1+2,3g); Griffiths — Wales (1); Hunte — Britain (3); Joynt — Britain (3); Nickle — Britain (+1), England (1); Neill — Cumbria (1); Prescott — GB Under-21s (2,1t,3g); Sullivan — Wales (3).

ST. HELENS 1994-95 MATCH ANALYSIS

Date	Com-petition	H/A	Opponent	Rlt	Score	Tries	Goals	Atten-dance	Referee
21.8.94	SBC	H	Doncaster	L	20-29	Hunte (2), Joynt, Loughlin	Loughlin (2)	7672	Presley
24.8.94	SBC	A	Warrington	L	10-31	Loughlin, Nickle	Goulding	—	—
28.8.94	SBC	A	Halifax	W	30-22	Goulding (2), Joynt, Fogerty, Hunte	Goulding (5)	—	—

(Continued)

113

Date	Competition	H/A	Opponent	Rlt	Score	Tries	Goals	Attendance	Referee
4.9.94	SBC	H	Salford	W	34-28	Hunte (2), Casey, Joynt, Nickle, Prescott	Goulding (5)	7239	Atkin
11.9.94	SBC	A	Workington T.	W	30-25	Pickavance (2), Fogerty, Goulding, Loughlin, Nickle	Goulding (3)	—	—
18.9.94	SBC	H	Castleford	W	47-14	Hunte (4), Sullivan (3), Gibbs	Goulding (7, 1dg)	7710	J. Connolly
25.9.94	SBC	H	Sheffield E.	W	26-10	Hunte (3), Loughlin, Prescott	Goulding (3)	7353	Cummings
2.10.94	SBC	A	Oldham	D	18-18	Goulding, Hunte, Prescott	Goulding (3)	—	—
9.10.94	SBC	H	Leeds	W	25-18	Sullivan (2), Hunte, Loughlin	Goulding (4, 1dg)	—	—
16.10.94	SBC	A	Bradford N.	W	51-12	Joynt (2), Prescott (2), Sullivan (2), Gibbs, Hunte, Loughlin	Goulding (7, 1dg)	9482	Holdsworth
1.11.94	Tour	H	Australia	L	14-32	Dwyer, Haigh	Martyn (3)	13,911	Morris
8.11.94	SBC	A	Doncaster	W	24-5	Gibbs (2), Goulding, Haigh, Loughlin	Goulding (2)	—	—
13.11.94	SBC	H	Halifax	W	18-14	Gibbs (2), Joynt, Loughlin	Goulding	9082	Smith
27.11.94	SBC	A	Salford	L	12-39	Prescott, Veivers	Goulding (2)	—	—
4.12.94	RT(2)	A	Huddersfield	W	52-11	Sullivan (4), Pickavance (3), Booth, Joynt, Neill	Goulding (5), Martyn	—	—
11.12.94	SBC	H	Workington T.	W	48-10	Sullivan (3), Prescott (2), Fogerty, Joynt, Martyn	Goulding (8)	6043	Smith
18.12.94	RT(3)	A	Batley	D	22-22	Haigh, Lyon, Martyn, Perelini	Goulding (3)	—	—
20.12.94	RT(3) Replay	H	Batley	W	50-22	Prescott (3), Griffiths (2), Goulding, Joynt, Martyn	Goulding (8), Martyn	4940	Cross
26.12.94	SBC	H	Wigan	L	25-32	Martyn (2), Lyon, Sullivan	Goulding (4, 1dg)	18,058	Smith
1.1.95	SBC	A	Widnes	W	20-10	Hunte, Fogerty, Martyn	Goulding (4)	—	—
8.1.95	RT(QF)	A	Wigan	L	22-24	Hunte, Lyon, Prescott	Goulding (5)	—	—
11.1.95	SBC	A	Wakefield T.	L	0-15	—	—	—	—
15.1.95	SBC	H	Featherstone R.	W	26-20	Elia, Fogerty, Haigh, Perelini	Goulding (5)	5339	Cross
22.1.95	SBC	H	Hull	W	54-18	Sullivan (3), Elia, Fogerty, Nickle, Northey, Perelini	Goulding (10), Elia	5595	Smith
29.1.95	SBC	A	Castleford	L	16-18	Veivers (2), Northey	Sullivan (2)	—	—
5.2.95	SBC	A	Sheffield E.	L	31-35	Cooper, Elia, Haigh, Lyon, Sullivan, Veivers	Sullivan (3), Veivers (dg)	—	—
11.2.95	CC(4)	A	Wigan	D	16-16	Hunte, Pickavance	Goulding (3, 1dg), Pickavance (dg)	—	—
15.2.95	CC(4) Replay	H	Wigan	L	24-40	Goulding, Joynt, Nickle, Pickavance	Goulding (3), Prescott	17,300	Holdsworth
19.2.95	SBC	H	Oldham	W	32-22	Northey (2), Hunte, Joynt, Sullivan, Veivers	Goulding (4)	5824	J. Connolly
12.3.95	SBC	A	Hull	W	43-32	Lyon (2), Nickle (2), Cunningham, Joynt, Northey, Sullivan	Goulding (5), Martyn (dg)	—	—
17.3.95	SBC	H	Bradford N.	W	36-27	Cunningham (2), Elia, Hunte, Joynt, Prescott	Goulding (6)	4949	Cummings
22.3.95	SBC	A	Leeds	W	31-20	Haigh, Hunte, Joynt, Nickle, Prescott	Goulding (5, 1dg)	—	—
26.3.95	SBC	A	Featherstone R.	L	27-34	Martyn (2), Cooper, Elia, Prescott	Goulding (3, 1dg)	—	—
2.4.95	SBC	H	Wakefield T.	W	56-14	Hunte (2), Martyn (2), Cunningham, Dwyer,Elia, Loughlin, Lyon, Morley	Goulding (8)	5697	Bates
14.4.95	SBC	A	Wigan	L	18-34	Cooper (2), Prescott	Goulding (3)	—	—
17.4.95	SBC	H	Widnes	W	54-22	Hunte (3), Goulding (2), Nickle (2), Elia, Martyn, Prescott	Prescott (4), Goulding	5974	Morris
21.4.95	SBC	H	Warrington	W	31-12	Cooper, Goulding, Hunte, Martyn, Perelini, Sullivan	Goulding (3), Martyn (dg)	5991	Cummings
7.5.95	PT(1)	H	Halifax	W	32-16	Prescott (2), Elia, Hunte, Lyon	Goulding (6)	7008	Holdsworth
14.5.95	PT(SF)	A	Leeds	L	26-30	Goulding, Hunte, Loughlin, Matautia, Prescott	Goulding (3)	—	—

114

SALFORD

Ground: The Willows (0161-737-6363)
First Season: 1896-97
Nickname: Red Devils
Chairman: John Wilkinson
Chief Exec: Dave Tarry
Honours: **Championship** Winners, 1913-14,
1932-33, 1936-37, 1938-39
Beaten finalists, 1933-34
Division One Champions, 1973-74,
1975-76
Division Two Champions, 1990-91
Challenge Cup Winners, 1937-38
Beaten finalists, 1899-1900,
1901-02, 1902-03, 1905-06, 1938-39,
1968-69
Regal Trophy Beaten finalists,
1972-73
Premiership Beaten finalists,
1975-76
Second Division Premiership
Winners, 1990-91
Lancashire Cup Winners, 1931-32,
1934-35, 1935-36, 1936-37, 1972-73
Beaten finalists, 1929-30, 1938-39,
1973-74, 1974-75, 1975-76, 1988-89,
1990-91
Lancashire League Winners,
1932-33, 1933-34, 1934-35, 1936-37,
1938-39
BBC2 Floodlit Trophy Winners,
1974-75

RECORDS
Match
Goals: 13 by Gus Risman v. Bramley, 5 Apr 1933
Gus Risman v. Broughton R.,
18 May 1940
David Watkins v. Keighley,
7 Jan 1972
Steve Rule v. Doncaster, 4 Sep 1981
Tries: 6 by Frank Miles v. Leeds, 5 Mar 1898
Ernest Bone v. Goole, 29 Mar 1902
Jack Hilton v. Leigh, 7 Oct 1939
Points: 39 by Jim Lomas v. Liverpool C.,
2 Feb 1907

Season
Goals: 221 by David Watkins, 1972-73
Tries: 46 by Keith Fielding, 1973-74
Points: 493 by David Watkins, 1972-73
Career
Goals: 1,241 by David Watkins, 1967-79
Tries: 297 by Maurice Richards, 1969-83
Points: 2,907 by David Watkins, 1967-79
Appearances: 496+2 by Maurice Richards,
1969-83
Highest score: 78-0 v. Liverpool C., 2 Feb 1907
Highest against: 70-6 at Wigan, 14 Mar 1993
Attendance: 26,470 v. Warrington (RL Cup),
13 Feb 1937

COACHING REGISTER
● **Since 1974-75**

Les Bettinson	Dec 73 - Mar 77
Colin Dixon	Mar 77 - Jan 78
Stan McCormick	Feb 78 - Mar 78
Alex Murphy	May 78 - Nov 80
Kevin Ashcroft	Nov 80 - Mar 82
Alan McInnes	Mar 82 - May 82
Malcolm Aspey	May 82 - Oct 83
Mike Coulman	Oct 83 - May 84
Kevin Ashcroft	May 84 - Oct 89
Kevin Tamati	Oct 89 - July 93
Garry Jack	July 94 - Mar 95
Andy Gregory	Mar 95 -

*Prop Phil Sumner, Salford's loan signing from Warrington
in March 1995.*

GREAT BRITAIN REGISTER
(28 players)

Bill Burgess	(1)	1969
Paul Charlton	(17+1)	1970-74
Mike Coulman	(2+1)	1971
George Curran	(6)	1946-48
Eddie Curzon	(1)	1910
Tom Danby	(3)	1950
Colin Dixon	(11+2)	1969-74
Alan Edwards	(7)	1936-37
Jack Feetham	(7)	1932-33
Keith Fielding	(3)	1974-77
Ken Gill	(5+2)	1974-77
Jack Gore	(1)	1926
Chris Hesketh	(21+2)	1970-74
Barney Hudson	(8)	1932-37
Emlyn Jenkins	(9)	1933-37
Jim Lomas	(5)	1908-10
Tom McKinney	(7)	1951-54
Alf Middleton	(1)	1929
Steve Nash	(8)	1977-82
Maurice Richards	(2)	1974
Gus Risman	(17)	1932-46
Jack Spencer	(1)	1907
Johnny Ward	(1)	1970
Silas Warwick	(2)	1907
Billy Watkins	(7)	1933-37
David Watkins	(2+4)	1971-74
Billy Williams	(2)	1929-32
Peter Williams	(1+1)	1989

1994-95 SIGNINGS REGISTER

Signed	Player	Club From
2.8.94	Gregory, Mike	Warrington
8.8.94	Panapa, Sam	Wigan
19.8.94	Eccles, Cliff	Rochdale H.
25.8.94	McPherson, Neil	Salford Academy
3.9.94	Causer, Paul	Salford Academy
9.9.94	*Marriott, Karl	Rochdale H.
11.9.94	Watson, Ian	Eccles ARL
10.10.94	Sinfield, Ian	Waterhead ARL
3.11.94	Williams, Jason	NZ
18.12.94	Wilson, Scott	Aus
22.1.95	Marsh, Steve	Blackbrook ARL
15.2.95	Blakeley, Michael	Leigh
29.3.95	*Myler, Rob	Warrington
29.3.95	*Sumner, Philip	Warrington
30.3.95	Martin, Scott	Leigh
22.5.95	Ratcliffe, David	Eccles ARL
22.5.95	Wade, Christopher	Salford Academy

Former Great Britain skipper Mike Gregory, an August 1994 Salford recruit from Warrington.

SALFORD 1994-95 PLAYERS' SUMMARY

	Date of Birth	App	T	G	D	Pts	Previous club	Signed
Birkett, Martin	16.9.65	10+4	2	1	—	10	Frizington ARL	7.12.89
Blakeley, Steve	17.10.72	24	12	79	2	208	Wigan	19.11.92
Blease, Ian	1.1.65	16+7	2	—	—	8	Folly Lane ARL	13.3.85
Brown, Shaun	19.10.69	9+1	1	6	1	17	Leigh East ARL	3.8.89
Coussons, Phil	2.8.73	7	2	—	—	8	Salford U-18s	11.2.92
Critchley, Jason	7.12.70	27+3	8	—	—	32	Widnes	4.8.92
Eccles, Cliff	4.9.67	31+1	1	—	—	4	Rochdale H.	19.8.94
Evans, Tex	25.1.64	5	1	—	—	4	Swinton	17.8.88
Forber, Paul	29.4.64	21	4	—	—	16	St. Helens	11.1.93
Ford, Phil	16.3.61	31	17	—	—	68	Leeds	28.8.92
Gregory, Andy	10.8.61	12+2	1	6	1	17	Leeds	16.11.93
Gregory, Mike	20.5.64	7+4	—	—	—	—	Warrington	2.8.94
Lee, Mark	27.3.68	26+1	5	—	1	21	St. Helens	8.1.90
McAvoy, Nathan	31.12.76	22+2	14	—	—	56	Eccles ARL	8.2.94
Mahon, Scott		17	6	5	—	34	Australia	
Marsden, Bob	28.2.66	16+10	2	—	—	8	Rochdale H.	7.10.93
Marshall, Wayne		4	—	—	—	—	Australia	
Martin, Scott	29.12.74	5	4	—	—	16	Leigh	30.3.95
Myler, Robert	4.3.70	4	1	4	—	12	Warrington	29.3.95
Naylor, Scott	2.2.72	19+6	8	—	—	32	Wigan	30.7.93
Panapa, Sam	14.5.62	31	14	—	—	56	Wigan	8.8.94
Potts, Ian	5.1.69	1	—	—	—	—		23.4.87
Quigley, Jonathan	6.6.73	17+5	4	—	—	16	Leigh Miners ARL	25.10.90
Randall, Craig	22.9.72	18+14	8	—	—	32	Leigh Miners ARL	21.5.91
Southern, Paul	18.3.76	4	—	—	—	—	Salford Academy	22.4.93
Sumner, Phil	14.6.71	0+1	—	—	—	—	Warrington	29.3.95
Tyrer, Gary	1.2.71	11	3	5	—	22	Orrell RU	1.12.92
Watson, Ian	27.10.76	4+1	—	3	—	6	Eccles ARL	11.9.94
Webster, Richard	9.7.68	10+7	4	—	—	16	Swansea RU	29.9.93
Williams, Jason		10	6	—	—	24	Australia	3.11.94
Wilson, Scott		2	—	—	—	—	Australia	18.12.94
Young, David	26.7.67	34	1	—	—	4	Leeds	25.4.91
TOTALS								
32 players			131	109	5	747		

Representative appearances 1994-95
Birkett — Cumbria (1); Ford — Wales (2+1); McAvoy — GB Under-21s (+1); Webster — Wales (+1); Young — Wales (3).

SALFORD 1994-95 MATCH ANALYSIS

Date	Competition	H/A	Opponent	Rlt	Score	Tries	Goals	Attendance	Referee
21.8.94	SBC	A	Wakefield T.	L	10-13	Blakeley	Blakeley (3)	—	—
28.8.94	SBC	H	Hull	W	33-28	Young, Forber, Blakeley (2), Ford	Blakeley (6), Brown (dg)	3247	Campbell
31.8.94	SBC	A	Widnes	L	16-24	Blakeley, Brown, Forber	Blakeley (2)	—	—
4.90.94	SBC	A	St. Helens	L	28-34	Birkett, Blakeley, Critchley, Ford, Mahon	Blakeley (4)	—	—
11.9.94	SBC	H	Featherstone R.	D	24-24	McAvoy (2), Coussons, Mahon	Mahon (2), Blakeley, Brown	3410	Cross
18.9.94	SBC	A	Leeds	L	20-26	Ford (2), McAvoy (2), Panapa	—	—	—
25.9.94	SBC	H	Halifax	L	12-24	Coussens, Randall	Brown (2)	4681	Gilmour
2.10.94	SBC	H	Doncaster	W	22-12	Ford (2), Critchley, Panapa	Mahon (2), Brown	3147	Presley
9.10.94	SBC	A	Castleford	L	6-34	Randall	Mahon	—	—
16.10.94	SBC	A	Wigan	L	22-52	Mahon (2), Ford, McAvoy	A. Gregory (3)	—	—
4.11.94	SBC	H	Wakefield T.	W	48-8	A. Gregory, Mahon, Forber, Blakeley, Randall, McAvoy, Naylor, Williams	Blakeley (8)	2637	Smith
13.11.94	SBC	A	Hull	L	16-29	McAvoy, Panapa, Randall	Blakeley (2)	—	—
27.11.94	SBC	H	St. Helens	W	39-12	Blakeley, Critchley, Ford, Lee, Mahon, Williams	Blakeley (7,1dg)	5558	J. Connolly
4.12.94	RT(2)	H	London B.	W	16-14	Forber, Ford, Panapa	Blakeley (2)	2088	Oddy
11.12.94	SBC	A	Featherstone R.	W	20-12	Williams (3)	Blakeley (4)	—	—
17.12.94	RT(3)	H	Warrington	L	24-31	Panapa, Randall, Critchley, McAvoy	Blakeley (4)	2189	J. Connolly
26.12.94	SBC	H	Oldham	L	12-16	Blakeley	Blakeley (4)	4984	Cross
1.1.95	SBC	A	Bradford N.	L	18-24	Blease (2), Webster	Blakeley (3)	—	—
8.1.95	SBC	H	Sheffield E.	W	24-20	Ford (2), Birkett, Naylor, Williams	Blakeley (2)	2427	Ollerton
22.1.95	SBC	A	Workington T.	L	0-34	—	—	—	—
5.2.95	SBC	A	Halifax	W	27-24	Naylor (2), Critchley, Panapa, Tyrer	A. Gregory (3, 1dg)	—	—
12.2.95	CC(4)	A	Hunslet	D	32-32	Ford (2), Blakeley, Marsden, Quigley, Tyrer	Blakeley (4)	—	—
15.2.95	CC(4) Replay	H	Hunslet	W	52-10	Webster (2), Blakeley, Ford, Critchley, Lee, McAvoy, Panapa, Tyrer	Blakeley (7), Birkett	1931	Ollerton
19.2.95	SBC	A	Doncaster	W	19-12	Blakeley, Critchley, McAvoy Panapa	Blakeley (1,1dg)	—	—
26.2.95	CC(5)	H	Featherstone R.	L	10-30	Lee (2)	Tyrer	4064	Campbell
1.3.95	SBC	H	Leeds	L	8-26	Naylor	Brown (2)	3271	Tennant
12.3.95	SBC	H	Castleford	L	16-48	Ford, Marsden, Naylor, Webster	—	2670	Campbell
15.3.95	SBC	H	Warrington	L	16-32	McAvoy (2), Panapa	Tyrer (2)	2590	Smith
19.3.95	SBC	A	Wigan	L	8-42	Lee	Tyrer (2)	7091	Campbell
26.3.95	SBC	A	Warrington	L	22-58	McAvoy (2), Eccles, Randall	Watson (3)	—	—
2.4.95	SBC	A	Sheffield E.	L	16-29	Evans, Myler, Panapa	Myler (2)	—	—
9.4.95	SBC	H	Workington T.	W	46-16	Panapa (3), Ford (2), Martin, Quigley, Randall	Blakeley (5), Myler (2)	2551	Tennant
14.4.95	SBC	A	Oldham	L	16-28	Panapa, Quigley	Blakeley (4)	—	—
17.4.95	SBC	H	Bradford N.	L	14-16	Martin (2), Naylor	Blakeley	2647	Asquith
23.4.95	SBC	H	Widnes	W	35-18	Blakeley, Critchley, Martin, Naylor, Quigley, Randall	Blakeley (5), Lee (dg)	3094	J. Connolly

SHEFFIELD EAGLES

Ground: Don Valley Stadium (0114-261-0326)
First Season: 1984-85
Nickname: Eagles
Chairman: Gary Hetherington
Secretary: Julie Bush
Honours: **Division Two** Champions, 1991-92
Second Division/Divisional Premiership Winners, 1988-89, 1991-92
Yorkshire Cup Beaten finalists, 1992-93

RECORDS

Match
Goals: 12 by Roy Rafferty at Fulham, 21 Sep 1986
Mark Aston v. Keighley C., 25 Apr 1992
Tries: 5 by Daryl Powell at Mansfield M., 2 Jan 1989
Points: 32 by Roy Rafferty at Fulham, 21 Sep 1986

Season
Goals: 148 by Mark Aston, 1988-89
Tries: 30 by Iva Ropati, 1991-92
Points: 307 by Mark Aston, 1988-89

Career
Goals: 622 by Mark Aston, 1986-
Tries: 114 by Daryl Powell, 1984-95
Points: 1,370 by Mark Aston, 1986-94
Appearances: 300+26 by Mark Gamson, 1984-
Highest score: 80-8 v. Wigan St. Patricks, 13 Nov 1988
Highest against: 80-2 v. Australia, 26 Oct 1994
Attendance: 7,984 v. Wakefield T. (Div. 1), 26 Sep 1990 — at Don Valley
8,636 v. Widnes (Div. 1), 8 Oct 1989 — at Bramall Lane, Sheffield U. FC

COACHING REGISTER
● **Since formation in 1984**

Alan Rhodes	Apr 84 - May 86
Gary Hetherington	July 86 - Apr 93
Bill Gardner	May 93 - Dec 93
Gary Hetherington	Dec 93 -

GREAT BRITAIN REGISTER
(3 players)

Mark Aston	(+1)	1991
Lee Jackson	(6)	1993-94
Daryl Powell	(19+9)	1990-94

1993-94 SIGNINGS REGISTER

Signed	Player	Club From
25.7.94	Glancy, John	Wakefield T.
6.8.94	Sodje, Bright	Hull K.R.
7.8.94	*Hutchinson, Rob	Hull K.R.
1.9.94	Senior, Keith	Eagles Academy
3.9.94	Trindall, Darrell	Aus
28.10.94	*Martin, Scott	Leigh
18.12.94	Lucchese, Laurent	Huddersfield

Eagles loose forward Anthony Farrell, an England debutant in 1995.

SHEFFIELD EAGLES 1994-95 PLAYERS' SUMMARY

	Date of Birth	App	T	G	D	Pts	Previous club	Signed
Briggs, Carl	29.7.74	18+7	2	22	10	62	Doncaster	1.7.92
Boothroyd, Alan	19.6.66	1+1	—	—	—	—	Bradford N.	
Broadbent, Paul	24.5.68	35	10	—	—	40	Lock Lane ARL	26.10.87
Carr, Paul	13.5.67	31+1	18	—	—	72	Hunslet	1.7.92
Chapman, Richard	5.9.75	1+1	—	—	—	—	Dewsbury Moor ARL	27.6.93
Cook, Michael	1.8.61	15+1	1	—	—	4	Hunslet Jnrs. ARL	28.2.87
Crowther, Matthew	6.5.74	1+1	1	—	—	4	Kippax ARL	11.9.91
Farrell, Anthony	17.1.69	26+1	11	—	—	44	Huddersfield	1.11.89
Gamson, Mark	17.8.65	27+4	5	—	—	20	Crigglestone ARL	27.7.84
Glancy, John	14.4.62	21+2	1	—	—	4	Wakefield T.	25.7.94
Hayes, Brad	22.4.67	6	2	—	—	8	Ryedale-York	11.3.94
Hughes, Ian	13.3.72	27+3	10	—	—	40	East Leeds	1.7.91
Hutchinson, Rob	20.9.68	3	—	—	—	—	Hull K.R.	7.8.94
Jackson, Lee	12.3.69	25+1	1	—	—	4	Hull	17.9.93
Laughton, Dale	10.10.70	2+2	—	—	—	—	Dodworth ARL	3.9.89
Lucchese, Laurent	4.4.73	12	—	6	—	12	Huddersfield	18.12.94
Mann, David	28.10.69	1	—	—	—	—	Dodworth ARL	20.8.92
Martin, Scott	29.12.74	3	—	—	—	—	Leigh	28.10.94
Mycoe, David	1.5.72	24+2	3	70	—	152	Crigglestone ARL	31.7.89
Picksley, Richard	29.12.70	4	1	—	—	4	Lock Lane ARL	31.7.89
Powell, Daryl	21.7.65	19+2	6	—	2	26	Redhill ARL	27.7.84
Price, Richard	26.6.70	33	10	—	1	41	Hull	19.3.91
Randall, Carl	22.12.71	1+4	1	—	—	4	Dodworth ARL	20.8.92
Reilly, Glen	26.1.74	0+2	—	—	—	—		13.12.91
Senior, Keith	24.4.76	20+3	3	—	—	12	Sheffield E. Academy	1.9.94
Sheridan, Ryan	24.5.75	28+2	16	—	—	64	Dewsbury Moor ARL	10.7.91
Sodje, Bright	21.4.66	28+2	10	—	—	40	Hull K.R.	6.8.94
Stott, Lynton	9.5.71	30+1	13	11	—	74	Woolston R. ARL	19.12.92
Summerill, Darren	26.4.73	1+5	—	—	—	—	Rossington ARL	8.11.93
Thompson, Alex	29.7.74	8+6	—	—	—	—	Crown Malet ARL	1.7.91
Trindall, Darrell		1	—	3	—	6	Australia	3.9.94
Turner, Darren	13.10.73	12+11	2	—	—	8	Leeds Academy	1.1.92
Young, Andy	4.8.66	4+9	1	—	—	4	Eastmoor ARL	18.11.87
TOTALS								
33 players			128	112	13	749		

Representative appearances 1994-95
Broadbent — England (1,1t); Farrell — England (1); Jackson — Britain (3), England (1);
Martin — GB Under-21s (1); Powell — Britain (2+1), England (2); Sheridan — GB Under-21s (1);
Thompson — GB Under-21s (2).

SHEFFIELD EAGLES 1994-95 MATCH ANALYSIS

Date	Com-petition	H/A	Opponent	Rlt	Score	Tries	Goals	Atten-dance	Referee
23.8.94	SBC	H	Bradford N.	L	8-26	Carr	Mycoe (2)	4672	R. Connolly
28.8.94	SBC	A	Wigan	L	16-40	Broadbent, Mycoe, Hayes	Mycoe (2)	—	—
4.9.94	SBC	A	Workington T.	W	31-6	Carr (2), Farrell (2), Hayes, Stott	Trindall (3), Briggs (dg)	—	—
11.9.94	SBC	A	Castleford	L	9-28	Broadbent, Hughes	Briggs (dg)	—	—
18.9.94	SBC	H	Warrington	W	29-8	Farrell, Price, Stott, Turner	Mycoe (6), Briggs (dg)	3037	Campbell
25.9.94	SBC	A	St. Helens	L	10-26	Picksley, Price	Mycoe	—	—
2.10.94	SBC	H	Widnes	L	0-22	—	—	2085	Morris
9.10.94	SBC	H	Hull	W	38-14	Carr (2), Broadbent, Farrell, Powell, Sodje, Stott	Mycoe (5)	2164	Cummings
16.10.94	SBC	A	Leeds	L	18-30	Carr, Price, Sheridan	Mycoe (3)	—	—
26.10.94	Tour	H	Australia	L	2-80	—	Mycoe	7450	Tennant
30.10.94	SBC	A	Halifax	L	20-24	Farrell, Senior, Sheridan, Sodje	Mycoe (2)	—	—
6.11.94	SBC	A	Bradford N.	L	4-40	Carr	—	—	—
11.11.94	SBC	H	Wigan	L	20-36	Sheridan (2), Carr, Sodje	Mycoe, Stott	2601	Campbell
27.11.94	SBC	H	Workington T.	W	34-29	Carr, Farrell, Glancy, Powell, Sodje, Stott	Mycoe (5)	1906	Presley
4.12.94	RT(2)	H	Leigh	W	46-10	Sodje (2), Stott (2), Carr, Crowther, Farrell, Powell, Price, Sheridan	Mycoe (3)	870	McGregor
9.12.94	SBC	H	Castleford	L	16-27	Carr, Powell, Mycoe	Stott (2)	1840	J. Connolly
18.12.94	RT(3)	A	Keighley C.	L	10-26	Hughes, Sheridan	Mycoe	—	—
26.12.94	SBC	H	Doncaster	W	30-22	Broadbent, Carr, Hughes, Price, Stott	Lucchese (5)	3039	Tennant
8.1.95	SBC	A	Salford	L	20-24	Carr, Farrell, Senior, Sheridan	Lucchese, Mycoe	—	—
11.1.95	SBC	A	Featherstone R.	W	24-14	Broadbent, Farrell, Powell, Senior	Briggs (4)	—	—
15.1.95	SBC	H	Wakefield T.	L	14-41	Carr, Farrell, Jackson	Briggs	2274	Asquith
22.1.95	SBC	A	Oldham	W	14-12	Carr, Stott	Briggs (2), Powell (2dg)	—	—
5.2.95	SBC	H	St Helens	W	35-31	Broadbent, Farrell, Powell, Price, Sheridan, Stott	Briggs (5, 1dg)	2705	Bates
12.2.95	CC(4)	A	Doncaster	W	22-12	Briggs, Gamson, Sheridan, Stott	Briggs (3)	—	—
19.2.95	SBC	A	Widnes	L	18-36	Broadbent, Stott	Briggs (5)	—	—
26.2.95	CC(5)	H	Widnes	L	7-19	Carr	Briggs (1, 1dg)	2295	R. Connolly
3.3.95	SBC	A	Hull	W	20-16	Broadbent, Cook, Randall	Stott (4)	—	—
12.3.95	SBC	A	Warrington	L	18-26	Price, Sheridan, Sodje	Stott (3)	—	—
19.3.95	SBC	H	Leeds	W	31-22	Hughes, Price, Sheridan, Sodje	Mycoe (6), Briggs (2dg), Price (dg)	4778	Smith
26.3.95	SBC	A	Wakefield T.	W	14-10	Price, Sheridan	Mycoe (3)	—	—
2.4.95	SBC	H	Salford	W	29-16	Gamson, Hughes, Sheridan, Turner	Mycoe (6), Briggs (dg)	1983	Kirkpatrick
9.4.95	SBC	H	Oldham	L	12-17	Broadbent, Stott	Briggs, Stott	2137	Bates
14.4.95	SBC	A	Doncaster	W	56-16	Gamson (2), Broadbent, Carr, Hughes, Price, Sodje, Stott, Young	Mycoe (10)	—	—
17.4.95	SBC	H	Featherstone R.	W	26-16	Hughes (2), Carr, Sheridan	Mycoe (5)	1882	J. Connolly
23.4.95	SBC	H	Halifax	W	32-24	Sheridan (2), Briggs, Mycoe, Sodje	Mycoe (5), Briggs (2dg)	2823	Asquith
7.5.95	PT(1)	A	Wigan	L	16-48	Hughes (2), Gamson	Mycoe (2)	—	—

SWINTON

Ground: Gigg Lane, Bury (0161-761-2328)
First Season: 1896-97
Nickname: Lions
Chairman: Malcolm White
General
  Manager: Tony Barrow
Honours: **Championship** Winners, 1926-27,
1927-28, 1930-31, 1934-35
Beaten finalists, 1924-25, 1932-33
War Emergency League Beaten
finalists, 1939-40
Division One Champions, 1962-63,
1963-64
Division Two Champions, 1984-85
Challenge Cup Winners,
1899-1900, 1925-26, 1927-28
Beaten finalists, 1926-27, 1931-32
Second Division Premiership
Winners, 1986-87
Beaten finalists, 1988-89
Lancashire Cup Winners, 1925-26,
1927-28, 1939-40, 1969-70
Beaten finalists, 1910-11, 1923-24,
1931-32, 1960-61, 1961-62, 1962-63,
1964-65, 1972-73
Lancashire League Winners,
1924-25, 1927-28, 1928-29, 1930-31,
1960-61
Lancashire War League Winners,
1939-40
Western Division Championship
Beaten finalists, 1963-64
BBC2 Floodlit Trophy
Beaten finalists, 1966-67

RECORDS

Match
Goals: 12 by Ken Gowers v. Liverpool C.,
3 Oct 1959
Tries: 5 by Morgan Bevan v. Morecambe,
10 Sep 1898
Billy Wallwork v. Widnes,
15 Dec 1900
Jack Evans v. Bradford N.,
30 Sep 1922
Hector Halsall v. St. Helens,
24 Jan 1925
Dick Cracknell v. Whitehaven Rec.,
11 Feb 1928
Randall Lewis v. Keighley,
12 Jan 1946
John Stopford v. Bramley,
22 Dec 1962
Alan Buckley v. Salford, 8 Apr 1964
Joe Ropati v. Nottingham C.,
21 Jan 1990
Points: 29 by Bernard McMahon v. Dewsbury,
15 Aug 1959

Season
Goals: 128 by Albert Blan, 1960-61
Tries: 42 by John Stopford, 1963-64
Points: 283 by Albert Blan, 1960-61

Career
Goals: 970 by Ken Gowers, 1954-73
Tries: 197 by Frank Evans, 1921-31
Points: 2,105 by Ken Gowers, 1954-73
Appearances: 593+8 by Ken Gowers, 1954-73
Highest score: 76-4 v. Pontefract, 8 Sep 1906
Highest against: 78-0 v. Wigan, 29 Sep 1992
Attendance: 26,891 v. Wigan (RL Cup),
12 Feb 1964 (at Station Road)
3,501 v. Wigan (Lancs Cup),
29 Sep 1992 (at Gigg Lane)

COACHING REGISTER
● **Since 1974-75**

Austin Rhodes	June 74 - Nov 75
Bob Fleet	Nov 75 - Nov 76
John Stopford	Nov 76 - Apr 77
Terry Gorman	June 77 - Nov 78
Ken Halliwell	Nov 78 - Dec 79
Frank Myler	Jan 80 - May 81
Tom Grainey	May 81 - Oct 83
Jim Crellin	Nov 83 - May 86
Bill Holliday Mike Peers	June 86 - Oct 87
Frank Barrow	Oct 87 - June 89
Jim Crellin	July 89 - July 91
Chris O'Sullivan	July 91 - Dec 91
Tony Barrow	Jan 92 -

GREAT BRITAIN REGISTER
(15 players)

Tom Armitt	(8)	1933-37
Alan Buckley	(7)	1963-66
Fred Butters	(2)	1929
Billy Davies	(1)	1968
Bryn Evans	(10)	1926-33
Frank Evans	(4)	1924
Jack Evans	(3)	1926
Ken Gowers	(14)	1962-66
Hector Halsall	(1)	1929
Martin Hodgson	(16)	1929-37
Ron Morgan	(2)	1963
Billo Rees	(11)	1926-29
Dave Robinson	(12)	1965-67
John Stopford	(12)	1961-66
Joe Wright	(1)	1932

1994-95 SIGNINGS REGISTER

Signed	Player	Club From
20.6.94	McCabe, Carl	Nutgrove ARL
30.6.94	Ogden, David	Leigh Rangers ARL
5.7.94	Shaw, Roger	West Park RU
25.7.94	Harthill, David	Warrington
25.8.94	Price-Jones, Gavin	Wagga M., Aus.
3.9.94	*Clayton, Richard	—
10.11.94	*Hudspith, Mark	Oldham
10.11.94	*Olsen, Ben	Oldham
12.11.94	Clark, Brett	Mayfield ARL
26.11.94	*Donegan, Austin	Salford
15.12.94	*Pickles, Damien	Huddersfield
13.1.95	*Chrimes, David	Oldham
18.1.95	*Forber, Gary	Highfield
22.1.95	*Connor, Ian	St. Helens
27.1.95	*Litherland, Roy	Halifax
4.2.95	Tanner, David	Keighley C.
31.3.95	Gunning, John	Leigh
31.3.95	*Measures, Neil	Leigh
6.4.95	Warburton, Steve	Rochdale H.

Swinton winger John Stopford in action for Great Britain during his 12-cap Test career.

SWINTON 1994-95 PLAYERS' SUMMARY

	Date of Birth	App	T	G	D	Pts	Previous club	Signed
Allison, Steve	22.5.74	1+2	—	—	—	—	Salford Academy	1.7.93
Ashall, Barry	1.9.71	12+2	5	1	1	23	Thatto Heath ARL	21.2.89
Ashcroft, Simon	27.6.70	22	14	—	—	56	Highfield	3.6.92
Ashurst, Chris	24.7.65	5+3	1	—	—	4	Widnes	8.6.93
Baines, Vinnie	18.11.73	3+1	—	—	—	—		11.9.93
Barrow, Paul	20.10.74	12+7	1	—	—	4		15.3.93
Barrow, Tony	19.10.71	32	9	—	—	36	Oldham	6.2.92
Chrimes, David	16.12.69	12+1	4	—	—	16	Oldham	13.1.95
Clark, Brett	1.11.61	11	6	—	—	24	Mayfield ARL	12.11.94
Clark, Jason	18.10.70	0+2	—	—	—	—	Oldham St. Annes ARL	30.8.90
Clayton, Richard	24.2.70	1	—	—	—	—	Chorley B.	21.3.94
Connor, Ian	21.3.70	8+2	2	—	—	8	St. Helens	22.1.95
Cooper, Carl	21.9.69	0+1	—	—	—	—	St. Helens	23.1.92
Earner, Adrian	19.11.66	21+3	—	—	—	—	Leigh	3.11.92
Errington, Craig	17.8.72	5+2	—	—	—	—	Folly Lane ARL	8.9.92
Evans, Jim	14.6.72	8	3	—	—	12	Folly Lane ARL	17.5.94
Forber, Gary	22.5.68	3+1	—	—	—	—	Highfield	18.1.95
Gartland, Paul	2.11.72	32	15	66	1	193	Wigan	9.7.93
Gunning, John	30.3.69	3+1	1	—	—	4	Leigh	31.3.95
Hansen, Shane	5.12.60	2	—	—	—	—	Salford	20.9.93
Harthill, David	19.4.74	6+1	—	—	—	—	Warrington	24.11.93
Hudspith, Mark	20.2.72	15+1	12	31	—	110	Oldham	10.11.94
Humphries, Tony	3.9.63	29+1	1	—	—	4	Rochdale H.	25.3.93
Kay, Paul	30.11.68	7	—	—	—	—	Batley	28.2.92
Kennett, Paul	7.1.71	4	1	—	—	4	Tondu RU	22.10.90
Ledger, Barry	19.6.62	9+1	6	1	—	26	Leigh	25.4.93
Lord, Paul	22.12.67	22+1	13	—	—	52	Wakefield T.	22.9.93
McCabe, Carl	10.8.76	1+3	—	—	—	—	Nutgrove ARL	20.6.94
Marsh, David	8.10.68	25+5	3	—	—	12	Widnes	20.5.93
Measures, Neil	11.1.71	2+1	—	—	—	—	Leigh	31.3.95
Olsen, Ben	17.3.65	4+2	1	—	—	4	Oldham	10.11.94
Pickles, Damien	2.12.70	5	2	—	—	8	Huddersfield	15.12.94
Price-Jones, Gavin	19.12.70	18+1	3	—	—	12	Australia	25.8.94
Prince, Glen	8.4.67	10+5	—	—	—	—	Langworthy ARL	9.5.91
Purcell, Andy		20+3	5	—	—	20	Australia	
Skeech, Ian	4.2.67	18+4	4	—	—	16	Newton-le-Willows RU	24.11.87
Tanner, David	29.9.65	11	1	—	—	4	Keighley C.	4.2.95
Turner, Stuart	13.11.69	3	—	—	—	—	Wigan	30.7.93
Warburton, Steve	6.2.69	6+1	1	—	—	4	Rochdale H.	6.4.95
Welsby, Gary	17.9.71	26	6	—	—	24	Thatto Heath ARL	25.2.93
Whittle, Danny	18.7.70	8+5	1	—	—	4	Nutgrove ARL	12.3.92
TOTALS								
41 players			121	99	2	684		

SWINTON 1994-95 MATCH ANALYSIS

Date	Competition	H/A	Opponent	Rlt	Score	Tries	Goals	Attendance	Referee
21.8.94	SD	H	Ryedale-York	W	19-18	Lord (2), T. Barrow	Gartland (3, 1dg)	552	Ollerton
4.9.94	SD	H	Huddersfield	W	20-18	Gartland (2), Lord, Marsh	Gartland (2)	1331	Burke
11.9.94	SD	A	Hull K. R.	L	0-50	—	—	—	—
18.9.94	SD	H	Bramley	W	24-22	Evans, Kennett, Price-Jones	Gartland (6)	631	Nicholson
25.9.94	SD	A	Carlisle	W	36-16	Evans, Gartland, Ledger, Skeech, Welsby	Gartland (7), Ashall	—	—
2.10.94	SD	A	London B.	L	29-40	Ledger (3), Ashall, T. Barrow	Gartland (4), Ashall (dg)	—	—
9.10.94	SD	H	Hunslet	W	46-20	Ashall (3), Skeech (2), Ashurst, Gartland, Ledger, Welsby	Gartland (5)	737	Oddy
16.10.94	SD	A	Batley	L	6-10	Gartland	Gartland	—	—
25.10.94	SD	A	Dewsbury	L	4-30	Lord	—	—	—
30.10.94	SD	H	Whitehaven	L	12-42	Ledger, Warburton	Gartland (2)	790	Asquith
6.11.94	SD	A	Ryedale-York	L	6-52	Lord	Ledger	—	—
13.11.94	SD	H	Dewsbury	L	12-24	T. Barrow, Price-Jones	Gartland (2)	906	Gilmour
27.11.94	RT(1)	H	Saddleworth R.	W	32-26	Ashcroft (2), Purcell (2), Olsen, Welsby	Gartland (4)	380	Morris
4.12.94	RT(2)	A	Leeds	L	24-54	Lord (2), P. Barrow, B. Clark	Gartland (4)	—	—
11.12.94	SD	A	Huddersfield	L	20-32	Lord (2), B. Clark	Gartland (4)	—	—
18.12.94	SD	H	Hull K. R.	L	22-38	B. Clark, Gartland, Marsh, Whittle	Gartland (3)	624	Lee
26.12.94	SD	A	Rochdale H.	L	18-24	Ashall, B. Clark	Hudspith (3), Gartland (2)	—	—
8.1.95	SD	A	Highfield	W	44-14	B. Clark (2), Hudspith (2), Pickles (2), T. Barrow, Gartland	Hudspith (6)	—	—
15.1.95	SD	H	Keighley C.	L	6-48	Welsby	Hudspith	2025	Kirkpatrick
22.1.95	CC(3)	H	Millom	W	30-10	T. Barrow (3), Hudspith, Humphries, Marsh	Hudspith (3)	463	Ollerton
25.1.95	SD	H	Leigh	W	28-4	Connor (2), Lord (2), Welsby	Hudspith (4)	600	Carter
29.1.95	SD	A	Bramley	L	10-30	Gartland, Lord	Hudspith	—	—
5.2.95	SD	H	Carlisle	W	40-18	Gartland (2), Ashcroft, Hudspith (3), Chrimes	Hudspith (6)	499	Atkin
19.2.95	CC(4)	H	Leigh	L	22-34	Hudspith (2), Evans, Gartland	Hudspith (3)	806	Presley
26.2.95	SD	H	London B.	L	26-38	Hudspith (3), Ashcroft, T. Barrow, Skeech	Hudspith	760	Steele
6.3.95	SD	A	Hunslet	L	4-6	Purcell	—	—	—
12.3.95	SD	A	Barrow	L	14-37	Chrimes (2), Lord	Hudspith	—	—
19.3.95	SD	H	Batley	L	16-24	Ashcroft, Chrimes, Gartland	Gartland, Hudspith	727	Atkin
26.3.95	SD	A	Whitehaven	W	10-6	Ashcroft, Hudspith	Hudspith	—	—
2.4.95	SD	H	Highfield	W	44-14	Ashcroft (4), T. Barrow, Gartland, Price-Jones, Purcell, Welsby	Gartland (4)	296	Asquith
9.4.95	SD	A	Keighley C.	L	6-42	Ashcroft	Gartland	—	—
14.4.95	SD	H	Rochdale H.	W	16-14	Ashcroft, Gartland	Gartland (4)	762	Presley
17.4.95	SD	A	Leigh	L	10-24	Gartland, Purcell	Gartland	—	—
23.4.95	SD	H	Barrow	W	28-13	Ashcroft (2), Gunning, Tanner	Gartland (6)	402	Presley

WAKEFIELD TRINITY

Ground: Belle Vue (01924-372445)
First Season: 1895-96
Nickname: Dreadnoughts
Chairman: Ted Richardson
Secretary; Brian Eccles
Honours: **Championship** Winners, 1966-67, 1967-68
Beaten finalists, 1959-60, 1961-62
Division Two Champions, 1903-04
Challenge Cup Winners, 1908-09, 1945-46, 1959-60, 1961-62, 1962-63
Beaten finalists, 1913-14, 1967-68, 1978-79
Regal Trophy Beaten finalists, 1971-72
Yorkshire Cup Winners, 1910-11, 1924-25, 1946-47, 1947-48, 1951-52, 1956-57, 1960-61, 1961-62, 1964-65, 1992-93
Beaten finalists, 1926-27, 1932-33, 1934-35, 1936-37, 1939-40, 1945-46, 1958-59, 1973-74, 1974-75, 1990-91
Yorkshire League Winners, 1909-10, 1910-11, 1945-46, 1958-59, 1959-60, 1961-62, 1965-66

RECORDS
Match
Goals: 13 by Mark Conway v. Highfield, 27 Oct 1992
Tries: 7 by Fred Smith v. Keighley, 25 Apr 1959
Keith Slater v. Hunslet, 6 Feb 1971
Points: 34 by Mark Conway v. Highfield, 27 Oct 1992
Season
Goals: 163 by Neil Fox, 1961-62
Tries: 38 by Fred Smith, 1959-60
David Smith, 1973-74
Points: 407 by Neil Fox, 1961-62
Career
Goals: 1,836 by Neil Fox, 1956-69 & 1970-74
Tries: 272 by Neil Fox, 1956-69 & 1970-74
Points: 4,488 by Neil Fox, 1956-69 & 1970-74
Appearances: 605 by Harry Wilkinson, 1930-49

Highest score: 90-12 v. Highfield, 27 Oct 1992
Highest against: 86-0 at Castleford, 17 Apr 1995
Attendance: 37,906 Leeds v. Huddersfield
(RL Cup SF), 21 Mar 1936
Home match: 30,676 v. Huddersfield
(RL Cup), 26 Feb 1921

COACHING REGISTER
● **Since 1974-75**

Peter Fox	June 74 - May 76
Geoff Gunney	June 76 - Nov 76
Brian Lockwood	Nov 76 - Jan 78
Ian Brooke	Jan 78 - Jan 79
Bill Kirkbride	Jan 79 - Apr 80
Ray Batten	Apr 80 - May 81
Bill Ashurst	June 81 - Apr 82
Ray Batten	May 82 - July 83
Derek Turner	July 83 - Feb 84
Bob Haigh	Feb 84 - May 84
Geoff Wraith	May 84 - Oct 84
David Lamming	Oct 84 - Apr 85
Len Casey	Apr 85 - June 86
Tony Dean	June 86 - Dec 86
Trevor Bailey	Dec 86 - Apr 87
David Topliss	May 87 - Apr 94
David Hobbs	May 94 - Jan 95
Paul Harkin/ Andy Kelly	Jan 95 -

A nine-month stay at Belle Vue for coach David Hobbs.

GREAT BRITAIN REGISTER
(46 players)

Jack Arkwright	(6)	1936-37
Kevin Ashcroft	(+1)	1974
Willie Aspinall	(1)	1966
Allan Bateman	(1+2)	1992-94
Billy Belshaw	(2)	1937
Nat Bentham	(2)	1929
John Bevan	(6)	1974-78
Tom Blinkhorn	(1)	1929
Ernie Brooks	(3)	1908
Jim Challinor	(3)	1958-60
Neil Courtney	(+1)	1982
Billy Cunliffe	(11)	1920-26
Jonathan Davies	(4)	1993-94
George Dickenson	(1)	1908
Billy Dingsdale	(3)	1929-33
Des Drummond	(2)	1987-88
Ronnie Duane	(3)	1983-84
Bob Eccles	(1)	1982
Kevin Ellis	(+1)	1991
Jim Featherstone	(6)	1948-52
Mark Forster	(2)	1987
Eric Fraser	(16)	1958-61
Laurie Gilfedder	(5)	1962-63
Bobby Greenough	(1)	1960
Andy Gregory	(1)	1986
Mike Gregory	(19+1)	1987-90
Gerry Helme	(12)	1948-54
Keith Holden	(1)	1963
Albert Johnson	(6)	1946-47
Ken Kelly	(2)	1980-82
Tom McKinney	(3)	1955
Joe Miller	(6)	1933-36
Alex Murphy	(1)	1971
Albert Naughton	(2)	1954
Terry O'Grady	(1)	1961
Harold Palin	(2)	1947
Ken Parr	(1)	1968
Albert Pimblett	(3)	1948
Ray Price	(9)	1954-57
Bob Ryan	(5)	1950-52
Ron Ryder	(1)	1952
Frank Shugars	(1)	1910
George Skelhorne	(7)	1920-21
George Thomas	(1)	1907
Derek Whitehead	(3)	1971
John Woods	(+1)	1987

1994-95 SIGNINGS REGISTER

Signed	Player	Club From
17.6.94	McGuire, Bruce	Sheffield E.
1.8.94	Murray, Anthony	Wigan
17.9.94	Davies, Emlyn	Rose Bridge ARL
4.10.94	Sculthorpe, Paul	Waterhead ARL
28.10.94	Barlow, Tukere	Waikato C., NZ
22.11.94	Gardner, John-Paul	Waterhead ARL
24.11.94	McAvoy, Robert	Glasson R. ARL
17.12.94	Heaton, Stephen	Warrington Academy
17.12.94	Milligan, Paul	Warrington Academy
28.3.95	Anders, Darren	Warrington Academy

New Zealander Kelly Shelford, maker of 37 appearances in 1994-95.

WARRINGTON 1994-95 PLAYERS' SUMMARY

	Date of Birth	App	T	G	D	Pts	Previous club	Signed
Barlow, Tukere	17.9.70	26	9	—	—	36	New Zealand	28.10.94
Bateman, Allan	6.3.65	28+1	17	—	—	68	Neath RU	28.9.90
Bennett, Andrew	23.7.73	6+22	8	—	—	32	Woolston R. ARL	10.8.90
Chambers, Gary	5.1.70	9+3	1	—	—	4	Kells ARL	15.2.88
Cullen, Paul	4.3.63	26	5	—	—	20	Crosfields ARL	25.11.80
Darbyshire, Paul	3.12.69	12+6	2	—	—	8	Wigan St. Patricks ARL	16.12.88
Davies, Jonathan	24.10.62	29	18	104	12	292	Widnes	6.7.93
Elliott, David	23.2.71	12+4	1	—	—	4	Kells ARL	21.5.90
Ellis, Kevin	29.5.65	7	2	—	—	8	Bridgend RU	18.6.90
Forster, Mark	25.11.64	40	24	—	—	96	Woolston R. ARL	27.11.81
Harris, Iestyn	25.6.76	39	18	38	—	148	Oldham St. Annes ARL	2.8.93
Hilton, Mark	31.3.75	16+10	—	—	—	—	Warrington Academy	13.8.92
Lee, Jason	16.1.71	5+1	1	—	—	4	Dudley Hill ARL	28.4.94
McGuire, Bruce	31.1.62	37	7	—	—	28	Sheffield E.	17.6.94
Mackey, Greg	20.10.61	30	7	—	3	31	Hull	18.8.92
Maloney, Francis	26.5.73	17+3	4	—	—	16	Featherstone R.	19.5.94
Myler, Robert	4.3.70	2	1	—	—	4	Widnes St. Maries ARL	2.10.89
Penny, Lee	24.9.74	31	9	—	—	36	Orrell St. James ARL	15.10.91
Phillips, Rowland	28.7.65	0+1	—	—	—	—	Neath RU	28.9.90
Roper, Jonathan	5.5.76	21	11	—	—	44	Hensingham ARL	5.5.93
Rudd, Chris	17.12.69	11+1	—	—	—	—	Kells ARL	15.2.88
Sanderson, Gary	21.2.67	27+10	7	—	—	28	Thatto Heath ARL	30.12.85
Sculthorpe, Paul	22.9.77	0+6	2	—	1	9	Waterhead ARL	4.10.94
Shelford, Kelly	4.5.66	36+1	12	—	1	49	New Zealand	5.10.91
Sumner, Phil	14.6.71	0+1	—	—	—	—	Wigan St. Patricks ARL	8.7.88
Tees, Gary	25.7.67	31+1	3	—	—	12	Barrow	5.12.90
Thursfield, John	22.10.69	11+1	1	—	—	4	ARL	9.9.86
Wainwright, Mike	25.2.75	11+5	2	—	—	8	Woolston R. ARL	9.5.92
Whitter, Damien	25.11.76	0+1	—	—	—	—	Wigan St. Patricks ARL	25.11.93
TOTALS								
29 players			165	142	17	961		

Representative appearances 1994-95

Bateman — Britain (+1), Wales (2,2t); Davies — Britain (1,1t,1g), Wales (2,7g,2dg); Elliott — Cumbria (1); Ellis — Wales (1): Harris — Wales (3,1t); Hilton — England (+1), GB Under-21s (2); Lee — Wales (+1); Phillips — Wales (1); Roper — Cumbria (1).

WARRINGTON 1994-95 MATCH ANALYSIS

Date	Com-petition	H/A	Opponent	Rlt	Score	Tries	Goals	Atten-dance	Referee
21.8.94	SBC	A	Hull	D	16-16	Forster, Shelford	Davies (4)	—	—
24.8.94	SBC	H	St. Helens	W	31-10	Forster (3), Bateman, Penny	Davies (5, 1dg)	7811	J. Connolly
28.8.94	SBC	H	Wakefield T.	W	31-10	McGuire, Davies, Forster, Bateman (2)	Davies (5), Mackey (1dg)	5417	Smith
4.9.94	SBC	A	Featherstone R.	L	10-26	Davies	Davies (3)	—	—
7.9.94	SBC	A	Bradford N.	L	10-16	Davies, Harris	Davies	—	—
11.9.94	SBC	H	Oldham	W	55-6	Ellis (2), Forster (2), Harris (2), Bateman, Chambers, Davies	Davies (9), Mackey (1dg)	5079	Cummings
18.9.94	SBC	A	Sheffield E.	L	8-29	McGuire	Davies (2)	—	—
25.9.94	SBC	A	Doncaster	W	30-8	Forster (2), Mackey (2), Harris	Harris (5)	—	—
7.10.94	SBC	H	Bradford N.	W	25-2	Bateman, Cullen, Davies, Thursfield	Davies (4, 1dg)	5618	J.. Connolly
16.10.94	SBC	H	Workington T.	W	64-12	Davies (2), Mackey (2), Maloney (2), Cullen, Forster, Harris, Penny, Shelford	Davies (10)	5181	Smith
6.11.94	SBC	H	Hull	W	22-8	Barlow, Darbyshire, Forster, Harris	Harris (3)	4958	Holdsworth
9.11.94	Tour	H	Australia	L	0-24	—	—	10,587	R. Connolly
13.11.94	SBC	A	Wakefield T.	W	32-26	Forster (4), Cullen, Shelford	Harris (4)	—	—
27.11.94	SBC	H	Featherstone R.	W	18-14	Forster, Harris, Penny, Roper	Harris	4891	Cross
4.12.94	RT(2)	H	Doncaster	W	44-14	Bateman (2), Barlow, Bennett, Forster, Harris, Maloney, Shelford	Harris (6)	3581	Asquith
7.12.904	SBC	A	Halifax	L	6-19	Mackey	Harris	—	—
11.12.94	SBC	A	Oldham	L	22-52	Bennett (2), Shelford (2)	Harris (3)	—	—
17.12.94	RT(3)	A	Salford	W	31-24	Bennett, Tees, Mackey, Shelford, Barlow	Harris (5)	—	—
26.12.94	SBC	H	Widnes	W	11-2	Maloney	Harris (3), Mackey (dg)	8304	Morris
1.1.95	SBC	A	Wigan	L	12-30	Cullen, Roper (2)	—	—	—
8.1.95	RT(QF)	A	Keighley C.	W	20-18	Barlow, Davies, Harris, Roper	Davies (2)	—	—
14.1.95	RT(SF)	A	Widnes	W	30-4	Forster (2), Harris (2), Myler	Davis (4, 2dg)	—	—
18.1.95	SBC	H	Castleford	W	25-24	Cullen, Davies, Roper	Davies (5, 3dg)	4551	J. Connolly
22.1.95	SBC	A	Leeds	L	0-30	—	—	—	—
28.1.95	RT(F)	N¹	Wigan	L	10-40	Forster (2)	Davies	(19,636)	Cummings
5.2.95	SBC	H	Doncaster	W	68-20	Davies (3), Harris (2), Barlow, Bateman, Bennett, Darbyshire, Forster, Mackey, Penny, Tees	Davies (8)	4082	Smith
12.2.95	CC(4)	H	Castleford	W	17-2	Barlow, Forster, McGuire	Davies (2, 1dg)	6063	Morris
19.2.95	SBC	H	Halifax	D	14-14	Bennett (2), Barlow	Davies	5214	Holdsworth
25.2.95	CC(5)	H	Oldham	L	6-17	Davies	Davies	4489	Holdsworth
12.3.95	SBC	H	Sheffield E.	W	26-18	Bateman (2), Harris (2), Roper	Davies (3)	3754	Lee
15.3.95	SBC	A	Salford	W	32-16	Bennett, Davies, McGuire, Penny, Shelford, Tees	Davies (4)	—	—
19.3.95	SBC	A	Workington T.	W	30-18	Roper (2), Bateman, Elliott, Shelford	Harris (5)	—	—
26.3.95	SBC	H	Salford	W	58-22	Bateman (2), Harris (2), Penny (2), Roper (2), Davies, Lee, McGuire	Davies (7)	4023	R. Connolly
31.3.95	SBC	A	Castleford	W	37-24	Barlow (2), Bateman, Davies, Harris, Wainwright	Davies (6, 1dg)	—	—
7.4.95	SBC	H	Leeds	L	11-17	Bateman, Wainwright	Davies (1, 1dg)	—	—
14.4.95	SBC	A	Widnes	W	37-16	Bateman, Davies, Forster, Penny, Roper, Shelford	Davies (6), Sculthorpe (dg)	—	—
17.4.95	SBC	H	Wigan	L	0-34	—	—	6687	Cummings
21.4.95	SBC	A	St. Helens	L	12-31	Penny, Sculthorpe	Harris (2)	—	—
7.5.95	PT(1)	A	Castleford	W	30-22	Batemen, McGuire, Sculthorpe, Shelford	Davies (6, 2dg)	—	—
12.5.95	PT(SF)	A	Wigan	L	20-50	Davies, McGuire, Shelford	Davies (4)	—	—

N¹ at Huddersfield

133

WHITEHAVEN

Ground: Recreation Ground (01946-592869)
First Season: 1948-49
Nickname: Warriors
Chairman: Derek Mossop
Secretary: Bill Madine

RECORDS

Match
Goals: 13 by Lee Anderson at Highfield,
25 Jan 1995
Tries: 6 by Vince Gribbin v. Doncaster,
18 Nov 1984
Points: 30 by Lee Anderson at Highfield,
25 Jan 1995

Season
Goals: 141 by John McKeown, 1956-57
Tries: 34 by Mike Pechey, 1994-95
Points: 291 by John McKeown, 1956-57

Career
Goals: 1,050 by John McKeown, 1948-61
Tries: 148 by Bill Smith, 1950-62
Points: 2,133 by John McKeown, 1948-61
Appearances: 417 by John McKeown, 1948-61
Highest score: 86-6 at Highfield, 25 Jan 1995
Highest against: 92-10 at Hull K.R., 18 Mar 1990
Attendance: 18,500 v. Wakefield T. (RL Cup),
19 Mar 1960

COACHING REGISTER
● **Since 1974-75**

Jeff Bawden	May 72 - May 75
Ike Southward	Aug 75 - June 76
Bill Smith	Aug 76 - Oct 78
Ray Dutton	Oct 78 - Oct 79
Phil Kitchin	Oct 79 - Jan 82
Arnold Walker	Jan 82 - May 82
Tommy Dawes	June 82 - May 83
Frank Foster	June 83 - June 85
Phil Kitchin	June 85 - Oct 87
John McFarlane	Oct 87 - May 88
Barry Smith	July 88 - Sep 89

Eric Fitzsimons	Oct 89 - Mar 90
Norman Turley	June 90 - Apr 91
Jackie Davidson	May 91 - June 92
Gordon Cottier	June 92 - May 93
Kurt Sorensen	May 93 -

GREAT BRITAIN REGISTER
(5 players)

Vince Gribbin	(1)	1985
Bill Holliday	(1)	1964
Dick Huddart	(4)	1958
Phil Kitchin	(1)	1965
Arnold Walker	(1)	1980

1994-95 SIGNINGS REGISTER

Signed	Player	Club From
4.7.94	Quirk, Les	St. Helens
22.8.94	Smith, Peter	Kells ARL
2.9.94	*Aspinall, Scott	Leigh
3.9.94	Armstrong, David	Whitehaven Academy
3.9.94	Blackwell, Mark	Whitehaven Academy
22.9.94	Clark, Neil	Hensingham ARL
1.10.94	Anderson, Lee	Kells ARL
7.10.94	*Atherton, Peter	St. Helens
10.2.95	*Scott, Ian	Leeds
17.2.95	*Waddell, Hugh	Carlisle
23.3.95	Lancaster, Paul	Egremont ARL

Forward Bill Holliday, capped for Great Britain in 1964 while with Whitehaven.

WHITEHAVEN 1994-95 PLAYERS' SUMMARY

	Date of Birth	App	T	G	D	Pts	Previous club	Signed
Anderson, Lee	1.10.69	27	4	103	1	223	Kells ARL	1.10.94
Anderson, Scott	9.12.70	5	—	—	—	—	Wath Brow ARL	10.1.94
Aspinall, Scott	26.4.75	5+3	—	—	—	—	Leigh	2.9.94
Atherton, Peter	29.12.70	26+3	4	—	—	16	St. Helens	7.10.94
Blackwell, Mark	14.2.75	0+1	—	—	—	—	Whitehaven Acad.	3.9.94
Blaney, Ged	17.6.65	16+2	3	—	—	12	Mirehouse ARL	8.1.89
Cameron, Graham		2	—	—	—	—		
Chambers, Craig	25.4.73	2	—	—	—	—	Kells ARL	6.8.93
Clark, Neil	7.10.64	2	—	—	—	—	Hensingham ARL	22.9.94
Dover, Peter	9.12.65	1+1	1	—	—	4	Flimby ARL	1.7.89
Dunn, Reg	23.5.68	26+2	3	—	1	13	Barrow	28.1.92
Fisher, Billy	27.10.62	35	1	—	—	4	St. Benedicts RU	20.7.81
Friend, Clayton	22.3.62	35	18	—	3	75	Carlisle	24.9.92
Gribbin, Vince	15.3.65	21+3	12	—	—	48	Hensingham ARL	23.7.82
Harrison, Mark		0+2	—	—	—	—		
Hetherington, Gary	5.7.65	29+4	2	—	—	8	Kells ARL	26.7.85
Jones, Simon		0+2	—	—	—	—		
Kiddie, Lee	2.1.75	3	2	—	—	8	Kells ARL	18.9.93
Lancaster, Paul	25.2.70	2+2	—	—	—	—	Egremont ARL	23.3.95
Lewthwaite, Graeme	5.7.72	14+1	9	—	—	36	Hensingham ARL	10.9.93
Maguire, Steve	12.8.63	22+6	2	40	—	88	Barrow	11.1.91
Morton, Graeme	15.1.73	30+1	2	—	—	8	Kells ARL	6.8.93
Pechey, Mike	16.12.68	34	34	—	—	136	Australia	29.8.93
Quirk, Les	6.3.65	25+1	15	—	—	60	St. Helens	4.7.94
Rose, Graham		2+3	1	2	—	8		
Routledge, John	7.2.65	23	18	—	—	72	Egremont RU	24.8.90
Ryan, Mark	31.7.64	3+3	1	—	—	4	Mirehouse ARL	10.11.87
Seeds, David	23.6.74	28	20	3	—	86	Kells ARL	7.9.93
Smith, Dennis		11+7	—	—	—	—	New Zealand	
Smith, Peter	13.8.66	33	9	—	—	36	Kells ARL	22.8.94
Sorensen, Kurt	8.11.56	1+13	1	—	—	4	Widnes	23.6.93
Waddell, Hugh	1.9.59	7+2	—	—	—	—	Carlisle	17.2.95
White, Nigel	30.10.65	21+10	9	—	—	36	Carlisle	
Wilson, Grant	25.7.75	3	—	—	—	—	Egremont ARL	18.5.94
TOTALS								
34 players			171	148	5	985		

Representative appearances 1994-95

L. Anderson — Cumbria (+1); Routledge — Cumbria (1); Seeds — Cumbria (1).

WHITEHAVEN 1994-95 MATCH ANALYSIS

Date	Com-petition	H/A	Opponent	Rlt	Score	Tries	Goals	Atten-dance	Referee
21.8.94	SD	A	Keighley C.	L	8-38	Gribbin, Quirk	—	—	—
28.8.94	SD	H	Leigh	W	16-8	Routledge, Gribbin	Maguire (4)	1054	Oddy
4.9.94	SD	H	Rochdale H.	W	24-10	Gribbin, Pechey, Routledge, Seeds, White	Maguire (2)	926	Asquith

(Continued)

135

Date	Com-petition	H/A	Opponent	Rlt	Score	Tries	Goals	Atten-dance	Referee
11.9.94	SD	A	Bramley	L	14-30	Gribbin, Pechey	Maguire (3)	—	—
18.9.94	SD	A	Batley	L	6-22	Morton	L. Anderson	—	—
25.9.94	SD	H	Barrow	W	26-18	Gribbin, Hetherington, Pechey, Seeds, White	L. Anderson (3)	915	Tennant
4.10.94	SD	H	Hull K. R.	W	28-14	Pechey (3), Hetherington, P. Smith	L. Anderson (4)	1008	Oddy
9.10.94	SD	A	Ryedale-York	W	48-18	Pechey (2), Routledge (2), Seeds (2), Friend, Gribbin, P. Smith	L. Anderson (6)	—	—
16.10.94	SD	H	Huddersfield	W	24-18	Friend, Gribbin, Pechey, P. Smith	L. Anderson (4)	1568	Burke
30.10.94	SD	A	Swinton	W	42-12	Friend (2), Pechey (2), Seeds (2), Atherton, Gribbin	McGuire (4), L. Anderson	—	—
6.11.94	SD	H	Keighley C.	L	8-38	Friend	Maguire (2)	2388	Cummings
13.11.94	SD	A	Leigh	W	30-10	Friend (2), Seeds (2), White	Maguire (5)	—	—
27.11.94	RT(1)	H	Thatto Heath	W	66-0	Quirk (3), Friend (2), Pechey (2), Atherton, Rose, Seeds, P. Smith, White	Maguire (9)	686	Redfearn
4.12.94	RT(2)	H	Featherstone R.	W	18-12	Pechey, Quirk	Maguire (5)	1248	Morris
11.12.94	SD	A	Rochdale H.	L	14-48	Pechey, White	Maguire (3)	—	—
18.12.94	RT(3)	H	Bradford N.	L	14-34	Blaney, Gribbin, Pechey	Seeds	1962	Cummings
31.12.94	SD	H	Carlisle	W	36-4	Pechey (2), Gribbin (2), Quirk, Routledge, Seeds	Maguire (2), Seeds (2)	1067	Smith
8.1.95	SD	H	Hunslet	W	27-14	Fisher, P. Smith, Sorensen, White	L. Anderson (5, 1dg)	1022	Lee
15.1.95	SD	A	Dewsbury	W	18-8	L. Anderson, Friend, Seeds	L. Anderson (3)	—	—
22.1.95	CC(3)	H	Moorends	W	64-12	Seeds (4), Quirk (3), Friend (2),Routledge (2), Pechey	L. Anderson (8)	637	Galtress
25.1.95	SD	A	Highfield	W*	86-6	Pechey (4), Kiddie (2), Seeds (2), L. Anderson, Blaney, Dover, Dunn, Quirk, P. Smith, Ryan	L. Anderson (13)	—	—
29.1.95	SD	H	Batley	W	30-8	Dunn,. Morton, Pechey, Quirk, Routledge	L. Anderson (5)	1326	Preseley
5.2.95	SD	A	Barrow	W	31-8	Routledge (2), Dunn, Friend, Seeds	L. Anderson (5), Friend (dg)	—	—
12.2.95	CC(4)	H	Wakefield T.	W	24-12	Friend,. Routledge, Seeds, P. Smith	L. Anderson (4)	2092	Smith
19.2.95	SD	A	Hull K.R.	W	12-6	Friend, Routledge	L. Anderson (2)	—	—
26.2.95	CC(5)	A	Hull K.R.	W	18-14	Routledge (2)	L. Anderson (5)	—	—
6.3.95	SD	H	Ryedale-York	W	20-13	Friend, Lewthwaite, P. Smith, Routledge	L. Anderson (2)	1303	Ollerton
12.3.95	CC(QF)	H	Featherstone R.	L	14-42	Pechey, Routledge	L. Anderson (3)	4119	Morris
15.3.95	SD	A	London B.	L	16-18	L. Anderson, Atherton, Pechey, Seeds	—	—	—
19.3.95	SD	A	Huddersfield	L	4-42	Atherton	—	—	—
26.3.95	SD	H	Swinton	L	6-10	—	L. Anderson (2), Maguire	1006	Holdsworth
2.4.95	SD	A	Hunslet	L	20-22	Blaney, Quirk, Routledge	L. Anderson (4)	—	—
9.4.95	SD	H	Dewsbury	W	37-12	Lewthwaite (2), Friend, Routledge, White, Pechey	L. Anderson (6), Friend (dg)	904	Redfearn
14.4.95	SD	H	Highfield	W	60-0	Pechey (5), Quirk (3), Lewthwaite (2), Maguire	L. Anderson (8)	786	Oddy
17.4.95	SD	A	Carlisle	L	13-16	Friend, Pechey	L. Anderson (2), Friend (dg)	—	—
19.4.95	SD	H	Bramley	W	50-6	Lewthwaite (4), White (2), L. Anderson, Gribbin, P. Smith	L. Anderson (7)	835	Tennant
23.4.95	SD	H	London B.	L	12-30	Maguire, Pechey	Rose (2)	1134	Holdsworth
8.5.95	SDP(1)	A	London B.	L	1-28	—	Dunn (dg)	—	—

*Abandoned after 63 minutes because of waterlogged pitch. Result stands.

WIDNES

Ground: Naughton Park (0151-495-2250)
First Season: 1895-96
Nickname: Chemics
Chairman: Jim Mills
General
Manager: Frank Myler
Honours: **Championship** Beaten finalists, 1935-36
Division One Champions, 1977-78, 1987-88, 1988-89
Challenge Cup Winners, 1929-30, 1936-37, 1963-64, 1974-75, 1978-79, 1980-81, 1983-84
Beaten finalists, 1933-34, 1949-50, 1975-76, 1976-77, 1981-82, 1992-93
Regal Trophy Winners, 1975-76, 1978-79, 1991-92
Beaten finalists, 1974-75, 1977-78, 1979-80, 1983-84, 1988-89
Premiership Winners, 1979-80, 1981-82, 1982-83, 1987-88, 1988-89, 1989-90
Beaten finalists, 1977-78, 1990-91
Lancashire Cup Winners, 1945-46, 1974-75, 1975-76, 1976-77, 1978-79, 1979-80, 1990-91
Beaten finalists, 1928-29, 1939-40, 1955-56, 1971-72, 1981-82, 1983-84
Lancashire League Winners, 1919-20
Western Division Championship Beaten finalists, 1962-63
Charity Shield Winners, 1988-89, 1989-90, 1990-91
World Club Challenge Winners, 1989-90
BBC2 Floodlit Trophy Winners, 1978-79
Beaten finalists, 1972-73, 1973-74

RECORDS
Match
Goals: 11 by Robin Whitfield v. Oldham, 28 Oct 1965
Tries: 5 by Eddie Cunningham v. Doncaster, 15 Feb 1981
John Basnett at Hunslet, 17 Oct 1981
John Basnett v. Hull K.R., 2 Nov 1986
David Hulme v. Dewsbury, 30 Nov 1986
Andy Currier v. Featherstone R., 25 Sep 1988
Martin Offiah v. Warrington, 15 Mar 1989
Points: 34 by Andy Currier v. Featherstone R., 25 Sep 1988
Jonathan Davies v. Whitehaven, 26 Aug 1990
Season
Goals: 140 by Mick Burke, 1978-79
Tries: 58 by Martin Offiah, 1988-89
Points: 342 by Jonathan Davies, 1990-91
Career
Goals: 1,083 by Ray Dutton, 1966-78
Tries: 234 by Mal Aspey, 1964-80
Points: 2,195 by Ray Dutton, 1966-78
Appearances: 587+4 by Keith Elwell, 1970-86
Highest score: 82-0 v. Dewsbury, 30 Nov 1986
Highest against: 60-5 at Oldham, 9 Apr 1928
Attendance: 24,205 v. St. Helens (RL Cup), 16 Feb 1961

COACHING REGISTER
● **Since 1974-75**

Vince Karalius	Jan 72 - May 75
Frank Myler	May 75 - May 78
Doug Laughton	May 78 - Mar 83
Harry Dawson } Colin Tyrer }	Mar 83 - May 83
*Vince Karalius } Harry Dawson }	May 83 - May 84
Eric Hughes	June 84 - Jan 86
Doug Laughton	Jan 86 - May 91
Frank Myler	June 91 - May 92
Phil Larder	May 92 - May 94
Tony Myler	May 94 -

Dawson quit as coach in March 1984 with Karalius continuing as team manager.

GREAT BRITAIN REGISTER

(46 players)

Mick Adams	(11+2)	1979-84
John Basnett	(2)	1984-86
Keith Bentley	(1)	1980
Mick Burke	(14+1)	1980-86
Frank Collier	(1)	1964
Andy Currier	(2)	1989-93
Jonathan Davies	(8+1)	1990-93
John Devereux	(6+2)	1992-93
Ray Dutton	(6)	1970
Keith Elwell	(3)	1977-80
Richard Eyres	(3+4)	1989-93
John Fieldhouse	(6)	1985-86
Ray French	(4)	1968
Les Gorley	(4+1)	1980-82
Andy Gregory	(8+1)	1981-84
Ian Hare	(1)	1967
Fred Higgins	(6)	1950-51
Harold Higgins	(2)	1937
Les Holliday	(3)	1991-92
Eric Hughes	(8)	1978-82
David Hulme	(7+1)	1988-89
Paul Hulme	(3+5)	1988-92
Albert Johnson	(4)	1914-20
Vince Karalius	(2)	1963
George Kemel	(2)	1965
Doug Laughton	(4)	1973-79
Joe Lydon	(9+1)	1983-85
Tommy McCue	(6)	1936-46
Steve McCurrie	(1)	1993
Jim Measures	(2)	1963
Jim Mills	(6)	1974-79
Paul Moriarty	(1+1)	1991-94
Frank Myler	(14+1)	1960-67
Tony Myler	(14)	1983-86
George Nicholls	(7)	1971-72
Martin Offiah	(20)	1988-91
Dennis O'Neill	(2+1)	1971-72
Mike O'Neill	(3)	1982-83
Harry Pinner	(1)	1986
Glyn Shaw	(1)	1980
Nat Silcock	(12)	1932-37
Stuart Spruce	(1)	1993
Alan Tait	(9)	1989-92
John Warlow	(3)	1971
Darren Wright	(+1)	1988
Stuart Wright	(7)	1977-78

1994-95 SIGNINGS REGISTER

Signed	Player	Club From
19.7.94	Thorniley, Tony	Warrington
20.7.94	Collier, Andrew	Leigh
3.8.94	Hansen, Lee	Leigh
5.8.94	Hicks, Neil	—
8.8.94	Myler, Paul	Warrington
15.8.94	O'Neill, Michael	Leeds
16.8.94	Davidson, Lee	Simms Cross ARL
30.8.94	Briers, James	Widnes St. Maries ARL
30.8.94	Brown, Jamie	Widnes St. Maries ARL
30.8.94	Kendrick, Philip	Rosebridge ARL
30.8.94	Rogers, Wesley	Waterhead ARL
1.9.94	*Knight, Mark	Chorley
10.9.94	Godwin, Iain	Widnes St. Maries ARL
18.9.94	Green, Jason	Rochdale H.
18.10.94	Singleton, Anthony	Barrow
25.11.94	*O'Brien, Darren	St. Helens
11.12.94	Edghill, Richard	Batley
28.12.94	Alvarez, Sean	—
17.2.95	Nuttie, Chris	—
6.3.95	Argent, Stephen	Halton Hornets ARL

Four tries in 18 appearances in 1994-95 for veteran Widnes half back David Hulme.

WIDNES 1994-95 PLAYERS' SUMMARY

	Date of Birth	App	T	G	D	Pts	Previous club	Signed
Ashton, Lee		3	1	—	—	4		
Barrow, Steve	8.12.75	0+1	—	—	—	—		1.8.93
Boscoe, Steve	12.9.76	1	—	—	—	—	St. Maries ARL	26.11.93
Broadbent, Gary	31.10.76	19	1	—	—	4	Barrow ARL	20.3.93
Cassidy, Jim		0+4	1	—	—	4		
Collier, Andy	3.6.68	29	4	—	1	17	Leigh	20.7.94
Davidson, Lee	14.4.75	1	—	—	—	—	Simms Cross ARL	16.8.94
Devereux, John	30.3.66	14	8	2	—	36	Bridgend RU	10.10.89
Green, Jason	19.1.72	23	5	—	—	20	Rochdale H.	18.9.94
Hadley, Adrian	1.3.63	28	11	68	—	180	Salford	4.8.92
Halliwell, Adrian	25.8.72	2+3	—	—	—	—		8.1.90
Hammond, Karle	25.4.74	34	—	—	—	108		23.7.90
Hansen, Lee	23.7.68	26	—	—	—	—	Leigh	3.8.94
Harris, Paul	18.4.74	0+2	1	—	—	4	St. Maries ARL	13.8.92
Hulme, David	6.2.64	18	4	—	—	16	Halton H. ARL	4.8.80
Hulme, Paul	19.4.66	25	4	—	—	16	Halton H. ARL	5.7.83
Hunter, Jason	2.7.71	8	2	—	—	8	Blackbrook ARL	13.9.93
Ireland, Andy	6.12.71	19+1	2	—	—	8	Golborne ARL	24.7.91
Kelly, Chris	29.8.73	2+1	—	—	—	—		23.7.90
Koloto, Emosi	23.1.65	11+2	2	—	—	8	New Zealand RU	21.10.88
McCurrie, Steve	2.7.73	31+1	12	—	1	49	Hensingham ARL	23.7.90
Makin, Craig	13.4.73	27+4	7	—	—	28	Orrell St. James ARL	10.1.92
Myler, Paul	11.11.72	17+4	—	—	—	—	Warrington	8.8.94
O'Neill, Mike	29.11.60	10+13	—	—	—	—	Leeds	15.8.94
Rogers, Wesley	3.11.77	3	—	8	—	16	Waterhead ARL	30.8.94
Ruane, David	24.9.63	25+9	3	—	—	12	Leigh	10.1.94
Singleton, Anthony	25.3.69	22+7	5	—	—	20	Barrow	21.1.94
Smith, David	15.3.68	12+9	—	—	—	—		5.6.87
Smith, Peter	1.9.73	16	5	—	—	20	Widnes T. ARL	6.9.91
Spruce, Stuart	3.1.71	15	5	—	—	20	Widnes T. ARL	8.1.90
Thorniley, Tony	10.10.66	3+4	—	—	—	—	Warrington	19.7.94
Tyrer, Christian	19.12.73	6+2	2	7	1	23	Leigh R. ARL	23.7.90
Walker, Scott	7.9.74	2+2	—	—	—	—	Hensingham ARL	8.2.92
Wright, Darren	17.1.68	29+1	7	—	—	28	Leigh M. ARL	23.3.85

TOTALS

			T	G	D	Pts		
34 players			111	100	5	649		

Representative appearances 1994-95
Devereux — Wales (2); Hadley — Wales (1+1); Hammond — GB Under-21s (1+1); McCurrie — England (+2), Cumbria (1).

WIDNES 1994-95 MATCH ANALYSIS

Date	Com-petition	H/A	Opponent	Rlt	Score	Tries	Goals	Atten-dance	Referee
21.8.94	SBC	H	Castleford	L	16-30	D. Hulme (2), Hammond	Hammond (2)	4323	Atkin
26.8.94	SBC	A	Doncaster	L	6-21	Wright	Tyrer	—	—
31.8.94	SBC	H	Salford	W	24-16	Hammond (2), Hadley, Wright	Tyrer (4)	3402	Smith
4.9.94	SBC	H	Halifax	W	17-10	Collier, Tyrer	Hadley (2), Tyrer (2, 1dg)	4234	Tennant
11.8.94	SBC	A	Bradford N.	L	4-48	Hadley	—	—	—
18.8.94	SBC	A	Wigan	L	12-46	Green, Makin	Hadley (2)	—	—
25.9.94	SBC	H	Leeds	L	10-48	Makin	Hadley (3)	5315	J. Connolly
2.10.94	SBC	A	Sheffield E.	W	22-0	Wright (2), Hammond, Spruce	Hadley (3)	—	—
9.10.94	SBC	H	Featherstone R.	W	28-18	Hadley, Hammond, Makin, Singleton	Hadley (6)	3976	Ollerton
14.10.94	SBC	A	Oldham	L	0-29	—	—	—	—
6.11.94	SBC	A	Castleford	L	6-26	Spruce	Hammond	—	—
13.11.94	SBC	H	Doncaster	D	12-12	McCurrie, Singleton	Hadley (2)	3573	Tennant
25.11.94	SBC	A	Halifax	L	10-27	Hadley, McCurrie	Hadley	—	—
4.12.94	RT(2)	A[1]	Highfield	W	50-2	P. Hulme (2), P. Smith (2), Spruce (2), Hadley, Hammond, Wright	Hadley (7)	—	—
11.12.94	SBC	H	Bradford N.	L	15-34	McCurrie, Ruane	Hadley (3), Collier (1dg)	3325	Holdsworth
18.12.94	RT(3)	H	Oldham	W	20-6	Collier, Hadley, McCurrie, Spruce	Hadley (2)	3517	Tennant
26.12.94	SBC	A	Warrington	L	2-11	—	Hadley	—	—
1.1.95	SBC	H	St Helens	L	10-20	Koloto, Hadley	Hadley	7382	Tennant
8.1.95	RT(4)	H	Bradford N.	W	23-10	Hammond (2), Hadley, Koloto	Hadley (3), McCurrie (dg)	4807	Morris
14.1.95	RT(SF)	H	Warrington	L	4-30	Broadbent	—	6181	Smith
22.1.95	SBC	H	Wakefield T.	L	4-20	—	Hadley (2)	3377	Redfearn
3.2.95	SBC	A	Leeds	L	4-36	P. Smith	—	—	—
12.2.95	CC(4)	A	Carlisle	W	40-2	Collier, Devereux, Hadley, Hammond, D. Hulme, McCurrie, P. Smith, Makin	Hadley (4)	—	—
15.2.95	SBC	H	Workington T.	W	23-0	Hammond (2), P. Hulme	Hadley (5), Hammond (dg)	2988	Asquith
19.2.95	SBC	H	Sheffield E.	W	36-18	Hammond (2), Devereux, Hadley, Makin	Hadley (8)	2969	Kirkpatrick
26.2.95	CC(5)	A	Sheffield E.	W	19-7	Hadley, Hammond, P. Smith	Hadley (3), Hammond (dg)	—	—
11.3.95	CC(QF)	H	Wigan	L	12-26	Hammond, Makin	Hadley (2)	6981	Smith
15.3.95	SBC	H	Wigan	L	12-46	Singleton, Wright	Hammond (2)	4705	Morris
19.3.95	SBC	H	Oldham	W	40-4	Devereux (2), Hammond (2), Ireland, McCurrie	Hadley (8)	3278	Tennant
24.3.95	SBC	H	Hull	W	42-18	Collier, Devereux, Green, Hammond, D. Hulme, Ireland Singleton, Wright	Hammond (5)	2522	J. Connolly
29.3.95	SBC	A	Hull	L	18-24	Devereux, Hammond , P. Hulme	Hammond (3)	—	—
2.4.95	SBC	A	Workington T.	L	16-18	Devereux, Green, Hunter	Hammond (2)	—	—
9.4.95	SBC	A	Wakefield T.	L	16-29	Devereux, Green, McCurrie, Ruane	—	—	—
14.4.95	SBC	H	Warrington	L	16-37	Makin, McCurrie, Ruane	Devereux (2)	5931	Smith
17.4.95	SBC	A	St. Helens	L	22-54	McCurrie (3), Green, Hunter	Rogers	—	—
20.4.95	SBC	A	Featherstone R.	L	20-32	McCurrie, Singleton, Tyrer	Rogers (4)	—	—
23.4.95	SBC	A	Salford	L	18-35	Ashton, Cassidy, Harris	Rogers (3)	—	—

[1] St Helens

WIGAN

Ground: Central Park (01942-31321)
First Season: 1895-96
Nickname: Riversiders
Chairman: Jack Robinson
Secretary: Mary Sharkey
Honours: **Championship** Winners, 1908-09, 1921-22, 1925-26, 1933-34, 1945-46, 1946-47, 1949-50, 1951-52, 1959-60
Beaten finalists, 1909-10, 1910-11, 1911-12, 1912-13, 1923-24, 1970-71
War Emergency League Winners, 1943-44
Beaten finalists, 1940-41
League Leaders Trophy Winners, 1970-71
Division One Champions, 1986-87, 1989-90, 1990-91, 1991-92, 1992-93, 1993-94, 1994-95
Challenge Cup Winners, 1923-24, 1928-29, 1947-48, 1950-51, 1957-58, 1958-59, 1964-65, 1984-85, 1987-88, 1988-89, 1989-90, 1990-91, 1991-92, 1992-93, 1993-94, 1994-95
Beaten finalists, 1910-11, 1919-20, 1943-44, 1945-46, 1960-61, 1962-63, 1965-66, 1969-70, 1983-84
Regal Trophy Winners, 1982-83, 1985-86, 1986-87, 1988-89, 1989-90, 1992-93, 1994-95
Beaten finalists, 1993-94
Premiership Winners, 1986-87, 1991-92, 1993-94, 1994-95
Beaten finalists, 1992-93
Lancashire Cup Winners, 1905-06, 1908-09, 1909-10, 1912-13, 1922-23, 1928-29, 1938-39, 1946-47, 1947-48, 1948-49, 1949-50, 1950-51, 1951-52, 1966-67, 1971-72, 1973-74, 1985-86, 1986-87, 1987-88, 1988-89, 1992-93
Beaten finalists, 1913-14, 1914-15, 1925-26, 1927-28, 1930-31, 1934-35, 1935-36, 1936-37, 1945-46, 1953-54, 1957-58, 1977-78, 1980-81, 1984-85
Lancashire League Winners, 1901-02, 1908-09, 1910-11, 1911-12, 1912-13, 1913-14, 1914-15, 1920-21, 1922-23, 1923-24, 1925-26, 1945-46, 1946-47, 1949-50, 1951-52, 1958-59, 1961-62, 1969-70
Lancashire War League Winners, 1940-41
Charity Shield Winners, 1985-86, 1987-88, 1991-92
Beaten finalists, 1988-89, 1989-90, 1990-91, 1992-93
World Club Challenge Winners, 1987-88, 1991-92, 1993-94
Beaten finalists, 1992-93
BBC2 Floodlit Trophy Winners, 1968-69
Beaten finalists, 1969-70

RECORDS
Match
Goals: 22 by Jim Sullivan v. Flimby & Fothergill, 14 Feb 1925
Tries: 10 by Martin Offiah v. Leeds, 10 May 1992
Shaun Edwards at Swinton, 29 Sep 1992
Points: 44 by Jim Sullivan v. Flimby & Fothergill, 14 Feb 1925

Season
Goals: 186 by Frano Botica, 1994-95
Tries: 62 by Johnny Ring, 1925-26
Points: 423 by Frano Botica, 1992-93
Career
Goals: 2,317 by Jim Sullivan, 1921-46
Tries: 478 by Billy Boston, 1953-68
Points: 4,883 by Jim Sullivan, 1921-46
Appearances: 774 by Jim Sullivan, 1921-46
Highest score: 116-0 v. Flimby & Fothergill, 14 Feb 1925
Highest against: 58-3 at Leeds, 14 Oct 1972
Attendance: 47,747 v. St. Helens (League), 27 Mar 1959

COACHING REGISTER
● **Since 1974-75**

Ted Toohey	May 74 - Jan 75
Joe Coan	Jan 75 - Sep 76
Vince Karalius	Sep 76 - Sep 79
Kel Coslett	Oct 79 - Apr 80
George Fairbairn	Apr 80 - May 81
Maurice Bamford	May 81 - May 82
Alex Murphy	June 82 - Aug 84
Colin Clarke	} Aug 84 - May 86
Alan McInnes	
Graham Lowe	Aug 86 - June 89
John Monie	Sep 89 - May 93
John Dorahy	June 93 - May 94
Graeme West	May 94 -

GREAT BRITAIN REGISTER

(88 players)

Ray Ashby	(1)	1965
Ernest Ashcroft	(11)	1947-54
Eric Ashton	(26)	1957-63
Bill Ashurst	(3)	1971-72
Frank Barton	(1)	1951
John Barton	(2)	1960-61
Jack Bennett	(1)	1926
Denis Betts	(24+1)	1990-94
Dai Bevan	(1)	1952
Billy Blan	(3)	1951
Dave Bolton	(23)	1957-63
Billy Boston	(31)	1954-63
Tommy Bradshaw	(6)	1947-50
Frank Carlton	(1)	1962
Brian Case	(6+1)	1984-88
Mick Cassidy	(+2)	1994
Norman Cherrington	(1)	1960
Colin Clarke	(7)	1965-73
Phil Clarke	(15+1)	1990-94
Percy Coldrick	(4)	1914
Frank Collier	(1)	1963
Gary Connolly	(7)	1993-94
Neil Cowie	(1)	1993
Jack Cunliffe	(4)	1950-54
Martin Dermott	(11)	1990-93
Shaun Edwards	(32+4)	1985-94
Joe Egan	(14)	1946-50
Roy Evans	(4)	1961-62
George Fairbairn	(14)	1977-80
Andrew Farrell	(5)	1993-94
Terry Fogerty	(1)	1967
Phil Ford	(1)	1985
Bill Francis	(4)	1967-77
Danny Gardiner	(1)	1965
Ken Gee	(17)	1946-51
Henderson Gill	(14+1)	1981-88
Andy Goodway	(12)	1985-90
Bobby Goulding	(5)	1990
John Gray	(5+3)	1974
Andy Gregory	(16)	1987-92
Steve Hampson	(11+1)	1987-92
Ellery Hanley	(23)	1985-91
Cliff Hill	(1)	1966
David Hill	(1)	1971
Jack Hilton	(4)	1950
Tommy Howley	(6)	1924
Bill Hudson	(1)	1948
Danny Hurcombe	(8)	1920-24
Bert Jenkins	(12)	1907-14
Ken Jones	(2)	1970
Roy Kinnear	(1)	1929
Nicky Kiss	(1)	1985

Doug Laughton	(11)	1970-71
Johnny Lawrenson	(3)	1948
Jim Leytham	(5)	1907-10
Ian Lucas	(1+1)	1991-92
Joe Lydon	(14+6)	1986-92
Barrie McDermott	(1+2)	1994
Billy McGinty	(4)	1992
Brian McTigue	(25)	1958-63
Barrie-Jon Mather	(+1)	1994
Joe Miller	(1)	1911
Jack Morley	(2)	1936-37
Martin Offiah	(13)	1992-94
Andy Platt	(17+1)	1989-93
Ian Potter	(7+1)	1985-86
Jack Price	(4)	1924
Dick Ramsdale	(8)	1910-14
Gordon Ratcliffe	(3)	1947-50
Johnny Ring	(2)	1924-26
Dave Robinson	(1)	1970
Jason Robinson	(4)	1993-94
Martin Ryan	(4)	1947-50
Billy Sayer	(7)	1961-63
Jim Sharrock	(4)	1910-11
Nat Silcock	(3)	1954
Dick Silcock	(1)	1908
Kelvin Skerrett	(6+2)	1992-93
David Stephenson	(5)	1982-87
Jim Sullivan	(25)	1924-33
Mick Sullivan	(19)	1957-60
Gwyn Thomas	(1)	1914
Johnny Thomas	(8)	1907-11
Shaun Wane	(2)	1985-86
Edward Ward	(3)	1946-47
Les White	(2)	1947
David Willicombe	(2)	1974
Billy Winstanley	(3)	1911

1994-95 SIGNINGS REGISTER

Signed	Player	Club From
1.7.94	McDermott, Barrie	Oldham
14.8.94	Walker, David	Blackbrook ARL
20.8.94	Paul, Henry	Auckland W., NZ
23.8.94	O'Connor, Terry	Salford
24.8.94	Tirac, Cael	Lezignan, Fr.
5.9.94	Roberts, Anthony	Leigh Rangers ARL
14.9.94	Baynes, Neil	Wigan St. Judes ARL
16.9.94	Cotton, Wesley	Wigan St. Judes ARL
22.9.94	Quinnell, Scott	Llanelli RU
23.9.94	Pendlebury, John	Leigh
9.10.94	George, Paul	Halton, Hornets ARL
14.11.94	Talbot, Ian	Wigan Academy
19.11.94	Grundy, Andrew	Wigan St. Judes ARL
6.2.95	Thompson, Ian	Hunslet Boys ARL
10.2.95	Morris, Michael	—

WIGAN 1994-95 PLAYERS' SUMMARY

	Date of Birth	App	T	G	D	Pts	Previous club	Signed
Atcheson, Paul	17.5.73	23+15	7	—	—	28	Widnes	8.10.92
Betts, Denis	14.9.69	37	20	—	—	80	Leigh R. ARL	6.10.86
Botica, Frano	3.8.63	31+2	9	186	—	408	New Zealand RU	15.6.90
Cassidy, Mick	3.7.73	25+12	6	—	—	24	Wigan St. Judes ARL	24.5.90
Clarke, Phil	16.5.71	25+1	7	—	—	28	Wigan St. Pats ARL	26.10.87
Connolly, Gary	22.6.71	43+2	30	—	—	120	St. Helens	1.8.93
Cowie, Neil	16.1.67	35+1	6	—	—	24	Rochdale H.	3.9.91
Craig, Andrew	16.3.76	0+1	—	—	—	—	Wigan Academy	1.11.93
Dermott, Martin	25.9.67	3	—	—	—	—	Wigan St. Pats ARL	7.11.84
Edwards, Shaun	17.10.66	34+1	20	1	1	83	Wigan St. Pats ARL	18.10.83
Farrell, Andrew	30.5.75	33+4	5	59	1	139	Orrell St. James ARL	19.10.92
Hall, Martin	5.12.68	42	13	—	—	52	Rochdale H.	11.1.93
Haughton, Simon	10.11.75	7+7	4	—	—	16	Dudley Hill ARL	10.11.92
Johnson, Andrew	14.6.74	1+4	2	—	—	8	St. Patricks ARL	22.9.92
Knowles, Matthew	2.9.75	1	—	—	—	—	Blackbrook ARL	3.10.92
Long, Sean	24.9.76	2+3	2	2	—	12	Wigan St. Judes ARL	1.11.93
Lydon, Joe	26.11.63	0+4	1	—	1	5	Widnes	20.1.86
McDermott, Barrie	22.7.72	8+5	4	—	—	16	Oldham	1.7.94
Mather, Barrie-Jon	15.1.73	6+8	6	—	—	24	Arnold School	14.8.91
Murdock, Craig	24.10.73	10	4	1	—	18	Hensingham ARL	19.8.93
O'Connor, Terry	13.10.71	18+9	1	—	—	4	Salford	23.8.94
Offiah, Martin	29.12.66	38	53	—	—	212	Widnes	3.1.92
Paul, Henry	10.2.74	38+5	19	25	—	126	Auckland W., NZ	18.8.94
Quinnell, Scott	20.8.72	8+3	5	—	—	20	Llanelli RU	22.9.94
Radlinski, Kris	9.4.76	17+4	18	—	—	72	Wigan Academy	25.5.93
Robinson, Jason	30.7.74	35	23	—	—	92	Hunslet P. ARL	31.7.91
Skerrett, Kelvin	22.5.66	25+1	6	—	—	24	Bradford N.	13.8.90
Stevens, Paul	7.10.74	1	—	—	—	—	Orrell St. James ARL	31.10.91
Tuigamala, Va'aiga	4.9.69	39	25	—	—	100	New Zealand RU	8.1.94
TOTALS								
29 players			296	274	3	1,735		

Representative appearances 1994-95

Atcheson — Wales (2,1t); Betts — Britain (3); Cassidy — Britain (+2), England (+1); Clarke — Britain (3), England (1); Connolly — Britain (3); Cowie — Wales (+2); Edwards — Britain (2); Farrell — Britain (3,2g); Hall — Wales (2); McDermott — Britain (1+2); Offiah — Britain (3); Robinson — Britain (3); England (1,1t); Skerrett — Wales (2).

WIGAN 1994-95 MATCH ANALYSIS

Date	Competition	H/A	Opponent	Rlt	Score	Tries	Goals	Attendance	Referee
21.8.94	SBC	A	Featherstone R.	W	36-24	Botica (2), Atcheson, Betts, Robinson, Skerrett	Botica (6)	—	—
28.8.94	SBC	H	Sheffield E.	W	40-16	Offiah (3), Edwards (3), McDermott	Botica (6)	13,627	Morris
4.9.95	SBC	A	Oldham	W	58-10	Offiah (4), Edwards (2), Robinson (2), Tuigamala (2), Betts	Paul (7)	—	—
9.9.95	SBC	H	Leeds	W	38-6	Robinson, Offiah (2), McDermott, Connolly, Edwards	Paul (7)	15,727	Smith
18.8.94	SBC	H	Widnes	W	46-12	Betts (3), Robinson (3), Edwards, Hall, McDermott	Paul (3), Farrell (2)	14,174	Presley
23.8.94	SBC	A	Castleford	W	31-28	Paul (2), Offiah, Robinson, Tuigamala	Botica (3), Farrell (2), Edwards (dg)	—	—
2.10.94	SBC	H	Wakefield T.	W	46-0	Connolly (3), Offiah (2), Paul (2), Murdock	Botica (4), Farrell (3)	12,889	Atkin
8.10.94	Tour	H	Australia	L	20-30	Connolly, Offiah, Robinson, Tuigamala	Botica, Farrell	20,057	Campbell
12.10.94	SBC	A	Workington T.	W	30-6	Connolly (2), Farrell, Offiah, Tuigamala	Botica (5)	—	—
16.10.94	SBC	H	Salford	W	52-22	Betts (2), Offiah (2), Robinson (2), Tuigamala (2), Connolly	Farrell (8)	12,740	Cummings
28.10.94	SBC	A	Hull	W	19-12	Offiah (2), Hall	Farrell (3), Lydon (dg)	—	—
11.11.94	SBC	A	Sheffield E.	W	36-20	Atcheson, Hall, Lydon, Offiah, Skerrett, Tuigamala	Farrell (6)	—	—
21.11.94	SBC	H	Featherstone R.	W	30-6	Betts, Cassidy, Offiah, Radlinski, Skerrett	Farrell (5)	10,646	Cummings
27.11.94	SBC	H	Oldham	W	46-0	Connolly (2), Atcheson, Betts, Edwards, Haughton, Paul, Radlinski, Tuigamala	Farrell (5)	13,276	Smith
4.12.94	RT(2)	H	Rochdale H.	W	34-12	Radlinski (3), Edwards, Farrell, Offiah	Farrell (5)	7493	Galtress
11.12.94	SBC	A	Leeds	L	28-33	Betts, Cowie, Hall, Offiah, Robinson, Tuigamala	Botica (2)	—	—
18.12.94	RT(3)	A	Hull	W	38-14	Offiah (3), Edwards, Farrell	Botica (9)	—	—
26.12.94	SBC	A	St. Helens	W	32-25	Tuigamala (2), Betts, Edwards, Offiah	Botica (6)	—	—
1.1.95	SBC	H	Warrington	W	30-12	Botica, Farrell, Robinson, Offiah, Haughton	Botica (5)	14,753	Holdsworth
8.1.95	RT(QF)	H	St. Helens	W	24-22	Paul (2), Skerrett	Botica (6)	23,278	Campbell
15.1.95	RT(SF)	H	Castleford	W	34-6	Offiah (3), Hall, Robinson	Botica (7)	13,006	Cummings
20.1.95	SBC	A	Bradford N.	W	14-10	Atcheson, Botica, Paul	Botica	—	—
24.1.95	SBC	A	Doncaster	W	28-10	Robinson (2), Atcheson, Betts	Botica (6)	—	—
28.1.95	RT(F)	N[1]	Warrington	W	40-10	Tuigamala (2), Botica, Connolly, McDermott, Offiah	Botica (8)	(19,636)	Cummings
5.2.95	SBC	H	Castleford	W	46-6	Offiah (3), Connolly (2), Cowie, Radlinski	Botica (9)	13,989	Campbell
11.2.95	CC(4)	H	St. Helens	D	16-16	Betts, Hall, Tuigamala	Botica (2)	15,714	Holdsworth
15.2.95	CC(4) Replay	A	St. Helens	W	40-24	Offiah (3), Clarke, Connolly, Paul, Robinson	Botica (6)	—	—
19.2.95	SBC	A	Wakefield T.	W	20-12	Cassidy, Offiah, Paul	Botica (4)	—	—
26.2.95	CC(5)	A	Batley	W	70-4	Offiah (3), Paul (2), Cassidy, Clarke, Connolly, Edwards, Skerrett, Tuigamala	Botica (10), Paul (3)	—	—
6.3.95	SBC	H	Workington T.	W	38-0	Cassidy, Connolly, Offiah, Paul, Quinnell, Robinson	Botica (7)	13,772	Holdsworth

(Continued)

Date	Competition	H/A	Opponent	Rlt	Score	Tries	Goals	Attendance	Referee
11.3.95	CC(QF)	A	Widnes	W	26-12	Betts, Cowie, Hall, Offiah	Botica (5)	—	—
15.3.95	SBC	A	Widnes	W	46-12	Offiah (3), Cowie (2), Clarke, Mather, Tuigamala	Botica (6), Edwards	—	—
19.3.95	SBC	A	Salford	W	42-8	Connolly (2), Atcheson, Cassidy, Murdock, Radlinski, Tuigamala	Paul (5), Long (2)	—	—
25.3.95	CC(SF)	N[1]	Oldham	W	48-20	Connolly (3), Betts (2), Tuigamala (2), Edwards, Mather	Botica (6)	(12,749)	Smith
29.3.95	SBC	A	Halifax	L	16-18	Edwards (2), Connolly	Botica (2)	—	—
2.4.95	SBC	H	Halifax	W	62-6	Clarke (2), Edwards (2), Botica, Cassidy, Connolly, Mather, Radlinski, Robinson, Tuigamala	Botica (6), Farrell (3)	15,771	Cummings
5.4.95	SBC	H	Doncaster	W	44-4	Johnson (2), Radlinski (2), Connolly, Long, Paul, Quinnell	Farrell (6)	9886	Holdsworth
9.4.95	SBC	H	Bradford N.	W	60-34	Hall (3), Clarke (2), Mather (2), Atcheson, Betts, Connolly, Tuigamala	Botica (8)	14,078	Campbell
14.4.95	SBC	H	St. Helens	W	34-18	Paul (2), Betts, Hall, Offiah, Tuigamala	Botica (5)	26,314	Holdsworth
17.4.95	SBC	A	Warrington	W	34-0	Botica (2), Radlinski (2), Connolly, Tuigamala	Botica (3), Farrell, Murdock	—	—
23.4.95	SBC	H	Hull	W	66-16	Quinnell (3), Murdock (2), Offiah (2), Cowie, Farrell, Long, Mather, O'Connor	Farrell (9)	11,494	Morris
29.4.95	CC(F)	N[2]	Leeds	W	30-10	Robinson (2), Hall, Paul, Tuigamala	Botica (5)	(78,550)	Smith
7.5.95	PT(1)	H	Sheffield E.	W	48-16	Offiah (3), Radlinski (2) Botica, Haughton, Paul	Botica (8)	9668	Campbell
12.5.95	PT(SF)	H	Warrington	W	50-20	Edwards (2), Robinson (2), Betts, Connolly, Offiah, Radlinski	Botica (9)	8426	Campbell
21.5.95	PT(F)	N[3]	Leeds	W	69-12	Connolly (3), Radlinski (3), Betts, Edwards, Hall, Paul, Haughton, Skerrett	Botica (10), Farrell (dg)	(30,160)	Cummings

N[1] at Huddersfield
N[2] at Wembley
N[3] at Manchester U. FC

Test loose forward Phil Clarke powers into the Widnes defence during a 1994-95 season in which he scored seven tries in 26 games.

WORKINGTON TOWN

Ground: Derwent Park (01900-603609)
First Season: 1945-46
Nickname: Town
Chairman: Kevan Gorge
Secretary: John Bell
Honours: **Championship** Winners, 1950-51
Beaten finalists, 1957-58
Division Two Champions, 1993-94
Challenge Cup Winners, 1951-52
Beaten finalists, 1954-55, 1957-58
Second Division/Divisional Premiership Winners 1993-94,
Beaten finalists, 1992-93
Lancashire Cup Winners, 1977-78
Beaten finalists, 1976-77, 1978-79, 1979-80
Western Division Championship Winners, 1962-63

RECORDS
Match
Goals: 13 by Dean Marwood v. Highfield,
1 Nov 1992; v. Leigh, 25 Feb 1995
Tries: 7 by Ike Southward v. Blackpool B.,
17 Sep 1955
Points: 42 by Dean Marwood v. Highfield,
1 Nov 1992; v. Leigh, 25 Feb 1995
Season
Goals: 186 by Lyn Hopkins, 1981-82
Tries: 49 by Johnny Lawrenson, 1951-52
Points: 438 by Lyn Hopkins, 1981-82
Career
Goals: 809 by Iain MacCorquodale, 1972-80
Tries: 274 by Ike Southward, 1952-59 & 1960-68
Points: 1,800 by Iain MacCorquodale, 1972-80
Appearances: 415+4 Paul Charlton, 1961-69 & 1975-80
Highest score: 94-4 v. Leigh, 26 Feb 1995
Highest against: 68-0 at Wigan, 18 Jan 1987
68-6 at Leigh, 8 Mar 1992
Attendance: 17,741 v. Wigan (RL Cup),
3 Mar 1965 — at Derwent Park
20,403 v. St. Helens (RL Cup),
8 Mar 1952 — at Borough Park

COACHING REGISTER
● **Since 1974-75**

Ike Southward	Aug 73 - June 75
Paul Charlton	June 75 - June 76
Ike Southward	June 76 - Feb 78
Sol Roper	Feb 78 - Apr 80
Keith Irving	Aug 80 - Oct 80
Tommy Bishop	Nov 80 - June 82
Paul Charlton	July 82 - Dec 82
Dave Cox	Mar 83 - Mar 83
Harry Archer/Bill Smith	May 83 - June 84
Bill Smith	June 84 - Apr 85
Jackie Davidson	Apr 85 - Jan 86
Keith Davies	Feb 86 - Mar 87
Norman Turley	Mar 87 - Apr 88
Maurice Bamford	July 88 - Dec 88
Phil Kitchin	Dec 88 - May 90
Ray Ashton	June 90 - Dec 91
Dean Williams	Dec 91 - Apr 92
Peter Walsh	May 92 -

GREAT BRITAIN REGISTER
(9 players)

Eddie Bowman	(4)	1977
Paul Charlton	(1)	1965
Brian Edgar	(11)	1958-66
Norman Herbert	(6)	1961-62
Vince McKeating	(2)	1951
Billy Martin	(1)	1962
Albert Pepperell	(2)	1950-51
Ike Southward	(4)	1958
George Wilson	(3)	1951

1994-95 SIGNINGS REGISTER

Signed	Player	Club From
1.7.94	McGinty, Billy	Wigan
14.7.94	Holgate, Stephen	Hensingham ARL
19.7.94	Chilton, James	Ellenborough ARL
19.7.94	Fawcett, Vince	Leeds
5.8.94	*Ellison, Danny	Wigan
25.8.94	Bibby, Dennis	Workington Academy
3.9.94	Grima, Andrew	Workington Academy
3.9.94	Keenan, Mark	Workington Academy
5.9.94	Beaumont, Jamie	Workington Academy
9.9.94	White, Kyle	Wests, Aus.
1.10.94	Banet, Vincent	XIII Catalan, Fr.
14.10.94	*O'Donnell, Gus	St. Helens
3.11.94	*Phillips, Rowland	Warrington
4.11.94	*Ellis, Kevin	Warrington
9.12.94	Pape, Kevin	Carlisle

WORKINGTON TOWN 1994-95 PLAYERS' SUMMARY

	Date of Birth	App	T	G	D	Pts	Previous club	Signed
Armstrong, Colin	26.1.63	27+6	4	3	—	22	Hull K.R.	3.10.90
Banet, Vincent	12.8.73	1	—	—	—	—	France	1.10.94
Burns, Paul	9.2.67	34+1	10	—	—	40	Barrow	16.8.92
Carter, Darren	8.1.72	7+2	3	—	—	12	Millom ARL	31.10.92
Chilton, Lee		4+3	—	—	—	—		
Cocker, Stuart	8.5.66	10	3	—	—	12	Oldham	27.8.93
Drummond, Des	17.6.58	29	8	—	—	32	Warrington	19.3.93
Ellis, Kevin	29.5.65	21	10	—	1	41	Warrington	4.11.94
Ellison, Danny	16.12.72	5	2	—	—	8	Wigan	5.8.94
Fawcett, Vince	13.11.70	33	16	—	—	64	Leeds	19.7.94
Gorley, Jonathan	21.7.71	4+4	2	—	—	8	Ellenborough R. ARL	24.8.93
Hepi, Brad	11.2.68	30+1	4	—	—	16	Carlisle	1.5.92
Holgate, Stephen	15.12.71	21+11	4	—	—	16	Hensingham ARL	14.7.94
Kay, Tony	16.4.64	4+1	1	—	—	4	Barrow	2.10.92
Kitchin, Wayne	26.11.70	3	—	—	—	—	Kells ARL	26.9.89
McGinty, Billy	6.12.64	17+1	2	—	—	8	Wigan	1.7.94
McKenzie, Phil	13.6.63	31	3	—	—	12	Widnes	4.2.93
Marwood, Dean	22.2.70	33	7	112	2	254	Barrow	23.12.91
Moore, Jason	27.12.70	0+4	—	—	—	—	Ellenborough ARL	21.6.93
Mulligan, Mark	6.3.70	31	16	2	3	71	Australia	17.9.92
O'Donnell, Gus	11.12.70	2	—	—	—	—	St. Helens	14.10.94
Oglanby, Martin	22.7.64	4	1	—	—	4	Glasson ARL	24.7.90
Pape, Kevin	17.12.61	19+2	11	—	—	44	Carlisle	9.12.94
Penrice, Paul	27.2.66	2+1	—	—	—	—	Gt. Clifton ARL	30.7.87
Phillips, Rowland	28.7.65	20+1	5	—	—	20	Warrington	3.11.94
Pickering, James	11.12.66	25+3	1	—	—	4	New Zealand	5.11.92
Riley, Peter	1.3.68	1+5	1	—	—	4	Gt. Clifton ARL	30.7.87
Schubert, Gary	18.9.66	8+12	1	—	—	4	Carlisle	9.8.91
Smith, Leigh	1.9.75	8+5	3	—	—	12	Hensingham ARL	27.3.94
White, Kyle	12.1.70	21+1	1	—	—	4	Australia	9.9.94
Williams, Barry	15.5.71	0+6	—	—	—	—	Carlisle	
TOTALS								
31 players			119	117	6	716		

Representative appearances 1994-95
Armstrong — Cumbria (1); Burns — Cumbria (1,1t); Holgate — England (1), Cumbria (+1); Marwood — Cumbria (1,2g).

WORKINGTON TOWN 1994-95 MATCH ANALYSIS

Date	Com- petition	H/A	Opponent	Rlt	Score	Tries	Goals	Atten- dance	Referee
19.8.94	SBC	H	Leeds	L	16-22	Burns, Oglanby	Marwood (4)	5007	R. Connolly
28.8.94	SBC	A	Castleford	L	14-26	Marwood, Kay	Marwood (3)	—	—
4.9.94	SBC	H	Sheffield E.	L	6-31	Cocker	Marwood	3636	Presley
11.9.94	SBC	H	St. Helens	L	25-30	Mulligan (2), Fawcett, Smith	Marwood (4), Mulligan (dg)	4551	Morris
18.9.94	SBC	H	Hull	W	18-8	Ellison (2), Cocker	Marwood (3)	3649	R. Connolly
25.9.94	SBC	A	Bradford N.	L	2-30	—	Marwood	—	—
4.10.94	SBC	A	Featherstone R.	L	0-46	—	—	—	—
12.10.94	SBC	H	Wigan	L	6-30	Holgate	Marwood	6634	Holdsworth
16.10.94	SBC	A	Warrington	L	12-64	Burns, Cocker	Armstrong (2)	—	—
30.10.94	SBC	H	Doncaster	W	19-16	Mulligan (2)	Marwood (5), Mulligan (dg)	3370	Ollerton
6..11.94	SBC	A	Leeds	L	16-42	Drummond, Fawcett, Holgate	Marwood (2)	—	—
13.11.94	SBC	H	Castleford	D	4-4	—	Marwood (2)	3248	Cross
27.11.94	SBC	A	Sheffield E.	L	29-34	Burns, Ellis, Fawcett, Marwood, McKenzie	Marwood (4), Mulligan (dg)	—	—
4.12.94	RT(2)	H	Wakefield T.	W	24-8	Fawcett, Drummond, Mulligan, Holgate	Marwood (4)	2349	Kirkpatrick
11.12.94	SBC	A	St. Helens	L	10-48	Pickering, Smith	Marwood	—	—
18.12.94	RT(3)	H	Leeds	L	14-18	Fawcett (2), Schubert	Marwood	3648	Presley
26.12.94	SBC	H	Wakefield T.	W	28-12	Mulligan (2), Ellis, Holgate, Phillips	Marwood (4)	3268	Ollerton
1.1.95	SBC	A	Oldham	L	10-20	Fawcett (2)	Marwood	—	—
13.1.95	SBC	H	Halifax	W	36-10	Armstrong, Burns, Ellis, Hepi, Marwood, Pape	Marwood (6)	2544	R. Connolly
22.1.95	SBC	H	Salford	W	34-0	Ellis (2), Fawcett (2), Burns, Pape	Marwood (5)	3325	Holdsworth
29.1.95	SBC	A	Hull	W	26-22	Drummond, Ellis, Hepi, Mulligan	Marwood (2), Mulligan (2), Armstrong	—	—
5.2.95	SBC	H	Bradford N.	W	32-14	Burns (2), Mulligan (2), Pape, Drummond	Marwood (4)	3956	Tennant
12.2.95	CC(4)	H	Hull	W	30-6	Burns, Drummond, Mulligan, Pape, Phillips	Marwood (5)	3081	Redfearn
15.2.95	SBC	A	Widnes	L	0-23	—	—	—	—
19.2.95	SBC	H	Featherstone R.	W	13-2	Drummond, Ellis	Marwood (2), Ellis (dg)	3489	R. Connolly
26.2.95	CC(5)	H	Leigh	W	94-4	Marwood (4), Fawcett (3), Mulligan (2), Pape (2), Burns, Ellis, Hepi, McGinty, Phillips, White	Marwood (13)	3436	J. Connolly
6.3.95	SB	A	Wigan	L	0-38	—	—	—	—
12.3.95	CC(QF)	A	Leeds	L	16-50	Ellis, Phillips	Marwood (4)	—	—
19.3.95	SBC	H	Warrington	L	18-30	Armstrong, McKenzie, Pape	Marwood (3)	3805	J. Connolly
26.3.95	SBC	A	Halifax	L	20-39	Burns, Carter, Drummond	Marwood (4)	—	—
2.4.95	SBC	H	Widnes	W	18-16	Drummond, Fawcett, Pape	Marwood (3)	2977	Presley
9.4.95	SBC	A	Salford	L	16-46	Armstrong, Carter, Mulligan	Marwood (2)	—	—
14.4.95	SBC	A	Wakefield T.	W	26-12	Carter, Gorley, McGinty, Pape	Marwood (4, 2dg)	—	—
17.4.95	SBC	H	Oldham	W	34-12	Gorley, Hepi, Mulligan, Pape, Smith	Marwood (7)	3158	Tennant
23.4.95	SBC	A	Doncaster	W	50-16	Fawcett (2), Armstrong, Ellis, McKenzie, Mulligan, Pape, Phillips, Riley	Marwood (7)	—	—

Bradford Northern skipper Deryck Fox who reached a milestone scoring his 100th career try in September 1994.

RECORDS

LEADING SCORERS FOR 1994-95

● Club and representative matches

TOP TEN TRIES

1. Martin Offiah (Wigan) 53
2. Greg Austin (Huddersfield) 52
3. Nick Pinkney (Keighley C.) 46
4. Ellery Hanley (Leeds) 41
5. David Plange (Hull K.R.) 35
6. Mike Pechey (Whitehaven) 34
7. Gary Connolly (Wigan) 30
8. John Bentley (Halifax) 29
   Alan Hunte (St. Helens) 29
   Scott Limb (Hunslet) 29

● Others with 20 or more: Paul Newlove (Bradford N.), Glen Tomlinson (Batley), 26; Leigh Deakin (Ryedale-York), Andy Eyres (Keighley C.), Va'aiga Tuigamala (Wigan) 25; Richard Blackmore (Castleford), Chris Churm (Rochdale H.), Jim Fallon (Leeds), Mark Forster (Warrington) 24; Steve Gibson (Rochdale H.), Simon Reynolds (Huddersfield), Jason Robinson (Wigan), Scott Roskell (London B.) 23; Gary Brown (Hull K.R.), Francis Cummins (Leeds), Dean Hanger (Huddersfield), Simon Irving (Keighley C.), Tony Smith (Castleford), Anthony Sullivan (St. Helens) 22; Steve Prescott (St. Helens), Mark Preston (Halifax), Eddie Rombo (Dewsbury), Ian Thomas (Huddersfield) 21; Denis Betts (Wigan), Shaun Edwards (Wigan), Davide Longo (Dewsbury), David Seeds (Whitehaven), Gary Thornton (Batley), Steve Walker (Batley), Martin Wood (Keighley C.) 20.

TOP TEN GOALS

● Including drop goals

1. Frano Botica (Wigan) 186
2. Bobby Goulding (St. Helens) 158
3. Simon Irving (Keighley C.) 152
4. Martin Strett (Rochdale H.) 150
5. John Schuster (Halifax) 144
6. Mike Fletcher (Hull K.R.) 142
7. Graham Holroyd (Leeds) 135
8. Deryck Fox (Bradford N.) 131
9. Simon Wilson (Batley) 127
10. Jonathan Davies (Warrington) 126

● Others with 100 or more: Dean Marwood (Workington T.) 116; Lee Crooks (Castleford) 111; Lee Anderson (Whitehaven) 104; Richard Agar (Dewsbury) 102.

TOP FIVE DROP GOALS

1. Jonathan Davies (Warrington) 14
2. Nigel Wright (Wakefield T.) 12
3. Carl Briggs (Sheffield E.) 10
4. Steve Dobson (Ryedale-York) 9
5. Bobby Goulding (St. Helens) 7

TOP TEN POINTS

	T	G	DG	Pts
1. Frano Botica (Wigan)	9	186	0	408
2. Simon Irving (Keighley C.)	22	152	0	392
3. John Schuster (Halifax)	19	142	2	362
4. Bobby Goulding (St. Helens)	11	151	7	353
5. Martin Strett (Rochdale H.)	12	148	2	346
6. Mike Fletcher (Hull K.R.)	9	142	0	320
7. Graham Holroyd (Leeds) ...	12	134	1	317
8. Jonathan Davies (Warrington)	19	112	14	314
9. Simon Wilson (Batley)	12	125	2	300
10. Deryck Fox (Bradford N.)..	4	128	3	275

Key:

SBC	....	Stones Bitter Championship
SD	....	Second Division
PT	....	Premiership Trophy
SDP	....	Second Division Premiership
RT	....	Regal Trophy
CC	....	Challenge Cup
N	....	Neutral venue
NA	....	Non-appearance

OUTSTANDING SCORING FEATS IN 1994-95

INDIVIDUAL

Most tries in a match:

9 by Greg Austin (Huddersfield) v. Blackpool G.	RT
5 by Nick Pinkney (Keighley C.) v. Hunslet	SD
Nick Pinkney (Keighley C.) at Highfield	SD
David Plange (Hull K.R.) v. Highfield	SD
Dean Hanger (Huddersfield) v. Blackpool G.	RT
Steve Ashcroft (Barrow) v. Nottingham C. ...	RT
Scott Limb (Hunslet) v. Highfield	SD
Mike Pechey (Whitehaven) v. Highfield	SD

Most goals in a match:

17 by Darren Carter (Barrow) v. Nottingham C. ..	RT
13 Lee Anderson (Whitehaven) at Highfield ...	SD
Dean Marwood (Workington T.) v. Leigh ...	CC
Simon Wilson (Batley) v. Leigh	SD
12 by Mike Fletcher (Hull K.R.) v. Highfield ...	SD
Phil Hellewell (Huddersfield) v. Blackpool G.	RT
Rod Wishart (Australia) at Sheffield E.	Tour
Simon Irving (Keighley C.) at Highfield......	SD
11 by Wilson Marsh (Oldham) v. Bramley	CC
Martin Strett (Rochdale H.) v. Highfield	SD
10 by Les Holliday (Dewsbury) v. Barrow	SD
Mike Blakeley (Leigh) at Highfield	SD
John Schuster (Halifax) at Doncaster	SBC
Jonathan Davies (Warrington) v. Work'ton T.	SBC
Bobby Goulding (St. Helens) v. Hull	SBC
Richard Pell (Hunslet) v. Wigan St. Patricks	CC
Richard Agar (Dewsbury) v. Kells	CC
Richard Agar (Dewsbury) at Highfield	SD
Frano Botica (Wigan) v. Leeds	PT
Frano Botica (Wigan) at Batley	CC
David Mycoe (Sheffield) at Doncaster	SBC

Most points in a match:

42 by Darren Carter (Barrow) v. Nottingham C. ..	RT
Dean Marwood (Workington T.) v. Leigh	CC
36 by Greg Austin (Huddersfield) v. Blackpool G.	RT

32 by Les Holliday (Dewsbury) v. Barrow .... SD
John Schuster (Halifax) at Doncaster .... SBC
30 by Lee Anderson (Whitehaven) at Highfield ... SD
Simon Irving (Keighley C.) v. Highfield ..... SD
Simon Wilson (Batley) v. Leigh .... SD

TEAM

Highest score:
Huddersfield 142 v. Blackpool G. 4 .... RT
● There was a total of 78 matches in which a team scored 50 points or more, compared with 57 in the previous season.

The previous highest number of 50-plus scores since the try value was increased from three to four points in 1983 was 73 in 1992-93.

Other 60-plus scores in 1994-95 were:

Home:
Barrow 138 v. Nottingham C. 0 .... RT
Workington T. 94 v. Leigh 4 CC
Castleford 86 v. Wakefield T. 0 .... SBC
Hull K.R. 78 v. Highfield 4 .... SD
Batley 78 v. Leigh 22 .... SD
Rochdale H. 78 v. Highfield 6 .... SD
Dewsbury 76 v. Barrow 8 .... SD
Huddersfield 74 v. Highfield 16 .... SD
Bradford N. 74 v. Doncaster 18 .... SBC
Dewsbury 72 v. Kells 12 CC
Oldham 70 v. Bramley 10 CC
Wigan 69 v. Leeds 12 .... PT
Keighley C. 68 v. Highfield 0 .... SD
Keighley C. 68 v. Chorley 0 CC
Warrington 68 v. Doncaster 20.......................... SBC
Ryedale-York 66 v. Highfield 6 .... SD
Batley 66 v. Highfield 0 .... SD
Keighley C. 66 v. Hunslet 10........................... SD
Whitehaven 66 v. Thatto Heath 0 .... RT
Wigan 66 v. Hull 16 .... SBC
Warrington 64 v. Workington T. 12 .... SBC
Hunslet 64 v. Wigan St. Patricks 4 CC
Whitehaven 64 v. Moorends 12 CC
Wigan 62 v. Halifax 6. .... SBC
Wigan 60 v. Bradford N. 34 .... SBC
London B. 60 v. Leigh 6 .... SD
Dewsbury 60 v. Highfield 0 .... SD
Whitehaven 60 v. Highfield 0 .... SD

Away:
Highfield 4 v. Keighley C. 104 (at Rochdale)........ SD
Highfield 6 v. Whitehaven 86* .... SD
Highfield 8 v. Leigh 80 .... SD
Sheffield E. 2 v. Australia 80 .... Tour
Doncaster 0 v. Halifax 72 .... SBC
Batley 4 v. Wigan 70 CC
Highfield 10 v. Hull K.R. 68 .... SD
Highfield 12 v. Dewsbury 68 .... SD
Hunslet 20 v. Hull K.R. 60 .... SD

*Match abandoned after 63 minutes because of water-logged pitch, but result stands.

Highest score by a losing team:
Doncaster 42 v. Hull 38 ....SBC
● There was a record total of 115 matches in which a team scored 20 points or more and lost. The old record of 86 since the increase in value of a try from three to four points in 1983 was set in 1993-94.

High-scoring draws:
Hunslet 32 v. Salford 32 CC
Salford 24 v. Featherstone R. 24 .... SBC
London B. 24 v. Huddersfield 24 .... SD
Batley 22 v. St. Helens 22 .... RT
Hull K.R. 22 v. Huddersfield 22 .... SD

● From the start of the 1983-84 season, the value of a try was raised from three to four points. It was decided officially that records for most points in a match, season or career would subsequently include the four-point try and that no attempt would be made to adjust existing records featuring the three-point try.
● Substitute appearances do not count towards players' full appearance records.
● Points and appearances in abandoned matches are included in records, except in League matches which are replayed. Although the abandoned League match points and appearances are included in players' overall totals they do not count towards League records.

RECORD FEATS IN 1994-95

AT A GLANCE

SIMON WILSON of Batley broke four club records with 127 goals and 300 points in a season plus 13 goals and 30 points in a match.

JOHN SCHUSTER of Halifax broke three records and joined the elite who have scored in every match throughout a season. The Western Samoan centre scored a club record 362 points in a season, including a match record of 32 and a Division One best of 326 points.

MARTIN STRETT of Rochdale Hornets broke two club records with 150 goals and 346 points in a season.

FRANK BOTICA of Wigan broke his own club goals record with 186 in a season; achieved two Regal Trophy final records with eight goals and 20 points; and equalled his own Premiership final records of 10 goals and 20 points.

NICK PINKNEY of Keighley Cougars scored a club record 45 tries in a season and twice equalled the match record of five tries.

MIKE PECHEY broke the Whitehaven tries in a season record with 34.

ELLERY HANLEY of Leeds scored a record 41 tries in a season by a forward.

GREG AUSTIN of Huddersfield scored a record-equalling 52 tries in a season by a centre, including a Regal Trophy match record of nine.

DARREN CARTER of Barrow set club match records with 17 goals and 42 points. The 17 goals also equalled the Regal Trophy record.

LEE ANDERSON of Whitehaven broke two club records with 13 goals and 30 points in a match.

DEAN MARWOOD of Workington Town equalled his own club match records of 13 goals and 42 points.

SCOTT ROSKELL of London Broncos equalled the club record of four tries in a match.

LES HOLLIDAY of Dewsbury scored a club match record of 32 points.

RICHARD PELL of Hunslet equalled the club record of 28 points in a match.

KRIS RADLINSKI and GARY CONNOLLY of Wigan became the first players to score a hat-trick of tries in the Premiership final.

ROD WISHART of Australia kicked a match record 12 goals by a Kangaroos tourist in Britain.

HUDDERSFIELD piled up the highest-ever score in any British competitive match with a 142-4 trouncing of Blackpool Gladiators. A day later BARROW equalled the winning margin with a 138-0 thrashing of Nottingham City.

KEIGHLEY COUGARS ran up a club and league match record score with their 104-4 Division Two defeat of HIGHFIELD at Rochdale. It was also Highfield's biggest defeat and equalled the record away score.

BATLEY twice ran up their highest score with a 66-0 defeat of Highfield followed by a 78-22 victory over Leigh.

CASTLEFORD achieved a club record winning margin with an 86-0 victory which was WAKEFIELD TRINITY'S worst defeat.

OLDHAM achieved their highest score with a 70-10 defeat of Bramley.

WHITEHAVEN ran up their highest score with an 86-6 win at Highfield.

WORKINGTON TOWN scored a club record 94-4 victory which was Leigh's biggest defeat.

HALIFAX achieved a Division One record winning away margin with a 72-0 victory at Doncaster.

WIGAN ran up the highest Regal Trophy final score with their 40-10 defeat of Warrington at Huddersfield.

WIGAN piled up the highest score in any final with their 69-12 defeat of Leeds in the Stones Bitter Premiership final.

WIGAN equalled the Division One record for the longest winning run from the start of a season with 13 and finished with a record haul of 1,735 points including a Division One record 1,148 points.

HULL went down to a club record 66-16 defeat at Wigan.

SHEFFIELD EAGLES suffered a club record defeat when they went down 80-2 against Australia.

HIGHFIELD conceded a record 1,604 league points.

NEW RECORDS IN DETAIL . . .

SIMON WILSON of Batley broke four club records during the season.

The stand off or full back scored a record 127 goals and 300 points in a season, including two drop goals and 12 tries. He also broke two match records with 13 goals and 30 points, including a try, in the 78-22 Division Two home

defeat of Leigh on 26 March.

The previous goals in a season record was held by full back Stan Thompson with 120 in 1958-59, while winger Jack Perry set the points record with 281 from 112 goals and 19 tries in 1950-51.

Wilson passed both records with three goals and a try in the 26-28 Division Two home defeat by Hunslet on 21 April.

The previous match records had been held by Steve Parrish with 10 goals in a 64-0 Division Three win at Nottingham City on 10 November 1991 and Perry with 26 points from seven goals and four tries in a 29-17 home league defeat of Liverpool City on 13 September 1952.

Wilson played in all 39 matches for Batley in 1994-95 when his scoring record was as follows:

	T	G	DG	Pts
Huddersfield ....(H)	0	4	0	8
Carlisle ....(H)	0	6	0	12
Highfield ....(H)	1	7	0	18
Ryedale-York ....(A)	0	0	0	0
Whitehaven ....(H)	0	0	0	0
London B. ....(A)	0	0	0	0
Rochdale H. ....(H)	0	0	0	0
Keighley C. ....(A)	1	4	2	14
Swinton ....(H)	0	1	0	2
Leigh ....(A)	1	0	0	4
Huddersfield ....(A)	0	3	0	6
Carlisle ....(A)	2	3	0	14
Ryedale-York ....(H)	0	0	0	0
Queens (RT) ....(H)	0	5	0	10
Ryedale-York (RT) ....(H)	0	6	0	12
Highfield ....(A)	1	5	0	14
St. Helens (RT) ....(A)	0	2	0	4
St. Helens (RT replay) ....(A)	1	5	0	14
Dewsbury ....(A)	0	0	0	0
Bramley ....(H)	0	3	0	6
Barrow ....(H)	0	4	0	8
Hull K.R. ....(H)	0	5	0	10
Shaw Cross (CC) ....(H)	0	2	0	4
Whitehaven ....(A)	0	1	0	2
London B. ....(H)	0	3	0	6
Beverley (CC) ....(A)	1	3	0	10
Rochdale H. ....(A)	0	3	0	6
Wigan (CC) ....(H)	0	0	0	0
Keighley C. ....(H)	0	2	0	4
Hunslet ....(A)	0	5	0	10
Swinton ....(A)	0	4	0	8
Leigh ....(H)	1	13	0	30
Barrow ....(A)	1	4	0	12
Hull K.R. ....(A)	0	6	0	12
Dewsbury ....(H)	1	7	0	18
Bramley ....(A)	0	1	0	2
Hunslet ....(H)	1	3	0	10
Dewsbury (SDP) ....(H)	0	4	0	8
Huddersfield (SDP) ....(H)	0	1	0	2
Totals				
39 appearances	**12**	**125**	**2**	**300**

JOHN SCHUSTER of Halifax broke three records and joined the elite who have scored in every match in a season.

The Western Samoan centre scored a club record 362 points, including a match record of 32 points in the 72-0 Division One win at Doncaster on 9 October.

His total included a Division One record 326 points from 18 tries, 126 goals and two drop goals.

The previous match record of 31 was set by stand off Bruce Burton with 14 goals and a try in the 76-8 Yorkshire Cup first round win at Hunslet on 27 August 1971.

Colin Whitfield held the old Halifax record of 298 points in a season with 21 tries and 105 goals plus four drop goals in 40 matches, including one substitute appearance, in 1986-87.

Schuster passed the record in the 39-20 Division One home defeat of Workington Town on 26 March, finishing with 19 tries and 144 goals, including two drop goals, in his total of 34 matches.

The previous Division One record of 295 points was set by Leigh stand off John Woods with 23 tries and 102 goals, including a drop goal, in 1983-84.

Schuster broke the record with 18 points in the 34-8 home defeat of Featherstone Rovers on 9 April.

His match-by-match figures were as follows:

	T	G	DG	Pts
Oldham .... (A)	0	6	0	12
St. Helens .... (H)	1	3	0	10
Widnes .... (A)	0	1	0	2
Hull .... (H)	1	7	0	18
Wakefield T. .... (H)	1	6	0	16
Salford .... (A)	1	4	0	12
Doncaster .... (A)	3	10	0	32
Australia (Tour) .... (H)	0	2	0	4
Featherstone R. .... (A)	1	3	0	10
Sheffield E. .... (H)	1	2	0	8
Oldham .... (H)	2	7	0	22
St. Helens .... (A)	0	3	0	6
Widnes .... (H)	1	5	0	14
Castleford (RT) .... (A)	0	5	0	10
Warrington .... (H)	1	3	0	10
Hull .... (A)	1	4	0	12
Bradford N. .... (H)	0	4	0	8
Leeds .... (A)	0	3	0	6
Workington T. .... (A)	0	1	0	2
Castleford .... (H)	1	3	0	10
Wakefield T. .... (A)	0	5	0	10
Salford .... (H)	1	2	0	8
Huddersfield (CC) .... (A)	0	7	0	14
Warrington .... (A)	0	3	0	6
Doncaster .... (H)	1	7	0	18
Castleford .... (A)	0	2	1	5
Workington T. .... (H)	0	7	1	15
Wigan .... (H)	0	5	0	10
Wigan .... (A)	0	1	0	2
Featherstone R............... (H)	1	7	0	18
Bradford N. .... (A)	0	3	0	6
Leeds .... (H)	0	5	0	10
Sheffield E. .... (A)	0	4	0	8
St. Helens (PT).............. (A)	1	2	0	8
Totals				
34 appearances	**19**	**142**	**2**	**362**

MARTIN STRETT of Rochdale Hornets broke two club records with 150 goals and 346 points in a season, including 12 tries and two drop goals in 33 appearances.

The previous goals record of 115 was set by Kevin Harcombe in 1985-86 and included one drop goal in 35 matches.

Strett broke the record with six goals in the 36-20 Division Two win at Leigh on 19 March.

The centre broke Steve Gartland's record of 276 points in 1992-93 with four points in the next match, a 20-26 Division Two home defeat by Huddersfield on 22 March. Gartland played in 35 matches with the half back's points total consisting of 17 tries and 105 goals, including two drop goals.

Strett's match-by-match facts were:

	T	G	DG	Pts
Barrow .... (A)	0	8	0	16
Keighley C. .... (H)	0	2	0	4
Whitehaven .... (A)	0	3	0	6
Carlisle .... (H)	1	5	0	14
Hull K.R. .... (A)	0	1	0	2
Hunslet .... (H)	1	7	0	18
Batley .... (A)	0	2	0	4
Huddersfield .... (A)	0	2	0	4
Leigh .... (H)	1	8	0	20
London B. .... (A)	0	1	1	3
Highfield .... (A)	0	4	0	8
Barrow .... (H)	0	6	0	12
Keighley C. .... (A)	0	2	1	5
Woolston R. (RT) .... (H)	0	5	0	10
Wigan (RT) .... (A)	0	4	0	8
Whitehaven .... (H)	0	6	0	12
Carlisle .... (A)	1	3	0	10
Swinton .... (H)	0	6	0	12
Dewsbury .... (H)	0	4	0	8
Ryedale-York .... (A)	0	6	0	12
Lock Lane (CC) .... (H)	3	6	0	24
Hull K.R. .... (H)	1	5	0	14
Hunslet .... (A)	1	3	0	10
Ryedale-York (CC).......... (A)	0	4	0	8
Batley .... (H)	1	5	0	14
Bramley .... (H)	0	2	0	4
Leigh .... (A)	0	6	0	12
Huddersfield .... (H)	0	2	0	4
Highfield .... (H)	1	11	0	26
Dewsbury .... (A)	0	5	0	10
Ryedale-York .... (H)	0	5	0	10
Swinton .... (A)	1	3	0	10
London B. .... (H)	NA			
Bramley .... (A)	0	6	0	12
Huddersfield (SDP) .... (A)	NA			
Totals				
33 appearances	**12**	**148**	**2**	**346**

FRANO BOTICA of Wigan broke his own club record of 186 goals in a season; achieved Regal Trophy final records with eight goals and 20 points; and equalled his own Premiership final records of 10 goals and 20 points.

The stand off's eight goals in the 40-10 Regal Trophy final defeat of Warrington at Huddersfield's Alfred McAlpine Stadium beat the six goals by Derek Whitehead (Warrington) v. Rochdale Hornets in 1973-74 and Lee Crooks (Castleford) v. Wigan in 1993-94.

Botica added a try to beat the 16 points by Castleford prop Crooks, who scored six goals and a try in the previous year's 33-2 defeat of Wigan.

The New Zealander's 10 goals and 20 points in the 69-12 Stones Bitter Premiership final defeat of Leeds at Old Trafford equalled both records he set when Wigan beat St. Helens 48-16 in the 1992 final at Old Trafford.

Botica's 10 goals took him past the Wigan record of 184 in 1992-93 when he played in 40 matches compared with only 31 plus two substitute appearances last season, missing 12 games.

He also scored nine tries for a total of 408 points, leaving him 15 points short of the club record he set in 1992-93.

Botica's record 186 goals in 1994-95 was achieved as follows:

Featherstone R.	(A)	6
Sheffield E.	(H)	6
Oldham	(A)	NA
Leeds	(H)	NA
Widnes	(H)	NA
Castleford	(A)	3
Wakefield T.	(H)	4
Australia (Tour)	(H)	1
Workington T.	(A)	5
Salford	(H)	NA
Hull	(A)	NA
Sheffield E.	(A)	NA
Featherstone R.	(H)	NA
Oldham	(H)	NA
Rochdale H. (RT)	(H)	NA
Leeds	(A)	2
Hull (RT)	(H)	9
St. Helens	(A)	6
Warrington	(H)	5
St. Helens (RT)	(A)	6
Castleford (RT)	(H)	7
Bradford N.	(A)	1
Doncaster	(A)	6
Warrington (RT)	(N^1)	8
Castleford	(H)	9
St. Helens (CC)	(H)	2
St. Helens (CC)	(A)	6
Wakefield T.	(A)	4
Batley (CC)	(A)	10
Workington T.	(H)	7
Widnes (CC)	(A)	5
Widnes	(A)	6
Salford	(A)	NA

Oldham (CC)	(N^1)	6
Halifax	(A)	2
Halifax	(H)	6
Doncaster	(H)	NA
Bradford N.	(H)	8
St. Helens	(H)	5
Warrington	(A)	3
Hull	(H)	NA
Leeds (CC)	(N^2)	5
Sheffield E. (PT)	(H)	8
Warrington (PT)	(H)	9
Leeds (PT)	(N^3)	10

Totals

33 appearances **186**

(N^1) At the Alfred McAlpine Stadium, Huddersfield
(N^2) At Wembley
(N^3) At Old Trafford

NICK PINKNEY of Keighley Cougars scored a club record 45 tries in a season and twice equalled the match record of five.

It was the second time the former Ryedale-York centre had broken theKeighley tries in a season record in two years.

He first broke the record that had stood for nearly 50 years in his first season with 31 in as many appearances and followed it with 45 in 37 matches last term.

The record went with two tries in the 24-12 Silk Cut Challenge Cup fourth round home defeat of Dewsbury on 12 February.

Pinkney equalled Keighley's match record with five in a 66-10 Division Two home defeat of Hunslet on 16 October and again in the 104-4 league away victory against Highfield at Rochdale Hornets' Spotland ground on 23 April.

He shares the record with centre Ike Jagger, who scored five in a 67-0 home league defeat of Castleford on 13 January 1906, and winger Sam Stacey in a 53-10 home league defeat of Liverpool City on 9 March 1907.

Pinkney also scored one try on his England debut and his match-by-match club record was achieved as follows:

Whitehaven	(H)	3
Rochdale H.	(A)	2
Ryedale-York	(H)	NA
London B.	(A)	0
Dewsbury	(H)	1
Bramley	(A)	0
Barrow	(A)	0
Batley	(H)	1
Hunslet	(H)	5
Carlisle	(H)	4
Whitehaven	(A)	2
Rochdale H.	(H)	1
Chorley (RT)	(H)	3
Bramley (RT)	(H)	2
Ryedale-York	(A)	1
Sheffield E. (RT)	(H)	0
Hull K.R.	(H)	1
Huddersfield	(A)	0

Warrington (RT)	(H)	1
London B.	(H)	0
Swinton	(A)	1
Chorley (CC)	(H)	1
Leigh	(H)	1
Bramley	(H)	1
Dewsbury (CC)	(H)	2
Barrow	(H)	1
Huddersfield (CC)	(H)	0
Batley	(A)	1
Highfield	(H)	NA
Hunslet	(A)	0
Dewsbury	(A)	0
Carlisle	(A)	0
Leigh	(A)	2
Swinton	(H)	NA
Hull K.R.	(A)	0
Huddersfield	(H)	1
Highfield	(A)	5
Hull K.R. (SDP)	(H)	0
London B. (SDP)	(H)	1
Huddersfield (SDP)	(N[1])	1

Totals

37 appearances **45**

(N[1]) At Old Trafford

MIKE PECHEY of Whitehaven scored a club record 34 tries in a season, beating the 31 by wing or centre Vince Gribbin in 1991-92. The Australian centre's total was totted up in 34 matches, while Gribbin made 27 appearances. Pechey broke the record with the last of five tries in a 60-0 Division Two home defeat of Highfield on 14 April.   His match-by-match figures for 1994-95 were:

Keighley C.	(A)	0
Leigh	(H)	NA
Rochdale H.	(H)	1
Bramley	(A)	1
Batley	(A)	0
Barrow	(H)	1
Hull K.R.	(H)	3
Ryedale-York	(A)	2
Huddersfield	(H)	1
Swinton	(A)	2
Keighley C.	(H)	0
Leigh	(A)	0
Thatto Heath (RT)	(H)	2
Featherstone R. (RT)	(H)	1
Rochdale H.	(A)	1
Bradford N. (RT)	(H)	1
Carlisle	(H)	2
Hunslet	(H)	0
Dewsbury	(A)	NA
Moorends (CC)	(H)	1
Highfield	(A)	4
Batley	(H)	1
Barrow	(A)	NA
Wakefield T. (CC)	(H)	0

Hull K.R.	(A)	0
Hull K.R. (CC)	(A)	0
Ryedale-York	(H)	0
Featherstone R. (CC)	(H)	1
London B.	(A)	1
Huddersfield	(A)	0
Swinton	(H)	NA
Hunslet	(A)	0
Dewsbury	(H)	1
Highfield	(H)	5
Carlisle	(A)	1
Bramley	(H)	0
London B.	(H)	1
London B. (SDP)	(A)	0

Totals

34 appearances **34**

ELLERY HANLEY of Leeds scored a record 41 tries in a season by a forward. The loose forward beat the old record of 40 tries by second row Bob Haigh, also of Leeds, in 1970-71.

Hanley played in 34 club matches, while Haigh achieved his record in 47 matches for Leeds plus one appearance each for Yorkshire and Great Britain without scoring.

The Leeds captain's total included his 100th for Leeds and his 400th in all matches (see MILESTONES).

Hanley's 41 tries were scored as follows:

Workington T.	(A)	0
Featherstone R.	(H)	1
Doncaster	(A)	0
Wigan	(A)	0
Salford	(H)	1
Widnes	(A)	1
Castleford	(H)	1
Australia (Tour)	(H)	NA
St. Helens	(A)	NA
Sheffield E.	(H)	NA
Wakefield T.	(H)	3
Workington T.	(H)	0
Featherstone R.	(A)	2
Doncaster	(H)	3
Swinton (RT)	(H)	2
Wigan	(H)	1
Workington T. (RT)	(A)	1
Hull	(A)	2
Halifax	(H)	2
Castleford (RT)	(H)	2
Oldham	(A)	1
Bradford N.	(H)	3
Warrington	(H)	0
Widnes	(H)	4
Bradford N. (CC)	(H)	2
Castleford	(A)	1
Ryedale-York (CC)	(H)	0
Salford	(A)	2
Workington T. (CC)	(H)	3
Sheffield E.	(A)	0

St. Helens	(H)	0
Bradford N.	(A)	1
Featherstone R. (CC)	(N¹)	2
Oldham	(H)	0
Warrington	(A)	1
Hull	(H)	0
Halifax	(A)	NA
Wakefield T.	(A)	NA
Wigan (CC)	(N²)	0
Bradford N. (PT)	(H)	NA
St. Helens (PT)	(H)	NA
Wigan (PT)	(N³)	NA
Totals		
34 appearances		**41**

(N¹) At Elland Road, Leeds
(N²) At Wembley
(N³) At Old Trafford

GREG AUSTIN of Huddersfield equalled Paul Newlove's record of 52 tries in a season by a centre and broke the Regal Trophy match record with nine tries.

The Australian played in all 39 matches for Huddersfield, while Newlove set the record after scoring 48 tries in 35 matches for Featherstone Rovers plus three tries in one match for Great Britain and another for England.

Austin broke the Regal Trophy match record with nine in Huddersfield's 142-4 first round home defeat of Blackpool Gladiators.

The previous record of six was shared by Whitehaven centre Vince Gribbin in a 64-0 home defeat of Doncaster on 18 November 1984 and Bradford Northern centre Steve McGowan in a 70-10 home victory over Barrow on 8 November 1992. Both were first round ties.

Austin also scored a drop goal during the season when his match-by-match try figures were as follows:

Batley	(A)	0
Barrow	(H)	2
Swinton	(A)	1
Hunslet	(H)	2
Leigh	(A)	1
Hull K.R.	(H)	0
Highfield	(A)	3
Rochdale H.	(H)	1
Whitehaven	(A)	2
Bramley	(A)	2
Batley	(H)	0
Barrow	(A)	2
Blackpool G. (RT)	(H)	9
St. Helens (RT)	(H)	0
Swinton	(H)	0
Hunslet	(A)	0
Ryedale-York	(A)	1
Keighley C.	(H)	0
Carlisle	(A)	2
London B.	(H)	1
Wigan St. Judes (CC)	(H)	3

Leigh	(H)	1
Hull K.R.	(A)	0
Halifax (CC)	(H)	2
Highfield	(H)	2
Keighley C. (CC)	(A)	1
Oldham (CC)	(A)	0
Whitehaven	(H)	2
Rochdale H.	(A)	0
Bramley	(H)	1
Dewsbury	(A)	4
Carlisle	(H)	2
London B.	(A)	1
Ryedale-York	(H)	1
Keighley C.	(A)	1
Dewsbury	(H)	1
Rochdale H. (SDP)	(H)	1
Batley (SDP)	(H)	0
Keighley C. (SDP)	(N¹)	0
Totals		
39 appearances		**52**

(N)¹ at Old Trafford

DARREN CARTER of Barrow set club match records with 17 goals and 42 points, including two tries, in the 138-0 Regal Trophy first round home defeat of National Conference League side Nottingham City on 27 November.

The second row, who achieved the feat while on loan from Workington Town, beat the Barrow goals record of 12 shared by Frank French v. Maryport (19 February 1938), Willie Horne v. Cardiff (8 September 1951), Steve Tickle v. Kent Invicta (8 April 1984) and Mike Kavanagh v. Blackpool Gladiators (21 March 1993).

The previous points record of 28 was held by Keith Jarrett v. Doncaster (25 August 1970), Steve Tickle v. Kent Invicta (8 April 1984), Dean Marwood at Runcorn Highfield (16 April 1989), Mike Kavanagh v. Blackpool Gladiators (21 March 1993).

Carter's 17 goals also equalled the Regal Trophy record set by Castleford's Geoff "Sammy" Lloyd in the 88-5 first round home defeat of Millom amateurs on 16 September 1973.

LEE ANDERSON of Whitehaven scored club records of 13 goals and 30 points, including a try, in the 86-6 Division Two win at Highfield on 25 January.

Although the match was abandoned after 63 minutes because of a waterlogged pitch the result and records stand.

The full back's 13 goals beat the 12 by Steve Maguire in an 80-6 Division Three home defeat of Nottingham City on 12 April 1992.

Maguire held the previous points record of 28, with the loose forward scoring 10 goals and two tries in a 72-0 Division Three home win over Highfield on 28 February 1993.

DEAN MARWOOD of Workington Town equalled his own club match records of 13 goals and 42 points in the 94-4 Silk

Cut Challenge Cup fifth round home defeat of Leigh on 26 February.

The scrum half also scored four tries, as he did when setting the club records in a 78-0 Division Three home defeat of Highfield on 1 November 1992.

SCOTT ROSKELL of London Broncos scored a club record-equalling four tries in the 38-6 Division Two win at Bramley on 19 March.

The centre equalled the record set by scrum half Mark Riley in a 62-6 home defeat of Highfield on 17 October 1993 and winger Mark Johnson in the 58-6 win at Highfield on 1 April 1994. Both were Division Two matches.

LES HOLLIDAY of Dewsbury broke a club match record that had stood for 75 years when he scored 32 points in the 76-8 Division Two home defeat of Barrow in the first-ever match at their new Crown Flatt Stadium on 11 September. The loose forward's tally consisted of 10 goals and three tries.

Winger Joe Lyman held the old record with 29 points from five tries and seven goals in the 56-0 home league defeat of Hull on 22 April 1919.

RICHARD PELL of Hunslet equalled the club match record of 28 points with 10 goals and two tries in the 64-4 Silk Cut Challenge Cup third round home defeat of Wigan St. Patricks amateurs on 22 January.

The prop equalled the record set by scrum half Tim Lumb, who scored three tries and eight goals in a 52-12 Division One home defeat of Runcorn Highfield on 7 October 1990.

KRIS RADLINKSI and GARY CONNOLLY of Wigan became the first players to score hat-tricks of tries in the Premiership Final.

Radlinski achieved the feat in 43 minutes followed by co-centre Connolly in the 69-12 defeat of Leeds at Old Trafford.

At 19 years six weeks, Radlinski also became the youngest player to win the Harry Sunderland Trophy as the Man of the Match.

ROD WISHART of Australia kicked a record 12 goals by a Kangaroos tourist in the 80-2 defeat of Sheffield Eagles on 26 October.

He beat the 11 goals by Eric Weissel in the 58-9 win on the 1928-29 tour and by Noel Pidding in the 58-8 win at Wakefield Trinity in 1952.

HUDDERSFIELD piled up the highest-ever score in any British competitive match with a 142-4 trouncing of National Conference League side Blackpool Gladiators in the first round of the Regal Trophy on 26 November.

The 26-try romp beat the previous highest score of 119-2, also achieved by Huddersfield with a record 27 tries at home to Swinton Park amateurs in a Challenge Cup first round home tie on 28 February 1914.

BARROW equalled Huddersfield's new record winning margin the following day with a 138-0 first round home defeat of national Conference side Nottingham City when they also scored 26 tries.

Barrow's previous record win was an 83-3 Challenge Cup first round home defeat of Maryport amateurs on 19 February 1938 when they scored 19 tries.

KEIGHLEY COUGARS ran up a club and league match record score with their 104-4 Division Two away defeat of HIGHFIELD at Rochdale Hornet's Spotland ground on 23 April.

It was also Highfield's biggest defeat and beat the record away score by any team.

Keighley scored 20 tries to beat their club record 86-0 defeats of Nottingham City (14 tries) in a Division Three home match on 1 November 1992 and of Highfield (15 tries) in a Challenge Cup first round home tie on 31 January 1993.

The previous record league score and still the widest margin was Leeds's 102-0 home defeat of Coventry on 12 April 1913 when they scored 24 tries.

Keighley beat the away record score set by Hull Kingston Rovers, who beat Nottingham City 100-6 in a Yorkshire Cup first round tie on 19 August 1990 at Doncaster's ground.

Nottingham switched the home tie because their own ground was not available.

Highfield switched their tie against Keighley to Rochdale because their own ground could not cope with the 4,500 crowd boosted by the Cougars big following.

BATLEY twice broke the club record score during the season.

First with a 66-0 (13 tries) Division Two home defeat of Highfield on 4 September.

It beat the 64-1 (13 tries) Regal Trophy first round home defeat of Leeds amateur club Queens on 31 October 1993 and 64-0 (11 tries) Division Three win at Nottingham City on 10 November 1991.

Then they scored a 78-22 (13 tries) Division Two home victory over Leigh on 26 March.

CASTLEFORD achieved a club record winning margin with their 86-0 Division One home victory on 17 April which was WAKEFIELD TRINITY'S worst defeat.

Castleford scored 17 tries compared with 18 when they gained their previous best winning margin of 88-5 against Millom amateurs in a John Player Trophy first round home tie on 16 September 1973.

Wakefield's previous biggest defeat was 72-6 in a Division One home match on 29 March 1987 against Wigan, who scored 14 tries.

OLDHAM achieved their highest score with a 70-10 Silk Cut Challenge Cup fourth round home defeat of Bramley on 12 February.

The 12-try victory beat Oldham's best of 67-6 at home to Liverpool City in a league match on 4 April 1959 when they scored 13 tries.

WHITEHAVEN ran up a club record score with their 86-6 (15 tries) victory at Highfield on 25 January. Although the match was abandoned after 63 minutes because of a waterlogged pitch the result and record stands.

It beat the previous record 80-6 (14 tries) Division Three home defeat of Nottingham City on 2 April 1992.

WORKINGTON TOWN scored a club record win of 94-4 as visiting LEIGH went down to their biggest defeat in the Silk Cut Challenge Cup fifth round on 26 February.

Town scored 17 tries to beat their previous highest scores of 78-0 (13 tries) at home to Highfield on 1 November 1992 and 78-12 (14 tries) at Blackpool Gladiators on 28 February 1993. Both were Division Three matches.

Leigh's previous biggest defeats were 70-6 at Castleford on 20 February 1994 and 70-16 at Hull on 24 April 1994. They conceded 13 tries in both Division One matches.

HALIFAX scored a Division One away record winning margin with their 72-0 (13 tries) victory at Doncaster on 9 October.

It beat Wigan's 72-6 (14 tries) win at Wakefield Trinity on 29 March 1987 and 66-0 (12 tries) win at Barrow on 1 October 1989.

The highest away score remains Castleford's 76-12 (14 tries) win at Rochdale Hornets on 3 March 1991.

WIGAN equalled the longest winning run at the start of a Division One season by winning their first 13 league matches before losing 28-33 at Leeds.

Widnes held the record with 13 wins at the start of 1981-82. They drew their next match and then lost for an opening 14-match unbeaten run which still stands.

WIGAN ran up a Regal Trophy final record score of 40-10 against Warrington at Huddersfield's Alfred McAlpine Stadium when they scored six tries. It beat the 33-2 (five tries) defeat Wigan suffered against Castleford at Leeds a year earlier, which remains the widest margin.

WIGAN registered the highest score in any final with their 69-12 defeat of Leeds in the Stones Bitter Premiership final at Old Trafford. They scored 12 tries to beat the record they set themselves with a 48-16 Premiership Final defeat of St. Helens at Old Trafford in 1992 when they scored seven tries.

WIGAN piled up a record 1,148 Division One points in their 30-match programme and finished with a record 1,735 points in all 45 matches. Their totals included records of 200 and 296 tries respectively.

Wigan held the previous Division One records of 174 tries and 941 points from 30 matches in 1986-87.

Leigh held the all-match records with 258 tries and 1,436 points from 43 matches in 1985-86 when they became Division Two champions.

Wigan also finished with the best Division One record of only two defeats, equalling their 56 points in 1986-87.

A breakdown of Wigan's record-breaking season, which included becoming the first team to achieve a modern-day Grand Slam — by winning all four of the present trophies in one campaign is as follows:

	Matches	T	G	DG	Pts
Division One	30	200	173	2	1,148
Challenge Cup	6	39	37	0	230
Regal Trophy	5	25	35	0	170
Premiership	3	28	27	1	167
Australia	1	4	2	0	20
Totals	**45**	**296**	**274**	**3**	**1,735**

HULL conceded a club record score when they lost 66-16 at Wigan, who scored 12 tries in the Division One match on 23 April. The previous highest score against Hull was 64-2 in a Division One match at St. Helens on 17 February 1988 when they let in 11 tries.

SHEFFIELD EAGLES suffered a club record defeat when they went down 80-2 against the Australian tourists on 26 October. They conceded 14 tries compared with the 11 when Sheffield sustained their previous biggest defeat of 62-11 at Warrington on 9 February 1986.

HIGHFIELD conceded a record 1,604 (298 tries) league points in 30 Division Two matches and 1,687 (313 tries) in all 33 matches. Nottingham City held the previous unwanted records with 1,323 (241 tries) points conceded in 26 Division Three matches in 1991-92 when their total deficits were 1,437 (261) in 28 matches.

MILESTONES . . .

ELLERY HANLEY of Leeds took his career total of tries to 401 with two in the 54-24 Regal Trophy second round home defeat of Swinton on 4 December.

The loose forward reached his century for Leeds with the first of three tries in the 50-16 Silk Cut Challenge Cup quarter-final home defeat of Workington Town on 12 March.

He then broke the British record of 40 tries in a season by a forward with one in the 17-11 Division One win at Warrington on 7 April (SEE NEW RECORDS IN DETAIL).

It proved to be Hanley's last season before extending his career in Australia and he finished with a British total of 428 tries in 498 matches, including six substitute appearances.

The tries total was made up of 106 for Leeds, 189 Wigan, 90 Bradford Northern and 43 in representative matches including 20 touchdowns in 36 Test and World Cup appearances for Great Britain.

He holds the Division One record for most league tries in a career with 279. His 44 league tries for Wigan in 1986-87 is another Division One record, having scored the previous best of 40 for Bradford in 1984-85.

Hanley's 63 tries in all matches in 1986-87 is the most by a non-winger in a season as he played mainly stand off and loose forward with the occasional game at centre.

Five tries for Wigan against Bradford Northern on 1 March 1987 is a Division One record for a forward. But his best match feat was six tries as a centre in a Silk Cut Challenge Cup-tie win at Rochdale Hornets on 24

February 1991. Including the above, plus nine four-try feats, Hanley has scored three tries or more in a match on 36 occasions.

Hanley's 428 tries put him sixth in the all-time list behind leader Brian Bevan (Warrington and briefly Blackpool Borough) who scored 796 between 1945 and 1964.

A former Corpus Christi, Leeds, amateur, Hanley turned professional as a 17-year-old with Bradford on 2 June 1978. He made his debut as a substitute, scoring a try in the 30-18 home Division One defeat of Rochdale Hornets on 26 November 1978.

He was then absent for a period and did not make his full debut until 16 August 1981 when he scored a try in the centre in a 33-5 Yorkshire Cup first round win at Halifax.

Wigan signed him in a then world record £150,000 deal on 16 September 1985, paying a then record £85,000 in cash plus the transfer of Phil Ford and Steve Donlan.

Hanley made his Wigan debut in the centre in a 32-10 Division One home victory over Widnes on 22 September 1985. After playing as a centre or stand off, Hanley switched to loose forward in February 1987.

The transfer record was broken again when Hanley moved to Leeds for £250,000 on 6 September 1991 and made his debut two days later in 20-14 Division One home defeat of Hull.

Hanley has also kicked 100 goals, including six drop goals, for a career total of 1,880 points.

His season-by-season tryscoring figures are as follows:

	App.	Tries
Bradford N.		
1978-79	0+1	1
1979-80	Did not play	
1980-81	Did not play	
1981-82	39	15
1982-83	19	10
1983-84	22	12 +1t GB, 1t Under-24s
1984-85	37	52 +2t GB, 1t England
Wigan		
1985-86	40	35 +2t GB, 1t York're
1986-87	38+1	59 +3t GB, 1t York're
1987-88	34	31 +4t GB, 1t York're
1988-89	38	25 +3t* GB, 1t York're
1989-90	19+1	10
1990-91	33	29
Leeds		
1991-92	19	9
1992-93	31	31 +2t GB, 1t England
1993-94	29+1	25
1994-95	34	41
Totals		
Bradford N.	117+1	90
Wigan	202+2	189
Leeds	113+1	106
Gt Britain	*36+1	*21
1984 Tour	9	8 Not inc 4t in 7 Tests
1988 Tour	5+1	7 Not inc 1t in 5 Tests

1992 Tour	1	0
England	2	2
Yorkshire	5	4
GB Under-24s	2	1
GRAND TOTALS	**492+6**	**428**

*Includes one appearance and a try against a World XIII that was not a Test match.

KEVIN PAPE of Workington Town scored the 200th try of his career with one in the 18-30 Stones Bitter Championship home defeat against Warrington on 19 March.

His total of 204 at the end of the season consisted of 11 for Workington, 192 for Carlisle and one for Cumbria in a total of 351 matches.

His 192 tries in 324 appearances for Carlisle are both club career records.

He is also the joint holder of the Carlisle match record with four in a 30-22 Silk Cut Challenge Cup first round home defeat of Rochdale Hornets on 11 February 1987. He scored four other hat-tricks for Carlisle but has yet to achieve the feat at Workington.

A former player with Cumbrian amateurs Glasson Rangers, Pape made his senior debut on 2 September 1984 when he scored a try in a 31-15 Division Two home defeat of Doncaster.

Pape's most prolific season was his last full term at Carlisle, scoring 24 tries in 1993-94. He has finished in the top ten only once, when reaching fifth after scoring 23 tries in 1987-88.

After 10 seasons at Carlisle, Pape moved to Workington and made his debut as a substitute in a 48-10 Division One defeat at St Helens on 11 December 1994.

He made his full debut in the centre a week later when Town lost 14-18 at home to Leeds in a Regal Trophy third round tie. After playing most of his career in the centre, Pape settled on the wing at Workington.

His season-by-season tryscoring totals are as follows:

	App.	Tries
Carlisle		
1984-85	31	19
1985-86	38	20
1986-87	34	22
1987-88	31	22 +1t Cumbria
1988-89	33	14
1989-90	27	16
1990-91	31	19
1991-92	27	9
1992-93	29	19
1993-94	36	24
1994-95	7	8
Workington Town		
1994-95	19+2	11
Totals		
Carlisle	324	192
Workington T.	19+2	11
Cumbria	5+1	1
GRAND TOTALS	**348+3**	**204**

159

RECORDS

DENIS BETTS reached a career century of tries with one in the 26-12 Silk Cut Challenge Cup quarter-final win at Widnes on 11 March.

The Great Britain forward left for a new career Down Under at the end of the season with a total of 106 tries, made up of 95 for Wigan and 11 in representative matches including five Test tries. His only hat-trick was scored in a league match against Widnes last season.

A former Leigh Rangers amateur, Betts made a tryscoring debut for Wigan as a substitute in a 68-0 Silk Cut Challenge Cup preliminary round home defeat of Workington Town on 18 January 1987.

He made one other substitute appearance before his full debut on the wing in a 14-6 Division One win at Salford on 17 January 1988.

Betts settled into the second row the following season and has been a regular ever since. His season-by-season try totals are as follows:

	App.	Tries	
Wigan			
1986-87	0+2	1	
1987-88	1+1	0	
1988-89	24+15	9	+1t GB Under-21s
1989-90	32+1	11	+1t GB Under-21s
1990-91	37+2	12	+1t GB
1991-92	42+1	19	+1t GB
1992-93	36	14	+1t GB
1993-94	18+5	9	
1994-95	37	20	
Totals			
Wigan	227+27	95	
Britain	24+1	5	
Tours (2)	8+3	4	(Not inc. Tests)
Lancashire	1	0	
GB U-21s	4	2	
GRAND TOTALS	**264+31**	**106**	

STUART COCKER scored the 100th try of his career while on loan to Batley from Workington Town.

The winger reached his century with one try in Batley's club record 78-22 Division Two home defeat of Leigh on 26 March.

At the end of the season he had totalled 104 tries, consisting of 50 for Huddersfield, eight for Oldham, 38 for Workington and eight for Batley. He has made a total of 145 appearances, including six as a substitute.

Cocker finished fifth in the try chart in 1993-94 with 35 for Workington, including a personal best of five at home to Barrow. He has also scored four in a match three times plus two hat-tricks.

A former Rugby Union player from the Morley area, Cocker made his senior league debut as a substitute with Huddersfield in a 17-14 Division Two home defeat of Bramley on 22 January 1989.

He made another four substitute appearances before making his full debut at stand off on 24 September 1989 when he scored two tries despite Huddersfield's 16-21

Division Two home defeat against Workington.

Oldham signed Cocker for the start of the 1992-93 season and he opened with two tries on his debut at centre in a 27-12 Division Two home defeat of London Crusaders on 30 August 1992.

He had just one season at Oldham before moving to Workington and making his debut as a centre in a 24-4 Division Two win at Batley on 5 September 1993. After 11 matches in the centre, Cocker played the rest of the season on the wing.

He played 10 matches for Town early last season before taking a break to concentrate on a family business. He returned on loan to Batley and scored two tries on his left wing debut in a 34-22 Division Two win at Hunslet on 12 March.

Cocker's season-by-season try totals are as follows:

	App.	Tries
Huddersfield		
1988-89	0+2	0
1989-90	22+4	13
1990-91	24	15
1991-92	22	22
Oldham		
1992-93	14	8
Workington Town		
1993-94	37	35
1994-95	10	3
Batley		
1994-95	10	8
Totals		
Huddersfield	68+6	50
Oldham	14	8
Workington T.	47	38
Batley	10	8
GRAND TOTALS	**139+6**	**104**

NICK PINKNEY of Keighley Cougars scored the 100th try of his career with the third of four in a 46-14 Division Two home defeat of Carlisle on 30 October.

The centre's end-of-season total of 131 comprised of 76 for Keighley, 54 for Ryedale-York, plus one on his England debut last season. He has played in a total of 165 matches.

He broke the Keighley tries in a season record with 31 in his first term of 1993-94 and increased it to 45 a year later. (see RECORDS)

Pinkney also equalled Keighley's match record with five in a 66-10 Division Two home defeat of Hunslet on 16 October 1994 and away to Highfield in a 104-4 Division Two win on 23 April 1995. He has scored six other hat-tricks for Keighley, including three four-try feats, plus one hat-trick for York.

A former amateur from Hull, Pinkney turned professional with Ryedale-York and made a tryscoring debut on the wing in a 28-10 Division Two home defeat of Chorley Borough on 24 November 1989.

After establishing himself as a centre he moved to Keighley for a club record £40,000 and scored three tries on his debut in a 38-8 Division Two home defeat of Whitehaven on 20 August 1994.

His season-by-season try totals are as follows:

Ryedale-York

	App.	Tries
1989-90	7	2
1990-91	31	14
1991-92	29	13
1992-93	28	25
Keighley C.		
1993-94	31	31
1994-95	37	45 + 1t England
Totals		
Ryedale-York.........	95	54
Keighley C.	68	76
England...............	1	1
GB Under-21	0+1	0
GRAND TOTALS	**164+1**	**131**

MARTIN WOOD of Keighley Cougars scored his 100th career try with one in the 52-12 Division Two win at Ryedale-York on 11 December.

The stand off or loose forward's end-of-season total of 113 tries was made up of 72 for Keighley, 36 for Halifax and five for Scarborough Pirates from a total of 175 appearances.

The former Streethouse amateur made his senior professional debut for Halifax as a substitute in a 21-12 Division One home defeat of Salford on 5 March 1989.

He made three more substitute appearances before starting at loose forward and scoring two tries in a 72-20 Division Two win at Nottingham City on 1 October 1989.

Wood moved to the now defunct Scarborough Pirates for a brief spell, scoring two tries on his debut at loose forward in a 16-17 Division Three home defeat against Dewsbury on 2 December 1991.

Keighley then signed Wood making his debut for them against Scarborough in an 18-16 Division Three home win on 17 February 1992. He again played loose forward.

Wood scored four tries in a match and another hat-trick for Halifax, with three hat-tricks for Keighley, including one four-try feat.

His season-by-season tryscoring figures are as folows:

Halifax

	App.	Tries
1988-89	0+2	1
1989-90	5+12	4
1990-91	29+9	31
1991-92	2+1	0
Scarborough P.		
1991-92	5+1	5
Keighley C.		
1991-92	11	6
1992-93	28	27
1993-94	33+1	19
1994-95	33+3	20

Totals

Halifax.................	36+24	36
Scarborough P.......	5+1	5
Keighley C.	105+4	72
GRAND TOTALS	**146+29**	**113**

JOHN BENTLEY of Halifax scored the 100th try of his career with one in the 40-20 Division One win at Oldham on 20 August.

His total of 128 tries at the end of the season had been scored in 195 matches including nine as substitute, and is made up of 74 for Halifax, 53 for Leeds and one for Great Britain. He has scored five hat-tricks for Halifax and two for Leeds.

A former Sale and England Rugby Union international, Bentley signed for Leeds and made his debut on the wing in a 24-6 Division one win at Salford on 27 November 1988.

He was transferred to Halifax for about £50,000 and made his debut at centre against Leeds, scoring a try in a 26-8 Division One home victory on 6 September 1992.

Bentley's season-by-season try totals are as follows:

Leeds

	App.	Tries
1988-89	21	15
1989-90	20+3	10
1990-91	21+3	9
1991-92	30+3	19 + 1t GB
Halifax		
1992-93	29	20
1993-94	30	25
1994-95	33	29
Totals		
Leeds.................	92+9	53
Halifax.................	92	74
Britain	2	1
England...............	1	0
GRAND TOTALS	**186+9**	**128**

DERYCK FOX of Bradford Northern scored the 100th try of his career with one in the 48-4 Division One home defeat of Widnes on 11 September.

The scrum half's total at the end of the season was 101 made up of 16 for Bradford, 78 for Featherstone Rovers and seven in representative matches including three Test tries for Great Britain.

He has totalled 446 appearances, including 12 as a substitute. Fox has scored one hat-trick each for Bradford and Featherstone, with a best season's total of 16 in 1987-88.

Featherstone signed Fox from St. John Fisher (Dewsbury) amateurs after his return from BARLA's 1983 Great Britain youth tour of New Zealand.

He made his senior debut as a substitute in Featherstone's 24-8 Yorkshire Cup first round defeat at Hull on 4 September 1983. His full debut came 14 days later in an 18-14 Division One win at Whitehaven.

Fox was transferred to Bradford in September 1993 for £140,000, then a record for Northern and the most paid by any club for a scrum half. He made a substitute debut for Bradford in a 34-22 Yorkshire Cup first round win at Bramley on 13 September 1993. His full debut was a week later when he kicked three goals in a 24-12 Division One win at Widnes.

His season-by-season try totals are as follows:

	App.	Tries	
Featherstone R.			
1983-84	30+2	6	
1984-85	34	6	+1t GB
1985-86	31	11	
1986-87	36	14	
1987-88	38	16	
1988-89	35	9	
1989-90	34	3	+1t Yorkshire
1990-91	33	12	
1991-92	36	1	+ 1t GB, 1t York'e
Bradford N.			
1992-93	23+1	5	
1993-94	39	8	
1994-95	34	3	
Totals			
Featherstone R.	307+2	78	
Bradford N.	96+1	16	
Great Britain	10+4	3	
Tours	12+5	2	(Not inc. Tests)
Great Britain U-21 .	1	0	
Yorkshire	8	2	
GRAND TOTALS	**434+12**	**101**	

STEVE GIBSON of Rochdale Hornets scored the 100th try of his career with one in the 36-10 Division Two win at Ryedale-York on 15 January.

The Australian full back's total of 107 at the end of the season was made up of 34 tries for Rochdale and 73 for Salford in an overall total of 224 appearances, including eight as a substitute.

A former player in the Brisbane League, he made his English debut for Salford as a full back in the 58-4 Lancashire Cup first round home defeat of Fulham on 13 September 1987.

After six seasons he moved to Rochdale as player-coach and made a tryscoring debut at full back in a 28-10 Division Two win at Bramley on 10 October 1993.

Gibson's best match tally is four tries, achieving the feat once each for Salford and Rochdale. He has also scored three hat-tricks.

His season-by-season totals are as follows:

	App.	Tries
Salford		
1987-88	31	13
1988-89	31	13
1989-90	26+3	13
1990-91	30+1	17
1991-92	32	15
1992-93	11+4	2
Rochdale H.		
1993-94	26	11
1994-95	29	23
Totals		
Salford	161+8	73
Rochdale H.	55	34
GRAND TOTALS	**216+8**	**107**

GRAHAM STEADMAN of Castleford scored his 100th try for the club in a 35-28 Division One defeat at Doncaster on 16 October. Steadman's try total of 108 at the end of the season was achieved in 186 matches, including six substitute appearances.

He has scored nine hat-tricks for Castleford, including a best match feat of four. His highest season's total is 29 in 1991-92 when he also scored twice for Great Britain to put him fifth in the try chart.

An amateur with Knottingley Welfare, Steadman also played for Knottingley Rugby Union club before turning professional with York in March 1982. In five seasons at York he scored 63 tries.

He moved to Featherstone Rovers in February 1986 and totalled 48 tries for them before being transferred to Castleford at the start of 1989-90 in a then world record deal. A transfer tribunal ordered Castleford to pay Featherstone £145,000 plus £25,000 after Steadman played for Great Britain.

He made his debut for Castleford at stand off in a 20-22 Division One home defeat by Featherstone on 3 September 1989. Originally a stand off, Steadman switched to full back on a regular basis in 1991-92.

Steadman's season-by-season try totals for Castleford are as follows:

	App.	Tries
1989-90	26	17
1990-91	32+1	23
1991-92	35+1	29
1992-93	24+1	9
1993-94	40	16
1994-95	23+3	14
Totals	**180+6**	**108**

LEE CROOKS took his points total for Castleford to 1,003 with his best match tally for the club of 20 from 10 goals in the 52-10 Division One home defeat of Hull on 27 November.

He then passed the 500-goals mark for the club with five in the 18-16 Stones Bitter Championship home defeat of St. Helens on 29 January.

Crooks reached 1,000 career goals with the last of four in a 27-6 Division One win at Featherstone Rovers on 14 April. His end-of-season total stood at 1,008 goals made up of 545 for Castleford, 400 Hull and 31 Leeds plus 32 in representative matches.

The former Great Britain forward began his professional career as a 17-year-old with Hull, making his debut in a 15-10 Division One home defeat of Salford on 30 November

162

1980. He moved to Leeds in June 1987 for a then world record £150,000. Crooks made his Leeds debut in the second row in a 38-12 Division One home defeat of Leigh on 30 August 1987 when he scored a try and two goals.

Castleford signed him for the same amount three years later and he made his debut at prop in a 39-12 Silk Cut Challenge Cup preliminary round defeat at St. Helens on 30 January 1990.

His season-by-season totals for Castleford are as follows:

	App.	T	G	Pts
1989-90	6+1	1	14	32
1990-91	31+1	4	61	138
1991-92	31+1	5	111	242
1992-93	34	2	112	232
1993-94	39	2	136(1)	279
1994-95	30+1	2	111	230
Totals	**171+4**	**16**	**545(1)**	**1,153**

( ) denotes drop goals included in total.

His season-by-season goals figures for other clubs are as follows:

	App.	Goals
Hull		
1980-81	3+2	—
1981-82	35+7	118(3)
1982-83	41	115(2)
1983-84	19+1	36
1984-85	33	27
1985-86	30	53(1)
1986-87	35+2	51(5)
Leeds		
1987-88	14+1	30(2)
1988-89	32	1
1989-90	9	—
Totals		
Hull	196+12	400(11)
Leeds	55+1	31(2)
Castleford	171+4	545(1)
Britain	17+2	18(1)
Tours	14+4	8Not incl. Tests
England	1	4
Yorkshire	3	2
Totals	**457+23**	**1,008**

SHAUN EDWARDS of Wigan reached the 1,000 points mark for the club with a try in the 34-12 Regal Trophy second round home defeat of Rochdale Hornets on 4 December.

The half back's total of 1,046 points at the end of the season was made up of 250 tries and 24 goals including one drop goal. He has played in 421 matches for Wigan, including 11 substitute appearances.

He scored his 250th try in the 69-12 Stones Bitter Premiership final defeat of Leeds at Old Trafford, Manchester.

His best match tally is 40 points from a club record-equalling 10 tries in a 78-0 Lancashire Cup second round away win aganst Swinton on 29 September 1992. They were both County Cup records and, playing at scrum half, his 10 tries were the most by a non-winger in any match. In addition, Edwards has thrice scored four tries in a match for Wigan, plus six other hat-tricks.

He was the game's top tryscorer in 1991-92 with 40, second in 1992-93 with 46, including three for Great Britain, and has finished in the top 10 on three other occasions.

The former schoolboy international signed for Wigan on his 17th birthday – 17 October 1983 – and made his debut at stand off in a 30-13 John Player Special Trophy first round home defeat of York on 6 November 1983.

Edwards has also scored 88 points in representative matches including 15 Test tries for Great Britain.

The half back's season-by-season scoring record for Wigan is as follows:

	App.	T	G	Pts
1983-84	24	6	1	26
1984-85	34	11	1	46
1985-86	33+3	14	0	56
1986-87	41	24	6	108
1987-88	32+2	17	0	68
1988-89	31+1	15	0	60
1989-90	32+1	25	10	120
1990-91	33+1	16	1	66
1991-92	37	40	2	164
1992-93	44	43	1(1)	173
1993-94	35+2	19	0	76
1994-95	34+1	20	2(1)	83
Totals	**410+11**	**250**	**24(2)**	**1,046**

( ) denotes drop goal included in total.

Having passed the 1,000-points mark in December 1994, Wigan skipper Shaun Edwards lifts the Silk Cut Challenge Cup at Wembley in April 1995.

LEADING SCORERS 1895-1977

	TRIES	GOALS	POINTS
1895-96	Hurst (Oldham) 28	Lorimer (Manningham).....35	Cooper (Bradford).......... 106
			Lorimer (Manningham)... 106
1896-97	Hannah (Hunslet)............19	Goldthorpe (Hunslet)........26	Rigg (Halifax)............... 112
		Sharpe (Liversedge)...........26	
1897-98	Hoskins (Salford).............30	Goldthorpe (Hunslet)........66	Goldthorpe (Hunslet)...... 135
1898-99	Williams (Oldham) 39	Goldthorpe (Hunslet)........67	Jaques (Hull)................ 169
1899-00	Williams (Oldham) 36	Cooper (Bradford).............39	Williams (Oldham) 108
1900-01	Williams (Oldham) 47	Goldthorpe (Hunslet)........44	Williams (Oldham) 141
1901-02	Wilson (Broughton R.) 38	James (Broughton R.)........75	Lomas (Salford) 172
1902-03	Evans (Leeds).................27	Goldthorpe (Hunslet)........48	Davies (Batley) 136
1903-04	Hogg (Broughton R.) 34	Lomas (Salford) 66	Lomas (Salford) 222
1904-05	Dechan (Bradford)...........31	Ferguson (Oldham)...........50	Lomas (Salford) 146
1905-06	Leytham (Wigan) 40	Ferguson (Oldham)...........49	Leytham (Wigan) 160
1906-07	Eccles (Halifax)...............41	Lomas (Salford) 86	Lomas (Salford) 280
1907-08	Leytham (Wigan) 44	Goldthorpe (Hunslet)...... 101	Goldthorpe (Hunslet)...... 217
1908-09	Miller (Wigan) 49	Lomas (Salford) 88	Lomas (Salford) 272
	Williams (Halifax) 49		
1909-10	Leytham (Wigan) 48	Carmichael (Hull K.R.) 78	Leytham (Wigan) 232
1910-11	Kitchen (Huddersfield) 41	Carmichael (Hull K.R.) .. 129	Carmichael (Hull K.R.) .. 261
1911-12	Rosenfeld (Huddersfield) 78	Carmichael (Hull K.R.) .. 127	Carmichael (Hull K.R.) ..254
1912-13	Rosenfeld (Huddersfield) 56	Carmichael (Hull K.R.) 93	Thomas (Wigan)............ 198
1913-14	Rosenfeld (Huddersfield) 80	Holland (Huddersfield) ... 131	Holland (Huddersfield) ... 268
1914-15	Rosenfeld (Huddersfield) 56	Gronow (Huddersfield) 136	Gronow (Huddersfield) 284
● Competitive matches suspended during war years			
1918-19	Francis (Hull)..................25	Kennedy (Hull) 54	Kennedy (Hull) 135
1919-20	Moorhouse (Huddersfield)....39	Gronow (Huddersfield) 148	Gronow (Huddersfield) 332
1920-21	Stone (Hull) 41	Kennedy (Hull) 108	Kennedy (Hull) 264
1921-22	Farrar (Oldham)...............49	Sullivan (Wigan)............ 100	Farrar (Oldham)............. 213
1922-23	Ring (Wigan) 41	Sullivan (Wigan)............ 161	Sullivan (Wigan)............ 349
1923-24	Ring (Wigan) 49	Sullivan (Wigan)............ 158	Sullivan (Wigan)............ 319
1924-25	Ring (Wigan) 54	Sullivan (Wigan)............ 138	Sullivan (Wigan)............ 282
1925-26	Ring (Wigan) 63	Sullivan (Wigan)............ 131	Sullivan (Wigan)............ 274
1926-27	Ellaby (St. Helens)...........55	Sullivan (Wigan)............ 149	Sullivan (Wigan)............ 322
1927-28	Ellaby (St. Helens)...........37	Thompson (Leeds)......... 106	Thompson (Leeds)......... 233
1928-29	Brown (Wigan) 44	Sullivan (Wigan)............ 107	Sullivan (Wigan)............ 226
	Mills (Huddersfield) 44		
1929-30	Ellaby (St. Helens)...........39	Thompson (Leeds)......... 111	Thompson (Leeds)......... 243
1930-31	Harris, E. (Leeds) 58	Sullivan (Wigan)............ 133	Sullivan (Wigan)............ 278
1931-32	Mills (Huddersfield) 50	Sullivan (Wigan)............ 117	Sullivan (Wigan)............ 249
1932-33	Harris, E. (Leeds) 57	Sullivan (Wigan)............ 146	Sullivan (Wigan)............ 307
1933-34	Brown (Salford) 45	Sullivan (Wigan)............ 194	Sullivan (Wigan)............ 406
1934-35	Morley (Wigan) 49	Sullivan (Wigan)............ 165	Sullivan (Wigan)............ 348
1935-36	Harris, E. (Leeds) 63	Sullivan (Wigan)............ 117	Sullivan (Wigan)............ 246
1936-37	Harris, E. (Leeds) 40	Sullivan (Wigan)............ 120	Sullivan (Wigan)............ 258
1937-38	Harris, E. (Leeds) 45	Sullivan (Wigan)............ 135	Sullivan (Wigan)............ 285

(continued)

	TRIES	GOALS	POINTS
1938-39	Markham (Huddersfield) 39	Sullivan (Wigan) 124	Risman (Salford) 267

● For the next six seasons emergency war-time competitions resulted in a reduction of matches and players were allowed to "guest" for other clubs

	TRIES	GOALS	POINTS
1939-40	Batten (Hunslet) 38	Hodgson (Swinton) 98	Hodgson (Swinton) 208
1940-41	Walters (Bradford N.) 32	Lockwood (Halifax) 70	Belshaw (Warrington) 174
1941-42	Francis (Barrow) 30	Lockwood (Halifax) 91	Lockwood (Halifax) 185
1942-43	Batten (Hunslet) 24	Lockwood (Halifax) 65	Lockwood (Halifax) 136
1943-44	Lawrenson (Wigan) 21	Horne (Barrow) 57	Horne (Barrow) 144
1944-45	Batten (Bradford N.) 41	Stott (Wakefield T.) 51	Stott (Wakefield T.) 129

● Normal peace-time rugby resumed

	TRIES	GOALS	POINTS
1945-46	Batten (Bradford N.) 35	Ledgard (Dewsbury).........89	Bawden (Huddersfield) 239
1946-47	Bevan (Warrington)...........48	Miller (Hull)................. 103	Bawden (Huddersfield) 243
1947-48	Bevan (Warrington)...........57	Ward (Wigan) 141	Ward (Wigan)................ 312
1948-49	Cooper (Huddersfield) 60	Ward (Wigan) 155	Ward (Wigan)................ 361
1949-50	Nordgren (Wigan)............57	Gee (Wigan) 133	Palin (Warrington) 290
		Palin (Warrington) 133	
1950-51	Bevan (Warrington)...........68	Cook (Leeds)................. 155	Cook (Leeds)................ 332
1951-52	Cooper (Huddersfield) 71	Ledgard (Leigh) 142	Horne (Barrow) 313
1952-53	Bevan (Warrington)...........72	Bath (Warrington) 170	Bath (Warrington) 379
1953-54	Bevan (Warrington)...........67	Metcalfe (St. Helens)...... 153	Metcalfe (St. Helens)...... 369
		Bath (Warrington) 153	
1954-55	Cooper (Huddersfield) 66	Ledgard (Leigh) 178	Ledgard (Leigh)............. 374
1955-56	McLean (Bradford N.)......61	Ledgard (Leigh) 155	Bath (Warrington) 344
1956-57	Boston (Wigan) 60	Jones (Leeds)................ 194	Jones (Leeds)................ 496
1957-58	Sullivan (Wigan) 50	Ganley (Oldham)............ 219	Ganley (Oldham)............ 453
1958-59	Vollenhoven (St. Helens) 62	Ganley (Oldham)............ 190	Griffiths (Wigan) 394
1959-60	Vollenhoven (St. Helens) 54	Rhodes (St. Helens) 171	Fox (Wakefield T.).......... 453
		Fox (Wakefield T.).......... 171	
1960-61	Vollenhoven (St. Helens) 59	Rhodes (St. Helens) 145	Rhodes (St. Helens) 338
1961-62	Boston (Wigan) 51	Fox (Wakefield T.).......... 183	Fox (Wakefield T.).......... 456
1962-63	Glastonbury (Work'ton T.) ...41	Coslett (St. Helens)........ 156	Coslett (St. Helens)........ 321
1963-64	Stopford (Swinton)...........45	Coslett (St. Helens)........ 138	Fox (Wakefield T.).......... 313
1964-65	Lake (Wigan).................40	Kellett (Hull K.R.) 150	Killeen (St. Helens) 360
1965-66	Killeen (St. Helens) 32	Killeen (St. Helens) 120	Killeen (St. Helens) 336
	Lake (Wigan).................32		
1966-67	Young (Hull K.R.) 34	Risman (Leeds) 163	Killeen (St. Helens) 353
	Howe (Castleford).............34		
1967-68	Millward (Hull K.R.)........38	Risman (Leeds) 154	Risman (Leeds)............. 332
1968-69	Francis (Wigan) 40	Risman (Leeds) 165	Risman (Leeds)............. 345
1969-70	Atkinson (Leeds).............38	Tyrer (Wigan) 167	Tyrer (Wigan) 385
1970-71	Haigh (Leeds).................40	Coslett (St. Helens)........ 193	Coslett (St. Helens)........ 395
	Jones (St. Helens)............40		
1971-72	Atkinson (Leeds).............36	Coslett (St. Helens)........ 214	Watkins (Salford) 473
	Lamb (Bradford N.).........36		
1972-73	Atkinson (Leeds).............39	Watkins (Salford) 221	Watkins (Salford) 493
1973-74	Fielding (Salford) 49	Watkins (Salford) 183	Watkins (Salford) 438
1974-75	Dunn (Hull K.R.) 42	Fox (Hull K.R.).............. 146	Fox (Hull K.R.)............. 333
1975-76	Richards (Salford)............37	Watkins (Salford) 175	Watkins (Salford) 385
1976-77	Wright (Widnes) 31	Lloyd (Castleford) 163	Lloyd (Castleford) 341

LEADING SCORERS 1977-94

TRIES

1977-78
Stuart Wright (Widnes) 33
Keith Fielding (Salford) 31
Eddie Cunningham (St. Helens)............................30
John Bevan (Warrington) 30
Steve Fenton (Castleford) 30
Green Vigo (Wigan)..29
Peter Glynn (St. Helens) 28
David Smith (Leeds)..28
Terry Morgan (York) 27
Bruce Burton (Castleford)...................................27

1978-79
Steve Hartley (Hull K.R.) 35
Stuart Wright (Widnes) 28
David Barends (Bradford N.) 25
Phil Lowe (Hull K.R.)..25
Paul Prendiville (Hull).......................................25
Keith Fielding (Salford) 24
David Redfearn (Bradford N.) 23
Roy Mathias (St. Helens) 22
Graham Bray (Hull)..21
Keiron O'Loughlin (Wigan)................................21
Clive Sullivan (Hull K.R.)...................................21

1979-80
Keith Fielding (Salford) 30
Steve Hubbard (Hull K.R.) 30
Geoff Munro (Oldham)......................................29
Ian Ball (Barrow)..27
Keith Bentley (Widnes)......................................27
Peter Glynn (St. Helens) 27
Roy Mathias (St. Helens) 27
John Bevan (Warrington) 26
David Redfearn (Bradford N.)..............................26
David Smith (Leeds)..24

1980-81
John Crossley (York)..35
Terry Richardson (Castleford)..............................28
Steve Hubbard (Hull K.R.) 25
Steve Hartley (Hull K.R.) 23
Paul McDermott (York) 23
Ian Slater (Huddersfield)....................................23
Des Drummond (Leigh) 20
Ian Ball (Barrow) 19
John Bevan (Warrington) 19
Peter Cramp (Huddersfield) 19
Gary Hyde (Castleford)......................................19
Denis Ramsdale (Wigan)....................................19

1981-82
John Jones (Workington T.)................................31
Des Drummond (Leigh) 26
John Basnett (Widnes)..26
Ray Ashton (Oldham)..26
Mick Morgan (Carlisle)......................................25
Steve Hartley (Hull K.R.) 23
Lyn Hopkins (Workington T.)..............................23
Terry Day (Hull) 23
Steve Evans (Hull) 22
David Hobbs (Featherstone R.) 21
David Moll (Keighley)..21

1982-83
Bob Eccles (Warrington) 37
Steve Evans (Hull) 28
John Crossley (Fulham) 27
Tommy David (Cardiff C.) 26
David Topliss (Hull) 24
Hussain M'Barki (Fulham)..................................23
Gary Hyde (Castleford)......................................22
Paul McDermott (York)......................................22
James Leuluai (Hull) 21
Phil Ford (Warrington) 20
Garry Clark (Hull K.R.) 20

1983-84
Garry Schofield (Hull) 38
Joe Lydon (Widnes)..28
Graham King (Hunslet) 28
John Woods (Leigh) 27
John Basnett (Widnes)..26
Carl Gibson (Batley) 26
Steve Herbert (Barrow)......................................25
Graham Steadman (York) 25
Gary Prohm (Hull K.R.)......................................25
Garry Clark (Hull K.R.) 24

1984-85
Ellery Hanley (Bradford N.) 55
Gary Prohm (Hull K.R.)......................................45
Henderson Gill (Wigan)......................................34
Barry Ledger (St. Helens) 30
Mal Meninga (St. Helens) 28
Vince Gribbin (Whitehaven) 27
Carl Gibson (Batley) 26
Gary Peacham (Carlisle) 25
Ged Byrne (Salford)..25
Steve Evans (Hull) 24
John Ferguson (Wigan) 24

1985-86
Steve Halliwell (Leigh) 49
Ellery Hanley (Wigan)..38
Peter Lister (Bramley)..34
John Henderson (Leigh) 31

Tommy Frodsham (Blackpool B.)............................30
Phil Fox (Leigh)...29
Stewart Williams (Barrow)................................27
Brian Garrity (Runcorn H.) 24
Carl Gibson (Leeds)..23
David Beck (Workington T.)..............................23

1986-87
Ellery Hanley (Wigan).......................................63
Garry Schofield (Hull).......................................37
Henderson Gill (Wigan).....................................32
Derek Bate (Swinton)..31
Phil Ford (Bradford N.).....................................30
John Henderson (Leigh)....................................27
Shaun Edwards (Wigan) 26
Brian Johnson (Warrington)..............................25
Joe Lydon (Wigan)...24
Brian Dunn (Rochdale H.) 23
Barry Ledger (St. Helens) 23
Kevin McCormack (St. Helens)..........................23

1987-88
Martin Offiah (Widnes) 44
Ellery Hanley (Wigan).......................................36
Garry Schofield (Leeds).....................................25
Carl Gibson (Leeds)..24
Andy Goodway (Wigan).....................................23
Kevin Pape (Carlisle) 23
Shaun Edwards (Wigan) 21
Des Foy (Oldham) 21
Peter Smith (Featherstone R.) 21
Chris Bibb (Featherstone R.)..............................20
Mark Conway (Wakefield T.) 20
Mark Elia (St. Helens) 20
Les Quirk (St. Helens) 20

1988-89
Martin Offiah (Widnes) 60
Barry Ledger (Leigh)...34
Derek Bate (Swinton)..32
Ellery Hanley (Wigan).......................................29
Peter Lister (Bramley).......................................28
Daryl Powell (Sheffield E.)................................28
Peter Lewis (Bramley).......................................26
Les Quirk (St. Helens) 24
Grant Anderson (Castleford) 24
Paul Burns (Barrow) 24

1989-90
Martin Offiah (Widnes) 45
Greg Austin (Hull K.R.).....................................38
Anthony Sullivan (Hull K.R.) 35
Mark Preston (Wigan).......................................33
Gerald Cordle (Bradford N.) 32
Steve Larder (Castleford) 29
Paul Lord (Oldham) 29
Shaun Edwards (Wigan) 26
Andy Goodway (Wigan).....................................26

John Cogger (Oldham) 24
St. John Ellis (Castleford) 24
Wilf George (Halifax)..24
Mark Lord (Rochdale H.) 24
Owen Simpson (Keighley) 24

1990-91
Martin Offiah (Widnes) 49
Greg Austin (Halifax)..47
Martin Wood (Halifax)......................................31
Adrian Hadley (Salford).....................................31
Jonathan Davies (Widnes) 30
Ellery Hanley (Wigan).......................................29
Les Quirk (St. Helens) 26
Alan Hunte (St. Helens) 26
Garry Schofield (Leeds) 25
Graham Steadman (Castleford)..........................23
Andy Currier (Widnes) 23
John Devereux (Widnes) 23

1991-92
Shaun Edwards (Wigan) 40
John Devereux (Widnes) 35
Iva Ropati (Oldham) 33
Greg Austin (Halifax)..33
Vince Gribbin (Whitehaven) 31
Graham Steadman (Castleford)..........................31
Martin Offiah (Wigan).......................................30
David Myers (Wigan)...29
Paul Newlove (Featherstone R.).........................28
Mark Preston (Halifax)......................................27

1992-93
Paul Newlove (Featherstone R.) 52
Shaun Edwards (Wigan) 46
Ellery Hanley (Leeds) 34
Owen Simpson (Featherstone R.) 34
Martin Offiah (Wigan).......................................32
Alan Hunte (St. Helens) 30
John Wasyliw (Keighley C.) 29
Martin Pearson (Featherstone R.).......................29
Greg Austin (Halifax)..27
Martin Wood (Keighley C.) 27

1993-94
Mark Johnson (London C.) 43
St. John Ellis (Castleford) 40
Paul Newlove (Bradford N.) 37
Martin Offiah (Wigan).......................................37
Stuart Cocker (Workington T.) 35
Nick Pinkney (Keighley C.)...............................31
Mark Riley (London C.).....................................30
Carl Hall (Bradford N.) 27
Darren Moxon (Batley)......................................27
Jason Critchley (Salford) 25
John Bentley (Halifax).......................................25
Ellery Hanley (Leeds) 25

GOALS

● including drop goals

1977-78

Geoff Pimblett (St. Helens)	178
Steve Hesford (Warrington)	158
John Woods (Leigh)	149
Iain MacCorquodale (Workington T.)	138
Paul Woods (Widnes)	122
David Watkins (Salford)	110
Keith Mumby (Bradford N.)	107
Geoff "Sammy" Lloyd (Castleford)	104
Neil Fox (Bradford N.)	95
Willie Oulton (Leeds)	80

1978-79

Geoff "Sammy" Lloyd (Hull)	172
Steve Hesford (Warrington)	170
Mick Burke (Widnes)	140
Iain MacCorquodale (Workington T.)	114
Geoff Pimblett (St. Helens)	105
Graham Beale (Keighley)	96
John Woods (Leigh)	96
Jimmy Birts (Halifax)	86
George Fairbairn (Wigan)	86
Paul Norton (Castleford)	82

1979-80

Steve Quinn (Featherstone R.)	163
Steve Hubbard (Hull K.R.)	138
Steve Rule (Salford)	134
Steve Hesford (Warrington)	128
Mick Burke (Widnes)	127
Ian Ball (Barrow)	119
Steve Diamond (Wakefield T.)	116
Eric Fitzsimons (Oldham)	108
Mick Parrish (Hunslet)	98
Jimmy Birts (Halifax)	97

1980-81

Steve Hesford (Warrington)	147
Steve Quinn (Featherstone R.)	123
Steve Diamond (Wakefield T.)	112
Mick Burke (Widnes)	110
Steve Hubbard (Hull K.R.)	109
Ian Ball (Barrow)	104
Jimmy Birts (Halifax)	100
Graham Beale (Keighley)	97
Mick Parrish (Oldham)	95
George Fairbairn (Wigan)	94

1981-82

Lyn Hopkins (Workington T.)	190
George Fairbairn (Hull K.R.)	168
Mick Parrish (Oldham)	164
John Woods (Leigh)	158
Steve Rule (Salford)	130
Kevin Dick (Leeds)	125
Steve Quinn (Featherstone R.)	120
Malcolm Agar (Halifax)	119
Lee Crooks (Hull)	118
Steve Hesford (Warrington)	116

1982-83

Steve Diamond (Fulham)	136
Eric Fitzsimons (Hunslet)	121
Lee Crooks (Hull)	120
Bob Beardmore (Castleford)	117
Steve Hesford (Warrington)	113
Steve Fenwick (Cardiff C.)	111
Ken Jones (Swinton)	110
Colin Whitfield (Wigan)	104
Shaun Kilner (Bramley)	104
Steve Quinn (Featherstone R.)	98

1983-84

Steve Hesford (Warrington)	142
Bob Beardmore (Castleford)	142
Lyn Hallett (Cardiff C.)	140
Eric Fitzsimons (Hunslet)	131
John Woods (Leigh)	124
Colin Whitfield (Wigan)	122
Ian Ball (Barrow)	104
Mick Parrish (Oldham)	101
Malcolm Agar (Halifax)	94
Steve Tickle (Barrow)	91

1984-85

Sean Day (St. Helens)	157
George Fairbairn (Hull K.R.)	141
Peter Wood (Runcorn H.)	126
Graham Steadman (York)	122
Clive Griffiths (Salford)	118
Mick Parrish (Oldham)	117
Garry Schofield (Hull)	105
David Creasser (Leeds)	102
Malcolm Agar (Halifax)	87
Ken Jones (Swinton)	87

1985-86

Chris Johnson (Leigh)	173
David Stephenson (Wigan)	128
David Noble (Doncaster)	118
Kevin Harcombe (Rochdale H.)	115
Shaun Kilner (Bramley)	110
John Dorahy (Hull K.R.)	101
John Woods (Bradford N.)	98
David Creasser (Leeds)	84
Dean Carroll (Carlisle)	83
Gary Smith (Workington T.)	83

1986-87

Paul Loughlin (St. Helens)	190
Paul Bishop (Warrington)	117
David Noble (Doncaster)	114
Colin Whitfield (Halifax)	109
Alan Platt (Hunslet)	102
Paul Topping (Swinton)	100
Chris Johnson (Leigh)	86
Martin Ketteridge (Castleford)	80
David Wood (Rochdale H.)	80
Steve Quinn (Featherstone R.)	77

1987-88

John Woods (Warrington)................................. 152
Steve Quinn (Featherstone R.)........................... 128
Kevin Harcombe (Wakefield T.)......................... 116
Paul Loughlin (St. Helens) 114
Gary Pearce (Hull) 111
Mike Smith (Springfield B.).............................. 98
David Stephenson (Leeds)................................ 95
Mike Fletcher (Hull K.R.) 94
David Hobbs (Bradford N.).............................. 83
Ken Jones (Salford) 79

1988-89

Mark Aston (Sheffield E.) 148
Martin Ketteridge (Castleford)........................... 129
David Hobbs (Bradford N.).............................. 118
Chris Johnson (Leigh)..................................... 117
Dean Marwood (Barrow).................................. 115
Paul Loughlin (St. Helens) 113
David Noble (Doncaster) 110
John Woods (Warrington)................................. 107
Andy Currier (Widnes).................................... 107
Steve Turner (Rochdale H.) 104

1989-90

Mike Fletcher (Hull K.R.) 199
Paul Loughlin (St. Helens) 145
Duncan Platt (Oldham) 126
Colin Maskill (Leeds)..................................... 114
Mark Conway (Wakefield T.) 107
David Hobbs (Bradford N.).............................. 104
Paul Eastwood (Hull)..................................... 101
Mark Aston (Sheffield E.) 99
Jonathan Davies (Widnes) 98
Steve Turner (Rochdale H.) 98

1990-91

Steve Kerry (Salford) 177
Frano Botica (Wigan)...................................... 126
Paul Eastwood (Hull)..................................... 119
Jonathan Davies (Widnes) 112
Simon Irving (Leeds)...................................... 99
Graham Sullivan (Ryedale-York) 94
Paul Loughlin (St. Helens) 94
Alan Platt (Halifax) 91
Barry Vickers (Carlisle).................................... 88
Tim Lumb (Hunslet)....................................... 85

1991-92

Frano Botica (Wigan)...................................... 161
Steve Carroll (Bramley).................................... 138
Deryck Fox (Featherstone R.) 115
Lee Crooks (Castleford) 113
David Hobbs (Bradford N.).............................. 110
Chris Vasey (Dewsbury)................................... 109
Paul Eastwood (Hull)..................................... 108
Steve Parrish (Batley)...................................... 106
Mark Aston (Sheffield E.) 104
Jonathan Davies (Widnes) 99

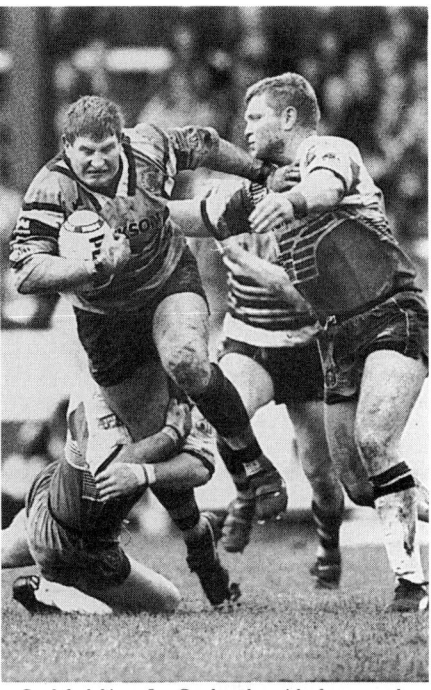

Castleford skipper Lee Crooks, a hat-trick of top ten goals appearances from 1992-94.

1992-93

John Wasyliw (Keighley C.)............................... 187
Frano Botica (Wigan)...................................... 184
Dean Marwood (Workington T.) 179
Martin Pearson (Featherstone R.) 145
Paul Bishop (Halifax) 118
Lee Crooks (Castleford) 116
Jonathan Davies (Widnes) 116
Steve Gartland (Rochdale H.) 105
Steve Maguire (Whitehaven) 95
Andy Precious (Hunslet)................................... 90

1993-94

Frano Botica (Wigan)...................................... 188
John Gallagher (London C.)............................... 159
Deryck Fox (Bradford N.)................................. 148
Lee Crooks (Castleford) 137
Jonathan Davies (Warrington) 132
Mark Conway (Dewsbury)................................ 130
Robert Turner (Doncaster)................................ 123
Mark Aston (Sheffield E.) 123
Graham Holroyd (Leeds) 103
Dean Marwood (Workington T.) 100

DROP GOALS

1977-78	Jim Fiddler (Bramley, Leigh)	10
1978-79	Norman Turley (Blackpool B.)	18
1979-80	Tony Dean (Hunslet)	18
1980-81	Arnold Walker (Whitehaven)	22
1981-82	Malcolm Agar (Halifax)	17
	Steve Donlan (Leigh)	17
1982-83	Harry Pinner (St. Helens)	13
1983-84	Lyn Hallett (Cardiff C.)	29
1984-85	Peter Wood (Runcorn H.)	28
1985-86	Paul Bishop (Warrington)	13
1986-87	Billy Platt (Mansfield M.)	18
1987-88	Wayne Parker (Hull K.R.)	15
1988-89	Gary Pearce (Hull)	16
1989-90	Paul Harkin (Bradford N.)	12
1990-91	Ray Ashton (Workington T.)	13
	Dean Carroll (Doncaster)	13
1991-92	Andy Ruane (Leigh)	17
1992-93	Paul Shuttleworth (Dewsbury)	11
1993-94	Jonathan Davies (Warrington)	14

POINTS

1977-78	Geoff Pimblett (St. Helens)	381
1978-79	Geoff "Sammy" Lloyd (Hull)	373
1979-80	Steve Quinn (Featherstone R.)	375
1980-81	Steve Hesford (Warrington)	310
1981-82	Lyn Hopkins (Workington T.)	446
1982-83	Steve Diamond (Fulham)	308
1983-84	John Woods (Leigh)	355
1984-85	Sean Day (St. Helens)	362
1985-86	Chris Johnson (Leigh)	400
1986-87	Paul Loughlin (St. Helens)	424
1987-88	John Woods (Warrington)	351
1988-89	Mark Aston (Sheffield E.)	307
1989-90	Mike Fletcher (Hull K.R.)	450
1990-91	Steve Kerry (Salford)	427
1991-92	Frano Botica (Wigan)	364
1992-93	John Wasyliw (Keighley C.)	490
1993-94	Frano Botica (Wigan)	422

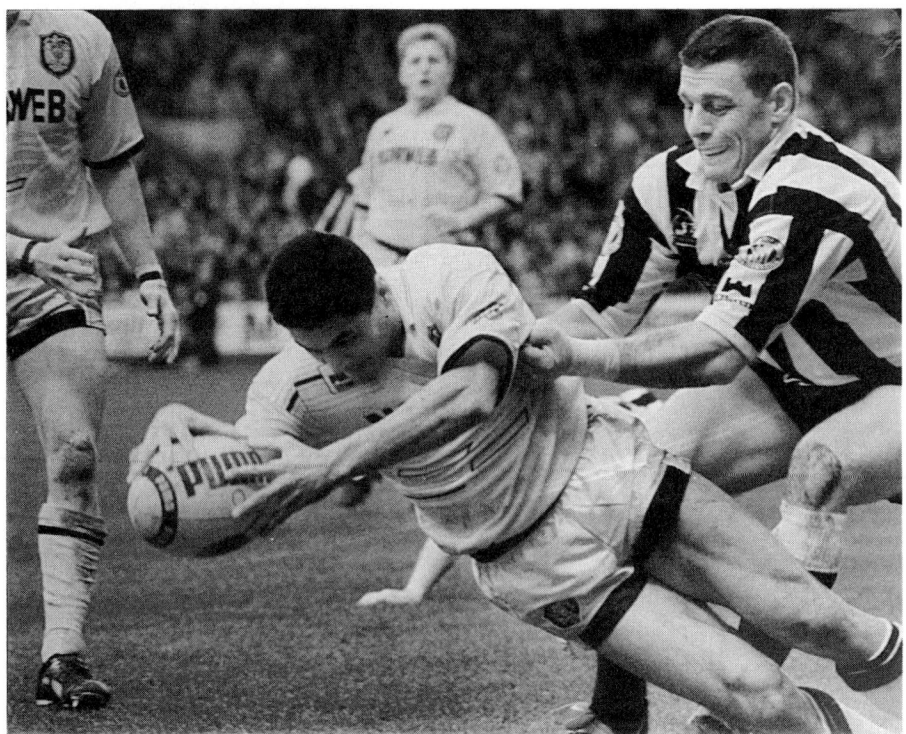

Wigan's former RU All Black Frano Botica, top points scorer in 1991-92, 1993-94 and 1994-95.

ALL-TIME RECORDS

Most goals in a match:
22 by Jim Sullivan (Wigan) v. Flimby & Fothergill (Challenge Cup), 14 February 1925

Most goals in a season:
DAVID WATKINS holds the record for most goals in a season with 221 — all for Salford — in 1972-73. Watkins played and scored a goal in every match that season as follows:

1972

Aug.	19	Leeds .... (H)	5
	23	Featherstone R. ....(A)	3
	26	Whitehaven ....(A)	4
	28	Swinton .... (H)	1
Sep.	1	Oldham ....(LC) (H)	10
	9	Leeds..................................... (A)	2
	15	Rochdale H. ....(LC) (H)	11
	17	Leigh .... (A)	6
	24	Barrow ....(JP) (A)	4
	29	Huyton..................................... (H)	10
Oct.	3	Oldham ....(FT) (A)	4
	6	Wigan ....(LC) (A)	4
	8	Blackpool B. ....(A)	5
	13	Blackpool B. ....(H)	8
	21	Swinton .... (LCF)	5
Nov.	5	Huyton ....(A)	8
	10	Rochdale H. ....(H)	6
	17	Warrington ....(A)	4
	19	New Zealand..........................(H)	10
	24	Dewsbury...................... (JP) (H)	4
	26	Workington T. ....(H)	6
Dec.	1	Barrow .... (H)	9
	10	Bradford N. ....(JP) (H)	9
	13	Oldham .... (A)	4
	15	Leigh ....(H)	3
	24	Bradford N. ....(A)	5
	26	Workington T. ....(A)	3
	30	Hull K.R. .... (JP) (A)	5

1973

Jan.	3	Bradford N. ....(H)	6
	7	Rochdale H. ....(A)	2
	12	Featherstone R. ....(H)	4
	28	Featherstone R. .... (RL Cup) (A)	4
Feb.	2	Whitehaven ....(H)	4
	11	Barrow ....(A)	5
	23	St. Helens ....(H)	3
Mar.	7	Widnes ....(A)	3
	9	Dewsbury.................................(H)	3
	16	St. Helens .... (A)	2
	24	Leeds........................(JP Final)	2
	30	Warrington .... (H)	1
Apr.	6	Widnes .... (H)	4
	13	Oldham .... (H)	3
	15	Dewsbury................................(A)	2
	17	Wigan ....(A)	3
	20	Swinton .... (A)	7
	23	Wigan .... (H)	3
	29	Rochdale H. ....(top 16) (H)	2

	App	Goals
League	34	147
Lancs Cup	4	30
John Player	5	24
Tour match	1	10
RL Cup....................................	1	4
Floodlit Cup	1	4
Top 16......................................	1	2
Totals	**47**	**221**

Fastest goals century:
Four players share the record of scoring the fastest 100 goals from the start of a season in terms of number of matches played. They are BERNARD GANLEY, DAVID WATKINS, STEVE QUINN and JOHN WASYLIW, who achieved the century in 18 matches.

Ganley reached 100 goals on 16 November 1957, after playing 17 matches for Oldham and one for Great Britain.

Watkins scored his 100th goal on 17 November 1972, all for Salford.

Quinn scored his 100th goal on 16 December 1979, all for Featherstone Rovers.

Wasyliw equalled the record with his 100th goal for Keighley Cougars on 31 January 1993.

Most goals in a career:
JIM SULLIVAN holds the record for most goals in a career with 2,867 between 1921-22 and 1945-46. He scored a century of goals in every season after leaving Welsh Rugby Union for Wigan until the war interrupted the 1939-40 campaign. The Test full back played all of his club rugby for Wigan apart from war-time appearances with Bradford Northern, Dewsbury and Keighley.

Sullivan's total includes 441 in representative matches, including three tours of Australasia. These figures are accepted by the Record Keepers' Club following research by James Carter and Malcolm Bentley.

Most one-point drop goals in a match:
5 by Danny Wilson (Swinton) v. Hunslet (John Player Special), 6 November 1983
Peter Wood (Runcorn H.) v.Batley, 21 October 1984
Paul Bishop (Warrington) at Wigan (Premiership semi-final), 11 May 1986

Most one-point drop goals in a season:
29 by Lyn Hallett (Cardiff C.) 1983-84

Most one-point drop goals in a career:
97 by Norman Turley (Warrington, Runcorn H., Swinton, Blackpool B., Rochdale H., Barrow, Workington T., Trafford B., Whitehaven) 1974-91

Longest successful goal kick:
ARTHUR ATKINSON of Castleford is credited with the longest successful goal kick, covering 75 yards (68.5 metres) to the posts. The centre's wind-assisted penalty kick was taken during Castleford's 20-10 league win at St. Helens on 26 October 1929.

Martin Hodgson of Swinton has often been credited with the longest successful kick, but his goal at Rochdale Hornets on 13 April 1940 was measured at 77¾ yards (71.06m) to beyond the posts where the ball landed. Reports at the time referred to a 58-yard (53m) goal.

● Details of the record kick were discovered following research by Graham Morris.

Most tries in a match:
11 by George West (Hull K.R.) v Brookland Rovers (Challenge Cup), 4 March 1905

Most tries in a career:
BRIAN BEVAN holds the record for most tries in a career with 796 between 1946 and 1964. His season-by-season record is:

1946-47	48
1947-48	57
1948-49	56
1949-50	33
1950-51	68
1951-52	51
1952-53	72
1953-54	67
1954-55	63
1955-56	57
1956-57	17
1957-58	46
1958-59	54
1959-60	40
1960-61	35
1961-62	15
1962-63	10
1963-64	7

Totals

Warrington	740
Blackpool Borough	17
Other Nationalities	26
Other representative matches	13
Grand Total	**796**

The Australian winger played his first game for Warrington on 17 November 1945 and his last on 23 April 1962 before having two seasons at Blackpool Borough. His last match for Borough was on 22 February 1964.

Most tries in a season:
ALBERT ROSENFELD holds the record for most tries in a season with 80 — all for Huddersfield — in 1913-14.

Rosenfeld's match-by-match record:

1913			
Sep.	6	York ....(A)	4
	8	Warrington ....(H)	2
	13	Leeds ....(H)	5
	20	Halifax ....(A)	1
	27	Batley...............................(A)	0
Oct.	4	Oldham ....(H)	2
	11	Rochdale H. ....(A)	0
	18	Bramley ....(YC)(H)	2
	25	Dewsbury............................(A)	4
Nov.	1	Halifax ....(YC)(A)	2
	8	Wigan ....(A)	1
	15	Dewsbury.......................(YC)(H)	3
	19	Bradford N. ....(H)	3
	22	Leeds................................(A)	3
	29	Bradford N. ....(Halifax, YCF)	1
Dec.	3	Halifax ....(H)	3
	6	Hunslet ....(A)	2
	13	Rochdale H. ....(H)	3
	20	Hull K.R. ....(A)	2
	25	Hull.................................(A)	1
	26	Wakefield T. ....(H)	3
	27	Hunslet ....(H)	0
1914			
Jan.	1	St. Helens ....(A)	0
	3	Warrington ....(A)	0
	10	York ....(H)	3
	17	Keighley.............................(A)	2
	24	Dewsbury............................(H)	1
	31	Batley...............................(H)	0
Feb.	7	Oldham ....(A)	0
	14	Bramley ....(H)	5
	21	Wigan ....(H)	3
	28	Swinton Park R. ....(RL Cup)(H)	7
Mar.	7	Wakefield T. ....(A)	2
	14	Hull K.R. ....(RL Cup)(A)	2
	18	Bramley..............................(A)	3
	21	Widnes ....(RL Cup)(H)	0
	25	Keighley ....(H)	3
	28	Hull K.R. ....(H)	1
	30	Bradford N. ....(A)	1
Apr.	4	Hull...........(Leeds, RL Cup SF)	0
	11	Hull...................(H) did not play	
	13	St. Helens ....(H)	0
	20	Hull...........(Play-off) (H) did not play	
	25	Salford ......(Leeds, Championship final)	0

	App	Tries
League	33	63
Yorks Cup	4	8
RL Cup	4	9
Play-off	1	0
Totals	**42**	**80**

Most points in a season:
LEWIS JONES holds the record for most points in a season with 496 from 194 goals and 36 tries for Leeds and representative teams in 1956-57.

Jones's match-by-match record:

For Leeds

1956			G	T	Pts
Aug.	17	Halifax.......................... (H)	3	0	6
	22	Bradford N. .... (A)	11	3	31
	25	Wigan..........................(A)	4	0	8
	27	Featherstone R. .... (H)	4	1	11
Sep.	1	Wakefield T. ....(YC) (A)	3	1	9
	8	Dewsbury ....(A)	6	0	12
	15	Warrington.................. (H)	7	0	14
	22	Huddersfield .... (A)	3	0	6
	29	York .... (H)	6	0	12
Oct.	6	Batley ....(A)	4	2	14
	13	Australia .... (H)	Did not play		
	20	Hull K.R. .... (A)	Did not play		
	27	Wigan .... (H)	2	0	4
Nov.	3	Hunslet....................... (A)	1	0	2
	10	Barrow........................ (H)	3	2	12
	17	Halifax........................ (A)	4	0	8
	24	Keighley .... (H)	3	3	15
Dec.	1	Barrow.........................(A)	4	0	8
	8	Bramley ....(A)	5	0	10
	15	Doncaster .... (H)	1	2	8
	22	Bradford N. ...(abandoned) (H)	1	1	5
	25	Batley .... (H)	8	1	19
	29	Keighley ....(A)	3	0	6
1957					
Jan.	5	Hull .... (H)	5	2	16
	12	Warrington...................(A)	0	3	9
	19	St. Helens .... (H)	5	1	13
	26	Doncaster .... (A)	Did not play		
Feb.	2	Huddersfield .... (H)	6	0	12
	9	Wigan...........(RL Cup) (H)	2	1	7
	16	York............................(A)	7	1	17
	23	Warrington.....(RL Cup) (H)	5	1	13
	27	Castleford .... (H)	4	1	11
Mar.	9	Halifax..........(RL Cup) (A)	5	0	10
	16	Wakefield T. .... (H)	5	1	13
	20	Bradford N. .... (H)	5	1	13
	23	Hull .... (A)	2	0	4
	30	Whitehaven ....(Odsal, RL Cup SF)	1	0	2
Apr.	3	Wakefield T. ....(A)	3	0	6
	6	St. Helens .... (A)	0	0	0
	12	Hull K.R. .... (H)	Did not play		
	13	Dewsbury .... (H)	6	2	18
	19	Hunslet....................... (H)	5	2	16
	20	Featherstone R. ....(A)	2	0	4
	22	Castleford .... (A)	2	0	4
	23	Bramley .... (H)	7	1	17
May	4	Oldham.......... (Play-off) (A)	3	0	6
	11	Barrow .....(Wembley, RL Cup final)	0	0	0

Representative matches
For Great Britain:

			G	T	Pts
Jan.	26	France ....(at Leeds)	9	1	21
Mar.	3	France ....(at Toulouse)	5	1	13
Apr.	10	France ....(at St. Helens)	7	1	17

For The Rest:
| Oct. | 3 | Britain XIII .... (at Bradford) | 4 | 0 | 8 |

For RL XIII:
| Oct. | 29 | Australia .... (Leigh) | 3 | 0 | 6 |

	App	G	T	Pts
League	36	147	30	384
RL Cup	5	13	2	32
Yorks Cup	1	3	1	9
Play-off	1	3	0	6
Representative	5	28	3	65
Totals	**48**	**194**	**36**	**496**

Most points in a match:
53 (11t,10g) by George West (Hull K.R.) v. Brookland Rovers (RL Cup), 4 March 1905

Most points in a career:
NEIL FOX holds the record for most points in a career with 6,220 between 1956 and 1979. This total does not include points scored during a spell of club rugby in New Zealand.

Fox was a month short of his 17th birthday when he made his debut for Wakefield Trinity on 10 April 1956. Apart from a brief time at Bradford Northern, Fox had 19 seasons at Wakefield before moving to a succession of clubs in later years.

After a long career as an international centre Fox moved into the forwards and played his last professional match for Bradford in their opening fixture of the 1979-80 season, on 19 August. That match enabled him to join the elite few who have played first team rugby at 40 years of age.

Fox's season-by-season tally is as follows:

	G	T	Pts
1955-56............................	6	0	12
1956-57............................	54	10	138
1957-58............................	124	32	344
1958-59............................	148	28	380
1959-60............................	171	37	453
1960-61............................	94	20	248
1961-62............................	183	30	456
1962 Tour			
Australasia	85	19	227
South Africa	19	4	50
1962-63............................	125	14	292
1963-64............................	125	21	313
1964-65............................	121	13	281
1965-66............................	98	11	229
1966-67............................	144	16	336
1967-68............................	98	18	250
1968-69............................	95	9	217
1969-70............................	17	5	49

(continued)

1970-71	110	12	256
1971-72	84	6	186
1972-73	138	8	300
1973-74	62	8	148
1974-75	146(1)	14	333
1975-76	102(1)	4	215
1976-77	79(1)	6	175
1977-78	95(1)	9	216
1978-79	50	4	112
1979-80	2	0	4

A breakdown of Fox's club and representative totals is as follows:

	App	G	T	Pts
Wakefield T.	574	1,836	272	4,488
Bradford N.	70	85(1)	12	205
Hull K.R.	59	212(2)	16	470
York	13	42	2	90
Bramley	23	73	6	164
Huddersfield	21	73(1)	5	160
Club Totals	**760**	**2,321(4)**	**313**	**5,577**
Yorkshire	17	60	9	147
Britain v. Australia	8	26	3	61
New Zealand	4	11	1	25
France	17	56	10	142
Other representative games including tour	22	101	22	268
Representative Totals	**68**	**254**	**45**	**643**
Grand Totals	**828**	**2,575(4)**	**358**	**6,220**

( ) Figures in brackets are one-point drop goals included in total.

Score-a-match:
The following players have appeared and scored in all of their club's matches in one season:

Jim Hoey (Widnes) 1932-33
Billy Langton (Hunslet) 1958-59
Stuart Ferguson (Leigh) 1970-71
David Watkins (Salford) 1972-73
David Watkins (Salford) 1973-74
John Woods (Leigh) 1977-78
Steve Quinn (Featherstone R.) 1979-80
Mick Parrish (Hunslet) 1979-80
John Gorton (Swinton) 1980-81
Mick Parrish (Oldham) 1981-82
Peter Wood (Runcorn H.) 1984-85
David Noble (Doncaster) 1986-87
Mark Aston (Sheffield E.) 1988-89
Mike Fletcher (Hull K.R.) 1989-90
Steve Carroll (Bramley) 1991-92
Paul Bishop (Halifax) 1992-93
John Wasyliw (Keighley C.) 1992-93
John Schuster (Halifax) 1994-95

Salford utility back David Watkins, holder of the record for the longest scoring run and a score-a-match exponent over two successive seasons.

Longest scoring run:
DAVID WATKINS holds the record for the longest scoring run, playing and scoring in 92 consecutive matches for Salford from 19 August 1972 to 25 April 1974. He totalled 403 goals, 41 tries and 929 points.

Longest run of appearances:
KEITH ELWELL holds the record for the longest run of appearances with one club with a total of 239 for Widnes. The consecutive run started at Wembley in the 1977 Challenge Cup final against Leeds on 7 May, and ended after he played in a Lancashire Cup tie at home to St. Helens on 5 September 1982. He was dropped for the match at Featherstone Rovers a week later. Although he went on as a substitute the record refers to full appearances only. Elwell played as a substitute in the next match and then made a full appearance before his run of all appearances ended at 242.

TEAM
Highest score:
Huddersfield 142 v. Blackpool Gladiators 4 (Regal Trophy)
..... 26 November 1994

Highest score away:
Highfield 4 v. Keighley Cougars 104 (Division Two played at Rochdale Hornets) ....23 April 1995

● The highest score on an opponent's ground is:
Blackpool Gladiators 5 v. Dewsbury 90 (Division Three)
.... 4 April 1993

Widest margin:
Runcorn Highfield 2 v. Leigh 88 (Division Two)
.... 15 January 1989

Widest margin:
As above and
Barrow 138 v. Nottingham City 0 (Regal Trophy)
..... 27 November 1994

Most points in all matches in a season:
1,735 by Wigan from 45 matches in 1994-95 as follows:
30 Division One matches 1,148
  6 Challenge Cup... 230
  5 Regal Trophy 170
  3 Premiership 167
  1 Australia.. 20

Most League points in a season:
1,156 by Leigh from 34 Division Two matches in 1985-86.

Longest winning run:
29 by Wigan from February to October 1987, as follows:
20 Division One, 3 Premiership, 4 Lancashire Cup, 1
Charity Shield and 1 World Club Challenge.

Longest unbeaten run:
43 Cup and League matches, including two draws, by
Huddersfield in 1914-19.
    They were unbeaten in the last 38 matches of 1914-15
and after the interruption of the First World War won their
next five competitive matches — four Yorkshire Cup ties
in 1918-19 and the first League match of 1919-20.

Longest winning run in the League:
31 matches by Wigan. Last 8 matches of 1969-70 and first
23 of 1970-71.
● In 1978-79 Hull won all of their 26 Division Two
matches, the only time a club has won all its League
matches in one season.

Longest losing run:
61 Cup and League matches by Runcorn Highfield from
January 1989 to February 1991. Made up of 55 Division
Two, 2 Challenge Cup, 2 Regal Trophy and 2 Lancs Cup.

Longest run without a win:
75 Cup and League matches by Runcorn Highfield from
October 1988 to March 1991. Made up of 67 Division
Two, 3 Challenge Cup, 3 Regal Trophy and 2 Lancs Cup.

Longest League losing run and run without a win:
Included in the above.
● Only three teams have lost all their matches in a season:
Liverpool City (1906-07)*, Runcorn Highfield (1989-90)
and Nottingham City (1991-92).
*Liverpool drew a League match against Bramley but this
was expunged from the records as the return fixture was
cancelled.

*Hull K.R.'s Mike Fletcher, who played and scored in
every match in 1989-90.*

CHARTS

The following are extended charts of outstanding scoring and appearance records established by British-based players.

*Denotes amateur or non-league team

EIGHT OR MORE TRIES IN A MATCH

11	George West (Hull K.R.) v. Brookland R.*	4 Mar. 1905
10	Lionel Cooper (Huddersfield) v. Keighley	17 Nov. 1951
	Martin Offiah (Wigan) v. Leeds	10 May 1992
	Shaun Edwards (Wigan) at Swinton	29 Sep. 1992
9	Ray Markham (Huddersfield) v. Featherstone R.	21 Sep. 1935
	Greg Austin (Huddersfield) v. Blackpool G.*	26 Nov. 1994
8	Dai Thomas (Dewsbury) v. Liverpool C.	13 Apr. 1907
	Albert Rosenfeld (Huddersfield) v. Wakefield T.	26 Dec. 1911
	Fred Webster (Leeds) v. Coventry	12 Apr. 1913
	Eric Harris (Leeds) v. Bradford N.	14 Sep. 1931
	Lionel Cooper (Huddersfield) v. Yorkshire Amateurs*	11 Sep. 1948
	Keith Williams (Halifax) v. Dewsbury	9 Nov. 1957

14 OR MORE GOALS IN A MATCH

22	Jim Sullivan (Wigan) v. Flimby & Fothergill*	14 Feb. 1925
18	Major Holland (Huddersfield) v. Swinton Park*	28 Feb. 1914
17	Geoff "Sammy" Lloyd (Castleford) v. Millom*	16 Sep. 1973
	Darren Carter (Barrow) v. Nottingham C.*	27 Nov. 1994
16	Paul Loughlin (St. Helens) v. Carlisle	14 Sep. 1986
15	Mick Stacey (Leigh) v. Doncaster	28 Mar. 1976
	John Wasyliw (Keighley C.) v. Nottingham C.	1 Nov. 1992
14	Alf Carmichael (Hull K.R.) v. Merthyr Tydfil	8 Oct. 1910
	Jim Kennedy (Hull) v. Rochdale H.	7 Apr. 1921
	Harold Palin (Warrington) v. Liverpool S.	13 Sep. 1950
	Joe Phillips (Bradford N.) v. Batley	6 Sep. 1952
	Bernard Ganley (Oldham) v. Liverpool C.	4 Apr. 1959
	Bruce Burton (Halifax) v. Hunslet	27 Aug. 1972
	Geoff "Sammy" Lloyd (Hull) v. Oldham	10 Sep. 1978
	Chris Johnson (Leigh) v. Keighley	30 Apr. 1986
	Steve Turner (Rochdale H.) v. Runcorn H.	5 Nov. 1989
	Mike Fletcher (Hull K.R.) v. Whitehaven	18 Mar. 1990
	Colin Armstrong (Hull K.R.) at Nottingham C.	19 Aug. 1990

On tour with Great Britain:

17	Ernest Ward v. Mackay (Australia)	2 Jul. 1946
15	Alf Wood v. South Australia	23 May 1914
	Jim Ledgard v. Wide Bay (Australia)	28 Jun. 1950
	Lewis Jones v. Southern New South Wales (Australia)	21 Aug. 1954
	Eric Fraser v. North Queensland (Australia)	29 Jun. 1958

35 POINTS OR MORE IN A MATCH

53 George West (Hull K.R.) v. Brookland R.★ .... 4 Mar. 1905
44 Jim Sullivan (Wigan) v. Flimby & Fothergill★ .... 14 Feb. 1925
43 Geoff "Sammy" Lloyd (Castleford) v. Millom★ .... 16 Sep. 1973
42 Dean Marwood (Workington T.) v. Highfield .... 1 Nov. 1992
   Dean Marwood (Workington T.)v. Leigh .... 26 Feb. 1995
   Darren Carter (Barrow) v. Nottingham C.★ .... 27 Nov. 1994
40 Paul Loughlin (St. Helens) v. Carlisle .... 14 Sep. 1986
   Martin Offiah (Wigan) v. Leeds .... 10 May 1992
   Shaun Edwards (Wigan) at Swinton .... 29 Sep. 1992
39 James Lomas (Salford) v. Liverpool C. .... 2 Feb. 1907
   Major Holland (Huddersfield) v. Swinton Park★ .... 28 Feb. 1914
38 John Woods (Leigh) v. Blackpool B. .... 11 Sep. 1977
   Bob Beardmore (Castleford) v. Barrow .... 22 Mar. 1987
   John Woods (Leigh) v. Ryedale-York .... 12 Jan. 1992
36 Jim Kennedy (Hull) v. Keighley .... 29 Jan. 1921
   Mick Stacey (Leigh) v. Doncaster .... 28 Mar. 1976
   John Woods (Bradford N.) v. Swinton .... 13 Oct. 1985
   Graham Steadman (Castleford) v. Salford .... 1 Apr. 1990
   John Wasyliw (Keighley C.) v. Nottingham C.★ .... 31 Oct. 1993
   Greg Austin (Huddersfield) v. Blackpool G,★ .... 26 Nov. 1994
35 Jim Bawden (Huddersfield) v. Swinton .... 20 Apr. 1946

Castleford's Graham Steadman (right), scorer of 36 points against Salford in April 1990.

50 TRIES OR MORE IN A SEASON

80 Albert Rosenfeld (Huddersfield)........1913-14
78 Albert Rosenfeld (Huddersfield)........1911-12
72 Brian Bevan (Warrington) 1952-53
71 Lionel Cooper (Huddersfield)..........1951-52
68 Brian Bevan (Warrington) 1950-51
67 Brian Bevan (Warrington) 1953-54
66 Lionel Cooper (Huddersfield)..........1954-55
63 Johnny Ring (Wigan) 1925-26
   Eric Harris (Leeds).......................1935-36
   Jack McLean (Bradford N.)............1951-52
   Brian Bevan (Warrington) 1954-55
   Ellery Hanley (Wigan) 1986-87
62 Tom Van Vollenhoven (St. Helens).....1958-59
61 Jack McLean (Bradford N.)............1955-56
60 Lionel Cooper (Huddersfield)..........1948-49
   Billy Boston (Wigan) 1956-57
   Martin Offiah (Widnes)..................1988-89
59 Lionel Cooper (Huddersfield)..........1950-51
   Jack McLean (Bradford N.)............1952-53
   Tom Van Vollenhoven (St. Helens).....1960-61
58 Eric Harris (Leeds)......................1930-31
57 Eric Harris (Leeds)......................1932-33
   Brian Bevan (Warrington) 1947-48
   Brian Nordgren (Wigan) 1949-50
   Brian Bevan (Warrington) 1955-56
56 Albert Rosenfeld (Huddersfield)........1912-13
   Albert Rosenfeld (Huddersfield)........1914-15
   Brian Bevan (Warrington) 1948-49
55 Alf Ellaby (St. Helens) 1926-27
   Ellery Hanley (Bradford N.) 1984-85
54 Stan Moorhouse (Huddersfield) 1911-12
   Johnny Ring (Wigan) 1924-25
   Brian Bevan (Warrington) 1958-59
   Billy Boston (Wigan) 1958-59
   Tom Van Vollenhoven (St. Helens).....1959-60
53 Ray Markham (Huddersfield) 1935-36
   Martin Offiah (Wigan)...................1994-95
52 Jack Harrison (Hull) 1914-15
   Frank Castle (Barrow) 1951-52
   Jack McLean (Bradford N.)............1953-54
   Paul Newlove (Featherstone R.) 1992-93
   Greg Austin (Huddersfield)............1994-95
51 Brian Bevan (Warrington) 1951-52
   Jim Lewthwaite (Barrow) 1956-57
   Billy Boston (Wigan) 1961-62
50 Ernest Mills (Huddersfield) 1931-32
   Lionel Cooper (Huddersfield)..........1952-53
   Mick Sullivan (H'field and Wigan) ...1957-58

170 GOALS OR MORE IN A SEASON

● Including drop goals

221 David Watkins (Salford) 1972-73
219 Bernard Ganley (Oldham)..............1957-58
214 Kel Coslett (St. Helens)...............1971-72
199 Mike Fletcher (Hull K.R.)...........1989-90
194 Jim Sullivan (Wigan) 1933-34
    Lewis Jones (Leeds) 1956-57
193 Kel Coslett (St. Helens)...............1970-71
    David Watkins (Salford) 1971-72
190 Bernard Ganley (Oldham)..............1958-59
    Lyn Hopkins (Workington T.).......1981-82
    Paul Loughlin (St. Helens)............1986-87
189 Bernard Ganley (Oldham)..............1956-57
188 Frano Botica (Wigan)...................1993-94
187 John Wasyliw (Keighley C.) 1992-93
186 Frano Botica (Wigan)...................1994-95
184 Frano Botica (Wigan)...................1992-93
183 Fred Griffiths (Wigan) 1961-62
    Neil Fox (Wakefield T.) 1961-62
    David Watkins (Salford) 1973-74
181 Billy Langton (Hunslet)................1958-59
179 Dean Marwood (Workington T.)......1992-93
178 Jim Ledgard (Leigh)....................1954-55
    Geoff Pimblett (St. Helens)...........1977-78
177 Steve Kerry (Salford)...................1990-91
176 Fred Griffiths (Wigan) 1958-59
175 David Watkins (Salford) 1975-76
173 Eddie Tees (Bradford N.) 1971-72
    Chris Johnson (Leigh)..................1985-86
172 Geoff "Sammy" Lloyd (Hull) 1978-79
171 Austin Rhodes (St. Helens)...........1959-60
    Neil Fox (Wakefield T.) 1959-60
170 Harry Bath (Warrington)..............1952-53
    Steve Hesford (Warrington)...........1978-79

Workington Town full back Lyn Hopkins, a top ten performer for goals in a season.

370 OR MORE POINTS IN A SEASON

496	Lewis Jones (Leeds)	1956-57
493	David Watkins (Salford)	1972-73
490	John Wasyliw (Keighley C.)	1992-93
476	David Watkins (Salford)	1971-72
456	Neil Fox (Wakefield T.)	1961-62
453	Bernard Ganley (Oldham)	1957-58
	Neil Fox (Wakefield T.)	1959-60
452	Kel Coslett (St. Helens)	1971-72
450	Mike Fletcher (Hull K.R.)	1989-90
446	Lyn Hopkins (Workington T.)	1981-82
438	David Watkins (Salford)	1973-74
427	Steve Kerry (Salford)	1990-91
424	Paul Loughlin (St. Helens)	1986-87
423	Frano Botica (Wigan)	1992-93
422	Frano Botica (Wigan)	1993-94
418	Dean Marwood (Workington T.)	1992-93
408	Frano Botica (Wigan)	1994-95
406	Jim Sullivan (Wigan)	1933-34
405	Martin Pearson (Featherstone R.)	1992-93
400	Chris Johnson (Leigh)	1985-86
399	Austin Rhodes (St. Helens)	1959-60
395	Kel Coslett (St. Helens)	1970-71
394	Fred Griffiths (Wigan)	1958-59
392	Simon Irving (Keighley C.)	1994-95
390	Fred Griffiths (Wigan)	1961-62
385	Colin Tyrer (Wigan)	1969-70
	David Watkins (Salford)	1975-76
384	Bernard Ganley (Oldham)	1956-57
	John Gallagher (London C.)	1993-94
383	Bernard Ganley (Oldham)	1958-59
381	Geoff Pimblett (St. Helens)	1977-78
380	Neil Fox (Wakefield T.)	1958-59
	Billy Langton (Hunslet)	1958-59
379	Harry Bath (Warrington)	1952-53
	Mick Parrish (Oldham)	1981-82
376	Nigel Stephenson (Dewsbury)	1972-73
375	Steve Quinn (Featherstone R.)	1979-80
374	Jim Ledgard (Leigh)	1954-55
373	Geoff "Sammy" Lloyd (Hull)	1978-79
372	John Woods (Leigh)	1981-82

John Woods, scorer of 372 points for Leigh in 1981-82.

300 TRIES OR MORE IN A CAREER

796	Brian Bevan (Warrington, Blackpool B.)	1945-1964
571	Billy Boston (Wigan, Blackpool B.)	1953-1970
446	Alf Ellaby (St. Helens, Wigan)	1926-1939
443	Eric Batten (Wakefield T., Hunslet, Bradford N., Featherstone R.)	1933-1954
441	Lionel Cooper (Huddersfield)	1947-1955
428	Ellery Hanley (Bradford N., Wigan, Leeds)	1978-
415	Johnny Ring (Wigan, Rochdale H.)	1922-1933
406	Clive Sullivan (Hull, Hull K.R., Oldham, Doncaster)	1961-1985
401	John Atkinson (Leeds, Carlisle)	1966-1983
399	Eric Harris (Leeds)	1930-1939
395	Tom Van Vollenhoven (St. Helens)	1957-1968
386	Albert Rosenfeld (Huddersfield, Wakefield T., Bradford N.)	1909-1924
383	Jim Lewthwaite (Barrow)	1943-1957
378	Martin Offiah (Widnes, Wigan)	1987-
374	Ike Southward (Workington T., Oldham, Whitehaven)	1952-1969
372	Barney Hudson (Salford)	1928-1946
358	Neil Fox (Wakefield T., Bradford N., Hull K.R., York, Bramley, Huddersfield)	1956-1979
342	Mick Sullivan (Huddersfield, Wigan, St. Helens, York, Dewsbury)	1952-1966
321	Johnny Lawrenson (Wigan, Workington T., Swinton)	1939-1954
319	Eric Ashton (Wigan)	1955-1969
314	Jim Leytham (Wigan)	1901-1912
312	Brian Nordgren (Wigan)	1946-1955
311	Alan Smith (Leeds)	1962-1983
310	Jim Lomas (Bramley, Salford, Oldham, York)	1902-1923
304	Alan Hardisty (Castleford, Leeds)	1958-1974
302	Maurice Richards (Salford)	1969-1983

Great Britain skipper Ellery Hanley scores a try in the first Test against Australia in Sydney in June 1988, one of 428 career touchdowns.

1,000 OR MORE GOALS IN A CAREER

2,867	Jim Sullivan (Wigan)	1921-1946
2,575	Neil Fox (Wakefield T., Bradford N., Hull K.R., York, Bramley, Huddersfield)	1956-1979
1,768	Cyril Kellett (Hull K.R., Featherstone R.)	1956-1974
1,698	Kel Coslett (St. Helens, Rochdale H.)	1962-1979
1,677	Gus Risman (Salford, Workington T., Batley)	1929-1954
1,591	John Woods (Leigh, Bradford N., Warrington, Rochdale H.)	1976-1992
1,578	Steve Quinn (York, Featherstone R.)	1970-1988
1,560	Jim Ledgard (Leeds, Dewsbury, Leigh)	1944-1961
1,478	Lewis Jones (Leeds)	1952-1964
1,398	Bernard Ganley (Oldham)	1951-1961
1,376	Ray Dutton (Widnes, Whitehaven)	1966-1981
1,342	David Watkins (Salford, Swinton, Cardiff C.)	1967-1983
1,306	George Fairbairn (Wigan, Hull K.R.)	1974-1990
1,272	Colin Tyrer (Leigh, Wigan, Barrow, Hull K.R.)	1962-1978
1,189	Frank Dyson (Huddersfield, Oldham)	1949-1965
1,179	Terry Clawson (Featherstone R., Bradford N., Hull K.R., Leeds, Oldham, York, Wakefield T., Huddersfield, Hull)	1957-1980
1,169	Steve Hesford (Warrington, Huddersfield B.)	1975-1986
1,154	Derek Whitehead (Swinton, Oldham, Warrington)	1964-1979
1,127	Geoff "Sammy" Lloyd (Castleford, Hull)	1970-1983
1,092	John McKeown (Whitehaven)	1948-1961
1,081	Vic Yorke (York)	1954-1967
1,075	Ken Gowers (Swinton)	1954-1973
1,044	Billy Langton (Hunslet)	1955-1966
1,030	Ron James (Halifax)	1961-1971
1,016	Iain MacCorquodale (Salford, Workington T., Fulham, Blackpool B., Rochdale H.)	1970-1982
1,008	Lee Crooks (Hull, Leeds, Castleford)	1980-

Iain MacCorquodale (left), scorer of 1,016 career goals, in action for Workington Town in the 1979 Lancashire Cup final against Widnes.

2,500 OR MORE POINTS IN A CAREER

6,220	Neil Fox (Wakefield T., Bradford N., Hull K.R., York, Bramley, Huddersfield)	1956-1979
6,022	Jim Sullivan (Wigan)	1921-1946
4,050	Gus Risman (Salford, Workington T., Batley)	1929-1954
3,985	John Woods (Leigh, Bradford N., Warrington, Rochdale H.)	1976-1992
3,686	Cyril Kellett (Hull K.R., Featherstone R.)	1956-1974
3,545	Kel Coslett (St. Helens, Rochdale H.)	1962-1979
3,445	Lewis Jones (Leeds)	1952-1964
3,438	Steve Quinn (York, Featherstone R.)	1970-1988
3,279	Jim Ledgard (Leeds, Dewsbury, Leigh)	1944-1961
3,117	David Watkins (Salford, Swinton, Cardiff C.)	1967-1982
2,902	Colin Tyrer (Leigh, Wigan, Barrow, Hull K.R.)	1962-1978
2,894	George Fairbairn (Wigan, Hull K.R.)	1974-1990
2,844	Bernard Ganley (Oldham)	1951-1961
2,786	Ray Dutton (Widnes, Whitehaven)	1966-1981
2,574	Terry Clawson (Featherstone R., Bradford N., Hull K.R., Leeds, Oldham, York, Wakefield T., Huddersfield, Hull)	1957-1980
2,561	Frank Dyson (Huddersfield, Oldham)	1949-1965

650 APPEARANCES OR MORE IN A CAREER

• Figures in brackets denote substitute appearances included in main total.

928	Jim Sullivan (Wigan)	1921-1946
873	Gus Risman (Salford, Workington T., Batley)	1929-1954
828 (28)	Neil Fox (Wakefield T., Bradford N., Hull K.R., York, Bramley, Huddersfield)	1956-1979
776 (57)	Jeff Grayshon (Dewsbury, Bradford N., Leeds, Featherstone R., Batley)	1969-
740 (46)	Graham Idle (Bramley, Wakefield T., Bradford N., Hunslet, Rochdale H., Sheffield E., Doncaster, Nottingham C., Highfield)	1969-1993
738 (25)	Colin Dixon (Halifax, Salford, Hull K.R.)	1961-1981
727 (9)	Paul Charlton (Workington T., Salford, Blackpool B.)	1961-1981
692 (24)	Keith Mumby (Bradford N., Sheffield E., Keighley C., Ryedale-York)	1973-1994
691 (1)	Ernie Ashcroft (Wigan, Huddersfield, Warrington)	1942-1962
688	Brian Bevan (Warrington, Blackpool B.)	1945-1964
683 (24)	John Wolford (Bramley, Bradford N., Dewsbury, Hunslet)	1962-1985
682	Joe Ferguson (Oldham)	1899-1923
679	Joe Oliver (Huddersfield, Batley, Hull, Hull K.R.)	1923-1945
669 (33)	John Joyner (Castleford)	1973-1992
665	George Carmichael (Hull K.R., Bradford N.)	1929-1950
663 (25)	John Holmes (Leeds)	1968-1989
662 (28)	Mal Aspey (Widnes, Fulham, Wigan, Salford)	1964-1983
651	Jack Miller (Warrington, Leigh)	1926-1947

Wigan coach Graeme West gets his hands on the 1995 Silk Cut Challenge Cup, completing his personal Grand Slam of the four domestic trophies starting with the 1994 Stones Bitter Premiership success.

CUPS

RUGBY LEAGUE CHALLENGE CUP

1995 Final

At the height of the Super League controversy, Wigan used the Silk Cut Challenge Cup final as the stage to confirm that they were in a league of their own.

The Riversiders and Leeds became the first two clubs to meet at Wembley in successive seasons. The Yorkshiremen arrived under the twin towers with virtually the same line-up which had experienced the occasion 12 months earlier, plus the confidence of having beaten Wigan once during the season en route to claiming runners-up spot in the Stones Bitter Championship.

But it turned out to be the same old story as rampant Wigan collected the Challenge Cup for a record-extending eighth season with a convincing 30-10 victory.

Leeds' biggest defeat in 16 Challenge Cup finals proved that the Loiners had learned nothing from the previous year's 26-16 reversal. All the old faults were again on show, allowing Wigan's forwards to develop a head of steam before moving in to try to halt them.

Wigan's Test props Kelvin Skerrett and Neil Cowie repeatedly drove down the middle, the supportive back three of Denis Betts, substitute Andrew Farrell and Phil Clarke turning the barrage into a cavalry charge.

Their steamrolling pack was completed by Welsh international Martin Hall, the epitome of the modern hooker with his impeccable defence and darting runs from acting half back. He exploited Leeds' weakness round the play-the-ball to nip in for a well deserved 52nd-minute try.

The Yorkshiremen paid a more spectacular price for slack marking at the play-the-ball when Leeds-born Jason Robinson zipped through near the centre spot to beat three defenders on a brilliant 50-metre run to the posts for a try four minutes after the interval which effectively ended the game as a contest

with Wigan leading 18-4.

Robinson also opened the try scoring with a superb piece of wing play in the 17th minute which defied his lack of match practice, having been laid up through injury for nearly a month. The Great Britain wingman, emulating his two-try Test debut performance at Wembley in October 1993, dashed 35 metres down the right flank for his first touchdown.

The brace of tries alone were enough to earn the Lance Todd Trophy as Man of the Match to emulate teammate Martin Offiah, whose two touchdowns were the main reasons for Leeds' defeat a year earlier.

Wigan were a team of stars, each posing individual problems for the harrassed Leeds side, who in turn were blunted on attack by a superb Wigan scrambling defence.

Leeds had massive problems trying to cope with the rumbling runs of former All Black Va'aiga Tuigamala, two or three players often being needed to pull down the powerful centre. The Western Samoan added a subtle touch with a dummy before charging in for Wigan's last try in the 64th minute.

While Tuigamala was the battering ram, full back Henry Paul was the spinning top. His inimitable style of evading the tackle sent him in for the second try after 25 minutes, having been fed the ball by the impressive Clarke.

Stand off Frano Botica contributed penetrative running and five goals, which took him past Neil Fox's record Wembley total of 39 points in three finals. The New Zealander's total of 46 points came in his fourth final, consisting of a record 21 goals plus a try.

Orchestrating the daunting Wigan side was scrum half and skipper Shaun Edwards, an inspiration with his ball distribution and tactical kicking. An injury doubt during the run-in to Wigan's record-extending 25th Challenge Cup final, Edwards lengthened his own Cup final records with a 10th appearance and ninth winners' medal.

Edwards remained the only player to have figured in all 42 of Wigan's record run of unbeaten Challenge Cup ties, including a draw, their last defeat in the competition being a first round 10-8 loss at Oldham in 1987.

Leeds, in their 10th Wembley final, made most of their mistakes on defence with full back Alan Tait taking much of the blame for his uncertainty when faced by a quick-breaking opponent. Yet it was typical of Leeds' enigmatic performance that Tait produced two daring catches under pressure and was their liveliest attacker.

New Zealand Test centre Kevin Iro was a constant threat and would have run amok against any other club defence than Wigan's. His wing partner Francis Cummins also ran strongly on occasion, while the aggressive Jim Fallon, on the other flank, made his presence felt on attack and defence.

Hooker James Lowes topped Leeds' tackle count with 28, kept himself busy on attack and claimed a well deserved try by sneaking in for their only touchdown two minutes from the end. Leeds were denied an earlier score when stand off Garry Schofield nipped in with an interception only to be recalled by referee Russell Smith for not standing square at the play-the-ball.

Leeds skipper Ellery Hanley was quiet throughout, having battled with a shoulder injury for the previous two weeks and never looked likely to be climbing the Wembley steps to receive the Challenge Cup for a record fourth time as captain . . . the other three times as skipper of Wigan!

In-goal judges were used for the first time at Wembley.

A victorious farewell to Wembley for Wigan duo Phil Clarke (left) and Denis Betts, both bound Down Under for Sydney Premiership club duty.

SILK CUT CHALLENGE CUP FINAL
29 April 1995   **Wembley**

WIGAN 30		**LEEDS 10**
Henry Paul	1.	Alan Tait
Jason Robinson	2.	Jim Fallon
Va'aiga Tuigamala	3.	Kevin Iro
Gary Connolly	4.	Craig Innes
Martin Offiah	5.	Francis Cummins
Frano Botica	6.	Garry Schofield
Shaun Edwards, Capt.	7.	Graham Holroyd
Kelvin Skerrett	8.	Harvey Howard
Martin Hall	9.	James Lowes
Neil Cowie	10.	Esene Faimalo
Denis Betts	11.	Gary Mercer
Mick Cassidy	12.	Richard Eyres
Phil Clarke	13.	Ellery Hanley, Capt.
Paul Atcheson	14.	George Mann
Andrew Farrell	15.	Neil Harmon

T: Robinson (2), Paul, Hall,
Tuigamala
G: Botica (5)
Substitutions:
Farrell for Cassidy (9 min.)
Atcheson for Skerrett (53 min.)
Referee: Russell Smith (Castleford)

T: Lowes
G: Holroyd (3)
Substitutions:
Mann for Howard (30 min.)
Harmon for Faimalo (53 min.)
Half-time: 12-4
Attendance: 78,550
Receipts: £2,040,000

Eight on the trot for 1995 Wembley victors Wigan.

1994-95 Round by Round

Beverley became the first amateur side for 86 years to eliminate a professional club from the Challenge Cup when the Humbersiders registered a 27-4 success at Highfield. Ironically, it was Beverley who last performed the feat with a 7-2 home defeat of Ebbw Vale in 1909. The victory by Beverley came in the third round in the second season of the new-look Silk Cut Challenge Cup competition. Amateur sides contested the first two rounds, 32 clubs in the National Conference League having home advantage in the first round, the second stage being drawn at random.

Those 16 winners then played away to the professional Second Division clubs. Seven professional sides registered 50 points or more, the widest margin being Keighley Cougars' 68-0 victory over Chorley, the 14 tries coming from 11 different players.

The First Division sides entered the fourth round in a random draw. Beverley came close to pulling off another shock when they led Second Division promotion favourites Batley 20-18 at the Boulevard midway through the second half, centre Scott Sullivan putting the amateurs ahead with a scintillating 90-metre try. Batley rallied with two tries in two minutes to record a 30-20 victory.

Holders Wigan snatched a late 16-16 draw at home to arch rivals St. Helens, who were denied victory when Bobby Goulding hit the post with a drop goal attempt five minutes from time. Saints held a 12-6 half-time lead before Wigan fought back with two second half tries. Wigan's Frano Botica rediscovered his kicking boots in the replay as the visitors raced into a 32-8 interval lead, St. Helens rallying before Martin Offiah completed his hat-trick of tries in a 40-24 Wigan victory. The shock of the round was Huddersfield's 36-30 home success over neighbours Halifax, who trailed 22-4 at the break. Huddersfield's biggest crowd at the McAlpine Stadium of 9,348 saw former Halifax centre Greg Austin score two tries. In another derby encounter, Leeds entertained Bradford Northern, whose 12-8 half-time deficit was scant reward for a dominating first period. While Northern became indisciplined, a try on either side of the interval revived Leeds, as skipper Ellery Hanley and Gary Mercer each collected two tries on the way to a 31-14 success.

The South Yorkshire derby was won 22-12 by visitors Sheffield Eagles, Doncaster's pitch of thick mud and heavy sand producing a high error rate. The home side were rocked by a try from Eagles half back Ryan Sheridan on the stroke of half-time and a 90-metre interception try by wingman Linton Stott 10 minutes after the re-start. Carlisle had only a Willie Richardson penalty goal to show in a 40-2 home defeat by Widnes, for whom Welshman John Devereux marked his return to senior team action for the first time in a year with the opening try. Featherstone Rovers skipper Steve Molloy had a hand in all eight tries in a 50-22 drubbing of lowly Barrow at Post Office Road, New Zealander Brett Rodgers claiming a hat-trick of tries. Salford led 32-16 at Hunslet before the Second Division outfit rallied to register three tries in the last 13 minutes for a 32-32 draw. In the replay, Hunslet were behind only 12-4 at the interval before Salford raced away to a 52-10 victory, inspired by a try and seven goals from Steve Blakeley.

Keighley Cougars scored five tries to one in the 24-12 home success over Dewsbury, England centre Nick Pinkney claiming two touchdowns. Hull K.R.'s 26-20 victory margin at London Broncos did not reflect their superiority, two of the visitors' five tries coming from full back Brown. Kiwi Wilson Marsh kicked 11 goals from 13 attempts to take the Silk Cut Award in Oldham's 70-10 home victory over Bramley, all but one of the 12 tries coming from the back division. Rochdale Hornets had keyman Wayne Reid sent off in the first half of their tie at Ryedale-York but trailed only 14-12 with two minutes left. Dean Thomas then clinched an 18-12 victory for Ryedale with a well-taken try.

Leigh got off to a flying start at Swinton with a 16-0 lead after only eight minutes before home full back Mark Hudspith inspired a revival with two tries, Scott Martin sealing a 34-22 Leigh victory with a try five minutes from the end. Warrington literally booted Castleford out of the competition, all of their three tries stemming from kicks. Internationals Jonathan Davies and Kelly Shelford were the inspiration in a 17-2 home victory. Division Two side Whitehaven claimed their second Division One scalp of the season with a 24-12 home success over Wakefield Trinity, after holding a 18-2 lead four minutes after the break. Hull, hit by injuries and flu, generally looked out of sorts as Workington Town ran in five tries to one in a 30-6 home victory.

In the fifth round, unfancied Oldham travelled to Warrington to pull off the shock victory of the round. Coach Andy Goodway drew on his experience of four successful Wembley appearances to inflict the Wire's first home defeat of the season by a club side. Davies opened the scoring with a try and a goal in the third minute before Oldham took control for a 17-6 success, Mike Kuiti taking the individual honours. In a top-of-the-table Second Division clash, leaders Keighley Cougars were thrashed 30-0 by visitors Huddersfield, who adapted better to the heavily-sanded pitch and were helped by the home side's high error rate. Sheffield Eagles opened the scoring against Widnes with a Carl Briggs drop goal before the visitors took firm control to score three first half tries and make the second period a formality en route to a convincing 19-7 victory. Salford and Featherstone Rovers were level 10-10 at the interval at the Willows, before the latter ran in 20 points without reply for a 30-10 success.

Visitors Wigan brought Second Division promotion favourites Batley down to earth with a 70-4 hammering, the Riversiders' 11-try display being highlighted by a point-a-minute first half tempo featuring a Martin Offiah hat-trick. Winger Jim Fallon grabbed four of Leeds' seven tries as they disposed of Second Division Ryedale-York 44-14 at Headingley with a workmanlike performance. Hull K.R. entertained Whitehaven and crashed out 18-14 in controversial style with two players sent off, Nick Halafihi and Andy Thompson, and four sent to the sin bin. Cumbrian neighbours Workington Town had an easier passage at home to Leigh, scoring 17 tries in a 94-4 win with top scorer Dean Marwood contributing a club record-equalling 13 goals and 42 points, featuring four touchdowns.

In the quarter-finals, Denis Betts scored his 100th career try as Wigan clocked up their 40th successive Silk Cut Challenge Cup tie without defeat with a hard earned 26-12 success at fast-improving Widnes, who were well led by Andy Ireland and Steve McCurrie. Featherstone Rovers reached their first semi-final since 1983 with a 42-14 victory at Whitehaven, marked by a four-try haul by Frenchman Frederic Banquet. Ellery Hanley scored his 100th try for Leeds in the 50-16 trouncing of visitors Workington Town and went on to register a hat-trick. Oldham reached their fourth Challenge Cup semi-final in 10 years with a 23-12 home defeat of Huddersfield, scrum half Martin Crompton scoring two first half tries.

The previous year's Wembley finalists, Leeds and Wigan, were kept apart in the semi-finals. Wigan made sure of an eighth successive final appearance with a comfortable 48-20 victory over a nervous Oldham, loose forward Phil Clarke taking the Silk Cut Award. Gary Connolly claimed a hat-trick in a nine-try Wigan display. A week later, Leeds cruised to a 39-22 success over Featherstone Rovers at Elland Road, Leeds. Hanley scored two tries to equal the record of 40 in a season set by Bob Haigh in 1970-71. Rovers, with former Leeds coach David Ward at the helm, made too many mistakes, Man of the Match rating being given to adventurous Leeds full Alan Tait.

1994-95 RESULTS

First Round

Askam	10	Moorends	15
Barrow Island	26	Norland	8
Beverley	8	Chequerfield	6
Blackbrook	26	West Bowling	14
Blackpool G.	27	Fryston	14
Chorley B.	12	Simms Cross	8
Dewsbury Celtic	6	Thatto Heath	22
Dudley Hill	54	Cardiff Institute	4
East Leeds	22	Wath Brown H.	14
Eastmoor	23	Upton & Frickley	22
Egremont	34	New Earswick A.B.	6
Greetland A.B.	12	Crosfield	6
Hemel Hempstead	52	Leeds Met. Univ.	0
Heworth	32	Littleborough	10
Leigh East	10	Bisons	16
Leigh Miners	7	Wigan St. Judes	10
Lock Lane	36	Orrell St. James	8
Mayfield	32	Park Amateurs	6
Milford	12	Thornhill	20
Millom	62	Northampton K.	4
Moldgreen	30	Embassy	14
Nottingham C.	0	Normanton	36
Oldham St. Annes	20	Kells	24
Oulton	12	Ovenden	8
Redhill	22	Ellenborough	28
Saddleworth R.	30	Skirlaugh	12
Shaw Cross	46	Fulham Travellers	20
Walney Central	4	Hensingham	14
West Hull	48	South London	10
Wigan St. Patricks	22	Worth Village	0
Woolston	26	Eccles	10
York Acorn	18	Crown Malet	25

Second Round

Barrow Island	19	West Hull	12
Beverley	14	Normanton	16
Bisons	8	East Leeds	33
Blackbrook	0	Chorley	23
Blackpool G.	0	Thornhill	28
Eastmoor	8	Dudley Hill	16
Ellenborough	23	Egremont	10
Hensingham	8	Heworth	14
Lock Lane	20	Mayfield	14
Millom	38	Saddleworth R.	16
Moorends	12	Thatto Heath	10
Oulton	12	Kells	14
Shaw Cross	9	Moldgreen	4
Wigan St. Judes	14	Hemel Hempstead	13
Wigan St. Patricks	42	Crown Malet	6
Woolston	14	Greetland A.R.	4
Replay			
Beverley	20	Normanton	10

Third Round

Barrow	56	East Leeds	0
Batley	32	Shaw Cross	4
Bramley	42	Woolston	2
Carlisle	34	Dudley Hill	4
Dewsbury	72	Kells	12
Highfield	4	Beverley	27
Huddersfield	44	Wigan St. Judes	10
Hull K.R.	58	Thornhill	6
Hunslet	64	Wigan St. Patricks	4
Keighley C.	68	Chorley	0
Leigh	40	Heworth	28
London B.	30	Ellenborough	10
Rochdale H.	48	Lock Lane	16
Ryedale-York	50	Barrow Island	20
Swinton	30	Millom	10
Whitehaven	64	Moorends	12

Wigan winger Jason Robinson (right) celebrates one of his two 1995 Wembley tries in a Lance Todd Trophy performance.

Fourth Round

Beverley	20	Batley	30
(at Hull)			
Carlisle	2	Widnes	40
Doncaster	12	Sheffield E.	22
Featherstone R.	50	Barrow	22
Huddersfield	36	Halifax	30
Hunslet	32	Salford	32
Keighley C.	24	Dewsbury	12
Leeds	31	Bradford N.	14
London B.	20	Hull K.R.	26
Oldham	70	Bramley	10
Ryedale-York	18	Rochdale H.	12
Swinton	22	Leigh	34
Warrington	17	Castleford	2
Whitehaven	24	Wakefield T.	12
Wigan	16	St. Helens	16
Workington T.	30	Hull	6

Replay

St. Helens	24	Wigan	40
Salford	52	Hunslet	10

Fifth Round

Batley	4	Wigan	70
Hull K.R.	14	Whitehaven	18
Keighley C.	0	Huddersfield	30
Leeds	44	Ryedale-York	14
Salford	10	Featherstone R.	30
Sheffield E.	7	Widnes	19
Warrington	6	Oldham	17
Workington T.	94	Leigh	4

Quarter-Finals

Leeds	50	Workington T.	16
Oldham	23	Huddersfield	12
Whitehaven	14	Featherstone R.	42
Widnes	12	Wigan	26

Semi-Finals

Wigan	48	Oldham	20
(at Huddersfield)			
Leeds	39	Featherstone R.	22
(at Elland Rd, Leeds)			

Final

Wigan	30	Leeds	10
(at Wembley)			

Leeds prop Harvey Howard on the defensive in the 1995 Wembley showpiece, his third successive final on the losing side.

1994-95 Prizes

Third Round	£2,700 to each Second Division club
Fourth Round	£2,700 to losers
Fifth Round	£4,300 to losers
Quarter-Finals	£6,900 to losers
Semi-Finals	£11,000 to losers
Runners-up	£20,500
Winners	£39,000

Total Prize Money	£254,000
Capital Development Fund	£146,000
Grand Total	£400,000

RUGBY LEAGUE CHALLENGE CUP FINAL PLAYERS' REGISTER

The following is an index of players who have appeared in the Rugby League Challenge Cup final in the last 20 seasons. It also includes the pre-1975 record of any listed player. W — winners, L — losers, D — draw. Substitute appearances in lower case letters. The year denotes the second half of the season. * denotes replay.

ADAMS, Mick: Widnes 75W, 76L, 77L, 79W, 81W, 82DL*, 84W
AGAR, Allan: Hull K.R. 80W
AH KUOI, Fred: Hull 85L
ANDERSON, Chris: Widnes 75W; Halifax 87W
ANDERSON, Grant: Castleford 92L
ANDERSON, Tony: Halifax 88L
ARKWRIGHT, Chris: St. Helens 87L
ASHCROFT, Kevin: Leigh 71W; Warrington 74W, 75L
ASHURST, Bill: Wigan 70L; Wakefield T. 79L
ASPEY, Malcolm: Widnes 75W, 77L, 79W
ATCHESON, Paul: Wigan 95w
ATKINSON, John: Leeds 68W, 71L, 72L, 77W, 78W

BANKS, Alan: Featherstone R. 83W
BARKER, Nigel: Featherstone R. 83W
BASNETT, John: Widnes 82DL*, 84W
BEARDMORE, Kevin: Castleford 86W
BEARDMORE, Bob: Castleford 86W
BEEVERS, Graham: Halifax 87W
BELL, Dean: Wigan 88W, 89W, 90W, 91W, 92W, 93W, 94W
BENTLEY, Keith: Widnes 81W
BENYON, Billy: St. Helens 66W, 72W, 76W
BETTS, Denis: Wigan 89w, 90W, 91W, 92W, 93W, 94W, 95W
BEVAN, John: Warrington 74W, 75L
BIRDSALL, Charlie: Hull 80L
BISHOP, Paul: Warrington 90L; St. Helens 91L
BLACKMORE, Richard: Castleford 92L
BLOOR, Darren: St. Helens 89l
BOTICA, Frano: Wigan 91W, 92W, 93W, 94W, 95W
BOWDEN, Reg: Widnes 75W, 76L, 77L, 79W
BRADLEY, Graeme: Castleford 92L
BRAY, Graham: Featherstone R. 74L; Hull 80L
BRIDGES, John "Keith": Featherstone R. 73W, 74L; Hull 83L
BRIGGS, Wilf: Warrington 75l
BURKE, John: Leeds 71L; Wakefield T. 79L
BURKE, Mick: Widnes 79W, 81W, 82DL*, 84W
BURKE, Tony: St. Helens 87L, 89L; Warrington 90L
BURTON, Chris: Hull K.R. 81L
BYRNE, Ged: Wigan 88w

CAMPBELL, Danny: Wigan 85w
CANNON, Mark: Wigan 84L
CASE, Brian: Wigan 84L, 85W, 88W
CASEY, Len: Hull K.R. 80W, 81L
CASSIDY, Mick: Wigan 94w, 95W
CHISNALL, Dave: Warrington 74W, 75L; St. Helens 78L
CHISNALL, Eric: St. Helens 72W, 76W
CLARK, Brett: St. Helens 87L
CLARK, Garry: Hull K.R. 86L
CLARKE, Phil: Wigan 91W, 92W, 93W, 94W, 95W
CONNOLLY, Gary: St. Helens 89L, 91l; Wigan 94W, 95W
CONROY, Tom: Warrington 75L
COOKSON, Phil: Leeds 72L, 77W, 78W
COOPER, Shane: St. Helens 89L, 91L
COSLETT, Kel: St. Helens 72W, 76W
COURTNEY, Neil: Wigan 85W
COWIE, Neil: Wigan 92w, 95W

CRANE, Mick: Leeds 78W; Hull 82Dw*, 83l
CROMPTON, Martin: Warrington 90L
CROOKS, Lee: Hull 82dW*, 83L, 85L; Castleford 92L
CROOKS, Steve: Hull K.R. 81L
CUMMINS, Francis: Leeds 94L, 95L
CUNNINGHAM, Eddie: St. Helens 76W, 78L; Widnes 81W, 82DL*
CURRIER, Andy: Widnes 93L

DARBYSHIRE, Paul: Warrington 90L
DAVIES, Jonathan: Widnes 93L
DAY, Terry: Hull 82D, 83l
DEAN, Tony: Hull 82W*
DEARDEN, Alan: Widnes 77L, 79W
DERMOTT, Martin: Wigan 90W, 91W, 92W, 93W, 94W
DEVEREUX, John: Widnes 93L
DIAMOND, Steve: Wakefield T. 79L
DICK, Kevin: Leeds 77W, 78w
DICKINSON, Roy: Leeds 77w, 78w
DIVORTY, Gary: Hull 85l
DIXON, Paul: Halifax 87W, 88L
DONLAN, Steve: Wigan 85W
DORAHY, John: Hull K.R. 86L
DRUMMOND, Des: Warrington 90L
DUKE, Tony: Hull 82W*
DUNN, Brian: Wigan 85W
DUTTON, Ray: Widnes 75W, 76L, 77L
DWYER, Bernard: St. Helens 89L, 91L
DYL, Les: Leeds 71l, 72L, 77W, 78W

EADIE, Graham: Halifax 87W, 88L
ECCLES, Graham: Leeds 77W, 78W
ECKERSLEY, David: Leigh 71W; Widnes 76L, 77L, 79W
EDWARDS, Shaun: Wigan 84L, 85W, 88W, 89W, 90W, 91W, 92W, 93W, 94W, 95W
ELIA, Mark: St. Helens 87L
ELLIS, St. John: Castleford 92L
ELVIN, Wayne: Wigan 84l
ELWELL, Keith: Widnes 75W, 76L, 77L, 79W, 81W, 82DL*, 84W
EMA, Asuquo: Hull K.R. 86L
ENGLAND, Keith: Castleford 86W, 92L
EVANS, Steve: Hull 82DW*, 83L, 85L
EVANS, Stuart: St. Helens 89l
EYRES, Richard: Widnes 93L; Leeds 94L, 95L

FAIMALO, Esene: Widnes 93L; Leeds 95L
FAIRBAIRN, George: Hull K.R. 86L
FAIRBANK, Dick: Halifax 88l
FALLON, Jim: Leeds 94L, 95L
FARRAR, Andrew: Wigan 93W
FARRAR, Vince: Featherstone R. 73W; Hull 80l
FARRELL, Andrew: Wigan 93w, 94W, 95w
FEARNLEY, Stan: Bradford N. 73L; Leeds 77W
FERGUSON, John: Wigan 85W
FIELDHOUSE, John: St. Helens 87L
FLETCHER, Andrew: Wakefield T. 79L
FORAN, John: Widnes 75W, 76L, 77l
FORBER, Paul: St. Helens 89L
FORD, Mike: Wigan 85W; Castleford 92L

FORSTER, Mark: Warrington 90L
FRANCIS, Bill: Wigan 70L; St. Helens 78L
FRENCH, Ian: Castleford 86W

GEORGE, Derek "Mick": Widnes 75W, 76L, 77l, 79W, 81W
GEORGE, Wilf: Halifax 87W
GIBBINS, Mick: Featherstone R. 83W
GILBERT, John: Featherstone R. 83W
GILDART, Ian: Wigan 90w
GILL, Henderson: Wigan 84L, 85W, 88W
GLYNN, Peter: St. Helens 76w, 78L
GOODWAY, Andy: Wigan 88W, 89w, 90W, 91w
GORDON, Parry: Warrington 74W, 75L
GORLEY, Les: Widnes 81W, 82DL*, 84W
GOULDING, Bobby: Wigan 90w, 91w; Widnes 93L
GREGORY, Andy: Widnes 81W, 82DL*, 84W; Wigan 88W, 89W, 90W, 91W, 92W
GREGORY, Mike: Warrington 90L
GRIFFITHS, Jonathan: St. Helens 91L
GROGAN, Bob: Halifax 88L
GROVES, Paul: St. Helens 89L, 91l
GWILLIAM, Ken: Salford 69L; St. Helens 78L

HAGGERTY, Roy: St. Helens 87L, 89L
HAGUE, Neil: Leeds 77W, 78W
HALL, David: Hull K.R. 80W, 81L
HALL, Martin: Wigan 95W
HAMPSON, Steve: Wigan 89W, 90W, 91W, 92w, 93W
HANCOCK, Brian: Hull 80l
HANDSCOMBE, Ray: Featherstone R. 83W
HANKINS, Steve: Featherstone R. 83W
HANLEY, Ellery: Wigan 88W, 89W, 90W, 91W; Leeds 94L, 95L
HARKIN, Kevin: Hull 82D, 83L
HARKIN, Paul: Hull K.R. 81L, 86L
HARMON, Neil: Warrington 90L; Leeds 94L, 95l
HARRISON, Des: Hull K.R. 86L
HARRISON, John: St. Helens 91L
HARRISON, Mick: Leeds 77W, 78W
HARTLEY, Steve: Hull K.R. 80W, 81L
HEATON, Jeff: St. Helens 72W, 76W
HEMSLEY, Kerry: Wigan 84L
HOBBS, David: Featherstone R. 83W
HOGAN, Phil: Hull K.R. 80w, 81L
HOLDING, Neil: St. Helens 87L, 89L
HOLDSTOCK, Roy: Hull K.R. 80W, 81L
HOLLIDAY, Les: Halifax 88L
HOLMES, John: Leeds 71L, 72L, 77W, 78W
HOLROYD, Graham: Leeds 94L, 95L
HORTON, Stuart: Castleford 86w
HOWARD, Harvey: Widnes 93L; Leeds 94L, 95L
HUBBARD, Steve: Hull K.R. 80W, 81L
HUDSON, Terry: Featherstone R. 83W
HUGHES, Eric: Widnes 75W, 76L, 77L, 79W, 81W, 82DL*, 84W
HULL, David: St. Helens 76W; Widnes 79w
HULME, David: Widnes 84w, 93L
HULME, Paul: Widnes 93L
HUNTE, Alan: St. Helens 91L
HYDE, Gary: Castleford 86W

IDLE, Graham: Wakefield T. 79L
INNES, Craig: Leeds 94L, 95L
IRO, Kevin: Wigan 88W, 89W, 90W, 91W; Leeds 94L, 95L
IRO, Tony: Wigan 88W, 89W

JACKSON, Bob: Warrington 90L
JAMES, Kevin: Hull 85L
JAMES, Mel: St. Helens 76w, 78L
JAMES, Neil: Halifax 87w, 88L
JENKINS, David: Widnes 76L
JOHNSON, Barry: Castleford 86W
JOHNSTON, Peter: Hull K.R. 86L
JONES, Les: St. Helens 72W, 76W, 78L
JOYNER, John: Castleford 86W
JULIFF, Brian: Wakefield T. 79L; Wigan 84l; Halifax 87w

KARALIUS, Tony: St. Helens 76W
KELLETT, Ken: Featherstone R. 73W, 83W
KELLY, Andy: Hull K.R. 86L
KEMBLE, Gary: Hull 82DW*, 83L, 85L
KENNY, Brett: Wigan 85W
KETTERIDGE, Martin: Castleford 86W, 92L
KISS, Nicky: Wigan 85W, 88W, 89W

LAMPKOWSKI, Mike: Wakefield T. 79L
LAUGHTON, Doug: Wigan 70L; Widnes 75W, 76L, 77L, 79W
LAWS, David: Hull K.R. 86L
LEDGER, Barry: St. Helens 87L
LEULUAI, James: Hull 82W*, 83L, 85L
LIPTROT, Graham: St. Helens 78L, 87L
LLOYD, Geoff "Sammy": Hull 80L, 82D
LOCKWOOD, Brian: Castleford 69W, 70W; Hull K.R. 80W; Widnes 81W, 82DL*
LORD, Gary: Castleford 86W
LOUGHLIN, Paul: St. Helens 87L, 89L, 91L
LOWE, Phil: Hull K.R. 80W, 81L
LOWES, James: Leeds 94L, 95L
LUCAS, Ian: Wigan 89W, 91W
LYDIAT, John: Hull K.R. 86L
LYDON, Joe: Widnes 84W; Wigan 88W, 89W, 90W, 92W, 93W
LYMAN, Paul: Featherstone R. 83w
LYON, David: Warrington 90L

McCALLION, Seamus: Halifax 87W, 88L
McCORMACK, Kevin: St. Helens 87L
McCURRIE, Alan: Wakefield T. 79L
McCURRIE, Steve: Widnes 93l
McGINTY, Billy: Warrington 90l; Wigan 92W
MANN, Duane: Warrington 90L
MANN, George: St. Helens 91L; Leeds 95l
MANTLE, John: St. Helens 66W, 72W, 76W
MARCHANT, Tony: Castleford 86W
MARSDEN, John: Featherstone R. 83W
MARTYN, Tommy: Warrington 75L
MATHER, Barrie-Jon: Wigan 94W
MATHIAS, Roy: St. Helens 76W, 78L
MERCER, Gary: Warrington 90L; Leeds 94L, 95L
MEREDITH, Martin: Halifax 88L
MILES, Gene: Wigan 92W
MILLER, Gavin: Hull K.R. 86L
MILLINGTON, John: Hull K.R. 80w, 81l
MILLS, Jim: Widnes 75W, 77L, 79W
MILLWARD, Roger: Hull K.R. 80W
MUGGLETON, John: Hull 85L
MURRELL, Brian: Leeds 77W
MUSCROFT, Peter: Hull K.R. 81L
MYERS, David: Wigan 91W; Widnes 93L

MYLER, John: Widnes 81w
MYLER, Tony: Widnes 82d

NEILL, Jonathan: St. Helens 91L
NELLER, Keith: Halifax 87W, 88L
NELSON, David: Castleford 92L
NELSON, Nick: Widnes 76L
NEWLOVE, John: Featherstone R. 73W, 74L; Hull 80L
NICHOLAS, Mike: Warrington 74W, 75l
NICHOLLS, George: St. Helens 76W, 78L
NIKAU, Tawera: Castleford 92L
NOONAN, Derek: Warrington 74W, 75L; St. Helens 76W, 78L
NORTON, Steve: Hull 80L, 82DW*, 83L, 85L

O'CONNOR, Michael: St. Helens 89L
OFFIAH, Martin: Wigan 92W, 93W, 94W, 95W
O'HARA, Dane: Hull 82D, 83L, 85L
O'LOUGHLIN, Keiron: Widnes 82DL*, 84W
O'NEILL, Dennis: Widnes 76l, 77L
O'NEILL, Julian: Widnes 93l
O'NEILL, Mike: Widnes 79w, 81W, 82DL*, 84W; Leeds 94l
O'NEILL, Steve: Widnes 82d, 84W
OULTON, Willie: Leeds 78W

PANAPA, Sam: Wigan 93w, 94w
PATRICK, Shaun: Hull 85L
PAUL, Henry: Wigan 95W
PENDLEBURY, John: Wigan 84L; Halifax 87W, 88L
PHILBIN, Barry: Warrington 74W, 75L
PHILBIN, Mike: Warrington 74W, 75L
PICKERILL, Clive: Hull 80L
PIMBLETT, Geoff: St. Helens 72W, 76W, 78L
PINNER, Harry: St. Helens 78L
PITCHFORD, Steve: Leeds 77W, 78W
PLANGE, David: Castleford 86W
PLATT, Andy: St. Helens 87L; Wigan 89W, 90W, 91W, 92W, 93W, 94W
POTTER, Ian: Wigan 85W, 88W, 89W
PRENDIVILLE, Paul: Hull 80L, 82DW*, 83L
PRESCOTT, Alan: Widnes 75W, 76L
PRESCOTT, Eric: Widnes 81W, 82DL*
PRESTON, Mark: Wigan 90W
PROCTOR, Paul: Hull K.R. 81l
PROHM, Gary: Hull K.R. 86L
PUCKERING, Neil: Hull 85L

QUINN, Steve: Featherstone R. 83W
QUIRK, Les: St. Helens 89L, 91L

RAMSDALE, Denis: Wigan 84L
RAMSEY, Bill: Hunslet 65L; Leeds 68W, 71L, 72L; Widnes 77L
RAYNE, Keith: Wakefield T. 79L
REYNOLDS, Frank: Warrington 75L
RIX, Grant: Halifax 87W
ROBINSON, Jason: Wigan 93W, 95W
ROBINSON, Steve: Halifax 88L
ROOCKLEY, David: Castleford 86w
ROPATI, Tea: St. Helens 91L
ROSE, Paul: Hull K.R. 80W; Hull 83L, 85L
ROUND, Paul: St. Helens 87l

SAMPSON, Dean: Castleford 92l
SANDERSON, Gary: Warrington 90L
SANDERSON, John "Sammy": Leeds 78W
SANDY, Jamie: Castleford 86W
SCHOFIELD, Garry: Hull 85l; Leeds 94L, 95L
SCOTT, Mick: Wigan 84L; Halifax 87W, 88l
SHAW, Glyn: Widnes 79W, 81w
SHEARD, Les: Wakefield T. 79L
SHELFORD, Adrian: Wigan 88W, 89W, 90W
SHERIDAN, Barry: Widnes 75W, 76l
SIDDALL, Gary: Featherstone R. 83w
SKERRETT, Kelvin: Wigan 92W, 93W, 94W, 95W
SKERRETT, Trevor: Wakefield T. 79L; Hull 82DW*, 83L
SLATTER, Tim: Featherstone R. 83W
SMITH, Alan: Leeds 68W, 72L, 77W
SMITH, David: Leeds 77w, 78W
SMITH, Gordon: Hull K.R. 86l
SMITH, Keith: Wakefield T. 79L
SMITH, Mike: Hull K.R. 80W, 81L, 86L
SMITH, Peter: Featherstone R. 83W
SMITH, Tony: Castleford 92l
SORENSEN, Kurt: Widnes 93L
SOUTHERNWOOD, Graham: Castleford 92L
SPRUCE, Stuart: Widnes 93L
STEADMAN, Graham: Castleford 92L
STEPHENS, Gary: Wigan 84L; Halifax 87W
STEPHENSON, David: Wigan 84L, 85W
STERLING, Paul: Hull 85L
STONE, Richard "Charlie": Featherstone R. 73W, 74l; Hull 80L, 82DW*, 83L
SULLIVAN, Clive: Hull K.R. 80W; Hull 82W*

TAIT, Alan: Leeds 94L, 95L
TAMATI, Howie: Wigan 84L
TAMATI, Kevin: Widnes 84W
THOMAS, Mark: Warrington 90l
TINDALL, Keith: Hull 80L, 82W*
TOPLISS, David: Wakefield T. 79L; Hull 82DW*, 83L
TUIGAMALA, Va'aiga: Wigan 94W, 95W

VASSILAKOPOULOS, Marcus: Leeds 94l
VAUTIN, Paul: St. Helens 89L
VEIVERS, Phil: St. Helens 87L, 89L, 91L

WALTERS, Graham: Hull 80L
WANBON, Bobby: Warrington 74w, 75L
WANE, Shaun: Wigan 88w
WARD, David: Leeds 77W, 78W
WARD, Kevin: Castleford 86W; St. Helens 91L
WATKINSON, David: Hull K.R. 80W, 81L, 86L
WEST, Graeme: Wigan 84L, 85W
WHITEHEAD, Derek: Warrington 74W, 75L
WHITFIELD, Colin: Wigan 84L; Halifax 87W, 88L
WHITFIELD, Fred: Widnes 84w
WHITTLE, Alan: Warrington 74W, 75L
WILBY, Tim: Hull 80L
WILEMAN, Ron: Hull 80L, 82D
WILKINSON, Ian: Halifax 88L
WILSON, Scott: Halifax 87W
WOOD, John: Widnes 76L
WOODS, Paul: Hull 80L
WRAY, Jon: Castleford 92L
WRIGHT, Darren: Widnes 93L
WRIGHT, Stuart: Widnes 77L, 79W, 81W, 82DL*, 84W

THE LANCE TODD TROPHY

The Lance Todd Trophy is presented to the Man of the Match in the Rugby League Challenge Cup final, the decision being reached by a ballot of members of the Rugby League Writers' Association present at the game.

Lance Todd made his name in Britain as a player with Wigan and as manager of Salford. His untimely death in a road accident on the return journey from a game at Oldham was commemorated by the introduction of the Lance Todd Trophy.

The award was instituted by Australian-born Harry Sunderland, Warrington director Bob Anderton and Yorkshire journalist John Bapty.

Around 1950, the Red Devils' Association at Salford, comprising players and officials who had worked with Todd, raised sufficient funds to provide a trophy and replica for each winner.

Hull's Tommy Harris is the only hooker to earn the title; and Ray Ashby and Brian Gabbitas the only players to share the honour.

Following the 1954 replay, it was decided by the Red Devils that in the future the trophy would be awarded for the Wembley game. In 1954, Gerry Helme had received the trophy for his performance in the Odsal replay. In the 1982 replay at Elland Road, Leeds, the Man of the Match award went to Hull skipper David Topliss, the Lance Todd Trophy having been awarded to Eddie Cunningham, of Widnes, in the drawn Wembley tie.

In 1990 Andy Gregory, of Wigan, became the first player to win the trophy twice at Wembley, having also won it two years earlier, a feat emulated by Martin Offiah in 1992 and 1994.

Ellery Hanley, Lance Todd Trophy winner in 1989 and skipper of beaten finalists Leeds in 1994 and 1995.

The Lance Todd Trophy Roll of Honour

Year	Winner	Team	Position
1946	Billy Stott	Wakefield Trinity (v Wigan)	Centre
1947	Willie Davies	Bradford Northern (v Leeds)	Stand off
1948	Frank Whitcombe	Bradford Northern (v Wigan)	Prop
1949	Ernest Ward	Bradford Northern (v Halifax)	Centre
1950	Gerry Helme	Warrington (v Widnes)	Scrum half

1951	Cec Mountford	Wigan (v Barrow)	Stand off
1952	Billy Ivison	Workington T. (v Featherstone R.)	Loose forward
1953	Peter Ramsden	Huddersfield (v St. Helens)	Stand off
1954	Gerry Helme	Warrington (v Halifax)	Scrum half
1955	Jack Grundy	Barrow (v Workington Town)	Second row
1956	Alan Prescott	St. Helens (v Halifax)	Prop
1957	Jeff Stevenson	Leeds (v Barrow)	Scrum half
1958	Rees Thomas	Wigan (v Workington Town)	Scrum half
1959	Brian McTigue	Wigan (v Hull)	Second row
1960	Tommy Harris	Hull (v Wakefield Trinity)	Hooker
1961	Dick Huddart	St. Helens (v Wigan)	Second row
1962	Neil Fox	Wakefield Trinity (v Huddersfield)	Centre
1963	Harold Poynton	Wakefield Trinity (v Wigan)	Stand off
1964	Frank Collier	Widnes (v Hull K.R.)	Prop
1965	Ray Ashby	Wigan	Full back
	Brian Gabbitas	Hunslet	Stand off
1966	Len Killeen	St. Helens (v Wigan)	Winger
1967	Carl Dooler	Featherstone Rovers (v Barrow)	Scrum half
1968	Don Fox	Wakefield Trinity (v Leeds)	Prop
1969	Malcolm Reilly	Castleford (v Salford)	Loose forward
1970	Bill Kirkbride	Castleford (v Wigan)	Second row
1971	Alex Murphy	Leigh (v Leeds)	Scrum half
1972	Kel Coslett	St. Helens (v Leeds)	Loose forward
1973	Steve Nash	Featherstone R. (v Bradford N.)	Scrum half
1974	Derek Whitehead	Warrington (v Featherstone Rovers)	Full back
1975	Ray Dutton	Widnes (v Warrington)	Full back
1976	Geoff Pimblett	St. Helens (v Widnes)	Full back
1977	Steve Pitchford	Leeds (v Widnes)	Prop
1978	George Nicholls	St. Helens (v Leeds)	Second row
1979	David Topliss	Wakefield Trinity (v Widnes)	Stand off
1980	Brian Lockwood	Hull K.R. (v Hull)	Prop
1981	Mick Burke	Widnes (v Hull K.R.)	Full back
1982	Eddie Cunningham	Widnes (v Hull)	Centre
1983	David Hobbs	Featherstone Rovers (v Hull)	Second row
1984	Joe Lydon	Widnes (v Wigan)	Centre
1985	Brett Kenny	Wigan (v Hull)	Stand off
1986	Bob Beardmore	Castleford (v Hull K.R.)	Scrum half
1987	Graham Eadie	Halifax (v St. Helens)	Full back
1988	Andy Gregory	Wigan (v Halifax)	Scrum half
1989	Ellery Hanley	Wigan (v St. Helens)	Loose forward
1990	Andy Gregory	Wigan (v Warrington)	Scrum half
1991	Denis Betts	Wigan (v St. Helens)	Second row
1992	Martin Offiah	Wigan (v Castleford)	Winger
1993	Dean Bell	Wigan (v Widnes)	Loose forward
1994	Martin Offiah	Wigan (v Leeds)	Winger
1995	Jason Robinson	Wigan (v Leeds)	Winger

CHALLENGE CUP RECORDS

ALL ROUNDS

TEAM
Highest score:
Huddersfield 119 v. *Swinton Park 2 1914

INDIVIDUAL
Most goals in a match:
22 by Jim Sullivan (Wigan) v. *Flimby and Fothergill
. . . . 1925

Most tries in a match:
11 by George West (Hull K.R.) v. *Brookland Rovers
. . . . 1905

Most points in a match:
53 (11t,10g) by George West (Hull K.R.) as above.

*Amateur teams

FINAL RECORDS

TEAM

Most wins: 16 by Wigan

Most finals: 25 by Wigan

Highest score:
Wakefield T. 38 v. Hull 5 1960

Widest margin:
Huddersfield 37 v. St. Helens 3 1915

Biggest attendance:
102,569 Warrington v. Halifax (Replay) at Bradford
. . . . 1954

Neil Fox, holder of the Challenge Cup record for most points in a final.

INDIVIDUAL
Most goals:
8 by Cyril Kellett (Featherstone R.) v. Bradford N.
. . . . 1973

Most tries:
3 by Bob Wilson (Broughton R.) v. Salford 1902
Stan Moorhouse (Huddersfield) v. Warrington . 1913
Tom Holliday (Oldham) v. Swinton 1927

Most points:
20 (2t,7g) by Neil Fox (Wakefield T.) v. Hull . . . 1960

WEMBLEY FACTS
WIGAN have made a record 21 appearances at Wembley and won there a record 15 times, including a record eight successive appearances from 1988.

A RECORD 10 overseas players trod the Wembley turf in 1985. Hull fielded six — a record for one club. The Airlie Birds sextet were Australians Peter Sterling and John Muggleton, plus New Zealanders Gary Kemble, James Leuluai, Dane O'Hara and Fred Ah Kuoi. Wigan added Australians John Ferguson and Brett Kenny together with New Zealanders Graeme West and Danny Campbell, who went on as substitute. South African Nick Du Toit was substitute back but did not play.

THE 1985 aggregates of 10 tries and 52 points were both record totals for a Challenge Cup final with Hull's 24 points the most by a losing side. There were also 10 tries in the 1915 final when Huddersfield beat St. Helens 37-3, which is the widest margin. Wakefield Trinity ran up the highest Cup final score when they beat Hull 38-5 in 1960.

WORLD RECORD receipts of £2,040,000 were taken at the 1995 final between Wigan and Leeds from a capacity crowd of 78,550.

SHAUN EDWARDS holds the record for most Cup-winning appearances at Wembley with nine from a record 10 appearances.
Edwards made his debut in Wigan's losing side of 1984, earning winners' medals in 1985 and from 1988-95 inclusive.

ERIC ASHTON captained a record six teams at Wembley — Wigan in 1958, 1959, 1961, 1963, 1965 and 1966. His record of three wins (in 1958, 1959, 1965) is shared with Derek Turner (Wakefield Trinity 1960, 1962, 1963), Alex Murphy (St. Helens 1966, Leigh 1971 and Warrington 1974), Ellery Hanley (Wigan 1989, 1990, 1991) and Dean Bell (Wigan 1992, 1993 and 1994), Hanley's and Bell's being the only three successive wins.

THE YOUNGEST player to appear in a Wembley Cup final was Francis Cummins who was 17 years and 200 days when he played on the wing for Leeds against Wigan in 1994. Shaun Edwards was the youngest captain at Wembley, leading Wigan to success in the 1988 final against Halifax at the age of 21 years, 6 months and 14 days. The youngest winner at Wembley was Wigan's Andrew Farrell, a substitute in the 1993 final against Widnes at 17 years, 11 months. The youngest forward to play at Wembley is Marcus Vassilakopoulos of Leeds who went on as a substitute against Wigan in 1994 at 17 years and seven months.

ALEX MURPHY has been a record six times to Wembley as a coach. He was a winner as player-coach with Leigh (1971) and Warrington (1974), but losing each time when confined to the bench with Warrington (1975), Wigan (1984) and St. Helens (1987 and 1989). Murphy also went twice solely as a player, with St. Helens in 1961 and 1966.

MOST WINS as a coach at Wembley is four, by John Monie (Wigan 1990, 1991, 1992 and 1993).

THE OLDEST player at Wembley was Gus Risman, who at 41 years, 29 days led Workington Town to victory over Featherstone Rovers in 1952. He played full back.

THE TALLEST players at Wembley were St. Helens second row man John Harrison who appeared in the 1991 final, and Barrie-Jon Mather who was at centre for Wigan in 1994. Both were 6ft 7in.

SCHOOLBOYS who have appeared in an Under-11 curtain-raiser at Wembley and gone on to play in the major final at the stadium are Joe Lydon, David Hulme, Mike Ford, Neil Puckering, David Plange, Denis Betts, Bobby Goulding and Phil Clarke. Lydon became the first to achieve the feat with Widnes in the 1984 final against Wigan, followed by teammate Hulme who went on as a 72nd-minute substitute. Both had played in the first schoolboys' curtain-raiser in 1975 — Lydon for Wigan, and Hulme for Widnes.

CYRIL KELLETT holds the record for most goals in a Challenge Cup final with his eight for Featherstone Rovers in 1973.

In the most remarkable exhibition of kicking seen at Wembley, the veteran full back was successful with every one of his attempts as Bradford Northern crashed 33-14.

Nine years earlier he scored only one for Hull Kingston Rovers in the 13-5 defeat by Widnes.

NEIL FOX piled up the most points in a Challenge Cup final in 1960. His 20 points helped Wakefield Trinity to a 38-5 defeat of Hull. Fox's points came from two tries and seven goals.

His three drop goals for Trinity in the 12-6 victory over Huddersfield two years later was another extraordinary feat in the days when the drop goal was a rarity.

NO player has scored a hat-trick of tries at Wembley, the feat being achieved only three times in the preceding era.

The last to do it was Oldham winger Tom Holliday in the 26-7 defeat of Swinton in 1927.

Bob Wilson, the Broughton Rangers centre and captain, was the first to score three tries, in the 25-0 victory over Salford in 1902.

In between, Stan Moorhouse's three-try feat accounted for all of Huddersfield's points when they beat Warrington 9-5 in 1913.

MANY great players have gone through an entire career without achieving their ambition of playing at Wembley. Hull's Mike Smith achieved it in his first senior game.

Smith made one of the most remarkable debuts in sporting history when he played in the second row of an injury-hit Boulevard side against Wakefield Trinity in 1960.

In contrast, Freddie Miller signed for Hull in 1932 and did not play at Wembley until 1952...two years after joining Featherstone Rovers.

A NOTABLE Wembley captain was Gus Risman who led two clubs to victory...14 years apart. He was captain of Salford when they beat Barrow in 1938. At 41, he led Workington Town to their triumph over Featherstone Rovers in 1952.

Mike O'Neill holds the record for the longest playing span at Wembley of 15 years. He was a playing substitute for Widnes in 1979 and had the same role with Leeds in 1994. He played in five finals.

PROBABLY the unluckiest Challenge Cup finalist was Dai Davies who appeared in four finals and was on the losing side each time. Three of those occasions were at Wembley with different clubs. He was a loser with Warrington (1933), Huddersfield (1935) and Keighley (1937). Before the Wembley era he was also in Warrington's beaten team of 1928.

Steve Norton and Lee Crooks played at Wembley four times and were never on the winning side. Norton was in the beaten Hull teams of 1980, 1983 and 1985 in addition to playing in the 1982 drawn final. In 1970 he was a non-playing substitute for Castleford, who won the Cup.

Crooks was in the beaten Hull sides of 1983 and 1985 plus the drawn final of 1982. He was then in Castleford's beaten 1992 team.

Norton and Crooks both won winners' medals in the 1982 replay.

Bill Ramsey was on the losing side in four Wembley finals but gained a winners' medal with Leeds in 1968. He picked up losers' medals with Hunslet (1965), Leeds (1971 and 1972) and Widnes (1977).

ELEVEN of last season's clubs have never appeared at Wembley. They are: Batley, Bramley, Carlisle, Doncaster, Highfield, London Broncos, Oldham, Rochdale Hornets, Sheffield Eagles, Swinton and Whitehaven.

Fate seems to be against Swinton and Oldham. In the five years preceding the move to Wembley, one or the other appeared in the final, twice meeting each other. Oldham played in four successive finals in that period. Swinton's run of three finals ended when the first Wembley took place in 1929. They got through to the final three years later ...only for it to be played at Wigan!

WEMBLEY ERA SEMI-FINALS

It is generally felt that it is better to have played at Wembley and lost than never to have played there at all. This makes the semi-final stage of the RL Challenge Cup almost as important as the final, with no consolation for the losers.

Of the 14 current clubs who have never appeared at Wembley, four have been beaten semi-finalists. They are Oldham (seven times), Rochdale Hornets (twice), Swinton and Whitehaven.

Probably the unluckiest are Oldham. They have reached the penultimate stage seven times without being able to realise their ambition. Oldham almost made it in 1964. After drawing 5-5 with Hull K.R., they were winning 17-14 in extra time of the replay when bad light stopped play and they were beaten in the third game.

Swinton did win a semi-final in 1932 but the final that year was switched from Wembley to Wigan!

There have been three occasions when Yorkshire has provided all four semi-finalists in one year — in 1962, 1973 and 1983. Four times have all four semi-finalists come from west of the Pennines — in 1930, 1989, 1990 and 1991.

Until 1962 the two semi-finals were always played on the same Saturday, but with four Yorkshire clubs competing for the first time it was decided to play one midweek. Both matches were played at Odsal Stadium, Bradford. The first was on a Wednesday evening — without floodlights — when 43,625 saw Wakefield Trinity beat Featherstone Rovers and on the following Saturday there were 31,423 to see Huddersfield beat Hull K.R.

The following year both semi-finals were again played on the same Saturday, but since then they have been staged on different Saturdays.

Some semi-final facts during the Wembley era are:

Biggest attendance: 69,898 Warrington v. Leeds at Bradford in 1950

Biggest aggregate: 104,453 in 1939 (Only other six-figure aggregate was 102,080 in 1951)

Record receipts: £177,161 St. Helens v. Wigan at Old Trafford, Manchester in 1990

Lowest attendance: 7,971 Featherstone R. v. Leigh at Leeds in 1974

Highest score and widest margin: Wigan 71 v. Bradford N. 10 in 1992

CHALLENGE CUP SEMI-FINALS

Year	Winners		Runners-up		Venue	Attendance	Receipts
1929	Dewsbury	9	Castleford	3	Huddersfield	25,000	£1,562
	Wigan	7	St. Helens Recs.	7	Swinton	31,000	£2,209
Replay	Wigan	13	St. Helens Recs.	12	Leigh	21,940	£1,437
1930	Widnes	10	Barrow	3	Warrington	25,500	£1,630
	St. Helens	5	Wigan	5	Swinton	37,169	£2,666
Replay	St. Helens	22	Wigan	10	Leigh	24,000	£1,657
1931	Halifax	11	St. Helens	2	Rochdale	21,674	£1,498
	York	15	Warrington	5	Leeds	32,419	£2,329
1932*	Leeds	2	Halifax	2	Huddersfield	31,818	£2,456
Replay	Leeds	9	Halifax	2	Wakefield	21,000	£1,417
	Swinton	7	Wakefield T.	4	Rochdale	21,273	£1,369
1933	Huddersfield	30	Leeds	8	Wakefield	36,359	£2,299
	Warrington	11	St. Helens	5	Swinton	30,373	£2,055
1934	Hunslet	12	Huddersfield	7	Wakefield	27,450	£1,797
	Widnes	7	Oldham	4	Swinton	17,577	£1,050

* Final was played at Wigan, not Wembley

Year	Winners		Runners-up		Venue	Attendance	Receipts
1935	Castleford	11	Barrow	5	Swinton	24,469	£1,534
	Huddersfield	21	Hull	5	Leeds	37,111	£2,753
1936	Leeds	10	Huddersfield	5	Wakefield	37,906	£2,456
	Warrington	7	Salford	2	Wigan	41,538	£2,796
1937	Keighley	0	Wakefield T.	0	Leeds	39,998	£2,793
Replay	Keighley	5	Wakefield T.	3	Huddersfield	14,400	£1,052
	Widnes	13	Wigan	9	Warrington	29,260	£1,972
1938	Barrow	4	Halifax	2	Huddersfield	31,384	£2,431
	Salford	6	Swinton	0	Belle Vue, Manchester	31,664	£2,396
1939	Halifax	10	Leeds	4	Bradford	64,453	£3,645
	Salford	11	Wigan	2	Rochdale	40,000	£2,154

● *During the war the semi-finals were two-legged and the finals were not played at Wembley*

Year	Winners		Runners-up		Venue	Attendance	Receipts
1946	Wakefield T.	7	Hunslet	3	Leeds	33,000	£4,991
	Wigan	12	Widnes	5	Swinton	36,976	£4,746
1947	Bradford N.	11	Warrington	7	Swinton	33,474	£4,946
	Leeds	21	Wakefield T.	0	Huddersfield	35,136	£6,339
1948	Bradford N.	14	Hunslet	7	Leeds	38,125	£7,437
	Wigan	11	Rochdale H.	0	Swinton	26,004	£4,206
1949	Bradford N.	10	Barrow	0	Swinton	26,572	£4,646
	Halifax	11	Huddersfield	10	Bradford	61,875	£8,638
1950	Warrington	16	Leeds	4	Bradford	69,898	£9,861
	Widnes	8	Bradford N.	0	Wigan	25,390	£3,936
1951	Barrow	14	Leeds	14	Bradford	57,459	£8,248
Replay	Barrow	28	Leeds	13	Huddersfield	31,078	£5,098
	Wigan	3	Warrington	2	Swinton	44,621	£7,358
1952	Featherstone R.	6	Leigh	2	Leeds	35,621	£6,494
	Workington T.	5	Barrow	2	Wigan	31,206	£4,782
1953	Huddersfield	7	Wigan	0	Bradford	58,722	£10,519
	St. Helens	9	Warrington	3	Swinton	38,059	£7,768
1954	Halifax	18	Hunslet	3	Bradford	46,961	£8,243
	Warrington	8	Leeds	4	Swinton	36,993	£7,596
1955	Barrow	9	Hunslet	6	Wigan	25,493	£4,671
	Workington T.	13	Featherstone R.	2	Leeds	33,499	£7,305
1956	Halifax	11	Wigan	10	Bradford	51,889	£9,054
	St. Helens	5	Barrow	5	Swinton	38,897	£7,793
Replay	St. Helens	10	Barrow	5	Wigan	44,731	£7,750
1957	Barrow	2	Leigh	2	Wigan	34,628	£6,340
Replay	Barrow	15	Leigh	10	Swinton	28,081	£5,695
	Leeds	10	Whitehaven	9	Bradford	49,094	£8,987
1958	Wigan	5	Rochdale H.	3	Swinton	28,597	£6,354
	Workington T.	8	Featherstone R.	2	Bradford	31,517	£6,325
1959	Wigan	5	Leigh	0	Swinton	27,906	£6,068
	Hull	15	Featherstone R.	5	Bradford	52,131	£9,776
1960	Wakefield T.	11	Featherstone R.	2	Bradford	55,935	£10,390
	Hull	12	Oldham	9	Swinton	27,545	£6,093
1961	St. Helens	26	Hull	9	Bradford	42,935	£9,231
	Wigan	19	Halifax	10	Swinton	35,118	£7,557
1962	Wakefield T.	9	Featherstone R.	0	Bradford	43,625	£8,496
	Huddersfield	6	Hull K.R.	0	Bradford	31,423	£6,685

Year	Winners		Runners-up		Venue	Attendance	Receipts
1963	Wakefield T.	5	Warrington	2	Swinton	15,565	£3,530
	Wigan	18	Hull K.R.	4	Leeds	21,420	£6,029
1964	Widnes	7	Castleford	7	Swinton	25,603	£5,541
Replay	Widnes	7	Castleford	5	Wakefield	28,739	£5,313
	Hull K.R.	5	Oldham	5	Leeds	28,823	£7,411
Replay	Hull K.R.	14	Oldham	17	Swinton	27,209	£5,929

● *Score after 80 minutes was 14-14, then bad light caused match to be abandoned after 12 minutes of extra time with Oldham winning 17-14*

Year	Winners		Runners-up		Venue	Attendance	Receipts
Second Replay	Hull K.R.	12	Oldham	2	Huddersfield	28,732	£6,183
1965	Wigan	25	Swinton	10	St. Helens	26,658	£6,384
	Hunslet	8	Wakefield T.	0	Leeds	21,262	£6,090
1966	St. Helens	12	Dewsbury	5	Swinton	13,046	£3,102
	Wigan	7	Leeds	2	Huddersfield	22,758	£5,971
1967	Featherstone R.	16	Leeds	8	Huddersfield	20,052	£6,276
	Barrow	14	Dewsbury	9	Swinton	13,744	£4,560
1968	Leeds	25	Wigan	4	Swinton	30,058	£9,845
	Wakefield T.	0	Huddersfield	0	Bradford	21,569	£6,196
Replay	Wakefield T.	15	Huddersfield	10	Leeds	20,983	£6,425
1969	Castleford	16	Wakefield T.	10	Leeds	21,497	£8,477
	Salford	15	Warrington	8	Wigan	20,600	£7,738
1970	Castleford	6	St. Helens	3	Swinton	18,913	£7,171
	Wigan	19	Hull K.R.	8	Leeds	18,495	£7,862
1971	Leeds	19	Castleford	8	Bradford	24,464	£9,120
	Leigh	10	Huddersfield	4	Wigan	14,875	£5,670
1972	St. Helens	10	Warrington	10	Wigan	19,300	£8,250
Replay	St. Helens	10	Warrington	6	Wigan	32,380	£12,604
	Leeds	16	Halifax	3	Bradford	16,680	£6,851
1973	Featherstone R.	17	Castleford	3	Leeds	15,369	£9,454
	Bradford N.	23	Dewsbury	7	Leeds	14,028	£9,221
1974	Warrington	17	Dewsbury	7	Wigan	11,789	£6,821
	Featherstone R.	21	Leigh	14	Leeds	7,971	£4,461
1975	Widnes	13	Wakefield T.	7	Bradford	9,155	£5,856
	Warrington	11	Leeds	4	Wigan	13,168	£9,581
1976	Widnes	15	Featherstone R.	9	Swinton	13,019	£9,078
	St. Helens	5	Keighley	4	Huddersfield	9,829	£6,113
1977	Leeds	7	St. Helens	2	Wigan	12,974	£11,379
	Widnes	14	Hull K.R.	5	Leeds	17,053	£16,068
1978	Leeds	14	Featherstone R.	9	Bradford	12,824	£11,322
	St. Helens	12	Warrington	8	Wigan	16,167	£13,960
1979	Widnes	14	Bradford N.	11	Swinton	14,324	£16,363
	Wakefield T.	9	St. Helens	7	Leeds	12,393	£14,195
1980	Hull K.R.	20	Halifax	7	Leeds	17,910	£31,650
	Hull	10	Widnes	5	Swinton	18,347	£29,415
1981	Widnes	17	Warrington	9	Wigan	12,624	£20,673
	Hull K.R.	22	St. Helens	5	Leeds	17,073	£30,616
1982	Hull	15	Castleford	11	Leeds	21,207	£41,867
	Widnes	11	Leeds	8	Swinton	13,075	£25,796
1983	Featherstone R.	11	Bradford N.	6	Leeds	10,784	£22,579
	Hull	14	Castleford	7	Elland Rd, L'ds	26,031	£65,498
1984	Wigan	14	York	8	Elland Rd, L'ds	17,156	£52,888
	Widnes	15	Leeds	4	Swinton	14,046	£37,183

Year	Winners		Runners-up		Venue	Attendance	Receipts
1985	Wigan	18	Hull K.R.	11	Elland Rd, L'ds	19,275	£70,192
	Hull	10	Castleford	10	Leeds	20,982	£64,163
Replay	Hull	22	Castleford	16	Leeds	20,968	£65,005
1986	Castleford	18	Oldham	7	Wigan	12,430	£38,296
	Hull K.R.	24	Leeds	24	Elland Rd, L'ds	23,866	£83,757
Replay	Hull K.R.	17	Leeds	0	Elland Rd, L'ds	32,485	£113,345
1987	St. Helens	14	Leigh	8	Wigan	13,105	£48,627
	Halifax	12	Widnes	8	Leeds	16,064	£61,260
1988	Wigan	34	Salford	4	Bolton W. FC	20,783	£95,876
	Halifax	0	Hull	0	Leeds	20,534	£82,026
Replay	Halifax	4	Hull	3	Elland Rd, L'ds	25,117	£113,679
1989	St. Helens	16	Widnes	14	Wigan	17,119	£70,411
	Wigan	13	Warrington	6	Man. C. FC	26,529	£144,056
1990	Wigan	20	St. Helens	14	Man. U. FC	26,489	£177,161
	Warrington	10	Oldham	6	Wigan	15,631	£80,500
1991	Wigan	30	Oldham	16	Bolton W. FC	19,057	£116,937
	St. Helens	19	Widnes	2	Wigan	16,109	£81,342
1992	Castleford	8	Hull	4	Leeds	14,636	£91,225
	Wigan	71	Bradford N.	10	Bolton W. FC	18,027	£131,124
1993	Widnes	39	Leeds	4	Wigan	13,823	£83,914
	Wigan	15	Bradford N.	6	Elland Rd, L'ds	20,085	£150,167
1994	Wigan	20	Castleford	6	Leeds	17,049	£115,842
	Leeds	20	St. Helens	8	Wigan	20,771	£135,722
1995	Wigan	48	Oldham	20	Huddersfield	12,749	£115,705
	Leeds	39	Featherstone R.	22	Elland Rd, L'ds	21,485	£175,245

NON-LEAGUE CLUBS IN THE CHALLENGE CUP

AMATEUR clubs were invited to compete in the 1986 Rugby League Challenge Cup after a five-year break. The League asked for two of the three county cup competition winners to enter the preliminary round.

The League later decided that from 1987 the Silk Cut Challenge Cup campaign would feature 38 teams, amateur clubs joining the professionals for a preliminary round of six ties. But amateur clubs were not invited to enter the 1993 tournament due to a prolonged dispute between the League and BARLA.

In 1993-94 the competition was expanded with the first round consisting of 64 amateur clubs, half of them from the National Conference League who had home advantage against the rest. The second round was also restricted to amateur clubs but with a random draw. Those 16 winners played away to Division Two professional opposition in the third round, before the Division One clubs entered in the fourth round.

In the early years of the Northern Union Challenge Cup — as it was then called — the line between professional and amateur was less clearly defined.

A variety of Leagues also make it difficult to set non-League clubs apart. Fifty-six clubs appeared in the inaugurating first round of 1897 and four others received byes. The complications continued until 1904 when the League format settled down and non-League clubs had to qualify for the first round.

The last amateur side to eliminate a senior team was Beverley, who won 27-4 at Highfield in the third round in 1995. Ironically, the previous non-league success was also Beverley who beat Ebbw Vale in 1909.

NON-LEAGUE CLUB VICTORIES OVER SENIOR CLUBS SINCE 1904

(Excluding preliminary rounds before 1908)
Non-League Clubs in Capitals

1905-06 *FEATHERSTONE R. 23 v. Widnes 2
(second round)

1907-08 WHITEH'N REC. 13 v. St. Helens 8
(Lost 33-5 at Merthyr Tydfil in second round)

1908-09 BEVERLEY 7 v. Ebbw Vale 2
(Lost 53-2 at Halifax in second round)

1945-46 SHARLSTON 12 v. Work'n Town 7
(1st leg) (Workington Town won 2nd leg 16-2)

1947-48
RISEHOW AND GILLHEAD 10 v. Keighley 2 (2nd leg)
(Keighley won 1st leg 11-0)

1994-95 Highfield 4 v. BEVERLEY 27
(third round, professional clubs excluded from first two rounds. Lost 20-30 to Batley in fourth round home tie at Hull).

*FEATHERSTONE ROVERS are the only non-League club to appear in the old third round when they lost 3-0 at Keighley. In the first round they beat BROOKLAND ROVERS 16-5.

There have been seven drawn clashes, with the professional club winning through each time. The last draw was in 1986-87 when KELLS drew 4-4 with Fulham at Whitehaven. Fulham won the replay 22-14 at Chiswick.

CHALLENGE CUP PROGRESS CHART
A 20-year review . . . .

Key: W — Winners. F — Beaten finalists. SF — Semi-final. P — Preliminary round.

	1994-95	1993-94*	1992-93	1991-92	1990-91	1989-90	1988-89	1987-88	1986-87	1985-86	1984-85	1983-84	1982-83	1981-82	1980-81	1979-80	1978-79	1977-78	1976-77	1975-76
BARROW	4	4	1	2	2	1	2	1	2	2	P	1	2	2	1	2	3	1	2	1
BATLEY	5	4	2	1	1	1	1	1	1	1	1	1	1	2	1	1	1	1	1	1
BLACKPOOL G.	2	1	P	1	1	2	2	2	1	2	1	1	1	1	1	1	1	1	1	1
BRADFORD N.	4	6	SF	SF	3	3	2	1	2	3	3	3	SF	3	1	3	SF	3	3	2
BRAMLEY	4	4	1	P	1	1	P	P	1	2	3	1	1	1	1	1	2	1	1	1
CARLISLE	4	4	1	P	P	1	2	1	2	1	1	P	1	1						
CASTLEFORD	4	SF	3	F	1	P	2	1	1	W	SF	3	SF	SF	2	2	3	3	3	1
CHORLEY B.	3	2	1	P	1	1														
DEWSBURY	4	4	1	2	1	2	1	1	1	1	1	1	1	1	2	1	2	1	3	1
DONCASTER	4	6	1	2	1	P	1	3	1	2	P	2	1	1	1	1	1	1	1	2
FEATHERSTONE R.	SF	6	1	3	1	1	3	2	1	1	P	1	W	P	3	1	1	SF	2	SF
HALIFAX	4	4	3	3	3	1	1	F	W	1	2	1	2	3	2	SF	1	1	1	1
HIGHFIELD	3	4	1	1	1	1	1	1	1	1	2	1	2	1	1	1	1	1	1	1
HUDDERSFIELD	6	4	2	P	P	P	1	P	1	1	1	1	1	1	1	2	3	3	1	1
HULL	4	5	P	SF	P	2	1	SF	3	1	F	2	F	W	2	F	3	2	2	1
HULL K.R.	5	5	3	1	1	1	3	3	3	F	SF	3	1	2	F	W	2	1	SF	2
HUNSLET	4	4	2	2	1	1	P	1	2	1	3	2	3	1	1	1	1	2	1	2
KEIGHLEY C.	5	5	2	1	2	2	2	2	2	1	1	1	1	1	2	1	2	1	1	SF
LEEDS	F	F	SF	2	2	P	3	2	3	SF	1	SF	2	SF	1	2	1	W	W	3
LEIGH	5	4	1	1	1	1	1	1	SF	3	2	1	1	3	2	1	2	1	1	3
LONDON B.	4	4	1	2	1	2	1	1	1	1	1	2	2	2	1					
NOTTINGHAM C.	1	1	1	P	1	1	1	2	2	P	1									
OLDHAM	SF	5	3	1	SF	SF	3	1	2	SF	1	2	1	2	3	2	2	2	1	3
ROCHDALE H.	4	4	2	1	2	2	1	2	1	2	2	1	1	2	1	2	2	1	2	1
RYEDALE-YORK	5	4	1	1	1	1	1	1	P	2	1	SF	1	1	2	2	1	1	1	2
ST. HELENS	4	SF	2	3	F	SF	F	3	F	2	1	3	3	1	SF	2	SF	F	SF	W
SALFORD	5	4	1	1	3	2	1	SF	1	1	2	1	2	1	3	3	1	2	2	2
SHEFFIELD E.	5	5	2	2	2	2	2	2	1	1										
SWINTON	4	4	P	1	1	1	1	1	P	P	1	P	2	1	1	1	1	2	2	1
WAKEFIELD T.	4	4	2	1	2	3	2	1	2	1	2	2	2	3	3	3	F	2	2	1
WARRINGTON	5	5	1	2	3	F	SF	2	1	2	2	2	3	1	SF	3	1	SF	1	3
WHITEHAVEN	6	5	1	1	2	3	1	P	3	1	1	1	1	1	1	1	1	1	1	1
WIDNES	6	6	F	1	SF	3	SF	3	SF	3	3	W	1	F	W	SF	W	3	F	F
WIGAN	W	W	W	W	W	W	W	W	1	3	W	F	1	2	1	1	2	2	2	2
WORKINGTON T.	6	5	1	3	2	1	P	1	P	1	2	2	3	2	2	1	1	2	3	2

* From 1993-94, Second Division clubs entered the new-style tournament in the third round, First Division clubs being exempt until the fourth round, there being six rounds before the semi-finals.

REGAL TROPHY

1994-95 Final

Huddersfield's new Alfred McAlpine Stadium went on show for the first time in a major final as Wigan put on a superb exhibition to lift the Regal Trophy in record-breaking fashion.

The Riversiders beat Warrington 40-10 to pass the record final score of 33-2 they had suffered against Castleford a year earlier. Stand off Frano Botica also set records with eight goals and 20 points.

The recapture of the Regal Trophy meant all the major prizes were in the Wigan trophy cabinet, having won the Silk Cut Challenge Cup, Stones Bitter Championship, Stones Bitter Premiership and the World Club Challenge in the previous season.

While Botica took the scoring honours, the Man-of-the-Match award went to loose forward Phil Clarke, who gave a copybook display on attack and defence. Another outstanding candidate was Western Samoan centre Va'aiga Tuigamala, scorer of two outstanding first-half tries. The fact that the powerful threequarter was off the field for 19 minutes in the second half did little to dilute his impact on the game.

A capacity crowd of nearly 20,000 witnessed vintage Wigan superiority in a commanding first half performance which brought a 28-4 interval lead from four tries and six goals. Warrington rallied in the second period and kept their line intact until the 76th minute.

Wigan blitzed the Wire in the opening half hour, scoring at the rate of almost a point a minute to lead 8-0 after seven minutes, 16-0 after 16, and 22-0 after 24.

Ironically, Warrington applied the first pressure, charging down Shaun Edwards' kick, skipper Greg Mackey chipping to the corner on the sixth tackle only for winger Rob Myler to be the victim of a perfect cover tackle by Clarke.

Wigan opened the scoring in the fifth minute with a penalty goal from Botica, who went on to kick eight from nine attempts. He revealed later that he had swapped his traditional pre-match kicking practice for a mental session behind the wheel of his car, visualising his technique while trapped in snow-hit traffic jams.

Wigan's first try was achieved Kangaroo-style with almost every player handling as the ball was swept across the field three times. Clarke then straightened the attack and fed supporting wingman Jason Robinson, who handed on for Tuigamala to score. Botica added the goal and a penalty soon after, before going in for a 16th minute try, which he again goaled.

The mighty Tuigamala powered through to put Gary Connolly over at the corner and Botica's goal gave Wigan a 22-0 lead.

Warrington struck back with a consolation try created by Kelly Shelford and Mackey, whose floating pass was collected by winger Mark Forster to touch down. Wigan bounced straight back with a piece of Henry Paul brilliance, the Kiwi chipping ahead to regain after a series of juggles for the supporting Clarke to send over Tuigamala for a 24-point interval lead.

Forster snatched his second touchdown in the 66th minute, again created by Shelford, substitute Barrie McDermott opening Wigan's second half try account with four minutes left. Martin Offiah rounded off the scoring with the last play of the day, celebrating in crowd-baiting style.

Edwards — a shock contestant after being ruled out through hamstring injury — collected the Regal Trophy and a prize cheque for £36,000 at the end of a memorable big match debut for the new £16 million stadium.

REGAL TROPHY FINAL

28 January 1995   **Huddersfield**

WIGAN   40   **WARRINGTON   10**

Henry Paul	1.	Jonathan Davies
Jason Robinson	2.	Mark Forster
Va'aiga Tuigamala	3.	Allan Bateman
Gary Connolly	4.	Iestyn Harris
Martin Offiah	5.	Robert Myler
Frano Botica	6.	Francis Maloney
Shaun Edwards, Capt.	7.	Greg Mackey, Capt.
Kelvin Skerrett	8.	Gary Tees
Martin Hall	9.	Tukere Barlow
Neil Cowie	10.	Bruce McGuire
Denis Betts	11.	Paul Cullen
Mick Cassidy	12.	Paul Darbyshire
Phil Clarke	13.	Kelly Shelford
Paul Atcheson	14.	Andrew Bennett
Barrie McDermott	15.	Gary Sanderson

T: Tuigamala (2), Botica, Connolly,
McDermott, Offiah
G: Botica (8)
McDermott for Cowie (Half-time)
Atcheson for Tuigamala (56 min.)
Half-time: 28-4
Attendance: 19,636

T: Forster (2)
G: Davies
Substitutions:
Sanderson for Darbyshire (18 min.)
Bennett for Barlow (66 min.)
Referee: Stuart Cummings (Widnes)

Wigan's Kiwi full back Henry Paul is collared during the 1994-95 Regal Trophy.

1994-95 Round by Round

In the first round, the 16 Second Division clubs entertained non-League opposition with Huddersfield demolishing former professional side Blackpool Gladiators 142-4, a record score for any first-class match. Greg Austin scored a Regal Trophy record nine tries. Huddersfield's 26 tries were equalled by Barrow in their 138-0 hammering of ex-Second Division outfit Nottingham City. Keighley Cougars and Whitehaven both passed the 50-mark as all the Second Division home sides progressed to the second round except Hunslet who were defeated 18-14 by French visitors St. Esteve. The closest contest was Highfield's 12-6 success over Halifax side Ovenden.

In the second round, Castleford and Halifax served up a classic encounter in the televised 10-try tie at Wheldon Road. Key men for the Tigers were Kiwis Richard Blackmore and Tony Kemp, scorers of three of their six touchdowns in a tense 32-26 victory. Second Division London Broncos came within two points of a draw at First Division Salford with only 10 minutes left, the Red Devils' experience helping them to hang on to a 16-14 lead. Another Second Division side, Whitehaven, went one better with a well earned 18-12 home success over First Division strugglers Featherstone Rovers, who lacked Frenchmen Daniel Divet and Frederic Banquet both of whom were on Test duty. Rovers led 6-4 at the break before winger Les Quirk scored seven minutes after the restart to inspire the Cumbrians. Neighbours Workington Town beat fellow relegation candidates Wakefield Trinity 24-8 at Derwent Park, with stand off Kevin Ellis in inspirational form and Vince Fawcett gaining Man-of-the-Match rating with two tries.

Glen Tomlinson scored a hat-trick as Batley beat Ryedale-York 36-8 at Mount Pleasant, while neighbours Dewsbury travelled to Carlisle to record a 30-16 victory. They led 24-0 at half-time before the Cumbrians registered three tries to one in the second period.

Bradford Northern scored seven tries, but only two goals, in the 32-6 defeat of French side St. Esteve at Odsal. Highfield's slim chances of beating Widnes in a home tie switched to St. Helens, were further reduced by the dismissal of centre Glyn Owen after 21 minutes. Widnes went on to score nine tries in a 50-2 victory.

Huddersfield crashed to their first home defeat of the season at the hands of St. Helens, Anthony Sullivan scoring four tries and Ian Pickavance registering a hat-trick in a 52-11 trouncing. Hull entertained Barrow and opened a 20-4 interval lead before losing their way to allow the Cumbrians to close the gap to four points. But Mark Hewitt sealed a 26-16 victory with a 78th minute try. Second Division leaders Keighley Cougars also led 20-4 at half-time in their home tie against Bramley. But they added only two more tries for a 28-4 success despite Bramley playing one man down throughout the second period following the dismissal of Dean Hall. Leeds skipper Ellery Hanley scored the 400th try of his career in the 54-24 triumph over Second Division visitors Swinton, Graham Holroyd contributing 26 points from two tries and nine goals.

Torrential rain for the last 50 minutes of Oldham's home tie against Hull K.R. slowed down the home side's scoring rate, the 28-0 defeat putting question marks against the Robins' potential as promotion candidates. Sheffield Eagles put on a 10-try display as visitors Leigh were disposed of 46-10, the contest being over at the interval with the Eagles leading 28-0. Crisis club Doncaster held a shock 14-12 half-time lead at Warrington before going down 44-14. Former Welsh Rugby Union international forward Scott Quinnell was given his Wigan debut in the home encounter with Second Division Rochdale Hornets. The visitors trailed only 16-10 at the interval before the dismissal of Brian McCarthy on the hour and Wigan finished 34-12 ahead.

In the third round, televised game home side Salford raced to a 24-10 half-time lead before Warrington hit back to win a thriller 31-24.

Second Division promotion candidates Batley entertained St. Helens and led 22-16 with only seconds left. Then Saints' David Lyon scored a try and a magnificent touchline conversion by Bobby Goulding secured a 22-22 draw. In the replay, Batley battled for an hour before the superior fitness of the Saints told in a 50-22 success. Visitors Castleford lodged complaints about the waterlogged pitch at Dewsbury's new Owl Lane ground but still managed to sail to a 30-2 victory in a weather-delayed tie. A full blooded encounter between Hull and visitors Wigan resulted in the sending off of the latter's Denis Betts for an alleged high tackle, plus five players sin-binned. Hull's hopes of a shock win were ended two minutes after the break when Andy Farrell touched down and Wigan coasted to a 38-14 victory.

Keighley Cougars skipper Steve Hall was the star of the show as the Second Division leaders disposed of First Division Sheffield Eagles 26-10 at Cougar Park. The Eagles paid the penalty for play-the-ball infringements with the sin binning of Paul Broadbent and Paul Carr. Veteran forward Paul Dixon scored two tries as Bradford Northern secured a 34-14 success at Whitehaven, the contest being over at half-time as Northern led 26-0. Widnes hooker Steve McCurrie took the Man-of-the-Match award in their 20-6 home success over Oldham, scoring the first of the Chemics' four tries after eight minutes. Goalkicking proved decisive in Workington Town's 18-14 home defeat by Leeds. Both teams scored three tries but Town's Dean Marwood hit the target only once from six attempts, while the visitors' Holroyd scored three from four shots.

In the quarter-finals, Second Division leaders Keighley Cougars were robbed of the scalp of First Division Warrington by a last ditch try and goal from Jonathan Davies which secured a 20-18 victory. The Cougars had opened a 10-point lead before losing Hall with a broken leg as they bid to reach their first Regal semi-final. In another of a series of classic derbies, Wigan beat St. Helens 24-22 at

David Lyon, third round tryscorer for St. Helens at Batley.

Central Park with Test prop Kelvin Skerrett being sent off shortly after scoring the match-clinching try. Wigan's star was Henry Paul, who scored two tries, made several crucial breaks and a try-saving tackle on Chris Joynt. Castleford found top form at Headingley to send Leeds' trophy hopes crashing. The Tigers scored five tries to two in a convincing 34-14 victory, Leeds' skipper Ellery Hanley contributing two consolation tries. Relegation-haunted Widnes, without a league win for three months, tore Bradford Northern to shreds at Naughton Park. They scored four tries in the first 17 minutes to secure a 23-10 success despite being down to 10 men at one stage with Paul Hulme sent off and brother David and Emosi Koloto in the sin bin.

High-flying Castleford were brought down to earth in the semi-finals with a 34-6 defeat at Wigan, Martin Offiah registering his fourth hat-trick of the season. The turning point was just before half-time when Castleford could have taken the lead but for a wild pass. Wigan bounced back to score at the other end for a 14-6 interval lead, adding a further 20 points without reply in the second period. Warrington's Davies continued his comeback after a 11-week absence through injury by contributing 10 points and creating two of the Wire's five tries in the 30-4 victory at Widnes. Teenage Welsh international Iestyn Harris added two tries.

1994-95 RESULTS

First Round

Barrow	138	Nottingham C.	0
Batley	38	Queens	8
Bramley	40	Mysons	14
Carlisle	25	Dudley Hill	12
Dewsbury	22	XIII Catalan	4
Highfield	12	Ovenden	6
Huddersfield	142	Blackpool G.	4
Hull K.R.	48	Hensingham	8
Hunslet	14	St. Esteve	18
Keighley C.	56	Chorley	0
Leigh	18	Leigh M.W.	12
London B.	34	Hemel Hempstead	16
Rochdale H.	34	Woolston R.	10
Ryedale-York	26	West Hull	9
Swinton	32	Saddleworth R.	26
Whitehaven	66	Thatto Heath	0

Second Round

Batley	36	Ryedale-York	8
Bradford N.	32	St. Esteve	6
Carlisle	16	Dewsbury	30
Castleford	32	Halifax	26
Highfield	2	Widnes	50
(at St. Helens)			
Huddersfield	11	St. Helens	52
Hull	26	Barrow	16
Keighley C.	28	Bramley	4
Leeds	54	Swinton	24
Oldham	28	Hull K.R.	0
Salford	16	London B.	14
Sheffield E.	46	Leigh	10
Warrington	44	Doncaster	14
Whitehaven	18	Featherstone R.	12
Wigan	34	Rochdale H.	12
Workington T.	24	Wakefield T.	8

Third Round

Batley	22	St. Helens	22
Dewsbury	2	Castleford	30
Hull	14	Wigan	38
Keighley C.	26	Sheffield E.	10
Salford	24	Warrington	31
Whitehaven	14	Bradford N.	34
Widnes	20	Oldham	6
Workington T.	14	Leeds	18

Replay

St. Helens	50	Batley	22

Fourth Round

Keighley C.	18	Warrington	20
Leeds	14	Castleford	34
Widnes	23	Bradford N.	10
Wigan	24	St. Helens	22

Semi-finals

Widnes	4	Warrington	30
Wigan	34	Castleford	6

Final

Wigan	40	Warrington	10
(at Huddersfield)			

1994-95 PRIZES

First Round .... £2,700 to each RFL club and two French clubs
£1,000 to each amateur club
Second Round........................ £2,700 to losers
Third Round .... £4,200 to losers
Quarter-finals........................ £6,500 to losers
Semi-finals ....£10,250 to losers
Runners-up £19,000
Winners £36,000

Total Prize Money	£246,000
Capital Development Fund	£164,000
Grand Total	£410,000

REGAL TROPHY ROLL OF HONOUR

Season	Winners		Runners-up		Venue	Attendance	Receipts
1971-72	Halifax	22	Wakefield T.	11	Bradford	7,975	£2,545
1972-73	Leeds	12	Salford	7	Huddersfield	10,102	£4,563
1973-74	Warrington	27	Rochdale H.	16	Wigan	9,347	£4,380
1974-75	Bradford N.	3	Widnes	2	Warrington	5,935	£3,305
1975-76	Widnes	19	Hull	13	Leeds	9,035	£6,275
1976-77	Castleford	25	Blackpool B.	15	Salford	4,512	£2,919
1977-78	Warrington	9	Widnes	4	St. Helens	10,258	£8,429
1978-79	Widnes	16	Warrington	4	St. Helens	10,743	£11,709
1979-80	Bradford N.	6	Widnes	0	Leeds	9,909	£11,560
1980-81	Warrington	12	Barrow	5	Wigan	12,820	£21,020
1981-82	Hull	12	Hull K.R.	4	Leeds	25,245	£42,987
1982-83	Wigan	15	Leeds	4	Elland Rd, Leeds	19,553	£49,027
1983-84	Leeds	18	Widnes	10	Wigan	9,510	£19,824
1984-85	Hull K.R.	12	Hull	0	Hull City FC	25,326	£69,555
1985-86	Wigan	11	Hull K.R.	8	Elland Rd, Leeds	17,573	£66,714
1986-87	Wigan	18	Warrington	4	Bolton W. FC	21,144	£86,041
1987-88	St. Helens	15	Leeds	14	Wigan	16,669	£62,232
1988-89	Wigan	12	Widnes	6	Bolton W. FC	20,709	£94,874
1989-90	Wigan	24	Halifax	12	Leeds	17,810	£73,688
1990-91	Warrington	12	Bradford N.	2	Leeds	11,154	£57,652
1991-92	Widnes	24	Leeds	0	Wigan	15,070	£90,453
1992-93	Wigan	15	Bradford N.	8	Elland Rd, Leeds	13,221	£90,204
1993-94	Castleford	33	Wigan	2	Leeds	15,626	£99,804
1994-95	Wigan	40	Warrington	10	McAlpine St'm, Hudd'd	19,636	£161,976

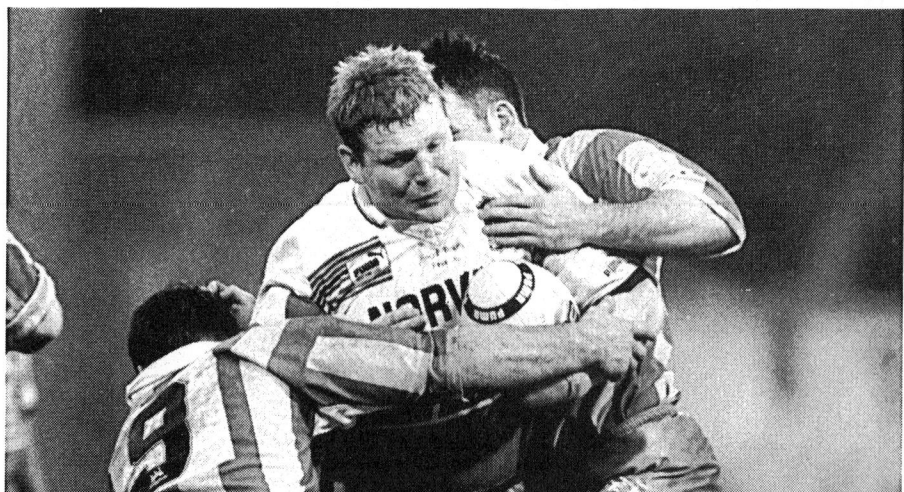

A Warrington twin tackle halts Wigan's Neil Cowie in the 1994-95 Regal final.

REGAL TROPHY FINAL ....
A REVIEW

1971-72
Halifax 22 Hepworth; Rayner, Davies (1t),
Willicombe (1t), Kelly (1t); Burton (5g), Baker
(Sanderson); Dewhirst, Hawksley, Callon (1t)
(Reeves), Fogerty, Martin, Halmshaw
Wakefield T. 11 Wraith (Ward); Slater (1t),
Marston, Hegarty, Major; Topliss (1t), Harkin;
Jeanes, Morgan, Lyons, Harrison (Spencer),
Valentine (1t), N. Fox (1g)
Referee: S. Shepherd (Oldham)
1972-73
Leeds 12 Holmes (1g); Alan Smith, Hynes,
Dyl, Atkinson (2t); Hardisty, Hepworth;
Clawson (2g) (Ward), Fisher (Pickup), Jeanes,
Haigh, Cookson, Eccles
Salford 7 Charlton; Colloby, Watkins (2g),
Hesketh, Richards; Gill (P. Ward), Banner;
Ramshaw, J. Ward, Mackay, Grice (Davies),
Kirkbride, Dixon (1t)
Referee: W.H. Thompson (Huddersfield)
1973-74
Warrington 27 Whitehead (1t, 6g); M. Philbin,
Noonan (2t), Reynolds (Pickup), Bevan (1t);
Whittle, Gordon; D. Chisnall (Nicholas 1t),
Ashcroft, Brady, Wright, Wanbon, B. Philbin
Rochdale H. 16 Crellin; Brelsford (2t), Brophy
(1t), Taylor (1t), Aspinall; Butler (Wood),
Gartland; Holliday (2g), Harris, Whitehead,
Fogerty, Sheffield, Halmshaw
Referee: D.G. Kershaw (York)
1974-75
Bradford N. 3 Carlton (1t); Francis, Ward,
Gant, D. Redfearn; Blacker, Seabourne; Earl,
Jarvis, Jackson, Joyce, Trotter, Fearnley
Widnes 2 Dutton (1g); A. Prescott, D. O'Neill,
Aspey, Anderson; Hughes, Bowden; Mills,
Elwell, Sheridan, Adams, Blackwood,
Laughton
Referee: G.F. Lindop (Wakefield)
1975-76
Widnes 19 Dutton (3g); A. Prescott, George,
Aspey, Jenkins (2t); Hughes, Bowden (1t, 1dg);
Mills, Elwell, Wood, Foran, Sheridan,
Adams (1t)
Hull 13 Stephenson; Macklin, Clark, Portz,
Hunter (1t); Hancock, Foulkes (Davidson);
Ramsey, Flanagan, Wardell, Boxall (2g),
Walker, Crane (2t)
Referee: J.V. Moss (Manchester)
1976-77
Castleford 25 Wraith (1t); Fenton, Joyner (1t),
P. Johnson (1t), Briggs; Burton (1t), Stephens
(1t); Khan, Spurr, A. Dickinson, Reilly, Lloyd
(5g), S. Norton
Blackpool B. 15 Reynolds; Robinson, Heritage,

Machen (1t), Pitman (Lamb); Marsh, Newall;
Hamilton, Allen (1t), Egan (1t, 3g), Gamble,
Groves (Hurst), M. Pattinson
Referee: M.J. Naughton (Widnes)
1977-78
Warrington 9 Finnigan; Hesford (3g), Benyon,
Wilson, Bevan (1t); K. Kelly, Gordon; Lester,
Dalgreen, Nicholas, Martyn, B. Philbin, Potter
Widnes 4 Eckersley; S. Wright, Aspey, George,
Woods (2g); Hughes, Bowden; Ramsey, Elwell,
Shaw (Dearden), Adams, Hull, Laughton
Referee: W.H. Thompson (Huddersfield)
1978-79
Widnes 16 Eckersley; S. Wright (1t), Aspey,
Hughes, Burke (3g); Moran, Bowden; Mills,
Elwell (2dg), Shaw, Dearden, Hull (1t), Adams
(2dg)
Warrington 4 Finnigan; M. Kelly, Hesford
(2g), Benyon, Sutton; K. Kelly (Hunter),
Gordon; Lester, Waller, Nicholas, Case,
Martyn, A. Gwilliam
Referee: G.F. Lindop (Wakefield)
1979-80
Bradford N. 6 Mumby (1g); Barends,
D. Redfearn, D. Parker (1t), Gant; Stephenson
(1dg), A. Redfearn; Thompson, Bridges,
Forsyth (I. Van Bellen), Grayshon, G. Van
Bellen (Ferres), Casey
Widnes 0 Eckersley; S. Wright, Aspey, George,
Burke; Hughes, Bowden; Hogan (Mills),
Elwell, Shaw, L. Gorley, Hull, Adams
Referee: W.H. Thompson (Huddersfield)
1980-81
Warrington 12 Hesford (2g, 2dg); Thackray,
I. Duane, Bevan (2t), M. Kelly; K. Kelly,
A. Gwilliam; Courtney, Waller, Case, Martyn,
Potter, Hunter (Eccles)
Barrow 5 Elliott; McConnell, French, Ball (1g),
Wainwright; Mason (1t), Cairns; D. Chisnall,
Allen (Szymala), Flynn, K. James, Kirkby,
Hadley
Referee: W.H. Thompson (Huddersfield)
1981-82
Hull 12 Banks; O'Hara, Harrison, Leuluai,
Prendiville; Day, Dean (1dg) (Harkin); Skerrett,
Wileman (1t), Stone, Crane, L. Crooks (4g),
Norton
Hull K.R. 4 Fairbairn (2g); Hubbard,
M. Smith, Hogan, Muscroft; Hartley, Harkin
(Burton); Holdstock (Millington), Watkinson,
Crooks, Lowe, Casey, Hall
Referee: G.F. Lindop (Wakefield)
1982-83
Wigan 15 Williams; Ramsdale, Stephenson,
Whitfield (4g, 1dg), Gill (1t) (Juliff 1t);
Foy, Fairhurst; Shaw, Kiss, Campbell, West
(Case), Scott, Pendlebury

Leeds 4 Hague; Campbell, Wilkinson, Dyl, Andy Smith; Holmes, Dick (2g); Dickinson, Ward, Burke, Sykes, W. Heron, D. Heron
Referee: R. Campbell (Widnes)
1983-84
Leeds 18 Wilkinson; Prendiville, Creasser (5g), Bell, Andy Smith; Holmes (1t), Dick (1t); Keith Rayne, Ward (Squire), Kevin Rayne, Moorby, Laurie, Webb
Widnes 10 Burke (1g); S. Wright, Keiron O'Loughlin, Lydon (1t), Linton (1t); Hughes, Gregory; S. O'Neill, Elwell, Tamati, L. Gorley, Whitfield, Adams
Referee: W.H. Thompson (Huddersfield)
1984-85
Hull K.R. 12 Fairbairn; Clark (1t), Robinson, Prohm (1t), Laws; M. Smith, Harkin; Broadhurst, Watkinson, Ema, Burton, Hogan (1t), Miller
Hull 0 Kemble (Schofield); S. Evans, Ah Kuoi, Leuluai, O'Hara; Topliss, Sterling; Edmonds (Dannatt), Patrick, Rose, L. Crooks, Proctor, Divorty
Referee: S. Wall (Leigh)
1985-86
Wigan 11 Hampson; Mordt, Stephenson (1g), Hanley, Gill (Edwards); Ella, M. Ford (1t); Dowling (1dg), Kiss, Wane (1t), West, Goodway, Potter (Du Toit)
Hull K.R. 8 Lydiat (1t); Clark, M. Smith, Dorahy, Laws (1t); G. Smith, Harkin; P. Johnston (Robinson), Watkinson, Ema, Burton, Kelly, Miller
Referee: J. Holdsworth (Kippax)
1986-87
Wigan 18 Hampson; Stephenson, Lydon, Bell (1t), Gill (2t, 1g); Hanley, Edwards; West, Dermott, Case, Roberts, Potter, Goodway (1t)
Warrington 4 Johnson; Meadows, Cullen, Ropati, Forster (1t); K. Kelly, Peters (R. Duane); Boyd, Tamati (Rathbone), Jackson, Sanderson, Roberts, M. Gregory
1987-88 J. Holdsworth (Kippax)
St. Helens 15 Veivers; Tanner, Loughlin (2t, 3g), Elia, Quirk; Cooper, Holding (1dg); Burke, Groves, Souto (Evans), Forber, Haggerty, Platt
Leeds 14 Gurr; Morris, Schofield, Jackson (1t), Basnett (Gibson); Creasser (1t, 3g), Ashton; Tunks, Maskill, Kevin Rayne (Fairbank), Powell, Medley, D. Heron
Referee: G.F. Lindop (Wakefield)
1988-89
Wigan 12 Hampson; Bell, K. Iro (1t), Lydon (2g) (Gregory), T. Iro; Byrne, Edwards; Shelford (Goodway), Dermott, Wane, Betts, Potter, Hanley (1t)

Widnes 6 Tait; Thackray, Currier (1g), D. Wright (1t), Offiah; A. Myler, D. Hulme; Sorensen, McKenzie, Grima, M. O'Neill, Koloto (P. Hulme), R. Eyres
Referee: J. Holdsworth (Kippax)
1989-90
Wigan 24 Lydon (2g); Marshall, K. Iro, Bell, Preston; Edwards (1t), Gregory; Lucas (Wane), Dermott, Platt, Betts, Gildart (Goodway 1t), Hanley (3t)
Halifax 12 Whitfield (Smith) (Scott); Riddlesden, T. Anderson, Hetherington, George; Dorahy, Lyons; Hill (1t), McCallion, Johnston, Bell, Milner, Holliday (4g)
Referee: D.G. Kershaw (Easingwold)
1990-91
Warrington 12 Lyon (4g); Drummond, Bateman, Thorniley, Forster; O'Sullivan, Ellis; Harmon (Phillips), Mann, Chambers (Thomas 1t), Mercer, McGinty, Cullen
Bradford N. 2 Wilkinson; Cordle, Shelford, Simpson, Marchant (Hellewell); Summers, Iti; Hobbs (1g), Noble, Hamer, Medley, Croft, Pendlebury
Referee: J. Smith (Halifax)
1991-92
Widnes 24 Tait (1t); Devereux, Currier, D. Wright, Sarsfield (Atcheson); Davies (1t, 3g, 1dg), Dowd; Sorensen (1t), P. Hulme, D. Smith, Howard, R. Eyres, Holliday (1t, 1dg) (Grima)
Leeds 0 Edwards; Ford, Creasser, Irving (Gibson), Bentley; Schofield, Goulding; Wane (Molloy), Gunn, O'Neill, Powell, Dixon, Divorty
Referee: B. Galtress (Bradford)
1992-93
Wigan 15 Hampson (1dg); Robinson (1t), Bell, Farrar, Offiah (Lydon); Botica (3g), Edwards (1t); Cowie, Dermott, Platt, Betts, McGinty, Clarke (Panapa)
Bradford N. 8 Watson; Marchant, McGowan (1t), Anderson (Mumby 1g), Simpson; Summers, Fox; Hobbs (1g), Noble (Clark), R. Powell, Medley, Fairbank, D. Heron
Referee: J. Holdsworth (Kippax)
1993-94
Castleford 33 Steadman; Ellis, Blackmore, Anderson (1t) (Hay), Middleton; Kemp (1 dg), Ford; Crooks (1t, 6g), Russell, Ketteridge (2t) (Sampson), Morrison, Smales, Nikau (1t)
Wigan 2 Lydon; Robinson, Mather, Connolly, Offiah; Botica (1g), Edwards (Panapa); Skerrett, Dermott, Platt, Cowie (Cassidy), Farrell, Clarke
Referee: D. Campbell (Widnes)

REGAL TROPHY MAN OF THE MATCH

Season	Winner	Team	Position
1971-72	Bruce Burton	Halifax (v. Wakefield T.)	Stand off
1972-73	Keith Hepworth	Leeds (v. Salford)	Scrum half
1973-74	Kevin Ashcroft	Warrington (v. Rochdale H.)	Hooker
1974-75	Barry Seabourne	Bradford N. (v. Widnes)	Scrum half
1975-76	Reg Bowden	Widnes (v. Hull)	Scrum half
1976-77	Gary Stephens	Castleford	Scrum half
	Howard Allen	Blackpool B.	Hooker
1977-78	Steve Hesford	Warrington (v. Widnes)	Winger
1978-79	David Eckersley	Widnes (v. Warrington)	Full back
1979-80	Len Casey	Bradford N. (v. Widnes)	Loose forward
1980-81	Tommy Martyn	Warrington (v. Barrow)	Second row
1981-82	Trevor Skerrett	Hull (v. Hull K.R.)	Prop
1982-83	Martin Foy	Wigan (v. Leeds)	Stand off
1983-84	Mark Laurie	Leeds (v. Widnes)	Second row
1984-85	Paul Harkin	Hull K.R. (v. Hull)	Scrum half
1985-86	Paul Harkin	Hull K.R. (v. Wigan)	Scrum half
1986-87	Andy Goodway	Wigan (v. Warrington)	Loose forward
1987-88	Paul Loughlin	St. Helens (v. Leeds)	Centre
1988-89	Ellery Hanley	Wigan (v. Widnes)	Loose forward
1989-90	Ellery Hanley	Wigan (v. Halifax)	Loose forward
1990-91	Billy McGinty	Warrington (v. Bradford N.)	Second row
1991-92	Les Holliday	Widnes (v. Leeds)	Loose forward
1992-93	Shaun Edwards	Wigan (v. Bradford N.)	Scrum half
1993-94	Martin Ketteridge	Castleford (v. Wigan)	Prop
1994-95	Phil Clarke	Wigan (v. Warrington)	Loose forward

Jubilant Wigan skipper Shaun Edwards shows off the 1994-95 Regal Trophy after the 40-10 victory over Warrington.

REGAL TROPHY FINAL PLAYERS' REGISTER

The following is an index of players who have appeared in the Regal Trophy final since its inauguration as the Player's No. 6 Trophy in 1971-72.
W — winners, L — losers. Substitute appearances in lower case letters. The year denotes the second half of the season.

ADAMS, Mick: Widnes 75L, 76W, 78L, 79W, 80L, 84L
AH KUOI, Fred: Hull 85L
ALLEN, Howard: Blackpool B. 77L; Barrow 81L
ANDERSON, Chris: Widnes 75L
ANDERSON, Grant: Castleford 94W
ANDERSON, Tony: Halifax 90L; Bradford N. 93L
ASHCROFT, Kevin: Warrington 74W
ASHTON, Ray: Leeds 88L
ASPEY, Mal: Widnes 75L, 76W, 78L, 79W, 80L
ASPINALL, Willie: Rochdale H. 74L
ATCHESON, Paul: Widnes 92w; Wigan 95w
ATKINSON, John: Leeds 73W

BAKER, Gordon: Halifax 72W
BALL, Ian: Barrow 81L
BANKS, Barry: Hull 82W
BANNER, Peter: Salford 73L
BARENDS, David: Bradford N. 80W
BARLOW, Tukere: Warrington 95L
BASNETT, John: Leeds 88L
BATEMAN, Allan: Warrington 91W, 95L
BELL, Dean: Leeds 84W; Wigan 87W, 89W, 90W, 93W
BELL, Peter: Halifax 90L
BENNETT, Andrew: Warrington 95l
BENTLEY, John: Leeds 92L
BENYON, Billy: Warrington 78W, 79L
BETTS, Denis: Wigan 89W, 90W, 93W, 95W
BEVAN, John: Warrington 74W, 78W, 81W
BLACKER, Mick: Bradford N. 75W
BLACKMORE, Richard: Castleford 94W
BLACKWOOD, Bob: Widnes 75L
BOTICA, Frano: Wigan 93W, 94L, 95W
BOWDEN, Reg: Widnes 75L, 76W, 78L, 79W, 80L
BOXALL, Keith: Hull 76L
BOYD, Les: Warrington 87L
BRADY, Brian: Warrington 74W
BRELSFORD, Norman: Rochdale H. 74L
BRIDGES, John "Keith": Bradford N. 80W
BRIGGS, Trevor: Castleford 77W
BROADHURST, Mark: Hull K.R. 85W
BROPHY, Tom: Rochdale H. 74L
BURKE, Mick: Widnes 79W, 80L, 84L
BURKE, Tony: Leeds 83L; St. Helens 88W
BURTON, Bruce: Halifax 72W; Castleford 77W
BURTON, Chris: Hull K.R. 82l, 85W, 86L
BUTLER, John: Rochdale H. 74L
BYRNE, Ged: Wigan 89W

CAIRNS, David: Barrow 81L
CALLON, David: Halifax 72W
CAMPBELL, Danny: Wigan 83W
CAMPBELL, Mark: Leeds 83l
CARLTON, Stuart: Bradford N. 75W
CASE, Brian: Warrington 79L, 81W; Wigan 83w, 87W
CASEY, Len: Bradford N. 80W; Hull K.R. 82L
CASSIDY, Mick: Wigan 94l, 95W
CHAMBERS, Gary: Warrington 91W
CHARLTON, Paul: Salford 73L
CHISNALL, Dave: Warrington 74W; Barrow 81L
CLARK, Garry: Hull K.R. 85W, 86L
CLARK, George: Hull 76L
CLARK, Trevor: Bradford N. 93l
CLARKE, Phil: Wigan 93W, 94L, 95W
CLAWSON, Terry: Leeds 73W
COLLOBY, Tony: Salford 73L
CONNOLLY, Gary: Wigan 94L, 95W
COOKSON, Phil: Leeds 73W
COOPER, Shane: St. Helens 88W
CORDLE, Gerald: Bradford N. 91L
COURTNEY, Neil: Warrington 81W
COWIE, Neil: Wigan 93W, 94L, 95W
CRANE, Mick: Hull 76L, 82W
CREASSER, David: Leeds 84W, 88L, 92L
CRELLIN, Jim: Rochdale H. 74L
CROFT, David: Bradford N. 91L
CROOKS, Lee: Hull 82W, 85L; Castleford 94W
CROOKS, Steve: Hull K.R. 82L
CULLEN, Paul: Warrington 87L, 91W, 95L
CURRIER, Andy: Widnes 89L, 92W

DALGREEN, John: Warrington 78W
DANNATT, Andy: Hull 85l
DARBYSHIRE, Paul: Warrington 95L
DAVIDSON, Chris: Hull 76l
DAVIES, Doug: Salford 73l
DAVIES, Jonathan: Widnes 92W; Warrington 95L
DAVIES, Phil: Halifax 72W
DAY, Terry: Hull 82W
DEAN, Tony: Hull 82W
DEARDEN, Alan: Widnes 78l, 79W
DERMOTT, Martin: Wigan 87W, 89W, 90W, 93W, 94L
DEVEREUX, John: Widnes 92W
DEWHIRST, Terry: Halifax 72W
DICK, Kevin: Leeds 83L, 84W
DICKINSON, Alan: Castleford 77W
DICKINSON, Roy: Leeds 83L
DIVORTY, Gary: Hull 85L; Leeds 92L

DIXON, Colin: Salford 73L
DIXON, Paul: Leeds 92L
DORAHY, John: Hull K.R. 86L; Halifax 90L
DOWD, Barry: Widnes 92W
DOWLING, Greg: Wigan 86W
DRUMMOND, Des: Warrington 91W
DUANE, Ian: Warrington 81W
DUANE, Ronnie: Warrington 87L
DU TOIT, Nick: Wigan 86w
DUTTON, Ray: Widnes 75L, 76W
DYL, Les: Leeds 73W, 83L

EARL, Kelvin: Bradford N. 75W
ECCLES, Bob: Warrington 81w
ECCLES, Graham: Leeds 73W
ECKERSLEY, David: Widnes 78L 79W, 80L
EDMONDS, Phil: Hull 85L
EDWARDS, Morvin: Leeds 92L
EDWARDS, Shaun: Wigan 86W, 87W, 89W, 90W, 93W, 94L, 95W
EGAN, Joe: Blackpool B. 77L
ELIA, Mark: St. Helens 88W
ELLA, Steve: Wigan 86W
ELLIOTT, David: Barrow 81L
ELLIS, Kevin: Warrington 91W
ELLIS, St. John; Castleford 94W
ELWELL, Keith: Widnes 75L, 76W, 78L, 79W, 80L, 84L
EMA, Asuquo: Hull K.R. 85W, 86L
EVANS, Steve: Hull 85L
EVANS, Stuart: St. Helens 88w
EYRES, Richard: Widnes 89L, 92W

FAIRBAIRN, George: Hull K.R. 82L, 85W
FAIRBANK, John: Leeds 88l
FAIRBANK, Karl: Bradford N. 93L
FAIRHURST, Jimmy: Wigan 83W
FARRAR, Andrew: Wigan 93W
FARRELL, Andrew: Wigan 94L
FEARNLEY, Stan: Bradford N. 75W
FENTON, Steve: Castleford 77W
FERRES, Steve: Bradford N. 80w
FINNIGAN, Derek: Warrington 78W, 79L
FISHER, Tony: Leeds 73W
FLANAGAN, Peter: Hull 76L
FLYNN, Malcolm: Barrow 81L
FOGERTY, Terry: Halifax 72W; Rochdale H. 74L
FORAN, John: Widnes 76W
FORBER, Paul: St. Helens 88W
FORD, Mike: Wigan 86W; Castleford 94W
FORD, Phil: Leeds 92L
FORSTER, Mark: Warrington 87L, 91W, 95L
FORSYTH, Colin: Bradford N. 80W
FOULKES, Kenny: Hull 76L
FOX, Deryck: Bradford N. 93L
FOX, Neil: Wakefield T. 72L
FOY, Martin: Wigan 83W

FRANCIS, Rudi: Bradford N. 75W
FRENCH, Nigel: Barrow 81L

GAMBLE, Paul: Blackpool B. 77L
GANT, Les: Bradford N. 75W, 80W
GARTLAND, Peter: Rochdale H. 74L
GEORGE, Derek "Mick": Widnes 76W, 78L, 80L
GEORGE, Wilf: Halifax 90L
GIBSON, Carl: Leeds 88L, 92l
GILDART, Ian: Wigan 90W
GILL, Henderson: Wigan 83W, 86W, 87W
GILL, Ken: Salford 73L
GOODWAY, Andy: Wigan 86W, 87W, 89w, 90w
GORDON, Parry: Warrington 74W, 78W, 79L
GORLEY, Les: Widnes 80L, 84L
GOULDING, Bobby: Leeds 92L
GRAYSHON, Jeff: Bradford N. 80W
GREGORY, Andy: Widnes 84L; Wigan 89w, 90W
GREGORY, Mike: Warrington 87L
GRICE, Alan: Salford 73L
GRIMA, Joe: Widnes 89L, 92w
GROVES, Ken: Blackpool B. 77L
GROVES, Paul: St. Helens 88W
GUNN, Richard: Leeds 92L
GURR, Marty: Leeds 88L
GWILLIAM, Alan: Warrington 79L, 81W

HADLEY, Derek: Barrow 81L
HAGGERTY, Roy: St. Helens 88W
HAGUE, Neil: Leeds 83l
HAIGH, Bob: Leeds 73W
HALL, David: Hull K.R. 82L
HALL, Martin: Wigan 95W
HALMSHAW, Tony: Halifax 72W; Rochdale H. 74L
HAMER, Jon: Bradford N. 91L
HAMILTON, Jim: Blackpool B. 77L
HAMPSON, Steve: Wigan 86W, 87W, 89W, 93W
HANCOCK, Brian: Hull 76L
HANLEY, Ellery: Wigan 86W, 87W, 89W, 90W
HARDISTY, Alan: Leeds 73W
HARKIN, Kevin: Wakefield T. 72L; Hull 82w
HARKIN, Paul: Hull K.R. 82L, 85W, 86L
HARMON, Neil: Warrington 91W
HARRIS, Iestyn: Warrington 95L
HARRIS, Ray: Rochdale H. 74L
HARRISON, Chris: Hull 82W
HARRISON, Peter: Wakefield T. 72L
HARTLEY, Steve: Hull K.R. 82L
HAWKSLEY, Roy: Halifax 72W
HAY, Andy: Castleford 94w
HEGARTY, John: Wakefield T. 72L
HELLEWELL, Phil: Bradford N. 911
HEPWORTH, Keith: Leeds 73W
HEPWORTH, Tony: Halifax 72W
HERITAGE, John: Blackpool B. 77L
HERON, David: Leeds 83L, 88L; Bradford N. 93L

HERON, Wayne: Leeds 83L
HESFORD, Steve: Warrington 78W, 79L, 81W
HESKETH, Chris: Salford 73L
HETHERINGTON, Brian: Halifax 90L
HILL, Brendan: Halifax 90L
HOBBS, David: Bradford N. 91L, 93L
HOGAN, Brian: Widnes 80L
HOGAN, Phil: Hull K.R. 82L, 85W
HOLDING, Neil: St. Helens 88W
HOLDSTOCK, Roy: Hull K.R. 82L
HOLLIDAY, Bill: Rochdale H. 74L
HOLLIDAY, Les: Halifax 90L; Widnes 92W
HOLMES, John: Leeds 73W, 83L, 84W
HOWARD, Harvey: Widnes 92W
HUBBARD, Steve: Hull K.R. 82L
HUGHES, Eric: Widnes 75L, 76W, 78L, 79W,
  80L, 84L
HULL, David: Widnes 78L, 79W, 80L
HULME, David: Widnes 89L
HULME, Paul: Widnes 89l, 92W
HUNTER, Eddie: Warrington 79l, 81W
HUNTER, Paul: Hull 76L
HURST, Phil: Blackpool B. 77l
HYNES, Syd: Leeds 73W

IRO, Kevin: Wigan 89W, 90W
IRO, Tony: Wigan 89W
IRVING, Simon: Leeds 92L
ITI, Brett: Bradford N. 91L

JACKSON, Bob: Warrington 87L
JACKSON, Peter: Leeds 88L
JACKSON, Phil: Bradford N. 75W
JAMES, Kevin: Barrow 81L
JARVIS, Francis: Bradford N. 75W
JEANES, David: Wakefield T. 72L; Leeds 73W
JENKINS, David: Widnes 76W
JOHNSON, Brian: Warrington 87L
JOHNSON, Phil: Castleford 77W
JOHNSTON, Lindsay: Halifax 90L
JOHNSTON, Peter: Hull K.R. 86L
JOYCE, Graham: Bradford N. 75W
JOYNER, John: Castleford 77W
JULIFF, Brian: Wigan 83w

KAHN, Paul: Castleford 77W
KELLY, Andy: Hull K.R. 86L
KELLY, Ken: Warrington 78W, 79L, 81W, 87L
KELLY, Mike: Halifax 72W
KELLY, Mike: Warrington 79L, 81W
KEMBLE, Gary: Hull 85L
KEMP, Tony: Castleford 94W
KETTERIDGE, Martin: Castleford 94W
KIRKBRIDE, Bill: Salford 73L
KIRKBY, Steve: Barrow 81L
KISS, Nicky: Wigan 83W, 86W
KOLOTO, Emosi: Widnes 89L

LAMB, Cliff: Blackpool B. 77l
LAUGHTON, Doug: Widnes 75L, 78L
LAURIE, Mark: Leeds 84W
LAWS, David: Hull K.R. 85W, 86L
LESTER, Roy: Warrington 78W, 79L
LEULUAI, James: Hull 82W, 85L
LINTON, Ralph: Widnes 84L
LLOYD, Geoff "Sammy": Castleford 77W
LOUGHLIN, Paul: St. Helens 88W
LOWE, Phil: Hull K.R. 82L
LUCAS, Ian: Wigan 90W
LYDIAT, John: Hull K.R. 86L
LYDON, Joe: Widnes 84L; Wigan 87W, 89W,
  90W, 93w, 94L
LYON, David: Warrington 91W
LYONS, John: Halifax 90L
LYONS, Steve: Wakefield T. 72L

McCALLION, Seamus: Halifax 90L
McCONNELL, Ralph: Barrow 81L
McDERMOTT, Barrie: Wigan 95w
McGINTY, Billy: Warrington 91W; Wigan 93W
McGOWAN, Steve: Bradford N. 93L
McGUIRE, Bruce: Warrington 95L
MACKAY, Graham: Salford 73L
McKENZIE, Phil: Widnes 89L
MACHEN, Paul: Blackpool B. 77L
MACKEY, Greg: Warrington 95L
MACKLIN, Alf: Hull 76L
MAJOR, Mick: Wakefield T. 72L
MALONEY, Francis: Warrington 95L
MANN, Duane: Warrington 91W
MARCHANT, Tony: Bradford N. 91L, 93L
MARSH, Ged: Blackpool B. 77L
MARSHALL, David: Wigan 90W
MARSTON, Jack: Wakefield T. 72L
MARTIN, John: Halifax 72W
MARTYN, Tommy: Warrington 78W, 79L, 81W
MASKILL, Colin: Leeds 88L
MASON, Mel: Barrow 81L
MATHER, Barrie-Jon: Wigan 94L
MEADOWS, Kevin: Warrington 87L
MEDLEY, Paul: Leeds 88L; Bradford N. 91L, 93L
MERCER, Gary: Warrington 91W
MIDDLETON, Simon: Castleford 94W
MILLER, Gavin: Hull K.R. 85W, 86L
MILLINGTON, John: Hull K.R. 82l
MILLS, Jim: Widnes 75L, 76W, 79W, 80l
MILNER, Richard: Halifax 90L
MOLLOY, Steve: Leeds 92l
MOORBY, Gary: Leeds 84W
MORAN, Dave: Widnes 79W
MORDT, Ray: Wigan 86W
MORGAN, Mick: Wakefield T. 72L
MORRIS, Steve: Leeds 88L
MORRISON, Tony: Castleford 94W
MUMBY, Keith: Bradford N. 80W, 93l

MUSCROFT, Peter: Hull K.R. 82L
MYLER, Rob: Warrington 95L
MYLER, Tony: Widnes 89L

NEWALL, Jackie: Blackpool B. 77L
NICHOLAS, Mike: Warrington 74w, 78W, 79L
NIKAU, Tawera: Castleford 94W
NOBLE, Brian: Bradford N. 91L, 93L
NOONAN, Derek: Warrington 74W
NORTON, Steve: Castleford 77W; Hull 82W

OFFIAH, Martin: Widnes 89L; Wigan 93W, 94L, 95W
O'HARA, Dane: Hull 82W, 85L
O'LOUGHLIN, Keiron: Widnes 84L
O'NEILL, Dennis: Widnes 75L
O'NEILL, Mike: Widnes 89L; Leeds 92L
O'NEILL, Steve: Widnes 84L
O'SULLIVAN, Chris: Warrington 91W

PANAPA, Sam: Wigan 93w, 94l
PARKER, Derek: Bradford N. 80W
PATRICK, Shaun: Hull 85L
PATTINSON, Malcolm: Blackpool B. 77L
PAUL, Henry: Wigan 95W
PENDLEBURY, John: Wigan 83W; Bradford N. 91L
PETERS, Steve: Warrington 87L
PHILBIN, Barry: Warrington 74W, 78W
PHILBIN, Mike: Warrington 74W
PHILLIPS, Rowland: Warrington 91w
PICKUP, Bill: Warrington 74w
PICKUP, Fred: Leeds 73w
PITMAN, Phil: Blackpool B. 77L
PLATT, Andy: St. Helens 88W; Wigan 90W, 93W, 94L
PORTZ, Steve: Hull 76L
POTTER, Ian: Warrington 78W, 81W; Wigan 86W, 87W, 89W
POWELL, Roy: Leeds 88L, 92L; Bradford N. 93L
PRENDIVILLE, Paul: Hull 82W; Leeds 84W
PRESCOTT, Alan: Widnes 75L, 76W
PRESTON, Mark: Wigan 90W
PROCTOR, Wayne: Hull 85L
PROHM, Gary: Hull K.R. 85W

QUIRK, Les: St. Helens 88W

RAMSDALE, Denis: Wigan 83W
RAMSEY, Bill: Hull 76L; Widnes 78L
RAMSHAW, Terry: Salford 73L
RATHBONE, Alan: Warrington 87l
RAYNE, Keith: Leeds 84W
RAYNE, Kevin: Leeds 84W, 88L
RAYNER, David: Halifax 72W
REDFEARN, Alan: Bradford N. 80W

REDFEARN, David: Bradford N. 75W, 80W
REEVES, Derek: Halifax 72w
REILLY, Malcolm: Castleford 77W
REYNOLDS, Doug: Blackpool B. 77L
REYNOLDS, Frank: Warrington 74W
RICHARDS, Maurice: Salford 73L
RIDDLESDEN, Eddie: Halifax 90L
ROBERTS, Ian: Wigan 87W
ROBERTS, Mark: Warrington 87L
ROBINSON, Doug: Blackpool B. 77L
ROBINSON, Ian: Hull K.R. 85W, 86l
ROBINSON, Jason: Wigan 93W, 94L, 95W
ROPATI, Joe: Warrington 87L
ROSE, Paul: Hull 85L
RUSSELL, Richard: Castleford 94W

SAMPSON, Dean: Castleford 94w
SANDERSON, Gary: Warrington 87L, 95l
SANDERSON, John "Sammy": Halifax 72w
SARSFIELD, Mark: Widnes 92W
SCHOFIELD, Garry: Hull 85l; Leeds 88L, 92L
SCOTT, Mick: Wigan 83W; Halifax 90l
SEABOURNE, Barry: Bradford N. 75W
SHAW, Glyn: Widnes 78L, 79W, 80L; Wigan 83W
SHEFFIELD, Bill: Rochdale H. 74L
SHELFORD, Adrian: Wigan 89W
SHELFORD, Darrall: Bradford N. 91L
SHELFORD, Kelly: Warrington 95L
SHERIDAN, Barry: Widnes 75L, 76W
SIMPSON, Roger: Bradford N. 91L, 93L
SKERRETT, Kelvin: Wigan 94L, 95W
SKERRETT, Trevor: Hull 82W
SLATER, Keith: Wakefield T. 72L
SMALES, Ian: Castleford 94W
SMITH, Alan: Leeds 73W
SMITH, Andy: Leeds 83L, 84W
SMITH, David: Widnes 92W
SMITH, Gordon: Hull K.R. 86L
SMITH, Mike: Hull K.R. 82L, 85W, 86L
SMITH, Steve: Halifax 90l
SORENSEN, Kurt: Widnes 89L, 92W
SOUTO, Peter: St. Helens 88W
SPENCER, Ray: Wakefield T. 72l
SPURR, Bob: Castleford 77W
SQUIRE, Kevin: Leeds 84w
STEADMAN, Graham: Castleford 94W
STEPHENS, Gary: Castleford 77W
STEPHENSON, David: Wigan 83W, 86W, 87W
STEPHENSON, Mike: Hull 76L
STEPHENSON, Nigel: Bradford N. 80W
STERLING, Peter: Hull 85L
STONE, Richard "Charlie": Hull 82W
SUMMERS, Neil: Bradford N. 91L, 93L
SUTTON, Dave: Warrington 79L
SYKES, Andy: Leeds 83L
SZYMALA, Eddie: Barrow 81l

TAIT, Alan: Widnes 89L, 92W
TAMATI, Kevin: Widnes 84L; Warrington 87L
TANNER, David: St. Helens 88W
TAYLOR, David: Rochdale H. 74L
TEES, Gary: Warrington 95L
THACKRAY, Rick: Warrington 81W; Widnes 89L
THOMAS, Mark: Warrington 91w
THOMPSON, Jimmy: Bradford N. 80W
THORNILEY, Tony: Warrington 91W
TOPLISS, David: Wakefield T. 72L; Hull 85L
TROTTER, Dennis: Bradford N. 75W
TUIGAMALA, Va'aiga: Wigan 95W
TUNKS, Peter: Leeds 88L

VALENTINE, Rob: Wakefield T. 72L
VAN BELLEN, Gary: Bradford N. 80W
VAN BELLEN, Ian: Bradford N. 80w
VEIVERS, Phil: St. Helens 88W

WAINWRIGHT, Tony: Barrow 81L
WALKER, Malcolm: Hull 76L
WALLER, Tony: Warrington 79L, 81W
WANBON, Bobby: Warrington 74W
WANE, Shaun: Wigan 86W, 89W, 90w; Leeds 92L
WARD, Bernard: Wakefield T. 72l
WARD, David: Leeds 73w, 83L, 84W
WARD, Johnny: Salford 73L
WARD, Phil: Salford 73l; Bradford N. 75W
WARDELL, Alan: Hull 76L
WATKINS, David: Salford 73L
WATKINSON, David: Hull K.R. 82L, 85W, 86L
WATSON, David: Bradford N. 93L
WEBB, Terry: Leeds 84W
WEST, Graeme: Wigan 83W, 86W, 87W
WHITEHEAD, Derek: Warrington 74W
WHITEHEAD, Stuart: Rochdale H. 74L
WHITFIELD, Colin: Wigan 83W; Halifax 90L
WHITFIELD, Fred: Widnes 84L
WHITTLE, Alan: Warrington 74W
WILEMAN, Ron: Hull 82W
WILKINSON, Ian: Leeds 83L, 84W;
Bradford N. 91L
WILLIAMS, Barry: Wigan 83W
WILLICOMBE, David: Halifax 72W
WILSON, Frank: Warrington 78W
WOOD, Harry: Rochdale H. 74l
WOOD, John: Widnes 76W
WOODS, Paul: Widnes 78L
WRAITH, Geoff: Wakefield T. 72L;
Castleford 77W
WRIGHT, Darren: Widnes 89L, 92W
WRIGHT, Dave: Warrington 74W
WRIGHT, Stuart: Widnes 78L, 79W, 80L, 84L

REGAL TROPHY RECORDS

ALL ROUNDS

TEAM

Highest score: Huddersfield 142 v. Blackpool G. 4 (1994-95)
Also widest margin win with Barrow 138 v.
Nottingham C. 0 (1994-95)
Biggest attendance: 25,326 Hull v. Hull K.R.
(at Hull C. FC) ....Final 1984-85

INDIVIDUAL

Most tries: 9 by Greg Austin (Huddersfield) v. Blackpool G.
(1994-95)
Most goals: 17 by Sammy Lloyd (Castleford) v.
Millom (1973-74)
17 by Darren Carter (Barrow) v.
Nottingham C. (1994-95)
Most points: 43 (3t,17g) by Sammy Lloyd (Castleford) v.
Millom (1973-74)

REGAL TROPHY FINAL RECORDS

TEAM

Most final appearances: 8 by Widnes and Wigan
Most wins: 7 by Wigan
Highest score: Wigan 40 v. Warrington 10 1994-95
Widest margin win: Castleford 33 v.
Wigan 2 1993-94
Biggest attendance: 25,326 Hull v. Hull K.R.
(at Hull C. FC) 1984-85
Biggest receipts: £161,976 Warrington v. Wigan
(at McAlpine Stad'm, Hudd'd) ... 1994-95

INDIVIDUAL

Most tries: 3 by Ellery Hanley (Wigan) v. Halifax
.... 1989-90
Most goals: 8 by Frano Botica (Wigan) v.
Warrington 1994-95
Most points: 20 (1t,8g) by Frano Botica (Wigan) v.
Warrington 1994-95

● *BEFORE 1977-78 the competition was known as the Player's No.6 Trophy, then the John Player Trophy. In 1983-84 it became the John Player Special Trophy, renamed the Regal Trophy in 1989-90. It was not until 1979-80 that semi-finals were played at neutral venues, reverting to home advantage in 1992-93.*

FRENCH CLUBS IN REGAL TROPHY
French clubs were admitted into the Regal tournament for the first time in 1992-93. The inaugural entrants were champions Carcassonne and XIII Catalan who qualified through a play-off. St. Esteve were the first French entrants to win a tie when they beat Hunslet 18-14 in the first round of the 1994-95 competition.

NON-LEAGUE CLUBS IN THE REGAL TROPHY

Amateur clubs have entered the Regal tournament in every season apart from a period between 1981 and 1984, plus 1992-93 when the League and BARLA were in dispute. Two figured in the first round up to 1979-80 and one the following season. They were then left out from 1981-82 because the number of professional clubs had grown beyond the mathematically suitable 32.

But the amateurs returned in 1984-85 with two clubs joining the professionals in a small preliminary round, the number being increased to three in 1989-90. A new-style format in 1993-94 saw the preliminary round scrapped, replaced by a full first round of 16 Second Division clubs, two French sides, the three professional clubs demoted in 1992-93 plus Hemel Hempstead and 10 selected amateur sides.

The professional clubs were given home advantage in ties against the non-league sides and French clubs.

The full list of amateur clubs' results up to 1991-92 — all first round matches except where stated (P) Preliminary (2) Second Round — is:

Season							Attendance
1971-72		Wigan	33	v	Ace Amateurs (Hull)	9	2,678
		Thames Board Mill (Warr.)	7	v	Huddersfield	27	1,175
1972-73		Bramley	26	v	Pilkington Recs. (St. Helens)	5	616
		Dewsbury	22	v	Dewsbury Celtic	4	1,897
1973-74		Whitehaven	26	v	Dewsbury Celtic	3	1,276
		Castleford	88	v	Millom (Cumbria)	5	1,031
1974-75		Whitehaven	32	v	Lock Lane (Castleford)	6	537
		Doncaster	15	v	Kippax White Swan	6	453
1975-76		Salford	57	v	Mayfield (Rochdale)	3	3,449
		Barrow	16	v	Pilkington Recs. (St. Helens)	9	612
1976-77		Halifax	24	v	Ovenden (Halifax)	4	3,680
		Salford	39	v	Ace Amateurs (Hull)	15	3,037
1977-78		N.D.L.B. (Hull)	4	v	New Hunslet	18	3,845
		Halifax	8	v	Cawoods (Hull)	9	1,168
	(2)	Wakefield T.	31	v	Cawoods (Hull)	7	3,380
1978-79		Leigh Miners Welfare	9	v	Halifax	21	1,621
		Milford (Leeds)	5	v	Dewsbury	38	3,129
1979-80		Pilkington Recs. (St. Helens)	9	v	Wigan	18	6,707
		Blackpool B.	6	v	West Hull	3	555
1980-81		Castleford	30	v	Pilkington Recs. (St. Helens)	17	2,823
1984-85	(P)	Myson (Hull)	2	v	Dewsbury	8	1,572
	(P)	Keighley	24	v	Dudley Hill (Bradford)	10	1,570
1985-86	(P)	Keighley	24	v	Jubilee (Featherstone)	6	1,007
	(P)	West Hull	10	v	Castleford	24	2,500
1986-87	(P)	Batley	2	v	Myson (Hull)	8	687
	(P)	Millom (Cumbria)	4	v	Wakefield T.	18	2,000
		Myson (Hull)	11	v	Swinton	18	1,648
1987-88	(P)	Featherstone R.	34	v	Thatto Heath (St. Helens)	16	1,045
	(P)	Heworth (York)	5	v	Swinton	32	1,063
1988-89	(P)	Wigan St. Patricks	36	v	Elland (Halifax)	2	2,510
		Sheffield E.	80	v	Wigan St. Patricks	8	621
1989-90	(P)	Batley	28	v	West Hull	14	844
	(P)	Crosfields (Warrington)	14	v	Workington T.	19	942
	(P)	Kells (Whitehaven)	2	v	Doncaster	28	2,127
1990-91	(P)	Dudley Hill (Bradford)	18	v	Dewsbury	24	970
	(P)	Saddleworth R. (Oldham)	35	v	Egremont (Cumbria)	18	900
		Rochdale H.	30	v	Saddleworth R. (Oldham)	10	2,434
1991-92	(P)	Saddleworth R. (Oldham)	0	v	Workington T.	30	1,650
	(P)	Leigh East	20	v	Chorley	10	1,393
		Bradford N.	76	v	Leigh East	0	1,613

REGAL TROPHY PROGRESS CHART

Key: W — Winners. F — Beaten finalists. SF — Semi-final. P — Preliminary round.

	1994-95	1993-94	1992-93	1991-92	1990-91	1989-90	1988-89	1987-88	1986-87	1985-86	1984-85	1983-84	1982-83	1981-82	1980-81	1979-80	1978-79	1977-78	1976-77	1975-76	1974-75	1973-74	1972-73	1971-72
BARROW	2	2	1	1	1	1	1	1	1	3	2	1	2	3	3	F	1	1	1	1	2	1	1	3
BATLEY	3	3	1	1	3	1	1	2	P	1	1	P	1	1	1	1	1	1	1	2	1	1	2	1
BLACKPOOL G.	(1)	(1)	P	1	1	1	2	3	2	1	1	1	2	P	2	2	1	1	F	1	1	1	1	3
BRADFORD N.	4	SF	F	3	F	2	SF	1	3	2	2	1	3	2	1	W	SF	SF	2	1	W	1	3	1
BRAMLEY	2	3	1	1	2	1	2	P	1	1	3	*	1	1	1	2	1	1	2	1	2	SF	2	2
CARLISLE	2	4	2	2	P	1	1	1	2	P	P	2	2	2										
CASTLEFORD	SF	W	SF	3	3	SF	2	2	2	1	2	1	1	2	SF	3	3	2	W	SF	1	2	1	2
CHORLEY B.	(1)	(1)	P	P	1	1																		
DEWSBURY	3	2	1	P	1	2	1	2	1	1	3	1	1	1	1	1	2	1	1	1	1	3	2	1
DONCASTER	2	2	1	2	2	1	2	1	2	2	1	1	1	1	1	1	1	1	1	2	1	1	1	
FEATHERSTONE R.	2	2	2	3	2	3	1	1	2	P	2	3	1	2	2	2	2	3	2	1	1	1	2	1
HALIFAX	2	3	2	2	P	F	2	2	2	1	SF	1	1	1	3	1	2	1	2	1	1	2	1	W
HIGHFIELD	2	2	P	1	1	1	1	1	1	1	2	2	P	1	1	1	1	1	1	2	1	1	1	
HUDDERSFIELD	2	2	P	1	1	2	1	1	P	1	1	1	2	2	2	1	1	3	1	3	1	1	2	2
HULL	3	4	SF	2	1	1	2	3	SF	3	F	2	2	W	SF	1	2	1	3	F	1	1	3	3
HULL K.R.	2	2	2	1	1	1	3	2	1	F	W	2	3	F	2	1	SF	1	1	3	SF	1	SF	2
HUNSLET	1	2	2	1	1	2	P	1	2	P	1	1	2	1	1	2	1	2	1	1	1	1		
KEIGHLEY C.	4	2	1	2	2	1	1	1	1	2	1	2	1	2	3	2	1	1	2	3	1	2		
LEEDS	4	2	1	F	2	3	1	F	1	1	SF	W	F	3	1	2	1	1	3	2	3	3	W	SF
LEIGH	2	3	3	P	2	1	3	2	3	SF	1	SF	2	1	3	3	3	3	SF	2	1	2	2	1
LONDON B.	2	4	2	1	1	1	P	P	1	1	1	1	1	2										
NOTTINGHAM C.	(1)	(1)	1	1	1	1	2	1	1	1														
OLDHAM	3	3	1	2	2	3	1	SF	1	2	2	1	1	SF	1	1	1	2	2	2	2	1	1	1
ROCHDALE H.	2	2	2	P	SF	1	2	1	1	1	2	1	2	1	1	1	1	1	1	1	1	F	1	2
RYEDALE-YORK	2	3	1	1	P	P	1	1	P	3	1	1	2	1	2	2	1	1	3	1	2	2	2	2
ST. HELENS	4	3	3	SF	3	SF	SF	W	3	SF	3	SF	2	1	1	2	2	2	2	3	1	SF	SF	SF
SALFORD	3	SF	1	SF	1	2	1	3	1	2	1	2	3	3	2	SF	2	2	2	SF	3	2	F	1
SCARBOROUGH P.			P																					
SHEFFIELD E.	3	2	1	2	P	3	2	1	2	1	1													
SWINTON	2	2	P	1	1	2	1	1	2	1	1	3	1	SF	1	1	1	1	1	3	1	3	1	
WAKEFIELD T.	2	2	1	2	2	P	3	2	2	2	P	1	1	1	1	SF	3	SF	1	2	2	3	2	F
WARRINGTON	F	4	2	1	W	P	3	3	F	3	1	2	SF	2	W	3	F	W	1	1	3	W	1	1
WHITEHAVEN	3	2	1	1	1	2	1	1	1	1	2	P	1	1	3	1	1	1	1	1	SF	2	1	2
WIDNES	SF	3	3	W	SF	2	F	1	SF	3	3	F	SF	3	3	F	W	F	SF	W	F	1	3	1
WIGAN	W	F	W	3	3	W	W	SF	W	W	2	3	W	1	1	2	2	3	2	2	2	2	1	3
WORKINGTON T.	3	2	3	1	1	1	P	1	1	1	1	1	2	1	3	2	2	3	3	1	2	1	1	

*Bramley withdrew from the Trophy while in liquidation, opponents Hull K.R. receiving a bye.
( ) Entrant as non-League side

PREMIERSHIP TROPHY

1995 Final

Mighty Wigan again rewrote the record books as they completed the first-ever modern day Grand Slam by humiliating Leeds with a 69-12 hammering at Manchester United's Old Trafford.

The Stones Bitter Premiership title – plus a prize cheque for £24,000 – was duly added to their 1994-95 roll of honour of the Challenge Cup, Championship and Regal trophies. Also in the showcase was the 1994 World Club Challenge trophy.

The rampant Riversiders completed the domestic whitewash in devastating style which was both marvellous and horrifying to watch.

Wigan's total annihilation of a Leeds side which had also been runners up in the league and at Wembley was bordering on perfection, achieved in breathtaking fashion. But it also confirmed that the cherry-and-whites were in a Super League of their own, a continuing worry for the state of the British game as Wigan took their trophy tally to 37 in 10 golden years.

The score was not only a record for the 21-year history of the Premiership final – topping Wigan's own thrashing of St. Helens 44-16 three years earlier – but also for any final in the game's history.

Frano Botica equalled his own three-year-old records for the final with another haul of 10 goals and 20 points. The goals bonanza took his season's tally to 186, beating the club record set by himself two years earlier. Botica's total of 408 points for the season, including nine tries, put him at the head of both the game's goals and points charts.

The devastating team performance heralded the departure to Australian club football of Botica, newly-crowned Man of Steel Denis Betts and Phil Clarke. But their impending absence was counterbalanced by the confirmation of more emergent talent off the Central Park production line.

Having made his full debut only the previous November, 19-year-old Kris Radlinski was switched from the wing to centre to deputise for Va'aiga Tuigamala, who had returned to New Zealand for his grandfather's funeral after the Silk Cut Challenge Cup final. Radlinski revelled in the Old Trafford romp, becoming the first player to score a hat-trick of tries in a Premiership final and the youngest to win the Harry Sunderland Trophy as Man of the Match.

The teenager opened the scoring with an eighth-minute try, all three touchdowns being the result of great support play and taking his season's tally to 18 in 21 matches.

Another prodigy, junior international second row man Simon Haughton, stepped off the bench in the 49th minute to add the final insult. The Yorkshireman turned the Leeds defence inside out with a rampaging 50-metre charge for Wigan's last try four minutes from the end.

After Radlinski registered the first Premiership final hat-trick, co-centre Gary Connolly became the second, collecting his threesome in a 32-minute spell. Connolly's second touchdown finished off the most spectacular of Wigan's 12 tries. Winger Jason Robinson triggered it off with one of his many dashes from the Wigan line. Botica took over and linked with the impressive Henry Paul before Connolly joined the attack and raced away to complete the 95-metre move.

With dejected Leeds fans streaming from the stadium after the hour with Wigan already past the half-century score, Andrew Farrell gave another twist of the dagger when he nonchalantly popped over a drop goal with the Riversiders already 62-12 ahead.

Leeds, missing the injured Ellery Hanley and the suspended Garry Schofield, had raised early hopes of making a game of it by drawing level at 6-6 with a Richard Eyres try in the 14th minute, their second touchdown coming in the 68th minute from stand off Craig Innes, some reward for a hardworking performance.

STONES BITTER PREMIERSHIP FINAL

21 May 1995   Old Trafford, Manchester

WIGAN 69   **LEEDS 12**

Wigan	No.	Leeds
Henry Paul	1.	Alan Tait
Jason Robinson	2.	Jim Fallon
Kris Radlinski	3.	Kevin Iro, Capt.
Gary Connolly	4.	Phil Hassan
Martin Offiah	5.	Francis Cummins
Frano Botica	6.	Craig Innes
Shaun Edwards, Capt.	7.	Graham Holroyd
Kelvin Skerrett	8.	Harvey Howard
Martin Hall	9.	James Lowes
Neil Cowie	10.	Esene Faimalo
Denis Betts	11.	George Mann
Andrew Farrell	12.	Richard Eyres
Phil Clarke	13.	Gary Mercer
Simon Haughton	14.	Marcus Vassilakopoulos
Mick Cassidy	15.	Neil Harmon

T: Radlinski (3), Connolly (3),
Skerrett, Edwards, Betts, Paul,
Hall, Haughton
G: Botica (10), Farrell (dg)
Substitutions:
Cassidy for Skerrett (20 min.)
Haughton for Farrell (49 min.)
Attendance: 30,160 (capacity)

T: Eyres, Innes
G: Holroyd (2)
Substitutions:
Harmon for Howard (29 mins.)
Vassilakopoulos for Hassan (Half-time)
Half-time: 36-6
Referee: Stuart Cummings (Widnes)
Receipts: £351,038

1995 Round by Round

In the four-tie first round, holders Wigan comfortably disposed of the challenge of eighth-placed Sheffield Eagles at Central Park with skipper Shaun Edwards the architect of a 48-16 victory. As the Riversiders mounted their bid for a first-ever Grand Slam, the Eagles opened a shock 12-0 lead through two Ian Hughes tries, both converted by David Mycoe, before Wigan duly rallied with Martin Offiah registering his ninth try hat-trick of the season. Warrington became the only side to win away with a 30-22 success at Castleford. The home side scored five tries to four but skipper Lee Crooks kicked only one goal from six attempts while Jonathan Davies struck eight from eight, including two drop goals. Castleford were also hit by the dismissal of Tony Kemp for dissent early in the second half.

In a West Yorkshire derby, Leeds beat Bradford Northern 50-30 on a sunny Friday evening, the summer rugby theory not being supported by a crowd of around 7,500, well below the five-figure Headingley average. Those present were treated to a 14-try attacking spectacular, highlighted by Kevin Iro's hat-trick of tries which included his 100th in British club football. St. Helens displayed their renowned free-flowing style of football but added a steadiness in defence to topple Halifax 32-16 at Knowsley Road. Saints full back Steve Prescott scored two scintillating tries with the inspirational Bobby Goulding adding six goals.

In the semi-finals, Wigan again ran riot with a 50-20 home triumph over Warrington after the Wire had provided resistance in the first half, trailing only 18-8 at the break. There were two-try celebrations for Edwards, to mark his new contract at Central Park, and Jason Robinson, a beneficiary of a £1m-plus deal Down Under. Leeds pulled off an Houdini act at Headingley after trailing 20-6 to St. Helens with Garry Schofield sent off for verbal abuse of the referee Stuart Cummings and Alan Tait sin-binned. Acting stand off George Mann inspired the comeback for Leeds to hang on to a 30-26 lead under last minute Saints' pressure.

1995 Results

First Round

Castleford	22	Warrington	30
Leeds	50	Bradford N.	30
St. Helens	32	Halifax	16
Wigan	48	Sheffield E.	16

Semi-Finals

Leeds	30	St. Helens	26
Wigan	50	Warrington	20

Final

Wigan	69	Leeds	12

(at Old Trafford, Manchester)

1995 Prizes

Winners: £24,000
Runners-up: £12,000

History

With the reintroduction of two divisions in 1973-74 the: was no longer a need for a play-off to decide tl championship.

However, it was decided to continue the tradition of a end-of-season play-off, the winners to receive the new instituted Premiership Trophy.

In the first season of the Premiership, 1974-75, the top 1 Division One clubs and the top four from Division Tv went into a first round draw, the luck of the draw operatir through to the final, played at a neutral venue.

The following season the play-off was reduced to the tc eight clubs in the First Division, the ties being decided on merit basis, i.e., 1st v. 8th, 2nd v. 7th, etc. At the semi-fin stage the highest placed clubs had the option of when to pl at home in the two-legged tie.

In 1978-79 the two-leg system was suspended because fixture congestion, and the higher-placed clubs had hon advantage right through to the neutrally staged final.

Two legs returned the following season, but were final abolished from 1980-81.

PREMIERSHIP ROLL OF HONOUR

Year	Winners		Runners-up		Venue	Attendance	Receipts
1975	Leeds (3)	26	St. Helens (1)	11	Wigan	14,531	£7,795
1976	St. Helens (4)	15	Salford (1)	2	Swinton	18,082	£13,138
1977	St. Helens (2)	32	Warrington (5)	20	Swinton	11,178	£11,626
1978	Bradford N. (2)	17	Widnes (1)	8	Swinton	16,813	£18,677
1979	Leeds (4)	24	Bradford N. (8)	2	Huddersfield	19,486	£21,291
1980	Widnes (2)	19	Bradford N. (1)	5	Swinton	10,215	£13,665
1981	Hull K.R. (3)	11	Hull (7)	7	Leeds	29,448	£47,529
1982	Widnes (3)	23	Hull (2)	8	Leeds	12,100	£23,749
1983	Widnes (5)	22	Hull (1)	10	Leeds	17,813	£34,145
1984	Hull K.R. (1)	18	Castleford (4)	10	Leeds	12,515	£31,769
1985	St. Helens (2)	36	Hull K.R. (1)	16	Elland Rd, Leeds	15,518	£46,950
1986	Warrington (4)	38	Halifax (1)	10	Elland Rd, Leeds	13,683	£50,879
1987	Wigan (1)	8	Warrington (3)	0	Old Trafford, Man'r	38,756	£165,166
1988	Widnes (1)	38	St. Helens (2)	14	Old Trafford, Man'r	35,252	£202,616
1989	Widnes (1)	18	Hull (4)	10	Old Trafford, Man'r	40,194	£264,242
1990	Widnes (3)	28	Bradford N. (4)	6	Old Trafford, Man'r	40,796	£273,877
1991	Hull (3)	14	Widnes (2)	4	Old Trafford, Man'r	42,043	£384,300
1992	Wigan (1)	48	St. Helens (2)	16	Old Trafford, Man'r	33,157	£389,988
1993	St. Helens (2)	10	Wigan (1)	4	Old Trafford, Man'r	36,598	£454,013
1994	Wigan (1)	24	Castleford (4)	20	Old Trafford, Man'r	35,644	£475,000
1995	Wigan (1)	69	Leeds (2)	24	Old Trafford, Man'r	30,160	£351,038

() denotes final League position

PREMIERSHIP FINAL . . . . A REVIEW

Initials are included where more than one player shared a surname in the club in the same era.

1974-75
Leeds 26 Holmes (2g) (Marshall 3g); Alan Smith (1t), Hynes (1t, 1dg) (Eccles), Dyl, Atkinson (2t); Mason (1t), Hepworth; Dickinson, Ward, Pitchford, Cookson, Batten, Haigh
St. Helens 11 G. Pimblett; L. Jones (1t), Wilson, Hull, Mathias (1t); Walsh, Heaton (1t); Warlow (Cunningham), A. Karalius, Mantle (K. Gwilliam), E. Chisnall, Nicholls, Coslett (1g)
Referee: W.H. Thompson (Huddersfield)
1975-76
St. Helens 15 G. Pimblett (3g); L. Jones, Glynn (1t), Noonan, Mathias; Benyon, Heaton (K. Gwilliam); Mantle, A. Karalius (1t), James, Nicholls, E. Chisnall (1t), Coslett
Salford 2 Watkins (2dg); Fielding, Richards, Hesketh, Graham; Butler, Nash; Coulman, Raistrick, Sheffield, Knighton (Turnbull), Dixon, E. Prescott
Referee: M.J. Naughton (Widnes)
1976-77
St. Helens 32 G. Pimblett (1t, 7g); L. Jones, Benyon (1t), Cunningham (1t), Mathias (1t); Glynn (Ashton), K. Gwilliam (1t); D. Chisnall, Liptrot, James (1t), Nicholls (A. Karalius), E. Chisnall, Pinner
Warrington 20 Finnegan; Curling, Bevan (Cunliffe), Hesford (4g), M. Kelly; A. Gwilliam (1t), Gordon (1t); Weavill (1t), Price, Case, Martyn (Peers), Lester, B. Philbin (1t)
Referee: G.F. Lindop (Wakefield)
1977-78
Bradford N. 17 Mumby (2g); Barends (1t), Roe (1t), Austin, D. Redfearn (1t); Wolford (1dg), A. Redfearn; I. Van Bellen (N. Fox), Raistrick, Thompson, Joyce (Forsyth), Trotter, Haigh (1t)
Widnes 8 Eckersley; S. Wright, Hughes, Aspey (2t), Woods (1g); Gill, Bowden; Mills, Elwell, Shaw (Ramsey) (George), Adams, Hull, Laughton
Referee: J.E. Jackson (Pudsey)
1978-79
Leeds 24 Hague; Alan Smith (1t), D. Smith (1t), Dyl (Fletcher), Atkinson; Dick (7g, 1dg), J. Sanderson; Harrison, Ward (1t), Pitchford, Joyce, Eccles (Adams), Cookson
Bradford N. 2 Mumby; D. Parker, Okulicz, Gant, Spencer; Ferres (1g), A. Redfearn; Thompson, Bridges, Forsyth (I. Van Bellen), Trotter (Mordue), J. Grayshon, Casey
Referee: W.H. Thompson (Huddersfield)

1979-80
Widnes 19 Burke (1g); S. Wright (1t), George, Aspey (1t), Bentley (1t); Eckersley (1dg), Bowden; Shaw, Elwell (1t, 1dg), M. O'Neill, L. Gorley (1t), Hull (Hogan), Adams
Bradford N. 5 Mumby (1g); MacLean (Ferres), D. Redfrn (1t), D. Parker, Gant; Stephenson, A. Redfearn; Thompson, Bridges, Forsyth, Clarkson (G. Van Bellen), J. Grayshon, Hale
Referee: W.H. Thompson (Huddersfield)
1980-81
Hull K.R. 11 Proctor; Hubbard (1g), M. Smith (1t), Hogan (1t), Muscroft; Hartley (1t), Harkin; Holdstock, Watkinson, Millington, Lowe, Casey, Hall (Burton)
Hull 7 Woods (2g); Peacham, Elliott, Wilby, Prendiville; Banks, Dean; Tindall, Wileman, Stone, Skerrett (Madley), Crane (1t), Norton
Referee: J. Holdsworth (Kippax)
1981-82
Widnes 23 Burke (1t, 4g); S. Wright (1t), Kieron O'Loughlin, Cunningham (A. Myler), Basnett (1t); Hughes (1t), Gregory; M. O'Neill, Elwell, Lockwood (Whitfield), L. Gorley, Prescott, Adams (1t)
Hull 8 Kemble; O'Hara (Day), Leuluai, S. Evans, Prendiville; Topliss, Harkin; Tindall, Wileman (Lloyd), Stone, Skerrett, L. Crooks (1t, 2g, 1dg), Norton
Referee: S. Wall (Leigh)
1982-83
Widnes 22 Burke; Linton, Hughes, Lydon (5g), Basnett (2t); A. Myler (1t), Gregory (1t) (D. Hulme); M. O'Neill, Elwell, L. Gorley, Whitfield (S. O'Neill), Prescott, Adams
Hull 10 Kemble; O'Hara (1t), Day (Solal), Leuluai, S. Evans; Topliss (1t), Dean; Skerrett, Bridges, Stone, Rose, L. Crooks (2g), Norton (Crane)
Referee: G.F. Lindop (Wakefield)
1983-84
Hull K.R. 18 Fairbairn; G. Clark, M. Smith (1t), Prohm (1t), Laws (1t); Dorahy (1t, 1g), Harkin; Holdstock, Rudd, Millington (Robinson), Burton (Lydiat), Broadhurst, Hall
Castleford 10 Roockley; Coen, Marchant, Hyde, Kear (1t); Robinson, R. Beardmore (3g); Ward, Horton, Connell, Crampton, B. Atkins, Joyner
Referee: R. Campbell (Widnes)
1984-85
St. Helens 36 Veivers (1t); Ledger (2t), Peters, Meninga (2t) (Allen), Day (4g); Arkwright, Holding; Burke (Forber), Ainsworth (1t), P. Gorley, Platt, Haggerty, Pinner (1t)

Hull K.R. 16 Fairbairn (1t, 2g); G. Clark, Robinson (1t), Prohm, Laws (1t); M. Smith, G. Smith (Harkin); Broadhurst, Watkinson, Ema (Lydiat), Kelly, Hogan, Hall
Referee: S. Wall (Leigh)

1985-86
Warrington 38 Paul Ford (Johnson 1t); Forster (1t), Cullen, R. Duane, Carbert; Bishop (1t, 5g), A. Gregory; Boyd (2t), Tamati (1t), Jackson (1t), Sanderson (McGinty), Roberts, M. Gregory
Halifax 10 Whitfield (3g) (Smith); Riddlesden, T. Anderson, C. Anderson (1t), S. Wilson; Crossley, Stephens; Scott, McCallion, G. Robinson, Juliff, James (Bond), Dixon
Referee: G.F. Lindop (Wakefield)

1986-87
Wigan 8 Hampson; Gill (1g), Stephenson (1g), Bell, Lydon (1t) (Russell); Edwards, Gregory; Case, Kiss, Wane (West), Goodway, Potter, Hanley
Warrington 0 Johnson; Drummond, Ropati, B. Peters, Forster; Cullen, Bishop; Tamati, Roberts (Eccles), Jackson, Humphries (M. Gregory), Sanderson, R. Duane
Referee: K. Allatt (Southport)

1987-88
Widnes 38 Platt (1g); Thackray (Tait 1t), Currier (4g), D. Wright (2t), Offiah; Dowd, D. Hulme (2t); Sorensen (1t), McKenzie (1t), Grima (S. O'Neill), M. O'Neill, P. Hulme, R. Eyres
St. Helens 14 Loughlin (3g); Ledger (1t), Tanner, Elia, Quirk; Bailey, Holding; Burke, Groves, Evans (Dwyer), Forber, Fieldhouse (Allen), Haggerty (1t)
Referee: J. Holdsworth (Kippax)

1988-89
Widnes 18 Tait; Davies (3g), Currier (1t) (Pyke), D. Wright (1t), Offiah (1t); D. Hulme (A. Myler), P. Hulme; Sorensen, McKenzie, Grima, M. O'Neill, Koloto, R. Eyres
Hull 10 Fletcher; Eastwood, Blacker, Price (Wilby), O'Hara; Pearce (3g), Windley (R. Nolan); Dannatt, L. Jackson, S. Crooks, Welham (1t), Sharp, Divorty
Referee: J. Holdsworth (Kippax)

1989-90
Widnes 28 Tait (2t); Davies (4g), Currier (2t), D. Wright, Offiah; D. Hulme, P. Hulme; Sorensen (A. Myler), McKenzie, M. O'Neill, Koloto (Grima), R. Eyres, Holliday (1t)
Bradford N. 6 Wilkinson; Cordle, McGowan (Cooper), Marchant (1t), Francis; Simpson, Harkin; Skerrett, Noble (Richards), Hobbs, Medley, Fairbank, Mumby (1g)
Referee: C. Morris (Huddersfield)

1990-91
Hull 14 Gay (1t); Eastwood (1g), McGarry (G. Nolan 1t), Webb, Turner; Mackey, Entat; Harrison, L. Jackson, Dannatt, Marlow (Busby), Walker (1t), Sharp
Widnes 4 Tait; Devereux, Currier, Davies, Offiah (1t); Dowd, D. Hulme; Sorensen, McKenzie (D. Wright), Grima, P. Hulme, Koloto (Howard), McCurrie
Referee: J. Holdsworth (Kippax)

1991-92
Wigan 48 Hampson (Myers 1t); Lydon, Bell, Miles (1t), Offiah (2t); Botica (10g), Edwards; Cowie, Dermott, Platt (1t), Betts (2t), McGinty (Panapa), Clarke
St. Helens 16 Veivers; Hunte, Connolly (Griffiths), Loughlin (1t, 2g), Sullivan (2t); Ropati, Bishop; Neill (Groves), Dwyer, Ward, Nickle, Mann, Cooper
Referee: J. Holdsworth (Kippax)

1992-93
St. Helens 10 Lyon; Riley, Connolly (1t), Loughlin (1t), Hunte; Ropati, O'Donnell (2dg); Neill, Dwyer, Mann (Griffiths), Joynt, Nickle, Cooper
Wigan 4 Atcheson; Robinson, Panapa, Farrar, Offiah; Botica, Edwards; Cowie, Dermott, Skerrett (Gildart), Cassidy (Forshaw 1t), Farrell, Clarke
Referee: J. Holdsworth (Kippax)

1993-94
Wigan 24 Atcheson; Robinson, Panapa (1t) (Lydon), Connolly, Offiah; Botica (1t, 4g), Edwards; Skerrett, Hall, Cowie (Cassidy), Betts (1t), Farrell (1t), Clarke
Castleford 20 Ellis; C. Smith, Blackmore, T. Smith, Middleton; Steadman (1t,2g), Ford; Crooks (2g) (Sykes, 1t), Russell, Sampson (1t), Ketteridge (Smales), Hay, Nikau
Referee: Stuart Cummings (Widnes)

PREMIERSHIP TROPHY FINAL PLAYERS' REGISTER
The following is an index of players who have appeared in the Premiership final since the first in 1975. W — winners, L — losers. Substitute appearances in lower case letters. The year denotes the second half of the season.

ADAMS, Bryan: Leeds 79w
ADAMS, Mick: Widnes 78L, 80W, 82W, 83W
AINSWORTH, Gary: St. Helens 85W
ALLEN, Shaun: St. Helens 85w, 88l
ANDERSON, Chris: Halifax 86L
ANDERSON, Tony: Halifax 86L
ARKWRIGHT, Chris: St. Helens 85W
ASHTON, Alan: St. Helens 77l
ASPEY, Malcolm: Widnes 78L, 80W
ATCHESON, Paul: Wigan 93L, 94W
ATKINS, Brett: Castleford 84L

ATKINSON, JOHN: Leeds 75W, 79W
AUSTIN, Jack: Bradford N. 78W

BAILEY, Mark: St. Helens 88L
BANKS, Barry: Hull 81L
BARENDS, David: Bradford N. 78W
BASNETT, John: Widnes 82W, 83W
BATTEN, Ray: Leeds 75W
BEARDMORE, Bob: Castleford 84L
BELL, Dean: Wigan 87W, 92W
BENTLEY, Keith: Widnes 80W
BENYON, Billy: St. Helens 76W, 77W
BETTS, Denis: Wigan 92W, 94W, 95W
BEVAN, John: Warrington 77L
BISHOP, Paul: Warrington 86W, 87L; St. Helens 92L
BLACKER, Brian: Hull 89L
BLACKMORE, Richard: Castleford 94L
BOND, Steve: Halifax 86l
BOTICA, Frano: Wigan 92W, 93L, 94W, 95W
BOWDEN, Reg: Widnes 78L, 80W
BOYD, Les: Warrington 86W
BRIDGES, John "Keith": Bradford N. 79L, 80L; Hull 83L
BROADHURST, Mark: Hull K.R. 84W, 85L
BURKE, Mick: Widnes 80W, 82W, 83W
BURKE, Tony: St. Helens 85W, 88L
BURTON, Chris: Hull K.R. 81w, 84W
BUSBY, Dean: Hull 91w
BUTLER, John: Salford 76L

CARBERT, Brian: Warrington 86W
CASE, Brian: Warrington 77L; Wigan 87W
CASEY, Len: Bradford N. 79L; Hull K.R. 81W
CASSIDY, Mick: Wigan 93L, 94w, 95w
CHISNALL, Dave: St. Helens 77W
CHISNALL, Eric: St. Helens 75L, 76W, 77W
CLARK, Garry: Hull K.R. 84W, 85L
CLARKE, Phil: Wigan 92W, 93L, 94W, 95W
CLARKSON, Geoff: Bradford N. 80L
COEN, Darren: Castleford 84L
CONNELL, Gary: Castleford 84L
CONNOLLY, Gary: St. Helens 92L, 93W; Wigan 94W, 95W
COOKSON, Phil: Leeds 75W, 79W
COOPER, David: Bradford N. 90l
COOPER, Shane: St. Helens 92L, 93W
CORDLE, Gerald: Bradford N. 90L
COSLETT, Kel: St. Helens 75L, 76W
COULMAN, Mike: Salford 76L
COWIE, Neil: Wigan 92W, 93L, 94W, 95W
CRAMPTON, Jimmy: Castleford 84L
CRANE, Mick: Hull 81L, 83l
CROOKS, Lee: Hull 82L, 83L; Castleford 94L
CROOKS, Steve: Hull 89L
CROSSLEY, John: Halifax 86L
CULLEN, Paul: Warrington 86W, 87L
CUMMINS, Francis: Leeds 95L
CUNLIFFE, Dave: Warrington 77l
CUNNINGHAM, Eddie: St. Helens 75l, 77W; Widnes 82W
CURLING, Denis: Warrington 77L
CURRIER, Andy: Widnes 88W, 89W, 90W, 91L

DANNATT, Andy: Hull 89L, 91W
DAVIES, Jonathan: Widnes 89W, 90W, 91L
DAY, Sean: St. Helens 85W
DAY, Terry: Hull 82l, 83L
DEAN, Tony: Hull 81L, 83L
DERMOTT, Martin: Wigan 92W, 93L
DEVEREUX, John: Widnes 91L
DICK, Kevin: Leeds 79W
DICKINSON, Roy: Leeds 75W
DIVORTY, Gary: Hull 89L
DIXON, Colin: Salford 76L
DIXON, Paul: Halifax 86L
DORAHY, John: Hull K.R. 84W
DOWD, Barry: Widnes 88W, 91L
DRUMMOND, Des: Warrington 87L
DUANE, Ronnie: Warrington 86W, 87L
DWYER, Bernard: St. Helens 88l, 92L, 93W
DYL, Les: Leeds 75W, 79W

EASTWOOD, Paul: Hull 89L, 91W
ECCLES, Bob: Warrington 87l
ECCLES, Graham: Leeds 75w, 79W
ECKERSLEY, David: Widnes 78L, 80W
EDWARDS, Shaun: Wigan 87W, 92W, 93L, 94W, 95W
ELIA, Mark: St. Helens 88L
ELLIOTT, David: Hull 81L
ELLIS, St. John: Castleford 94L
ELWELL, Keith: Widnes 78L, 80W, 82W, 83W
EMA, Asuquo: Hull K.R. 85L
ENTAT, Patrick: Hull 91W
EVANS, Steve: Hull 82L, 83L
EVANS, Stuart: St. Helens 88L
EYRES, Richard: Widnes 88W, 89W, 90W; Leeds 95L

FAIMALO, Esene: Leeds 95L
FAIRBAIRN, George: Hull K.R. 84W, 85L
FAIRBANK, Karl: Bradford N. 90L
FALLON, Jim: Leeds 95L
FARRAR, Andrew: Wigan 93L
FARRELL, Andrew: Wigan 93L, 94W, 95W
FERRES, Steve: Bradford N. 79L, 80l
FIELDHOUSE, John: St. Helens 88L
FIELDING, Keith: Salford 76L
FINNEGAN, Derek: Warrington 77L
FLETCHER, Paul: Hull 89L
FLETCHER, Paul: Leeds 79w
FORBER, Paul: St. Helens 85w, 88L
FORD, Mike: Castleford 94L
FORD, Paul: Warrington 86W
FORSHAW, Mike: Wigan 93l
FORSTER, Mark: Warrington 86W, 87L
FORSYTH, Colin: Bradford N. 78w, 79L, 80L
FOX, Neil: Bradford N. 78w
FRANCIS, Richard: Bradford N. 90L

GANT, Les: Bradford N. 79L, 80L
GAY, Richard: Hull 91W
GEORGE, Derek "Mick": Widnes 78l, 80W
GILDART, Ian: Wigan 93l
GILL, Henderson: Wigan 87W
GILL, Ken: Widnes 78L
GLYNN, Peter: St. Helens 76W, 77W
GOODWAY, Andy: Wigan 87W

GORDON, Parry: Warrington 77L
GORLEY, Les: Widnes 80W, 82W, 83W
GORLEY, Peter: St. Helens 85W
GRAHAM, Gordon: Salford 76L
GRAYSHON, Jeff: Bradford N. 79L, 80L
GREGORY, Andy: Widnes 82W, 83W;
    Warrington 86W; Wigan 87W
GREGORY, Mike: Warrington 86W, 871
GRIFFITHS, Jonathan: St. Helens 92l, 93w
GRIMA, Joe: Widnes 88W, 89W, 90w, 91L
GROVES, Paul: St. Helens 88L, 921
GWILLIAM, Alan: Warrington 77L
GWILLIAM, Ken: St. Helens 75l, 76w, 77W

HAGGERTY, Roy: St. Helens 85W, 88L
HAGUE, Neil: Leeds 79W
HAIGH, Bob: Leeds 75W; Bradford N. 78W
HALE, Gary: Bradford N. 80L
HALL, David: Hull K.R. 81W, 84W, 85L
HALL, Martin: Wigan 94W, 95W
HAMPSON, Steve: Wigan 87W, 92W
HANLEY, Ellery: Wigan 87W
HARKIN, Kevin: Hull 82L
HARKIN, Paul: Hull K.R. 81W, 84W, 85l;
    Bradford N. 90L
HARMON, Neil: Leeds 95l
HARRISON, Karl: Hull 91W
HARRISON, Mick: Leeds 79W
HARTLEY, Steve: Hull K.R. 81W
HASSAN, Phil: Leeds 95L
HAUGHTON, Simon: Wigan 95w
HAY, Andy: Castleford 94L
HEATON, Jeff: St. Helens 75L, 76W
HEPWORTH, Keith: Leeds 75W
HESFORD, Steve: Warrington 77L
HESKETH, Chris: Salford 76L
HOBBS, David: Bradford N. 90L
HOGAN, Brian: Widnes 80w
HOGAN, Phil: Hull K.R. 81W, 85L
HOLDING, Neil: St. Helens 85W, 88L
HOLDSTOCK, Roy: Hull K.R. 81W, 84W
HOLLIDAY, Les: Widnes 90W
HOLROYD, Graham: Leeds 95L
HOLMES, John: Leeds 75W
HORTON, Stuart: Castleford 84L
HOWARD, Harvey: Widnes 91l; Leeds 95L
HUBBARD, Steve: Hull K.R. 81W
HUGHES, Eric: Widnes 78L, 82W, 83W
HULL, David: St. Helens 75L; Widnes 78L, 80W
HULME, David: Widnes 83w, 88W, 89W, 90W, 91L
HULME, Paul: Widnes 88W, 89W, 90W, 91L
HUMPHRIES, Tony: Warrington 87L
HUNTE, Alan: St. Helens 92L, 93W
HYDE, Gary: Castleford 84L
HYNES, Syd: Leeds 75W

INNES, Craig: Leeds 95L
IRO, Kevin: Leeds 95L

JACKSON, Bob: Warrington 86W, 87L
JACKSON, Lee: Hull 89L, 91W
JAMES, Mel: St. Helens 76W, 77W
JAMES, Neil: Halifax 86L

JOHNSON, Brian: Warrington 86w, 87L
JONES, Les: St. Helens 75L, 76W, 77W
JOYCE, Graham: Bradford N. 78W; Leeds 79W
JOYNER, John: Castleford 84L
JOYNT, Chris: St. Helens 93W
JULIFF, Brian: Halifax 86L

KARALIUS, Tony: St. Helens 75L, 76W, 77w
KEAR, John: Castleford 84L
KELLY, Andy: Hull K.R. 85L
KELLY, Mike: Warrington 77L
KEMBLE, Gary: Hull 82L, 83L
KETTERIDGE, Martin: Castleford 94L
KISS, Nicky: Wigan 87W
KNIGHTON, John: Salford 76L
KOLOTO, Emosi: Widnes 89W, 90W, 91L

LAUGHTON, Doug: Widnes 78L
LAWS, David: Hull K.R. 84W, 85L
LEDGER, Barry: St. Helens 85W, 88L
LESTER, Roy: Warrington 77L
LEULUAI, James: Hull 82L, 83L
LINTON, Ralph: Widnes 83W
LIPTROT, Graham: St. Helens 77W
LLOYD, Geoff "Sammy": Hull 821
LOCKWOOD, Brian: Widnes 82W
LOUGHLIN, Paul: St. Helens 88L, 92L, 93W
LOWE, Phil: Hull K.R. 81W
LOWES, James: Leeds 95L
LYDIAT, John: Hull K.R. 84w, 85l
LYDON, Joe: Widnes 83W; Wigan 87W, 92W, 94w
LYON, David: St. Helens 93W

McCALLION, Seamus: Halifax 86L
McCURRIE, Steve: Widnes 91L
McGARRY, Damien: Hull 91W
McGINTY, Billy: Warrington 86w; Wigan 92W
McGOWAN, Steve: Bradford N. 90L
McKENZIE, Phil: Widnes 88W, 89W, 90W, 91L
MACKEY, Greg: Hull 91W
MacLEAN, Ian: Bradford N. 80L
MADLEY, Ian: Hull 811
MANN, George: St. Helens 92L, 93W; Leeds 95L
MANTLE, John: St. Helens 75L, 76W
MARCHANT, Tony: Castleford 84L;
    Bradford N. 90L
MARLOW, Ian: Hull 91W
MARSHALL, David: Leeds 75w
MARTYN, Tommy: Warrington 77L
MASON, Mel: Leeds 75W
MATHIAS, Roy: St. Helens 75L, 76W, 77W
MEDLEY, Paul: Bradford N. 90L
MENINGA, Mal: St. Helens 85W
MERCER, Gary: Leeds 95L
MIDDLETON, Simon: Castleford 94L
MILES, Gene: Wigan 92W
MILLINGTON, John: Hull K.R. 81W, 84W
MILLS, Jim: Widnes 78L
MORDUE, David: Bradford N. 79l
MUMBY, Keith: Bradford N. 78W, 79L, 80L, 90L
MUSCROFT, Peter: Hull K.R. 81W
MYERS, David: Wigan 92w
MYLER, Tony: Widnes 82w, 83W, 89w, 90w

NASH, Steve: Salford 76L
NEILL, Jonathan: St. Helens 92L, 93W
NICHOLLS, George: St. Helens 75L, 76W, 77W
NICKLE, Sonny: St. Helens 92L, 93W
NIKAU, Tawera: Castleford 94L
NOBLE, Brian: Bradford N. 90L
NOLAN, Gary: Hull 91w
NOLAN, Rob: Hull 891
NOONAN, Derek: St. Helens 76W
NORTON, Steve: Hull 81L, 82L, 83L

O'DONNELL, Gus: St. Helens 93W
OFFIAH, Martin: Widnes 88W, 89W, 90W, 91L;
    Wigan 92W, 93L, 94W, 95W
O'HARA, Dane: Hull 82L, 83L, 89L
OKULICZ, Eddie: Bradford N. 79L
O'LOUGHLIN, Kieron: Widnes 82W
O'NEILL, Mike: Widnes 80W, 82W, 83W,
    88W, 89W, 90W
O'NEILL, Steve: Widnes 83w, 88w

PANAPA, Sam: Wigan 92w, 93L, 94W
PARKER, Derek: Bradford N. 79L, 80L
PAUL, Henry: Wigan 95W
PEACHAM, Gary: Hull 81L
PEARCE, Gary: Hull 89L
PEERS, Mike: Warrington 771
PETERS, Barry: Warrington 87L
PETERS, Steve: St. Helens 85W
PHILBIN, Barry: Warrington 77L
PIMBLETT, Geoff: St. Helens 75L, 76W, 77W
PINNER, Harry: St. Helens 77W, 85W
PITCHFORD, Steve: Leeds 75W, 79W
PLATT, Andy: St. Helens 85W; Wigan 92W
PLATT, Duncan: Widnes 88W
POTTER, Ian: Wigan 87W
PRENDIVILLE, Paul: Hull 81L, 82L
PRESCOTT, Eric: Salford 76L; Widnes 82W, 83W
PRICE, Joe: Warrington 77L
PRICE, Richard; Hull 89L
PROCTOR, Paul: Hull K.R. 81W
PROHM, Gary: Hull K.R. 84W, 85L
PYKE, Derek: Widnes 89w

QUIRK, Les: St. Helens 88L

RADLINSKI, Kris: Wigan 95W
RAISTRICK, Dean: Salford 76L; Bradford N. 78W
RAMSEY, Bill: Widnes 781
REDFEARN, Alan: Bradford N. 78W, 79L, 80L
REDFEARN, David: Bradford N. 78W, 80L
RICHARDS, Craig: Bradford N. 90l
RICHARDS, Maurice: Salford 76L
RIDDLESDEN, Eddie: Halifax 86L
RILEY, Mike: St. Helens 93W
ROBERTS, Mark: Warrington 86W, 87L
ROBINSON, Geoff: Halifax 86L
ROBINSON, Ian: Hull K.R. 84w, 85L
ROBINSON, Jason: Wigan 93L, 94W, 95W
ROBINSON, Steve: Castleford 84L
ROE, Peter: Bradford N. 78W
ROOCKLEY, David: Castleford 84L
ROPATI, Joe: Warrington 87L

ROPATI, Tea: St. Helens 92L, 93W
ROSE, Paul: Hull 83L
RUDD, Chris: Hull K.R. 84W
RUSSELL, Richard: Wigan 87w; Castleford 94L

SAMPSON, Dean: Castleford 94L
SANDERSON, Gary: Warrington 86W, 87L
SANDERSON, John "Sammy": Leeds 79W
SCOTT, Mick: Halifax 86L
SHARP, Jon: Hull 89L, 91W
SHAW, Glyn: Widnes 78L, 80W
SHEFFIELD, Bill: Salford 76L
SIMPSON, Roger: Bradford N. 90L
SKERRETT, Kelvin: Bradford N. 90L; Wigan 93L,
    94W, 95W
SKERRETT, Trevor: Hull 81L, 82L, 83L
SMALES, Ian: Castleford 94l
SMITH, Alan: Leeds 75W, 79W
SMITH, Chris: Castleford 94L
SMITH, David: Leeds 79W
SMITH, Gordon: Hull K.R. 85L
SMITH, Mike: Hull K.R. 81W, 84W, 85L
SMITH, Steve: Halifax 861
SMITH, Tony: Castleford 94L
SOLAL, Patrick: Hull 831
SORENSEN, Kurt: Widnes 88W, 89W, 90W, 91W
SPENCER, Alan: Bradford N. 79L
STEADMAN, Graham: Castleford 94L
STEPHENS, Gary: Halifax 86L
STEPHENSON, David: Wigan 87W
STEPHENSON, Nigel: Bradford N. 80L
STONE, Richard "Charlie": Hull 81L, 82L, 83L
SULLIVAN, Anthony: St. Helens 92L
SYKES, Nathan: Castleford 94l

TAIT, Alan: Widnes 88w, 89W, 90W, 91L; Leeds 95L
TAMATI, Kevin: Warrington 86W, 87L
TANNER, David: St. Helens 88L
THACKRAY, Rick: Widnes 88W
THOMPSON, Jimmy: Bradford N. 78W, 79L, 80L
TINDALL, Keith: Hull 81L, 82L
TOPLISS, David: Hull 82L, 83L
TROTTER, Dennis: Bradford N. 78W, 79L
TURNBULL, Sam: Salford 761
TURNER, Neil: Hull 91W

VAN BELLEN, Gary: Bradford N. 801
VAN BELLEN, Ian: Bradford N. 78W, 791
VASSILAKOPOULOS, Marcus: Leeds 951
VEIVERS, Phil: St. Helens 85W, 92L

WALKER, Russ: Hull 91W
WALSH, John: St. Helens 75L
WANE, Shaun: Wigan 87W
WARD, David: Leeds 75W, 79W
WARD, Kevin: Castleford 84L; St. Helens 92L
WARLOW, John: St. Helens 75L
WATKINS, David: Salford 76L
WATKINSON, David: Hull K.R. 81W, 84W, 85L
WEAVILL, Dave: Warrington 77L
WEBB, Brad: Hull 91W
WELHAM, Paul: Hull 89L
WEST, Graeme: Wigan 87w

WHITFIELD, Colin: Halifax 86L
WHITFIELD, Fred: Widnes 82w, 83W
WILBY, Tim: Hull 81L, 89l
WILEMAN, Ronnie: Hull 81L, 82L
WILKINSON, Ian: Bradford N. 90L
WILSON, Frank: St. Helens 75L
WILSON, Scott: Halifax 86L
WINDLEY, Phil: Hull 89L
WOLFORD, John: Bradford N. 78W
WOODS, Paul: Widnes 78L; Hull 81L
WRIGHT, Darren: Widnes 88W, 89W, 90W, 911
WRIGHT, Stuart: Widnes 78L, 80W, 82W

THE HARRY SUNDERLAND TROPHY

The trophy, in memory of the famous Queenslander, a former Australian tour manager, broadcaster and journalist, is presented to the Man of the Match in the end-of-season Championship or Premiership final.

The award is donated and judged by the Rugby League Writers' Association and is sponsored by Stones Bitter.

The Harry Sunderland Trophy Roll of Honour

Year	Winner	Team	Position
1965	Terry Fogerty	Halifax (v. St. Helens)	Second row
1966	Albert Halsall	St. Helens (v. Halifax)	Prop
1967	Ray Owen	Wakefield T. (v. St. Helens)	Scrum half
1968	Gary Cooper	Wakefield T. (v. Hull K.R.)	Full back
1969	Bev Risman	Leeds (v. Castleford)	Full back
1970	Frank Myler	St. Helens (v. Leeds)	Stand off
1971	Bill Ashurst	Wigan (v. St. Helens)	Second row
1972	Terry Clawson	Leeds (v. St. Helens)	Prop
1973	Mick Stephenson	Dewsbury (v. Leeds)	Hooker
1974	Barry Philbin	Warrington (v. St. Helens)	Loose forward
1975	Mel Mason	Leeds (v. St. Helens)	Stand off
1976	George Nicholls	St. Helens (v. Salford)	Second row
1977	Geoff Pimblett	St. Helens (v. Warrington)	Full back
1978	Bob Haigh	Bradford N. (v. Widnes)	Loose forward
1979	Kevin Dick	Leeds (v. Bradford N.)	Stand off
1980	Mal Aspey	Widnes (v. Bradford N.)	Centre
1981	Len Casey	Hull K.R. (v. Hull)	Second row
1982	Mick Burke	Widnes (v. Hull)	Full back
1983	Tony Myler	Widnes (v. Hull)	Stand off
1984	John Dorahy	Hull K.R. (v. Castleford)	Stand off
1985	Harry Pinner	St. Helens (v. Hull K.R.)	Loose forward
1986	Les Boyd	Warrington (v. Halifax)	Prop
1987	Joe Lydon	Wigan (v. Warrington)	Winger
1988	David Hulme	Widnes (v. St. Helens)	Scrum half
1989	Alan Tait	Widnes (v. Hull)	Full back
1990	Alan Tait	Widnes (v. Bradford N.)	Full back
1991	Greg Mackey	Hull (v. Widnes)	Stand off
1992	Andy Platt	Wigan (v. St. Helens)	Prop
1993	Chris Joynt	St. Helens (v. Wigan)	Second row
1994	Sam Panapa	Wigan (v. Castleford)	Centre
1995	Kris Radlinski	Wigan (v. Leeds)	Centre

PREMIERSHIP RECORDS First staged 1975
ALL ROUNDS
TEAM
Highest score: Wigan 74 v. Leeds 6 .... Semi-final 1992
(Also widest margin)
Biggest attendance: 42,043 Hull v. Widnes
(at Old Trafford, Manchester)......... Final 1991
INDIVIDUAL
Most goals:
10 by Frano Botica (Wigan) v. St. Helens ...... Final 1992
Frano Botica (Wigan) v. Leeds.............. Final 1995
Most tries:
10 by Martin Offiah (Wigan) v. Leeds
.... Semi-final 1992
Most points:
40 (10t) by Martin Offiah (Wigan) v. Leeds
.... Semi-final 1992

PREMIERSHIP FINAL
TEAM
Most appearances: 8 by Widnes
Most wins: 6 by Widnes
Highest score:
Wigan 69 v. Leeds 12 (also widest margin).............1995
Biggest attendance:
42,043 Hull v. Widnes
(at Old Trafford, Manchester).................1991
INDIVIDUAL
Most tries: 3 by Kris Radlinski (Wigan) v. Leeds.....1995
Gary Connolly (Wigan) v. Leeds....................1995
Most goals:
10 by Frano Botica (Wigan) v. St. Helens 1992
Frano Botica (Wigan) v. Leeds.....................1995
Most points:
20 (10g) by Frano Botica (Wigan) v. St. Helens 1992
Frano Botica (Wigan) v. Leeds.....................1995

Wigan celebrate the first modern Grand Slam haul after collecting the 1995 Stones Bitter Premiership Trophy for the third time in four years.

Wigan centre Kris Radlinski dives over en route to the first-ever hat-trick of tries in a Premiership final in the 1995 Old Trafford showpiece.

Leeds stand off Craig Innes (right), with teammate Richard Eyres in support, moves in on Wigan second row man Andrew Farrell in the 1995 Premiership showdown.

SECOND DIVISION PREMIERSHIP TROPHY

1995 Final

Keighley Cougars completed the most successful season in the club's 93-year history by adding a first-ever knockout trophy to their 1994-95 Second Division Championship title.

The dynamic Cougars lifted the Stones Bitter Second Division Premiership Trophy with an emphatic 26-6 defeat of third-placed Huddersfield in the play-off finals at Manchester United's Old Trafford.

The Second Division League and Premiership double crowned Keighley's rebuilding programme, based on Cougarmania, launched four years earlier when the club was virtually down and out.

Coach Phil Larder, who surprised many pundits by stepping down from the First Division to take control at Cougar Park, saw his gameplan carried out to near perfection after Huddersfield had built a 6-0 lead through two Greg Pearce penalty goals and drop goals from Steve Kerry and Greg Austin.

Keighley opened their scoring account on the half hour with a penalty goal from Simon Irving. The first of four tries came two minutes later from loose forward Martin Wood, who went on to earn the Tom Bergin Trophy as Man of the Match.

Darren Appleby made the initial break near the centre spot with Wood in support, taking the ball 30 metres out to break Huddersfield full back Phil Hellewell's tackle and go over near the posts. Irving added the goal to put the Cougars 8-6 ahead and in control. Hooker Jason Ramshaw added a 35th minute drop goal to extend the lead to 9-6 at the break.

Wood continued to be a major force as stand off Daryl Powell increased his influence, fully justifying the club record £135,000 paid to Sheffield Eagles for the Test player.

Powell added a touch of First Division class to an already impressive team, setting a tremendous example with his hard-driving runs and ability to get the ball away. He rounded off his third Second Division Premiership final by claiming Keighley's third try, taking advantage of a hesitant defence expecting his usual pass by powering over from close range.

The Cougars' most spectacular try went to England centre Nick Pinkney, who extended his new club tryscoring record for the season to 45 with a typical defence-splitting burst. Former Hull forward Gareth Cochrane was the creator, popping out a gem of a pass to send Pinkney sprinting 45 clear metres to the line.

Wingman Andy Eyres grabbed Keighley's final try, slipping past a defender within inches of the touchline to dive over in the corner in the 66th minute. The pass came from Ramshaw, who rounded off an excellent all-round game by adding his second drop goal, a towering effort from 30 metres out.

The hooker also headed the tackle count, 33, with substitute Shane Tupaea, who went on after five minutes to replace Brendan Hill, a victim of a hamstring injury.

Behind them Australian Appleby completed a dominating half back partnership with Powell, while Namibian Andre Stoop fielded well at full back and ran strongly out of defence.

Despite their early lead, Huddersfield never looked like repeating their 30-0 Silk Cut Challenge Cup win at Keighley earlier in the year, Australian prop Dave King going nearest to a try when crashing over the line and being prevented from grounding the ball just before the interval.

Keighley kept a close watch on Australian centre Austin, who needed just one try to finish as joint leader of the season's try chart with Wigan's Martin Offiah. A 53rd try would also have broken the record for a centre in one season, held by Paul Newlove. Ex-Keighley man Austin almost got it in the last seconds when Stoop crashed him down just short of the line.

STONES BITTER SECOND DIVISION PREMIERSHIP FINAL

21 May 1995   Old Trafford, Manchester

KEIGHLEY COUGARS 26   **HUDDERSFIELD 6**

Keighley Cougars		Huddersfield
Andre Stoop	1.	Phil Hellewell
Andy Eyres	2.	Ben Barton
Nick Pinkney	3.	Darrall Shelford
Simon Irving (Capt.)	4.	Greg Austin (Capt.)
Keith Dixon	5.	Simon Reynolds
Daryl Powell	6.	Dean Hanger
Darren Appleby	7.	Steve Kerry
Brendan Hill	8.	Dave King
Jason Ramshaw	9.	Lee St. Hilaire
Ian Gately	10.	Andy Pucill
Darren Fleary	11.	Basil Richards
Gareth Cochrane	12.	Gary Senior
Martin Wood	13.	Greg Pearce
David Larder	14.	Mick Taylor
Shane Tupaea	15.	Gary Coulter

T: Wood, Pinkney, Powell, Eyres
G: Irving (4), Ramshaw (2dg)
Substitutions:
Tupaea for Hill (5 min.)
Larder for Tupaea (67 min.)
Half-time: 9-6

G: Pearce (2), Kerry (dg), Austin (dg)
Substitutions:
Taylor for Senior (48 min.)
Coulter for Richards (57 min.)
Referee: Russell Smith (Castleford)

1995 Round by Round

The closest contest of the four-tie first round was at Mount Pleasant where Batley beat Heavy Woollen derby rivals Dewsbury 20-16 in a controversial finish. The sounding of a hooter in the crowd 15 seconds from the end halted a Dewsbury move and left coach Tony Fisher fuming, although gaining some satisfaction at the close scoreline after a 40-6 league drubbing by Batley a couple of weeks earlier. Second Division champions Keighley Cougars disposed of Hull K.R. 42-16 at Cougar Park in a contest marred by a 68th minute brawl involving nearly all the players. Keighley prop Brendan Hill was sent off, with sin bin punishment for team-mate Shane Tupaea and Rovers' Tim Lumb and Lee Marsden. On the footballing front, there was a brace of tries each for Cougar backs Keith Dixon, Simon Irving and Daryl Powell.

Huddersfield's Australian centre Greg Austin registered a 52nd try to equal the record for a centre in a season set by Paul Newlove in 1992-93 as visitors Rochdale Hornets were beaten 36-10. Whitehaven travelled to London to suffer a 28-1 defeat at the hands of the Broncos, conceding four tries.

In the semi-finals, Huddersfield visited Batley to record a 13-6 success based on a blistering opening spell of 10 points in as many minutes. Overseas imports Austin and Dean Hanger were outstanding as only Paul Harrison stood out in a below-par Gallant Youths outfit. Keighley Cougars qualified for a first appearance in a major final for 43 years with a convincing 38-4 victory over London Broncos at Cougar Park. While the Cougars registered six tries, with two for Martin Wood, the success was built on a foundation of sound defensive especially in the first half.

1995 Results
First Round
Batley	20	Dewsbury	16
Huddersfield	36	Rochdale H.	10
Keighley C.	42	Hull K.R.	16
London B.	28	Whitehaven	1

Semi-Finals
Batley	6	Huddersfield	13
Keighley C.	38	London B.	4

Final
Keighley C.	26	Huddersfield	6

(at Old Trafford, Manchester)

1995 Prizes
Winners:	£14,000
Runners-up:	£7,000

History
A Second Division Premiership tournament was introduced for the first time in 1986-87, Manchester United's Old Trafford being selected as a new fixed venue for a double-header final. With the introduction of a Third Division in 1991-92, the top eight Division Three clubs played off to visit the top four Second Division clubs, the second tier event being renamed the Divisional Premiership. But three divisions lasted only two seasons and the Second Division Premiership returned in 1994.

SECOND DIVISION PREMIERSHIP
ROLL OF HONOUR

Year	Winners		Runners-up		Venue
1987	Swinton (2)	27	Hunslet (1)	10	Old Trafford, Manchester
1988	Oldham (1)	28	Featherstone R. (2)	26	Old Trafford, Manchester
1989	Sheffield E. (3)	43	Swinton (5)	18	Old Trafford, Manchester
1990	Oldham (3)	30	Hull K.R. (1)	29	Old Trafford, Manchester
1991	Salford (1)	27	Halifax (2)	20	Old Trafford, Manchester
†1992	Sheffield E. (1)	34	Oldham (3)	20	Old Trafford, Manchester
†1993	Featherstone R. (1)	20	Workington T. (*2)	16	Old Trafford, Manchester
1994	Workington T. (1)	30	London C. (3)	22	Old Trafford, Manchester
1995	Keighley C. (1)	26	Huddersfield (3)	6	Old Trafford, Manchester

( )Denotes Second Division position
(*)Denotes Third Division position
† Divisional Premiership, three-division era

THE TOM BERGIN TROPHY

The trophy, in honour of the late president of the Rugby League Writers' Association and former editor of the *Salford City Reporter*, is presented to the Man of the Match in the end-of-season Second Division, later Divisional, Premiership final. The award is donated and judged by the Association and sponsored by Stones Bitter.

Year	Winner	Team	Position
1987	Gary Ainsworth	Swinton (v. Hunslet)	Hooker
1988	Des Foy	Oldham (v. Featherstone R.)	Centre
1989	Mark Aston	Sheffield E. (v. Swinton)	Stand off
1990	Mike Ford	Oldham (v. Hull K.R.)	Scrum half
1991	Steve Kerry	Salford (v. Halifax)	Scrum half
1992	Daryl Powell	Sheffield (v. Oldham)	Centre
1993	Paul Newlove	Featherstone R. (v. Workington T.)	Centre
1994	Dean Marwood	Workington T. (v. London C.)	Scrum half
1995	Martin Wood	Keighley C. (v. Huddersfield)	Loose forward

SECOND DIVISION/DIVISIONAL PREMIERSHIP. . . . A REVIEW

1986-87
Swinton 27 Viller; Bate (1t), Topping (Ratcliffe), Brown, Rippon (3g); Snape, Lee (1t); Grima (1t), Ainsworth (1t), Muller, Derbyshire (1t), M. Holliday (Allen), L. Holliday (1dg)
Hunslet 10 Kay; Tate, Penola, Irvine, Wilson; Coates, King; Sykes, Gibson (Senior), Bateman (2t), Platt (1g) (Mason), Bowden, Jennings
Referee: J. McDonald (Wigan)

1987-88
Oldham 28 Burke (Irving); Round, D. Foy (2t), McAlister (4g), Meadows (1t); Walsh (1t), Ford; Sherratt (Warnecke), Sanderson, Waddell, Hawkyard, Graham, Flanagan (1t)
Featherstone R. 26 Quinn (5g); Bannister (1t), Sykes (1t), Banks, Marsh (Crossley); Steadman (2t), Fox; Siddall (Bastian), K. Bell, Harrison, Hughes, Smith, Lyman
Referee: R. Whitfield (Widnes)

1988-89
Sheffield E. 43 Gamson; Cartwright, Dickinson, Powell (3t), Young; Aston (1t, 7g, 1dg), Close (Evans); Broadbent (1t), Cook (1t), Van Bellen, Nickle, Fleming (McDermott 1t), Smiles
Swinton 18 Topping; Ranson (1t), Viller (Maloney), Snape, Bate; Frodsham (1t), Hewitt; Mooney, Melling (1t), S. O'Neill, Ainsworth, Allen (Horrocks), J. Myler (3g)
Referee: R. Whitfield (Widnes)

1989-90
Oldham 30 Platt (1g) (Martyn 1t); Irving (1t), Hyde (2g), Henderson (1t), Lord (1t); Brett Clark, Ford (1t); Casey (Newton), Ruane (1t), Fieldhouse, Round, McAlister, Russell
Hull K.R. 29 Lightfoot; G. Clark (1t), M. Fletcher (4g), Austin, Sullivan; Parker (2t, 1dg), Bishop (Irvine); Niebling, Rudd, Ema, Des Harrison (1t) (Armstrong), Thompson, Lyman (1t)
Referee: R. Whitfield (Widnes)

1990-91
Salford 27 Gibson; Evans (1t), Gilfillan (1t), Birkett, Hadley (Dean); Cassidy (1dg), Kerry (2t, 4g, 1dg); Worrall, Lee (1dg), Hansen, Bradshaw (Sherratt), Blease, Burgess
Halifax 20 Smith; Wood (1t), W. Wilson (1t), Austin, Silva (Platt 2g); Lyons, R. Southernwood (1t); Hill (1t), Ramshaw, Bell (Scott), Brown, Milner, Keebles
Referee: B. Galtress (Bradford)

1991-92
Sheffield E. 34 Mycoe (1t); Gamson, McAlister, Powell (3t), Plange; Price, Aston (5g); Broadbent, Cook, Waddell, Laughton (Lumb 1t), Hughes (Mumby 1t), Farrell

Oldham 20 Platt (1t); Ranson (1t), Nicklin, Ropati, Tyrer; Russell (Warburton), Martyn (2g); Sherratt, Pachniuk, Newton (1t), Joynt, Tupaea (Street), Byrne (1t)
Referee: S. Cummings (Widnes)

1992-93
Featherstone R. 20 Pearson (4g); Butt, Manning, Newlove (2t), Simpson (Roebuck); Daunt; Casey (Gunn), Wilson, Taekata, G.S. Price, Smales, Tuuta
Workington T. 16 Mulligan; Drummond, Kay, Hepi, Smith; Byrne, Marwood (4g); Pickering, McKenzie (1t), Riley (Schubert), Scott, Armstrong, Kitchin (Oglanby 1t)
Referee: J. Connolly (Wigan)

1993-94
Workington T. 30 Mulligan (1t); Drummond (1t), Kay (1t), Burns, Cocker (2t); Kitchin, Marwood (3g); Pickering (Riley), McKenzie, C. Armstrong, Hepi, Oglanby, Byrne (1t) (Penrice)
London C. 22 Stoop; Gallagher (3g), Roskell, Campbell (1t), Johnson (3t); McIvor, Riley (Luxon); Whiteley, Carter (Smith), Rotheram, Rosolen, Stewart, Ramsey
Referee: J. Connolly (Wigan)

Huddersfield prop Dave King powers into the Keighley defence in the 1995 Old Trafford final.

It's a 1994-95 Second Division double for Keighley Cougars as they revel in Old Trafford glory.

SECOND DIVISION/DIVISIONAL PREMIERSHIP TROPHY FINAL PLAYERS' REGISTER

The following is an index of players who have appeared in the Second Division Premiership final since the first in 1987. It also includes the Divisional finals of 1992 and 1993 when Third Division clubs were included in the competition. W – winners, L – losers. Substitute appearances in lower case letters. The year denotes the second half of the season.

AINSWORTH, Gary: Swinton 87W, 89L
ALLEN, John: Swinton 87w, 89L
APPLEBY, Darren: Keighley C. 95W
ARMSTRONG, Colin: Hull K.R. 90l; Workington T. 93L, 94W
ASTON, Mark: Sheffield E. 89W, 92W
AUSTIN, Greg: Hull K.R. 90L; Halifax 91L; Huddersfield 95L

BANKS, Alan: Featherstone R. 88L
BANNISTER, Andy: Featherstone R. 88L
BARTON, Ben: Huddersfield 95L
BASTIAN, John: Featherstone R. 88l
BATE, Derek: Swinton 87W, 89L
BATEMAN, Andy: Hunslet 87L
BELL, Keith: Featherstone R. 88L
BELL, Peter: Halifax 91L
BIRKETT, Martin: Salford 91W
BISHOP, David: Hull K.R. 90L

BLEASE, Ian: Salford 91W
BOWDEN, Chris: Hunslet 87L
BRADSHAW, Arthur: Salford 91W
BROADBENT, Paul: Sheffield E. 89W, 92W
BROWN, Jeff: Swinton 87W
BROWN, Peter: Halifax 91L
BURGESS, Andy: Salford 91W
BURKE, Mick: Oldham 88W
BURNS, Paul: Workington T. 94W
BUTT, Ikram: Featherstone R. 93W
BYRNE, Ged: Oldham 92L; Workington T. 93L, 94W

CAMPBELL, Logan: London C. 94L
CARTER, Scott: London C. 94L
CARTWRIGHT, Phil: Sheffield E. 89W
CASEY, Leo: Oldham 90W; Featherstone R. 93W
CASSIDY, Frank: Salford 91W
CLARK, Brett: Oldham 90W
CLARK, Garry: Hull K.R. 90L
CLOSE, David: Sheffield E. 89W
COATES, Ged: Hunslet 87L
COCHRANE, Gareth: Keighley C. 95W
COCKER, Stuart: Workington T. 94W
COOK, Mick: Sheffield E. 89W, 92W
COULTER, Gary: Huddersfield 95l
CROSSLEY, John: Featherstone R. 88l

DAUNT, Brett: Featherstone R. 93W
DEAN, Mick: Salford 91w
DERBYSHIRE, Alan: Swinton 87W

DICKINSON, Andy: Sheffield E. 89W
DIXON, Keith: Keighley C. 95W
DRUMMOND, Des: Workington T. 93L, 94W
EMA, Asuquo: Hull K.R. 90L
EVANS, Steve: Sheffield E. 89w
EVANS, Tex: Salford 91W
EYRES, Andy: Keighley C. 95W

FARRELL, Anthony: Sheffield E. 92W
FIELDHOUSE, John: Oldham 90W
FLANAGAN, Terry: Oldham 88W
FLEARY, Darren: Keighley C. 95W
FLEMING, Mark: Sheffield E. 89W
FLETCHER, Mike: Hull K.R. 90L
FORD, Mike: Oldham 88W, 90W
FOX, Deryck: Featherstone R. 88L
FOY, Des: Oldham 88W
FRODSHAM, Tommy: Swinton 89L

GALLAGHER, John: London C. 94L
GAMSON, Mark: Sheffield E. 89W, 92W
GATELY, Ian: Keighley C. 95W
GIBSON, Phil: Hunslet 87L
GIBSON, Steve: Salford 91W
GILFILLAN, John: Salford 91W
GRAHAM, Mal: Oldham 88W
GRIMA, Joe: Swinton 87W
GUNN, Richard: Featherstone R. 93w

HADLEY, Adrian: Salford 91W
HANSEN, Shane: Salford 91W
HANGER, Dean: Huddersfield 95L
HARRISON, Des: Hull K.R. 90L
HARRISON, Karl: Featherstone R. 88L
HAWKYARD, Colin: Oldham 88W
HELLEWELL, Phil: Huddersfield 95L
HENDERSON, John: Oldham 90W
HEPI, Brad: Workington T. 93L, 94W
HEWITT, Tony: Swinton 89L
HILL, Brendan: Halifax 91L; Keighley C. 95W
HOLLIDAY, Les: Swinton 87W
HOLLIDAY, Mike: Swinton 87W
HORROCKS, John: Swinton 89l
HUGHES, Ian: Sheffield E. 92W
HUGHES, Paul: Featherstone R. 88L
HYDE, Gary: Oldham 90W

IRVINE, Jimmy: Hunslet 87L; Hull K.R. 90l
IRVING, Richard: Oldham 88w, 90W
IRVING, Simon: Keighley C. 95W

JENNINGS, Graeme: Hunslet 87L
JOHNSON, Mark: London C. 94L
JOYNT, Chris: Oldham 92L

KAY, Andy: Hunslet 87L
KAY, Tony: Workington T. 93L, 94W
KING, Graham: Hunslet 87L
KING, Dave: Huddersfield 95L
KEEBLES, Mick: Halifax 91L
KERRY, Steve: Salford 91W; Huddersfield 95L

KITCHIN, Wayne: Workington T. 93L, 94W
LAUGHTON, Dale: Sheffield E. 92W
LARDER, David: Keighley C. 95w
LEE, Mark: Salford 91W
LEE, Martin: Swinton 87W
LORD, Paul: Oldham 90W
LIGHTFOOT, David: Hull K.R. 90L
LUMB, Tim: Sheffield E. 92w
LUXON, Geoff: London C. 94l
LYMAN, Paul: Featherstone R. 88L;
   Hull K.R. 90L
LYONS, John: Halifax 91L
McALISTER, Charlie: Oldham 88W, 90W;
   Sheffield E. 92W
McDERMOTT, Paul: Sheffield E. 89w
McIVOR, Dixon: London C. 94L
McKENZIE, Phil: Workington T. 93L, 94W
MALONEY, Dave: Swinton 89l
MALONEY, Francis: Featherstone R. 93W
MANNING, Terry: Featherstone R. 93W
MARSH, Richard: Featherstone R. 88L
MARTYN, Tommy: Oldham 90w, 92L
MARWOOD, Dean: Workington T. 93L, 94W
MASON, Keith: Hunslet 87l
MEADOWS, Kevin: Oldham 88W
MELLING, Alex: Swinton 89L
MILNER, Richard: Halifax 91L
MOONEY, Frank: Swinton 89L
MULLER, Roby: Swinton 87W
MULLIGAN, Mark: Workington T. 93L, 94W
MUMBY, Keith: Sheffield E. 92w
MYCOE, David: Sheffield E. 92W
MYLER, John: Swinton 89L

NEWLOVE, Paul: Featherstone R. 93W
NEWTON, Keith: Oldham 90w, 92L
NICKLE, Sonny: Sheffield E. 89W
NICKLIN, Vince: Oldham 92L
NIEBLING, Bryan: Hull K.R. 90L

OGLANBY, Martin: Workington T. 93l, 94W
O'NEILL, Steve: Swinton 89L

PACHNIUK, Richard: Oldham 92L
PARKER, Wayne: Hull K.R. 90L
PEARCE, Greg: Huddersfield 95L
PEARSON, Martin: Featherstone R. 93W
PENOLA, Colin: Hunslet 87L
PENRICE, Paul: Workington T. 94w
PICKERING, James: Workington T. 93L, 94W
PINKNEY, Nick: Keighley C. 95W
PLANGE, David: Sheffield E. 92W
PLATT, Alan: Hunslet 87L; Halifax 91l
PLATT, Duncan: Oldham 90W, 92L
POWELL, Daryl: Sheffield E. 89W, 92W;
   Keighley C. 95W
PRICE, Gary S.: Featherstone R. 93W
PRICE, Richard: Sheffield E. 92W
PUCILL, Andy: Huddersfield 95L

QUINN, Steve: Featherstone R. 88L
RAMSEY, Neville: London C. 94L
RAMSHAW, Jason: Halifax 91L; Keighley C. 95W
RANSON, Scott: Swinton 89L; Oldham 92L
RATCLIFFE, Alan: Swinton 87w
REYNOLDS, Simon: Huddersfield 95L
RICHARDS, Basil: Huddersfield 95L
RILEY, Mark: London C. 94L
RILEY, Peter: Workington T. 93L, 94w
RIPPON, Andy: Swinton 87W
ROEBUCK, Neil: Featherstone R. 93w
ROPATI, Iva: Oldham 92L
ROSKELL, Scott: London C. 94L
ROSOLEN, Steve: London C. 94L
ROTHERAM, Dave: London C. 94L
ROUND, Paul: Oldham 88W, 90W
RUANE, Andy: Oldham 90W
RUDD, Chris: Hull K.R. 90L
RUSSELL, Richard: Oldham 90W, 92L

ST. HILAIRE, Lee: Huddersfield 95L
SANDERSON, Ian: Oldham 88W
SCHUBERT, Gary: Workington T. 93l
SCOTT, Ian: Workington T. 93L
SCOTT, Mick: Halifax 91l
SENIOR, Gary: Hunslet 87l; Huddersfield 95L
SHERRATT, Ian: Oldham 88W, 92L; Salford 91w
SHELFORD, Darrall: Huddersfield 95L
SIDDALL, Gary: Featherstone R. 88L
SILVA, Matthew: Halifax 91L
SIMPSON, Owen: Featherstone R. 93W
SMALES, Ian: Featherstone R. 93W
SMILES, Warren: Sheffield E. 89W
SMITH, Kris: London C. 94l
SMITH, Gary: Workington T. 93L
SMITH, Peter: Featherstone R. 88L
SMITH, Steve: Halifax 91L
SNAPE, Steve: Swinton 87W, 89L
SOUTHERNWOOD, Roy: Halifax 91L
STEADMAN, Graham: Featherstone R. 88L
STEWART, Sam: London C. 94L
STOOP, Andre: London C. 94L; Keighley C. 95W
STREET, Tim: Oldham 92l
SULLIVAN, Anthony: Hull K.R. 90L
SYKES, Andy: Hunslet 87L
SYKES, David: Featherstone R. 88L

TAEKATA, Wayne: Featherstone R. 93W
TATE, Phil: Hunslet 87L
TAYLOR, Mick: Huddersfield 95l
THOMPSON, Andy: Hull K.R. 90L
TOPPING, Paul: Swinton 87W, 89L
TUPAEA, Shane: Oldham 92L; Keighley C. 95w
TUUTA, Brendon: Featherstone R. 93W
TYRER, Sean: Oldham 92L

VAN BELLEN, Gary: Sheffield E. 89W
VILLER, Mark: Swinton 87W, 89L

WADDELL, Hugh: Oldham 88W;
   Sheffield E. 92W
WALSH, Peter: Oldham 88W
WARBURTON, Steve: Oldham 92l
WARNECKE, Gary: Oldham 88w
WHITELEY, Chris: London C. 94L
WILSON, Mark: Featherstone R. 93W
WILSON, Warren: Hunslet 87L; Halifax 91L
WOOD, Martin: Halifax 91L; Keighley C. 95W
WORRALL, Mick: Salford 91W

YOUNG, Andy: Sheffield E. 89W

SECOND DIVISION/DIVISIONAL PREMIERSHIP RECORDS
First staged 1987
ALL ROUNDS
TEAM
Highest score: Sheffield E. 72 v. Keighley C. 14......1992
(Also widest margin)
Biggest attendance: 5,885 Halifax v. Leigh............1991
(Not including final)
INDIVIDUAL
Most goals:
12 by Mark Aston (Sheffield E.) v. Keighley C. 1992
Most tries:
4 by Martin Wood (Halifax) v. Fulham 1991
Most points:
26 (3t, 7g) by Martin Pearson (Featherstone R.) v.
                                    Ryedale-York 1993

FINAL ONLY
TEAM
Most appearances: 3 by Oldham
Most wins: 2 by Oldham, Sheffield E.
Highest score:
Sheffield E. 43 v. Swinton 18 1989
(Also widest margin)

INDIVIDUAL
Most goals:
8 by Mark Aston (Sheffield E.) v. Swinton............1989
Most tries:
3 by Daryl Powell (Sheffield E.) v. Swinton...........1989
   Daryl Powell (Sheffield E.) v. Oldham...........1992
   Mark Johnson (London C.) v. Workington T ...1994
Most points:
19 (1t,7g,1dg) by Mark Aston (Sheffield E. v. Swinton)
                                   1989

CHARITY SHIELD
● From 1985-86 to 1992-93, the Charity Shield was contested between the previous season's Challenge Cup winners and Division One Champions. When Wigan won both trophies in 1990 and 1991 they met the previous season's Premiership final winners. When Wigan won the Championship, Challenge Cup and Premiership in 1992, they met the previous season's Division One title runners-up.

CHARITY SHIELD ROLL OF HONOUR

Year	Winners		Runners-up		Venue	Attendance
1985-86	Wigan	34	*Hull K.R.	6	Isle of Man	4,066
1986-87	*Halifax	9	Castleford	8	Isle of Man	3,276
1987-88	*Wigan	44	Halifax	12	Isle of Man	4,804
1988-89	*Widnes	20	Wigan	14	Isle of Man	5,044
1989-90	*Widnes	27	Wigan	22	Liverpool FC	17,263
1990-91	†Widnes	24	*Wigan	8	Swansea C. FC	11,178
1991-92	*Wigan	22	†Hull	8	Gateshead	10,248
1992-93	#St. Helens	17	*Wigan	0	Gateshead	7,364

*Denotes previous season's Champions; † Premiership winners; unmarked, Challenge Cup winners; # Championship runners-up

CHARITY SHIELD .... A REVIEW

1985-86
Wigan 34 Hampson; P. Ford, Stephenson (7g), Donlan (2t), Gill (2t); Edwards, M. Ford (1t); Courtney (Mayo), Kiss, Campbell, West (Lucas), Du Toit, Wane
Hull K.R. 6 Fairbairn (Lydiat 1g); Clark (1t), Robinson, Prohm, Laws; M. Smith, G. Smith; Des Harrison, Watkinson, Ema, Kelly (Rudd), Burton, Hogan
Referee: R. Campbell (Widnes)

1986-87
Halifax 9 Smith (Wilson); Riddlesden, Whitfield (1t), Hague (1dg), George (1t); C. Anderson, Stephens; Dickinson, McCallion, Juliff, Scott (James), Bell, Dixon
Castleford 8 Roockley; Plange, Lord (1t), Irwin (R. Southernwood), Spears; Joyner (Fletcher), R. Beardmore; Ward, K. Beardmore, Johnson, Ketteridge (2g), Mountain, England
Referee: G.F. Lindop (Wakefield)

First-ever Charity Shield winners Wigan celebrate their 34-6 victory over Hull K.R. at Douglas on the Isle of Man in August 1985.

241

1987-88
Wigan 44 Hampson (2t); Stephenson (8g), Byrne (Russell), Bell (2t), Gill (1t); Edwards (2t), Gregory; West, Kiss, Case, Gildart (Wane), Potter, Goodway
Halifax 12 Eadie (2g); Taylor, Wilson, T. Anderson, George; Simpson (Juliff 1t), Stephens; Dickinson, Pendlebury, Beevers, James, Scott (Bell), Dixon (1t)
Referee: J. Holdsworth (Kippax)
1988-89
Widnes 20 Tait; Thackray, Currier (4g), D. Wright (1t), Offiah (1t); Dowd, D. Hulme; Sorensen, McKenzie (1t), Grima (Pyke), M. O'Neill, P. Hulme, R. Eyres
Wigan 14 Hampson; Gill, Lydon (1t, 1g), Bell, Preston (Lucas); Byrne, Gregory; Shelford (Betts), Kiss, Case, T. Iro (2t), Wane, Goodway
Referee: R. Tennant (Castleford)
1989-90
Widnes 27 Tait (1dg); Kebbie (1t), Davies (1t, 5g), D. Wright, Offiah (1t); A. Myler, D. Hulme (1t); Sorensen, P. Hulme, Grima (Pyke), M. O'Neill, Koloto, R. Eyres
Wigan 22 Hampson; Bell (Gilfillan), K. Iro (1t), Lydon (1t, 5g), Preston; Byrne, Gregory; Lucas, Kiss, Platt (1t) (Stazicker), Betts, Gildart, Goodway
Referee: J. Holdsworth (Kippax)
1990-91
Widnes 24 Tait; Devereux (1t), Currier, Davies (3t, 2g), Offiah (1t); A. Myler, D. Hulme; Ashurst (D. Wright), McKenzie, Grima, P. Hulme (Sorensen), Koloto, Holliday
Wigan 8 Gilfillan; Myers, Bell, Byrne, Preston; Botica (1t, 2g) (Edwards), Goulding; Skerrett, Bridge, Wane, Gildart (Forshaw), Platt, Betts
Referee: C. Morris (Huddersfield)

1991-92
Wigan 22 Hampson; Myers (1t), Bell (2t), Lydon, Botica (3g); Edwards (1t), Gregory; Lucas (Gildart), Dermott, Skerrett, Betts, Platt (Forshaw), Goodway
Hull 8 Feather; Eastwood (2g), Blacker, G. Nolan (1t), Turner; Hanlan, Mackey; Durham (Dixon), L. Jackson, Marlow, McNamara (Jones), Walker, Busby
Referee: R. Whitfield (Widnes)
1992-93
St. Helens 17 Hunte; Riley, Connolly, Ropati (1t, 2g), Sullivan (1t); Griffiths, O'Donnell (1dg) (Quirk); Neill, Dwyer, Ward, Harrison, Mann (Forber), Cooper (1t)
Wigan 0 Hampson; Panapa, Bell, Lydon (Myers), Offiah; Botica, Crompton; Lucas, Cassidy, Skerrett (Goodway), Betts, McGinty, Clarke
Referee: S. Cummings (Widnes)

CHARITY SHIELD RECORDS

TEAM
Most appearances: 7 Wigan
Most wins: 3 Widnes, Wigan
Highest score: Wigan 44 v. Halifax 12 1987
(Also widest margin)
Biggest attendance:
17,263 Widnes v. Wigan (at Liverpool FC) 1989

INDIVIDUAL
Most tries:
3 by Jonathan Davies (Widnes) v. Wigan 1990
Most goals:
8 by David Stephenson (Wigan) v. Halifax 1987
Most points:
16 (8g) by David Stephenson (Wigan) v. Halifax ... 1987
(3t,2g) Jonathan Davies (Widnes) v. Wigan 1990

MAN OF THE MATCH AWARDS

Season	Winner	Team	Position
1985-86	Shaun Edwards	Wigan (v. Hull K.R.)	Stand off
1986-87	Chris Anderson	Halifax (v. Castleford)	Stand off
1987-88	Shaun Edwards	Wigan (v. Halifax)	Stand off
1988-89	Phil McKenzie	Widnes (v. Wigan)	Hooker
1989-90	Denis Betts	Wigan (v. Widnes)	Second row
1990-91	Jonathan Davies	Widnes (v. Wigan)	Centre
1991-92	Dean Bell	Wigan (v. Hull)	Centre
1992-93	Alan Hunte	St. Helens (v. Wigan)	Full back

● From 1987 it became the Jack Bentley Trophy in memory of the former *Daily Express* Rugby League journalist.

WORLD CLUB CHALLENGE

ROLL OF HONOUR

Year	Winners		Runners-up		Venue	Attendance	Receipts
1987	Wigan	8	Manly-Warringah	2	Wigan	36,895	£131,000
1989	Widnes	30	Canberra	18	Old Trafford, Man'r	30,786	£207,764
1991	Wigan	21	Penrith	4	Anfield, Liverpool	20,152	£179,797
1992	Brisbane B.	22	Wigan	8	Wigan	17,746	£170,911
1994	Wigan	20	Brisbane B.	14	Brisbane	54,220	$448,041

A REVIEW. . .

1987-88

Wigan 8 Hampson; Russell, Stephenson (4g), Lydon, Gill; Edwards, Gregory; Case (Lucas), Kiss, Wane, Goodway, Potter, Hanley

Manly 2 Shearer; Ronson, Williams (Ticehurst), O'Connor (1g), Davis; Lyons, Hasler; Daley, Cochrane, Gately (Brokenshire), Gibbs, Cunningham (Shaw), Vautin

Referee: J. Holdsworth (Kippax)

1989-90

Widnes 30 Tait; Currier, Davies (1t, 3g), D. Wright (1t), Offiah (2t); A. Myler (Dowd), D. Hulme; Grima (Moriarty), McKenzie, Pyke, Sorensen, P. Hulme (1t), R. Eyres (1t)

Canberra 18 Belcher; Wood (2g), Meninga (1t) (Martin), Daley, Ferguson; O'Sullivan (1t, 1g), Stuart; Jackson (Lowry), Walters (1t), Lazarus, Lance, Coyne, Clyde

Referee: F. Desplas (France)

1991-92

Wigan 21 Hampson; Myers (1t), Panapa (1t), Lydon (1dg), Botica (6g); Edwards, Gregory; Skerrett (Cowie) (Lucas), Dermott, Platt, Betts, McGinty (Gildart), Clarke (Forshaw)

Penrith 4 Barwick (B. Alexander); Willis (1t) (Smith), Bradley, B. Izzard, Mackay; Carter, G. Alexander; Lee (G. Izzard), Simmons, Dunn, Clarke, Cartwright, Van Der Voort (Xuereb)

Referee: A. Sablayrolles (France)

1992-93

Brisbane B. 22 O'Neill (1t) (Plowman); Carne, Renouf, Johns (Currie), Hancock (2t); Kevin Walters, Langer (Plath); Lazarus, Kerrod Walters (1t), Gee (Ryan), Gillmeister, Hohn, Matterson (3g)

Wigan 8 Stoop (Crompton); Robinson, Bell, Farrar, Offiah; Botica (2g), Edwards (1t); Skerrett (Lucas), Dermott, Platt (Cowie), Betts, McGinty (Panapa), Clarke

Referee: D. Hale (New Zealand)

1993-94

Wigan 20 Connolly; Robinson (1t), Panapa, Mather (1t) (Atkinson), Offiah; Botica (4g), Edwards; Cowie, Dermott (Hall), McGinty (Cassidy), Betts (1t), Farrell, Clarke

Brisbane B. 14 Carne; Sailor (1t), Renouf (Ryan), Johns, Hancock (1t); Kevin Walters (Plath) (McKenna), Langer; Lazarus, Kerrod Walters, Gee (Gonea), Hohn, Carn, O'Neill (1t,1g)

Referee: Greg McCallum (Australia)

MAN OF THE MATCH AWARDS

1987: Shaun Wane (Wigan)
1989: David Hulme (Widnes)
1991: Frano Botica (Wigan)
1992: Terry Matterson (Brisbane B.)
1994: Shaun Edwards (Wigan)

Wigan prop Shaun Wane, the inaugural World Club Challenge Man of the Match, against Manly in 1987.

Wigan skipper and Man of the Match Shaun Edwards leads the celebrations after the Riversiders' memorable 20-14 World Club Challenge triumph in Brisbane in June 1994, the first time the World Club title had been contested Down Under.

Injured Keighley Cougars skipper Steve Hall holds the Stones Bitter Second Division Championship Bowl after clinching the title with a league record 104-4 defeat of Highfield.

LEAGUE

LEAGUE

1994-95 CHAMPIONSHIP

Amid the controversy regarding the advent of the new-style Super League, Wigan proved to be in a class of their own by lifting the traditional Championship Trophy in record-breaking fashion.

The Riversiders were crowned Stones Bitter Champions for a record-extending sixth successive season, equalling their own record of 56 points from a possible 60, only suffering defeat away at Halifax and Leeds. Ironically, in each defeat, Wigan scored more tries than their opponents.

Wigan confirmed their superiority by becoming the first club to score more than 1,000 points in a Division One campaign, including a record 200 tries. The Central Park outfit finished seven points clear of nearest rivals Leeds, themselves seven points ahead of third-placed Castleford.

The 56-point haul equalled Wigan's tally of 1986-87, their first season of being coached by New Zealander Graham Lowe. This 1994-95 triumph was under the guidance of fellow Kiwi Graeme West, making his Stones Bitter Championship debut as coach, having taken over the reins from sacked John Dorahy at the end of the previous season for Stones Bitter Premiership and World Club Challenge success.

The comfortable margin of Championship glory contrasted with the previous two campaigns, both won on point scoring difference. In 1993-94, Wigan topped joint leaders Bradford Northern and Warrington, while a year earlier arch rivals St. Helens shared equal billing.

Wigan had begun the season with a Division One record opening sequence of 13 successive wins before losing 33-28 at Leeds in a classic encounter.

They clinched the title and a Stones Bitter prize cheque for £60,000 with two games remaining, the trophy being presented after their 34-18 victory at home to St. Helens on Good Friday.

While basking in the glory of high-scoring prowess, Wigan also gained immense satisfaction from their defensive record, conceding only 386 points in the 30-match campaign, 140 less than second-best defenders Leeds. Thus Wigan's average score for the Championship campaign was 38-12.

The same clubs filled the top eight places as the previous season but with a reshuffle below table-toppers Wigan, Warrington and Bradford Northern, joint leaders in 1993-94, dropped to sixth and seventh places respectively, while Leeds climbed five rungs to runners-up spot.

Outside of the top eight, Workington Town gained the honours for most improved side, the 1993-94 Second Division champions clinching ninth position in the Championship with 12 wins and a draw. The Cumbrians were inspired by the early season capture of on-loan Warrington duo Kevin Ellis and Rowland Phillips, both Welsh internationals.

Fellow promoted side Doncaster took the headlines in the opening weeks of the season, claiming three victories in their first four matches. Tony Fisher's charges opened their first-ever campaign in the First Division since formation in 1951 with a shock 29-20 win at St. Helens, followed up a week later with a 21-6 home success over Widnes. A creditable 16-6 defeat by Leeds at Tattersfield preceded a 22-10 home success over Wakefield Trinity, leaving the Dons in fifth place in the Stones Bitter Championship table.

There were to be only two more victories, plus a draw, as the club plunged into financial administration amid the sacking of Fisher after a two-year reign. Doncaster finished the season at the foot of the table with 11 points, surrounded by talks of being taken over by Sheffield Eagles to form a club to serve South Yorkshire with a twin-town base.

Hull finished second to bottom, two points adrift of troubled Widnes. That poor finish saw both clubs placed in the new-style Division One outside the elite Super League.

Five of the bottom six clubs made coaching

changes during the campaign. Featherstone Rovers sacked Australian Steve Martin and brought in David Ward from Batley; Salford parted company with Australian Garry Jack and promoted scrum half Andy Gregory; Wakefield Trinity released David Hobbs and appointed duo Paul Harkin and Andy Kelly; Hull fired New Zealander Tony Gordon and put Phil Windley and Russ Walker in joint control with Windley eventually taking over on his own account; while Doncaster upgraded assistant Ian Brooke to replace Fisher.

In the Second Division, the title decider came on the final matchday of the season, ambitious Keighley Cougars clinching the title and £30,000 prize money with a club and league match record 104-4 victory over Highfield at Rochdale Hornets' Spotland ground.

The landslide victory beat Keighley's previous highest scores of 86-0, versus Highfield in January 1993 and Nottingham City in November 1992, both at home. It topped the previous best league match score of 102-0 in Leeds' defeat of Coventry in April 1913.

Batley, having missed out on promotion in the last match of the season 12 months earlier, secured runners-up spot two points behind the Cougars and five ahead of third-placed

Huddersfield, playing at the impressive Alfred McAlpine Stadium for the first time.

London Broncos finished in the top four for the second successive season, gaining controversial Super League status on geographical location.

With former New Zealand Test star Kurt Sorensen settling into the coaching role, Whitehaven climbed from 10th to fifth place, but relegated duo Hull K.R. and Leigh did not make the customary impact on the lower echelon.

Rovers hung on to eighth spot to qualify for the Second Division Premiership. Leigh, finished 11th with 12 victories in 30 matches, achieved under three different coaches. Australian Steve Simms was headhunted by Halifax to be replaced by former assistant coach Denis Ramsdale, who resigned after a short stint to be succeeded by former Wigan and Great Britain prop Ian Lucas.

Hunslet responded to new coach Steve Ferres, in his first full season, to gain 16 victories compared to the previous campaign's three. Cumbrian duo Carlisle and Barrow filled the last three places along with Highfield. The Merseysiders finished at the bottom for a third successive year with only one win, conceding a record 1,604 points.

Keighley loose forward Martin Wood incites "Cougarmania" during their run-in to the Second Division title.

FINAL TABLES 1994-95

STONES BITTER CHAMPIONSHIP

	P.	W.	D.	L.	FOR				AGAINST				Pts.
					Dg.	Gls.	Trs.	Pts.	Dg.	Gls.	Trs.	Pts.	
Wigan	30	28	0	2	2	173	200	1148	2	62	65	386	56
Leeds	30	24	1	5	3	120	155	863	8	85	87	526	49
Castleford	30	20	2	8	4	138	148	872	10	85	96	564	42
St. Helens	30	20	1	9	9	124	159	893	8	98	109	640	41
Halifax	30	18	2	10	6	126	131	782	4	85	98	566	38
Warrington	30	18	2	10	11	111	130	753	6	94	94	570	38
Bradford N.	30	17	1	12	1	115	145	811	8	93	114	650	35
Sheffield E.	30	15	0	15	12	101	108	646	5	93	127	699	30
Workington T.	30	12	1	17	6	90	88	538	3	112	129	743	25
Oldham	30	11	1	18	6	90	87	534	8	127	121	746	23
Featherstone R.	30	10	1	19	0	99	96	582	7	118	111	687	21
Salford	30	10	1	19	5	90	107	613	3	112	137	775	21
Wakefield T.	30	9	0	21	14	72	69	434	5	119	141	807	18
Widnes	30	8	1	21	3	79	80	481	9	123	128	767	17
Hull	30	7	1	22	8	103	95	594	6	141	148	880	15
Doncaster	30	5	1	24	5	72	80	469	3	156	173	1007	11

SECOND DIVISION

	P.	W.	D.	L.	FOR				AGAINST				Pts.
					Dg.	Gls.	Trs.	Pts.	Dg.	Gls.	Trs.	Pts.	
Keighley C.	30	23	2	5	2	144	171	974	5	52	57	337	48
Batley	30	23	0	7	4	111	132	754	3	70	70	423	46
Huddersfield	30	19	3	8	4	121	156	870	5	87	90	539	41
London B.	30	20	1	9	2	89	138	732	8	70	83	480	41
Whitehaven	30	19	0	11	4	113	134	766	3	76	88	507	38
Rochdale H.	30	18	0	12	5	134	133	805	4	88	91	544	36
Dewsbury	30	17	1	12	4	114	128	744	6	82	92	538	35
Hull K.R.	30	16	1	13	2	125	143	824	6	79	88	516	33
Ryedale-York	30	15	2	13	14	99	127	720	6	84	107	602	32
Hunslet	30	16	0	14	7	88	107	611	5	109	140	783	32
Leigh	30	12	0	18	2	94	108	622	3	124	134	787	24
Swinton	30	12	0	18	2	85	101	576	2	121	131	768	24
Bramley	30	10	0	20	4	67	104	554	1	97	115	655	20
Carlisle	30	8	0	22	2	86	93	546	5	116	160	877	16
Barrow	30	6	0	24	7	79	71	449	3	122	141	811	12
Highfield	30	1	0	29	0	34	39	224	0	206	298	1604	2

1994-95 PRE-SEASON BETTING FOR THE CHAMPIONSHIPS
Coral's pre-season betting:
For the Stones Bitter Championship: 8-11 Wigan; 5-1 Bradford N.; 6-1 Leeds; 13-2 St. Helens; 10-1 Warrington; 16-1 Castleford; 25-1 Halifax; 33-1 Featherstone R.; 50-1 Hull; 80-1 Salford; 100-1 Sheffield E.; Workington T.; 250-1 Oldham, Wakefield T.; 500-1 Widnes; 750-1 Doncaster.
For the Second Division Championship: 3-10 London B.; 11-2 Keighley C.; 13-2 Hull K.R.; 16-1 Batley, Dewsbury; 20-1 Huddersfield; 25-1 Leigh; 50-1 Ryedale-York, Whitehaven; 80-1 Rochdale H.; 250-1 Barrow, Swinton; 400-1 Carlisle; 1,000-1 Hunslet; 1,500 Bramley; 2,000-1 Highfield.

TWO DIVISION CHAMPIONSHIP ROLL OF HONOUR

	FIRST DIVISION	**SECOND DIVISION**
1902-03	Halifax	Keighley
1903-04	Bradford	Wakefield Trinity
1904-05	Oldham	Dewsbury
1962-63	Swinton	Hunslet
1963-64	Swinton	Oldham
1973-74	Salford	Bradford Northern
1974-75	St. Helens	Huddersfield
1975-76	Salford	Barrow
1976-77	Featherstone Rovers	Hull
1977-78	Widnes	Leigh
1978-79	Hull Kingston Rovers	Hull
1979-80	Bradford Northern	Featherstone Rovers
1980-81	Bradford Northern	York
1981-82	Leigh	Oldham
1982-83	Hull	Fulham
1983-84	Hull Kingston Rovers	Barrow
1984-85	Hull Kingston Rovers	Swinton
1985-86	Halifax	Leigh
1986-87	Wigan	Hunslet
1987-88	Widnes	Oldham
1988-89	Widnes	Leigh
1989-90	Wigan	Hull Kingston Rovers
1990-91	Wigan	Salford
1991-92	Wigan	Sheffield Eagles
1992-93	Wigan	Featherstone Rovers
1993-94	Wigan	Workington Town
1994-95	Wigan	Keighley Cougars

THIRD DIVISION CHAMPIONS

1991-92	Huddersfield
1992-93	Keighley Cougars

RELEGATION AND PROMOTION

Since reintroduction of two divisions in 1973-74.

● Figure in brackets indicates position in division.

	RELEGATED	PROMOTED
1973-74	Oldham (13) Hull K.R. (14) Leigh (15) Whitehaven (16)	Bradford Northern (1) York (2) Keighley (3) Halifax (4)
1974-75	York (13) Bramley (14) Rochdale Hornets (15) Halifax (16)	Huddersfield (1) Hull K.R. (2) Oldham (3) Swinton (4)
1975-76	Dewsbury (13) Keighley (14) Huddersfield (15) Swinton (16)	Barrow (1) Rochdale Hornets (2) Workington Town (3) Leigh (4)
1976-77	Rochdale Hornets (13) Leigh (14) Barrow (15) Oldham (16)	Hull (1) Dewsbury (2) Bramley (3) New Hunslet (4)
1977-78	Hull (13) New Hunslet (14) Bramley (15) Dewsbury (16)	Leigh (1) Barrow (2) Rochdale Hornets (3) Huddersfield (4)
1978-79	Barrow (13) Featherstone Rovers (14) Rochdale Hornets (15) Huddersfield (16)	Hull (1) New Hunslet (2) York (3) Blackpool Borough (4)
1979-80	Wigan (13) Hunslet (14) York (15) Blackpool Borough (16)	Featherstone Rovers (1) Halifax (2) Oldham (3) Barrow (4)
1980-81	Halifax (13) Salford (14) Workington Town (15) Oldham (16)	York (1) Wigan (2) Fulham (3) Whitehaven (4)
1981-82	Fulham (13) Wakefield Trinity (14) York (15) Whitehaven (16)	Oldham (1) Carlisle (2) Workington Town (3) Halifax (4)
1982-83	Barrow (13) Workington Town (14) Halifax (15) Carlisle (16)	Fulham (1) Wakefield Trinity (2) Salford (3) Whitehaven (4)

1983-84	Fulham (13)	Barrow (1)
	Wakefield Trinity (14)	Workington Town (2)
	Salford (15)	Hunslet (3)
	Whitehaven (16)	Halifax (4)
1984-85	Barrow (13)	Swinton (1)
	Leigh (14)	Salford (2)
	Hunslet (15)	York (3)
	Workington Town (16)	Dewsbury (4)
1985-86	York (14)	Leigh (1)
	Swinton (15)	Barrow (2)
	Dewsbury (16)	Wakefield Trinity (3)
1986-87	Oldham (13)	Hunslet (1)
	Featherstone Rovers (14)	Swinton (2)
	Barrow (15)	
	Wakefield Trinity (16)	
1987-88	Leigh (12)	Oldham (1)
	Swinton (13)	Featherstone Rovers (2)
	Hunslet (14)	Wakefield Trinity (3)
1988-89	Oldham (12)	Leigh (1)
	Halifax (13)	Barrow (2)
	Hull K.R. (14)	Sheffield Eagles (3)
1989-90	Leigh (12)	Hull K.R. (1)
	Salford (13)	Rochdale Hornets (2)
	Barrow (14)	Oldham (3)
1990-91	Oldham (12)	Salford (1)
	Sheffield Eagles (13)	Halifax (2)
	Rochdale Hornets (14)	Swinton (3)

	FIRST DIVISION	**SECOND DIVISION**	**THIRD DIVISION**
1991-92	Down: Featherstone R. (13)	Up: Sheffield E. (1)	Up: Huddersfield (1)
	Swinton (14)	Leigh (2)	Bramley (2)
		Down: Ryedale-York (7)	
		Workington Town (8)	
1992-93	Salford (13)	Up: Featherstone R. (1)	Keighley C. (1)
	Hull K.R. (14)	Oldham (2)	Workington T. (2)

● Reverted to two divisions with only Featherstone and Oldham moving divisions.

	RELEGATED	**PROMOTED**
1993-94	Hull K.R. (15)	Workington Town (1)
	Leigh (16)	Doncaster (2)
1994-95	Hull (15)	Keighley Cougars (1)
	Doncaster (16)	Batley (2)

● Promotion and relegation not carried out following formation of Super League and two other divisions.

● League match records do not include scores in abandoned matches that were replayed.

FIRST DIVISION RECORDS
Since reintroduction in 1973

INDIVIDUAL

Match records

Most tries:
6 Shane Cooper (St. Helens) v. Hull, 17 February 1988

Most goals: 13 Geoff Pimblett (St. Helens) v. Bramley, 5 March 1978

Most points: 38 (4t,11g) Bob Beardmore (Castleford) v. Barrow, 22 March 1987

Season records

Most tries: 44 Ellery Hanley (Wigan)   1986-87
Most goals: 130 Steve Hesford (Warrington)   1978-79
Most points: 326 (18t,126g,2dg) John Schuster (Halifax) 1994-95

TEAM

Highest score and widest margin: Leeds 90 v. Barrow 0, 11 February 1990

Highest away score: Rochdale H. 12 v. Castleford 76, 3 March 1991

Widest away margin: Doncaster 0 v. Halifax 72, 9 October 1994

Most points by losing team: Hunslet 40 v. Barrow 41, 9 September 1984

Scoreless draw: Wigan 0 v. Castleford 0, 26 January 1974

Highest score draw: Leeds 46 v. Sheffield E. 46, 10 April 1994

Best opening sequence: 13 wins then a draw by Widnes 1981-82; 13 wins by Wigan 1994-95

Longest winning run: 25 by St. Helens. Won last 13 of 1985-86 and first 12 of 1986-87 (Also longest unbeaten run)

Longest losing run: 20 by Whitehaven 1983-84; Rochdale H. 1990-91

Longest run without a win: 23, including 3 draws, by Whitehaven 1981-82 (Also worst opening sequence)

Biggest attendance: 29,839 Wigan v. St. Helens, 9 April 1993

Top ten Division One career tries
279 Ellery Hanley (Bradford N., Wigan, Leeds)
207 Martin Offiah (Widnes, Wigan)
178 Phil Ford (Warrington, Wigan, Bradford N., Leeds, Salford)
167 Garry Schofield (Hull, Leeds)
165 Keith Fielding (Salford)
157 Shaun Edwards (Wigan)
144 David Smith (Wakefield T., Leeds, Bradford N.)
139 Stuart Wright (Wigan, Widnes)
136 Roy Mathias (St. Helens)
134 Des Drummond (Leigh, Warrington, Workington T.)

Most Division One career goals
862 John Woods (Leigh, Bradford N., Warrington)

Most Division One career points
2,150 John Woods (Leigh, Bradford N., Warrington)

20 Division One tries in a season

1973-74	36	Keith Fielding (Salford)
	29	Roy Mathias (St. Helens)
	21	David Smith (Wakefield T.)
1974-75	21	Maurice Richards (Salford)
	21	Roy Mathias (St. Helens)
1975-76	26	Maurice Richards (Salford)
	20	David Smith (Wakefield T.)
1976-77	22	David Topliss (Wakefield T.)
	21	Keith Fielding (Salford)
	21	Ged Dunn (Hull K.R.)
	20	David Smith (Leeds)
	20	Stuart Wright (Widnes)
1977-78	26	Keith Fielding (Salford)
	25	Steve Fenton (Castleford)
	24	Stuart Wright (Widnes)
	20	David Smith (Leeds)
	20	Bruce Burton (Castleford)
	20	John Bevan (Warrington)
1978-79	28	Steve Hartley (Hull K.R.)
1979-80	24	Keith Fielding (Salford)
	21	Roy Mathias (St. Helens)
	21	Steve Hubbard (Hull K.R.)
	20	David Smith (Leeds)
1980-81	20	Steve Hubbard (Hull K.R.)
1981-82		David Hobbs (Featherstone R.) was top scorer with 19 tries.
1982-83	22	Bob Eccles (Warrington)
	20	Steve Evans (Hull)
1983-84	28	Garry Schofield (Hull)
	23	John Woods (Leigh)
	22	James Leuluai (Hull)
1984-85	40	Ellery Hanley (Bradford N.)
	34	Gary Prohm (Hull K.R.)
	23	Henderson Gill (Wigan)
	22	Barry Ledger (St. Helens)
	22	Mal Meninga (St. Helens)
1985-86	22	Ellery Hanley (Wigan)
1986-87	44	Ellery Hanley (Wigan)
	24	Phil Ford (Bradford N.)
	24	Henderson Gill (Wigan)
	23	Garry Schofield (Hull)
	21	John Henderson (Leigh)
1987-88	33	Martin Offiah (Widnes)
	22	Ellery Hanley (Wigan)
1988-89	37	Martin Offiah (Widnes)
	20	Grant Anderson (Castleford)
1989-90	28	Martin Offiah (Widnes)
	25	Mark Preston (Widnes)
	20	Steve Larder (Castleford)
1990-91	22	Martin Offiah (Widnes)
	22	Les Quirk (St. Helens)
	20	Ellery Hanley (Wigan)
1991-92	31	John Devereux (Widnes)
	27	Greg Austin (Halifax)
	25	Shaun Edwards (Wigan)
	23	Mark Preston (Halifax)
1992-93	24	Shaun Edwards (Wigan)
	23	Ellery Hanley (Leeds)
	20	Martin Offiah (Wigan)
	20	Alan Hunte (St. Helens)
1993-94	30	St. John Ellis (Castleford)
	26	Martin Offiah (Wigan)
	24	Jason Critchley (Salford)
	23	Paul Newlove (Bradford N.)
	21	John Bentley (Halifax)
	20	Anthony Sullivan (St. Helens)

1994-95 33 Martin Offiah (Wigan)
           29 Ellery Hanley (Leeds)
           26 John Bentley (Halifax)
           25 Alan Hunte (St. Helens)
           23 Paul Newlove (Bradford N.)
           21 Mark Preston (Halifax)

Top Division One goalscorers

1973-74	126	David Watkins (Salford)
1974-75	96	Sammy Lloyd (Castleford)
1975-76	118	Sammy Lloyd (Castleford)
1976-77	113	Steve Quinn (Featherstone R.)
1977-78	116	Steve Hesford (Warrington)
1978-79	130	Steve Hesford (Warrington)
1979-80	104	Steve Hubbard (Hull K.R.)
1980-81	96	Steve Diamond (Wakefield T.)
1981-82	110	Steve Quinn (Featherstone R.)
		John Woods (Leigh)
1982-83	105	Bob Beardmore (Castleford)
1983-84	106	Steve Hesford (Warrington)
1984-85	114	Sean Day (St. Helens)
1985-86	85	David Stephenson (Wigan)
1986-87	120	Paul Loughlin (St. Helens)
1987-88	95	John Woods (Warrington)
1988-89	95	David Hobbs (Bradford N.)
1989-90	96	Paul Loughlin (St. Helens)
1990-91	85	Paul Eastwood (Hull)
1991-92	86	Frano Botica (Wigan)
1992-93	107	Frano Botica (Wigan)
1993-94	123	Frano Botica (Wigan)
1994-95	128	John Schuster (Halifax)

Top Division One points-scorer 1994-95
326 (18t,126g,2dg) John Schuster (Halifax)

SECOND DIVISION RECORDS
Since reintroduction in 1973

INDIVIDUAL

Match records

Most tries: 6 Ged Dunn (Hull K.R.) v. New Hunslet,
    2 February 1975; David Kettlestring (Ryedale-York)
    at Keighley, 11 March 1990; Greg Austin (Halifax) v.
    Trafford B., 7 April 1991

Most goals: 15 Mick Stacey (Leigh) v. Doncaster,
    28 March 1976

Most points: 38 (4t,13g) John Woods (Leigh) v.
    Blackpool B., 11 September 1977; 38 (4t,11g) John
    Woods (Leigh) v. Ryedale-York, 12 January 1992

Season records

Most tries: 48 Steve Halliwell (Leigh) 1985-86

Most goals: 167 Mike Fletcher (Hull K.R.) 1989-90

Most points: 395 (22t,163g,3dg) Lyn Hopkins
    (Workington T.) 1981-82

TEAM

Highest score: Highfield 4 v. Keighley C. 104 (played at
    Rochdale H.), 23 April 1995 (Also widest margin)

Highest score on opponents' ground: Runcorn H. 2 v.
    Leigh 88, 15 January 1989

Most points by losing team:
    Dewsbury 36 v. Rochdale H. 34, 9 October 1988;
    Oldham 50 v. Keighley 34, 12 November 1989
    Swinton 40 v. Hunslet 34, 24 April 1994

Highest score draw: Huddersfield B. 32 v. Keighley 32,
    17 April 1986

Scoreless draw: Dewsbury 0 v. Rochdale H. 0,
    30 January 1983; Whitehaven 0 v. Workington T. 0,
    28 December 1993

Longest winning run: 30 by Leigh in 1985-86. Hull won
    all 26 matches in 1978-79

Longest losing run: 55 by Runcorn H. (9 in 1988-89, all
    28 in 1989-90 and 18 in 1990-91)

Longest run without a win: 67, inc 2 draws, by
    Runcorn H. (19 in 1988-89, all 28 in 1989-90 and
    20 in 1990-91)

Biggest attendance: 12,424 Hull v. New Hunslet,
    18 May 1979

1994-95 Top Division Two scorers

Most tries: 36 Greg Austin (Huddersfield)

Most goals: 131 Martin Strett (Rochdale H.)

Most points: 296 (9t,129g,2dg) Martin Strett
    (Rochdale H.)
    296 (16t,116g) Simon Irving (Keighley C.)

THIRD DIVISION RECORDS
Two seasons only, 1991-92 and 1992-93

INDIVIDUAL

Match records

Most tries: 6 Steve Rowan (Barrow) at Nottingham C.,
    15 November 1992

Most goals: 15 John Wasyliw (Keighley C.) v.
    Nottingham C., 1 November 1992

Most points: 42 (4t,13g) Dean Marwood (Workington T.)
    v. Highfield, 1 November 1992

Season records

Most tries: 31 Vince Gribbin (Whitehaven) 1991-92

Most goals: 146 John Wasyliw (Keighley C.) 1992-93

Most points: 380 (22t,146g) John Wasyliw (Keighley C.)
    1992-93

TEAM

Highest score: Blackpool G. 5 v. Dewsbury 90, 14 April
    1993 (Also highest away score)

Widest margin: Keighley C. 86 v. Nottingham C. 0,
    1 November 1992

Most points by losing team: Hunslet 33 v. Doncaster 32,
    16 February 1992

Highest score draw: None of 20-20 or more

Scoreless draw: None

Longest winning run: 14 by Keighley C. 1992-93
    (Also longest unbeaten)

Longest losing run: 27 by Nottingham C. All 26 in
    1991-92 and first of 1992-93 (Also longest without win)

Biggest attendance: 5,226 Keighley C. v. Batley, 9 April
    1993

THE 22-SEASON TABLE

St. Helens have been the most consistently successful club over 22 seasons of Division One rugby in terms of total points gained. Although St. Helens have won the title only once since the reintroduction of two divisions in 1973 they head a 22-season table with 831 points from 636 matches.

The Saints are also the only club to finish in the top eight throughout the 22 seasons. The only other clubs to have remained in Division One are Widnes, Leeds, Warrington and Castleford.

Bradford Northern, Hull and Leigh were all Division Two champions who went on to win the Division One title a few years after being promoted, while Hull Kingston Rovers, Halifax and Wigan are other former lower grade clubs who later won the major championship.

The highest place gained by a newly-promoted club is third by Hull in 1979-80 after winning the Division Two title with a 100 per cent record the previous season.

Division One champions who were relegated a few seasons after winning the Division One title were Salford, Featherstone Rovers, Leigh, Halifax and Hull K.R.

The records of the five clubs who have appeared in Division One throughout the 22 seasons are as follows:

FIRST DIVISION SCORING

The following table shows the scoring totals for each season since the inauguration of two divisions in 1973-74:

DIVISION ONE

Season	Matches each club played	Goals	1-Point drop goals	Tries	Pts
1973-74	30	1,508	—	1,295	6,901
1974-75	30	1,334	48	1,261	6,499
1975-76	30	1,498	53	1,331	7,042
1976-77	30[1]	1,435	91	1,423	7,230
1977-78	30[2]	1,402	99	1,443	7,232
1978-79	30	1,367	119	1,448	7,197
1979-80	30	1,389	131	1,349	6,956
1980-81	30	1,439	147	1,342	7,051
1981-82	30	1,486	132	1,354	7,166
1982-83	30	1,369	64	1,386	6,960
1983-84	30	1,472	108	1,479	8,968
1984-85	30	1,464	84	1,595	9,392
1985-86	30	1,296	80	1,435	8,412
1986-87	30	1,412	90	1,607	9,342
1987-88	26	1,070	75	1,170	6,895
1988-89	26	1,107	80	1,154	6,910
1989-90	26	1,198	80	1,295	7,656
1990-91	26	1,115	58	1,189	7,044
1991-92	26	1,026	46	1,178	6,810
1992-93	26	1,082	57	1,215	7,081
1993-94	30	1,488	107	1,699	9,879
1994-95	30	1,703	95	1,878	11,013

[1] Salford & Leeds played 29 matches — their final match was abandoned and not replayed. This match was expunged from league records.
[2] Featherstone R. & Bradford N. played 29 matches — their final match was cancelled following Featherstone's strike.

	P.	W.	D.	L.	F.	A.	Pts
1. St. Helens	636	403	25	208	13,769	9,341	831
2. Widnes	636	387	21	228	11,895	9,074	795
3. Leeds	635	371	27	237	12,593	9,893	769
4. Warrington	636	351	23	262	11,495	9,502	725
5. Castleford	636	340	31	265	12,696	10,230	711

●Although Wigan have had only 21 seasons in Division One they have totalled 813 points from 606 matches.

CHAMPIONSHIP PLAY-OFFS

Following the breakaway from the English Rugby Union, 22 clubs formed the Northern Rugby Football League. Each club played 42 matches and Manningham won the first Championship as league leaders in 1895-96.

This format was then abandoned and replaced by the Yorkshire Senior and Lancashire Senior Combination leagues until 1901-02 when 14 clubs broke away to form the Northern Rugby League with Broughton Rangers winning the first Championship.

The following season two divisions were formed with the Division One title going to Halifax (1902-03), Bradford (1903-04), who won a play-off against Salford 5-0 at Halifax after both teams tied with 52 points, and Oldham (1904-05).

In 1905-06 the two divisions were merged with Leigh taking the Championship as league leaders. They won the title on a percentage basis as the 31 clubs did not play the same number of matches. The following season the top four play-off was introduced as a fairer means of deciding the title.

The top club played the fourth-placed, the second

meeting the third, with the higher club having home advantage. The final was staged at a neutral venue.

It was not until 1930-31 that all clubs played the same number of league matches, but not all against each other, the top four play-off being a necessity until the reintroduction of two divisions in 1962-63.

This spell of two division football lasted only two seasons and the restoration of the one-league Championship table brought about the introduction of a top-16 play-off, this format continuing until the reappearance of two divisions in 1973-74.

Since then the Championship Trophy has been awarded to the leaders of the First Division, with the Second Division champions receiving a silver bowl. A Third Division was introduced for two years from 1991-92.

Slalom Lager launched a three-year sponsorship deal of the Championship and the Premiership in 1980-81 in a £215,000 package, extending the deal for another three years from 1983-84 for £270,000. From 1986-87, the sponsorship was taken over by brewers Bass, under the Stones Bitter banner, in a new £400,000 three-year deal, twice renewed through until 1996.

CHAMPIONSHIP PLAY-OFF FINALS

Season	Winners		Runners-up		Venue	Attendance	Receipts
Top Four Play-Offs							
1906-07	Halifax	18	Oldham	3	Huddersfield	13,200	£722
1907-08	Hunslet	7	Oldham	7	Salford	14,000	£690
Replay	Hunslet	12	Oldham	2	Wakefield	14,054	£800
1908-09	Wigan	7	Oldham	3	Salford	12,000	£630
1909-10	Oldham	13	Wigan	7	Broughton	10,850	£520
1910-11	Oldham	20	Wigan	7	Broughton	15,543	£717
1911-12	Huddersfield	13	Wigan	5	Halifax	15,000	£591
1912-13	Huddersfield	29	Wigan	2	Wakefield	17,000	£914
1913-14	Salford	5	Huddersfield	3	Leeds	8,091	£474
1914-15	Huddersfield	35	Leeds	2	Wakefield	14,000	£750
COMPETITION SUSPENDED DURING WAR-TIME							
1919-20	Hull	3	Huddersfield	2	Leeds	12,900	£1,615
1920-21	Hull	16	Hull K.R.	14	Leeds	10,000	£1,320
1921-22	Wigan	13	Oldham	2	Broughton	26,000	£1,825
1922-23	Hull K.R.	15	Huddersfield	5	Leeds	14,000	£1,370
1923-24	Batley	13	Wigan	7	Broughton	13,729	£968
1924-25	Hull K.R.	9	Swinton	5	Rochdale	21,580	£1,504
1925-26	Wigan	22	Warrington	10	St. Helens	20,000	£1,100
1926-27	Swinton	13	St. Helens Recs.	8	Warrington	24,432	£1,803
1927-28	Swinton	11	Featherstone R.	0	Oldham	15,451	£1,136
1928-29	Huddersfield	2	Leeds	0	Halifax	25,604	£2,028
1929-30	Huddersfield	2	Leeds	2	Wakefield	32,095	£2,111
Replay	Huddersfield	10	Leeds	0	Halifax	18,563	£1,319
1930-31	Swinton	14	Leeds	7	Wigan	31,000	£2,100
1931-32	St. Helens	9	Huddersfield	5	Wakefield	19,386	£943
1932-33	Salford	15	Swinton	5	Wigan	18,000	£1,053
1933-34	Wigan	15	Salford	3	Warrington	31,564	£2,114
1934-35	Swinton	14	Warrington	3	Wigan	27,700	£1,710
1935-36	Hull	21	Widnes	2	Huddersfield	17,276	£1,208

Season	Winners		Runners-up		Venue	Attendance	Receipts
1936-37	Salford	13	Warrington	11	Wigan	31,500	£2,000
1937-38	Hunslet	8	Leeds	2	Elland Rd., Leeds	54,112	£3,572
1938-39	Salford	8	Castleford	6	Man. C. FC	69,504	£4,301

WAR-TIME EMERGENCY PLAY-OFFS
For the first two seasons the Yorkshire League and Lancashire League champions met in a two-leg final as follows:

1939-40	Swinton	13	Bradford N.	21	Swinton	4,800	£237
	Bradford N.	16	Swinton	9	Bradford	11,721	£570
	Bradford N. won 37-22 on aggregate						
1940-41	Wigan	6	Bradford N.	17	Wigan	11,245	£640
	Bradford N.	28	Wigan	9	Bradford	20,205	£1,148
	Bradford N. won 45-15 on aggregate						

For the remainder of the war the top four in the War League played-off as follows:

1941-42	Dewsbury	13	Bradford N.	0	Leeds	18,000	£1,121
1942-43	Dewsbury	11	Halifax	3	Dewsbury	7,000	£400
	Halifax	13	Dewsbury	22	Halifax	9,700	£683

Dewsbury won 33-16 on aggregate but the Championship was declared null and void because they had played an ineligible player

1943-44	Wigan	13	Dewsbury	9	Wigan	14,000	£915
	Dewsbury	5	Wigan	12	Dewsbury	9,000	£700
	Wigan won 25-14 on aggregate						
1944-45	Halifax	9	Bradford N.	2	Halifax	9,426	£955
	Bradford N.	24	Halifax	11	Bradford	16,000	£1,850
	Bradford N. won 26-20 on aggregate						
1945-46	Wigan	13	Huddersfield	4	Man. C. FC	67,136	£8,387
1946-47	Wigan	13	Dewsbury	4	Man. C. FC	40,599	£5,895
1947-48	Warrington	15	Bradford N.	5	Man. C. FC	69,143	£9,792
1948-49	Huddersfield	13	Warrington	12	Man. C. FC	75,194	£11,073
1949-50	Wigan	20	Huddersfield	2	Man. C. FC	65,065	£11,500
1950-51	Workington T.	26	Warrington	11	Man. C. FC	61,618	£10,993
1951-52	Wigan	13	Bradford N.	6	Huddersfield Town FC	48,684	£8,215
1952-53	St. Helens	24	Halifax	14	Man. C. FC	51,083	£11,503
1953-54	Warrington	8	Halifax	7	Man. C. FC	36,519	£9,076
1954-55	Warrington	7	Oldham	3	Man. C. FC	49,434	£11,516
1955-56	Hull	10	Halifax	9	Man. C. FC	36,675	£9,179
1956-57	Oldham	15	Hull	14	Bradford	62,199	£12,054
1957-58	Hull	20	Workington T.	3	Bradford	57,699	£11,149
1958-59	St. Helens	44	Hunslet	22	Bradford	52,560	£10,146
1959-60	Wigan	27	Wakefield T.	3	Bradford	83,190	£14,482
1960-61	Leeds	25	Warrington	10	Bradford	52,177	£10,475
1961-62	Huddersfield	14	Wakefield T.	5	Bradford	37,451	£7,979

TWO DIVISIONS 1962-63 and 1963-64

Top Sixteen Play-Offs

1964-65	Halifax	15	St. Helens	7	Swinton	20,786	£6,141
1965-66	St. Helens	35	Halifax	12	Swinton	30,634	£8,750
1966-67	Wakefield T.	7	St. Helens	7	Leeds	20,161	£6,702
Replay	Wakefield T.	21	St. Helens	9	Swinton	33,537	£9,800
1967-68	Wakefield T.	17	Hull K.R.	10	Leeds	22,586	£7,697
1968-69	Leeds	16	Castleford	14	Bradford	28,442	£10,130
1969-70	St. Helens	24	Leeds	12	Bradford	26,358	£9,791
1970-71	St. Helens	16	Wigan	12	Swinton	21,745	£10,200
1971-72	Leeds	9	St. Helens	5	Swinton	24,055	£9,513
1972-73	Dewsbury	22	Leeds	13	Bradford	18,889	£9,479

TABLES

The first Northern Rugby Football League table was formed in 1895 following the historic breakaway from the English Rugby Union by 22 clubs.

There had been several meetings by rebel clubs in the North at which the key issue was their desire to pay players for any money they lost through taking time off work to play.

When this broken-time payment was rejected by the English RU the famous breakaway meeting took place at the George Hotel, Huddersfield, on Thursday 29 August 1895.

The meeting was attended by 21 clubs, but Dewsbury decided not to become part of the new Northern Rugby Football Union and they were replaced by Stockport.

Runcorn joined shortly afterwards to provide a 22-club league which played its first matches on 7 September 1895.

The league formula has gone through many changes since then – including one, two and three division formats – which can be charted through the following list of tables:

● AFTER the breakaway from the English Rugby Union, 22 clubs formed the Northern Union and played each other home and away.

1895-96

		P	W	D	L	F	A	Pts
1	Manningham	42	33	0	9	367	158	66
2	Halifax	42	30	5	7	312	139	65
3	Runcorn	42	24	8	10	314	143	56
4	Oldham	42	27	2	13	374	194	56
5	Brighouse R.	42	22	9	11	247	129	53
6	Tyldesley	42	21	8	13	260	164	50
7	Hunslet	42	24	2	16	279	207	50
8	Hull	42	23	3	16	259	158	49
9	Leigh	42	21	4	17	214	269	46
10	Wigan	42	19	7	16	245	147	45
11	Bradford	42	18	9	15	254	175	45
12	Leeds	42	20	3	19	258	247	43
13	Warrington	42	17	5	20	198	240	39
14	St. Helens*	42	15	8	19	195	230	36
15	Liversedge	42	15	4	23	261	355	34
16	Widnes	42	14	4	24	177	323	32
17	Stockport	42	12	8	22	171	315	32
18	Batley	42	12	7	23	137	298	31
19	Wakefield T.	42	13	4	25	156	318	30
20	Huddersfield	42	10	4	28	194	274	24
21	Broughton R.	42	8	8	26	165	244	24
22	Rochdale H.	42	4	8	30	78	388	16

*Deducted 2 points for playing ineligible player.

● So many clubs had joined the Northern Union that it was decided to abandon the one league system and introduce two county leagues.

LANCASHIRE SENIOR COMPETITION

1896-97

		P	W	D	L	F	A	Pts
1	Broughton R.	26	19	5	2	201	52	43
2	Oldham	26	20	2	4	243	59	42
3	Tyldesley	26	15	2	9	159	80	32
4	Runcorn	26	13	5	8	134	62	31
5	Stockport	26	14	2	10	157	137	30
6	Swinton	26	12	5	9	125	82	29
7	Warrington	26	11	5	10	100	124	27
8	Leigh	26	11	4	11	105	147	26
9	St. Helens	26	10	4	12	122	160	24
10	Widnes	26	10	3	13	113	164	23
11	Wigan	26	8	7	11	73	118	23
12	Rochdale H.	26	8	1	17	121	167	17
13	Salford	26	3	5	18	76	191	11
14	Morecambe	26	3	0	23	52	238	6

YORKSHIRE SENIOR COMPETITION

		P	W	D	L	F	A	Pts
1	Brighouse R.	30	22	4	4	213	68	48
2	Manningham	30	21	4	5	291	129	46
3	Halifax	30	18	4	8	219	112	40
4	Hunslet	30	16	4	10	211	138	36
5	Hull	30	15	6	9	152	125	36
6	Batley	30	15	5	10	164	126	35
7	Bradford	30	15	3	12	170	157	33
8	Wakefield T.	30	13	4	13	172	154	30
9	Castleford	30	11	6	13	178	161	28
10	Huddersfield	30	10	7	13	142	179	27
11	Liversedge	30	13	0	17	176	233	26
12	Leeds	30	10	4	16	115	123	24
13	Leeds Parish Ch.	30	9	4	17	129	162	22
14	Bramley	30	9	3	18	101	193	21
15	Holbeck	30	7	4	19	86	223	18
16	Heckmondwike	30	3	4	23	72	308	10

1897-98

LANCASHIRE SENIOR COMPETITION

		P	W	D	L	F	A	Pts
1	Oldham	26	23	1	2	295	94	47
2	Swinton	26	20	3	3	321	83	43
3	Widnes	26	19	1	6	251	114	39
4	Salford*	26	16	3	7	275	182	33
5	Broughton R.	26	13	4	9	183	108	30
6	Wigan	26	11	1	14	124	173	23
7	Leigh*	26	11	2	13	176	170	22
8	St. Helens	26	10	2	14	161	192	22
9	Warrington	26	10	2	14	131	178	22
10	Runcorn	26	9	2	15	142	184	20
11	Stockport	26	8	2	16	154	253	18
12	Tyldesley	26	8	1	17	111	281	17
13	Rochdale H.	26	7	0	19	146	247	14
14	Morecambe	26	4	2	20	74	285	10

*Deducted 2 points for fielding an ineligible player.

1898-99

LANCASHIRE SENIOR COMPETITION

		P	W	D	L	F	A	Pts
1	Broughton R.	26	21	0	5	277	74	42
2	Oldham	26	20	0	6	385	58	40
3	Salford	26	18	2	6	206	113	38
4	Widnes	26	17	2	7	196	113	36
5	Leigh	26	17	0	9	168	125	34
6	Swinton*	26	16	2	8	228	79	32
7	Runcorn	26	15	2	9	193	113	32
8	St. Helens	26	12	3	11	168	180	27
9	Warrington	26	11	1	14	134	217	23
10	Rochdale H.	26	9	3	14	112	216	21
11	Stockport	26	5	1	20	102	317	11
12	Tyldesley	26	3	5	18	82	240	11
13	Wigan	26	4	2	20	66	238	10
14	Morecambe	26	2	1	23	47	281	5

*Deducted 2 points for a breach of professional rules.

YORKSHIRE SENIOR COMPETITION

		P	W	D	L	F	A	Pts
1	Hunslet	30	22	4	4	327	117	48
2	Bradford	30	23	2	5	319	139	48
3	Batley	30	17	3	10	234	111	37
4	Halifax	30	16	3	11	193	164	35
5	Manningham	30	15	4	11	276	181	34
6	Castleford	30	16	1	13	256	208	33
7	Wakefield T.	30	16	1	13	248	214	33
8	Leeds Parish Ch..	30	15	1	14	187	213	31
9	Leeds	30	13	4	13	186	171	30
10	Huddersfield	30	12	3	15	208	170	27
11	Hull	30	11	4	15	192	187	26
12	Bramley	30	11	4	15	156	199	26
13	Brighouse R.	30	9	5	16	143	172	23
14	Holbeck	30	11	0	19	171	310	22
15	Heckmondwike	30	9	2	19	148	315	20
16	Liversedge	30	3	1	26	76	449	7

YORKSHIRE SENIOR COMPETITION

		P	W	D	L	F	A	Pts
1	Batley	30	23	2	5	279	75	48
2	Hull	30	23	1	6	429	101	47
3	Bradford	30	21	0	9	330	139	42
4	Leeds Parish Ch.	30	20	2	8	201	114	42
5	Hunslet	30	16	5	9	314	140	37
6	Huddersfield	30	15	3	12	169	147	33
7	Manningham*	30	15	2	13	222	212	30
8	Halifax	30	15	0	15	156	158	30
9	Wakefield T.	30	11	6	13	209	161	28
10	Brighouse R.	30	12	2	16	114	191	26
11	Leeds	30	11	3	16	127	186	25
12	Castleford	30	10	4	16	159	214	24
13	Holbeck	30	10	4	16	134	220	24
14	Bramley	30	7	3	20	62	266	17
15	Liversedge	30	5	3	22	131	439	13
16	Heckmondwike	30	4	4	22	70	343	12

*Deducted 2 points for a breach of professional rules.

1897-98
CHAMPIONSHIP PLAY-OFF
At Headingley, Leeds

	T	G	P		T	G	P
HUNSLET	1	1	5	BRADFORD	0	1	2

1899-1900

1900-01

LANCASHIRE SENIOR COMPETITION

		P	W	D	L	F	A	Pts
1	Runcorn	26	22	2	2	232	33	46
2	Oldham	26	21	1	4	340	75	43
3	Swinton	26	19	1	6	210	108	39
4	St. Helens	26	16	3	7	207	119	35
5	Widnes	26	12	4	10	174	146	28
6	Warrington	26	12	1	13	174	128	25
7	Broughton R.*	26	13	1	12	132	138	25
8	Salford	26	12	0	14	196	176	24
9	Stockport	26	10	2	14	126	136	22
10	Leigh	26	8	5	13	119	211	21
11	Rochdale H.*	26	9	1	16	90	181	17
12	Millom	26	7	1	18	112	234	15
13	Wigan	26	7	1	18	73	230	15
14	Tyldesley	26	2	1	23	66	336	5

*Two points deducted for a breach of professional rules.

LANCASHIRE SENIOR COMPETITION

		P	W	D	L	F	A	Pts
1	Oldham	26	22	1	3	301	67	45
2	Swinton	26	21	2	3	283	66	44
3	Runcorn	26	20	0	6	240	100	40
4	Broughton R.	26	17	2	7	211	84	36
5	Salford	26	15	0	11	229	149	30
6	Warrington	26	12	3	11	149	126	27
7	Leigh	26	12	2	12	157	143	26
8	Barrow	26	10	2	14	140	169	22
9	Wigan	26	8	3	15	98	227	19
10	Rochdale H.	26	8	2	16	103	257	18
11	Millom	26	8	0	18	85	194	16
12	Stockport	26	6	3	17	102	184	15
13	St. Helens*	26	6	2	18	82	228	12
14	Widnes	26	6	0	20	85	271	12

*Two points deducted for a breach of the professional rules.

YORKSHIRE SENIOR COMPETITION

		P	W	D	L	F	A	Pts
1	Bradford	30	24	2	4	324	98	50
2	Batley	30	21	6	3	219	72	48
3	Halifax	30	20	3	7	193	120	43
4	Wakefield T.	30	18	5	7	203	120	41
5	Huddersfield	30	17	4	9	181	110	38
6	Hull K.R.*	30	15	5	11	181	129	32
7	Hull	30	15	0	15	249	154	30
8	Hunslet	30	14	2	14	182	168	30
9	Manningham	30	13	3	14	207	203	29
10	Bramley	30	13	0	17	121	190	26
11	Castleford	30	11	3	16	155	199	25
12	Brighouse R.	30	9	3	18	80	231	21
13	Holbeck*	30	8	4	18	138	236	18
14	Leeds Parish Ch.	30	7	3	20	135	207	17
15	Leeds	30	7	3	20	103	225	17
16	Liversedge	30	5	1	24	94	303	11

*Two points deducted for a breach of professional rules.

YORKSHIRE SENIOR COMPETITION

		P	W	D	L	F	A	Pts
1	Bradford*	30	26	1	3	387	100	51
2	Halifax	30	22	3	5	309	147	47
3	Hunslet	30	20	0	10	252	142	40
4	Batley	30	17	5	8	166	131	39
5	Hull*	30	19	1	10	291	141	37
6	Huddersfield	30	17	1	12	241	130	35
7	Brighouse R.	30	16	0	14	194	162	32
8	Hull K.R.	30	15	2	13	195	169	32
9	Wakefield T.	30	14	3	13	242	148	31
10	Leeds Parish Ch.	30	12	6	12	115	108	30
11	Bramley	30	12	5	13	138	163	29
12	Manningham	30	9	1	20	115	258	19
13	Leeds	30	7	3	20	144	255	17
14	Holbeck*	30	7	3	20	110	263	15
15	Castleford	30	5	4	21	92	331	14
16	Liversedge	30	2	2	26	43	386	6

*Two points deducted for a breach of the professional rules.

TABLES

● Fourteen clubs resigned from the two county leagues to form a new Northern Rugby League.

1901-02

		P	W	D	L	F	A	Pts
1	Broughton R.	26	21	1	4	285	112	43
2	Salford*	26	15	3	8	235	125	31
3	Runcorn*	26	15	2	9	185	101	30
4	Swinton**	26	16	0	10	226	121	28
5	Halifax	26	12	4	10	142	165	28
6	Bradford*	26	14	1	11	201	157	27
7	Warrington*	26	14	0	12	162	150	26
8	Hull	26	11	2	13	166	193	24
9	Oldham	26	10	2	14	190	169	22
10	Leigh	26	11	0	15	158	162	22
11	Hunslet**	26	13	0	13	164	207	22
12	Batley	26	8	4	14	136	198	20
13	Huddersfield	26	8	2	16	122	262	18
14	Brighouse R.	26	3	1	22	74	324	7

*Two points deducted **four points deducted for breaches of professional rules

1902-03

FIRST DIVISION

		P	W	D	L	F	A	Pts
1	Halifax	34	23	3	8	199	85	49
2	Salford	34	20	5	9	244	130	45
3	Swinton	34	18	7	9	254	119	43
4	Runcorn	34	19	4	11	239	139	42
5	Broughton R.	34	17	7	10	222	97	41
6	Oldham	34	20	0	14	200	128	40
7	Bradford	34	16	5	13	220	161	37
8	Warrington	34	14	7	13	148	164	35
9	Hunslet	34	16	3	15	185	220	35
10	Hull	34	16	2	16	204	192	34
11	Batley	34	15	4	15	176	214	34
12	Leigh	34	12	5	17	136	178	29
13	Widnes	34	13	2	19	131	167	28
14	Hull K.R.	34	13	2	19	155	215	28
15	Huddersfield	34	13	2	19	116	196	28
16	Wigan	34	10	6	18	125	174	26
17	St. Helens	34	9	2	23	125	309	20
18	Brighouse R.	34	7	4	23	79	270	18

SECOND DIVISION

		P	W	D	L	F	A	Pts
1	Keighley	34	27	2	5	270	92	56
2	Leeds	34	26	1	7	334	98	53
3	Millom	34	22	3	9	238	118	47
4	Rochdale H.	34	20	6	8	323	88	46
5	Holbeck	34	20	5	9	213	83	45
6	Barrow	34	22	0	12	230	140	44
7	Wakefield T.	34	18	2	14	263	196	38
8	Bramley	34	16	4	14	179	151	36
9	Birkenhead W.	34	14	6	14	125	140	34
10	Manningham	34	14	5	15	141	170	33
11	Lancaster	34	13	4	17	123	214	30
12	Normanton	34	12	4	18	160	228	28
13	York	34	11	4	19	111	190	26
14	South Shields	34	10	2	22	158	264	22
15	Castleford	34	9	4	21	105	268	22
16	Dewsbury	34	8	5	21	123	245	21
17	Morecambe	34	9	2	23	88	220	20
18	Stockport	34	5	1	28	69	348	11

1903-04

FIRST DIVISION

		P	W	D	L	F	A	Pts
1	Bradford	34	25	2	7	303	96	52
2	Salford	34	25	2	7	366	108	52
3	Broughton R.	34	21	4	9	306	142	46
4	Hunslet	34	22	1	11	250	157	45
5	Oldham	34	20	3	11	215	110	43
6	Leeds	34	19	5	10	211	145	43
7	Warrington	34	17	3	14	214	153	37
8	Hull K.R.	34	17	2	15	191	167	36
9	Halifax	34	14	3	17	125	148	31
10	Wigan	34	11	6	17	177	174	28
11	Swinton	34	12	4	18	139	215	28
12	Batley	34	12	3	19	139	241	27
13	Hull	34	12	3	19	148	258	27
14	Widnes	34	11	5	18	126	243	27
15	Leigh	34	10	5	19	174	250	25
16	Runcorn	34	11	2	21	151	245	24
17	Keighley	34	8	5	21	129	319	21
18	Huddersfield	34	10	0	24	160	353	20

CHAMPIONSHIP PLAY-OFF
At Hanson Lane, Halifax

	T	G	P		T	G	P
BRADFORD	1	1	5	SALFORD	0	0	0

SECOND DIVISION

		P	W	D	L	F	A	Pts
1	Wakefield T	32	27	1	4	389	57	55
2	St. Helens	32	23	3	6	328	105	49
3	Holbeck	32	24	1	7	256	120	49
4	Rochdale H.	32	22	2	8	319	104	46
5	York	32	20	1	11	244	97	41
6	Brighouse R.	32	19	3	10	192	136	41
7	Castleford	32	18	3	11	185	194	39
8	Bramley	32	16	4	12	181	180	36
9	Barrow	32	16	3	13	219	162	35
10	Pontefract	32	14	6	12	174	150	34
11	Dewsbury	32	12	3	17	185	205	27
12	Millom	32	12	2	18	185	209	26
13	Lancaster	32	8	2	22	129	291	18
14	Birkenhead	32	7	0	25	75	334	14
15	South Shields	32	6	1	25	140	336	13
16	Morecambe	32	5	3	24	72	287	13
17	Normanton	32	4	0	28	105	411	8

PROMOTION PLAY-OFF
at Huddersfield

	T	G	P		T	G	P
ST. HELENS	1	2	7	HOLBECK	0	0	0

1904-05

FIRST DIVISION

		P	W	D	L	F	A	Pts
1	Oldham	34	25	1	8	291	158	51
2	Bradford	34	23	2	9	294	156	48
3	Broughton R.	34	22	2	10	295	175	46
4	Leeds	34	20	4	10	232	150	44
5	Warrington	34	20	2	12	220	150	42
6	Salford	34	19	2	13	276	204	40
7	Wigan	34	18	1	15	230	195	37
8	Hull	34	15	4	15	224	214	34
9	Hunslet	34	16	1	17	240	216	33
10	Halifax	34	15	2	17	204	155	32
11	Leigh	34	14	3	17	165	209	31
12	Hull K.R.	34	15	0	19	200	220	30
13	Swinton	34	13	2	19	155	196	28
14	Wakefield T.	34	13	2	19	154	211	28
15	Batley	34	12	3	19	160	228	27
16	Widnes	34	13	1	20	128	280	27
17	St. Helens	34	9	1	24	168	351	19
18	Runcorn	34	7	1	26	133	301	15

SECOND DIVISION

		P	W	D	L	F	A	Pts
1	Dewsbury	26	22	2	2	247	48	46
2	Barrow	26	22	0	4	286	68	44
3	York	26	18	3	5	205	76	39
4	Keighley	26	15	2	9	259	94	32
5	Huddersfield	26	14	2	10	231	143	30
6	Rochdale H.	26	11	4	11	154	145	26
7	Millom	26	12	0	14	139	173	24
8	Pontefract	26	10	1	15	156	175	21
9	Castleford	26	9	3	14	104	199	21
10	Normanton	26	9	1	16	105	228	19
11	Brighouse R.	26	8	1	17	111	169	17
12	Lancaster	26	8	1	17	106	257	17
13	Morecambe	26	7	2	17	88	272	16
14	Bramley	26	5	2	19	95	239	12

● Birkenhead resigned from the League after four games. These are not included in the league table. Birkenhead lost all four matches, conceding 93 points, with none scored.

● With the ending of two divisions the clubs again formed one major league. Clubs from the same county all played each other and arranged inter-county fixtures. Not all clubs played the same number of matches and so positions were decided on a percentage basis.

● A top four play-off was introduced for the first time to decide the championship. The top club played the fourth, and the second met the third with the higher placed club having ground advantage. The final was at a neutral venue.

1905-06

		P	W	D	L	F	A	Pts	%
1	Leigh	30	23	2	5	245	130	48	80.00
2	Hunslet	32	25	0	7	370	148	50	78.12
3	Leeds	34	25	2	7	377	123	52	76.47
4	Oldham	40	28	2	10	446	125	58	72.50
5	Keighley	28	19	1	8	255	164	39	69.64
6	Wigan	34	22	1	11	441	167	45	66.17
7	Hull K.R.	36	22	3	11	246	218	47	65.27
8	Broughton R.	34	21	1	12	400	222	43	63.23
9	Halifax	38	20	8	10	261	232	48	63.15
10	Runcorn	30	17	3	10	264	136	37	61.66
11	Huddersfield	30	17	2	11	224	174	36	60.00
12	Bradford	34	19	2	13	371	199	40	58.82
13	Swinton	32	17	3	12	203	168	37	57.81
14	St. Helens	30	16	1	13	244	212	33	55.00
15	Warrington	38	19	3	16	270	184	41	53.94
16	Wakefield T.	32	13	4	15	188	262	30	46.87
17	Hull	36	16	1	19	304	220	33	45.83
18	Salford	34	14	3	17	272	270	31	45.58
19	Pontefract	28	11	1	16	211	196	23	41.07
20	Batley	34	11	5	18	173	215	27	39.70
21	Widnes	28	10	2	16	129	242	22	39.28
22	Dewsbury	36	13	2	21	162	252	28	38.88
23	Bramley	26	9	2	15	126	246	20	38.46
24	York	34	11	2	21	170	249	24	35.29
25	Barrow	32	9	4	19	138	324	22	34.37
26	Normanton	24	4	2	18	50	280	10	20.83
27	Millom	20	3	2	15	77	328	8	20.00
28	Castleford	20	3	2	15	45	325	8	20.00
29	Rochdale H.	32	3	6	23	105	327	12	18.75
30	Morecambe	26	2	4	20	99	282	8	15.38
31	Brighouse R.	26	3	2	21	87	333	8	15.38

1906-07

		P	W	D	L	F	A	Pts	%
1	Halifax	34	27	2	5	649	229	56	82.35
2	Oldham	34	26	1	7	457	227	53	77.94
3	Runcorn	30	23	0	7	546	216	46	76.66
4	Keighley	24	17	1	6	431	231	35	72.91
5	Wigan	34	23	1	10	656	278	47	69.11
6	Leeds	30	19	2	9	424	301	40	66.66
7	Hunslet	32	21	0	11	520	354	42	65.62
8	Warrington	34	21	1	12	554	304	43	63.23
9	Broughton R.	30	17	1	12	496	235	35	58.33
10	Salford	32	18	0	14	462	349	36	56.25
11	Barrow	26	13	1	12	333	356	27	51.92
12	Widnes	20	9	1	10	221	320	19	47.50
13	Hull K.R.	32	15	0	17	390	366	30	46.87
14	Dewsbury	28	12	1	15	393	377	25	44.64
15	Leigh	28	12	1	15	318	311	25	44.64
16	Wakefield T.	28	12	1	15	348	409	25	44.64
17	Swinton	32	14	0	18	308	380	28	43.75
18	Bradford	30	12	2	16	387	367	26	43.33
19	Huddersfield	32	13	0	19	469	477	26	40.62
20	Rochdale H.	26	9	1	16	292	312	19	36.53
21	Batley	24	8	1	15	228	326	17	35.41
22	St. Helens	26	9	0	17	374	353	18	34.61
23	Hull	32	11	0	21	337	515	22	34.37
24	York	24	5	0	19	217	514	10	20.83
25	Bramley	20	1	0	19	85	466	2	5.00
26	Liverpool C.	30	0	0	30	76	1398	0	0.00

Pontefract resigned from the league after 8 matches and their record was expunged from the table. Their record was as follows:

P8　W3　L5　F63　A154　37.50%

CHAMPIONSHIP PLAY-OFF
Semi-finals

Halifax	9	Keighley	4
Oldham	11	Runcorn	3

FINAL
At Fartown, Huddersfield

	T	G	P		T	G	P
HALIFAX	4	3	18	OLDHAM	1	0	3

1907-08

		P	W	D	L	F	A	Pts	%
1	Oldham	32	28	2	2	396	121	58	90.62
2	Hunslet	32	25	1	6	389	248	51	79.68
3	Broughton R.	30	23	1	6	421	191	47	78.33
4	Wigan	32	23	1	8	501	181	47	73.43
5	Halifax	34	22	1	11	483	275	45	66.17
6	Hull K.R.	32	21	0	11	460	307	42	65.62
7	Warrington	30	18	3	9	431	156	39	65.00
8	Wakefield T.	32	20	1	11	422	322	41	64.06
9	Salford	32	19	3	10	344	187	41	64.06
10	Batley	32	20	0	12	360	306	40	62.05
11	Keighley	32	17	1	14	320	356	35	54.68
12	Bradford N.	32	17	0	15	313	350	34	53.12
13	Runcorn	30	15	0	15	255	219	30	50.00
14	Barrow	32	15	0	17	244	272	30	46.87
15	Huddersfield	32	14	1	17	439	330	29	45.31
16	Hull	34	15	0	19	349	323	30	44.11
17	Rochdale H.	30	13	0	17	232	290	26	43.33
18	Dewsbury	32	13	1	18	290	358	27	42.18
19	Leigh	30	11	1	18	279	362	23	38.33
20	Leeds	32	10	1	21	270	397	21	32.81
21	Swinton	30	9	1	20	180	316	19	31.66
22	York	30	9	0	21	284	437	18	30.00
23	Merthyr Tydfil	30	8	1	21	229	400	17	28.33
24	Widnes	30	6	4	20	179	335	16	26.66
25	St. Helens	32	7	3	22	228	500	17	26.56
26	Ebbw Vale	30	6	2	22	153	426	14	23.33
27	Bramley	32	5	1	26	188	674	11	17.18

1908-09

		P	W	D	L	F	A	Pts	%
1	Wigan	32	28	0	4	706	207	56	87.50
2	Halifax	34	28	1	5	526	174	57	83.82
3	Oldham	32	26	0	6	488	176	52	81.25
4	Batley	32	23	3	6	412	176	49	76.56
5	Huddersfield	34	21	3	10	504	292	45	66.17
6	Wakefield T.	31	20	1	10	471	318	41	66.12
7	Salford	32	20	1	11	455	309	41	64.06
8	Merthyr Tydfil	18	11	1	6	184	156	23	63.88
9	Broughton R.	32	19	1	12	420	330	39	60.93
10	Warrington	32	18	2	12	473	266	38	59.37
11	Runcorn	28	16	1	11	271	191	33	58.92
12	Hunslet	32	18	1	13	361	299	37	57.81
13	Hull	34	19	1	14	487	366	39	57.35
14	Ebbw Vale	24	12	1	11	249	269	25	52.08
15	Leeds	32	15	1	16	398	355	31	48.43
16	Hull K.R.	32	14	1	17	429	423	29	45.31
17	St. Helens	28	11	3	14	312	421	25	44.64
18	York	32	13	1	18	394	510	27	42.18
19	Dewsbury	30	12	1	17	350	324	25	41.66
20	Keighley	30	12	1	17	338	355	25	41.66
21	Leigh	28	11	0	17	214	308	22	39.28
22	Swinton	32	11	1	20	258	440	23	35.93
23	Bradford N.	32	11	0	21	324	451	22	34.37
24	Mid-Rhondda	18	5	1	12	111	214	11	30.55
25	Rochdale H.	30	8	2	20	195	384	18	30.00
26	Barrow	32	9	1	22	245	507	19	29.69
27	Widnes	28	6	3	19	197	359	15	26.78
28	Treherbert	18	4	1	13	81	212	9	25.00
29	Barry	18	3	0	15	76	445	6	16.66
30	Bramley	26	3	0	23	162	582	6	11.53
31	Aberdare	17	1	0	16	134	406	2	5.88

CHAMPIONSHIP PLAY-OFF
Semi-finals

Hunslet	28	Broughton R.	3
Oldham	12	Wigan	5

FINAL
At Weaste, Salford

	T	G	P		T	G	P
HUNSLET	1	2	7	OLDHAM	1	2	7

FINAL REPLAY
At Belle Vue, Wakefield

	T	G	P		T	G	P
HUNSLET	2	3	12	OLDHAM	0	1	2

CHAMPIONSHIP PLAY-OFF
Semi-finals

Halifax	3	Oldham	3
Wigan	18	Batley	2

Semi-final Replay

Oldham	8	Halifax	2

FINAL
At Weaste, Salford

	T	G	P		T	G	P
WIGAN	1	2	7	OLDHAM	1	0	3

1909-10

		P	W	D	L	F	A	Pts	%
1	Oldham	34	29	2	3	604	184	60	88.23
2	Salford	31	24	1	6	387	210	49	79.03
3	Wigan	30	23	1	6	545	169	47	78.33
4	Wakefield T.	32	24	0	8	435	242	48	75.00
5	Keighley	28	19	0	9	382	242	38	67.85
6	Leeds	34	21	1	12	451	317	43	63.26
7	Warrington	34	20	2	12	408	252	42	61.76
8	Huddersfield	34	21	0	13	477	301	42	61.76
9	Halifax	34	21	0	13	395	269	42	61.76
10	St. Helens	31	18	2	11	468	367	38	61.29
11	Hull K.R.	35	19	1	15	410	376	39	55.71
12	Leigh	32	15	5	12	218	206	35	54.68
13	Hull	36	19	0	17	456	373	38	52.77
14	Batley	33	16	2	15	313	201	34	51.51
15	Hunslet	32	16	0	16	321	347	32	50.00
16	Runcorn	30	14	1	15	232	317	29	48.33
17	Ebbw Vale	24	9	2	13	156	211	20	41.66
18	Widnes	28	10	3	15	152	244	23	41.07
19	Rochdale H.	32	13	0	19	272	376	26	40.62
20	Dewsbury	30	11	1	18	253	338	23	38.33
21	Swinton	30	10	2	18	203	306	22	36.66
22	Broughton R.	34	10	2	22	295	498	22	32.35
23	Bradford N.	34	9	1	24	176	388	19	27.94
24	York	30	6	1	23	269	473	13	21.66
25	Bramley	29	6	0	23	181	532	12	20.68
26	Barrow	28	5	1	22	146	377	11	19.64
27	Merthyr Tydfil	21	2	1	18	94	354	5	11.90
28	Treherbert	12	0	0	12	55	289	0	0.00

1910-11

		P	W	D	L	F	A	Pts	%
1	Wigan	34	28	1	5	650	205	57	83.82
2	Oldham	34	28	1	5	441	210	57	83.82
3	Wakefield T.	33	24	1	8	493	264	49	74.24
4	Widnes	30	19	3	8	310	137	41	68.33
5	Hull K.R.	33	21	3	9	587	294	45	68.18
6	Hunslet	34	21	0	13	431	389	42	61.76
7	Huddersfield	36	22	0	14	702	293	44	61.11
8	Hull	36	20	3	13	453	347	43	59.72
9	Warrington	31	15	5	11	284	303	35	56.45
10	Dewsbury	30	16	0	14	284	333	32	53.33
11	Swinton	34	18	0	16	333	262	36	52.94
12	Leeds	33	16	2	15	385	340	34	51.51
13	Rochdale H.	34	17	1	16	355	320	35	51.47
14	Halifax	36	18	1	17	371	328	37	51.38
15	Keighley	29	14	1	14	246	447	29	50.00
16	Salford	32	14	2	16	335	337	30	46.87
17	Batley	31	14	1	16	272	223	29	46.77
18	Broughton R.	32	14	1	17	208	338	29	45.31
19	St. Helens	34	14	1	19	377	449	29	42.64
20	Leigh	32	13	0	19	219	355	26	40.63
21	Barrow	32	11	1	20	272	395	23	35.94
22	Runcorn	30	9	3	18	230	331	21	35.00
23	Bradford N.	32	10	1	21	173	390	21	32.81
24	York	30	9	0	21	273	423	18	30.00
25	Ebbw Vale	30	9	0	21	178	297	18	30.00
26	Merthyr Tydfil	18	5	0	13	90	335	10	27.77
27	Coventry	32	6	1	25	288	524	13	20.31
28	Bramley	32	5	1	26	150	521	11	17.18

CHAMPIONSHIP PLAY-OFF
Semi-finals

Oldham	12	Wakefield T.	6
Salford	6	Wigan	17

FINAL
At Wheater's Field, Broughton

	T	G	P		T	G	P
OLDHAM	3	2	13	WIGAN	1	2	7

PLAY-OFF FOR FIRST PLACE
At Belle Vue, Wakefield

Wigan	11	Oldham	3

CHAMPIONSHIP PLAY-OFF
Semi-finals

Oldham	15	Wakefield T.	12
Wigan	16	Widnes	0

FINAL
At Wheater's Field, Broughton

	T	G	P		T	G	P
OLDHAM	4	4	20	WIGAN	1	2	7

1911-12

		P	W	D	L	F	A	Pts	%
1	Huddersfield	36	31	1	4	996	238	63	87.50
2	Wigan	34	27	1	6	483	215	55	80.88
3	Hull K.R.	34	25	0	9	597	294	50	73.52
4	Hunslet	34	24	1	9	554	286	49	72.05
5	Oldham	34	23	1	10	562	299	47	69.11
6	Wakefield T.	34	22	1	11	447	405	45	66.17
7	St. Helens	32	21	0	11	527	283	42	65.62
8	Dewsbury	32	18	1	13	403	341	37	57.81
9	Broughton R.	34	19	1	14	322	254	39	57.35
10	Hull	38	20	3	15	449	335	43	56.57
11	Leeds	34	19	0	15	467	331	38	55.83
12	Widnes	32	16	3	13	301	242	35	54.68
13	Leigh	32	17	1	14	309	296	35	54.68
14	Halifax	34	17	3	14	377	282	37	54.41
15	Batley	32	17	0	15	267	268	34	53.12
16	Rochdale H.	34	16	0	18	335	397	32	47.05
17	York	32	14	1	17	307	418	29	45.31
18	Warrington	32	13	2	17	288	296	28	43.75
19	Barrow	30	12	1	17	263	425	25	41.66
20	Salford	32	11	4	17	269	324	26	40.62
21	Swinton	32	11	3	18	266	356	25	39.06
22	Keighley	28	10	1	17	253	431	21	37.50
23	Coventry	34	6	2	26	208	646	14	20.58
24	Runcorn	28	5	1	22	147	369	11	19.64
25	Ebbw Vale	30	4	3	23	168	520	11	18.33
26	Bradford N.	36	4	0	32	250	657	8	11.11
27	Bramley	30	1	3	26	133	740	5	8.33

1912-13

		P	W	D	L	F	A	Pts	%
1	Huddersfield	32	28	0	4	732	217	56	87.50
2	Wigan	34	28	0	6	702	249	56	82.35
3	Hull K.R.	32	23	1	8	469	273	47	73.43
4	Dewsbury	34	23	1	10	534	230	47	69.11
5	Hunslet	34	22	2	10	468	252	46	67.66
6	Broughton R.	30	17	4	9	303	173	38	63.33
7	Salford	30	19	0	11	245	182	38	63.33
8	Wakefield T.	33	20	2	11	348	350	42	63.33
9	Batley	32	18	1	13	379	218	37	57.81
10	Leeds	34	19	1	14	497	281	39	57.36
11	Oldham	32	17	2	13	341	273	36	56.24
12	Rochdale H.	34	17	2	15	327	277	36	52.94
13	Hull	34	16	3	15	318	328	35	51.47
14	Widnes	32	15	2	15	333	319	32	50.00
15	Swinton	32	15	1	16	248	256	31	48.44
16	St. Helens	32	14	1	17	370	331	29	45.31
17	Bradford N.	34	14	2	18	253	336	30	44.12
18	Warrington	32	13	2	17	214	278	28	43.75
19	Runcorn	30	11	0	19	209	347	22	36.66
20	York	29	10	0	19	256	465	20	34.48
21	Halifax	32	10	2	20	269	367	22	34.38
22	Barrow	30	9	2	19	235	351	20	33.33
23	Leigh	30	8	0	22	153	321	16	26.67
24	Keighley	28	4	3	21	143	419	11	19.64
25	Bramley	31	4	1	26	172	686	9	14.52
26	Coventry	27	0	1	26	157	896	1	1.85

The Wakefield T. v. Coventry and Bramley v. York games were cancelled by permission of the League committee.

CHAMPIONSHIP PLAY-OFF
Semi-finals

| Huddersfield | 27 | Hunslet | 3 |
| Wigan | 41 | Hull K.R. | 3 |

FINAL
At Thrum Hall, Halifax

	T	G	P		T	G	P
HUD'SFIELD	3	2	13	WIGAN	1	1	5

CHAMPIONSHIP PLAY-OFF
Semi-finals

| Huddersfield | 30 | Dewsbury. | 3 |
| Wigan | 16 | Hull K.R. | 3 |

FINAL
At Belle Vue, Wakefield

	T	G	P		T	G	P
HUD'SFIELD	7	4	29	WIGAN	0	1	2

TABLES

1913-14

	P	W	D	L	F	A	Pts	%
1 Huddersfield	34	28	2	4	830	258	58	85.29
2 Salford	32	25	1	6	320	140	51	79.69
3 Wigan	34	25	2	7	676	252	52	76.47
4 Hull	34	24	1	9	507	264	49	72.06
5 Barrow	30	20	0	10	335	256	40	66.66
6 Hull K.R.	34	20	2	12	393	298	42	61.76
7 Rochdale H.	34	18	4	12	356	270	40	58.83
8 Widnes	32	17	1	14	262	241	35	54.69
9 Leeds	34	18	1	15	342	290	37	54.42
10 Hunslet	34	18	1	15	437	397	37	54.42
11 Warrington	34	17	2	15	280	332	36	52.94
12 Dewsbury	36	18	2	16	378	377	38	52.78
13 Swinton	30	15	1	14	243	232	31	51.66
14 Oldham	34	17	0	17	403	265	34	50.00
15 Batley	32	14	3	15	253	276	31	48.43
16 Broughton R.	32	14	0	18	235	264	28	43.75
17 Wakefield T.	34	12	3	19	257	382	27	39.71
18 Halifax	32	12	1	19	359	320	25	39.06
19 St. Helens	32	12	1	19	376	440	25	39.06
20 Leigh	30	10	0	20	165	329	20	33.33
21 Runcorn	30	10	0	20	165	442	20	33.33
22 Keighley	30	9	1	20	159	385	19	31.64
23 Bramley	30	7	0	23	163	464	14	23.33
24 Bradford N.	34	7	1	26	223	492	15	22.06
25 York	34	6	0	28	237	688	12	17.65

CHAMPIONSHIP PLAY-OFF

Semi-finals

Huddersfield	23	Hull	5
Salford	16	Wigan	5

FINAL

At Headingley, Leeds

	T	G	P		T	G	P
SALFORD	1	1	5	HUD'SFIELD	1	0	3

1914-15

	P	W	D	L	F	A	Pts	%
1 Huddersfield	34	28	4	2	888	235	60	88.24
2 Wigan	32	25	1	6	679	206	51	79.69
3 Leeds	34	24	3	7	486	207	51	75.02
4 Rochdale H.	34	24	2	8	306	194	50	73.53
5 Hull	36	24	1	11	705	301	49	68.06
6 Broughton R.	30	18	1	11	308	289	37	61.66
7 St. Helens	32	19	0	13	368	342	38	59.37
8 Halifax	34	18	3	13	342	268	39	57.36
9 Oldham	34	17	4	13	375	301	38	55.89
10 Wakefield T.	32	17	1	14	309	340	35	54.69
11 Hull K.R.	34	17	2	15	374	324	36	52.94
12 Widnes	32	14	3	15	291	292	31	48.44
13 Warrington	32	14	3	15	242	323	31	48.44
14 Batley	34	15	1	18	229	288	31	45.59
15 Leigh	31	14	0	17	252	185	28	45.16
16 Swinton	30	13	1	16	171	240	27	45.00
17 Dewsbury	32	12	2	18	310	353	26	40.62
18 Hunslet	32	12	0	20	298	356	24	37.50
19 Bradford N.	32	11	1	20	249	464	23	35.93
20 Bramley	32	11	1	20	143	474	23	35.93
21 Salford	30	8	4	18	134	313	20	33.33
22 Barrow	32	10	1	21	288	363	21	32.81
23 York	32	9	2	21	261	422	20	31.25
24 Keighley	30	6	2	22	120	542	14	29.37
25 Runcorn	27	0	1	26	84	590	1	1.85

CHAMPIONSHIP PLAY-OFF

Semi-finals

Wigan	4	Leeds	15
Huddersfield	33	Rochdale H.	2

FINAL

At Belle Vue, Wakefield

	T	G	P		T	G	P
HUD'SFIELD	7	7	35	LEEDS	0	1	2

Competitive Matches suspended during First World War from 1915-16 to 1917-18

● The ban on competitive football was removed in September 1918, officially organised games commencing in January 1919, on a regional basis.

1918-19

LANCASHIRE LEAGUE

	P	W	D	L	F	A	Pts	%
1 Rochdale H.	13	10	0	3	109	53	20	76.92
2 Leigh	12	8	2	2	99	31	18	75.00
3 Wigan	11	7	1	3	164	87	15	68.18
4 Warrington	17	10	1	6	145	105	21	61.76
5 Barrow	5	3	0	2	52	66	6	60.00
6 Widnes	12	7	0	5	120	83	14	58.33
7 Salford	15	7	0	8	107	95	14	46.66
8 Oldham	14	6	1	7	159	121	13	46.43
9 St. Helens	9	3	0	6	29	109	6	33.33
10 St. Helens Rec.	13	3	2	8	75	134	8	30.77
11 Broughton R.	14	4	0	10	80	144	8	28.70
12 Swinton	15	3	1	11	64	179	7	23.33

YORKSHIRE LEAGUE

	P	W	D	L	F	A	Pts	%
1 Hull	16	13	0	3	392	131	26	81.25
2 Leeds	16	10	1	5	183	112	21	65.62
3 Bramley	14	8	1	5	140	89	17	60.71
4 Halifax	15	8	1	6	187	82	17	56.66
5 Dewsbury	13	5	4	4	150	100	14	53.85
6 Batley	15	7	1	7	77	117	15	50.00
7 Hull K.R.	14	5	2	7	129	139	12	42.85
8 Wakefield T.	14	4	2	8	73	156	10	35.71
9 York	4	1	0	3	18	141	2	25.00
10 Hunslet	13	3	0	10	97	262	6	23.03
11 Bradford N.	10	2	0	8	51	168	4	20.00

1919-20

		P	W	D	L	F	A	Pts	%
1	Huddersfield	34	29	0	5	759	215	58	85.29
2	Hull	34	25	1	8	587	276	51	75.00
3	Leeds	32	23	0	9	445	208	46	71.87
4	Widnes	30	21	1	8	250	115	43	71.67
5	Barrow	32	22	1	9	477	202	45	70.31
6	Halifax	34	23	1	10	390	168	47	69.12
7	Rochdale H.	34	22	1	11	363	203	45	66.18
8	Oldham	34	21	1	12	333	226	43	63.23
9	Dewsbury	32	18	2	12	299	262	38	59.37
10	Warrington	30	15	2	13	236	198	32	53.33
11	St. Helens Rec.	28	13	3	12	329	196	29	51.79
12	Batley	32	15	2	15	223	319	32	50.00
13	Wigan	32	15	1	16	281	266	31	48.44
14	Leigh	28	12	2	14	175	228	26	46.43
15	Salford	32	14	1	17	202	269	29	45.31
16	St. Helens	30	12	2	16	278	285	26	43.33
17	Swinton	30	12	1	17	201	274	25	41.67
18	Wakefield T.	32	11	4	17	229	494	26	40.62
19	Hull K.R.	32	10	2	20	250	325	22	34.37
20	Bramley	30	8	4	18	163	372	20	33.33
21	York	30	8	1	21	213	422	17	28.33
22	Hunslet	34	9	0	25	167	384	18	26.47
23	Broughton R.	32	7	2	23	184	460	16	25.00
24	Bradford N.	32	7	1	24	177	479	15	23.44
25	Keighley	32	6	0	26	106	471	12	18.75

1920-21

		P	W	D	L	F	A	Pts	%
1	Hull K.R.	32	24	1	7	432	233	49	76.56
2	Hull	36	27	0	9	722	267	54	75.00
3	Halifax	38	27	0	11	492	184	54	71.05
4	Wigan	34	23	1	10	435	238	47	69.12
5	Swinton	34	22	1	11	289	250	45	66.18
6	Dewsbury	34	20	3	11	349	233	43	63.23
7	York	30	18	1	11	280	225	37	61.67
8	Leeds	34	20	1	13	380	209	41	60.29
9	Broughton R.	30	16	3	11	283	164	35	58.33
10	Rochdale H.	34	18	2	14	311	301	38	55.88
11	Widnes	30	15	2	13	231	252	32	53.33
12	Barrow	32	17	0	15	328	254	34	53.12
13	Warrington	34	17	2	15	295	289	36	52.94
14	Huddersfield	36	18	2	16	376	283	38	52.78
15	St. Helens Rec.	30	15	1	14	299	201	31	51.67
16	Batley	32	16	1	15	312	225	33	51.56
17	St. Helens	30	14	0	16	254	304	28	46.67
18	Oldham	34	13	3	18	267	254	29	42.65
19	Wakefield T.	34	14	1	19	253	426	29	42.65
20	Leigh	32	10	3	19	173	316	23	35.94
21	Bramley	30	9	0	21	153	371	18	30.00
22	Hunslet	32	8	1	23	190	298	17	26.56
23	Bradford N.	32	6	1	25	177	656	13	20.31
24	Keighley	34	5	0	29	159	655	10	14.71
25	Salford	32	2	2	28	111	463	6	9.37

CHAMPIONSHIP PLAY-OFF
Semi-finals

Huddersfield	7	Widnes	5
Hull	11	Leeds	0

FINAL
At Headingley, Leeds

	T	G	P		T	G	P
HULL	1	0	3	HUD'SFIELD	0	1	2

CHAMPIONSHIP PLAY-OFF
Semi-finals

Hull	27	Halifax	10
Hull K.R.	26	Wigan	4

FINAL
At Headingley, Leeds

	T	G	P		T	G	P
HULL	4	2	16	HULL K.R.	2	4	14

1921-22

		P	W	D	L	F	A	Pts	%
1	Oldham	36	29	1	6	521	201	59	81.94
2	Wigan	32	22	1	9	446	159	45	70.31
3	Hull	38	25	0	13	538	326	50	65.79
4	Huddersfield	36	23	1	12	608	271	47	65.28
5	Leeds	38	24	1	13	583	289	49	64.47
6	Batley	38	23	2	13	381	299	48	63.16
7	Rochdale H.	34	20	2	12	352	225	42	61.76
8	Halifax	36	21	2	13	418	218	44	61.11
9	Leigh	34	19	3	12	295	228	41	60.29
10	York	36	21	1	14	311	231	43	59.72
11	Hull K.R.	38	21	0	17	420	356	42	55.26
12	St. Helens Rec.	36	19	1	16	417	315	39	54.17
13	Dewsbury	36	19	1	16	290	339	39	54.17
14	Barrow	34	18	0	16	311	321	36	52.94
15	Warrington	36	16	1	19	285	418	33	45.83
16	Widnes	32	13	3	16	227	240	29	45.31
17	Wakefield T.	36	16	0	20	335	313	32	44.44
18	Broughton R.	32	13	2	17	284	247	28	43.75
19	Hunslet	36	13	5	18	215	400	31	43.05
20	Swinton	34	14	0	20	248	312	28	41.18
21	Bramley	34	13	2	19	251	496	28	41.18
22	St. Helens	34	12	1	21	255	399	25	36.76
23	Salford	34	9	4	21	164	312	22	32.35
24	Featherstone R.	36	10	2	24	280	463	22	30.55
25	Keighley	36	4	1	31	134	581	9	12.50
26	Bradford N.	34	2	1	31	134	744	5	7.35

1922-23

		P	W	D	L	F	A	Pts	%
1	Hull	36	30	0	6	587	304	60	83.33
2	Huddersfield	34	26	0	8	644	279	52	76.47
3	Swinton	36	27	0	9	467	240	54	75.00
4	Hull K.R.	36	26	1	9	597	231	53	73.61
5	Wigan	36	25	2	9	721	262	52	72.22
6	Leigh	32	22	0	10	378	281	44	68.75
7	Oldham	36	24	0	12	389	236	48	66.66
8	Leeds	38	24	2	12	502	297	50	65.78
9	Rochdale H.	36	22	0	14	389	355	44	61.11
10	York	34	17	5	12	254	252	39	57.35
11	St. Helens Rec	36	19	0	17	319	292	38	52.77
12	Featherstone R.	34	17	1	16	413	368	35	51.47
13	Wakefield T.	36	17	2	17	349	306	36	50.00
14	Batley	36	16	2	18	347	372	34	47.22
15	Warrington	36	17	0	19	348	410	34	47.22
16	Barrow	36	16	0	20	339	444	32	44.44
17	Salford	36	14	2	20	263	421	30	41.66
18	Hunslet	38	14	2	22	316	371	30	39.47
19	St. Helens	34	13	0	21	364	427	26	38.23
20	Halifax	38	14	1	23	272	442	29	38.15
21	Dewsbury	36	12	3	21	337	440	27	37.50
22	Widnes	34	11	1	22	195	350	23	33.82
23	Keighley	38	12	1	25	236	449	25	32.89
24	Broughton R.	32	10	1	21	230	319	21	32.81
25	Wigan Highfield	32	7	1	24	208	432	15	23.43
26	Bradford N.	34	6	1	27	180	676	13	19.11
27	Bramley	36	5	2	29	184	572	12	16.66

CHAMPIONSHIP PLAY-OFF

Semi-finals

Oldham	13	Huddersfield	5
Wigan	27	Hull	8

FINAL

At The Cliff, Broughton

	T	G	P		T	G	P
WIGAN	1	5	13	OLDHAM	0	1	2

CHAMPIONSHIP PLAY-OFF

Semi-finals

Huddersfield	16	Swinton	5
Hull	2	Hull K.R.	16

FINAL

At Headingley, Leeds

	T	G	P		T	G	P
HULL K.R.	3	3	15	HUD'SFIELD	1	1	5

1923-24		P	W	D	L	F	A	Pts	%
1	Wigan	38	31	0	7	824	228	62	81.57
2	Batley	36	24	3	9	432	287	51	70.83
3	Oldham	36	23	2	11	579	296	48	66.66
4	Leigh	34	20	3	11	407	250	43	63.23
5	Huddersfield	36	21	1	14	481	352	43	59.72
6	St. Helens Rec.	32	19	0	13	363	255	38	59.37
7	Swinton	34	20	0	14	346	312	40	58.82
8	Rochdale H.	36	19	4	13	318	330	42	58.33
9	York	36	18	5	13	323	258	41	56.94
10	Hunslet	36	18	5	13	328	332	41	56.94
11	Hull K.R.	36	19	2	15	408	377	40	55.55
12	Leeds	38	20	0	18	448	350	40	52.63
13	Halifax	38	20	0	18	360	357	40	52.63
14	Widnes	34	16	3	15	275	245	35	51.47
15	Broughton R.	34	15	4	15	286	251	34	50.00
16	St. Helens	34	16	0	18	332	522	32	47.05
17	Hull	38	17	1	20	439	447	35	46.05
18	Dewsbury	36	15	3	18	279	289	33	45.83
19	Wakefield T.	36	15	2	19	313	358	32	44.44
20	Warrington	36	16	0	20	341	395	32	44.44
21	Barrow	36	15	1	20	366	372	31	43.05
22	Keighley	36	14	1	21	291	427	29	40.27
23	Featherstone R.	36	12	3	21	348	545	27	37.50
24	Wigan Highfield	36	12	0	24	324	428	24	33.33
25	Salford	34	8	1	25	175	466	17	25.00
26	Bradford N.	34	8	0	26	190	524	16	23.52
27	Bramley	34	7	0	27	228	528	14	20.58

1924-25		P	W	D	L	F	A	Pts	%
1	Swinton	36	30	0	6	499	224	60	83.33
2	Hull K.R.	34	25	3	6	492	171	53	77.94
3	Wigan	36	27	1	8	784	258	55	76.38
4	St. Helens Rec.	38	26	3	9	564	267	55	72.36
5	Oldham	34	21	1	12	533	248	43	68.23
6	Leeds	36	21	3	12	341	278	45	62.50
7	Huddersfield	36	21	1	14	458	351	43	59.72
8	Dewsbury	36	20	2	14	310	269	42	58.33
9	Warrington	36	19	2	15	427	386	40	55.55
10	St. Helens	34	17	3	14	325	381	37	54.41
11	Batley	36	19	1	16	441	350	39	54.16
12	Rochdale H.	36	18	2	16	348	331	38	52.77
13	Hunslet	36	19	0	17	411	369	38	52.77
14	Wakefield T.	36	17	1	18	337	316	35	48.61
15	Keighley	36	17	1	18	305	420	35	48.51
16	Barrow	34	16	1	17	288	336	33	48.52
17	Featherstone R.	34	15	0	19	322	364	30	44.11
18	Hull	36	14	3	19	368	422	31	43.05
19	Salford	34	13	3	18	160	399	29	42.64
20	Leigh	34	13	1	20	328	433	27	39.70
21	Halifax	38	14	2	22	317	431	30	39.47
22	Broughton R.	34	12	1	21	244	429	25	36.76
23	York	36	12	1	23	272	351	25	34.72
24	Wigan Highfield	32	10	1	21	224	432	21	32.81
25	Widnes	34	10	1	23	257	462	21	30.83
26	Bradford N.	38	8	4	26	285	584	20	26.31
27	Bramley	36	2	2	32	174	572	6	8.33

1925-26		P	W	D	L	F	A	Pts	%
1	Wigan	38	29	3	6	641	310	61	80.26
2	Warrington	36	27	1	8	472	279	55	76.38
3	Swinton	36	26	2	8	442	223	54	75.00
4	Hull	38	24	3	11	547	329	51	67.10
5	St. Helens Rec.	36	23	2	11	437	278	48	66.66
6	Hull K.R.	34	20	3	11	416	320	43	63.23
7	Oldham	34	19	3	12	431	251	41	60.29
8	Wakefield T.	36	21	1	14	445	317	43	59.72
9	Leeds	36	20	2	14	526	311	42	58.33
10	St. Helens	34	18	2	14	410	282	38	55.88
11	Batley	38	20	2	16	325	296	42	55.26
12	York	36	19	0	17	359	350	38	52.77
13	Halifax	38	19	2	17	364	323	40	52.63
14	Barrow	36	17	3	16	313	303	37	51.38
15	Featherstone R.	32	15	2	15	362	362	32	50.00
16	Dewsbury	36	18	0	18	310	402	36	50.00
17	Widnes	34	15	0	19	339	397	30	44.11
18	Huddersfield	36	14	2	20	365	474	30	41.66
19	Wigan Highfield	32	12	1	19	280	323	25	39.06
20	Hunslet	36	14	0	22	389	435	28	38.88
21	Salford	34	11	4	19	246	393	26	38.23
22	Rochdale H.	36	13	1	22	320	414	27	37.50
23	Bradford N.	38	14	0	24	306	580	28	36.84
24	Leigh	32	8	2	22	270	435	18	28.12
25	Broughton R.	34	9	0	25	316	510	18	26.47
26	Keighley	36	9	1	26	290	577	19	26.38
27	Bramley	34	3	0	31	152	588	6	8.82

1923-24 CHAMPIONSHIP PLAY-OFF
Semi-finals

Batley	38	Oldham	0
Wigan	27	Leigh	0

FINAL

At The Cliff, Broughton

	T	G	P		T	G	P
BATLEY	3	2	13	WIGAN	1	2	7

1924-25 CHAMPIONSHIP PLAY-OFF
Semi-finals

Swinton	20	St. Helens Rec.	2
Hull K.R.	13	Wigan	4

FINAL

At The Athletic Ground, Rochdale

	T	G	P		T	G	P
HULL K.R.	1	3	9	SWINTON	1	1	5

1925-26 CHAMPIONSHIP PLAY-OFF
Semi-finals

Warrington	11	Swinton	8
Wigan	34	Hull	0

FINAL

At Knowsley Road, St. Helens

	T	G	P		T	G	P
WIGAN	6	2	22	WARRINGTON	2	2	10

269

1926-27

		P	W	D	L	F	A	Pts	%
1	St. Helens Rec.	38	29	3	6	544	235	61	80.26
2	Swinton	38	29	2	7	471	275	60	78.98
3	Wigan	40	29	0	11	691	366	58	72.50
4	St. Helens	34	23	1	10	538	283	47	69.11
5	Hull	38	25	1	12	434	317	51	67.10
6	Hull K.R.	36	21	5	10	456	244	47	65.27
7	Leigh	36	23	1	12	404	331	47	65.27
8	Rochdale H.	36	23	0	13	378	285	46	63.88
9	Leeds	40	23	1	16	582	371	47	58.75
10	Hunslet	42	24	1	17	533	380	49	58.33
11	Featherstone R.	38	21	1	16	504	369	43	56.57
12	Dewsbury	38	20	3	15	344	284	43	56.57
13	Oldham	38	19	4	15	489	346	42	55.26
14	Halifax	40	19	4	17	411	289	42	52.50
15	Wakefield T.	36	17	3	16	386	330	37	51.38
16	Warrington	38	18	1	19	409	524	37	48.68
17	Barrow	38	18	0	20	311	412	36	47.36
18	York	36	16	1	19	368	519	33	45.83
19	Batley	36	14	2	20	317	325	30	41.66
20	Salford	36	14	2	20	306	353	30	41.66
21	Broughton R.	36	14	1	21	369	392	29	40.27
22	Keighley	36	14	1	21	242	469	29	40.27
23	Huddersfield	40	16	0	24	414	562	32	40.00
24	Widnes	34	11	0	23	283	479	22	32.35
25	Wigan Highfield	34	9	1	24	239	383	19	27.94
26	Bramley	36	8	1	27	200	636	17	23.61
27	Pontypridd	32	7	1	24	223	447	15	23.43
28	Bradford N.	36	6	0	30	288	652	12	16.66
29	Castleford	36	5	1	30	274	550	11	15.27

1927-28

		P	W	D	L	F	A	Pts	%
1	Swinton	36	27	3	6	439	189	57	79.16
2	Leeds	42	32	0	10	619	307	64	76.19
3	Featherstone R.	36	25	1	10	387	234	51	70.83
4	Hunslet	40	28	0	12	546	308	56	70.00
5	St. Helens Rec.	36	24	0	12	499	251	48	66.66
6	Oldham	36	23	1	12	422	261	47	65.27
7	Wigan Highfield	32	19	1	12	272	240	39	60.93
8	Wigan	40	24	0	16	601	345	48	60.00
9	Leigh	34	20	0	14	298	236	40	58.82
10	Wakefield T.	40	22	2	16	476	355	46	57.50
11	St. Helens	36	19	1	16	485	336	39	54.17
12	Huddersfield	40	21	1	18	475	341	43	53.75
13	Hull K.R.	38	17	5	16	342	333	39	51.31
14	Halifax	40	19	2	19	341	328	40	50.00
15	Dewsbury	38	17	3	18	334	329	37	48.68
16	Bradford N.	32	13	2	17	204	333	28	43.75
17	Warrington	36	14	2	20	352	483	30	41.66
18	Barrow	34	13	1	20	249	337	27	39.70
19	Batley	38	14	2	22	264	466	30	39.47
20	Hull	38	12	6	20	312	347	30	39.47
21	York	36	13	1	22	233	350	27	37.50
22	Keighley	36	13	1	22	230	415	27	37.50
23	Widnes	32	11	0	21	196	418	22	34.37
24	Rochdale H.	34	11	1	22	192	448	23	33.82
25	Castleford	32	9	3	20	217	389	21	32.81
26	Salford	32	9	1	22	220	434	19	29.68
27	Broughton R.	32	8	0	24	285	450	16	25.00
28	Bramley	32	7	0	25	175	402	14	21.87

Pontypridd resigned from the League in October and their record was expunged from the table. They had played eight matches as follows:

P8 W1 L7 F46 A149 12.50%

1926-27 CHAMPIONSHIP PLAY-OFF
Semi-finals

St. Helens Rec.	33	St. Helens	0
Swinton	23	Wigan	3

FINAL
At Wilderspool, Warrington

	T	G	P		T	G	P
SWINTON	3	2	13	ST. HELENS REC 2	1	8

1927-28 CHAMPIONSHIP PLAY-OFF
Semi-finals

Leeds	12	Featherstone R.	15
Swinton	12	Hunslet	2

FINAL
At Watersheddings, Oldham

	T	G	P		T	G	P
SWINTON	3	1	11	F'STONE R.	0	0	0

1928-29

		P	W	D	L	F	A	Pts	%
1	Huddersfield	38	26	4	8	476	291	56	73.68
2	Hull K. R.	40	27	3	10	436	239	57	71.25
3	Leeds	38	26	2	10	695	270	54	71.05
4	Salford	34	23	2	9	395	222	48	70.58
5	Wigan	38	26	1	11	636	308	53	69.73
6	Swinton	36	23	2	11	429	249	48	66.66
7	Warrington	36	22	2	12	568	295	46	63.88
8	St. Helens Rec.	38	22	1	15	545	374	45	59.21
9	Oldham	36	18	4	14	439	343	40	55.55
10	St. Helens	38	19	4	15	460	381	42	55.26
11	Hunslet	38	19	4	15	539	356	42	55.26
12	Hull	40	20	4	16	458	395	44	55.00
13	Leigh	34	17	3	14	285	279	37	54.41
14	Wigan Highfield	32	16	1	15	262	333	33	51.56
15	Dewsbury	36	17	2	17	380	387	36	50.00
16	Wakefield T.	40	17	4	19	400	461	38	47.50
17	Halifax	40	18	3	19	379	399	39	48.75
18	Barrow	32	13	2	17	396	387	28	43.75
19	Batley	38	14	2	22	278	442	30	39.47
20	Broughton R.	30	11	1	18	235	401	23	38.33
21	Castleford	34	11	4	19	268	369	26	38.23
22	York	34	12	0	22	259	409	24	35.29
23	Bramley	34	11	2	21	241	437	24	35.29
24	Widnes	34	11	2	21	222	439	24	35.29
25	Featherstone R.	38	10	4	24	277	451	24	31.57
26	Rochdale H.	34	10	0	24	235	434	20	29.41
27	Keighley	34	8	2	24	209	422	18	26.47
28	Bradford N.	38	5	3	30	242	871	13	17.10

Carlisle City resigned from the League in November and their record was expunged from the table. They had played 10 matches as follows:

P10   W1   L9   F59   A166   10%

CHAMPIONSHIP PLAY-OFF
Semi-finals

Huddersfield	13	Salford	5
Hull K.R.	4	Leeds	7

FINAL
At Thrum Hall, Halifax

	T	G	P		T	G	P
HUD'SFIELD	0	1	2	LEEDS	0	0	0

1929-30

		P	W	D	L	F	A	Pts	%
1	St. Helens	40	27	1	12	549	295	55	68.75
2	Huddersfield	38	25	2	11	510	317	52	68.42
3	Salford	36	23	3	10	397	214	49	68.05
4	Leeds	40	25	2	13	672	302	52	65.00
5	Dewsbury	38	23	3	12	415	282	49	64.47
6	Hull K.R.	38	22	4	12	396	290	48	63.15
7	Wigan	38	23	1	14	590	303	47	61.84
8	Warrington	36	21	1	14	483	389	43	59.72
9	Hunslet	38	21	3	14	535	358	45	59.21
10	Oldham	38	20	4	14	393	306	44	57.89
11	Halifax	40	21	1	18	384	348	43	53.75
12	Hull	38	19	2	17	417	399	40	52.63
13	St. Helens Rec.	36	17	3	16	355	414	37	51.38
14	Swinton	36	17	2	17	332	220	36	50.00
15	Widnes	32	15	2	15	309	266	32	50.00
16	Wigan Highfield	32	16	0	16	257	266	32	50.00
17	Wakefield T.	40	19	1	20	399	428	39	48.75
18	Leigh	32	15	0	17	309	296	30	46.87
19	York	36	16	1	19	277	328	33	45.83
20	Keighley	36	14	2	20	244	427	30	41.66
21	Broughton R.	34	14	0	20	271	437	28	41.17
22	Rochdale H.	34	13	2	19	258	442	28	41.17
23	Featherstone R.	36	12	3	21	255	398	27	37.50
24	Bramley	36	10	5	21	199	399	25	34.72
25	Barrow	32	10	2	20	352	388	22	34.37
26	Castleford	36	10	2	24	230	535	22	30.55
27	Batley	36	7	2	27	221	543	16	22.22
28	Bradford N.	38	7	2	29	299	718	16	21.05

CHAMPIONSHIP PLAY-OFF
Semi-finals

Huddersfield	15	Salford	10
St. Helens	6	Leeds	10

FINAL
At Belle Vue, Wakefield

	T	G	P		T	G	P
HUD'SFIELD	0	1	2	LEEDS	0	1	2

FINAL REPLAY
At Thrum Hall, Halifax

	T	G	P		T	G	P
HUD'SFIELD	2	2	10	LEEDS	0	0	0

TABLES

● With all clubs playing the same number of matches, positions no longer needed to be decided on a percentage basis. All the clubs still did not meet each other and the play-offs continued.

1930-31

		P	W	D	L	F	A	Pts
1	Swinton	38	31	2	5	504	156	64
2	Leeds	38	29	1	8	695	258	59
3	Wigan	38	28	2	8	657	199	58
4	Oldham	38	27	4	7	464	178	58
5	Huddersfield	38	27	2	9	545	272	56
6	Halifax	38	25	3	10	405	283	53
7	St. Helens	38	25	1	12	502	344	51
8	Hunslet	38	24	2	12	573	278	50
9	Salford	38	23	3	12	420	256	49
10	Warrington	38	23	2	13	447	291	48
11	York	38	23	1	14	441	361	47
12	St. Helens Rec.	38	21	2	15	436	243	44
13	Hull K.R.	38	21	0	17	345	399	42
14	Wakefield T.	38	20	0	18	510	438	40
15	Wigan Highfield	38	17	3	18	398	435	37
16	Hull	38	17	2	19	398	428	36
17	Broughton R.	38	15	5	18	376	366	35
18	Dewsbury	38	14	2	22	418	406	30
19	Barrow	38	12	6	20	350	481	30
20	Castleford	38	15	0	23	351	539	30
21	Leigh	38	11	3	24	248	479	25
22	Widnes	38	11	2	25	245	450	24
23	Batley	38	11	1	26	245	505	23
24	Rochdale H.	38	10	2	26	330	557	22
25	Keighley	38	8	0	30	212	705	16
26	Featherstone R.	38	7	1	30	265	536	15
27	Bramley	38	5	3	30	251	636	13
28	Bradford N.	38	4	1	33	227	809	9

1931-32

		P	W	D	L	F	A	Pts
1	Huddersfield	38	30	1	7	636	368	61
2	St. Helens	38	29	2	7	699	279	60
3	Leeds	38	27	1	10	603	307	55
4	Hunslet	38	27	1	10	672	359	55
5	Salford	38	26	2	10	551	211	54
6	Swinton	38	26	1	11	523	253	53
7	Wigan	38	22	2	14	559	361	46
8	Warrington	38	22	2	14	495	412	46
9	York	38	22	2	14	455	382	46
10	Wakefield T.	38	21	3	14	545	388	45
11	Oldham	38	20	2	16	461	437	42
12	Rochdale H.	38	19	2	17	458	458	40
13	St. Helens Rec.	38	18	1	19	523	523	37
14	Hull K.R.	38	18	0	20	409	413	36
15	Dewsbury	38	17	2	19	421	467	36
16	Halifax	38	17	1	20	432	379	35
17	Batley	38	16	1	21	358	433	33
18	Broughton R.	38	16	1	21	351	382	33
19	Featherstone R.	38	15	2	21	374	415	32
20	Widnes	38	14	4	20	363	458	32
21	Hull	38	14	3	21	415	461	31
22	Castleford	38	14	1	23	402	515	29
23	Barrow	38	14	1	23	368	560	29
24	Leigh	38	13	2	23	353	487	28
25	Bramley	38	12	1	25	333	751	25
26	Keighley	38	10	0	28	228	630	20
27	Wigan Highfield	38	6	2	30	350	707	14
28	Bradford N.	38	5	1	32	313	854	11

CHAMPIONSHIP PLAY-OFF
Semi-finals

Leeds	13	Wigan	0
Swinton	16	Oldham	3

FINAL
At Central Park, Wigan

	T	G	P		T	G	P
SWINTON	2	4	14	LEEDS	1	2	7

CHAMPIONSHIP PLAY-OFF
Semi-finals

Huddersfield	12	Hunslet	9
St. Helens	9	Leeds	0

FINAL
At Belle Vue, Wakefield

	T	G	P		T	G	P
ST. HELENS	1	3	9	HUD'FIELD	1	1	5

1932-33

		P	W	D	L	F	A	Pts
1	Salford	38	31	2	5	751	165	64
2	Swinton	38	26	2	10	412	247	54
3	York	38	24	4	10	571	273	52
4	Wigan	38	25	2	11	717	411	52
5	Warrington	38	26	0	12	625	426	52
6	Barrow	38	24	2	12	508	332	50
7	Hunslet	38	23	0	15	529	365	46
8	Castleford	38	21	4	13	403	326	46
9	Huddersfield	38	21	0	17	504	333	42
10	Leeds	38	20	2	16	544	423	42
11	St. Helens	38	20	2	16	554	494	42
12	Widnes	38	19	2	17	446	406	40
13	Broughton R.	38	18	4	16	289	322	40
14	Oldham	38	19	1	18	438	464	39
15	Rochdale H.	38	19	1	18	497	533	39
16	St. Helens Rec.	38	16	4	18	419	416	36
17	Keighley	38	16	3	19	418	428	35
18	Hull	38	16	2	20	467	460	34
19	Wakefield T.	38	15	4	19	370	483	34
20	Halifax	38	16	1	21	434	392	33
21	Hull K.R.	38	15	0	23	383	490	30
22	Bradford N.	38	14	2	22	377	587	30
23	Leigh	38	15	0	23	364	610	30
24	Dewsbury	38	14	0	24	361	503	28
25	Batley	38	12	1	25	293	450	25
26	Featherstone R.	38	8	2	28	302	594	18
27	Wigan Highfield	38	8	2	28	240	734	18
28	Bramley	38	6	1	31	219	768	13

1933-34

		P	W	D	L	F	A	Pts
1	Salford	38	31	1	6	715	281	63
2	Wigan	38	26	0	12	739	334	52
3	Leeds	38	26	0	12	597	376	52
4	Halifax	38	26	0	12	457	340	52
5	York	38	24	1	13	481	370	49
6	Hunslet	38	23	1	14	608	441	47
7	Widnes	38	21	4	13	393	324	46
8	Warrington	38	22	1	15	508	370	45
9	Swinton	38	22	1	15	418	322	45
10	Hull	38	21	3	14	553	438	45
11	Keighley	38	22	1	15	429	367	45
12	Huddersfield	38	20	1	17	500	330	41
13	St. Helens	38	20	0	18	550	500	40
14	London Highfield	38	20	0	18	509	489	40
15	Oldham	38	17	3	18	400	520	37
16	Castleford	38	17	1	20	476	468	35
17	Rochdale H.	38	17	0	21	442	524	34
18	St. Helens Rec.	38	16	1	21	455	477	33
19	Hull K.R.	38	16	1	21	444	482	33
20	Batley	38	16	1	21	390	436	33
21	Leigh	38	15	2	21	479	537	32
22	Wakefield T.	38	15	2	21	332	404	32
23	Broughton R.	38	15	1	22	415	495	31
24	Barrow	38	15	0	23	375	464	30
25	Dewsbury	38	12	1	25	313	587	25
26	Bramley	38	11	1	26	367	790	23
27	Bradford N.	38	8	0	30	337	714	16
28	Featherstone R.	38	4	0	34	232	734	8

CHAMPIONSHIP PLAY-OFF
Semi-finals

Salford	14	Wigan	2
Swinton	11	York	4

FINAL
At Central Park, Wigan

	T	G	P		T	G	P
SALFORD	3	3	15	SWINTON	1	1	5

CHAMPIONSHIP PLAY-OFF
Semi-finals

Salford	28	Halifax	3
Wigan	14	Leeds	10

FINAL
At Wilderspool, Warrington

	T	G	P		T	G	P
WIGAN	3	3	15	SALFORD	1	0	3

TABLES

1934-35

		P	W	D	L	F	A	Pts
1	Swinton	38	30	1	7	468	175	61
2	Warrington	38	28	3	7	445	253	59
3	Wigan	38	26	4	8	790	290	56
4	Salford	38	27	1	10	478	272	55
5	Leeds	38	26	2	10	531	321	54
6	Hull	38	25	0	13	562	430	50
7	Huddersfield	38	22	3	13	552	379	47
8	York	38	21	3	14	527	374	45
9	Castleford	38	20	3	15	512	355	43
10	St. Helens Rec.	38	21	1	16	431	404	43
11	Hunslet	38	21	0	17	549	461	42
12	Keighley	38	20	2	16	398	479	42
13	Broughton R.	38	20	1	17	451	357	41
14	Halifax	38	18	4	16	380	314	40
15	Liverpool S.	38	18	2	18	399	287	38
16	Wakefield T.	38	18	1	19	494	331	37
17	Widnes	38	18	0	20	395	339	36
18	Oldham	38	15	4	19	358	447	34
19	Rochdale H.	38	16	1	21	395	521	33
20	Barrow	38	15	1	22	396	460	31
21	St. Helens	38	14	3	21	278	377	31
22	Dewsbury	38	14	2	22	307	501	30
23	Hull K.R.	38	13	1	24	414	514	27
24	Leigh	38	13	0	25	311	589	26
25	Bradford N.	38	11	1	26	321	580	23
26	Batley	38	9	1	28	306	603	19
27	Featherstone R.	38	6	0	32	293	804	12
28	Bramley	38	4	1	33	337	861	9

1935-36

		P	W	D	L	F	A	Pts
1	Hull	38	30	1	7	607	306	61
2	Liverpool S.	38	27	2	9	426	248	56
3	Widnes	38	25	4	9	433	190	54
4	Wigan	38	25	1	12	543	328	51
5	Salford	38	25	0	13	481	261	50
6	Broughton R.	38	23	3	12	461	315	49
7	York	38	22	4	12	490	309	48
8	Leeds	38	23	2	13	534	385	48
9	Huddersfield	38	23	0	15	580	356	46
10	Barrow	38	21	3	14	436	297	45
11	Warrington	38	21	3	14	414	325	45
12	Castleford	38	22	0	16	503	366	44
13	Halifax	38	20	3	15	410	380	43
14	Swinton	38	19	3	16	432	318	41
15	Oldham	38	20	1	17	377	351	41
16	Hunslet	38	20	1	17	390	405	41
17	Batley	38	19	2	17	408	516	40
18	Keighley	38	18	2	18	320	374	38
19	Bradford N.	38	16	2	20	374	392	34
20	Rochdale H.	38	17	0	21	380	439	34
21	Acton & Willesden	38	13	4	21	382	529	30
22	Wakefield T.	38	13	2	23	348	436	28
23	St. Helens	38	13	1	24	272	399	27
24	Streatham & Mitcham	38	12	2	24	390	520	26
25	Bramley	38	12	2	24	348	644	26
26	St. Helens Rec.	38	11	1	26	261	483	23
27	Leigh	38	10	2	26	224	506	22
28	Hull K.R.	38	9	3	26	306	472	21
29	Dewsbury	38	6	2	30	246	569	14
30	Featherstone R.	38	5	4	29	269	625	14

CHAMPIONSHIP PLAY-OFF
Semi-finals

Swinton	10	Salford	2
Warrington	9	Wigan	0

FINAL
At Central Park, Wigan

	T	G	P		T	G	P
SWINTON	2	4	14	WARRINGTON	1	0	3

CHAMPIONSHIP PLAY-OFF
Semi-finals

Hull	13	Wigan	2
Liverpool S.	9	Widnes	10

FINAL
At Fartown, Huddersfield

	T	G	P		T	G	P
HULL	3	6	21	WIDNES	0	1	2

274

1936-37

		P	W	D	L	F	A	Pts
1	Salford	38	29	3	6	529	196	61
2	Warrington	38	28	3	7	468	189	59
3	Leeds	38	28	1	9	627	262	57
4	Liverpool S.	38	26	3	9	425	226	55
5	Wigan	38	26	0	12	591	336	52
6	Castleford	38	25	2	11	490	325	52
7	Hull	38	24	2	12	535	312	50
8	Wakefield T.	38	23	1	14	442	372	47
9	Barrow	38	20	5	13	481	325	45
10	St. Helens Rec.	38	21	2	15	410	343	44
11	Huddersfield	38	21	1	16	671	405	43
12	Hunslet	38	21	0	17	512	405	42
13	Oldham	38	20	1	17	437	343	41
14	Halifax	38	19	3	16	329	418	41
15	Bradford N.	38	19	2	17	429	360	40
16	Swinton	38	19	2	17	366	312	40
17	Broughton R.	38	18	3	17	363	353	39
18	Keighley	38	19	0	19	395	356	38
19	Hull K.R.	38	17	1	20	414	387	35
20	Widnes	38	17	1	20	270	308	35
21	Rochdale H.	38	15	1	22	311	468	31
22	St. Helens	38	13	4	21	343	431	30
23*	Streatham & Mitcham	38	14	0	24	366	339	28
24	York	38	14	0	24	412	536	28
25	Batley	38	12	2	24	352	590	26
26	Dewsbury	38	12	1	25	295	514	25
27	Bramley	38	10	1	27	323	667	21
28	Leigh	38	5	4	29	237	615	14
29	Newcastle	38	5	1	32	300	890	11
30	Featherstone R.	38	5	0	33	317	858	10

*Streatham & Mitcham disbanded after playing 26 matches. The 12 unplayed matches were recorded as wins for their would be opponents.

1937-38

		P	W	D	L	F	A	Pts
1	Hunslet	36	25	3	8	459	301	53
2	Leeds	36	25	2	9	530	227	52
3	Swinton	36	24	2	10	392	198	50
4	Barrow	36	25	0	11	447	260	50
5	Warrington	36	23	1	12	534	286	47
6	Salford	36	23	1	12	493	293	47
7	Castleford	36	23	1	12	481	320	47
8	Widnes	36	22	2	12	475	210	46
9	Wigan	36	22	1	13	478	329	45
10	Wakefield T.	36	21	3	12	476	346	45
11	Oldham	36	21	2	13	392	276	44
12	Bradford N.	36	20	4	12	439	355	44
13	Hull	36	19	3	14	479	364	41
14	Halifax	36	19	2	15	531	393	40
15	Batley	36	17	2	17	392	367	36
16	Keighley	36	17	2	17	267	318	36
17	Liverpool S.	36	17	1	18	284	324	35
18	York	36	15	5	16	381	492	35
19	Broughton R.	36	16	2	18	394	413	34
20	Dewsbury	36	15	1	20	388	407	31
21	St. Helens	36	14	3	19	370	476	31
22	St. Helens Rec.	36	15	1	20	353	471	31
23	Huddersfield	36	14	1	21	499	502	29
24	Hull K.R.	36	13	1	22	354	476	27
25	Rochdale H.	36	9	1	26	338	567	19
26	Featherstone R.	36	8	2	26	311	606	18
27	Leigh	36	7	3	26	203	597	17
28	Newcastle	36	2	4	30	206	750	8
29	Bramley	36	2	2	32	221	643	6

CHAMPIONSHIP PLAY-OFF
Semi-finals

Salford	15	Liverpool S.	7
Warrington	12	Leeds	2

FINAL
At Central Park, Wigan

	T	G	P		T	G	P
SALFORD	1	5	13	WARRINGTON	1	4	11

CHAMPIONSHIP PLAY-OFF
Semi-finals

Hunslet	13	Barrow	7
Leeds	5	Swinton	2

FINAL
At Elland Road, Leeds

	T	G	P		T	G	P
HUNSLET	2	1	8	LEEDS	0	1	2

TABLES

1938-39

		P	W	D	L	F	A	Pts
1	Salford	40	30	3	7	551	191	63
2	Castleford	40	29	3	8	502	287	61
3	Halifax	40	28	3	9	544	349	59
4	Huddersfield	40	28	2	10	647	345	58
5	Leeds	40	25	4	11	509	291	54
6	Swinton	40	26	1	13	418	286	53
7	Warrington	40	26	0	14	520	329	52
8	Barrow	40	24	3	13	380	287	51
9	Wigan	40	25	0	15	566	365	50
10	Widnes	40	22	3	15	453	274	47
11	Wakefield T.	40	20	5	15	501	320	45
12	Hull	40	21	3	16	460	364	45
13	Keighley	40	21	1	18	361	384	43
14	Oldham	40	20	2	18	405	289	42
15	Hunslet	40	19	4	17	344	390	42
16	Bradford N.	40	19	1	20	493	392	39
17	Hull K.R.	40	18	3	19	441	448	39
18	York	40	18	2	20	485	554	38
19	Liverpool S.	40	18	1	21	291	298	38
20	Broughton R.	40	18	1	21	408	447	37
21	St. Helens	40	17	0	23	387	494	34
22	Featherstone R.	40	13	2	25	292	541	28
23	Batley	40	11	1	28	270	537	23
24	St. Helens Rec.	40	11	0	29	311	504	22
25	Bramley	40	8	5	27	348	630	21
26	Leigh	40	7	3	30	237	667	17
27	Dewsbury	40	5	2	33	252	557	12
28	Rochdale H.	40	4	0	36	261	817	8

1939-40

WAR EMERGENCY LEAGUE
YORKSHIRE SECTION

		P	W	D	L	F	A	Pts
1	Bradford	28	21	0	7	574	302	42
2	Huddersfield	28	19	1	8	545	340	39
3	Hull	28	18	0	8	378	265	36
4	Halifax	28	17	0	11	462	339	34
5	Hunslet	28	16	1	11	430	339	33
6	Castleford	28	16	1	11	364	300	33
7	Featherstone R.	28	15	0	13	373	365	30
8	Wakefield T.	28	14	0	14	479	314	28
9	Leeds	28	14	0	14	390	330	28
10	Hull K.R.	27	13	0	14	343	434	26
11	Dewsbury	27	11	2	14	291	406	24
12	York	28	10	3	15	349	467	23
13	Batley	27	8	0	19	255	406	16
14	Keighley	27	6	2	19	221	476	14
15	Bramley	28	4	0	24	248	617	8

LANCASHIRE SECTION

		P	W	D	L	F	A	Pts
1	Swinton	22	17	0	5	378	158	34
2	Salford	22	16	2	4	328	171	34
3	Wigan	22	16	1	5	301	157	33
4	Widnes	22	15	2	5	305	176	32
5	Warrington	22	11	1	10	281	258	21
6	St. Helens	22	11	1	10	288	224	23
7	Barrow	22	10	1	11	303	286	21
8	Oldham	21	8	2	11	241	242	18
9	Rochdale H.	21	8	0	13	197	306	16
10	Leigh	22	6	1	15	188	346	13
11	Liverpool S.	22	4	3	15	152	350	11
12	Broughton R.	22	2	0	20	153	441	4

CHAMPIONSHIP PLAY-OFF
Semi-finals

Castleford	21	Halifax	4
Salford	15	Huddersfield	0

FINAL
At Maine Road, Manchester

	T	G	P		T	G	P
SALFORD	2	1	8	CASTLEFORD	2	0	6

CHAMPIONSHIP FINAL
First Leg

	T	G	P		T	G	P
SWINTON	3	2	13	BRADFORD N.	5	3	21

Second Leg

	T	G	P		T	G	P
BRADFORD N.	4	2	16	SWINTON	1	3	9

Aggregate: Bradford N. 37 Swinton 22

1940-41 WAR EMERGENCY LEAGUE
YORKSHIRE LEAGUE

		P	W	D	L	F	A	Pts
1	Bradford N.	25	23	1	1	469	126	47
2	Hull	26	20	0	6	341	227	40
3	Huddersfield	25	14	2	9	422	297	30
4	Leeds	25	14	1	10	372	235	29
5	Halifax	22	14	0	8	357	229	28
6	Hunslet	25	14	0	11	328	279	28
7	Featherstone R.	24	14	0	10	255	255	28
8	Wakefield T.	23	12	0	11	237	214	24
9	Castleford	24	11	0	13	224	239	22
10	Dewsbury	23	6	2	15	238	301	14
11	Keighley	26	5	1	20	200	447	11
12	Bramley	21	5	1	15	129	364	11
13	York	23	5	0	18	227	388	10
14	Batley	20	5	0	15	148	344	10

LANCASHIRE LEAGUE

		P	W	D	L	F	A	Pts
1	Wigan	16	15	1	0	297	71	31
2	Warrington	16	13	0	3	236	42	26
3	St. Helens	14	10	1	3	280	83	21
4	Salford	14	9	0	5	216	95	18
5	Oldham	16	6	1	9	161	205	13
6	Swinton	13	6	0	7	121	132	12
7	Liverpool S.	14	2	1	11	147	270	5
8	Broughton R.	10	0	0	10	71	247	0
9	Leigh	13	0	0	13	62	446	0

CHAMPIONSHIP FINAL
First Leg

	T	G	P			T	G	P
WIGAN	2	0	6	BRADFORD N.		5	1	17

Second Leg

	T	G	P			T	G	P
BRADFORD N.	6	5	28	WIGAN		3	0	9

Aggregate: Bradford N. 45 Wigan 15

1941-42 WAR EMERGENCY LEAGUE

		P	W	D	L	F	A	Pts	%
1	Dewsbury	24	19	1	4	431	172	39	81.25
2	Bradford N.	17	13	1	3	318	130	27	79.41
3	Halifax	17	13	0	4	262	139	26	76.47
4	Hull	18	12	0	6	265	146	24	66.66
5	Hunslet	18	10	0	8	212	177	20	55.55
6	Wigan	20	11	0	9	241	207	22	55.00
7	Oldham	20	11	0	9	209	209	22	55.00
8	Leeds	23	12	1	10	245	213	25	54.34
9	Huddersfield	23	12	0	11	355	276	24	52.17
10	Keighley	23	12	0	11	224	306	24	52.17
11	Wakefield T.	19	9	0	10	195	215	18	47.36
12	Featherstone R.	18	8	0	10	166	181	16	44.44
13	St. Helens	19	8	0	11	217	270	16	42.10
14	Castleford	20	8	0	12	195	253	16	40.00
15	York	22	6	0	16	231	386	12	27.27
16	Batley	18	3	1	14	133	269	7	19.44
17	Bramley	19	0	0	19	104	454	0	0.00

CHAMPIONSHIP PLAY-OFF
Semi-finals

Bradford N.	15	Halifax	8
Dewsbury	32	Hull	18

FINAL
At Headingley, Leeds

	T	G	P			T	G	P
DEWSBURY	3	2	13	BRADFORD N.		0	0	0

1942-43 WAR EMERGENCY LEAGUE

		P	W	D	L	F	A	Pts	%
1	Wigan	16	13	0	3	301	141	26	81.25
2	Dewsbury	16	12	1	3	270	117	25	78.12
3	Bradford N.	19	13	1	5	312	183	27	71.05
4	Halifax	19	13	0	6	297	149	26	68.42
5	Leeds	17	11	1	5	337	145	23	67.64
6	Huddersfield	18	12	0	6	215	189	24	66.66
7	Wakefield T.	19	11	1	7	267	192	23	60.52
8	Featherstone R.	19	10	1	8	179	138	21	55.26
9	Keighley	18	5	2	11	145	235	12	33.33
10	Batley	15	4	0	11	159	294	8	26.66
11	Hull	15	4	0	11	125	295	8	26.66
12	Oldham	19	4	0	15	142	306	8	21.05
13	York	17	3	1	13	109	311	7	20.58
14	St. Helens	15	2	0	13	108	273	4	13.33

CHAMPIONSHIP PLAY-OFF
Qualifying Game

Bradford N.	16	Huddersfield	13

Semi-finals

Dewsbury	3	Bradford N.	8
Wigan	4	Halifax	13

Bradford N. were disqualified for fielding an ineligible player.

FINAL
First Leg

	T	G	P			T	G	P
DEWSBURY	3	1	11	HALIFAX		1	0	3

Second Leg

	T	G	P			T	G	P
HALIFAX	3	2	13	DEWSBURY		6	2	22

Aggregate: Dewsbury 33 Halifax 16
Championship declared null and void because Dewsbury fielded an ineligible player.

277

1943-44

WAR EMERGENCY LEAGUE

		P	W	D	L	F	A	Pts	%
1	Wakefield T.	22	19	0	3	359	97	38	86.36
2	Wigan	21	17	0	4	302	143	34	80.95
3	Hull	21	15	0	6	236	189	30	71.42
4	Dewsbury	22	15	1	6	304	169	31	70.45
5	Halifax	22	15	0	7	279	166	30	68.18
6	Bradford N.	19	11	1	7	292	125	23	60.52
7	Leeds	21	12	1	8	262	252	25	59.52
8	Hunslet	22	12	0	10	287	245	24	54.54
9	Barrow	22	11	0	11	315	199	22	50.00
10	Keighley	21	9	0	12	151	218	18	42.85
11	Huddersfield	21	7	1	13	223	230	15	35.71
12	Oldham	21	7	0	14	137	371	14	33.33
13	Featherstone R.	22	6	0	16	202	229	12	27.27
14	Batley	21	5	1	15	180	299	11	26.19
15	York	22	5	1	16	197	471	11	25.00
16	St. Helens	20	1	0	19	125	446	2	5.00

CHAMPIONSHIP PLAY-OFF

Semi-finals

Wakefield T.	5	Dewsbury	11
Wigan	27	Hull	10

FINAL
First Leg

	T	G	P		T	G	P
WIGAN	3	2	13	DEWSBURY	1	3	9

Second Leg

	T	G	P		T	G	P
DEWSBURY	1	1	5	WIGAN	2	3	12

Aggregate: Wigan 25 Dewsbury 14

1944-45

WAR EMERGENCY LEAGUE

		P	W	D	L	F	A	Pts	%
1	Bradford N.	20	17	0	3	337	69	34	85.00
2	Halifax	16	13	1	2	288	78	27	84.37
3	Wakefield T.	23	17	0	6	380	203	34	73.91
4	Wigan	24	17	1	6	302	138	35	72.91
5	Barrow	23	15	1	7	221	167	31	67.39
6	Castleford	23	14	2	7	274	139	30	65.21
7	Dewsbury	22	11	1	10	243	213	23	52.27
8	Batley	22	10	2	10	186	241	22	50.00
9	Huddersfield	24	8	6	10	281	252	22	45.83
10	Leeds	23	9	2	12	221	236	20	43.47
11	Hunslet	21	7	2	12	164	245	16	38.09
12	Hull	23	8	1	14	193	281	17	36.95
13	Oldham	23	8	1	14	189	282	17	36.95
14	Featherstone R.	22	8	0	14	153	229	16	36.36
15	Keighley	21	7	0	14	114	283	14	33.33
16	St. Helens	23	4	1	18	177	394	9	19.56
17	York	23	4	1	18	153	426	9	19.56

CHAMPIONSHIP PLAY-OFF

Semi-finals

Bradford N.	18	Wigan	15
Halifax	17	Wakefield T	11

FINAL
First Leg

	T	G	P		T	G	P
HALIFAX	1	3	9	BRADFORD N.	0	1	2

Second Leg

	T	G	P		T	G	P
BRADFORD N.	6	3	24	HALIFAX	1	4	11

Aggregate: Bradford N. 26 Halifax 20

1945-46

		P	W	D	L	F	A	Pts
1	Wigan	36	29	2	5	783	219	60
2	Huddersfield	36	27	1	8	688	286	55
3	Wakefield T.	36	26	0	10	707	283	52
4	Bradford N.	36	24	3	9	544	288	51
5	Barrow	36	22	4	10	535	363	48
6	Dewsbury	36	23	0	13	396	210	46
7	Hunslet	36	21	4	11	525	306	46
8	Salford	36	23	0	13	415	342	46
9	Batley	36	21	4	11	418	403	46
10	Warrington	36	21	3	12	430	343	45
11	Castleford	36	22	0	14	326	298	44
12	Widnes	36	19	3	14	449	272	41
13	Featherstone R.	36	19	1	16	407	395	39
14	Halifax	36	19	0	17	374	374	38
15	Oldham	36	18	0	18	352	403	36
16	Broughton R.	36	16	3	17	352	399	35
17	Hull	36	16	2	18	482	451	34
18	Hull K.R.	36	15	3	18	375	459	33
19	Workington T.	36	15	0	21	358	421	30
20	St. Helens	36	13	1	22	398	527	27
21	Swinton	36	9	5	22	338	528	23
22	Keighley	36	9	2	25	307	640	20
23	Leeds	36	9	1	26	351	581	19
24	Rochdale H.	36	9	1	26	221	513	19
25	Bramley	36	9	0	27	271	620	18
26	Liverpool S.	36	5	2	29	263	700	12
27	York	36	4	1	31	328	769	9

CHAMPIONSHIP PLAY-OFF

Semi-finals

Wigan	18	Bradford N.	4
Huddersfield	8	Wakefield T.	3

FINAL
At Maine Road, Manchester

	T	G	P		T	G	P
WIGAN	3	2	13	HUD'SFIELD	0	2	4

1946-47

		P	W	D	L	F	A	Pts
1	Wigan	36	29	1	6	567	196	59
2	Dewsbury	36	27	1	8	411	158	55
3	Widnes	36	26	2	8	284	149	54
4	Leeds	36	25	2	9	573	305	52
5	Warrington	36	26	0	10	432	236	52
6	Bradford N.	36	24	3	9	525	300	51
7	Huddersfield	36	24	2	10	572	332	50
8	Oldham	36	22	2	12	376	243	46
9	Leigh	36	21	0	15	319	238	42
10	Wakefield T.	36	20	2	14	399	357	42
11	Workington T.	36	19	2	15	345	267	40
12	Barrow	36	18	4	14	385	371	40
13	Castleford	36	19	1	16	398	354	39
14	Hunslet	36	17	2	17	355	355	36
15	Hull	36	17	0	19	388	370	34
16	Hull K.R.	36	15	3	18	359	455	33
17	Batley	36	15	1	20	398	390	31
18	Belle Vue R.	36	14	3	19	388	375	31
19	St. Helens	36	14	1	21	425	366	29
20	Halifax	36	13	2	21	281	440	28
21	York	36	12	2	22	327	549	26
22	Salford	36	11	2	23	280	401	24
23	Liverpool S.	36	11	1	24	322	497	23
24	Swinton	36	11	1	24	262	466	23
25	Keighley	36	10	1	25	299	509	21
26	Featherstone R.	36	9	1	26	217	477	19
27	Rochdale H.	36	9	0	27	223	430	18
28	Bramley	36	5	0	31	232	706	10

CHAMPIONSHIP PLAY-OFF
Semi-finals

Wigan	21	Leeds	11
Dewsbury	5	Widnes	2

FINAL
At Maine Road, Manchester

	T	G	P		T	G	P
WIGAN	3	2	13	DEWSBURY	0	2	4

1947-48

		P	W	D	L	F	A	Pts
1	Wigan	36	31	1	4	776	258	63
2	Warrington	36	30	1	5	688	232	61
3	Huddersfield	36	26	2	8	669	240	54
4	Bradford N.	36	26	0	10	549	310	52
5	Workington T.	36	22	4	10	426	236	48
6	Hunslet	36	21	4	11	449	239	46
7	Widnes	36	21	1	14	331	228	43
8	St. Helens	36	20	2	14	476	305	42
9	Leeds	36	20	2	14	588	409	42
10	Wakefield T.	36	20	2	14	496	378	42
11	Salford	36	20	1	15	347	443	41
12	Hull	36	19	1	16	454	301	39
13	Castleford	36	19	1	16	456	383	39
14	Leigh	36	18	1	17	374	452	37
15	Dewsbury	36	17	2	17	232	301	36
16	Oldham	36	17	1	18	306	385	35
17	Belle Vue R.	36	17	0	19	333	358	34
18	Halifax	36	16	0	20	309	449	32
19	Swinton	36	15	1	20	316	403	31
20	Keighley	36	15	1	20	295	432	31
21	Barrow	36	14	2	20	336	419	30
22	Rochdale H.	36	11	2	23	231	311	24
23	Bramley	36	12	0	24	330	482	24
24	Batley	36	11	1	24	281	482	23
25	Hull K.R.	36	10	1	25	303	470	21
26	Liverpool S.	36	8	1	27	192	550	17
27	Featherstone R.	36	6	0	30	270	724	12
28	York	36	4	1	31	216	849	9

CHAMPIONSHIP PLAY-OFF
Semi-finals

Wigan	3	Bradford N.	15
Warrington	17	Huddersfield	5

FINAL
At Maine Road, Manchester

	T	G	P		T	G	P
WARRINGTON	3	3	15	BRADFORD N.	1	1	5

TABLES

1948-49		P	W	D	L	F	A	Pts
1	Warrington	36	31	0	5	728	247	62
2	Wigan	36	28	1	7	802	286	57
3	Huddersfield	36	27	0	9	626	290	54
4	Barrow	36	25	1	10	459	252	51
5	Widnes	36	24	2	10	358	188	50
6	Batley	36	23	0	13	404	348	46
7	Salford	36	20	5	11	371	267	45
8	Workington T.	36	22	1	13	437	318	45
9	Swinton	36	21	3	12	354	305	45
10	Bradford N.	36	22	0	14	344	298	44
11	St. Helens	36	20	1	15	481	282	41
12	Wakefield T.	36	19	1	16	570	396	39
13	Hull	36	19	0	17	375	416	38
14	Leeds	36	18	1	17	490	478	37
15	Keighley	36	17	3	16	299	336	37
16	Hunslet	36	17	0	19	366	377	34
17	Hull K.R.	36	17	0	19	386	457	34
18	Leigh	36	14	5	17	290	330	33
19	Castleford	36	16	0	20	382	356	32
20	Dewsbury	36	15	1	20	355	346	31
21	Belle Vue R.	36	14	1	21	290	414	29
22	Rochdale H.	36	12	3	21	230	335	27
23	Oldham	36	12	3	21	283	450	27
24	Bramley	36	12	2	22	362	546	26
25	Halifax	36	11	3	22	258	372	25
26	Featherstone R.	36	9	3	24	305	519	21
27	Whitehaven	36	6	2	28	216	597	14
28	York	36	5	2	29	194	597	12
29	Liverpool S.	36	3	2	31	145	758	8

1949-50		P	W	D	L	F	A	Pts
1	Wigan	36	31	1	4	853	320	63
2	Huddersfield	36	28	1	7	694	362	57
3	Swinton	36	25	4	7	516	261	54
4	Halifax	36	25	0	11	496	251	50
5	Salford	36	24	2	10	427	306	50
6	Leigh	36	24	1	11	459	269	49
7	St. Helens	36	23	2	11	540	260	48
8	Leeds	36	24	0	12	602	365	48
9	Dewsbury	36	23	0	13	468	266	46
10	Workington T.	36	22	1	13	514	319	45
11	Warrington	36	22	0	14	579	367	44
12	Castleford	36	20	0	16	429	386	40
13	Keighley	36	20	0	16	375	390	40
14	Wakefield T.	36	19	0	17	523	447	38
15	Hunslet	36	18	1	17	405	317	37
16	Widnes	36	16	4	16	373	318	36
17	Belle Vue R.	36	16	2	18	388	393	34
18	Oldham	36	15	4	17	395	410	34
19	Hull	36	15	3	18	364	527	33
20	Barrow	36	14	1	21	393	464	29
21	Bradford N.	36	14	1	21	335	413	29
22	Hull K.R.	36	14	1	21	305	474	29
23	Whitehaven	36	11	4	21	262	432	26
24	Batley	36	10	0	26	346	555	20
25	Featherstone R.	36	9	2	25	299	550	20
26	Bramley	36	6	1	29	258	676	13
27	Rochdale H.	36	5	2	29	200	547	12
28	York	36	6	0	30	274	807	12
29	Liverpool S.	36	4	0	32	198	820	8

CHAMPIONSHIP PLAY-OFF
Semi-finals

Warrington	23	Barrow	8
Wigan	5	Huddersfield	14

FINAL
At Maine Road, Manchester

	T	G	P		T	G	P
HUD'SFIELD	3	2	13	WARRINGTON	2	3	12

CHAMPIONSHIP PLAY-OFF
Semi-finals

Huddersfield	9	Swinton	0
Wigan	5	Halifax	5

Replay

Halifax	2	Wigan	18

FINAL
At Maine Road, Manchester

	T	G	P		T	G	P
WIGAN	4	4	20	HUD'SFIELD	0	1	2

1950-51

		P	W	D	L	F	A	Pts
1	Warrington	36	30	0	6	738	250	60
2	Wigan	36	29	1	6	774	288	59
3	Workington T.	36	27	0	9	734	328	54
4	Leigh	36	24	2	10	420	288	50
5	Leeds	36	24	0	12	678	441	48
6	St. Helens	36	22	1	13	527	359	45
7	Hunslet	36	22	1	13	526	361	45
8	Batley	36	21	1	14	391	400	43
9	Huddersfield	36	20	2	14	575	410	42
10	Wakefield T.	36	19	3	14	587	521	41
11	Halifax	36	20	0	16	523	407	40
12	Belle Vue R.	36	19	2	15	427	374	40
13	Dewsbury	36	19	2	15	440	327	40
14	Bradford N.	36	19	0	17	406	404	38
15	Oldham	36	17	2	17	403	347	36
16	Keighley	36	16	3	17	359	442	35
17	Swinton	36	16	1	19	395	435	33
18	Hull	36	15	2	19	351	499	32
19	Salford	36	15	1	20	380	419	31
20	Barrow	36	14	2	20	385	518	30
21	Whitehaven	36	13	3	20	257	411	29
22	Rochdale H.	36	14	1	21	321	534	29
23	Hull K.R.	36	12	2	22	450	699	26
24	Bramley	36	11	3	22	380	530	25
25	Castleford	36	12	1	23	376	548	25
26	Featherstone R.	36	12	1	23	375	562	25
27	Widnes	36	10	1	25	265	382	21
28	York	36	8	1	27	266	706	17
29	Liverpool S.	36	2	1	33	193	712	5

CHAMPIONSHIP PLAY-OFF
Semi-finals

Wigan	5	Workington T.	8
Warrington	15	Leigh	9

FINAL
At Maine Road, Manchester

	T	G	P		T	G	P
WORK'N. T.	6	4	26	WARRINGTON	3	1	11

1951-52

		P	W	D	L	F	A	Pts
1	Bradford N.	36	28	1	7	758	325	57
2	Wigan	36	27	1	8	750	296	55
3	Hull	36	26	1	9	552	393	53
4	Huddersfield	36	26	0	10	785	446	52
5	Oldham	36	25	1	10	558	331	51
6	Warrington	36	24	1	11	622	396	49
7	Leigh	36	23	2	11	489	365	48
8	Workington T.	36	23	0	13	540	344	46
9	Hunslet	36	22	1	13	559	404	45
10	Barrow	36	21	2	13	697	345	44
11	Doncaster	36	21	1	14	422	371	43
12	Widnes	36	20	2	14	491	395	42
13	Leeds	36	19	2	15	578	514	40
14	Swinton	36	18	3	15	432	382	39
15	Salford	36	18	2	16	454	386	38
16	Wakefield T.	36	19	0	17	596	518	38
17	Batley	36	18	1	17	440	498	37
18	Dewsbury	36	18	0	18	419	439	36
19	Whitehaven	36	16	4	16	280	356	36
20	St. Helens	36	16	2	18	426	358	34
21	Halifax	36	16	2	18	474	403	34
22	Featherstone R.	36	14	2	20	431	470	30
23	Belle Vue R.	36	12	3	21	351	446	27
24	York	36	12	3	21	363	583	27
25	Hull K.R.	36	10	1	25	416	708	21
26	Rochdale H.	36	10	1	25	328	585	21
27	Bramley	36	10	1	25	300	577	21
28	Castleford	36	8	1	27	370	579	17
29	Keighley	36	8	1	27	351	617	17
30	Cardiff	36	5	0	31	342	1,024	10
31	Liverpool C.	36	4	0	32	199	915	8

CHAMPIONSHIP PLAY-OFF
Semi-finals

Wigan	13	Hull	9
Bradford N.	18	Huddersfield	15

FINAL
At Leeds Road, Huddersfield

	T	G	P		T	G	P
WIGAN	3	2	13	BRADFORD N.	0	3	6

TABLES

1952-53

		P	W	D	L	F	A	Pts
1	St. Helens	36	32	2	2	769	273	66
2	Halifax	36	29	2	5	620	309	60
3	Bradford N.	36	28	0	8	700	329	56
4	Huddersfield	36	27	2	7	747	366	56
5	Barrow	36	27	1	8	585	322	55
6	Leeds	36	24	0	12	690	452	48
7	Leigh	36	23	2	11	556	377	48
8	Oldham	36	22	2	12	599	280	46
9	Warrington	36	20	1	15	733	486	41
10	Whitehaven	36	19	3	14	465	486	41
11	Wigan	36	19	2	15	673	414	40
12	Hunslet	36	20	0	16	485	358	40
13	Salford	36	20	0	16	508	441	40
14	Swinton	36	18	0	18	441	401	36
15	Hull	36	17	2	17	461	451	36
16	Workington T.	36	16	2	18	453	460	34
17	Keighley	36	16	1	19	465	547	33
18	Wakefield T.	36	16	0	20	410	595	32
19	Dewsbury	36	15	1	20	410	440	31
20	Castleford	36	15	0	21	392	502	30
21	Batley	36	14	2	20	405	579	30
22	Rochdale H.	36	13	3	20	443	536	29
23	Widnes	36	13	2	21	336	478	28
24	Featherstone R.	36	12	1	23	415	535	25
25	York	36	10	0	26	370	496	20
26	Doncaster	36	10	0	26	377	665	20
27	Belle Vue R.	36	10	0	26	301	705	20
28	Hull K.R.	36	9	1	26	337	646	19
29	Bramley	36	6	0	30	293	898	12
30	Liverpool C.	36	4	0	32	225	837	8

1953-54

		P	W	D	L	F	A	Pts
1	Halifax	36	30	2	4	538	219	62
2	Warrington	36	30	1	5	663	311	61
3	St. Helens	36	28	2	6	672	297	58
4	Workington T.	36	29	0	7	604	333	58
5	Hull	36	25	0	11	685	349	50
6	Huddersfield	36	24	0	12	689	417	48
7	Wigan	36	23	1	12	688	392	47
8	Barrow	36	23	0	13	574	377	46
9	Bradford N.	36	22	0	14	628	414	44
10	Leeds	36	22	0	14	766	517	44
11	Wakefield T.	36	19	1	16	671	508	39
12	Oldham	36	17	4	15	504	366	38
13	Leigh	36	19	0	17	547	459	38
14	Featherstone R.	36	18	2	16	478	431	38
15	Hunslet	36	19	0	17	455	451	38
16	Widnes	36	16	3	17	420	431	35
17	York	36	17	0	19	412	401	34
18	Keighley	36	15	3	18	473	533	33
19	Rochdale H.	36	14	3	19	404	457	31
20	Dewsbury	36	14	3	19	432	508	31
21	Whitehaven	36	14	1	21	362	544	29
22	Salford	36	13	2	21	370	438	28
23	Swinton	36	13	1	22	341	513	27
24	Batley	36	13	1	22	367	658	27
25	Bramley	36	11	3	22	437	746	25
26	Castleford	36	11	1	24	437	728	23
27	Belle Vue R.	36	7	2	27	307	714	16
28	Doncaster	36	5	2	29	340	840	12
29	Hull K.R.	36	5	2	29	298	737	12
30	Liverpool C.	36	4	0	32	304	777	8

CHAMPIONSHIP PLAY-OFF
Semi-finals

Halifax	18	Bradford N.	16
St. Helens	46	Huddersfield	0

FINAL
At Maine Road, Manchester

	T	G	P		T	G	P
ST. HELENS	6	3	24	HALIFAX	2	4	14

CHAMPIONSHIP PLAY-OFF
Semi-finals

Halifax	18	Workington T.	7
Warrington	11	St. Helens	0

FINAL
At Maine Road, Manchester

	T	G	P		T	G	P
WARRINGTON	0	4	8	HALIFAX	1	2	7

1954-55

		P	W	D	L	F	A	Pts
1	Warrington	36	29	2	5	71`8	321	60
2	Oldham	36	29	2	5	633	313	60
3	Leeds	36	26	2	8	667	378	54
4	Halifax	36	26	1	9	579	269	53
5	Wigan	36	26	1	9	643	328	53
6	Leigh	36	25	2	9	738	399	52
7	St. Helens	36	25	1	10	631	337	51
8	Barrow	36	24	0	12	581	386	48
9	Featherstone R.	36	23	1	12	572	424	47
10	Workington T.	36	23	0	13	573	391	46
11	Huddersfield	36	22	0	14	790	483	44
12	Rochdale H.	36	20	3	13	396	346	43
13	York	36	21	0	15	439	374	42
14	Hunslet	36	20	0	16	582	477	40
15	Whitehaven	36	18	3	15	406	424	39
16	Wakefield T.	36	18	0	18	589	577	36
17	Bradford N.	36	17	2	17	476	475	36
18	Keighley	36	18	0	18	433	543	36
19	Hull	36	16	3	17	547	486	35
20	Swinton	36	16	1	19	398	451	33
21	Castleford	36	13	4	19	518	516	30
22	Widnes	36	13	0	23	325	478	26
23	Bramley	36	11	1	24	434	602	23
24	Liverpool C.	36	11	1	24	402	582	23
25	Hull K. R.	36	10	0	26	347	756	20
26	Salford	36	7	3	26	279	527	17
27	Doncaster	36	8	1	27	346	664	17
28	Batley	36	7	0	29	278	677	14
29	Blackpool B.	36	7	0	29	303	759	14
30	Belle Vue R.	36	7	0	29	248	666	14
31	Dewsbury	36	5	0	31	255	717	10

1955-56

		P	W	D	L	F	A	Pts	%*
1	Warrington	34	27	1	6	712	349	55	80.88
2	Halifax	36	28	2	6	761	306	58	80.55
3	St. Helens	34	27	0	7	766	351	54	79.41
4	Hull	36	25	1	10	720	458	51	70.83
5	Wigan	34	22	2	10	596	402	46	67.64
6	Featherstone R.	36	23	2	11	579	464	48	66.66
7	Barrow	34	21	2	11	676	506	44	64.70
8	Bradford N.	36	22	2	12	622	455	46	63.88
9	Oldham	34	20	0	14	658	455	40	58.82
10	Swinton	34	19	2	13	441	373	40	58.82
11	Leigh	34	19	2	13	588	565	40	58.82
12	Leeds	36	21	0	15	698	564	42	58.33
13	York	36	20	0	16	503	472	40	55.55
14	Huddersfield	36	18	1	17	606	544	37	51.37
15	Workington T.	34	17	0	17	532	520	34	50.00
16	Keighley	36	18	0	18	495	525	36	50.00
17	Wakefield T.	36	17	0	19	581	539	34	47.22
18	Hunslet	36	17	0	19	511	588	34	47.22
19	Bramley	34	16	0	18	535	605	32	47.05
20	Rochdale H.	34	15	0	19	475	514	30	44.11
21	Whitehaven	34	14	1	19	482	499	29	42.64
22	Salford	34	13	1	20	391	575	27	39.70
23	Widnes	34	11	0	23	403	519	22	32.35
24	Hull K. R.	36	11	1	24	365	747	23	31.94
25	Doncaster	34	7	5	22	349	592	19	27.94
26	Blackpool B.	34	9	0	25	449	745	18	26.47
27	Castleford	36	9	0	27	462	751	18	25.00
28	Liverpool C.	34	8	0	26	375	685	16	23.52
29	Dewsbury	34	8	0	26	315	700	16	23.52
30	Batley	34	7	1	26	367	645	15	22.05

*Positions decided on percentage basis after Belle Vue Rangers withdrew shortly before the start of the season.

CHAMPIONSHIP PLAY-OFF
Semi-finals

Warrington	17	Halifax	9
Oldham	25	Leeds	6

FINAL
At Maine Road, Manchester

	T	G	P		T	G	P
WARRINGTON	1	2	7	OLDHAM	1	0	3

CHAMPIONSHIP PLAY-OFF
Semi-finals

Halifax	23	St. Helens	8
Warrington	0	Hull	17

FINAL
At Maine Road, Manchester

	T	G	P		T	G	P
HULL	2	2	10	HALIFAX	3	0	9

1956-57

		P	W	D	L	F	A	Pts
1	Oldham	38	33	0	5	893	365	66
2	Hull	38	29	2	7	764	432	60
3	Barrow	38	29	0	9	702	481	58
4	Leeds	38	28	0	10	818	490	56
5	St. Helens	38	25	3	10	902	355	53
6	Wigan	38	26	0	12	750	417	52
7	Hunslet	38	26	0	12	688	417	52
8	Wakefield T.	38	23	1	14	747	545	47
9	Huddersfield	38	23	0	15	667	533	46
10	Warrington	38	21	1	16	571	565	43
11	York	38	21	0	17	641	538	42
12	Halifax	38	21	0	17	559	514	42
13	Salford	38	19	2	17	518	499	40
14	Workington T.	38	20	0	18	494	516	40
15	Featherstone R.	38	19	0	19	612	504	38
16	Rochdale H.	38	19	0	19	510	611	38
17	Leigh	38	18	1	19	684	608	37
18	Whitehaven	38	18	1	19	598	646	37
19	Swinton	38	18	0	20	576	594	36
20	Keighley	38	17	1	20	494	534	35
21	Bradford N.	38	17	0	21	479	672	34
22	Bramley	38	14	2	22	558	632	30
23	Widnes	38	15	0	23	439	526	30
24	Blackpool B.	38	14	0	24	470	875	28
25	Castleford	38	11	2	25	488	739	24
26	Hull K.R.	38	11	2	25	395	672	24
27	Liverpool C.	38	9	1	28	356	854	19
28	Batley	38	8	0	30	399	700	16
29	Dewsbury	38	5	1	32	391	818	11
30	Doncaster	38	3	0	35	321	835	6

CHAMPIONSHIP PLAY-OFF
Semi-finals

Hull	45	Barrow	14
Oldham	22	Leeds	12

FINAL
At Odsal, Bradford

	T	G	P		T	G	P
OLDHAM	3	3	15	HULL	2	4	14

1957-58

		P	W	D	L	F	A	Pts
1	Oldham	38	33	1	4	803	415	67
2	St Helens	38	32	0	6	842	336	64
3	Workington T.	38	28	2	8	685	356	58
4	Hull	38	27	2	9	920	431	56
5	Wigan	38	27	0	11	815	430	54
6	Halifax	38	25	2	11	819	441	52
7	Leigh	38	24	0	14	625	457	48
8	Featherstone R.	38	23	1	14	608	497	47
9	Wakefield T.	38	22	2	14	729	477	46
10	Widnes	38	23	0	15	608	453	46
11	Hunslet	38	22	1	15	611	569	45
12	York	38	19	4	15	627	489	42
13	Warrington	38	19	1	18	669	529	39
14	Leeds	38	18	1	19	657	662	37
15	Salford	38	18	1	19	471	542	37
16	Hull K.R.	38	17	2	19	477	570	36
17	Whitehaven	38	17	1	20	559	579	35
18	Huddersfield	38	17	1	20	531	675	35
19	Rochdale H.	38	17	1	20	466	642	35
20	Bradford N.	38	16	2	20	574	593	34
21	Barrow	38	16	2	20	579	688	34
22	Keighley	38	15	2	21	576	527	32
23	Bramley	38	14	2	22	477	728	30
24	Swinton	38	13	3	22	506	589	29
25	Blackpool B.	38	12	0	26	488	726	24
26	Batley	38	10	0	28	434	722	20
27	Liverpool C.	38	9	1	28	442	728	19
28	Dewsbury	38	6	4	28	375	946	16
29	Castleford	38	7	1	30	445	893	15
30	Doncaster	38	4	0	34	246	971	8

CHAMPIONSHIP PLAY-OFF
Semi-finals

Oldham	8	Hull	20
St. Helens	13	Workington T.	14

FINAL
At Odsal, Bradford

	T	G	P		T	G	P
HULL	4	4	20	WORK'N T.	1	0	3

1958-59

		P	W	D	L	F	A	Pts
1	St. Helens	38	31	1	6	1,005	450	63
2	Wigan	38	29	0	9	894	491	58
3	Hunslet	38	27	3	8	819	493	57
4	Oldham	38	28	1	9	791	477	57
5	Wakefield T.	38	27	1	10	790	393	55
6	Swinton	38	27	1	10	691	442	55
7	Hull	38	25	1	12	796	413	51
8	Widnes	38	23	0	15	672	474	46
9	Warrington	38	22	0	16	780	585	44
10	Bradford N.	38	20	2	16	593	563	42
11	York	38	20	1	17	621	622	41
12	Halifax	38	19	2	17	695	594	40
13	Featherstone R.	38	18	3	17	597	613	39
14	Leeds	38	19	0	19	608	653	38
15	Keighley	38	18	1	19	560	629	37
16	Leigh	38	18	0	20	585	562	36
17	Barrow	38	18	0	20	573	602	36
18	Hull K.R.	38	18	0	20	542	619	36
19	Huddersfield	38	18	0	20	573	677	36
20	Workington T.	38	16	3	19	499	585	35
21	Whitehaven	38	17	0	21	659	627	34
22	Salford	38	16	1	21	603	680	33
23	Bramley	38	15	1	22	409	579	31
24	Blackpool B.	38	15	0	23	477	753	30
25	Castleford	38	13	0	25	527	732	26
26	Rochdale H.	38	11	1	26	398	649	23
27	Batley	38	10	1	27	433	679	21
28	Liverpool C.	38	8	0	30	476	954	16
29	Dewsbury	38	7	0	31	378	859	14
30	Doncaster	38	5	0	33	329	924	10

1959-60

		P	W	D	L	F	A	Pts
1	St. Helens	38	34	1	3	947	343	69
2	Wakefield T.	38	32	0	6	831	348	64
3	Hull	38	28	1	9	758	474	57
4	Wigan	38	27	2	9	828	390	56
5	Featherstone R.	38	27	0	11	730	437	54
6	Whitehaven	38	22	3	13	594	533	47
7	Warrington	38	22	2	14	650	482	46
8	Swinton	38	22	2	14	654	503	46
9	Oldham	38	22	1	15	744	461	45
10	Hunslet	38	21	3	14	595	488	45
11	Leigh	38	20	4	14	600	502	44
12	Huddersfield	38	21	1	16	603	510	43
13	Hull K.R.	38	20	1	17	517	575	41
14	Leeds	38	20	0	18	641	573	40
15	Salford	38	19	2	17	629	583	40
16	Batley	38	18	3	17	476	506	39
17	Widnes	38	18	1	19	598	519	37
18	Castleford	38	18	0	20	561	630	36
19	Workington T.	38	18	0	20	448	530	36
20	Keighley	38	17	1	20	575	659	35
21	York	38	17	0	21	579	698	34
22	Halifax	38	15	2	21	627	561	32
23	Rochdale H.	38	15	0	23	435	519	30
24	Barrow	38	13	1	24	422	562	27
25	Bramley	38	10	2	26	393	673	22
26	Bradford N.	38	9	3	26	450	645	21
27	Liverpool C.	38	9	3	26	383	720	21
28	Blackpool B.	38	9	1	28	400	819	19
29	Dewsbury	38	4	1	33	337	982	9
30	Doncaster	38	2	1	35	284	1,084	5

CHAMPIONSHIP PLAY-OFF
Semi-finals

St. Helens	42	Oldham	4
Wigan	11	Hunslet	22

FINAL
At Odsal, Bradford

	T	G	P		T	G	P
ST. HELENS	8	10	44	HUNSLET	4	5	22

CHAMPIONSHIP PLAY-OFF
Semi-finals

St. Helens	9	Wigan	19
Wakefield T.	24	Hull	4

FINAL
At Odsal, Bradford

	T	G	P		T	G	P
WIGAN	5	6	27	WAKEFIELD T.	1	0	3

1960-61

		P	W	D	L	F	A	Pts
1	Leeds	36	30	0	6	620	258	60
2	Warrington	36	27	1	8	701	269	55
3	Swinton	36	27	1	8	647	271	55
4	St. Helens	36	27	0	9	773	304	54
5	Wigan	36	26	0	10	689	334	52
6	Leigh	36	26	0	10	588	299	52
7	Wakefield T.	36	26	0	10	576	326	52
8	Oldham	36	25	1	10	667	359	51
9	Featherstone R.	36	23	1	12	520	403	47
10	Workington T.	36	21	0	15	515	468	42
11	Hull	36	20	1	15	606	448	41
12	Hull K. R.	36	19	2	15	472	462	40
13	Halifax	36	19	1	16	500	436	39
14	Huddersfield	36	18	2	16	449	429	38
15	Hunslet	36	18	0	18	442	415	36
16	Whitehaven	36	17	2	17	448	478	36
17	Castleford	36	16	2	18	465	502	34
18	York	36	16	2	18	502	547	34
19	Batley	36	16	1	19	343	415	33
20	Widnes	36	16	0	20	396	514	32
21	Blackpool B.	36	14	3	19	405	443	31
22	Bramley	36	12	1	23	333	517	25
23	Salford	36	11	2	23	341	689	24
24	Bradford N.	36	10	2	24	312	580	22
25	Keighley	36	10	1	25	349	553	21
26	Barrow	36	9	2	25	305	578	20
27	Dewsbury	36	8	3	25	296	573	19
28	Rochdale H.	36	9	0	27	296	733	18
29	Liverpool C.	36	5	1	30	296	768	11
30	Doncaster	36	3	0	33	287	768	6

CHAMPIONSHIP PLAY-OFF
Semi-finals

Leeds	11	St. Helens	4
Warrington	13	Swinton	5

FINAL
At Odsal, Bradford

	T	G	P		T	G	P
LEEDS	5	5	25	WARRINGTON	2	2	10

1961-62

		P	W	D	L	F	A	Pts
1	Wigan	36	32	1	3	885	283	65
2	Wakefield T.	36	32	1	3	822	288	65
3	Featherstone R.	36	28	1	7	621	370	57
4	Huddersfield	36	25	2	9	494	351	52
5	Workington T.	36	25	0	11	658	362	50
6	Widnes	36	25	0	11	508	309	50
7	Leeds	36	25	0	11	593	390	50
8	Hull K.R.	36	24	0	12	513	451	48
9	St. Helens	36	23	0	13	606	302	46
10	Oldham	36	22	1	13	643	344	45
11	Swinton	36	21	1	14	527	326	43
12	Castleford	36	21	0	15	501	369	42
13	Bramley	36	19	4	13	450	393	42
14	Warrington	36	19	2	15	576	435	40
15	Halifax	36	18	3	15	400	334	39
16	Hull	36	18	1	17	573	415	37
17	Leigh	36	17	0	19	388	497	34
18	Barrow	36	14	1	21	423	558	29
19	Keighley	36	13	2	21	365	467	28
20	York	36	12	1	23	462	531	25
21	Salford	36	12	1	23	385	740	25
22	Whitehaven	36	11	2	23	383	539	24
23	Blackpool B.	36	11	1	24	335	600	23
24	Rochdale H.	36	9	4	23	317	595	22
25	Hunslet	36	10	1	25	350	582	21
26	Batley	36	9	2	25	255	538	20
27	Dewsbury	36	8	2	26	260	543	18
28	Doncaster	36	8	1	27	294	668	17
29	Liverpool C.	36	6	0	30	224	753	12
30	Bradford N.	36	5	1	30	288	766	11

CHAMPIONSHIP PLAY-OFF
Semi-finals

Wigan	11	Huddersfield	13
Wakefield T.	13	Featherstone R.	8

FINAL
At Odsal, Bradford

	T	G	P		T	G	P
HUD'SFIELD	2	4	14	WAKEFIELD	1	1	5

1970-71

		P	W	D	L	F	A	Pts
1	Wigan	34	30	0	4	662	308	60
2	St. Helens	34	29	0	5	748	231	58
3	Leeds	34	28	0	6	856	352	56
4	Leigh	34	26	0	8	636	380	52
5	Wakefield T.	34	24	1	9	760	330	49
6	Keighley	34	21	0	13	448	375	42
7	Salford	34	20	1	13	641	432	41
8	Hull	34	20	1	13	610	444	41
9	Workington T.	34	20	1	13	504	467	41
10	Halifax	34	20	0	14	538	497	40
11	Dewsbury	34	17	3	14	474	406	37
12	Castleford	34	18	0	16	467	403	36
13	Hull K.R.	34	18	0	16	447	524	36
14	Batley	34	16	2	16	492	411	34
15	Huddersfield	34	16	2	16	440	434	34
16	Oldham	34	12	7	15	487	434	31
17	Bramley	34	15	1	18	385	528	31
18	Widnes	34	14	2	18	439	422	30
19	York	34	14	1	19	428	451	29
20	Featherstone R.	34	14	1	19	572	635	29
21	Barrow	34	14	0	20	479	483	28
22	Warrington	34	13	2	19	449	657	28
23	Swinton	34	13	0	21	404	505	26
24	Huyton	34	11	2	21	229	508	24
25	Rochdale H.	34	9	3	22	318	533	21
26	Blackpool B.	34	10	1	23	380	647	21
27	Bradford N.	34	8	2	24	339	662	18
28	Doncaster	34	7	3	24	306	695	17
29	Whitehaven	34	8	1	25	298	698	17
30	Hunslet	34	6	1	27	355	739	13

CHAMPIONSHIP PLAY-OFF
First Round

Hull	14	Workington T.	3
Keighley	7	Dewsbury	20
Leeds	28	Batley	0
Leigh	10	Hull K.R.	5
Salford	33	Halifax	3
St. Helens	28	Huddersfield	5
Wakefield T.	10	Castleford	4
Wigan	12	Oldham	7

Second Round

Leeds	37	Salford	22
Leigh	5	Wakefield T.	8
St. Helens	30	Hull	5
Wigan	36	Dewsbury	12

Semi-finals

St. Helens	22	Leeds	7
Wigan	49	Wakefield T.	15

FINAL
At Station Road, Swinton

	T	G	P		T	G	P
ST. HELENS	2	5	16	WIGAN	2	3	12

1971-72

		P	W	D	L	F	A	Pts
1	Leeds	34	28	2	4	750	325	58
2	Bradford N.	34	26	2	6	724	357	54
3	St. Helens	34	26	1	7	661	297	53
4	Wigan	34	25	0	9	702	314	50
5	Salford	34	25	0	9	720	338	50
6	Swinton	34	23	2	9	554	368	48
7	Featherstone R.	34	23	1	10	632	372	47
8	Rochdale H.	34	21	1	12	429	306	43
9	Wakefield T.	34	21	0	13	587	414	42
10	Castleford	34	20	1	13	488	368	41
11	Widnes	34	19	3	12	476	388	41
12	Dewsbury	34	18	2	14	431	352	38
13	Oldham	34	18	1	15	573	480	37
14	Hull K.R.	34	18	0	16	432	498	36
15	Warrington	34	16	3	15	537	397	35
16	Leigh	34	17	0	17	421	407	34
17	Huddersfield	34	17	0	17	394	435	34
18	Barrow	34	16	2	16	375	508	34
19	Hull	34	16	0	18	488	495	32
20	York	34	15	2	17	465	498	32
21	Halifax	34	14	0	20	398	564	28
22	Bramley	34	13	0	21	333	542	26
23	Whitehaven	34	12	0	22	394	523	24
24	Workington	34	11	2	21	303	533	24
25	Blackpool B.	34	11	0	23	351	560	22
26	Keighley	34	8	0	26	330	740	16
27	Huyton	34	7	1	26	277	610	15
28	Batley	34	5	2	27	249	628	12
29	Doncaster	34	5	0	29	234	729	10
30	Hunslet	34	2	0	32	300	662	4

CHAMPIONSHIP PLAY-OFF
First Round

Bradford N.	37	Warrington	0
Featherstone R.	14	Castleford	18
Leeds	40	Leigh	2
Rochdale H.	18	Wakefield T.	13
St. Helens	25	Hull K.R.	5
Salford	23	Dewsbury	7
Swinton	11	Widnes	15
Wigan	18	Oldham	8

Second Round

Bradford N.	22	Castleford	12
Leeds	20	Widnes	9
St. Helens	17	Rochdale H.	5
Wigan	9	Salford	21

Semi-finals

Bradford N.	10	St. Helens	14
Leeds	10	Salford	0

FINAL
At Station Road, Swinton

	T	G	P		T	G	P
LEEDS	1	3	9	ST HELENS	1	1	5

1972-73

		P	W	D	L	F	A	Pts
1	Warrington	34	27	2	5	816	400	56
2	Featherstone R.	34	27	0	7	768	436	54
3	Leeds	34	26	1	7	810	324	53
4	St. Helens	34	24	2	8	623	298	50
5	Wakefield T.	34	25	0	9	814	398	50
6	Salford	34	25	0	9	723	383	50
7	Castleford	34	25	0	9	704	404	50
8	Dewsbury	34	23	0	11	534	354	46
9	Oldham	34	20	2	12	604	349	42
10	Hull K.R.	34	20	1	13	731	522	41
11	Rochdale H.	34	20	1	13	438	426	41
12	Widnes	34	19	0	15	592	458	38
13	Leigh	34	18	2	14	479	390	38
14	Bramley	34	18	1	15	452	453	37
15	Whitehaven	34	18	1	15	408	512	37
16	Wigan	34	17	1	16	577	491	35
17	York	34	17	1	16	586	575	35
18	Halifax	34	17	0	17	543	562	34
19	Batley	34	15	0	19	537	600	30
20	Keighley	34	15	0	19	451	505	30
21	Swinton	34	14	1	19	441	458	29
22	Workington T.	34	12	1	21	444	464	25
23	Bradford N.	34	12	0	22	582	685	24
24	Huddersfield	34	10	2	22	465	598	22
25	Hull	34	11	0	23	494	693	22
26	Barrow	34	7	0	27	351	775	14
27	Doncaster	34	6	0	28	298	911	12
28	Hunslet	34	5	0	29	371	916	10
29	Blackpool B.	34	4	0	30	324	972	8
30	Huyton	34	3	1	30	243	879	7

CHAMPIONSHIP PLAY-OFF

First Round

Castleford	24	Hull K.R.	12
Dewsbury	29	Oldham	14
Featherstone R.	14	Whitehaven	4
Leeds	45	Bramley	8
St. Helens	29	Leigh	14
Salford	10	Rochdale H.	14
Wakefield T.	33	Widnes	6
Warrington	30	Wigan	15

Second Round

Featherstone R.	7	Dewsbury	26
Leeds	30	Castleford	5
St. Helens	28	Wakefield T.	0
Warrington	16	Rochdale H.	9

Semi-finals

Leeds	7	St. Helens	2
Warrington	7	Dewsbury	12

FINAL

At Odsal, Bradford

	T	G	P		T	G	P
DEWSBURY	4	5	22	LEEDS	3	2	13

1973-74

FIRST DIVISION

		P	W	D	L	F	A	Pts
1	Salford	30	23	1	6	632	299	47
2	St. Helens	30	22	2	6	595	263	46
3	Leeds	30	20	1	9	554	378	41
4	Widnes	30	18	1	11	431	329	37
5	Warrington	30	16	1	13	414	368	33
6	Dewsbury	30	16	1	13	389	474	33
7	Wakefield T.	30	16	0	14	470	411	32
8	Featherstone R.	30	14	2	14	443	397	30
9	Castleford	30	12	4	14	420	411	28
10	Rochdale H.	30	13	2	15	379	415	28
11	Wigan	30	12	3	15	427	364	27
12	Bramley	30	11	3	16	344	457	25
13	Oldham	30	12	1	17	341	494	25
14	Hull K.R.	30	9	2	19	428	552	20
15	Leigh	30	7	0	23	326	655	14
16	Whitehaven	30	7	0	23	308	634	14

SECOND DIVISION

		P	W	D	L	F	A	Pts
1	Bradford N.	26	24	0	2	607	221	48
2	York	26	21	0	5	429	219	42
3	Keighley	26	20	0	6	439	250	40
4	Halifax	26	18	0	8	460	298	36
5	Workington T.	26	17	0	9	421	310	34
6	Hull	26	16	0	10	465	256	32
7	Swinton	26	15	0	11	405	276	30
8	Batley	26	12	0	14	286	311	24
9	Barrow	26	11	0	15	214	291	22
10	Huddersfield	26	9	0	17	363	394	18
11	New Hunslet	26	7	0	19	272	418	14
12	Blackpool B.	26	7	0	19	272	585	14
13	Doncaster	26	3	0	23	158	684	6
14	Huyton	26	2	0	24	182	460	4

TABLES

1974-75

FIRST DIVISION

		P	W	D	L	F	A	Pts
1	St. Helens	30	26	1	3	561	229	53
2	Wigan	30	21	0	9	517	341	42
3	Leeds	30	19	1	10	581	359	39
4	Featherstone R.	30	19	1	10	431	339	39
5	Widnes	30	18	1	11	382	305	37
6	Warrington	30	17	1	12	428	356	35
7	Bradford N.	30	16	1	13	393	376	33
8	Castleford	30	14	3	13	480	427	31
9	Salford	30	14	1	15	451	351	29
10	Wakefield T.	30	12	5	13	440	419	29
11	Keighley	30	13	0	17	400	424	26
12	Dewsbury	30	11	0	19	350	506	22
13	York	30	10	0	20	359	498	20
14	Bramley	30	9	0	21	338	493	18
15	Rochdale H.	30	8	0	22	219	400	16
16	Halifax	30	5	1	24	269	676	11

1975-76

FIRST DIVISION

		P	W	D	L	F	A	Pts
1	Salford	30	22	1	7	555	350	45
2	Featherstone R.	30	21	2	7	526	348	44
3	Leeds	30	21	0	9	571	395	42
4	St. Helens	30	19	1	10	513	315	39
5	Wigan	30	18	3	9	514	399	39
6	Widnes	30	18	1	11	448	369	37
7	Wakefield T.	30	17	0	13	496	410	34
8	Hull K.R.	30	17	0	13	446	472	34
9	Castleford	30	16	1	13	589	398	33
10	Warrington	30	15	2	13	381	456	32
11	Bradford N.	30	13	1	16	454	450	27
12	Oldham	30	11	1	18	380	490	23
13	Dewsbury	30	10	1	19	287	484	21
14	Keighley	30	7	0	23	274	468	14
15	Huddersfield	30	5	0	25	370	657	10
16	Swinton	30	3	0	27	238	581	6

SECOND DIVISION

		P	W	D	L	F	A	Pts
1	Huddersfield	26	21	0	5	489	213	42
2	Hull K.R.	26	20	1	5	628	249	41
3	Oldham	26	19	0	7	406	223	38
4	Swinton	26	17	1	8	399	254	35
5	Workington T.	26	16	0	10	371	275	32
6	Whitehaven	26	14	1	11	285	234	29
7	Huyton	26	12	2	12	301	291	26
8	Hull	26	12	1	13	344	309	25
9	Barrow	26	11	2	13	338	315	24
10	Leigh	26	11	1	14	302	348	23
11	New Hunslet	26	10	2	14	309	384	22
12	Blackpool B.	26	7	1	18	261	417	15
13	Batley	26	4	1	21	197	520	9
14	Doncaster	26	1	1	24	147	745	3

SECOND DIVISION

		P	W	D	L	F	A	Pts
1	Barrow	26	20	3	3	366	213	43
2	Rochdale H.	26	19	3	4	347	200	41
3	Workington T.	26	18	4	4	519	228	40
4	Leigh	26	19	1	6	571	217	39
5	Hull	26	19	1	6	577	278	39
6	New Hunslet	26	15	1	10	371	308	31
7	York	26	12	1	13	447	394	25
8	Bramley	26	11	1	14	344	370	23
9	Huyton	26	10	0	16	242	373	20
10	Whitehaven	26	8	2	16	253	347	18
11	Halifax	27	7	1	18	322	460	15
12	Batley	26	6	1	19	228	432	13
13	Blackpool B.	26	6	1	19	224	460	13
14	Doncaster	26	2	0	24	195	726	4

1976-77

FIRST DIVISION

		P	W	D	L	F	A	Pts
1	Featherstone R.	30	21	2	7	568	334	44
2	St. Helens	30	19	1	10	547	345	39
3	Castleford	30	19	1	10	519	350	39
4	Hull K.R.	30	18	1	11	496	415	37
5	Warrington	30	18	0	12	532	406	36
6	Salford	*29	17	1	11	560	402	35
7	Wigan	30	15	2	13	463	416	32
8	Bradford N.	30	15	2	13	488	470	32
9	Leeds	•29	14	2	13	467	439	30
10	Widnes	30	15	0	15	403	393	30
11	Wakefield T.	30	13	2	15	487	480	28
12	Workington T.	30	13	1	16	352	403	27
13	Rochdale H.	30	11	0	19	367	449	22
14	Leigh	30	8	1	21	314	634	17
15	Barrow	30	8	0	22	345	628	16
16	Oldham	30	7	0	23	322	666	14

*The Salford v. Leeds match was abandoned after a fatal injury to Chris Sanderson (Leeds) and not replayed. Leeds were winning 5-2 after 38 mins. but the match was declared null and void.

1977-78

FIRST DIVISION

		P	W	D	L	F	A	Pts
1	Widnes	30	24	2	4	613	241	50
2	**Bradford N.	29	21	2	6	500	291	44
3	St. Helens	30	22	1	7	678	384	45
4	Hull K.R.	30	16	3	11	495	419	35
5	Wigan	30	17	1	12	482	435	35
6	Salford	30	16	0	14	470	446	32
7	Featherstone R.	29	15	2	12	443	452	32
8	Leeds	30	15	1	14	512	460	31
9	Warrington	30	15	0	15	561	367	30
10	Castleford	30	13	2	15	515	583	28
11	Workington T.	30	11	4	15	406	519	26
12	Wakefield T.	30	12	1	17	393	450	25
13	Hull	30	10	3	17	358	480	23
14	New Hunslet	30	11	0	19	318	518	22
15	Bramley	30	5	4	21	281	608	14
16	Dewsbury	30	2	2	26	207	579	6

**Bradford N. second on percentage as last game was cancelled following Featherstone's strike.

SECOND DIVISION

		P	W	D	L	F	A	Pts
1	Hull	26	22	1	3	599	238	45
2	Dewsbury	26	19	2	5	429	199	40
3	Bramley	26	19	0	7	464	377	38
4	New Hunslet	26	17	3	6	411	231	37
5	York	26	17	0	9	422	279	34
6	Keighley	26	16	1	9	486	235	33
7	Huddersfield	26	13	0	13	397	329	26
8	Whitehaven	26	11	1	14	290	346	23
9	Huyton	26	11	0	15	302	402	22
10	Halifax	26	10	0	16	301	429	20
11	Swinton	26	8	2	16	261	406	18
12	Batley	26	7	1	18	262	461	15
13	Blackpool B.	26	5	.1	20	233	464	11
14	Doncaster	26	1	0	25	243	704	2

SECOND DIVISION

		P	W	D	L	F	A	Pts
1	Leigh	26	21	0	5	538	231	42
2	Barrow	26	21	0	5	521	234	42
3	Rochdale H.	26	21	0	5	437	200	42
4	Huddersfield	26	18	0	8	502	324	36
5	York	26	16	2	8	447	286	34
6	Oldham	26	17	0	9	419	325	34
7	Keighley	26	11	3	12	357	337	25
8	Swinton	26	11	1	14	369	385	23
9	Whitehaven	26	10	2	14	277	326	22
10	Huyton	26	9	2	15	250	352	20
11	Doncaster	26	9	0	17	304	528	18
12	Batley	26	5	1	20	233	496	11
13	Blackpool B.	26	5	1	20	262	543	11
14	Halifax	26	2	0	24	182	531	4

TABLES

1978-79

FIRST DIVISION

		P	W	D	L	F	A	Pts
1	Hull K.R.	30	23	0	7	616	344	46
2	Warrington	30	22	0	8	521	340	44
3	Widnes	30	21	2	7	480	322	44
4	Leeds	30	19	1	10	555	370	39
5	St. Helens	30	16	2	12	485	379	34
6	Wigan	30	16	1	13	484	411	33
7	Castleford	30	16	1	13	498	469	33
8	Bradford N.	30	16	0	14	523	416	32
9	Workington T.	30	13	3	14	378	345	29
10	Wakefield T.	30	13	1	16	382	456	27
11	Leigh	30	13	1	16	406	535	27
12	Salford	30	11	2	17	389	435	24
13	Barrow	30	9	2	19	368	536	20
14	Featherstone R.	30	8	1	21	501	549	17
15	Rochdale H.	30	8	0	22	297	565	16
16	Huddersfield	30	7	1	22	314	725	15

SECOND DIVISION

		P	W	D	L	F	A	Pts
1	Hull	26	26	0	0	702	175	52
2	New Hunslet	26	21	1	4	454	218	43
3	York	26	17	1	8	426	343	35
4	Blackpool B.	26	15	3	8	321	272	33
5	Halifax	26	15	2	9	312	198	32
6	Dewsbury	26	15	0	11	368	292	30
7	Keighley	26	12	2	12	357	298	26
8	Bramley	26	12	1	13	375	342	25
9	Oldham	26	10	1	15	297	435	21
10	Whitehaven	26	8	3	15	297	408	19
11	Swinton	26	7	2	17	349	452	16
12	Doncaster	26	7	0	19	259	547	14
13	Huyton	26	3	3	20	261	513	9
14	Batley	26	4	1	21	194	479	9

1979-80

FIRST DIVISION

		P	W	D	L	F	A	Pts
1	Bradford N.	30	23	0	7	448	272	46
2	Widnes	30	22	1	7	546	293	45
3	Hull	30	18	3	9	454	326	39
4	Salford	30	19	1	10	495	374	39
5	Leeds	30	19	0	11	590	390	38
6	Leigh	30	16	1	13	451	354	33
7	Hull K.R.	30	16	1	13	539	445	33
8	St. Helens	30	15	2	13	505	410	32
9	Warrington	30	15	2	13	362	357	32
10	Wakefield T.	30	14	2	14	435	466	30
11	Castleford	30	13	2	15	466	475	28
12	Workington T.	30	12	2	16	348	483	26
13	Wigan	30	9	3	18	366	523	21
14	Hunslet	30	7	1	22	346	528	15
15	York	30	6	1	23	375	647	13
16	Blackpool B.	30	5	0	25	230	613	10

SECOND DIVISION

		P	W	D	L	F	A	Pts
1	Featherstone R.	26	21	2	3	724	280	44
2	Halifax	26	19	3	4	463	213	41
3	Oldham	26	19	3	4	513	276	41
4	Barrow	26	18	1	7	582	280	37
5	Whitehaven	26	15	1	10	397	276	31
6	Dewsbury	26	13	2	11	408	343	28
7	Rochdale H.	26	9	5	12	315	373	23
8	Swinton	26	11	1	14	331	436	23
9	Batley	26	10	2	14	232	370	22
10	Bramley	26	10	1	15	330	451	21
11	Keighley	26	10	0	16	342	396	20
12	Huddersfield	26	10	0	16	363	423	20
13	Huyton	26	5	0	21	209	555	10
14	Doncaster	26	1	1	24	196	733	3

1980-81

SLALOM LAGER CHAMPIONSHIP

		P	W	D	L	F	A	Pts
1	Bradford N.	30	20	1	9	447	345	41
2	Warrington	30	19	1	10	459	330	39
3	Hull K.R.	30	18	2	10	509	408	38
4	Wakefield T.	30	18	2	10	544	454	38
5	Castleford	30	18	2	10	526	459	38
6	Widnes	30	16	2	12	428	356	34
7	Hull	30	17	0	13	442	450	34
8	St. Helens	30	15	1	14	465	370	31
9	Leigh	30	14	1	15	416	414	29
10	Leeds	30	14	0	16	388	468	28
11	Barrow	30	13	0	17	405	498	26
12	Featherstone R.	30	12	0	18	467	446	24
13	Halifax	30	11	0	19	385	450	22
14	Salford	30	10	1	19	473	583	21
15	Workington T.	30	9	3	18	335	457	21
16	Oldham	30	7	2	21	362	563	16

1981-82

SLALOM LAGER CHAMPIONSHIP

		P	W	D	L	F	A	Pts
1	Leigh	30	24	1	5	572	343	49
2	Hull	30	23	1	6	611	273	47
3	Widnes	30	23	1	6	551	317	47
4	Hull K.R.	30	22	1	7	565	319	45
5	Bradford N.	30	20	1	9	425	332	41
6	Leeds	30	17	1	12	514	418	35
7	St. Helens	30	17	1	12	465	415	35
8	Warrington	30	14	2	14	403	468	30
9	Barrow	30	13	0	17	408	445	26
10	Featherstone R.	30	12	1	17	482	493	25
11	Wigan	30	12	0	18	424	435	24
12	Castleford	30	10	1	19	486	505	21
13	Fulham	30	9	1	20	365	539	19
14	Wakefield T.	30	9	1	20	341	526	19
15	York	30	4	2	24	330	773	10
16	Whitehaven	30	2	3	25	224	565	7

SECOND DIVISION

		P	W	D	L	F	A	Pts
1	York	28	23	0	5	649	331	46
2	Wigan	28	20	3	5	597	293	43
3	Fulham	28	20	0	8	447	237	40
4	Whitehaven	28	19	1	8	409	250	39
5	Huddersfield	28	18	1	9	429	310	37
6	Swinton	28	17	2	9	440	302	36
7	Keighley	28	14	1	13	445	501	29
8	Hunslet	28	13	1	14	447	430	27
9	Bramley	28	13	1	14	433	431	27
10	Rochdale H.	28	13	0	15	406	418	26
11	Batley	28	12	0	16	328	405	24
12	Dewsbury	28	11	1	16	346	364	23
13	Doncaster	28	5	0	23	250	562	10
14	Blackpool B.	28	4	1	23	212	419	9
15	Huyton	28	2	0	26	211	796	4

SECOND DIVISION

		P	W	D	L	F	A	Pts
1	Oldham	32	30	0	2	734	276	60
2	Carlisle	32	28	0	4	649	296	56
3	Workington T.	32	24	0	8	777	311	48
4	Halifax	32	22	0	10	516	340	44
5	Salford	32	20	1	11	656	433	41
6	Hunslet	32	18	1	13	481	452	37
7	Keighley	32	18	0	14	514	426	36
8	Cardiff C.	32	17	1	14	566	549	35
9	Dewsbury	32	16	0	16	357	464	32
10	Swinton	32	15	0	17	514	418	30
11	Huddersfield	32	13	1	18	370	523	27
12	Bramley	32	13	0	19	381	513	26
13	Rochdale H.	32	10	1	21	361	484	21
14	Batley	32	8	0	24	357	596	16
15	Blackpool B.	32	7	0	25	341	608	14
16	Doncaster	32	5	1	26	319	793	11
17	Huyton	32	5	0	27	296	707	10

1982-83

SLALOM LAGER CHAMPIONSHIP

		P	W	D	L	F	A	Pts
1	Hull	30	23	1	6	572	293	47
2	Hull K.R.	30	21	1	8	496	276	43
3	Wigan	30	20	3	7	482	270	43
4	St. Helens	30	19	1	10	516	395	39
5	Widnes	30	18	2	10	534	357	38
6	Leeds	30	18	2	10	480	443	38
7	Castleford	30	18	1	11	629	458	37
8	Oldham	30	15	2	13	346	320	32
9	Bradford N.	30	14	2	14	381	314	30
10	Leigh	30	13	3	14	488	374	29
11	Warrington	30	13	2	15	423	410	28
12	Featherstone R.	30	10	4	16	350	447	24
13	Barrow	30	11	1	18	472	505	23
14	Workington T.	30	6	2	22	318	696	14
15	Halifax	30	5	1	24	221	651	11
16	Carlisle	30	2	0	28	252	751	4

SECOND DIVISION

		P	W	D	L	F	A	Pts
1	Fulham	32	27	1	4	699	294	55
2	Wakefield T.	32	25	2	5	672	381	52
3	Salford	32	24	0	8	686	363	48
4	Whitehaven	32	20	3	9	464	298	43
5	Bramley	32	20	1	11	560	369	41
6	Hunslet	32	17	5	10	553	448	39
7	Swinton	32	19	1	12	549	454	39
8	Cardiff C.	32	17	2	13	572	444	36
9	Keighley	32	15	5	12	470	423	35
10	York	32	15	0	17	516	455	30
11	Blackpool B.	32	13	1	18	381	433	27
12	Huddersfield	32	13	1	18	397	524	27
13	Rochdale H.	32	10	5	17	361	469	25
14	Dewsbury	32	8	1	23	325	507	17
15	Batley	32	6	1	25	305	719	13
16	Huyton	32	6	0	26	250	687	12
17	Doncaster	32	2	1	29	307	799	5

1983-84

SLALOM LAGER CHAMPIONSHIP

		P	W	D	L	F	A	Pts
1	Hull K.R.	30	22	2	6	795	421	46
2	Hull	30	22	1	7	831	401	45
3	Warrington	30	19	2	9	622	528	40
4	Castleford	30	18	3	9	686	438	39
5	Widnes	30	19	1	10	656	457	39
6	St. Helens	30	18	1	11	649	507	37
7	Bradford N.	30	17	2	11	519	379	36
8	Leeds	30	15	3	12	553	514	33
9	Wigan	30	16	0	14	533	465	32
10	Oldham	30	15	2	13	544	480	32
11	Leigh	30	14	0	16	623	599	28
12	Featherstone R.	30	11	2	17	464	562	24
13	Fulham	30	9	1	20	401	694	19
14	Wakefield T.	30	7	0	23	415	780	14
15	Salford	30	5	0	25	352	787	10
16	Whitehaven	30	3	0	27	325	956	6

SECOND DIVISION

		P	W	D	L	F	A	Pts
1	Barrow	34	32	0	2	1126	332	64
2	Workington T.	34	24	2	8	714	504	50
3	Hunslet	34	24	0	10	900	597	48
4	Halifax	34	23	2	9	722	539	48
5	Blackpool B.	34	20	3	11	615	466	43
6	Swinton	34	21	0	13	764	437	42
7	York	34	19	2	13	743	570	40
8	Bramley	34	16	2	16	584	545	34
9	Kent Invicta	34	17	0	17	595	700	34
10	Huddersfield	34	15	3	16	600	545	33
11	Cardiff C.	34	15	1	18	710	717	31
12	Rochdale H.	34	13	3	18	551	667	29
13	Batley	34	13	0	21	477	738	26
14	Dewsbury	34	12	0	22	526	698	24
15	Carlisle	34	12	0	22	539	780	24
16	Huyton	34	9	2	23	431	760	20
17	Keighley	34	7	3	24	425	728	17
18	Doncaster	34	2	1	31	384	1083	5

1984-85

SLALOM LAGER CHAMPIONSHIP

		P	W	D	L	F	A	Pts
1	Hull K.R.	30	24	0	6	778	391	48
2	St. Helens	30	22	1	7	920	508	45
3	Wigan	30	21	1	8	720	459	43
4	Leeds	30	20	1	9	650	377	41
5	Oldham	30	18	1	11	563	439	37
6	Hull	30	17	1	12	733	550	35
7	Widnes	30	17	0	13	580	517	34
8	Bradford N.	30	16	1	13	600	500	33
9	Featherstone R.	30	15	0	15	461	475	30
10	Halifax	30	12	2	16	513	565	26
11	Warrington	30	13	0	17	530	620	26
12	Castleford	30	12	1	17	552	518	25
13	Barrow	30	9	1	20	483	843	19
14	Leigh	30	8	2	20	549	743	18
15	Hunslet	30	7	1	22	463	952	15
16	Workington T.	30	2	1	27	297	935	5

1985-86

SLALOM LAGER CHAMPIONSHIP

		P	W	D	L	F	A	Pts
1	Halifax	30	19	6	5	499	365	44
2	Wigan	30	20	3	7	776	300	43
3	St. Helens	30	20	2	8	729	503	42
4	Warrington	30	20	1	9	665	393	41
5	Widnes	30	19	3	8	520	454	41
6	Leeds	30	15	3	12	554	518	33
7	Hull K.R.	30	16	1	13	507	500	33
8	Hull	30	15	2	13	616	508	32
9	Oldham	30	13	4	13	524	549	30
10	Salford	30	14	0	16	508	561	28
11	Castleford	30	12	1	17	551	585	25
12	Bradford N.	30	11	1	18	447	473	23
13	Featherstone R.	30	9	3	18	419	616	21
14	York	30	9	0	21	413	592	18
15	Swinton	30	8	0	22	371	648	16
16	Dewsbury	30	5	0	25	313	847	10

SECOND DIVISION

		P	W	D	L	F	A	Pts
1	Swinton	28	24	1	3	727	343	49
2	Salford	28	20	3	5	787	333	43
3	York	28	21	1	6	717	430	43
4	Dewsbury	28	21	1	6	539	320	43
5	Carlisle	28	19	0	9	547	437	38
6	Whitehaven	28	16	3	9	496	385	35
7	Batley	28	17	0	11	489	402	34
8	Fulham	28	16	1	11	521	526	33
9	Mansfield M.	28	15	0	13	525	398	30
10	Blackpool B.	28	15	0	13	486	434	30
11	Wakefield T.	28	12	2	14	450	459	26
12	Rochdale H.	28	12	2	14	436	466	26
13	Huddersfield B.	28	12	1	15	476	476	25
14	Runcorn H.	28	11	1	16	462	538	23
15	Keighley	28	11	0	17	495	567	22
16	Bramley	28	9	2	17	439	492	20
17	Sheffield E.	28	8	0	20	424	582	16
18	Doncaster	28	6	2	20	353	730	14
19	Southend I.	28	4	0	24	347	690	8
20	Bridgend	28	1	0	27	258	966	2

SECOND DIVISION

		P	W	D	L	F	A	Pts
1	Leigh	34	33	0	1	1156	373	66
2	Barrow	34	27	0	7	1012	398	54
3	Wakefield T.	34	24	1	9	680	435	49
4	Whitehaven	34	22	0	12	619	479	44
5	Rochdale H.	34	21	0	13	763	485	42
6	Blackpool B.	34	20	0	14	769	570	40
7	Batley	34	18	3	13	567	450	39
8	Bramley	34	17	1	16	608	663	35
9	Fulham	34	16	1	17	679	709	33
10	Doncaster	34	16	1	17	611	650	33
11	Carlisle	34	15	2	17	585	682	32
12	Sheffield E.	34	14	1	19	516	617	29
13	Workington T.	34	13	0	21	684	723	26
14	Hunslet	34	11	3	20	594	795	25
15	Huddersfield B.	34	8	4	22	542	841	20
16	Runcorn H.	34	9	2	23	489	790	20
17	Keighley	34	9	2	23	401	918	20
18	Mansfield	34	2	1	31	383	1080	5

● The increase of the Second Division to 20 clubs resulted in a complicated fixture formula to arrive at a manageable 28 matches each.

TABLES

STONES BITTER CHAMPIONSHIP

		P	W	D	L	F	A	Pts
1	Wigan	30	28	0	2	941	193	56
2	St. Helens	30	20	1	9	835	465	41
3	Warrington	30	20	1	9	728	464	41
4	Castleford	30	20	0	10	631	429	40
5	Halifax	30	17	1	12	553	487	35
6	Hull K.R.	30	16	0	14	446	531	32
7	Bradford N.	30	15	1	14	555	550	31
8	Widnes	30	14	0	16	598	613	28
9	Salford	30	14	0	16	509	656	28
10	Leigh	30	13	1	16	549	610	27
11	Hull	30	13	1	16	538	650	27
12	Leeds	30	13	0	17	565	571	26
13	Oldham	30	13	0	17	554	679	26
14	Featherstone R.	30	8	1	21	498	776	17
15	Barrow	30	7	2	21	456	725	16
16	Wakefield T.	30	4	1	25	386	943	9

● A two-up, four-down promotion and relegation formula introduced for this one season to pave the way for a new 14-club Stones Bitter Championship in 1987-88.

STONES BITTER CHAMPIONSHIP

		P	W	D	L	F	A	Pts
1	Widnes	26	20	0	6	641	311	40
2	St. Helens	26	18	0	8	672	337	36
3	Wigan	26	17	2	7	621	327	36
4	Bradford N.	26	18	0	8	528	304	36
5	Leeds	26	15	3	8	577	450	33
6	Warrington	26	14	2	10	531	416	30
7	Castleford	26	13	0	13	505	559	26
8	Halifax	26	12	0	14	499	437	24
9	Hull K.R.	26	11	1	14	420	480	23
10	Hull	26	11	0	15	364	595	22
11	Salford	26	10	0	16	368	561	20
12	Leigh	26	9	0	17	416	559	18
13	Swinton	26	4	2	20	390	780	10
14	Hunslet	26	4	2	20	363	779	10

SECOND DIVISION

		P	W	D	L	F	A	Pts
1	Hunslet	28	25	0	3	722	218	50
2	Swinton	28	23	1	4	713	323	47
3	Whitehaven	28	21	1	6	577	304	43
4	Doncaster	28	20	1	7	586	388	41
5	Rochdale H.	28	19	1	8	519	369	39
6	Sheffield E.	28	17	0	11	625	426	34
7	Bramley	28	16	0	12	407	440	32
8	Carlisle	28	15	1	12	463	446	31
9	Blackpool B.	28	14	0	14	530	477	28
10	York	28	11	0	17	492	537	22
11	Runcorn H.	28	10	1	17	391	533	21
12	Fulham	28	8	2	18	461	632	18
13	Batley	28	9	0	19	335	528	18
14	Workington T.	28	9	0	19	405	652	18
15	Huddersfield B.	28	8	0	20	456	673	16
16	Mansfield M.	28	8	0	20	366	592	16
17	Dewsbury	28	8	0	20	328	563	16
18	Keighley	29	7	0	21	366	641	14

● A new complicated fixture formula intoduced, which continued until three divisions came in 1991-92

SECOND DIVISION

		P	W	D	L	F	A	Pts
1	Oldham	28	23	1	4	771	335	47
2	Featherstone R.	28	21	2	5	712	353	44
3	Wakefield T.	28	20	1	7	666	315	41
4	Springfield B.	28	18	0	10	448	356	36
5	Sheffield E.	28	16	1	11	490	429	33
6	York	28	15	1	12	558	526	31
7	Mansfield M.	28	15	1	12	439	412	31
8	Keighley	28	15	0	13	497	428	30
9	Barrow	28	14	2	12	382	397	30
10	Workington T.	28	15	0	13	380	441	30
11	Carlisle	28	14	1	13	388	444	29
12	Runcorn H.	28	14	0	14	420	469	28
13	Whitehaven	28	10	1	17	417	452	21
14	Bramley	28	10	1	17	400	600	21
15	Dewsbury	28	10	0	18	417	519	20
16	Doncaster	28	9	2	17	406	512	20
17	Fulham	28	10	0	18	382	559	20
18	Rochdale H.	28	10	0	18	322	514	20
19	Huddersfield B.	28	7	1	20	383	597	15
20	Batley	28	6	1	21	305	523	13

1988-89

STONES BITTER CHAMPIONSHIP

		P	W	D	L	F	A	Pts
1	Widnes	26	20	1	5	726	345	41
2	Wigan	26	19	0	7	543	434	38
3	Leeds	26	18	0	8	530	380	36
4	Hull	26	17	0	9	427	355	34
5	Castleford	26	15	2	9	601	480	32
6	Featherstone R.	26	13	1	12	482	545	27
7	St. Helens	26	12	1	13	513	529	25
8	Bradford N.	26	11	1	14	545	518	23
9	Wakefield T.	26	11	1	14	413	540	23
10	Salford	26	11	0	15	469	526	22
11	Warrington	26	10	0	16	456	455	20
12	Oldham	26	8	1	17	462	632	17
13	Halifax	26	6	1	19	335	535	13
14	Hull K.R.	26	6	1	19	408	636	13

1989-90

STONES BITTER CHAMPIONSHIP

		P	W	D	L	F	A	Pts
1	Wigan	26	20	0	6	699	349	40
2	Leeds	26	18	0	8	704	383	36
3	Widnes	26	16	2	8	659	423	34
4	Bradford N.	26	17	0	9	614	416	34
5	St. Helens	26	17	0	9	714	544	34
6	Hull	26	16	1	9	577	400	33
7	Castleford	26	16	0	10	703	448	32
8	Warrington	26	13	1	12	424	451	27
9	Wakefield T.	26	12	1	13	502	528	25
10	Featherstone R.	26	10	0	16	479	652	20
11	Sheffield E.	26	9	1	16	517	588	19
12	Leigh	26	9	1	16	442	642	19
13	Salford	26	4	1	21	421	699	9
14	Barrow	26	1	0	25	201	1133	2

SECOND DIVISION

		P	W	D	L	F	A	Pts
1	Leigh	28	26	0	2	925	338	52
2	Barrow	28	21	1	6	726	326	43
3	Sheffield E.	28	19	1	8	669	362	39
4	York	28	17	1	10	585	383	35
5	Swinton	28	16	2	10	621	482	34
6	Doncaster	28	17	0	11	599	464	34
7	Whitehaven	28	15	2	11	522	378	32
8	Keighley	28	16	0	12	551	525	32
9	Rochdale H.	28	15	0	13	655	677	30
10	Bramley	28	14	1	13	600	514	29
11	Carlisle	28	14	1	13	512	441	29
12	Batley	28	13	3	12	461	416	29
13	Dewsbury	28	13	0	15	518	626	26
14	Hunslet	28	12	1	15	473	540	25
15	Fulham	28	10	0	18	464	650	20
16	Chorley B.	28	9	1	18	408	533	19
17	Workington T.	28	9	1	18	365	549	19
18	Huddersfield	28	9	1	18	400	615	19
19	Mansfield M.	28	4	1	23	308	769	9
20	Runcorn H.	28	2	1	25	224	998	5

SECOND DIVISION

		P	W	D	L	F	A	Pts
1	Hull K.R.	28	25	0	3	1102	190	50
2	Rochdale H.	28	24	0	4	977	422	48
3	Oldham	28	24	0	4	879	325	48
4	Ryedale-York	28	20	1	7	653	338	41
5	Halifax	28	20	0	8	741	360	40
6	Swinton	28	20	0	8	673	405	40
7	Dewsbury	28	19	1	8	503	411	39
8	Fulham	28	16	2	10	496	488	34
9	Doncaster	28	15	2	11	533	399	32
10	Trafford B.	28	15	0	13	551	551	30
11	Huddersfield	28	14	0	14	469	441	28
12	Batley	28	13	0	15	466	478	26
13	Bramley	28	11	0	17	413	623	22
14	Hunslet	28	10	0	18	431	585	20
15	Chorley	28	10	0	18	399	618	20
16	Whitehaven	28	10	0	18	396	710	20
17	Carlisle	28	9	0	19	511	625	18
18	Workington T.	28	6	0	22	311	708	12
19	Keighley	28	6	0	22	436	837	12
20	Nottingham C.	28	4	0	24	323	1032	8
21	Runcorn H.	28	0	0	28	218	935	0

1990-91

STONES BITTER CHAMPIONSHIP

		P	W	D	L	F	A	Pts
1	Wigan	26	20	2	4	652	313	42
2	Widnes	26	20	0	6	635	340	40
3	Hull	26	17	0	9	513	367	34
4	Castleford	26	17	0	9	578	442	34
5	Leeds	26	14	2	10	602	448	30
6	St. Helens	26	14	1	11	628	533	29
7	Bradford N.	26	13	1	12	434	492	27
8	Featherstone R.	26	12	1	13	533	592	25
9	Warrington	26	10	2	14	404	436	22
10	Wakefield T.	26	10	2	14	356	409	22
11	Hull K.R.	26	9	3	14	452	615	21
12	Oldham	26	10	0	16	481	562	20
13	Sheffield E.	26	7	2	17	459	583	16
14	Rochdale H.	26	1	0	25	317	912	2

SECOND DIVISION

		P	W	D	L	F	A	Pts
1	Salford	28	26	1	1	856	219	53
2	Halifax	28	24	0	4	941	311	48
3	Swinton	28	21	2	5	523	370	44
4	Ryedale-York	28	20	2	6	559	294	42
5	Leigh	28	18	1	9	698	372	37
6	Workington T.	28	18	1	9	497	323	37
7	Fulham	28	17	2	9	450	338	36
8	Carlisle	28	16	2	10	613	425	34
9	Doncaster	28	16	0	12	507	434	32
10	Hunslet	28	13	2	13	519	438	28
11	Huddersfield	28	13	1	14	493	477	27
12	Whitehaven	28	13	0	15	412	592	26
13	Keighley	28	12	0	16	456	588	24
14	Dewsbury	28	10	1	17	410	455	21
15	Trafford B.	28	10	0	18	508	618	20
16	Batley	28	10	0	18	337	466	20
17	Barrow	28	8	2	18	415	705	18
18	Chorley	28	7	1	20	388	721	15
19	Bramley	28	7	1	20	379	726	15
20	Runcorn	28	3	1	24	351	779	7
21	Nottingham C.	28	2	0	26	284	945	4

1991-92

STONES BITTER CHAMPIONSHIP

		P	W	D	L	F	A	Pts
1	Wigan	26	22	0	4	645	307	44
2	St. Helens	26	17	2	7	550	388	36
3	Castleford	26	15	2	9	558	365	32
4	Warrington	26	15	0	11	507	431	30
5	Leeds	26	14	1	11	515	408	29
6	Wakefield T.	26	13	1	12	400	435	27
7	Halifax	26	12	0	14	618	566	24
8	Widnes	26	12	0	14	511	477	24
9	Hull K.R.	26	12	0	14	379	466	24
10	Salford	26	11	0	15	480	507	22
11	Bradford N.	26	11	0	15	476	513	22
12	Hull	26	11	0	15	468	526	22
13	Featherstone R.	26	11	0	15	449	570	22
14	Swinton	26	3	0	23	254	853	6

SECOND DIVISION

		P	W	D	L	F	A	Pts
1	Sheffield	28	21	1	6	816	396	43
2	Leigh	28	21	0	7	617	401	42
3	Oldham	28	18	2	8	558	421	38
4	London C.	28	14	0	14	428	483	28
5	Rochdale H.	28	12	2	14	619	489	26
6	Carlisle	28	12	1	15	490	466	25
7	Ryedale-York	28	5	2	21	338	749	12
8	Workington T.	28	4	2	22	310	771	10

● Clubs played each other four times, two home and two away.

THIRD DIVISION

		P	W	D	L	F	A	Pts
1	Huddersfield	26	23	0	3	869	257	46
2	Bramley	26	21	0	5	675	258	42
3	Dewsbury	26	19	1	6	794	279	39
4	Batley	26	18	2	6	641	279	38
5	Barrow	26	17	1	8	663	355	35
6	Doncaster	26	15	2	9	567	362	32
7	Keighley C.	26	15	2	9	587	420	32
8	Hunslet	26	16	0	10	654	553	32
9	Scarborough P.	26	10	0	16	483	499	20
10	Whitehaven	26	9	0	17	510	595	18
11	Highfield	26	9	0	17	406	646	18
12	Chorley B.	26	4	0	22	290	842	8
13	Trafford B.	26	2	0	24	306	941	4
14	Nottingham	26	0	0	26	164	1323	0

1992-93

STONES BITTER CHAMPIONSHIP

		P	W	D	L	F	A	Pts
1	Wigan	26	20	1	5	744	327	41
2	St. Helens	26	20	1	5	632	345	41
3	Bradford N.	26	15	0	11	553	434	30
4	Widnes	26	15	0	11	549	446	30
5	Leeds	26	14	2	10	595	522	30
6	Castleford	26	14	1	11	544	401	29
7	Halifax	26	13	0	13	557	505	26
8	Warrington	26	12	1	13	487	450	25
9	Hull	26	10	1	15	381	535	21
10	Sheffield E.	26	10	1	15	405	627	21
11	Leigh	26	9	2	15	410	630	20
12	Wakefield T.	26	8	2	16	405	535	18
13	Salford	26	9	0	17	498	725	18
14	Hull K.R.	26	7	0	19	321	599	14

SECOND DIVISION

		P	W	D	L	F	A	Pts
1	Featherstone R.	28	24	1	3	996	352	49
2	Oldham	28	20	1	7	753	503	41
3	Huddersfield	28	15	0	13	565	548	30
4	Rochdale H.	28	14	0	14	622	607	28
5	London C.	28	12	2	14	534	562	26
6	Swinton	28	10	0	18	409	636	20
7	Carlisle	28	6	3	19	454	721	15
8	Bramley	28	7	1	20	328	732	15

● Clubs played each other four times, two home and two away.

THIRD DIVISION

		P	W	D	L	F	A	Pts
1	Keighley C.	24	21	0	3	917	288	42
2	Workington T.	24	19	0	5	835	237	38
3	Dewsbury	24	18	0	6	718	291	36
4	Ryedale-York	24	17	0	7	747	335	34
5	Whitehaven	24	16	0	8	696	328	32
6	Batley	24	16	0	8	508	268	32
7	Doncaster	24	14	0	10	564	469	28
8	Hunslet	24	14	0	10	554	498	28
9	Highfield	24	6	0	18	310	915	12
10	Barrow	24	5	0	19	476	625	10
11	Chorley B.	24	5	0	19	317	781	10
12	Blackpool G.	24	4	0	20	302	958	8
13	Nottingham C.	24	1	0	23	181	1132	2

1993-94

STONES BITTER CHAMPIONSHIP

		P	W	D	L	F	A	Pts
1	Wigan	30	23	0	7	780	403	46
2	Bradford N.	30	23	0	7	784	555	46
3	Warrington	30	23	0	7	628	430	46
4	Castleford	30	19	1	10	787	466	39
5	Halifax	30	17	2	11	682	581	36
6	Sheffield E.	30	16	2	12	704	671	34
7	Leeds	30	15	2	13	673	680	32
8	St. Helens	30	15	1	14	704	537	31
9	Hull	30	14	2	14	536	530	30
10	Widnes	30	14	0	16	523	642	28
11	Featherstone R.	30	13	1	16	651	681	27
12	Salford	30	11	0	19	554	650	22
13	Oldham	30	10	1	19	552	651	21
14	Wakefield T.	30	9	1	20	458	708	19
15	Hull K.R.	30	9	0	21	493	782	18
16	Leigh	30	2	1	27	370	912	5

SECOND DIVISION

		P	W	D	L	F	A	Pts
1	Workington T.	30	22	2	6	760	331	46
2	Doncaster	30	22	1	7	729	486	45
3	London C.	30	21	2	7	842	522	44
4	Batley	30	21	1	8	707	426	43
5	Huddersfield	30	20	0	10	661	518	40
6	Keighley C.	30	19	1	10	856	472	39
7	Dewsbury	30	18	1	11	766	448	37
8	Rochdale H.	30	18	0	12	704	532	36
9	Ryedale-York	30	17	1	12	662	516	35
10	Whitehaven	30	14	4	12	571	437	32
11	Barrow	30	13	1	16	581	743	27
12	Swinton	30	11	0	19	528	681	22
13	Carlisle	30	9	0	21	540	878	18
14	Hunslet	30	3	1	26	445	814	7
15	Bramley	30	3	0	27	376	957	6
16	Highfield	30	1	1	28	267	1,234	3

1994-95

STONES BITTER CHAMPIONSHIP

		P	W	D	L	F	A	Pts
1	Wigan	30	28	0	2	1148	386	56
2	Leeds	30	24	1	5	863	526	49
3	Castleford	30	20	2	8	872	564	42
4	St. Helens	30	20	1	9	893	640	41
5	Halifax	30	18	2	10	782	566	38
6	Warrington	30	18	2	10	753	570	38
7	Bradford N.	30	17	1	12	811	650	35
8	Sheffield E.	30	15	0	15	646	699	30
9	Workington T.	30	12	1	17	538	743	25
10	Oldham	30	11	1	18	534	746	23
11	Featherstone R.	30	10	1	19	582	687	21
12	Salford	30	10	1	19	613	775	21
13	Wakefield T.	30	9	0	21	434	807	18
14	Widnes	30	8	1	21	481	767	17
15	Hull	30	7	1	22	594	880	15
16	Doncaster	30	5	1	24	469	1007	11

SECOND DIVISION

		P	W	D	L	F	A	Pts
1	Keighley C.	30	23	2	5	974	337	48
2	Batley	30	23	0	7	754	423	46
3	Huddersfield	30	19	3	8	870	539	41
4	London B.	30	20	1	9	732	480	41
5	Whitehaven	30	19	0	11	766	507	38
6	Rochdale H.	30	18	0	12	805	544	36
7	Dewsbury	30	17	1	12	744	538	35
8	Hull K.R.	30	16	1	13	824	516	33
9	Ryedale-York	30	15	2	13	720	602	32
10	Hunslet	30	16	0	14	611	783	32
11	Leigh	30	12	0	18	622	787	24
12	Swinton	30	12	0	18	576	768	24
13	Bramley	30	10	0	20	554	655	20
14	Carlisle	30	8	0	22	546	877	16
15	Barrow	30	6	0	24	449	811	12
16	Highfield	30	1	0	29	224	1604	2

International coaching debutants Ellery Hanley (right) and assistant Gary Hetherington, in charge of Great Britain for the 1994 John Smith's Tests against Australia, and of England for the 1995 John Smith's European Championship.

COACHES

COACHES

INDEX OF COACHES

The following is an index of the 275 coaches who have held first team coaching posts since the start of the 1974-75 season to 1 June 1995.

It includes the alphabetical listing of British clubs they coached in the period.

Seven new coaches were added to the list during the past 12 months when 14 clubs made at least one change.

Although some clubs appoint team managers with a coach as his assistant, the list refers only to the man generally recognised as being in overall charge of team affairs.

A caretaker coach, who stands in while the club is seeking a permanent appointment, is only listed if he takes charge for more than a few matches.

For a list of each club's appointments since 1974 see CLUBS section.

Ray Abbey (Dewsbury)
Jack Addy (Dewsbury, Huddersfield B.)
Allan Agar (Bramley, Carlisle, Featherstone R., Rochdale H.)
Gary Ainsworth (Trafford B.)
Dave Alred (Bridgend)
Chris Anderson (Halifax)
Harry Archer (Workington T.)
Chris Arkwright (Highfield)
Kevin Ashcroft (Leigh, Salford, Warrington)
Eric Ashton (St. Helens)
Ray Ashton (Bramley, Workington T.)
Bill Ashurst (Runcorn H., Wakefield T.)
Mal Aspey (Salford)
John Atkinson (Carlisle)
Jack Austin (Hunslet)

Trevor Bailey (Scarborough P., Wakefield T.)
Maurice Bamford (Bramley, Dewsbury, Halifax, Huddersfield, Leeds, Wigan, Workington T.)
Frank Barrow (Oldham, Swinton)
Tony Barrow (Oldham, Swinton, Warrington)
Ray Batten (Wakefield T.)
Jeff Bawden (Whitehaven)
Mel Bedford (Huddersfield)
Cameron Bell (Carlisle)
Billy Benyon (Leigh, St. Helens, Warrington)
Les Bettinson (Salford)
Charlie Birdsall (Rochdale H.)
Alan Bishop (Runcorn H.)

Tommy Bishop (Barrow, Leigh, Workington T.)
Mick Blacker (Halifax, Huddersfield, Mansfield M.)
Tommy Blakeley (Blackpool B.)
Dick Bonser (Rochdale H.)
Reg Bowden (Fulham, Warrington)
Carl Briscoe (Chorley B.)
Drew Broatch (Hunslet)
Ian Brooke (Bradford N., Doncaster, Huddersfield, Wakefield T.)
Arthur Bunting (Hull, Hull K.R.)
Mark Burgess (Nottingham C.)
Dave Busfield (Dewsbury)

Len Casey (Hull, Scarborough P., Wakefield T.)
Jim Challinor (Oldham)
Paul Charlton (Carlisle, Workington T.)
Eddie Cheetham (Leigh)
Dave Chisnall (Runcorn H.)
Colin Clarke (Leigh, Wigan)
Terry Clawson (Featherstone R.)
Noel Cleal (Hull)
Malcolm Clift (Leeds)
Joe Coan (Wigan)
John Cogger (Runcorn H.)
Gary Cooper (York)
Kel Coslett (Rochdale H., St. Helens, Wigan)
Gordon Cottier (Whitehaven)
Keith Cotton (Featherstone R.)
Mike Coulman (Salford)
Les Coulter (Keighley)
Dave Cox (Batley, Castleford, Dewsbury, Huyton, Oldham, Workington T.)
Jim Crellin (Blackpool B., Halifax, Leigh, Mansfield M., Rochdale H., Swinton)
Terry Crook (Batley, Dewsbury)
Steve Crooks (Hull K.R., Ryedale-York)

Arthur Daley (Runcorn H.)
Paul Daley (Batley, Featherstone R., Hunslet, York)
Jackie Davidson (Whitehaven, Workington T.)
Keith Davies (Workington T.)
Tommy Dawes (Barrow, Carlisle, Whitehaven)
Harry Dawson (Widnes)
Tony Dean (Hull, Wakefield T.)
Henry Delooze (Rochdale H.)
Steve Dennison (Mansfield M.)
Robin Dewhurst (Leeds)
Bakary Diabira (Blackpool B., Keighley)
Tommy Dickens (Blackpool B., Leigh)
Roy Dickinson (Bramley)
Colin Dixon (Halifax, Keighley, Salford)
Mal Dixon (York)

John Dorahy (Halifax, Wigan)
David Doyle-Davidson (Hull, York)
Ray Dutton (Whitehaven)

Graham Eadie (Halifax)
Bob Eccles (Blackpool G., Chorley)
Derek Edwards (Doncaster)
Joe Egan Jnr. (Blackpool B.)

George Fairbairn (Huddersfield, Hull K.R., Wigan)
Vince Farrar (Featherstone R.)
Albert Fearnley (Batley, Blackpool B., Keighley)
Steve Ferres (Hunslet)
John Fieldhouse (Oldham)
Tony Fisher (Bramley, Dewsbury, Doncaster,
    Keighley)
Eric Fitzsimons (Oldham, Rochdale H.,
    Whitehaven)
Bob Fleet (Swinton)
Geoff Fletcher (Huyton, Runcorn H.)
Terry Fogerty (Rochdale H.)
Chris Forster (Bramley, Huddersfield B.)
Derek Foster (Ryedale-York)
Frank Foster (Barrow, Whitehaven)
Kenny Foulkes (Hull)
Don Fox (Batley)
Harry Fox (Halifax)
Neil Fox (Huddersfield)
Peter Fox (Bradford N., Bramley, Featherstone R.,
    Leeds, Wakefield T.)
Bill Francis (Oldham)
Roy Francis (Bradford N., Leeds)

Paul Gamble (Blackpool G.)
Bill Gardner (Sheffield E.)
Brian Gartland (Oldham)
Steve Gibson (Rochdale H.)
Stan Gittins (Blackpool B., Chorley, Rochdale H.,
    Springfield B.)
Andy Goodway (Oldham)
Bill Goodwin (Fulham, Kent Invicta)
Tony Gordon (Hull, London C.)
Terry Gorman (Huyton, Swinton)
Keith Goulding (Featherstone R., Huddersfield,
    York)
Mal Graham (Oldham)
Tom Grainey (Leigh, Swinton)
Jeff Grayshon (Batley, Dewsbury)
Lee Greenwood (Keighley, Mansfield M./
    Nottingham C.)
Andy Gregory (Salford)
Gary Grienke (London B.)
Geoff Gunney (Wakefield T.)

John Joyner, appointed coach of Castleford in May 1993.

Bob Haigh (Wakefield T.)
Derek Hallas (Halifax)
Ken Halliwell (Swinton)
Alan Hardisty (Dewsbury, Halifax, York)
Paul Harkin (Wakefield T.)
Arnold Hema (Nottingham C.)
Graham Heptinstall (Doncaster)
Alan Hepworth (Batley)
Keith Hepworth (Bramley, Hull)
Gary Hetherington (Sheffield E.)
Ron Hill (Dewsbury)
David Hobbs (Bradford N., Wakefield T.)
Neil Holding (Rochdale H.)
Bill Holliday (Swinton)
Stewart Horton (Ryedale-York)
Eric Hughes (Rochdale H., St. Helens, Widnes)
Syd Hynes (Leeds)

Bob Irving (Blackpool B.)
Keith Irving (Workington T.)

Garry Jack (Salford)
Dennis Jackson (Barrow)
Francis Jarvis (Huddersfield)
Peter Jarvis (Bramley, Hunslet)
Graeme Jennings (Hunslet)
Barry Johnson (Bramley)
Brian Johnson (Warrington)
Willie Johnson (Highfield)
Allen Jones (Huddersfield B.)
Lewis Jones (Dewsbury)
John Joyner (Castleford)

Vince Karalius (Widnes, Wigan)
Paul Kavanagh (Barrow)
John Kear (Bramley)
Arthur Keegan (Bramley)
Ivor Kelland (Barrow)
Alan Kellett (Carlisle, Halifax, Keighley)
Andy Kelly (Wakefield T.)
Bill Kenny (Doncaster)
Bill Kindon (Leigh)
Bill Kirkbride (Mansfield M., Rochdale H.,
    Wakefield T., York)
Phil Kitchin (Whitehaven, Workington T.)

Dave Lamming (Wakefield T.)
Steve Lane (Kent Invicta)
Phil Larder (Keighley C., Widnes)
Doug Laughton (Leeds, Widnes)
Roy Lester (Carlisle, Fulham)
Bob Lindner (Oldham)
Alan Lockwood (Dewsbury)
Brian Lockwood (Batley, Huddersfield,
    Wakefield T.)
Paul Longstaff (Rochdale H.)
Graham Lowe (Wigan)
Phil Lowe (York)
Trevor Lowe (Batley, Doncaster)
Ken Loxton (Bramley)
Ian Lucas (Leigh)
Geoff Lyon (Blackpool B.)

Mike McClennan (St. Helens)
Stan McCormick (Salford)
John McFarlane (Whitehaven)
Alan McInnes (Salford, Wigan)
John Mantle (Blackpool B., Cardiff C., Leigh)
Steve Martin (Featherstone R.)
Jack Melling (Blackpool G.)
Roger Millward (Halifax, Hull K.R.,
    Ryedale-York)
John Monie (Wigan)
Mick Morgan (Carlisle)
Geoff Morris (Doncaster)
David Mortimer (Huddersfield)
Alex Murphy (Huddersfield, Leigh, St. Helens,
    Salford, Warrington, Wigan)
Frank Myler (Oldham, Rochdale H., Swinton,
    Widnes)
Tony Myler (Widnes)

Steve Nash (Mansfield M.)
Steve Norton (Barrow)

Former Great Britain and Wigan prop Ian Lucas, who took over as coach of Leigh in December 1994.

Chris O'Sullivan (Swinton)

Les Pearce (Bramley, Halifax)
Mike Peers (Blackpool G., Chorley B./Trafford B.,
    Highfield, Swinton)
Geoff Peggs (Keighley)
George Pieniazek (Batley, Featherstone R.)
Billy Platt (Mansfield M.)
Harry Poole (Hull K.R.)

Denis Ramsdale (Barrow, Leigh)
Bill Ramsey (Hunslet)
Terry Ramshaw (Oldham)
Keith Rayne (Batley)
Rod Reddy (Barrow)
Graham Rees (Blackpool B.)
Peter Regan (Rochdale H.)
Malcolm Reilly (Castleford, Halifax, Leeds)
Alan Rhodes (Doncaster, Sheffield E.)
Austin Rhodes (Swinton)
Bev Risman (Fulham)
Ken Roberts (Halifax)
Don Robinson (Bramley)
Don Robson (Doncaster)
Peter Roe (Barrow, Halifax, Keighley)
Sol Roper (Workington T.)

Cougarised . . . Phil Larder left Widnes to join Second Division Keighley Cougars in May 1994.

Roy Sabine (Keighley)
Dave Sampson (Castleford, Doncaster,
    Nottingham C.)
Barry Seabourne (Bradford N., Huddersfield,
    Keighley)
Les Sheard (Huddersfield)
Danny Sheehan (York)
John Sheridan (Doncaster)
Royce Simmons (Hull)
Steve Simms (Halifax, Leigh)
Tommy Smales [*Scrum half*] (Featherstone R.)
Tommy Smales [*Forward*] (Batley, Bramley,
    Dewsbury, Doncaster, Featherstone R.)
Peter Smethurst (Leigh, Oldham)
Barry Smith (Whitehaven)
Bill Smith (Whitehaven, Workington T.)
Brian Smith (Huddersfield)
Brian Smith [*Australian*] (Hull)
Norman Smith (Dewsbury)
Kurt Sorensen (Whitehaven)
Ike Southward (Whitehaven, Workington T.)
Graham Starkey (Oldham, Rochdale H.)
Gary Stephens (York)
Nigel Stephenson (Huddersfield, Hunslet)
Dave Stockwell (Batley, Bramley)
John Stopford (Swinton)
Ted Strawbridge (Doncaster)
Ross Strudwick (Fulham/London C., Halifax)
Clive Sullivan (Doncaster, Hull)
Phil Sullivan (Fulham)

Kevin Tamati (Salford)
John Taylor (Chorley B.)
Bob Tomlinson (Huddersfield)
Ted Toohey (Wigan)

David Topliss (Wakefield T.)
Peter Tunks (Oldham)
Norman Turley (Trafford B., Whitehaven,
    Workington T.)
Derek Turner (Wakefield T.)
Colin Tyrer (Widnes)

Darryl Van de Velde (Castleford)
Don Vines (Doncaster)

Hugh Waddell (Carlisle)
Arnold Walker (Whitehaven)
Russ Walker (Hull)
Trevor Walker (Batley)
Peter Walsh (Workington T.)
David Ward (Batley, Featherstone R., Hunslet,
    Leeds)
John Warlow (Bridgend)
David Watkins (Cardiff C.)
Bernard Watson (Dewsbury)
Graeme West (Wigan)
Neil Whittaker (Huddersfield B.)
Mel Wibberley (Nottingham C.)
Ron Willey (Bradford N.)
Dean Williams (Workington T.)
Frank Wilson (Runcorn H.)
Phil Windley (Hull)
John Wolford (Hunslet)
Jeff Woods (Bridgend)
John Woods (Leigh)
Paul Woods (Runcorn H.)
Geoff Worrall (Barrow)
Geoff Wraith (Wakefield T.)

Billy Yates (Doncaster)

DOSSIER OF 1994-95 COACHES

The following is a dossier of the British coaching and playing careers of coaches holding first team posts from June 1994 to 1 June 1995. Overseas details are not included.

● BF — beaten finalist.

CHRIS ARKWRIGHT
Highfield:	Apr. 91 - Aug. 91
Highfield:	Sep. 94 -

Played for: St. Helens, Highfield

TONY BARROW
Warrington:	Mar. 86 - Nov. 88 (Premier winners & BF, John Player BF, Lancs. Cup BF)
Oldham:	Nov. 88 - Jan. 91 (Promotion, Lancs. Cup BF, Div. 2 Premier winners)
Swinton:	Jan. 92 -

Played for: St. Helens, Leigh

IAN BROOKE
Bradford N.:	Jan. 73 - Sep. 75 (Div. 2 Champs, RL Cup BF, John Player Trophy Winners)
Wakefield T.:	Jan. 78 - Jan. 79
Huddersfield:	July 79 - Mar. 80
Doncaster:	Dec. 94 -

Played for: Wakefield T., Bradford N.

PAUL CHARLTON
Workington T.:	June 75 - June 76 (Promotion)
Workington T.	July 82 - Dec. 82
Carlisle:	Dec. 94 -

Played for: Workington T., Salford

STEVE CROOKS
Ryedale-York	Nov. 92 - May 94
Hull K.R.	May 94 -

Played for: Hull K.R., Hull, York

GEORGE FAIRBAIRN
Wigan:	Apr. 80 - May 81 (Promotion)
Hull K.R.:	May 91 - May 94
Huddersfield:	June 94 - (Div. 2 Premier BF)

Played for: Wigan, Hull K.R.

STEVE FERRES
Hunslet:	Jan. 94 -

Played for: Bramley, York, Dewsbury, Bradford N., Carlisle, Kent I., Keighley, Batley, Sheffield E.

TONY FISHER
Bramley:	Nov. 87 - Feb. 89
Keighley:	June 90 - Sep. 91
Doncaster:	Nov. 92 - Dec. 94 (Promotion)
Dewsbury:	Apr. 95 -

Played for: Bradford N., Leeds, Castleford

PETER FOX
Featherstone R.:	Jan. 71 - May 74 (RL Cup winners & BF)
Wakefield T.:	June 74 - May 76 (Yorks. Cup BF)
Bramley:	Sep. 76 - Apr. 77 (Promotion)
Bradford N.:	Apr. 77 - May 85 (Div. 1 champs (2), Yorks. Cup winners & BF (2), Premier winners & BF (2), John Player winners)
Leeds:	May 85 - Dec. 86
Featherstone R.:	May 87 - Oct. 91 (Promotion, Div. 2 Premier BF, Yorks. Cup BF)
Bradford N.:	Oct. 91 - (Regal Trophy BF)
England:	1977 (2 matches)
Great Britain:	1978 (3 Tests v. Australia)
Yorkshire:	1985-86 to 1991-92

Played for: Featherstone R., Batley, Hull K.R., Wakefield T.

STEVE GIBSON (Australian)
Rochdale H.:	Oct. 93-

Played for: Salford, Rochdale H.

ANDY GOODWAY
Oldham:	May 94 -

Played for: Oldham, Wigan, Leeds

TONY GORDON (New Zealander)
London C.:	Feb. 93 - May 94 (Div. 2 Premier BF)
Hull:	May 94 - Dec. 94

JEFF GRAYSHON
Dewsbury:	May 78 - Oct. 78
Batley:	Oct. 94 - (Promotion)

Played for: Dewsbury, Bradford N., Leeds, Featherstone R., Batley

In at Salford . . . Andy Gregory promoted from assistant to player-coach in March 1995.

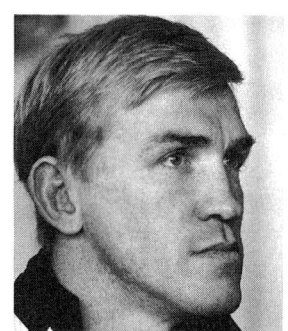

Out at Salford . . . ex-Australia Test full back Garry Jack parted company with the Willows in March 1995 after a 20-month reign as coach.

ANDY GREGORY
Salford: Mar. 95 -
Played for: Widnes, Warrington, Wigan, Leeds, Salford

GARY GRIENKE (Australian)
London B.:   May 94 -
Played for: St. Helens

PAUL HARKIN
Wakefield T.:   Jan. 95 -
Played for: Hull K.R., Bradford N.,
Featherstone R., Leeds, Halifax, Hunslet

GARY HETHERINGTON
Sheffield E.:   July 86 - May 93 (Div. 2 champs,
                  Promotion (2),
                  Div. 2 Premier winners,
                  Divisional Premier winners,
                  Yorks. Cup BF)
Sheffield E.:   Dec. 93 -
Great Britain
  Under-21s: Sep. 94 -
Played for: York, Leeds, Kent I., Sheffield E.

DAVID HOBBS
Bradford N.:   Mar. 90 - Oct. 91 (Premier BF,
                  Regal BF, Yorks. Cup BF)
Wakefield T.:   May 94 - Jan. 95
Played for: Featherstone R., Oldham, Bradford N.,
Wakefield T.

STEWART HORTON
Ryedale-York: Jan. 95 -
Played for: Castleford, Ryedale-York

ERIC HUGHES
Widnes: June 84 - Jan. 86
Rochdale H.   June 87 - June 88
St. Helens: Jan. 94 -
Played for: Widnes, St. Helens, Rochdale H.

GARRY JACK (Australian)
Salford: July 93 - Mar. 95
Played for: Sheffield E., Salford

BRIAN JOHNSON (Australian)
Warrington: Nov. 88 - (Lancs. Cup winners,
                  RL Cup BF, Regal winners &
                  BF)
Played for: Warrington

JOHN JOYNER
Castleford: May 93 - (Regal Trophy winners,
                  Premier BF)
Played for: Castleford

ANDY KELLY
Wakefield T.:   Jan. 95 -
Played for: Wakefield T., Huddersfield, Hull K.R.

Roger Millward, holding the coaching reins at Ryedale-York for seven months before being replaced by skipper Stewart Horton.

PHIL LARDER

Widnes:	May 92 - May 94 (RL Cup BF)
Keighley C.:	May 94 - (Div. 2 Champs, Div. 2 Premier winners)
Great Britain Under-21s:	1990-91, 1991-92

Played for: Oldham, Whitehaven

DOUG LAUGHTON

Widnes:	May 78 - Mar. 83 (RL Cup winners (2) & BF, Lancs. Cup winners (2) & BF, John Player winners & BF, Premier winners (2), Floodlit Trophy winners)
Widnes:	Jan. 86 - May 91 (Div. 1 champs (2), Premier winners (3) & BF, Charity Shield winners (3), John Player BF, Lancs. Cup winners, World Club Challenge winners)
Leeds:	May 91 - (Regal Trophy BF, RL Cup BF (2), Premier BF)
Lancashire:	1982-83, 1988-89, 1989-90

Played for: Wigan, St. Helens, Widnes

IAN LUCAS

Leigh:	Dec. 94 -

Played for: Wigan

STEVE MARTIN (Australian)

Featherstone R.:	Sep. 92 - Oct. 94 (Div. 2 champs, Divisional Premier winners)

Played for: Barrow, Leeds

ROGER MILLWARD

Hull K.R.:	Mar. 77 - May 91 (Div. 1 champs (3), RL Cup winners & BF(2), John Player winners & BF(2), Premier winners (2) & BF, Yorks. Cup winners & BF(2), Floodlit Trophy winners & BF, Charity Shield BF, Div. 2 champs, Div. 2 Premier BF)
Halifax:	May 91 - Dec. 92
Ryedale-York:	June 94 - Dec. 94

Played for: Castleford, Hull K.R.

TONY MYLER

Widnes:	May 94 -

Played for: Widnes

MIKE PEERS

Swinton:	June 86 - Oct. 87 (Promotion, Div. 2 Premier winners)
Springfield B./ Chorley B./ Trafford B.:	Aug. 87 - May 91
Blackpool G.:	Jan. 93 - Feb. 93
Highfield:	Apr. 93 - Sep. 94

Played for: Warrington, Swinton

DENIS RAMSDALE

Barrow:	May 93 - Sep. 94
Leigh:	Sep. 94 - Nov. 94

Played for: Wigan

MALCOLM REILLY

Castleford:	Dec. 74 - May 87 (RL Cup winners, John Player winners, Premier BF, Yorks. Cup winners (3) & BF (2), Charity Shield BF, Floodlit Trophy winners)
Leeds:	Aug. 88 - Sep. 89 (Yorks. Cup winners)
Halifax:	Jan. 93 - Sep. 94
Great Britain:	Jan. 87 - Aug. 94
Under-21s:	1986-87, 1987-88, 1989-90, 1991-92, 1992-93

Played for: Castleford

PETER ROE

Keighley:	Sep. 85 - July 86
Halifax:	Aug. 90 - May 91 (Promotion, Div. 2 Premier BF)
Keighley C.:	Sep. 91 - Apr. 94 (Div. 3 champs)
Barrow:	Sep. 94 -

Played for: Keighley, Bradford N., York, Hunslet

STEVE SIMMS (Australian)

Leigh:	Nov. 92 - Sep. 94
Halifax:	Sep. 94 -

NORMAN SMITH

Dewsbury:	Aug. 93 - Apr. 95

Played for: Bramley, Dewsbury

KURT SORENSEN (New Zealander)

Whitehaven:	May 93 -
Cumbria:	1994-95

Played for: Widnes, Wigan, Whitehaven

HUGH WADDELL

Carlisle:	Apr. 94 - Dec. 94

Played for: Blackpool B., Oldham, Leeds, Sheffield E., Swinton, Wakefield T., Carlisle

RUSS WALKER

Hull:	Dec. 94 - May 95

Played for: Barrow, Hull

PETER WALSH (Australian)

Workington T.:	Apr. 92 - (Div. 2 champs, Div. 2 Premier winners, Divisional Premier BF)
Cumbria:	1994-95

Played for: Oldham

Graeme West, six-time trophy winner since taking control at Wigan in May 1994.

DAVID WARD

Hunslet:	July 86 - Apr. 88 (Div. 2 champs, Div. 2 Premier BF)
Hunslet:	Jan. 89 - May 89
Leeds:	Sep. 89 - May 91
Batley:	May 91 - Oct. 94
Featherstone R.:	Oct. 94 -

Played for: Leeds, Workington T.

GRAEME WEST (New Zealander)

Wigan:	May 94 - (Premier winners (2), World Club Challenge winners, Div 1 champs, Regal Trophy winners, RL Cup winners)

Played for: Wigan

PHIL WINDLEY

Hull:	Dec. 94 -

Played for: Hull

313

REPRESENTATIVE REGISTER

The following is a list of international and county coaches since 1974-75.

GREAT BRITAIN
Jim Challinor	Dec. 71 - Aug. 74
	(Inc. tours)
David Watkins	1977 World Championship
Peter Fox	1978
Eric Ashton	1979 tour
Johnny Whiteley	Aug. 80 - Nov. 82
Frank Myler	Dec. 82 - Aug. 84
	(Inc. tour)
Maurice Bamford	Oct. 84 - Dec. 86
Malcolm Reilly	Jan. 87 - Aug. 94
	(Inc. tours)
Ellery Hanley	Aug. 94 - May 95

ENGLAND
Alex Murphy	Jan. 75 - Nov. 75
	(Inc. World Championship tour)
Peter Fox	1976-77
Frank Myler	1977-78
Eric Ashton	1978-79, 1979-80
Johnny Whiteley	1980-81, 1981-82
Reg Parker	1984-85
(Mgr)	
Malcolm Reilly	1992-93
Ellery Hanley	1994-95

WALES
Les Pearce	Jan. 75 - Nov. 75
	(Inc. World Championship tour)
David Watkins Bill Francis	} 1976-77
Kel Coslett Bill Francis	} 1977-78
Kel Coslett	1978-79 to 1981-82
David Watkins	1982-83, 1984-85
Clive Griffiths	1991-92, 1992-93, 1993-94, 1994-95

GREAT BRITAIN UNDER-24s
Johnny Whiteley	1976-82
Frank Myler	1983-84

GREAT BRITAIN UNDER-21s
Maurice Bamford	Oct. 84 - Dec. 86
Malcolm Reilly	1986-87, 1987-88, 1989-90, 1991-92, 1992-93, 1993-94
David Topliss	1988-89
Phil Larder	1990-91, 1991-92
Gary Hetherington	1994-95

CUMBRIA
Ike Southward	1975-76
Frank Foster	1976-77 to 1977-78
Sol Roper	1978-79
Frank Foster	1979-80
Phil Kitchin	1980-81 to 1981-82
Frank Foster	1982-83
Jackie Davidson	1985-86
Phil Kitchin	1986-87 to 1991-92
Gordon Cottier	1992-93
Peter Walsh/ Kurt Sorensen	1994-95

LANCASHIRE
Alex Murphy	1973-74 to 1977-78
Eric Ashton	1978-79 to 1979-80
Tom Grainey	1980-81 to 1981-82
Doug Laughton	1982-83
Alex Murphy	1985-86 to 1987-88
Doug Laughton	1988-89 to 1989-90
Ray Ashton	1991-92

YORKSHIRE
Johnny Whiteley	1970-71 to 1979-80
Arthur Keegan	1980-81
Johnny Whiteley	1981-82 to 1982-83
Peter Fox	1985-86 to 1991-92

OTHER NATIONALITIES
Dave Cox	1974-75 to 1975-76

An historic photograph of the first-ever presentation of the Rugby League World Cup. Great Britain skipper Dave Valentine holds aloft the inaugural trophy after their shock 16-12 triumph over hosts France in the November 1954 play-off, after the two countries finished joint top of the four-nation table.

WORLD CUP

The staging of the Halifax Centenary World Cup in Britain in October 1995 is the 11th tournament and the biggest with 10 competing countries.

Launched in 1954, the 10 previous World Cups have all involved Australia, France, Great Britain and New Zealand – except in 1975 when Great Britain was split into England and Wales – plus Papua New Guinea in the 1985-88 and 1989-92 competitions.

The entrants in the 1995 Centenary World Cup were Australia, England, Fiji, France, New Zealand, Papua New Guinea, South Africa, Tonga, Wales and Western Samoa.

World Cup success has been tasted by only Australia, seven times, and Great Britain, who shared the first six tournaments, the Kangaroos winning the last four in succession.

The Centenary World Cup's 10 countries were divided into three groups, the top two from a group of four meeting the top team from each of two groups of three in the semi-finals.

The World Cup has been organised under five different formats, including the 1995 event. In 1954, 1957 and 1960, the round-robin tournament was decided on league placings, although a play-off was necessary in the inaugural World Cup, staged in France, when the hosts and Great Britain both finished level on five points. "No-hopers" Britain lifted the trophy with an historic 16-12 victory in Paris in front of more than 30,000 people.

A top-two play-off final was introduced for the 1968, 1970 and 1972 World Cups which were played in Australia and New Zealand, Britain and France respectively. In 1975 the World Cup was staged over two legs, the first Down Under and the second in Europe, Australia heading the final table. The 1977 tourney reverted to a top-two play-off final.

The French League put forward a new extended format for the re-introduction of the World Cup a decade later. One Test of each series staged over a three-year cycle qualified for World Cup points, the top two countries in the final league table contesting the World Cup final.

The first of the two extended format tournaments opened in July 1985 with the final being played in October 1988. The following World Cup kicked off in July 1989 and was completed in October 1992.

However, while the qualifying ties were drawn out, both finals made a tremendous impact. A crowd of more than 47,000 watched the 1988 World Cup final between Australia and New Zealand at Eden Park, Auckland, while a world record international attendance of 73,631 witnessed the 1992 final between Australia and Great Britain at Wembley.

Great Britain wingman Mick Sullivan in action against New Zealand at Bradford in the 1960 World Cup, having appeared in the 1954 and 1957 tournaments.

1954   Played in France   WON BY GREAT BRITAIN

- Decided on league placings, but a play-off was necessary when Britain and France finished level top with five points.

Great Britain	Australia	France	New Zealand
Manager: G. Shaw	Managers: J. McMahon	Manager: A. Blain	Manager: T. McKenzie
	S. O'Neil	Coaches: J. Duhau	Coach: J. Amos
	Coach: V. Hey	R. Duffort	
D. Valentine (Huddersfield), Capt.	C. Churchill, Capt.	Puig-Aubert, Capt.	C. Eastlake, Capt.
W. Banks (Huddersfield)	R. Banks	J. Audobert	H. Anderson
H. Bradshaw (Huddersfield)	R. Bull	G. Benausse	A. Atkinson
G. Brown (Leeds)	H. Crocker	V. Cantoni	J. Austin
R. Coverdale (Hull)	B. Davies	A. Carrere	D. Blanchard
G. Helme (Warrington)	P. Diversi	R. Contrastin	J. Bond
F. Kitchen (Leigh)	D. Flannery	J. Crespo	J. Butterfield
P. Jackson (Barrow)	D. Hall	J. Delaye	N. Denton
J. Ledgard (Leigh)	G. Hawick	R. Guilhem	J. Edwards
A. Naughton (Warrington)	K. Holman	A. Jiminez	L. Erikson
D. Robinson (Wakefield T.)	K. Kearney	J. Krawzyk	I. Grey
D. Rose (Leeds)	K. McCaffery	J. Merquey	C. Johnson
R. Rylance (Huddersfield)	I. Moir	J. Pambrun	G. McDonald
S. Smith (Hunslet)	K. O'Shea	F. Rinaldi	R. McKay
M. Sullivan (Huddersfield)	N. Pidding	A. Save	W. McLennan
J. Thorley (Halifax)	N. Provan	C. Teisseire	G. Menzies
B. Watts (York)	A. Watson	G. Verdier	W. Sorensen
J. Whiteley (Hull)	H. Wells	M. Voron	J. Yates

FRANCE 22   NEW ZEALAND 13
Paris: 30 October   13,240

France: Puig-Aubert (5g); Contrastin (1t), Merquey, Jiminez, Cantoni; Benausse, Teisseire; Krawzyk, Audobert (1t), Rinaldi, Pambrun, Delaye (1t), Crespo (1t)
New Zealand: Anderson; Edwards (1t), Eastlake (1t), McKay (1t), Menzies; Sorensen, Erikson; McLennan, Blanchard, Johnson, Yates, Bond (2g), Atkinson
Referee: C.F. Appleton (England)

GREAT BRITAIN 28   AUSTRALIA 13
Lyon: 31 October   10,250

Britain: Ledgard (5g); Rose (1t), Jackson (2t), Sullivan, Kitchen (1t), Brown (2t), Helme; Thorley, Smith, Coverdale, Watts, Robinson, Valentine
Australia: Churchill; Pidding (2g), Wells (2t), Watson, Moir; McCaffery, Holman; Bull, Kearney (1t), Hall, Provan, Davies, Diversi
Referee: R. Guidicelli (France)

AUSTRALIA 34   NEW ZEALAND 15
Marseilles: 7 November   20,000

Australia: Churchill; Flannery, Watson (3t), Wells, Pidding (5g); Banks, Hawick (1t); Davies, Kearney (1t), Bull (1t), O'Shea (1t), Crocker, Diversi (1t)

New Zealand: Denton; Edwards, McKay (6g), Eastlake, Menzies; Sorensen, Erikson (1t); McLennan, Blanchard, Johnson, Butterfield, Yates, Atkinson
Referee: R. Guidicelli (France)

GREAT BRITAIN 13   FRANCE 13
Toulouse: 7 November   37,471

Britain: Ledgard (2g); Rose (1t), Jackson, Naughton, Sullivan; Brown (1t), Helme (1t); Thorley, Smith, Coverdale, Watts, Robinson, Valentine
France: Puig-Aubert (2g); Contrastin (2t), Merquey, Jiminez, Cantoni; Benausse, Crespo; Krawzyk (1t), Audobert, Rinaldi, Delaye, Pambrun, Guilhem
Referee: C.F. Appleton (England)

GREAT BRITAIN 26   NEW ZEALAND 6
Bordeaux: 11 November   14,000

Britain: Ledgard (1t,4g); Rose (1t), Jackson (1t), Sullivan, Kitchen (2t); Brown (1t), Helme; Thorley, Smith, Coverdale, Watts, Robinson, Valentine
New Zealand: Gray; Edwards, McKay (3g), Eastlake, Austin; Sorensen, Erikson; McLennan, Blanchard, Bond, Butterfield, McDonald, Atkinson
Referee: R. Guidicelli (France)

FRANCE 15   AUSTRALIA 5
Nantes: 11 November   13,000

France: Puig-Aubert (3g); Contrastin (1t),
Merquey (1t), Teisseire, Cantoni (1t); Jiminez,
Crespo; Rinaldi, Audobert, Krawzyk, Save,
Pambrun, Verdier
Australia: Churchill; Flannery, Hawick,
Watson, Pidding (1g); Banks, Holman; Davies,
Kearney, Bull, O'Shea (1t), Crocker, Diversi
Referee: C.F. Appleton (England)

Final Table
	P	W	D	L	F	A	Pts
Great Britain	3	2	1	0	67	32	5
France	3	2	1	0	50	31	5
Australia	3	1	0	2	52	58	2
New Zealand	3	0	0	3	34	82	0

1957   Played in Australia   WON BY AUSTRALIA
● Decided on league points

PLAY OFF
GREAT BRITAIN 16   FRANCE 12
Paris: 13 November   30,368

Britain: Ledgard (2g); Rose (1t), Jackson,
Naughton, Sullivan; Brown (2t), Helme (1t);
Thorley, Smith, Coverdale, Watts, Robinson,
Valentine
France: Puig-Aubert (3g); Contrastin (1t),
Merquey, Teisseire, Cantoni (1t); Jiminez,
Crespo; Krawzyk, Audobert, Rinaldi,
Pambrun, Save, Verdier
Referee: C.F. Appleton (England)

Great Britain	Australia	France	New Zealand
Managers: W. Fallowfield	Manager: N.C. Robinson	Manager: A. Blain	Manager: K. Blow
H. Rawson	Coach: R. Poole	Coach: J. Duhau	Coach: W. Telford
A. Prescott (St. Helens), Capt.	R. Poole, Capt.	J. Merquey, Capt.	C. Johnson, Capt.
E. Ashton (Wigan)	K. Barnes	A. Appelian	R. Ackland
W. Boston (Wigan)	B. Carlson	G. Benausse	V. Bakalich
A. Davies (Oldham)	B. Clay	G. Berthomieu	K. Bell
J. Grundy (Barrow)	B. Davies	H. Delhoste	S. Belsham
G. Gunney (Hunslet)	G. Hawick	F. Ferrero	J. Butterfield
T. Harris (Hull)	K. Holman	J. Foussat	P. Creedy
P. Jackson (Barrow)	K. Kearney	G. Husson	R. Griffiths
L. Jones (Leeds)	K. McCaffery	R. Jean	B. Hadfield
S. Little (Oldham)	W. Marsh	A. Jiminez	W. McLennan
T. McKinney (St. Helens)	I. Moir	F. Levy	H. Maxwell
G. Moses (St. Helens)	K. O'Shea	R. Medus	G. Menzies
R. Price (Warrington)	N. Provan	A. Parent	K. Pearce
A. Rhodes (St. Helens)	R. Ritchie	A. Rives	R. Percy
J. Stevenson (Leeds)	D. Schofield	J. Rouqueyrol	J. Riddell
M. Sullivan (Huddersfield)	T. Tyquin	A. Save	W. Sorensen
D. Turner (Oldham)	A. Watson	G. Verdier	G. Turner
J. Whiteley (Hull)	H. Wells	M. Voron	J. Yates

GREAT BRITAIN 23   FRANCE 5
Sydney: 15 June   50,007

Britain: Moses; Boston (1t), Jackson (1t),
Davies, Sullivan (2t); Jones (4g);
Stevenson (1t); Prescott, Harris, Little,
Grundy, Gunney, Turner
France: Rives; Husson, Jiminez, Merquey (1t),
Voron; Benausse (1g), Jean; Ferrero, Appelian,
Berthomieu, Save, Parent, Rouqueyrol
Referee: D. Lawler (Australia)

AUSTRALIA 25   NEW ZEALAND 5
Brisbane: 15 June   29,636

Australia: Barnes (5g); Moir (1t), Wells (1t),
Poole, Carlson (1t); Hawick, Holman; Marsh,
Kearney, Davies, O'Shea (1t), Provan (1t), Clay
New Zealand: Creedy; Bakalich, Sorensen (1g),
Ackland, Hadfield; Menzies, Belsham; McLennan,
Butterfield, Maxwell, Johnson (1t), Yates, Percy
Referee: V. Belsham (New Zealand)

AUSTRALIA 31   GREAT BRITAIN 6
Sydney: 17 June   57,955
Australia: Carlson (4g); Watson, Wells (1t),
Poole, Moir (2t); Clay (1t), McCaffery (2t);
Marsh, Kearney, Davies (1g), O'Shea (1t),
Provan, Schofield
Britain: Moses; Boston, Ashton, Davies,
Sullivan; Jones (3g), Stevenson; Prescott,
Harris, Little, Whiteley, Grundy, Turner
Referee: V. Belsham (New Zealand)

FRANCE 14   NEW ZEALAND 10
Brisbane: 17 June   28,000
France: Rives; Husson, Merquey, Voron,
Foussat (2t); Benausse (4g), Jean; Delhoste,
Appelian, Medus, Berthomieu, Parent,
Rouqueyrol
New Zealand: Creedy (1g); Bakalich, Sorensen,
(1t, 1g), Ackland, Hadfield (1t); Menzies,
Belsham; McLellan, Butterfield, Maxwell,
Johnson, Yates, Percy
Referee: D. Lawler (Australia)

AUSTRALIA 26   FRANCE 9
Sydney: 22 June   35,158
Australia: Carlson (1t, 7g); Watson, Poole (1t),
Wells, Moir; Clay, McCaffery; Marsh (1t),
Kearney, Davies, O'Shea (1t), Provan,
Schofield
1960   Played in England   WON BY GREAT BRITAIN
● Decided on league places

France: Rives; Husson, Jiminez, Foussat,
Voron; Benausse (1t, 3g), Jean; Ferrero,
Appelian, Delhoste, Medus, Parent, Levy
Referee: V. Belsham (New Zealand)

GREAT BRITAIN 21   NEW ZEALAND 29
Sydney: 25 June   14,263
Britain: Moses; Ashton, Jackson (1t),
Jones (1t, 3g), Sullivan (1t); Rhodes, Stevenson;
Prescott, McKinney, Little (1t), Grundy (1t),
Gunney, Turner
New Zealand: Creedy; Hadfield (1t),
Sorensen (7g), Turner (1t), Griffiths;
Menzies (1t), Belsham; McLennan (1t),
Butterfield, Yates, Maxwell, Johnson,
Riddell (1t)
Referee: D. Lawler (Australia)

Final Table

	P	W	D	L	F	A	Pts
Australia	3	3	0	0	82	20	6
Great Britain	3	1	0	2	50	65	2
New Zealand	3	1	0	2	44	60	2
France	3	1	0	2	28	59	2

Great Britain	Australia	France	New Zealand
Manager: W. Fallowfield	Managers: P. Duggan, J. O'Toole Coach: K. Barnes	Manager: A. Blain Coaches: R. Duffort, D. Duhau	Manager: G. Plant, T. Skinner Coach: T. Hardwick
E. Ashton (Wigan), Capt.	K. Karnes, Capt.	J. Barthe, Capt.	C. Johnson, Capt.
W. Boston (Wigan)	D. Beattie	A. Boldini	R. Ackland
J. Challinor (Warrington)	R. Boden	A. Casas	J. Butterfield
A. Davies (Oldham)	A. Brown	J. Dubon	M. Cooke
E. Fraser (Warrington)	R. Bugden	R. Erramouspe	R. Cooke
R. Greenhough (Warrington)	B. Carlson	G. Fages	N. Denton
T. Harris (Hull)	R. Gasnier	Y. Gourbal	C. Eastlake
V. Karalius (St. Helens)	B. Hambly	R. Gruppi	R. Griffiths
B. McTigue (Wigan)	K. Irvine	J. Guiraud	B. Hadfield
A. Murphy (St. Helens)	N. Kelly	A. Lacaze	T. Kilkelly
F. Myler (Widnes)	L. Morgan	C. Mantoulan	H. Maxwell
A. Rhodes (St. Helens)	R. Mossop	A. Marty	G. Menzies
B. Shaw (Hunslet)	B. Muir	J. Merquey	L. Oliff
J. Shaw (Halifax)	G. Parcell	Y. Mezard	G. Phillips
M. Sullivan (Wigan)	J. Raper	L. Poletti	T. Reid
D. Turner (Wakefield T.)	E. Rasmussen	A. Quaglio	N. Roberts
J. Whiteley (Hull)	W. Rayner	R. Rey	W. Sorensen
J. Wilkinson (Wakefield T.)	H. Wells	A. Vadon	G. Turner

GREAT BRITAIN 23   NEW ZEALAND 8
Bradford: 24 September   20,577
Britain: Fraser (4g); Greenhough, Ashton (1t),
Davies (1t), Sullivan; Myler (1t), Murphy (1t);
Wilkinson, Harris, McTigue (1t), Karalius,
Whiteley, Turner
New Zealand: Eastlake; Hadfield (1t), Turner,
Sorensen (1g), Denton; Menzies, Roberts;
Maxwell, Butterfield, Johnson, Aukland,
Kilkelly, M. Cooke (1t)
Referee: E. Martung (France)

AUSTRALIA 12   FRANCE 12
Wigan: 24 September   20,278
Australia: Carlson (2g); Morgan, Gasnier (1t),
Wells, Irvine; Brown, Muir; Beattie, Kelly (1t),
Mossop, Hambly, Rasmussen, Raper (1t)
France: Pelotti; Dubon, Rey, Mantoulan,
Gruppi (2t); Merquey, Fages; Quaglio, Casas,
Boldini, Barthe, Erramouspe, Lacaze (3g)
Referee: E. Clay (England)

GREAT BRITAIN 33   FRANCE 7
Swinton: 1 October   22,923
Britain: Fraser (6g); Challinor, Rhodes (2t),
Davies (2t), Sullivan (1t); Myler (1t), Murphy;
Wilkinson (1t), J. Shaw, McTigue, B. Shaw,
Karalius, Whiteley
France: Poletti; Dubon (1t), Rey, Mantoulan,
Gruppi; Merquey, Guiraud; Quaglio, Casas,
Erramouspe, Barthe, Mezard, Lacaze (2g)
Referee: E. Martung (France)

AUSTRALIA 21   NEW ZEALAND 15
Leeds: 1 October   10,773
Australia: Barnes; Carlson (3t,3g), Wells (1t),
Gasnier (1t), Irvine; Brown, Muir; Beattie,
Kelly, Parcell, Hambly, Mossop, Raper

New Zealand: Phillips; Hadfield (1t),
Turner, Eastlake (3g), Denton;
Menzies (1t), Roberts; Maxwell, Butterfield,
Johnson, Ackland, Oliff, M. Cooke
Referee: E. Clay (England)

GREAT BRITAIN 10   AUSTRALIA 3
Bradford: 8 October   32,773
Britain: Rhodes (2g); Boston (1t), Ashton
Davies, Sullivan; (1t); Myler, Murphy;
Wilkinson, J. Shaw, McTigue, B. Shaw,
Turner, Karalius
Australia: Barnes; Boden, Gasnier, Wells,
Carlson (1t); Brown, Muir; Beattie, Kelly,
Parcell, Mossop, Rasmussen, Hambly
Referee: E. Martung (France)

NEW ZEALAND 9   FRANCE 0
Wigan: 8 October   2,876
New Zealand: Phillips; Hadfield, Turner,
Griffiths, Eastlake (3g); Menzies, Roberts;
Reid (1t), Butterfield, Johnson, Ackland, Oliff,
M. Cooke
France: Poletti; Dubon, Rey, Mantoulon,
Gruppi; Merquey, Fages; Boldini, Vadon,
Quaglio, Barthe, Erramouspe, Lacaze
Referee: E. Clay (England)

Final Table

	P	W	D	L	F	A	Pts
Great Britain	3	3	0	0	66	18	6
Australia	3	2	0	1	37	37	4
New Zealand	3	1	0	2	32	44	2
France	3	0	0	3	19	55	0

1968   Played in Australia and New Zealand   WON BY AUSTRALIA
● Decided by top two in league table meeting in play-off final

Great Britain	Australia	France	New Zealand
Managers: W. Fallowfield	Manager: A. Kingston	Managers: J. Guiraud	Manager: D. Wilson
C. Hutton	Coach: H. Bath	F. Soubie	Coach: B. Barchard
B. Risman (Leeds), Capt.	J. Raper, Capt.	Coach: R. Lacoste	J. Bond, Capt.
K. Ashcroft (Leigh)	A. Beetson	G. Ailleres, Capt.	E. Carson
J. Atkinson (Leeds)	A. Branson	A. Alesina	J. Clarke
T. Bishop (St. Helens)	R. Coote	Y. Begou	O. Danielson

I. Brooke (Wakefield T.)
A. Burwell (Hull KR)
M. Clark (Leeds)
D. Edwards (Castleford)
P. Flanagan (Hull KR)
R. French (Widnes)
R. Haigh (Wakefield T.)
R. Millward (Hull KR)
A. Morgan (Featherstone R.)
C. Renilson (Halifax)
M. Shoebottom (Leeds)
C. Sullivan (Hull)
J. Warlow (St. Helens)
C. Watson (St. Helens)
C. Young (Hull KR)

B.Fitzsimmons
R.Fulton
J.Greaves
B.James
F.Jones
J.King
G.Langlands
D.Manteit
E.Rasmussen
J.Rhodes
E.Simms
W.Smith
R.Thornett
L.Williamson
J.Wittenberg

J.Capdouze
J.Clar
J.Cros
A.Ferren
M.Frattini
R.Garrigues
J.Gruppi
J.Lecompte
J.Ledru
H.Marracq
H.Mazard
M.Mohmer
F.DeNadan
D.Pelerin
C.Sabatie
V.Serrano

J.Dixon
S.Dunn
J.Ellwood
A.Kriletich
B.Lee
C.McMaster
R.Mineham
C.O'Neil
D.Parkman
P.Shultz
H.Sinel
G.Smith
R.Tait
H.Tatana
E.Wiggs

AUSTRALIA 25   GREAT BRITAIN 10

Sydney: 25 May   62,256

Australia: Simms (8g); Rhodes, Greaves, Langlands, King; Branson, Smith (1t): Beetson, Jones, Wittenberg, Coote (1t), Thornett, Raper (1t)
Britain: Risman (2g); Brooke (1t), Shoebottom, Burwell, Sullivan (1t); Millward, Bishop; Clark, Ashcroft, Watson, French, Haigh, Renilson
Referee: J. Percival (New Zealand)

FRANCE 15   NEW ZEALAND 10

Auckland: 25 May   18,000

France: Cros; Pellerin, Molinier, Lecompte, Ferren; Capdouze (1t,5g), Garrigues (1g); Aillieres, Begou, Sabatie, De Nadai, Marracq, Clar
New Zealand: Tait; Mincham, Sinel, Schultz, Wiggs (5g); Bond, Clarke; Danielson, O'Neil, Smith, Lee, Dixon, Kriletich. Sub: Tatana
Referee: C. Pearce (Australia)

AUSTRALIA 31   NEW ZEALAND 12

Brisbane: 1 June   23,608

Australia: Simms (8g); Rhodes (1t), Greaves, Langlands, King (2t); Branson, Smith; Wittenberg, Jones (1t), Rasmussen, Coote (1t), Thornett, Raper. Sub: Fulton
New Zealand: Ellwood; Mincham, Dunn (1t), Schultz (1t), Wiggs (3g); Bond, Clarke; Smith, O'Neil, Tatana, Lee, Dixon, Kriletich. Sub: Tait
Referee: J. Percival (New Zealand)

FRANCE 7   GREAT BRITAIN 2

Auckland: 2 June   15,760

France: Cros; Pelerin, Molinier, Lecompte, Ledru (1t); Capdouze (1g), Garrigues (1g); Aillieres, Begou, Sabatie, Marracq, Mazard, Clar
Britain: Risman (1g); Sullivan, Brooke, Burwell, Atkinson; Millward, Bishop; Clark, Flanagan, Watson, Morgan, Haigh, Renilson. Sub: Warlow
Referee: C. Pearce (Australia)

AUSTRALIA 37   FRANCE 4

Brisbane: 8 June   32,662

Australia: Simms (5g); James, Rhodes, Greaves (1t); Williamson (2t); Fulton (2t), Smith (1t,3g); Wittenberg, Fitzsimmons, Beetson, Coote (1t), Manteit, Raper
France: Cros; Ferren, Moliner, Gruppi, Ledru; Capdouze (2g), Frattini; Sabatie, Begou, Serrano, Alesina, Mazard, Clar. Sub: De Nadai
Referee: J. Percival (New Zealand)

GREAT BRITAIN 38   NEW ZEALAND 14

Sydney: 8 June   14,105

Britain: Risman (7g); Sullivan (3t), Brooke (1t), Burwell (2t), Atkinson; Millward, Bishop; Clark, Flanagan, Warlow, French, Morgan (1t), Renilson. Subs: Shoebottom (1t), Watson
New Zealand: Ellwood; Mincham, Dunn, Schultz (2t), Wiggs (4g); Tait, Carson; McMaster, O'Neil, Smith, Sinel, Lee, Kriletich. Sub: Dixon
Referee: C. Pearce (Australia)

Final Table

	P	W	D	L	F	A	Pts
Australia	3	3	0	0	93	26	6
France	3	2	0	1	26	49	4
Great Britain	3	1	0	2	50	46	2
New Zealand	3	0	0	3	36	84	0

FINAL

AUSTRALIA 20   FRANCE 2
Sydney: 10 June   54,290

Australia: Simms (4g); Williamson (2t), Langlands, Greaves (It), Rhodes; Fulton, Smith; Wittenberg, Jones, Beetson, Thornett, Raper, Coote (1t). Sub: Rasmussen.

France: Cros; Pelerin, Gruppi, Lecompte, Ledru; Capdouze (1g), Garrigues; Sabatie, Begou, Ailleres, De Nadai, Marracq, Clar
Referee: J. Percival (New Zealand)

1970   Played in England   WON BY AUSTRALIA
● Decided by top two in league table meeting in play-off final

Great Britain	Australia	France	New Zealand
Managers: J. Harding	Managers: J. Arthurson	Managers:	Manager: C. Mountford
Coach: J. Whiteley	J. Quinn		Coach: L. Blanchard
	Coach: H. Bath	Coach: H. Bath	
F. Myler (St. Helens), Capt.	R. Coote, Capt.	J. Clar, Capt.	F. Christian, Capt.
K. Ashcroft (Leigh)	R. Branighan	R. Biffi	M. Brereton
J. Atkinson (Leeds)	J. Brown	E. Bonal	W. Burgoyne
P. Charlton (Salford)	J. Cootes	F. Bonet	E. Carson
D. Chisnall (Leigh)	R. Costello	J. Cabero	G. Cooksley
R. Dutton (Widnes)	R. Fulton	J. Capdouze	W. Deacon
A. Fisher (Bradford N./Leeds)	M. Harris	R. Coquand	D. Gailey
R. Haigh (Leeds)	R. McCarthy	G. Cremouxx	L. Graham
D. Hartley (Castleford)	R. McTaggart	J. Cros	J. Greengrass
K. Hepworth (Castleford)	J. O'Neill	R. Garrigues	E. Heatley
C. Hesketh (Salford)	R. O'Reilly	J. Gruppi	E. Kereopa
S. Hynes (Leeds)	D. Pittard	G. Guiraud	A. Kritletich
K. Jones (Wigan)	P. Sait	S. Marsolan	D. Ladner
D. Laughton (Wigan)	E. Simms	H. Mazard	B. Lowther
M. Reilly (Castleford)	W. Smith	M. Molinier	R. McGuinn
M. Shoebottom (Leeds)	G. Sullivan	F. de Nadai	C. O'Neil
A. Smith (Leeds)	R. Turner	D. Pelerin	G. Smith
J. Thompson (Featherstone R.)	E. Walters	A. Ruiz	J. Whittaker
C. Watson (St. Helens)	L. Williamson	C. Sabatie	G. Woollard

AUSTRALIA 47   NEW ZEALAND 11
Wigan: 21 October   9,586

Australia: Simms (10g,1t); Williamson, Cootes (2t), Fulton (1t), Branighan (1t); Pittard, Smith (1t); O'Neill, Walters, O'Reilly, McCarthy (1t), Sait, Coote (1t). Sub: Turner (1t)
New Zealand: Ladner (4g); McGuinn, Christian, Lowther, Brereton; Woollard, Cooksley; Smith (1t), O'Neil, Gailey, Deacon, Heatley, Kritletich. Subs: Greengrass, Graham
Referee: W. H. Thompson (England)

GREAT BRITAIN 11   AUSTRALIA 4
Leeds: 24 October   15,084

Britain: Dutton (3g); Smith, Hynes (1t, 1g), Myler, Atkinson; Shoebottom, Hepworth; Hartley, Fisher, Watson, Thompson, Laughton, Reilly
Australia: Simms (1g); Harris, Branighan, Fulton (1g), Williamson; Pittard, Smith; O'Neill, Walters, O'Reilly, McCarthy, Sait, Sullivan
Referee: G. F. Lindop (England)

NEW ZEALAND 16   FRANCE 15
Hull: 25 October   3,824

New Zealand: Ladner (5g); Whittaker, Christian, Lowther, Brereton (1t); Woollard, Cooksley (1t); Greengrass, O'Neil, Gailey, Smith, Kereopa, Kriletich. Subs: Graham, Deacon
France: Cros; Marsolan (2t), Molinier, Ruiz, Bonal (1t); Capdouze (3g), Garrigues; Sabatie, Cabero, Bonet, Mazard, Biffi, Clar.
Sub: de Nadai
Referee: W. H. Thompson (England).

GREAT BRITAIN 6   FRANCE 0
Castleford: 28 October   8,958

Britain: Dutton (3g); Jones, Hynes, Myler, Atkinson; Shoebottom, Hepworth; Hartley, Ashcroft, Watson, Thompson, Laughton, Reilly
France: Cros; Marsolan, Molinier, Ruiz, Bonal; Capdouze, Guiraud; Sabatie, Cabero, de Nadai, Mazard, Cremoux, Clar. Subs: Pelerin, Bonet
Referee: G. F. Lindop (England)

GREAT BRITAIN 27   NEW ZEALAND 17

Swinton: 31 October   5,609

Britain: Dutton (6g); Jones, Hynes (1t),
Hesketh (1t), Atkinson (1t); Shoebottom,
Hepworth; Chisnall, Ashcroft, Watson (1t),
Thompson, Haigh, Laughton (1t).
Sub: Charlton
New Zealand: Ladner (4g); Whittaker,
Christian (1t), Lowther, Brereton; Woollard,
Cooksley; Greengrass, O'Neil, Keropa, Smith (1t),
Heatley, Kriletich (1t).
Sub: Graham
Referee: G. F. Lindop (England)

FRANCE 17   AUSTRALIA 15

Bradford: 1 November   6,215

France: Cros; Marsolan (2t), Molinier, Gruppi,
Pelerin; Capdouze (1t,3g), Garrigues (1g); Sabatie,
Cabero, Bonet, de Nadai, Biffi, Clar
Australia: Simms (3g); Branighan, Cootes (2t),
Fulton (1t), Williamson; Pittard, Smith; McTaggart,
Walters, O'Reilly, McCarthy, Sait, Coote.
Subs: Turner, Sullivan
Referee: W. H. Thompson (England)

Final Table

	P	W	D	L	F	A	Pts
Great Britain	3	3	0	0	44	21	6
Australia	3	1	0	2	66	39	2
France	3	1	0	2	32	37	2
New Zealand	3	1	0	2	44	89	2

FINAL

GREAT BRITAIN 7   AUSTRALIA 12

Leeds: 7 November   18,776

Britain: Dutton (1g); Smith, Hynes (1g), Myler,
Atkinson (1t); Shoebottom, Hepworth; Hartley,
Fisher, Watson, Thompson, Laughton, Reilly.
Subs: Hesketh, Haigh
Australia: Simms (3g); Williamson (1t), Cootes (1t),
Sait, Harris; Fulton, Smith; O'Neill, Turner,
O'Reilly, McCarthy, Costello, Coote.
Subs: Branighan, Walters
Referee: G. F. Lindop (England)

1972   Played in France   WON BY GREAT BRITAIN
● Decided by top two in league table meeting in play-off final

Great Britain	Australia	France	New Zealand
Managers: W. Spaven	Manager: A. Kingston	Managers: F. Soubie	Manager: T. Wellsmore
Coach: J. Challinor	J. Clark		Coach: D. Barchard
	Coach: H. Bath		
C. Sullivan (Hull) Capt.	G. Langlands, Capt.	F. de Nadai, Capt.	F. Christian, Capt.
J. Atkinson (Leeds)	A. Beetson	M. Anglade	M. Brereton
P. Charlton (Salford)	R. Branighan	E. Bonal	W. Burgoyne
T. Clawson (Leeds)	J. Elford	J. Bonal	A. Coll
C. Dixon (Salford)	R. Fulton	J. Franc	W. Collicoat
C. Hesketh (Salford)	J. Grant	M. Frattini	G. Cooksley
J. Holmes (Leeds)	M. Harris	J. Garzino	M. Eade
D. Jeanes (Leeds)	F. Jones	S. Gleyzes	D. Gailey
R. Irving (Oldham)	S. Knight	B. Guilhem	P. Gurnick
A. Karalius (St. Helens)	R. McCarthy	J. M. Imbert	D. Mann
B. Lockwood (Castleford)	J. O'Neill	S. Marsolan	M. Mohi
P. Lowe (Hull KR)	R. O'Reilly	M. Mazare	P. Orchard
S. Nash (Featherstone R.)	T. Raudonikis	M. Molinier	J. O'Sullivan
G. Nicholls (Widnes)	P. Sait	A. Rodriguez	R. Paul
D. O'Neill (Widnes)	G. Starling	A. Ruiz	B. Tracey
D. Redfearn (Bradford N.)	G. Stevens	J. Sauret	R. Walker
M. Stephenson (Dewsbury)	G. Sullivan	V. Serrano	J. Whittaker
D. Topliss (Wakefield T.)	E. Walters	R. Toujas	D. Williams
J. Walsh (St. Helens)	D. Ward	C. Zalduendo	J. Wilson

FRANCE 20   NEW ZEALAND 9
Marseilles: 28 October   20,748
France: Toujas; Marsolan, Molinier, Ruiz (1t),
J. Bonal (2t,1g); Guilhem (4g), Frattini (1dg);
de Nadai, Franc, Garzino, Serrano, Gleyzes,
Anglade. Sub: Zalduendo
New Zealand: Whittaker; Orchard (2t), O'Sullivan,
Christian, Brereton (1t); Williams, Tracey; Mohi,
Burgoyne, Paul, Gailey, Gurnick, Eade.
Subs: Cooksley, Coll
Referee: G. Jameau (France)

GREAT BRITAIN 27   AUSTRALIA 21
Perpignan: 29 October   6,324
Britain: Charlton; Sullivan (1t), Hesketh, Walsh,
Atkinson (1t); O'Neill (1t), Nash; Clawson (6g),
Stephenson (1t), Jeanes, Lowe (1t), Lockwood,
Nicholls. Sub: Holmes
Australia: Langlands (4g); Harris, Branighan,
Sterling, Knight; Fulton (3t), Raudonikis (1t);
O'Neill, Walters, Beetson, McCarthy (1dg), Elford,
Sullivan. Subs: Ward, Sait
Referee: M. Teisseire (France)

AUSTRALIA 9   NEW ZEALAND 5
Paris: 1 November   8,000
Australia: Langlands; Grant, Branighan (1g),
Starling, Knight; Fulton (1t,1dg), Ward (1t);
O'Neill, Walters, O'Reilly, Sullivan, Elford, Sait.
Sub: Stevens
New Zealand: Wilson (1g); Orchard, Brereton,
Christian, Whittaker (1t); Williams, Tracey; Mann,
Burgoyne, Gailey, Eade, Paul, Gurnick.
Sub: Walker
Referee: M. J. Naughton (England)

GREAT BRITAIN 13   FRANCE 4
Grenoble: 1 November   5,321
Britain: Charlton; Sullivan (1t), Hesketh, Walsh,
Atkinson; O'Neill, Nash; Clawson (2g), Stephenson,
Lockwood, Lowe (2t), Dixon, Nicholls
France: Toujas; Marsolan, Molinier, Ruiz, J. Bonal
(1g); Guilhem, Imbert; de Nadai, Franc, Sauret,
Serrano (1g), Gleyzes, Rodriguez. Sub: Zalduendo
Referee: F. Gril (France)

GREAT BRITAIN 53   NEW ZEALAND 19
Pau: 4 November   7,500
Britain: Charlton (1t); Sullivan (1t), Hesketh (1t),
Walsh, Atkinson (2t); Holmes (2t,10g), Nash (1t);
Jeanes (1t), Stephenson (1t), Lockwood, Lowe,
Irving, Nicholls (1t). Subs: Redfearn, Karalius
New Zealand: Wilson (2g); Orchard, Brereton,
Christian, Whittaker (1t); Williams (1t), Tracey;
Mann, Burgoyne (1t), Gailey, Eade (1t), Coll (1t),
Gurnick. Subs: Collicoat, Walker
Referee: G. Jameau (France)

AUSTRALIA 31   FRANCE 9
Toulouse: 5 November   10,332
Australia: Langlands; Grant, Harris (2t), Starling,
Branighan (5g); Fulton (1t), Ward; O'Neill (1t),
Walters (1t), O'Reilly, Beetson, Stevens, Sait (2t)
France: Toujas; Marsolan, Molinier, Mazare,
Frattini; Ruiz (1t), J. Bonal (3g); Zalduendo, Franc,
Garzino, Serrano, Gleyzes, de Nadai.
Subs: Guilhem, Anglade
Referee: M. J. Naughton (England)

Final Table

	P	W	D	L	F	A	Pts
Great Britain	3	3	0	0	93	44	6
Australia	3	2	0	1	61	41	4
France	3	1	0	2	33	53	2
New Zealand	3	0	0	3	33	82	0

FINAL
GREAT BRITAIN 10   AUSTRALIA 10
Lyons: 11 November   4,231
● 10-10 after 80 minutes. Extra time of
20 minutes produced no further score. Britain
awarded trophy because of higher position in
league table.

Britain: Charlton; Sullivan (1t), Hesketh,
Walsh, Atkinson; Holmes, Nash; Clawson (2g),
Stephenson (1t), Jeanes, Lowe, Lockwood,
Nicholls. Sub: Irving
Australia: Langlands; Grant, Harris, Starling,
Branighan (2g); Fulton, Ward; O'Neill (1t),
Walters, O'Reilly, Beetson (1t), Stevens,
Sullivan
Referee: G. Jameau (France)

1975　Played in all five countries　WON BY AUSTRALIA
● Decided on league places

England
In Australia and New Zealand
Manager: W. Oxley
Coach: A. Murphy
R. Millward (Hull KR), Capt.
J. Atkinson (Leeds)
J. Bridges (Featherstone R.)
D. Chisnall ((St. Helens)
E. Chisnall (St. Helens)
P. Cookson (Leeds)
M. Coulman (Salford)
G. Dunn (Hull KR)
L. Dyl (Leeds)
G. Fairbairn (Wigan)
K. Fielding (Salford)
K. Gill (Salford)
P. Gordon (Warrington)
T. Martyn (Warrington)
M. Morgan (Wakefield T.)
S. Nash (Featherstone R.)
G. Nicholls (St. Helens)
D. Noonan (Warrington)
S. Norton (Castleford)
J. Walsh (St. Helens)

The following players also appeared
in the World Cup but did not tour
Down Under:
M. Adams (Widnes), P. Charlton (Salford),
D. Eckersley (St. Helens), C. Forsyth (Bradford N.)
J. Gray (Wigan), J. Holmes (Leeds),
E. Hughes (Widnes), R. Irving (Wigan),
P. Jackson (Bradford N.), B. Philbin (Warrington),
D. Redfearn (Bradford N.),
J. Thompson (Featherstone R.), S. Wright (Wigan)

Wales
In Australia and New Zealand
Manager: R. Simpson
Coach: L. Pearce
D. Watkins (Salford), Capt.
P. Banner (Salford)
B. Butler (Swinton)
K. Coslett (St. Helens)
E. Cunningham (S. Helens)
C. Dixon (Salford)
R. Evans (Swinton)
A. Fisher (Leeds)
W. Francis (Wigan)
J. Mantle (St. Helens)
R. Mathias (St. Helens)
J. Mills (Widnes)
M. Nicholas (Warrington)
P. Rowe (Blackpool B.)
C. Sullivan (Hull KR)
D. Treasure (Oldham)
G. Turner (Hull KR)
R. Wanbon (Warrington)
D. Willicombe (Wigan)
F. Wilson (St. Helens)

The following players also appeared
in the World Cup but did not tour
Down Under:
J. Bevan (Warrington), S. Gallacher (Keighley),
B. Gregory (Wigan), M. James (St. Helens),
C. Jones (Leigh), M. Murphy (Bradford N.),
M. Richards (Salford), R. Wallace (York)

Australia
In England, Wales
and France
Managers: R. Abbott,
　　　　　 J. Cairns
Coach: G. Langlands
A. Beetson, Capt.
J. Brass
M. Cronin
G. Eadie
D. Fitzgerald
R. Higgs
J. Lang
I. Mackay
A. McMahon
J. Mayes
J. Peard
G. Pierce
G. Piggins　　　　(*cont.*)

France
In Australia
and New Zealand
Manager: R. Forges
Coach: Puig Aubert
J. Calle, Capt.
M. Anglade
E. Bonal
M. Cassins
B. Curt
F. de Nadai
A. Dumas
Z. Gleyzes
A. Gonzales
D. Hermet
J. M. Imbert
V. Kaminski
M. Maique　　　(*cont.*)

New Zealand
In England, Wales
and France
Manager: B. Watson
Coach: G. Menzies
K. Stirling, Capt.
F. Ah Kuoi
R. Baxendale
L. Beehre
A. Coll
W. Collicoat
T. Conroy
B. Dickison
M. Eade
A. Gordon
J. Greengrass
P. Gurnick
R. Jarvis　　　(*cont.*)

L. Platz
J. Porter
J. Quayle
T. Randall
T. Raudonikis
J. Rhodes
S. Rogers
I. Schubert
G. Veivers

*The following players also
appeared in the World Cup
but did not tour Europe:*

C. Anderson, R. Branighan,
R. Coote, J. Donnelly, T. Fahey,
R. Fulton, M. Harris,
G. Langlands, J. O'Neill,
T. Pickup, R. Sait, G. Stevens,
R. Strudwick, D. Wright
Non-playing substitute:
J. Payne

M. Mayorgas
A. Ruiz
R. Terrats
F. Tranier
C. Zalduendo

*The following players also
appeared in the World Cup
but did not tour Down Under:*

Y. Alvernhe, J. Bosc, G. Buchi,
P. Chauvet, P. Clergeau, M. De
Matos, F. Duthill, G. Garcia,
J. Grechi, B. Guilhem, M. Laffargue,
J. Lacoste, M. Molinier,
M. Moussard, M. Pillan,
J. Sauret, V. Serrano,
C. Thenegal, J. Tremoulille,
G. Vigouroux,
Non-playing substitutes:
J. Castel, G. Laskawieck

P. Orchard
L. Proctor
J. Smith
D. Sorensen
K. Sorensen
D. Williams

*The following players also
appeared in the World Cup
but did not tour Europe:*

M. Brereton, J. Hibbs, P. Matete,
D. Munro, J. O'Sullivan,
G. West, J. Whittaker

FRANCE 14   WALES 7
Toulouse: 2 March   7,563

France: Tranier; E. Bonal, Molinier,
Terrats (1t), Curt (1t); Lacoste (1dg),
Imbert (1dg); De Nadai, Kaminski,
Serrano (3g), Gleyzes, Hermet, Anglade.
Sub: Castel
Wales: Francis; Mathias, Willicombe,
Wilson (1t), Richards; Watkins, Banner;
Murphy, Evans, Butler, Mantle, Dixon,
Coslett (2g), Sub: Wallace
Referee: G. F. Lindop (England)

ENGLAND 20   FRANCE 2
Leeds: 16 March   10,842

England: Charlton; Fielding (2t), Noonan, Dyl,
Atkinson; Gill, Millward (1t); D. Chisnall,
Gray (4g), Jackson, Martyn, Nicholls, Philbin.
Sub: Morgan (1t)
France: Tranier; E. Bonal, Molinier, Terrats,
Curt; Lacoste, Imbert; De Nadai, Kamininski,
Serrano (1g), Gleyzes, Hermet, Anglade
Referee: K. Page (Australia)
Replaced by H. G. Hunt (England) after 25
minutes because of illness.

AUSTRALIA 36   NEW ZEALAND 8
Brisbane: 1 June   10,000

Australia: Langlands (2t); Anderson,
Fulton (1t), Cronin (2t,6g), Fahey; Pickup,
Strudwick; Randall (1t), Lang, Wright,
Stevens, Platz (1t), Coote.
Sub: Branighan (1t), Sait

New Zealand: Collicoat (1g); Brereton,
O'Sullivan, Whittaker (1t), Orchard; Williams,
Stirling (1t); West, Conroy, Hibbs, Coll,
Baxendale, Eade
Referee: F. Escande (France)

WALES 12   ENGLAND 7
Brisbane: 10 June   6,000

Wales: Francis; Sullivan (1t), Willicombe,
Watkins (3g), Mathias; Treasure (1t), Banner;
Mills, Fisher, Wanbon, Cunningham, Dixon,
Coslett. Subs: Wilson, Mantle
England: Fairbairn (2g); Fielding, Noonan,
Dyl, Atkinson; Millward, Nash; D. Chisnall,
Morgan, Coulman, E. Chisnall, Nicholls,
Norton. Subs: Gill, Martyn (1t)
Referee: D. Lancashire (Australia)

AUSTRALIA 30   WALES 13
Sydney: 14 June   25,386

Australia: Langlands (1t); Harris (1t),
Fulton (1t), Cronin (9g), Rhodes; Pickup,
Raudonikis (1t); Randall, Lang, O'Neill, Platz,
Stevens, Sait. Sub: Donnelly
Wales: Francis; Sullivan, Watkins (5g),
Willicombe, Mathias; Turner, Treasure; Mills,
Fisher (1t), Wanbon, Cunningham, Mantle,
Coslett. Subs: Wilson, Rowe
Referee: F. Escande (France)

NEW ZEALAND 27   FRANCE 0
Christchurch: 15 June   2,500

New Zealand: Whittaker; Orchard, O'Sullivan,
Williams, Munro; Jarvis (2t), Stirling (1t);
Greengrass, Conroy (1t), D. Sorensen (6g), Coll,
Baxendale, Eade (1t), Subs: Collicoat, Proctor

France: Tranier; Dumas, Terrats, Ruiz,
E. Bonal; Calle, Imbert; Zalduendo, Gonzales,
Cassins, Gleyzes, De Nadai, Mayorgas
Referee: L. Bruyeres (Australia)

NEW ZEALAND 17   ENGLAND 17
Auckland: 21 June   12,000
New Zealand: Whittaker; Orchard (1t),
O'Sullivan, Williams (2t), Munro; Jarvis,
Stirling; Greengrass, Conroy, D. Sorensen (4g),
Coll, Baxendale, Eade. Subs: Collicoat, Proctor
England: Fairbairn (2t,4g); Fielding, Walsh,
Dyl, Atkinson (1t); Gill, Nash; D. Chisnall,
Bridges, E. Chisnall, Nicholls, Cookson,
Norton. Sub: Morgan
Referee: L. Bruyeres (Australia)

AUSTRALIA 26   FRANCE 6
Brisbane: 22 June   9,000
Australia: Langlands; Harris (2t), Fulton (2t),
Cronin (1t,4g), Rhodes; Pickup (1t),
Raudonikis; Beetson, Lang, Donnelly, Platz,
Randall, Coote
France: Tranier; Dumas, Ruiz, Terrats, Curt;
Calle (3g), Imbert; De Nadai, Kaminski,
Cassins, Maique, Gleyzes, Anglade.
Sub: Zalduendo
Referee: J. Percival (New Zealand)

AUSTRALIA 10   ENGLAND 10
Sydney: 28 June   33,858
Australia: Langlands; Rhodes, Fulton,
Cronin (2g), Harris; Pickup, Raudonikis;
Beetson, Lang, Randall, Stevens, Platz,
Coote (1t). Subs: Anderson (1t), Donnelly.
England: Fairbairn (2g); Fielding, Walsh, Dyl,
Dunn (1t); Millward, Nash; Coulman, Bridges,
Morgan, Nicholls, Cookson, Norton.
Subs: Gill (It), E. Chisnall
Referee: J. Percival (New Zealand)

NEW ZEALAND 13   WALES 8
Auckland: 28 June   9,368
New Zealand: Collicoat (5g); Orchard (1t),
O'Sullivan, Williams, Munro; Jarvis, Stirling;
Proctor, Conroy, D. Sorensen, Coll, Baxendale,
Eade
Wales: Francis (1t); Mathias, Willicombe,
Watkins (1g), Sullivan; Treasure, Banner;
Mills (1t), Fisher, Wanbon, Mantle, Dixon,
Coslett. Sub: Butler
Referee: L. Bruyeres (Australia)

WALES 16   ENGLAND 22
Warrington: 20 September   5,034
Wales: Francis; Sullivan, Watkins (5g),
Wilson, Bevan; Treasure, Banner (1t); Mantle,
Fisher, James, Gregory, Cunningham,
Coslett (1t). Subs: Turner, Rowe
England: Fairbairn (6g); Fielding (1t),
Hughes (1t), Holmes (1t), Atkinson; Gill,
Millward; Hogan, Bridges (1dg), Forsyth,
Irving, Grayshon, Norton.
Subs: Eckersley, Nicholls
Referee: M. Cailol (France)

NEW ZEALAND 8   AUSTRALIA 24
Auckland: 27 September   20,000
New Zealand: Collicoat (4g); Orchard, Matete,
Williams, Ah Kuoi; Jarvis, Stirling;
Greengrass, Conroy, D. Sorensen, Coll,
Baxendale, Eade. Subs: Smith, K. Sorensen
Australia: Eadie; Rhodes, Cronin (1t,6g),
Brass, Schubert (1t); Peard, Mayes; Veivers,
Piggins, Mackay, Platz, Higgs (1t), Quayle (1t).
Subs: Raudonikis, Fitzgerald
Referee: G. F. Lindop (England)

FRANCE 2   ENGLAND 48
Bordeauxx: 11 October   1,581
France: De Matos; Grechi, Ruiz, Terrats,
Laffargue; Calle (1g), Imbert; Garcia, Duthill,
Gonzales, Bosc, Tremoulille, Buchi.
Subs: Thenegal, Vigouroux
England: Fairbairn (4g); Fielding (4t),
Hughes (1t), Holmes (2t), Dunn (2t); Gill (1t),
Millward (2g); Hogan (1t), Bridges,
Forsyth (1t), Grayshon, Irving, Norton.
Subs: Nicholls, Eckersley
Referee: J. Percival (New Zealand)

FRANCE 12   NEW ZEALAND 12
Marseilles: 17 October   10,000
France: Pillon; Grechi, Ruiz, Guilhem (3g),
Chauvet (2t); Calle, Imbert; Thenegal,
Gonzales, Zalduendo, Sauret, Tremoulille,
Terrats. Sub: Moussard
New Zealand: Collicoat (3g); Orchard,
Williams, Smith, Dickison; Jarvis (1t), Stirling;
Greengrass, Conroy, Proctor (1t), Coll,
Baxendale, Gurnick. Sub: Gordon
Referee: W. H. Thompson (England)

WALES 6   AUSTRALIA 18
Swansea: 19 October   11,112

Wales: Watkins (3g); Mathias, Francis, Wilson, Bevan, Turner, Banner; Mills, Fisher, Mantle, Cunningham, Dixon, Coslett. Sub: Rowe
Australia: Eadie; McMahon, Cronin (3g), Rogers, Schubert (3t); Peard (1t), Mayes; Beetson, Piggins, Veivers, Randall, Higgs, Quayle.
Subs: Mackay, Porter
Referee: J. Percival (New Zealand)

ENGLAND 27   NEW ZEALAND 12
Bradford: 25 October   5,937

England: Fairbairn (3g); Wright (1t), Hughes (1t), Holmes, Dunn (1t); Gill (3t), Millward; Hogan, Bridges, Forsyth, Grayshon, Adams, Norton (1t). Subs: Dyl, Nicholls
New Zealand: Collicoat (2g); Orchard, Smith (1t), Williams, Dickison; Jarvis, Stirling; Proctor, Conroy, Greengrass, Baxendale, Coll, Eade. Subs: Gordon (1t,1g), Gurnick
Referee: A. Lacaze (France)

FRANCE 2   AUSTRALIA 41
Perpignan: 26 October   10,440

France: Pillon; Grechi, Ruiz, Guilhem (1g), Chauvert; Calle, Imbert; Zalduendo, Gonzales, Thenegal, Sauret, Tremouille, Terrats.
Subs: Clergeau, Moussard
Australia: Eadie (1t,7g); Rhodes (1t), Rogers (2t), Brass, Porter; Peard (1t), Raudonikis (1t); Beetson, Lang, Randall (1t), Higgs (1t), Platz (1t), Pierce.
Sub: Schubert
Referee: J. Percival (New Zealand)

ENGLAND 16   AUSTRALIA 13
Wigan: 1 November   9,393

England: Fairbairn (5g); Dunn, Holmes (1t), Dyl, Redfearn; Gill, Millward; Hogan, Bridges, Thompson, Grayshon (1t), Irving, Norton.
Sub: Hughes, Adams
Australia: Eadie; Schubert (3t), Brass, Cronin (2g), Rhodes; Peard, Mayes; Beetson, Piggins, Mackay, Higgs, Randall, Pierce. Sub: Rogers
Referee: J. Percival (New Zealand)

WALES 25   NEW ZEALAND 24
Swansea: 2 November   2,645

Wales: Watkins (5g); Mathias, Wilson, Willicombe (1t), Bevan (1t); Francis (2t), Banner; Mills, Fisher, Murphy, Mantle (1t), Gallacher, Gregory. Sub: Jones
New Zealand: Collicoat (1g); Orchard (1t), Ah Kuoi, Williams, Gordon (1t,5g); Jarvis, Smith; D. Sorensen, Conroy, Greengrass (1t), K. Sorensen, Coll (1t), Gornick.
Subs: Proctor, Dickison
Referee: G. Jarneau (France)

WALES 23   FRANCE 2
Salford: 6 November   2,247

Wales: Watkins (4g); Mathias, Wilson, Williscombe (1t), Bevan (1t); Francis (1t), Banner (1t); Mantle, Evans, Murphy, Gregory (1t), Gallagher, Jones.
Subs: Turner, Butler
France: Calle; Grechi, Terrats, Guilhem (1g), Curt; Lacoste, Imbert; Alvernhe, Gonzales, Moossard, Tremouille, Sauret, Mayorgas. Sub: Maique
Referee: G. F. Lindop (England)

Final Table

	P	W	D	L	F	A	Pts
Australia	8	6	1	1	198	69	13
England	8	5	2	1	167	84	12
Wales	8	3	0	5	110	130	6
New Zealand	8	2	2	4	121	149	6
France	8	1	1	6	40	204	3

1977   Played in Australia and New Zealand   WON BY AUSTRALIA
● Decided by top two in league table meeting in play-off final.

Great Britain	Australia	France	New Zealand
Manager: R. Parker	Managers: D. Hall	Manager: P. De Jean	Manager: D. Barchard
Coach: D. Watkins	C. Brown	Coach: Y. Begou	Coach: R. Ackland
	Coach: T. Fearnley		
R. Millward (Hull K.R.), Capt.	A. Beetson, Capt.	J. Calle, Capt.	T. Coll, Capt.
E. Bowman (Workington T.)	G. Crear	G. Alard	F. Ah Kuoi
L. Casey (Hull K.R.)	M. Cronin	C. Baile	R. Baxendale
L. Dyl (Leeds)	G. Eadie	H. Bonnet	W. Collicoat
K. Elwell (Widnes)	T. Fahey	J. Bourret	G. Filipaina
G. Fairbairn (Wigan)	D. Fitzgerald	J. Brial	K. Fisher
K. Fielding (Salford)	R. Gartner	M. Caravaca	M. Graham
W. Francis (Wigan)	N. Geiger	M. Cassin	Whetu Henry
K. Gill (Salford)	M. Harris	M. Chantal	Whare Henry
A. Hodkinson (Rochdale H.)	R. Higgs	P. Chauvet	C. Jordan
P. Hogan (Barrow)	J. Kolc	J. Cologni	M. O'Donnell
J. Holmes (Leeds)	A. McMahon	H. Daniel	D. O'Hara
S. Lloyd (Castleford)	J. Peard	J. Garcia	L. Proctor
S. Nash (Salford)	G. Pierce	J. Guigue	A. Rushton
G. Nicholls (St. Helens)	T. Randall	J. Imbert	J. Smith
S. Pitchford (Leeds)	T. Raudonikis	J. M. Imbert	D. Sorensen
P. Smith (Featherstone R.)	R. Reddy	C. Laskaweic	K. Sorensen
J. Thompson (Featherstone R.)	M. Thomas	G. Lepine	J. Whittaker
D. Ward (Leeds)	G. Veivers	J. Mayorgas	D. Williams
S. Wright (Widnes)		M. Moussard	
		J. Moya	
		G. Rodriguez	
		J. Roosebrouck	
		A. Ruiz	
		P. Saboureau	
		J. Sauret	
		K. Terrats	

NEW ZEALAND 12   AUSTRALIA 27
Auckland: 29 May   18,000

New Zealand: Collicoat (3g); O'Hara,
Filipaina, Jordan, Fisher; Williams, Smith (1t);
Whetu Henry, Rushton (1t), D. Sorensen,
K. Sorensen, Coll, Whare Henry
Australia: Eadie; Harris (1t), Cronin (6g), Thomas
(1t), McMahon (2t); Peard (1t), Raudonikis;
Veivers, Geiger, Fitzgerald, Randall, Higgs, Pierce
Referee: W. H. Thompson (England)

GREAT BRITAIN 23   FRANCE 4
Auckland: 5 June   10,000

Britain: Fairbairn (7g); Fielding, Holmes,
Dyl (1t), Wright (1t); Millward (1t), Nash;
Thompson, Ward, Pitchford, Nicholls,
Bowman, Hogan. Subs: Casey, Gill
France: Guigue; Moya, Laskawieic, Ruiz,
Chauvet; Calle (2g), Allurd; Cassin, Bonnet,
Daniel, Sauret, Cologni, Roosebrouck.
Sub: Rodriguez
Referee: R. Cooper (New Zealand)

AUSTRALIA 21   FRANCE 9
Sydney: 11 June   13,321

Australia: Eadie (2t); McMahon (1t), Cronin (3g),
Thomas, Fahey; Peard, Raudonikis; Veivers (1t),
Geiger, Fitzgerald (1t), Randall, Beetson, Reddy.
Subs: Gartner, Higgs
France: Guigue; Moya, Bourret, Terrats,
Laskaweic (1t); Calle (3g), Allard; Cassin, Garcia,
Chantal, Sauret, Caravaca, Roosebrouck.
Subs: J. M. Imbert, Rodriguez
Referee: W. H. Thompson (England)

NEW ZEALAND 12   GREAT BRITAIN 30
Christchurch: 12 June   9,000

New Zealand: Collicoat (3g); Fisher (1t),
Ah Kuoi, Filipaina, Whittaker (1t); Williams,
Smith; Proctor, Rushton, Whetu Henry,
K. Sorensen, Coll, Whare Henry. Sub: Graham
Britain: Fairbairn (6g); Wright (2t), Holmes,
Dyl, Francis; Millward (1t), Nash; Thompson,
Ward, Pitchford, Nicholls (1t), Bowman (1t),
Hogan (1t). Sub: Casey
Referee: M. Caillol (France)

AUSTRALIA 19   GREAT BRITAIN 5
Brisbane: 18 June   27,000

Australia: Eadie (2t); McMahon, Cronin (5g); Thomas, Fahey; Peard, Raudonikis; Fitzgerald, Geiger, Veivers, Beetson, Randall (1t), Pierce. Sub: Higgs

Britain: Fairbairn (1g); Wright, Francis, Dyl, Fielding; Millward (1t), Nash; Thompson, Ward, Pitchford, Nicholls, Bowman, Hogan. Subs: Smith, Holmes
Referee: M. Caillol (France)

NEW ZEALAND 28   FRANCE 20
Auckland: 19 June   8,000

New Zealand: O'Donnell; Fisher (1t), Ah Kuoi, Williams, Whittaker; Jordan (1t,8g), Smith (1t); Proctor, Rushton, Whetu Henry, Coll, K. Sorensen, Graham (1t)
France: Calle; Moya (4g), Ruiz, Terrats, Guige (1t); Alard, J. M. Imbert; Cassin, Garcia, Sauret, Caravaca, Cologni (2t), Roosebrouck (1t). Subs: J. Imbert, Moussard
Referee: D. Lancashire (Australia)

Final Table

	P	W	D	L	F	A	Pts
Australia	3	3	0	0	67	26	6
Great Britain	3	2	0	1	58	35	4
New Zealand	3	1	0	2	52	77	2
France	3	0	0	3	33	72	0

FINAL
AUSTRALIA 13   GREAT BRITAIN 12
Sydney: 25 June   24,457

Australia: Eadie; McMahon (1t), Cronin (2g), Gartner (1t), Harris; Peard, Kolc (1t); Veivers, Geiger, Randall, Beetson, Higgs, Pierce. Sub: Fitzgerald

Britain: Fairbairn (3g); Wright, Holmes, Dyl, Francis; Millward, Nash; Thompson, Elwell, Pitchford (1t), Casey, Bowman, Hogan. Subs: Gill (1t), Smith
Referee: W. H. Thompson (England)

1985-88 Won by AUSTRALIA

● One match in each Test series between the countries designated as a World Cup match. The top two teams in league table at the end of the home-away series meeting in play-off final.

NEW ZEALAND 18   AUSTRALIA 0
Auckland: 7 July 1985   19,000

New Zealand: Kemble; Bell, Prohm, Leuluai (1t), O'Hara; Filipaina (3g), Friend (2t); Wright, H. Tamati, K. Tamati, Graham, K. Sorensen, McGahan. Subs: Ropati, Cowan
Australia: Jack; Ribot, Meninga, Ella, Ferguson; Lewis, Hasler; Tunks, Elias, Roach, Vautin, Wynn, Pearce. Subs: Close, Dowling
Referee: J. Rascagneres (France)

GREAT BRITAIN 6   NEW ZEALAND 6
Elland Road, Leeds: 9 November 1985   22,209

Britain: Burke (Widnes); Drummond (Leigh), Schofield (Hull), Edwards (Wigan), Lydon (Widnes); Hanley (Wigan), Fox (Featherstone R.); Grayshon (Leeds), Watkinson (Hull KR), Fieldhouse (Widnes), Goodway (Wigan), Potter (Wigan), Pinner (St. Helens). Subs: L. Crooks (Hull, 3g), Arkwright (St. Helens)
New Zealand: Kemble; Williams, Bell, Leuluai, O'Hara; Ah Kuoi, Friend; K. Tamati, Wallace, D. Sorensen (1g), Graham (1t), K. Sorensen, Prohm. Subs: Filipaina, McGahan
Referee: B. Gomersall (Australia)

FRANCE 0   NEW ZEALAND 22
Perpignan: 7 December 1985   5,000

France: Pallares; Ratier, Berge, Palisses, Couston; Espugna, Guasch; Chantal, Bernabe, Titeux, Montgaillard, Palanque, G. Laforgue. Subs: Perez, Rabot
New Zealand: Kemble (1t); Bell, Ah Kuoi, Leuluai, O'Hara; Filipaina (3g), Friend; K. Sorensen (1t), Wallace, D. Sorensen, McGahan (2t), Wright, O'Regan. Subs: Elia, Todd
Referee: R. Campbell (England)

FRANCE 10   GREAT BRITAIN 10
Avignon: 16 February 1986   4,000

France: Dumas (1t,3g); Couston, Maury, Fourquet, Laroche; Espugna, Entat; Chantal, Baco, Titeux, G. Laforgue, Palanque, Bernabe. Subs: Rabot, Berge
Britain: Burke (Widnes); Drummond (Leigh), Schofield (Hull), Hanley (Wigan, 1t), Gill (Wigan); A. Myler (Widnes), Fox (Featherstone R.); L. Crooks (Hull, 3g), Watkinson (Hull KR), Wane (Wigan), Potter (Wigan), Fieldhouse (Widnes), Pinner (St. Helens)
Referee: K. Roberts (Australia)

AUSTRALIA 32   NEW ZEALAND 12
Brisbane: 29 July   22,811
Australia: Jack; O'Connor (1t,4g), Miles (1t),
Kenny (2t), Kiss; Lewis (1t), Sterling (1t);
Roach, Simmons, Tunks, Cleal, Folkes, Pearce.
Subs: Lamb, Niebling
New Zealand: Kemble; Williams (2t), Ropati,
Prohm, O'Hara; Filipaina (2g), Freeman; Todd,
Harvey, K. Sorensen, Graham, McGahan, O'Regan.
Subs: Cooper, Wright
Referee: R. Whitfield (England)

PAPUA NEW GUINEA 24   NEW ZEALAND 22
Port Moresby: 17 August 1986   15,000
Papua New Guinea: Kovae (4g); Katsir,
Atoi (1t), Numapo, Kerekere; Haili (2t), Kila; Tep,
Heni, Lomutopa, Ako (1t), Waketsi, Taumaku.
Subs: Saea, Andy
New Zealand: Kemble; Crequer, Williams,
J. Ropati (1t), O'Hara; Cooper, Freeman; Shelford,
Wallace (1t), Brown (1t,3g), Wright, McGahan (1t),
O'Regan. Subs: Leuluai, Stewart
Referee: K. Roberts (Australia)

PAPUA NEW GUINEA 12   AUSTRALIA 62
Port Moresby: 4 October 1986   17,000
Papua New Guinea: Kovae (2g); Katsir, Atoi,
Numapo (2t), Kerekere; Haili, Kila; Tep, Heni,
Lomutopa, Ako (1t), Waketsi, Taumaku.
Subs: Saea, Andy
Australia: Jack (1t); O'Connor (2t,7g), Miles,
C. Mortimer (1t), Kiss (2t); Lewis (1t), Hasler (1t);
Roach (1t), Simmons, Niebling, Dunn, Cleal (2t),
Lindner (1t). Subs: Meninga, Sironen
Referee: N. Kesha (New Zealand)

GREAT BRITAIN 15   AUSTRALIA 24
Wigan: 22 November 1986   20,169
Britain: Lydon (Wigan, 2g); Gill (Wigan, 1g),
Schofield (Hull, 2t,1dg), Stephenson (Wigan),
Basnett (Widnes); A. Myler (Widnes), A. Gregory
(Warrington); Ward (Castleford), Watkinson
(Hull KR), Crooks (Hull), Burton (Hull KR),
Goodway(Wigan),Pinner(Widnes).Sub:Potter(Wigan)
Australia: Jack; Shearer (1t), Kenny, Miles (1t),
O'Connor (4g); Lewis (1t), Sterling; Dowling,
Simmons, Dunn, Meninga, Niebling, Lindner (1t).
Subs: Davidson, Lamb
Referee: J. Rascagneres (France)

Papua New Guinea half back Tuksy Karu, who competed in the 1989-92 World Cup tournament.

FRANCE 0   AUSTRALIA 52
Carcassonne: 13 December 1986   3,000
France: Wozniack; Rodriguez, Fourquet,
F. Laforgue, Ratier; Palisses, Scicchitano; Chantal,
Bernabe, Titeux, G. Laforgue, Verdes, Gestas.
Subs: Dumas, Storer
Australia: Jack (3t); Shearer (4t), Kenny, Miles,
O'Connor (1t,6g); Lewis, Sterling; Dowling,
Simmons, Dunn, Folkes (1t), Niebling (1t),
Lindner. Subs: Lamb, Davidson
Referee: G. F. Lindop (England)

GREAT BRITAIN 52   FRANCE 4
Leeds: 24 January 1987   6,567
Britain: Lydon (Wigan, 1t,8g); Forster (Warrington,
1t), Schofield (Hull), Stephenson (Wigan), Gill
(Wigan); Hanley (Wigan, 2t), Edwards (Wigan, 2t);
Hobbs (Oldham), K. Beardmore (Castleford),
L. Crooks (Hull), Goodway (Wigan, 1t), Haggerty
(St. Helens), M. Gregory (Warrington, 2t).
Subs: Creasser (Leeds), England (Castleford)
France: Perez (2g); Couston, Palisses, Ratier, Pons;
Espugna, Dumas; Storer, Mantese, Rabot, Verdes,
Palanque, Bernabe. Subs: Rocci, Titeux
Referee: M. Stone (Australia)

GREAT BRITAIN 42 PAPUA NEW GUINEA 0
Wigan: 24 October 1987 9,121

Britain: Hampson (Wigan); Drummond (Warrington), Stephenson (Wigan, 7g), Lydon (Wigan, 1t), Ford (Bradford N., 1t); Edwards (Wigan, 2t), Gregory (Wigan); Ward (Castleford), Groves (St. Helens), Case (Wigan), Medley (Leeds, 1t), Goodway (Wigan), Hanley (Wigan, 1t). Subs: Woods (Warrington), Fairbank (Bradford N.)
Papua New Guinea: Kovae; Saea, Atoi, Numapo, Krewanty; Haili, Kila; Tep, Heni, Lomutopa, Kombra, Waketsi, Taumaku.
Subs: Kitimun, Gaius
Referee: F. Desplas (France)

FRANCE 21 PAPUA NEW GUINEA 4
Carcassonne: 15 November 1987 5,000

France: Pougeau; Ratier (1t), Delaunay, Fraisse (2t), Pons (1t); Moliner, Bourrel (2g,1dg); Rabot, Khedimi, Ailleres, Montgaillard, Divet, G. Laforgue. Subs: Dumas, Verdes
Papua New Guinea: Kovae (1t); Krewanty, Saea, Atoi, Morea; Numapo, Kila; Lomutop, Heni, Taumaku, Waketsi, Ako, Kouoru.
Subs: Haili, Kombra
Referee: J. Holdsworth (England)

PAPUA NEW GUINEA 22
GREAT BRITAIN 42
Port Moresby: 22 May 1988 12,077

Papua New Guinea: Kovae (2t); Saea, Morea, Numapo (3g), Krewanty (1t); Haili, Kila; Rop (1t), Matmillo, Bom, Kombra, Evei, Kouoru.
Subs: Rombuk, Lapan
Britain: Loughlin (St. Helens, 7g); Ford (Bradford N.), Schofield (Leeds, 2t), Stephenson (Leeds, 1t), Gill (Wigan, 2t); Edwards (Wigan), A. Gregory (Wigan); Ward (Castleford), K. Beardmore (Castleford), Case (Wigan), Medley (Leeds, 1t), M. Gregory (Warrington, 1t), Hanley (Wigan).
Subs: D. Hulme (Widnes), Dixon (Halifax)
Referee: G. McCallum (Australia)

AUSTRALIA 12 GREAT BRITAIN 26
Sydney: 9 July 1988 15,994

Australia: Jack; Ettingshausen, O'Connor (2g), Jackson, Currie; Lewis (1t),Sterling; Bella, Conescu,

Backo (1t), Fullerton-Smith, Vautin, Pearce.
Subs: Belcher, Lindner
Britain: P. Ford (Bradford N., 1t); Gill (Wigan, 2t), Stephenson (Leeds), Loughlin (St. Helens, 3g), Offiah (Widnes, 1t); D. Hulme (Widnes), A. Gregory (Wigan); Ward (Castleford), P. Hulme (Widnes), Waddell (Oldham), M. Gregory (Warrington, 1t), Powell (Leeds), Hanley (Wigan). Sub: Case (Wigan)
Referee: F. Desplas (France)

NEW ZEALAND 66
PAPUA NEW GUINEA 14
Auckland: 10 July 1988 8,392

New Zealand: Williams (1t); S. Horo (3t), Bell, K. Iro (3t), Mercer (2t); Cooper, Friend; Brown (9g), Wallace (1t), Shelford (1t), Graham (1t), Stewart, M. Horo. Subs: Freeman, Faimalo
Papua New Guinea: Kovae (1t); Krewanty, Numapo (3g), Atoi, Morea; Haili, Kila; Ben-Moide, Marmillo (1t), Bom, Evei, Kombra, Kouoru.
Subs: Wanega, Kouru,
Referee: G. McCallum (Australia)

NEW ZEALAND 12 GREAT BRITAIN 10
Christchurch: 17 July 1988 8,525

New Zealand: Williams; S. Horo, Bell, K. Iro, Mercer; Cooper, Friend; Brown (2g), Wallace, Shelford, Graham, Stewart, M. Horo.
Sub: Freeman (2t)
Britain: P.Ford (Bradford N.); Gill (Wigan), Stephenson (Leeds), Loughlin (St. Helens, 1t,1g), Offiah (Widnes); D. Hulme (Widnes, 1t), A. Gregory (Wigan); K. Ward (Castleford), K. Beardmore (Castleford), Waddell (Oldham), M. Gregory (Warrington), Powell (Leeds), Hanley (Wigan). Sub: P. Hulme (Widnes)
Referee: M. Stone (Australia)

AUSTRALIA 70 PAPUA NEW GUINEA 8
Wagga Wagga: 20 July 1988 11,685

Australia: Jack (1t); O'Connor (4t,7g), Jackson, Meninga (2t), Currie (1t); Lewis (1t), Langer (2t); Daley, Conescu (1t), Dunn, Miller (1t), Fullerton-Smith (1t), Pearce. Subs: Hasler, Vautin
Papua New Guinea: Wanega; Krewanty, Kovae, Numapo (2g), Morea (1t); Atoi, Haili; Rombuk, Matmillo, Ben-Moide, Kombra, Evei, Gispe.
Subs: Karara, Kuno
Referee: N. Kesha (New Zealand)

Final Table

	P	W	D	L	F	A	Pts
Australia	7	5	0	2	252	91	12*
New Zealand	7	4	1	2	158	86	11*
Great Britain	8	4	2	2	203	90	10
Papua New Guinea	7	1	0	6	84	325	4*
France	5	1	1	3	35	140	3

*Awarded two points in lieu of non-fulfilment of French fixtures Down Under.

FINAL

AUSTRALIA 25   NEW ZEALAND 12

Eden Park, Auckland, 9 October 1988   47,363

Australia: Jack; Shearer (1t), Farrar, McGaw, O'Connor (4g); Lewis, Langer (2t); Dunn, Elias (1dg), Roach, Sironen, Miller (1t), Pearce.
Subs: Lamb, Gillespie
New Zealand: Mercer; T. Iro (1t), K. Iro (1t), Bell, Elia; Freeman, Friend; Brown (2g), Wallace, Shelford, Graham, K. Sorensen, M. Horo.
Subs: Cooper, Stewart
Referee: G. Ainui (Papua New Guinea)

Second row forward Mark Graham, skipper of 1988 World Cup finalists New Zealand.

1989-92   WON BY AUSTRALIA

- One match in each Test series between the countries designated as a World Cup match. The top two teams in the league table at the end of the home – away series meeting in the play-off final.

NEW ZEALAND 14   AUSTRALIA 22

Auckland: 23 July 1989   15,000

New Zealand: Williams; Mercer (1t), K. Iro, Kemp, Elia (1t); K. Shelford (3g), Freeman; Todd, D. Mann, Goulding, Stewart, M. Horo, McGahan.
Subs: Sherlock, Tuuta
Australia: Belcher; Hancock, Shearer (1t), Currie, O'Connor (1t,2g); Lewis, Hasler; Backo, Kerrod Walters, Roach, Meninga (1t,1g), Clyde (1t), Vautin. Sub: McGuire
Referee: R. Tennant (England)

GREAT BRITAIN 10   NEW ZEALAND 6

Wigan: 11 November 1989   20,346

Great Britain: Tait (Widnes, 1t); Ford (Leeds), Newlove (Featherstone R.), Loughlin (St. Helens, 1g), Offiah (Widnes, 1t); Edwards (Wigan), D. Hulme (Widnes); Skerrett (Bradford N.), P. Hulme (Widnes), Platt (Wigan), Goodway (Wigan), Powell (Leeds), M. Gregory (Warrington). Subs: Lydon (Wigan), England (Castleford)
New Zealand: Kemp; K. Iro, Bell, Williams, Mercer: K. Shelford (1t,1g), Freeman; Todd, D. Mann, Faimalo, K. Sorensen, Stewart, McGahan. Subs: Leota, Clark
Referee: G. McCallum (Australia)

FRANCE 0   NEW ZEALAND 34

Carcassonne: 3 December 1989   4,208

France: Pougeau; Chiron, Fourquet, Fraisse, Pons; Dumas, Entat; Rabot, Khedemi, Storer, Cabestany, Divet, Bernabe. Subs: Courty, Biennes
New Zealand: Kemp (1t); Watson (3t), Bell (1t), Williams (1t), Mercer; Clark, Freeman; Todd, D. Mann, G. Mann, Kuiti (1t), Stewart, McGahan. Subs: Sherlock (3g), K. Shelford
Referee: R. Whitfield (England)

PAPUA NEW GUINEA 8   GREAT BRITAIN 40
Port Moresby: 2 June 1990   5,969
Papua New Guinea: Wanega; Krewanty, Boge,
Numapo (2g), Morea; Haru, Ongugo (1t),
Lomutopa, Matmillo, Evei, Gispe, Taumaku,
Angara. Subs: Tiri, Itam
Great Britain: Tait (Widnes); Eastwood (Hull, 1t),
Davies (Widnes, 6g), D. Powell (Sheffield E., 1t),
Gibson (Leeds, 2t); Schofield (Leeds, 1t), Goulding
(Wigan, 1t); R. Powell (Leeds), L. Jackson (Hull),
England (Castleford), Betts (Wigan), Dixon (Leeds,
1t), M. Gregory (Warrington). Subs: Fox
(Featherstone R.), Clarke (Wigan)
Referee: D. Hale (New Zealand)

AUSTRALIA 34   FRANCE 2
Parkes: 27 June 1990   12,384
Australia: Belcher (1g); O'Connor, Meninga (1t),
McGaw (2t), Shearer (1t); Daley (1t), Langer; Bella,
Kerrod Walters, Roach, Sironen, Gillespie, Mackay
(3t). Subs: Ettingshausen, Carroll
France: Caster: Ratier, Samitou, Delaunay, Pons;
Dumas (1g), Entat; Rabot, Lope, Butignol,
Cabestany, Divet, Valero. Sub: Ruiz
Referee: G. Ainui (Papua New Guinea)

NEW ZEALAND 21   GREAT BRITAIN 18
Christchurch: 15 July 1990   3,133
New Zealand: Ridge (6g); Panapa, K. Iro, Williams,
T. Iro; Kemp (1t), Freeman; Brown, D. Mann,
Todd, Nikau (1t), M. Horo, McGahan (1dg).
Subs: M. Edwards, Lonergan
Great Britain: Lydon (Wigan); Davies (Widnes, 3g),
Gibson (Leeds), D. Powell (Sheffield E.), Offiah
(Widnes, 1t); Schofield (Leeds, 1t), Goulding
(Wigan); Skerrett (Bradford N.), Dermott (Wigan),
England (Castleford), Betts (Wigan), R. Powell
(Leeds, 1t), M. Gregory (Warrington).
Subs: Irwin (Castleford), Dixon (Leeds)
Referee: B. Harrigan (Australia)

PAPUA NEW GUINEA 10
NEW ZEALAND 18
Port Moresby: 11 August 1990   10,000
Papua New Guinea: Wanega; Krewanty, Boge,
Numapo (1g), Haru; Soga (1t), Ongugo; Ako,
M. Matmillo, Evei, Angara, Paglipari, Elara.
Subs: Waine (1t), Tiri

New Zealand: Ridge (3g); Panapa (1t), Watson (1t),
Tuimavave, T. Iro; Nixon, Freeman; Brown,
D. Mann, Todd, Nikau, Lonergan (1t), Kuiti.
Subs: M. Edwards, Patton, G. Mann, Leota
Referee: B. Harrigan (Australia)

GREAT BRITAIN 0   AUSTRALIA 14
Elland Road, Leeds: 24 November 1990 32,500
Great Britain: Hampson (Wigan): Eastwood (Hull),
D. Powell (Sheffield E.), Gibson (Leeds), Offiah
(Widnes); Schofield (Leeds), A. Gregory (Wigan);
Harrison (Hull), L. Jackson (Hull), Platt (Wigan),
Betts (Wigan), Dixon (Leeds), Hanley (Wigan).
Subs: Davies (Widnes), M. Gregory (Warrington),
R. Powell (Leeds)
Australia: Belcher; Ettingshausen (1t),
Meninga (1t,1g), Daley, Shearer; Lyons, Stuart;
Roach, Elias (1t), Lazarus, Sironen, Lindner,
Mackay. Subs: Alexander, Hasler, Sargent, Gillespie
Referee: A. Sablayrolles (France)

FRANCE 10   AUSTRALIA 34
Perpignan: 9 December 1990   3,428
France: Fraisse; Pons (1t), Bret, Delaunay, Bouzer;
Molier, Entat (1t); Tisseyre (1g), Valero, Buttignol,
Divet, Lope, Verdes. Subs: Bienes, Marginet
Australia: Belcher; Alexander (1t,3g), Meninga (1t),
Shearer (1t), Ettingshausen (1t); Lyons, Stuart;
Roach (1t), Elias, Lazarus, Sironen, Lindner,
Mackay (2t). Subs: Johns, Sargent, Hasler, Gillespie
Referee: J. Holdsworth (England)

FRANCE 10   GREAT BRITAIN 45
Perpignan: 27 January 1991   3,965
France: Auroy (1t); Remirez, Fraisse (1t), Delaunay,
Pons; Dumas, Entat; Tisseyre (1g), Valero,
Buttignol, Magnac, Verdes, Molinier.
Subs: Chamorin, Bienes, Baba
Great Britain: Hampson (Wigan); Eastwood (Hull,
6g), D. Powell (Sheffield E.), Gibson (Leeds), Offiah
(Widnes, 2t); Schofield (Leeds, 2t, 1dg), Edwards
(Wigan, 2t); Lucas (Wigan), L. Jackson (Hull), Platt
(Wigan, 1t), Betts (Wigan, 1t), Holliday
(Widnes), Hanley (Wigan). Subs: Aston
(Sheffield E.), S. Ellis (Castleford), Eyres (Widnes),
Fairbank (Bradford N.)
Referee: G. McCallum (Australia)

NEW ZEALAND 32   FRANCE 10
Christchurch: 23 June 1991   2,000

New Zealand: Botica (6g); Panapa (1t), McCracken, Watson (1t), Blackmore (1t); K. Shelford (1t), Freeman; Todd, D. Mann, Brown, Koloto, Lonergan, Nikau. Subs: Friend (1t), Patton, G. Mann, Mercer
France: Fages; Garcia, Despin, Bienes, Pons; Dumas (3g), Entat; Storer, Valero, Buttignol, Boyals, Cabestany, Verdes (1t).
Subs: Bernabe, Palisses, Romano, Viscay
Referee: G. Ainui (Papua New Guinea)

PAPUA NEW GUINEA 18   FRANCE 20
Goroka: 7 July 1991   11,485

Papua New Guinea: Wanega (5g); Krewanty, Gela (1t), Kamiak, Rena; Haru, Ongugo; Naipao (1t), Bate, Unagi, Daki, Tiri, Gispe. Subs: J. Kouoru, Kola, Soga, Paglipari
France: Auroy; Garcia (1t), Despin (1t), Bienes (1t), Pons; Fages, Entat; Boyals, Torreilles (4g), Buttignol, Plante, Cabestany, Verdes.
Subs: Chamorin, Delpech
Referee: C. Morris (England)

NEW ZEALAND 12   AUSTRALIA 40
Brisbane: 31 July 1991   29,139

New Zealand: Botica (2g); Blackmore (1t), McCracken (1t), K. Iro, Watson; Freeman, Friend; Todd, D. Mann, Brown, G. Mann, Mercer, Nikau. Subs: Patton, Williams, Koloto, Faimalo
Australia: Ettingshausen (1t); Carne (1t), Meninga (1t,6g), Daley (1t), Wishart (1t): P. Jackson, Langer; Salvatori, S. Walters (1t), Bella, Gillespie, Geyer, Clyde (1t).
Subs: Johns, Roberts, Hasler, Cartwright
Referee: J. Holdsworth (England)

PAPUA NEW GUINEA 6   AUSTRALIA 40
Port Moresby: 13 October 1991   14,500

Papua New Guinea: Boge (1g); Palangat, Kouoru, Sinemau, Wagambie; Haru (1t), Karara; Unagi, Moi, Naipo, Daki, Paglipari, Gispe.
Subs: Uradok, Lapan, Ngaffin, Hoffman
Australia: Belcher (1t); Wishart (1t), Meninga (1t,2g), Ettingshausen (1t), Carne (3t); P. Jackson (1t), Toovey; Lazarus, Kerrod Walters, Bella, Roberts, Clyde (1t), Fittler.
Subs: Lyons, Johns, Coyne, Kevin Walters
Referee: D. Hale (New Zealand)

GREAT BRITAIN 56   PAPUA NEW GUINEA 4
Wigan: 9 November 1991   4,193

Great Britain: Hampson (Wigan); Newlove (Featherstone R., 1t), D. Powell (Sheffield E., 1t), Davies (Widnes, 8g), Sullivan (St. Helens, 1t); Schofield (Leeds, 1t), Edwards (Wigan); Harrison (Halifax), Dermott (Wigan), Platt (Wigan), Betts (Wigan, 1t), Moriarty (Widnes, 2t), M. Jackson (Wakefield T., 2t). Subs: Connolly (St. Helens), Fox (Featherstone R.), Fairbank (Bradford N., 1t), Price (Wakefield T.)
Papua New Guinea: Wanega; Kouoru, Wagambie, Boge, Itam; Karu (2g), Haru; Unagi, Paglipari, Ngaffin, Naipao, Hoffman, Gispe.
Subs: Tiri, Lapan, Daki, Palangat
Referee: B. Harrigan (Australia)

FRANCE 28   PAPUA NEW GUINEA 14
Carcassonne: 24 November 1991   1,440

France: Ballery; Garcia (1t), Despin, Bienes, Pons (1t); Dumas (1t,4g), Entat; Viloni, Lope, Ailleres, Mountgaillard, Divet (1t), Bonnafous (1t). Subs: Fages, Alesina, Storer, Baba
Papua New Guinea: Wanega; Itam (1t), Wagambie, Boge, Kouoru; Karu (2g), Haru (1t,1g); Naipao, Matmillo, Ngaffin, Tiri, Paglipari, Gispe. Subs: Palangat, Lapan, Angra, Hoffman
Referee: C. Morris (England)

GREAT BRITAIN 36   FRANCE 0
Hull: 7 March 1992   5,250

Great Britain: Steadman (Castleford); Eastwood (Hull, 1t,6g), Connolly (St. Helens), Bateman (Warrington), Hunte (St. Helens, 1t); D. Powell (Sheffield E.), Edwards (Wigan); Crooks (Castleford), Dermott (Wigan, 1t), Skerrett (Wigan), Betts (Wigan), Fairbank (Bradford N.), Holliday (Widnes, 1t). Subs: Fox (Bradford N., 1t), Platt (Wigan, 1t), McNamara (Hull)
France: Limongi; Sirvent, Chamorin, Fages, Pons; Dumas, Entat; Ailleres, Valero, Viloni, Llong, Bonnafous, Pech. Subs: Torreilles, Lope, Bomati, Marginet
Referee: E. Ward (Australia)

AUSTRALIA 16   GREAT BRITAIN 10
Brisbane: 3 July 1992   32,313

Australia: Ettingshausen; Carne, Fittler, Meninga (1t,4g), Hancock; Daley (1t), Langer; Lazarus, S. Walters, Harragon, Sironen, Lindner, Clyde. Subs: Gillespie, Kevin Walters, Cartwright, Johns
Great Britain: Steadman (Castleford); Eastwood (Hull, 3g), D. Powell (Sheffield E.), Newlove (Featherstone R.), Offiah (Wigan, 1t); Schofield (Leeds), Edwards (Wigan); Skerrett (Wigan), Dermott (Wigan), Platt (Wigan), Betts (Wigan), McGinty (Wigan), Clarke (Wigan). Subs: Connolly (St. Helens), P. Hulme (Widnes), Harrison (Halifax), Lydon (Wigan)
Referee: D. Hale (New Zealand)

NEW ZEALAND 66
PAPUA NEW GUINEA 10
Auckland: 5 July 1992   3,000

New Zealand: Ridge (1t,4g); Hoppe (1t), K. Iro (1t), Kemp (1t), Blackmore (3t); Clark (2t), Freeman (1t); Stuart (1t), D. Mann (1t), Todd, Hill (1t), Pongia, Nikau. Subs: Halligan (3g), Tuuta, T. Ropati, Woods
Papua New Guinea: Boge (1g); Tani, Joseph, Wagambie, Uradok (2t); Karu, Emil; Bire, Matmillo, Ngafin, Yer, Naipao, Gispe. Subs: Piel, Sinemau, Angra, Lapan
Referee: G. McCallum (Australia)

AUSTRALIA 36   PAPUA NEW GUINEA 14
Townsville: 15 July 1992   12,470

Australia: Carne (1t); G. Mackay (2t), Fittler (1t), Meninga (4g), Hancock; Daley (1t), Langer; Lazarus, S. Walters, Gillespie, Sironen, Lindner, B. Mackay. Subs: Sargent (1t), Johns (1t), Kevin Walters, Cartwright
Papua New Guinea: Boge (1g); Uradok, Joseph (1t), Sinemau, Wagmabie; Karu (1t), Emil (1t); Bire, Matmillo, Ngaffin, Ben-Moide, Naipao, Gispe. Subs: Yer, Angra, Eremas, Lapan
Referee: D. Hale (New Zealand)

FINAL TABLE

	P	W	D	L	F	A	Pts
Australia	8	8	0	0	236	68	16
Great Britain	8	5	0	3	215	79	10
New Zealand	8	5	0	3	203	120	10
France	8	2	0	6	80	247	4
Papua New Guinea	8	0	0	8	84	304	0

FINAL
GREAT BRITAIN 6   AUSTRALIA 10
Wembley: 24 October 1992   73,631

Great Britain: Lydon (Wigan); Hunte (St. Helens), Connolly (St. Helens), Schofield (Leeds), Offiah (Wigan); Edwards (Wigan), Fox (Bradford N., 3g); Ward (St. Helens), Dermott (Wigan), Platt (Wigan), Betts (Wigan), Clarke (Wigan), Hanley (Leeds). Subs: Devereux (Widnes), Tait (Leeds), Skerrett (Wigan), Eyres (Widnes)
Australia: Brasher; Carne, Renouf (1t), Meninga (3g), Hancock; Fittler, Langer; Lazarus, S. Walters, Sargent, Sironen, Lindner, Clyde. Subs: Gillespie, Kevin Walters, Cartwright
Referee: D. Hale (New Zealand)

WORLD CUP ROLL OF HONOUR

Year	Host Country	Winners	Runners-up
1954	France	Great Britain	France
1957	Australia	Australia	Great Britain
1960	England	Great Britain	Australia
1968	Australia and New Zealand	Australia	France
1970	England	Australia	Great Britain
1972	France	Great Britain	Australia
1975	Both Hemispheres	Australia	England*
1977	Australia and New Zealand	Australia	Great Britain
1985-88	Both Hemispheres	Australia	New Zealand
1989-92	Both Hemispheres	Australia	Great Britain

England and Wales entered the tournament, rather than Great Britain.

Australia skipper Mal Meninga, for whom the 1994 Kangaroo tour was a record fourth trip, a record second as captain and a finale to an illustrious playing career.

1994 KANGAROOS

1994 KANGAROO TOUR REVIEW

For the third consecutive Anglo-Aussie series, Great Britain succeeded in winning one of the opening two Tests but failed to clinch the decider, leaving world champions Australia to celebrate 21 years of Ashes domination.

The Kangaroos' 18th visit contained only one defeat on the 14-match John Smith's tour itinerary, a shock 8-4 reversal at the hands of Great Britain in the first Test at Wembley.

Otherwise the Australians rampaged through Britain creating landmarks galore, including a record Test crowd, record Test and tour receipts, a 50th consecutive tour victory outside of the Test arena and a record scoring average.

The eight-week tour also provided major milestones for two of the game's international stalwarts. Australian skipper Mal Meninga said farewell to an illustrious Anglo-Aussie playing career while Great Britain's Garry Schofield bounced back from being dropped for the first John Smith's Test to earn a record-equalling 46th Test cap.

But the publicity-generating visit of the Australians also hit the headlines for wrong reasons when Kangaroo forward Dean Pay had a routine drug test proved positive, no action being taken by the Australian Rugby League as the drug was said to have been contained in a remedy for colds.

One of the most significant chapters of the tour was written a month before the Kangaroos landed in Britain. On 22 August, Great Britain coach Malcolm Reilly dropped a bombshell by announcing his appointment as coach of Australian club Newcastle Knights from the following November, despite being contracted to both the national side and Halifax.

Initial reaction from the Rugby Football League and Halifax was that Reilly might by permitted to continue his duties until the end of the John Smith's Test series, which coincided with his departure Down Under.

But five days later Reilly quit the Great Britain post. Over the weekend speculation mounted that a new three-man team was in the frame with assistant coach Phil Larder being promoted to coach, former Great Britain skipper Ellery Hanley acting as his right hand man and ex-New Zealand, Wigan and Manly coach Graham Lowe – a Kiwi – being appointed as manager.

Larder, a tour assistant coach in 1988, 1990 and 1992, ruled himself out by refusing to work with a non-Briton. On 29 August, Hanley was named by the League's Board of Directors as the new Great Britain coach, while retaining his role as player and assistant coach with Leeds.

Four days later Sheffield Eagles chairman and coach, Gary Hetherington, was chosen as assistant coach, Hull director Steve Watson being invited to continue as manager having been in charge for six unbeaten Tests over 18 months. Watson caused havoc by accepting, then declining before re-accepting the job inside a matter of hours.

The Australian tour squad of 28 players and nine management arrived in Britain only days after the Grand Final. The original tour itinerary scheduled the Kangaroos to open in midweek against high profile Leeds, followed by a weekend game at Wigan. A late addition provided Cumbria with a Sunday fixture which became a low key pipeopener in non-stop driving rain. The green-and-golds set the tempo for a high scoring tour by running in 52 points despite the foul weather and lack of match practice, taking the tally to the 100-mark by blitzing Leeds 48-6, a record against the club, three days later.

Only Wigan and Halifax provided any stern resistance in the build up to Wembley, the Kangaroos averaging 38 points per match to be declared odds-on favourites for first Test glory.

Britain tore up the form book, overcoming injuries and the loss of skipper Shaun Edwards, sent off for a high tackle after only 25 minutes, to register a shock four-point success based on defensive teamwork and the individual brilliance of Man-of-the-Match Jonathan Davies, hooker Lee Jackson and substitute Bobby Goulding.

The Australians did not stay down for long, bouncing back four days later to register the second highest score in Kangaroo history by hammering Sheffield Eagles 80-2 at the Don Valley Stadium. They put 46 points past Wales and disposed of a gutsy St. Helens side 32-14 before arriving at Manchester United's Old Trafford for the second John Smith's Test.

The euphoria of Wembley spilled over into the pre-match build up as a sell out near-44,000 crowd raised the rafters to welcome the British squad into the stadium. The British followers had little else to cheer for the rest of the afternoon.

The mighty Meninga recovered from a lacklustre performance at Wembley to break the deadlock with an interception, a thundering 60-metre run and a perfectly timed pass to wing partner Andrew Ettingshausen, who dived in at the corner. Recalled scrum half Ricky Stuart orchestrated a remaining hour of brilliance as the visitors ran in seven tries to a consolation solitary effort by substitute Paul Newlove.

The Australians continued to run in tries for the remaining four tour matches, which were also marked by exemplary defence, the Kangaroos conceding only one try in 320 minutes of football.

Thus the green-and-golds drove into Elland Road Stadium in Leeds with a finely-tuned, free-scoring machine, while Hanley presented a reshuffled line-up featuring loose forward and vice-captain Phil Clarke as a controversial selection at stand off.

The gamble did not pay off as Clarke was forced to retire with an ankle injury in the first quarter. Australia soaked up a sustained spell of pressure early in the second half, when leading by only five points, to run in two converted tries in the final 10 minutes to seal a comfortable 23-4 victory. Meninga received the John Smith's Trophy and Australia retained the Ashes which had been in their grip since the 1973 Kangaroo tour.

Off the field, the tour was again a tremendous success. A total of 257,277 saw the 14 matches, an average of 18,377 spectators being second only to the record 19,995 for 13 matches in 1990.

There was a British Test record of 57,034 at Wembley included in a record 143,432 for the series, which featured capacity crowds at Old Trafford and Elland Road. The three Tests earned record receipts of £2,326,154. Receipts for the full tour totalled £3,083,790, the Australians taking home a record profit share of £1,102,735.

On the field, the Kangaroos achieved the best-ever attack record, averaging over 38 points a match. The 40-0 whitewash of high-riding Bradford Northern in the 12th fixture was the Australian's 50th consecutive victory in non-Test football in Britain. The run which began on the 1978 tour now covered 51 matches, including three warm-up games to the 1992 World Cup final, as follows:

1978 Tour		
Hull	won	34-2
Salford	won	14-2
Wigan	won	28-2
St. Helens	won	26-4
York	won	29-2
1982 Tour		
Hull K.R.	won	30-10
Wigan	won	13-9
Barrow	won	29-2
St. Helens	won	32-0
Leeds	won	31-4
Wales (Cardiff)	**won**	**37-7**
Leigh	won	44-4
Bradford N.	won	13-6
Cumbria (Carlisle)	**won**	**41-2**
Fulham	won	22-5
Hull	won	13-7
Widnes	won	19-6
1986 Tour		
Wigan	won	26-18
Hull K.R.	won	46-10
Leeds	won	40-0
Cumbria (Barrow)	**won**	**48-12**
Halifax	won	36-2
St. Helens	won	32-8
Oldham	won	22-16
Widnes	won	20-4
Hull	won	48-0
Bradford N.	won	38-0
1990 Tour		
St. Helens	won	34-4
Wakefield T.	won	36-18
	(continued)	

Wigan	won	34-6
Cumbria (Workington)	**won**	**42-10**
Leeds	won	22-10
Warrington	won	26-6
Castleford	won	28-8
Halifax	won	36-18
Hull	won	34-4
Widnes	won	15-8
1992 World Cup		
Huddersfield	won	66-2
Sheffield E.	won	52-22
Cumbria (Workington)	**won**	**44-0**
1994 Tour		
Cumbria (Workington)	**won**	**52-8**
Leeds	won	48-6
Wigan	won	30-20
Castleford	won	38-12
Halifax	won	26-12
Sheffield E.	won	80-2
Wales (Cardiff)	**won**	**46-4**
St. Helens	won	32-14
Warrington	won	24-0
Bradford N.	won	40-0
Great Britain U-21s (Gateshead)	**won**	**54-10**

In that third Test, former Great Britain skipper Schofield went on as a 23rd minute substitute to record his 46th appearance at Test level since making his international debut in 1984, equalling the record number of caps held by winger Mick Sullivan between 1954 and 1963.

Schofield, who had captained Great Britain in 12 of the previous 13 Tests, was omitted from the squad for the first Test, being recalled for substitute duty in the second encounter only because of injuries, going on after half-time.

The controversy surrounding Pay's positive drug test was compounded by the British League being upset at their Australian counterpart's lack of action after the banned substance pseudo-epherdrine was found in the forward's system by random testing after the Wembley Test.

Pay claimed that he suffered cold symptoms before the match and received a chemist-bought remedy from the tour doctor. Although the drug was contained in most cold cures bought over the counter, it was banned by the International Olympic Committee. Pay played as a substitute at Wembley and was in the second row for the other two Tests.

The League's response to the Test series defeat was to call for an up-grading of youth rugby development within minutes of the final whistle at Elland Road, resulting in the launch of "Project 2000" less than a month later.

Meninga rounded off his farewell season at the age of 34 by lifting the John Smith's Trophy two months after receiving the Winfield Cup at the Sydney Grand Final. The popular centre was presented with a memento at almost every fixture on a record fourth Kangaroo tour, featuring a record second captaincy. He rounded off his playing career to take up an administrative role with his club Canberra Raiders by making a record 46th Australian Test and World Cup appearance in the French Test at Beziers. It includes a record 15 Test-only appearances against Great Britain, which he achieved in the third Test at Elland Road.

BRITISH TOUR RESULTS

Date	Result	Score	Opposition	Venue	Attendance
Oct. 2	Won	52-8	Cumbria	Workington	4,277
Oct. 5	Won	48-6	Leeds	Leeds	18,581
Oct. 8	Won	30-20	Wigan	Wigan	20,057
Oct. 12	Won	38-12	Castleford	Castleford	11,073
Oct. 16	Won	26-12	Halifax	Halifax	8,352
Oct. 22	Lost	4-8	GREAT BRITAIN	Wembley	57,034
Oct. 26	Won	80-2	Sheffield Eagles	Sheffield	7,423
Oct. 30	Won	46-4	Wales	Cardiff C. FC	8,729
Nov. 1	Won	32-14	St. Helens	St. Helens	13,911
Nov. 5	Won	38-8	GREAT BRITAIN	Manchester U. FC	43,930
Nov. 9	Won	24-0	Warrington	Warrington	11,244
Nov. 13	Won	40-0	Bradford N.	Bradford	9,080
Nov. 15	Won	54-10	Great Britain Under-21s	Gateshead	4,118
Nov. 20	Won	23-4	GREAT BRITAIN	Elland Road, Leeds	39,468

BRITISH TOUR SUMMARY

					FOR				AGAINST		
P	W	D	L	T	G	D	Pts	T	G	Dr	Pts
14	13	0	1	96	75	1	535	17	20	0	108

BRITISH TEST SUMMARY

					FOR				AGAINST		
P	W	D	L	T	G	D	Pts	T	G	Dr	Pts
3	2	0	1	11	10	1	65	2	6	0	20

FRENCH TOUR RESULTS

Date	Result	Score	Opposition	Venue	Attendance
Nov. 24	Won	42-17	**President's XIII**	Evry	1,500

T: Hill (2), Florimo (2), Mullins, Furner, Serdaris. G: Furner (7)

Nov. 27	Won	60-16	**Roussillon-Catalan XIII**	Perpignan	4,500

T: Renouf (3), Mullins (2), Smith, Meninga, Clyde, Menzies, Fittler, Daley. G: Wishart (8)

Nov. 30	Won	64-9	**France B**	Avignon	1,500

T: Hill (2), Harragon (2), Sailor (2), Menzies (2) Florimo, Brasher, Pay
G: Brasher (10)

Dec. 4	Won	74-0	**FRANCE**	Bezier	6,000

France:
Frantz Martial; David Fraisse, Frederic Serret, Pierre Chamorin, Frederic Banquet; Jean-Marc Garcia, Patrick Entat; Hadj Boudebza, Thierry Valero, Frederic Teixedo, Daniel Divet, Didier Cabestany (Capt.), Pascal Jampy. Subs: Claude Sirvent, Mathieu Khedemi, Karl Jaavuo, Jacques Pech (All played)
Australia:
Mullins (2t); Ettingshausen (3t), Meninga (Capt.) (1t), Renouf (2t), Wishart (1t, 11g); Daley (1t), Stuart (1t); Lazarus, S. Walters, Roberts, Pay, Clyde, Fittler. Subs: Brasher, Langer, Harragon (1t), Fairleigh (1t) (All played)
Referee: Bill Harrigan (Australia)

FRENCH TEST SUMMARY

					FOR				AGAINST		
P	W	D	L	T	G	D	Pts	T	G	Dr	Pts
4	4	0	0	42	36	0	240	5	10	2	42

BRITISH TOUR RECORDS

Biggest attendance: 57,034 v Great Britain first Test at Wembley
Highest score (and widest margin): 80-2 v. Sheffield Eagles
Highest score against: 20 by Wigan
Most tries in a match: 3 by Allan Langer v Leeds; by Andrew Ettingshausen v Leeds; by Andrew Ettingshausen v Sheffield E.
Most goals in a match: 12 by Rod Wishart v Sheffield E.
Most points in a match: 28 by Rod Wishart v Sheffield E.
Most tries on tour: 12 by Andrew Ettingshausen
Most goals on tour: 52 by Rod Wishart
Most points on tour: 132 by Rod Wishart
Most appearances: 11 by David Fairleigh (including seven as substitute) and Wendell Sailor (including three as substitute)
Most full appearances: 9 by Andrew Ettingshausen (+1), Brad Fittler (+1) and Brett Mullins

Sent off: Paul Sironen v St. Helens. Severe Caution.
Sin-bin: Tim Brasher (4), v Cumbria, Warrington and GB U-24 (2); Brett Mullins (2) v Leeds and Halifax; Ian Roberts v Wigan; Brad Fittler v Halifax; Wendell Sailor v Sheffield E; Glen Lazarus v Sheffield E.; Paul Sironen v Wales; David Fairleigh v Wales; Kevin Walters v St. Helens; Steve Walters v Great Britain, second Test.
Opponents sent off: Shaun Edwards (Great Britain, first Test). Suspended three matches and fined £1,000.
Opponents sin-bin: Gary Mercer (Leeds); Kelvin Skerrett (Wigan); Kevin Ellis (Wales); Phil Ford (Wales); Tommy Martyn (St. Helens); Barrie McDermott (Great Britain, second Test).
Opponent cited: Barrie McDermott (Wigan). Two matches, fined £1,000.

TOUR PARTY

Manager: Geoff Carr
Coach: Bobby Fulton
Doctor: Nathan Gibbs
Trainers: Brian Hollis, Dave Ryan, Frank Ponnisi

Business Manager: Ron Wilkinson
Assistant Coach: Sean McRae
Physiotherapist: Mark Bevan

Player	Club	IN BRITAIN					IN FRANCE					TOUR TOTALS				
		App	Sub	T	G	Pts	App	Sub	T	G	Pts	App	Sub	T	G	Pts
BRASHER, Tim	Balmain	7	2	5	1	22	2	2	1	10	24	9	4	6	1	46
CLYDE, Bradley	Canberra	6	–	4	–	16	2	–	1	–	4	8	–	5	–	20
DALEY, Laurie	Canberra	7	–	3	1	14	2	–	2	–	8	9	–	5	1	22
ETTINGSHAUSEN, Andrew	Cronulla	9	1	12	–	48	1	–	3	–	12	10	1	15	–	60
FAIRLEIGH, David	North Sydney	4	7	4	–	16	2	1	1	–	4	6	8	5	–	20
FITTLER, Brad	Penrith	9	1	1	–	4	2	–	1	–	4	11	1	2	–	8
FLORIMO, Greg	North Sydney	5	5	5	–	20	2	–	3	–	12	7	5	8	–	32
FURNER, David	Canberra	5	3	1	17	38	1	–	1	7	18	6	3	2	24	56
HANCOCK, Michael	Brisbane B.	4	1	2	–	8	2	–	–	–	–	6	1	2	–	8
HARRAGON, Paul	Newcastle	4	1	–	–	–	2	1	3	–	12	6	2	3	–	12
HILL, Terry	Manly	6	–	3	–	12	2	–	4	–	16	8	–	7	–	28
LANGER, Allan	Brisbane B.	7	3	5	–	20	1	1	–	–	–	8	4	5	–	20
LAZARAUS, Glenn	Brisbane B.	8	1	–	–	–	3	–	–	–	–	11	1	–	–	–
McGREGOR, Paul	Illawarra	3	–	2	–	8	–	–	–	–	–	3	–	2	–	8
MENINGA, Mal	Canberra	8	–	2	4	16	2	–	2	–	8	10	–	4	4	24
MENZIES, Steve	Manly	5	3	6	–	24	2	1	3	–	12	7	4	9	–	36
MULLINS, Brett	Canberra	9	–	6	–	24	3	–	5	–	20	12	–	11	–	44
PAY, Dean	Canterbury	6	3	3	–	12	3	1	1	–	4	9	4	4	–	16
RENOUF, Steve	Brisbane B.	7	–	7	–	28	2	–	5	–	20	9	–	12	–	48
ROBERTS, Ian	Manly	6	1	1	–	4	2	1	–	–	–	8	2	1	–	4
SAILOR, Wendell	Brisbane B.	8	3	7	–	28	2	–	2	–	8	10	3	9	–	36
SERDARIS, Jim	Wests	6	–	2	–	8	2	–	1	–	4	8	–	3	–	12
SIRONEN, Paul	Balmain	8	1	–	–	–	1	–	–	–	–	9	1	–	–	–
SMITH, Jason	Canterbury	7	–	3	–	12	2	–	1	–	4	9	–	4	–	16
STUART, Ricky	Canberra	6	2	–	(1)	1	2	1	1	–	4	8	3	1	(1)	5
WALTERS, Kevin	Brisbane B.	7	2	2	–	8	2	–	–	–	–	9	2	2	–	8
WALTERS, Steve	Canberra	7	–	3	–	12	1	2	–	–	–	8	2	3	–	12
WISHART, Rod	Illawarra	8	1	7	52	132	2	–	1	19	42	10	1	8	71	174

(1) Indicates drop goal.

Scrum half Ricky Stuart, one of the stars of the 1994 John Smith's tour by Australia, running by Kangaroo colleague Bradley Clyde.

JOHN SMITH'S TOUR...
MATCH BY MATCH

2 October

Workington

CUMBRIA	**8**
AUSTRALIA	**52**

1. Brasher
2. Sailor
3. McGregor
4. Hill
5. Wishart
6. Florimo
7. K. Walters
8. Roberts
9. Serdaris
10. Lazarus (Fairleigh, 21 min.)
11. Sironen, Capt
12. Menzies
13. Fittler
T: Fairleigh (2), Sailor (2), Brasher, McGregor, Menzies, Roberts, Serdaris
G: Wishart (8)

Cumbria

Routledge (Whitehaven); Seeds (Whitehaven), Pape (Carlisle), Burns (Workington T.), Roper (Warrington); Birkett (Salford), Marwood (Workington T.); Neill (St. Helens), McCurrie (Widnes), Walker (Hull), Armstrong (Workington T.), Elliott (Warrington), Knox (Carlisle).
Subsitutes: Anderson (Whitehaven) for Routledge; Holgate (Workington T.) for Elliott; Shaw (Barrow) for Pape; L. Smith (Workington T.) for Burns.
T: Burns
G: Marwood (2)
Half-time: 8-22
Referee: John Connolly (Wigan)
Attendance: 4,277

Winger Sailor, one of five players wearing the Australian jersey for the first time, touched down twice to lay an early claim for a Test debut at Wembley.

Both tries by the Brisbane Bronco were long-range efforts, the first from 60 yards and the second from 90 yards, as the Kangaroos ran in nine tries with one consolation Cumbrian touchdown in reply.

Second row man Menzies, a tryscorer, took the John Smith's Man of the Match award as the Cumbrians battled bravely to bridge the obvious gap in class, finding themselves 16 points down in less than seven minutes.

5 October

LEEDS	**6**
AUSTRALIA	**48**

1. Mullins
2. Ettingshausen (Sailor, 67 min.)
3. Meninga, Capt. (K. Walters, 68 min.)
4. Renouf
5. Hancock
6. Daley
7. Langer
8. Pay
9. Serdaris
10. Sironen (Fairleigh, half-time)
11. Furner
12. Smith (Menzies, 47 min.)
13. Fittler
T: Ettingshausen (3), Langer (3), Meninga, Menzies, Renouf
G: Furner (6)

Leeds

Tait; Fallon, Iro, Innes, Cummins; Schofield, Entat (Holroyd); Harmon (Fozzard), Lowes (Vassilakopoulos), Faimalo, Mann, Eyres, Mercer.
T: Tait
G: Cummins
Half-time: 2-26
Referee: Russell Smith (Castleford)
Attendance: 18,581

The rampant Kangaroos chalked up a record score against Leeds to take their tour tally to 100 points in only their second match.

A near-Test line-up thrilled a Headingley crowd of more than 18,000 with a display of scintillating support play, Ettingshausen returning to his former club to register a hat-trick of tries, a scoring feat emulated by scrum half Langer.

The Australians ran in nine tries for the second successive match, Leeds replying with a solitary touchdown by full back Tait, a Great Britain Test candidate.

Leeds, who trailed 26-2 at the interval, could not be faulted for effort but there was such a huge difference in speed of thought and movement, the home side lamenting the lack of a speedy support player.

8 October

WIGAN   **20**
AUSTRALIA   **30**

1. Mullins
2. Hancock
3. Meninga, Capt. (Brasher, 2 min.)
4. Renouf
5. Sailor
6. Daley
7. Stuart
8. Pay
9. Walters, S.
10. Roberts
11. Sironen (Fairleigh, half-time)
12. Clyde
13. Fittler (Menzies, 75 min.)
T: Clyde, Daley, Hancock, Mullins, Pay, Renouf
G: Meninga (2), Daley

Wigan
Connolly; Robinson, Paul, Tuigamala, Offiah; Botica (Atcheson), Edwards; Skerrett (McDermott) (O'Connor), Hall, Cowie (Cassidy), Betts, Farrell, Clarke.
T: Connolly, Offiah, Robinson, Tuigamala
G: Botica, Farrell
Half-time: 6-26
Referee: David Campbell (Widnes)
Attendance: 20,057

In a contest billed as the "Fourth Test", the awesome Australians sent out an ominous warning to Great Britain as they swept aside world club champions Wigan.

The Kangaroos fielded a virtual Test line-up against a full-strength Wigan 17-man outfit which contained 11 players in the Great Britain squad.

Wigan, unbeaten since April, were far from disgraced and actually had the better of the scoring in the second period, but they never looked likely to overhaul Australia's commanding 26-6 half-time lead.

Kangaroo half backs Daley and Stuart were individual stars in a tremendous all-round performance. Robinson shone for the Riversiders, who lost Skerrett with a broken thumb. The Australian management cited Wigan forward McDermott for a high tackle which put Test forward Sironen out of action for the whole of the second half. McDermott was later banned for two matches and fined £1,000.

12 October

CASTLEFORD   **12**
AUSTRALIA   **38**

1. Brasher (Sailor, 72 min.)
2. Ettingshausen
3. Hill
4. McGregor
5. Wishart
6. K. Walters
7. Langer, Capt. (Stuart, half-time)
8. Lazarus
9. Serdaris
10. Harragon
11. Smith (Menzies, 72 min.)
12. Furner (Fairleigh, 72 min.)
13. Florimo
T: Wishart (2), Ettingshausen, Langer, McGregor, Serdaris, K. Walters
G: Wishart (5)

Castleford
Goddard; C. Smith, Blackmore, Eden (McAllister), Wray; Kemp, T. Smith; Crooks (Sykes), Russell (Darley), Sampson (Morris), Ketteridge, Hay, Smales.
T: Blackmore, Eden, C. Smith
Half-time: 4-22
Referee: John Connolly (Wigan)
Attendance: 11,073

Castleford succeeded in making life more difficult for the Kangaroos but still failed to stop them adding seven more tries to record their 31st touchdown and fourth successive victory.

The Wheldon Road side performed better than the scoreline suggested, creating three well-taken tries. But the Yorkshiremen did not add a goal and were punished for every mistake, particularly through slack marking at the play-the-ball where the Australians took advantage to score three times.

Wingman Wishart contributed two tries and five goals for an 18-point tally, while tour debutant hooker Serdaris again took the eye as tryscorer and creator.

Kangaroo prop Harragon took the field for the first time on the tour after suspension, but the front row honours were taken by Castleford's Sampson, bidding to catch the attention of the watching Great Britain management.

16 October

HALIFAX   **12**
AUSTRALIA   **26**

1. Mullins (K. Walters, 72 min.)
2. Brasher
3. Meninga, Capt.
4. Ettinghshausen
5. Sailor
6. Daley
7. Stuart
8. Lazarus (Pay, half-time)
9. Langer
10. Harragon (Roberts, half-time)
11. Sironen
12. Clyde (Florimo, 51 min.)
13. Fittler
T: Sailor (2), Clyde, Ettingshausen, Florimo
G: Meninga (2), Brasher

Halifax

Hampson; Bentley, Schuster, Hallas, Preston (Smith);
Hagan (Harland), Parker; Harrison, Southernwood
(Lawless), Fieldhouse, Moriarty (Greenwood),
Perrett, Divorty.
T: Bentley, Smith
G: Schuster (2)
Half-time: 6-12
Referee: John Holdsworth (Kippax)
Attendance: 8,352

The 14-point victory margin flattered the Kangaroos
as Halifax's brave performance injected hope into the
British camp six days before the first John Smith's
Test at Wembley.

The Thrum Hallers gave Australia their most
demanding examination of the tour so far, rattling
the visitors for the first hour, a third major handling
error in the 60th minute gifting the green-and-golds
with the comfort of a 12-point margin.

With Steve Walters and Serdaris both injured, the
Kangaroos shared the hooking role between half backs
Langer and Stuart, while their composure was
unsettled by trips to the sin bin for Mullins, for
dissent, and Fittler, for obstruction.

Pin-up winger Sailor claimed two tries to place
himself firmly in the frame for Wembley selection.
Well led by skipper Harrison, Halifax proved to the
British management that by taking the game to the
Australians, the world champions could be made to
look fallible.

Halifax second row forward Mark Perrett grapples with Kangaroo substitute Greg Florimo.

345

FIRST TEST

Great Britain provided the heroes and a villain in an epic Wembley triumph to rank among the best against-the-odds victories in Test history.

The Lions roared to a dramatic 8-4 success in the first John Smith's Test, inspired by the individual brilliance of the likes of full back Jonathan Davies, hooker Lee Jackson and substitute Bobby Goulding.

But the tense win was based on the courage and determination of the full British ranks, the versatility of the squad responding to the challenge of major disruption.

The villainy came from newly-installed skipper Shaun Edwards, who became the first Rugby League international player to be sent off at Wembley and the first British captain to be dismissed in 109 Test encounters between the two countries.

His early bath was destined to be a turning point, coming in only the 25th minute when both sides were bidding for early supremacy in a 0-0 deadlock situation.

Two minutes earlier, Britain had lost stand off Daryl Powell with a dead leg, bringing on debutant prop forward Barrie McDermott and moving loose forward Phil Clarke to the number six role.

Edwards was dismissed by Australian referee Graham Annesley for a one-arm high tackle on Kangaroo second row man Bradley Clyde during a sweeping move which looked likely to produce the first try of the game. Clyde went to the blood bin for treatment, returned just before half-time, but collapsed during the interval and was taken to hospital for a precautionary brain scan, being later discharged.

Within minutes of the sending off of his main playmaker, new Great Britain coach Ellery Hanley pulled off a masterstroke by replacing second row forward Andrew Farrell with scrum half Goulding. The mischievous Goulding, an in-form squad selection, immediately inspired Britain with his fiery, but controlled, enthusiasm.

That traumatic five minutes of transformation through injury and dismissal was followed by 12-man Britain taking the lead through a Davies penalty goal on the half hour.

Six minutes later came the opening try by the mercurial Davies, which was to seal his rating as John Smith's Man of the Match. It was a classic piece of play as a dummy took him into the clear near halfway. Perfectly controlled pace took the Warrington star away from his equally speedy opposite number Brett Mullins, who was left grasping fresh air as the home full back dived in at the corner.

Britain's enforced policy of all-change continued after the break when Davies had to retire with a shoulder injury in the 58th minute, Gary Connolly moving to full back to be replaced at centre by substitute Allan Bateman.

With 10 minutes left, Britain suffered a lapse of concentration, Steve Renouf's 71st minute touchdown threatening the physical and mental powers of the home side. The Lions regained their composure and sealed a victory to rank alongside the Rorke's Drift Test of 1914 and the Battle of Brisbane of 1958 when the irrepressible Goulding stepped forward two minutes from time to score a penalty goal.

Davies' nearest rival to Man of the Match rating was hooker Jackson, who outplayed Australia at their own game of having a quick-breaking acting half back at the play-the-ball, proving to be sharper and more penetrative than opposite number Steve Walters. In addition, Jackson topped the tackle count of either side with a massive 42, epitomising the defensive effort of the beleaguered Lions.

Hanley's first-ever Test selection had been based on adaptability, his controversial choices paying off handsomely, particularly St. Helens clubmates Alan Hunte and Chris Joynt, both playing out their regular positions.

While Bobby Fulton heaped praise on Great Britain, Hanley warned: "Australia are a class act and will be coming back stronger than ever."

FIRST JOHN SMITH'S TEST

22 October 1994   **Wembley**

GREAT BRITAIN 8		**AUSTRALIA** 4
Jonathan Davies (Warrington)	1.	Brett Mullins
Jason Robinson (Wigan)	2.	Andrew Ettingshauscn
Gary Connolly (Wigan)	3.	Mal Meninga, Capt.
Alan Hunte (St. Helens)	4.	Steve Renouf
Martin Offiah (Wigan)	5.	Wendell Sailor
Daryl Powell (Sheffield E.)	6.	Laurie Daley
Shaun Edwards (Wigan) Capt.	7.	Allan Langer
Karl Harrison (Halifax)	8.	Ian Roberts
Lee Jackson (Sheffield E.)	9.	Steve Walters
Chris Joynt (St. Helens)	10.	Paul Harragon
Denis Betts (Wigan)	11.	Paul Sironen
Andrew Farrell (Wigan)	12.	Bradley Clyde
Phil Clarke (Wigan)	13.	Brad Fittler
Bobby Goulding (St. Helens)	14.	Ricky Stuart
Barrie McDermott (Wigan)	15.	Tim Brasher
Allan Bateman (Warrington)	16.	Dean Pay
Mick Cassidy (Wigan)	17.	David Furner

T: Davies
G: Davies, Goulding
Substitutions:
McDermott for Powell (23 min.)
Goulding for Farrell (31 min.)
Bateman for Davies (58 min.)
Cassidy for Harrison (61 min.)
Attendance: 57,034
Receipts: £1,107,423

T: Renouf

Substitutions:
Furner for Clyde (27 min.)
Pay for Sironen (52 min.)
Stuart for Daley (56 min.)
Half-time: 6-0
Referee: Graham Annesley (Australia)

Scorechart

Minute	Score	GB	Aus
30:	Davies (P)	2	0
36:	Davies (T)	6	0
71:	Renouf (T)	6	4
78:	Goulding (P)	8	4
	Scrums	4	7
	Penalties	7	6

Australia coach Bob Fulton, dejected after the shock 8-4 defeat.

Kangaroo tour top tryscorer Andrew Ettingshausen up-ends Great Britain centre Alan Hunte in the first John Smith's Test at Wembley.

26 October

SHEFFIELD EAGLES   2
AUSTRALIA   80

1. Mullins (Sailor, 54 min.)
2. Brasher
3. McGregor (Ettingshausen, 21 min.)
4. Hill
5. Wishart
6. K. Walters
7. Stuart, Capt.
8. Lazarus
9. S. Walters
10. Pay
11. Fairleigh
12. Menzies
13. Smith (Florimo, 19 min.)
T: Ettingshausen (3), Menzies (2), Mullins (2),
   S. Walters (2), Brasher, Florimo, Pay, K. Walters,
   Wishart
G: Wishart (12)

Sheffield E.
Hayes; Stott, Price, Gamson, Picksley; Mycoe (Sodje),
Sheridan; Broadbent (Boothroyd), Turner (Randall),
Thompson, Carr (Briggs), Hughes, Farrell
G: Mycoe
Half-time: 2-22
Referee: Ray Tennant (Castleford)
Attendance: 7,423

Sheffield Eagles, lacking their Great Britain duo of
skipper Powell and hooker Jackson, suffered the
backlash from Australia's shock defeat in the first
John Smith's Test four days earlier.

The Kangaroos bounced back to free-scoring form
to register their biggest win of the tour and the second
highest-ever in Britain, the tour record being a 92-7
hammering of Bramley in 1921-22.

Ironically, the Eagles opened the scoring after four
minutes with a Mycoe penalty goal, only to trail 22-2
at the interval.

Any hopes of a Sheffield revival were quashed when
the high-speed Kangaroos ran in three times within
10 minutes of the restart, Ettingshausen registering
his second hat-trick of tries. Winger Wishart's 12
goals broke a tour record that had stood since 1929.

Kangaroo hooker Steve Walters en route to one of his two tries at Don Valley Stadium.

WALES INTERNATIONAL

Odds-on favourites Australia, fielding a virtual Test side, set off on course for a massacre of a Wales side robbed of two Great Britain stars through injury and hit by the loss of two key players inside the first 10 minutes of the John Smith's International.

The Kangaroos built a 30-0 half-time lead and Wales, to their credit, shored their breached defence in the second period to slow down the scoring rate and keep the green-and-golds below the half-century mark.

The writing was on the wall with the expected pre-match announcement that skipper Jonathan Davies and Warrington colleague Allan Bateman had failed fitness tests, having starred in Britain's 8-4 victory at Wembley a week earlier.

After only eight minutes of the Ninian Park encounter, Wales suffered another sickening blow when centre John Devereux, in only his second game of the season, suffered a compound fracture of the jaw. The Widnes threequarter, obviously rusty from lack of match practice, mistimed his head-on tackle on powerful Australian skipper Mal Meninga.

Subsequent video analysis confirmed that there had been no illegal use of the forearm or elbow. A minute later stand-in skipper David Young was forced to leave the field for 12 stitches to a cut above the eye, not returning until the second half, and the double injury blow caused feelings to run high.

The tension spilled over in the 15th minute when a clash between Welsh stand off Kevin Ellis and Kangaroo second row man Paul Sironen sparked off a brawl, briefly involving most of the 26 players. Ellis and Sironen were sent to the sin bin by referee John Connolly, to be joined five minutes later by Wales full back Phil Ford, for showing dissent.

Young's return to the fray for a 25-minute spell immediately after the break summed up the Welsh performance which lacked nothing in spirit, despite its technical deficiencies. On a grey, rain-sodden afternoon, the Australians were simply too slick, sealing victory with three tries in eight minutes midway through the first half.

Centre Steve Renouf, complemented a creative display by scoring two of Australia's eight tries, to take the John Smith's Man of the Match award, ahead of outstanding loose forward Brad Fittler and high-scoring winger Rod Wishart, who added a touchdown to his seven goals.

A crowd of less than 9,000, obviously restricted by the foul weather, was treated to a solitary Welsh try, albeit a questionable one. When Bradford Northern's Gerald Cordle, on for the injured Devereux, seemed to palm Ellis's kick forward, fellow substitute Daio Powell pounced for the touchdown.

Amid the gloom of the weather and the scoreline, Wales found some solace in the encouraging performance of teenager Iestyn Harris, making his international debut with the added responsibility of replacing Davies as stand off and goalkicker. Fellow newcomer centre Scott Gibbs also gave a solid performance.

Australia's second half display was hampered not only by the resilience of the Welsh but also a bout of injuries. Their policy decision to name only three substitutes instead of the permitted four, coupled with David Fairleigh's trip to the sin bin, meant that they spent much of the second half with only 12 men.

However, Fittler still managed to make a late impact, a superb pass sending in Renouf on the hour, Fittler taking Allan Langer's pass after Sironen was stopped on the line to score the final touchdown.

SECOND JOHN SMITH'S TEST

5 November 1994   **Old Trafford, Manchester**

GREAT BRITAIN   8

Graham Steadman (Castleford)	1.	
Jason Robinson (Wigan)	2.	
Gary Connolly (Wigan)	3.	
Alan Hunte (St. Helens)	4.	
Martin Offiah (Wigan)	5.	
Daryl Powell (Sheffield E.)	6.	
Bobby Goulding (St. Helens)	7.	
Karl Harrison (Halifax)	8.	
Lee Jackson (Sheffield E.)	9.	
Chris Joynt (St. Helens)	10.	
Denis Betts (Wigan)	11.	
Andrew Farrell (Wigan)	12.	
Phil Clarke (Wigan), Capt.	13.	
Garry Schofield (Leeds)	14.	
Barrie McDermott (Wigan)	15.	
Paul Newlove (Bradford N.)	16.	
Mick Cassidy (Wigan)	17.	

AUSTRALIA   38

1.	Brett Mullins
2.	Andrew Ettingshausen
3.	Mal Meninga, Capt.
4.	Steve Renouf
5.	Rod Wishart
6.	Laurie Daley
7.	Ricky Stuart
8.	Glenn Lazarus
9.	Steve Walters
10.	Ian Roberts
11.	Dean Pay
12.	Bradley Clyde
13.	Brad Fittler
14.	Allan Langer
15.	Tim Brasher
16.	Greg Florimo
17.	Paul Sironen

T: Newlove

G: Goulding (2)
Substitutions:
Schofield for Powell (Half-time)
Newlove for Hunte (Half-time)
McDermott for Harrison (49 min.)
Cassidy for Joynt (58 min.)
Half-time: 4-18
Attendance: 43,930

T: Mullins (2), Clyde, Daley,
Ettingshausen, Renouf
G: Wishart (7)
Substitutions:
Florimo for Roberts (16 min.)
Langer for Florimo (53 min.)
Sironen for Daley (69 min.)
Referee: Graham Annesley (Australia)
Receipts: £634,467

Scorechart

Minute	Score	GB	Aus
5:	Goulding (P)	2	0
9:	Wishart (P)	2	2
12:	Goulding (P)	4	2
27:	Ettingshausen (T)	4	6
32:	Clyde (T)		
	Wishart (G)	4	12
36:	Mullins (T)		
	Wishart (G)	4	18
43:	Daley (T)		
	Wishart (G)	4	18
51:	Wishart (G)	4	24
60:	Newlove (T)	8	26
65:	Renouf (T)		
	Wishart (G)	8	32
70:	Mullins (T)		
	Wishart (G)	8	38
	Scrums	2	4
	Penalties	13	10

Australia centre Steve Renouf, a 65th minute tryscorer at Old Trafford.

9 November

WARRINGTON   **0**
AUSTRALIA   **24**

1. Brasher
2. Sailor
3. Hill
4. Florimo
5. Hancock
6. K. Walters
7. Langer, Capt.
8. Sironen
9. Serdaris
10. Fairleigh (Lazarus, half-time)
11. Furner
12. Menzies
13. Smith

T: Sailor (2), Brasher, Hill, Menzies
G: Furner (2)

Warrington
Penny; Forster, Harris (Rudd), Roper, Lee; Maloney, Mackey; Tees (Hilton), Barlow (Bennett), McGuire, Cullen, Sanderson (Sumner), Darbyshire
Half-time: 0-14
Referee: Bob Connolly (Wigan)
Attendance: 11,244

Warrington, one of the last club sides to inflict defeat on the Australian tourists back in 1978, became Australia's 49th successive victim outside of the Test arena.

The Australians staved off the challenge of a committed Warrington outfit by nilling them for the first time in 15 tour encounters.

But the Kangaroos' latest triumph was marred in the closing stages by a brawl involving several players from both sides which ended with visiting full back Brasher being sent to the sin bin.

The Wire had several key men missing, including Test star Davies, but gave as good as they got in a no-holds contest, particularly in the first quarter when there was no score. But three tries in a devastating 11-minute spell turned the match dramatically in the Australians' favour, winger Sailor adding two more tries to his tour tally.

13 November

BRADFORD N.   **0**
AUSTRALIA   **40**

1. Mullins
2. Ettingshausen
3. Meninga, Capt. (Furner, 64 min.)
4. Renouf (Hancock, half-time)
5. Wishart
6. Daley
7. Stuart (Langer, 62 min.)
8. Lazarus
9. S. Walters
10. Pay (Fairleigh, half-time)
11. Smith
12. Clyde
13. Fittler

T: Smith (2), Clyde, Ettingshausen, Fairleigh, Hancock, Renouf, Wishart
G: Wishart (4)

Bradford N.
Simpson; Hall, Fraisse, Newlove, Myers; Summers, Fox; Powell, Russell (Donohue), Clegg, Greenwood (Winterburn), McDermott (Heron), Medley (Hamer)
Half-time: 0-18
Referee: Stuart Cummings (Widnes)
Attendance: 9,080

Australia completed an amazing half-century of victories in non-Test matches against British opposition with a one-sided win over the previous season's Championship runners-up.

This 50th landmark consisted of 47 consecutive tour matches since defeat by Widnes back in 1978, supplemented by three-warm up victories before their 1992 World Cup final triumph.

The Kangaroos fielded 12 of their likely Test team against a Northern side lying second in the league table. The only member of the side not sure of featuring in the third John Smith's Test was packman Smith, and, as if to emphasise their strength in depth, the two-try Canterbury second row man proved one of their most effective performers.

The Odsal rout meant that the Kangaroos had within five days met the two sides pipped by points difference for the previous season's league title and scored a total of 64 points without reply.

15 November

Gateshead

GREAT BRITAIN UNDER-21s   10
AUSTRALIA   54

1. Brasher
2. Sailor
3. Hill
4. Ettingshausen
5. Hancock (Wishart, half-time)
6. K. Walters
7. Langer, Capt.
8. Smith (Fittler, 65 min.)
9. Serdaris
10. Fairleigh
11. Menzies
12. Furner
13. Florimo
T: Florimo (2), Hill (2), Brasher, Ettingshausen,
   Fairleigh, Langer, Menzies
G: Furner (9)

Great Britain Under-21s
Steve Prescott (St. Helens); Chris Smith (Castleford),
Richard Goddard (Castleford), Karle Hammond
(Widnes), Francis Cummins (Leeds); Nigel Wright
(Wakefield T.), Ryan Sheridan (Sheffield E.); Alex
Thompson (Sheffield E.), John Clarke (Oldham),
Mark Hilton (Warrington), Mark Perrett (Halifax),
Lee Harland (Halifax), Scott Martin (Sheffield E.).
Substitutes: Mark Hewitt (Hull) for Wright; Nathan
McAvoy (Salford) for Goddard; Jez Cassidy (Hull)
for Perrett; Nathan Sykes (Castleford) for Hilton.
T: Prescott
G: Prescott (3)
Half-time: 4-18
Referee: Steve Presley (Castleford)
Attendance: 4,118

Great Britain Under-21s emerged with some credit
even though the youngsters failed to prevent the
Australians breaking the 500-point barrier in the
13th game of their John Smith's tour.

The Kangaroos scored two tries, both from centre
Hill, in the opening nine minutes and threatened to
open the floodgates. But the Under-21s refused to
become downhearted and kept the first half score
down to a respectable 18-4.

The Australians' ability to produce tries at vital
times ensured Britain would never get too close and
as the young home side tired, the Kangaroos went on
a scoring spree in the last quarter.

The Under-21s were well served by full back
Prescott, who scored all their 10 points with a try and
three goals, plus scrum half Sheridan and hooker
Clarke. Australian full back Brasher had the dubious
distinction of being sent to the sin bin twice for
dissent.

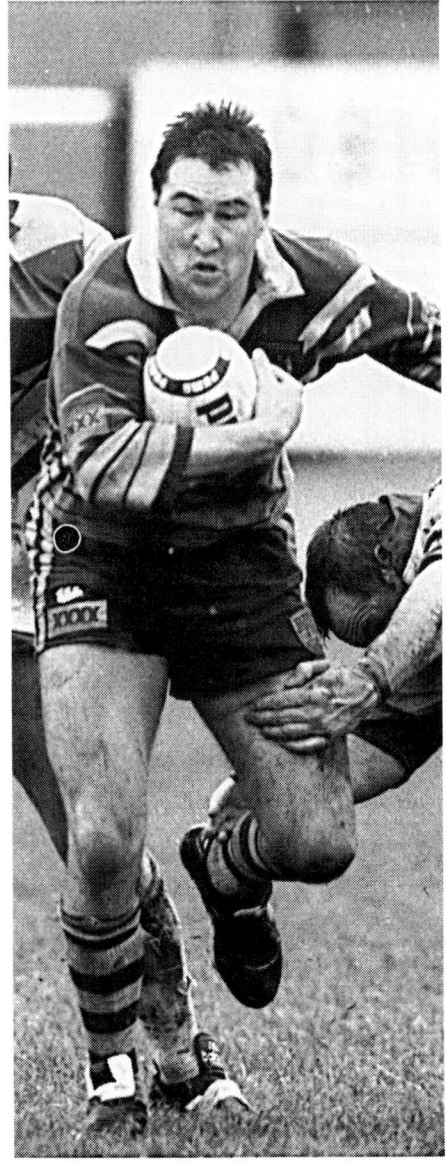

*Kangaroo centre Terry Hill, a two-try performer
at Gateshead.*

THIRD TEST

The outcome of the bold experiment of playing loose forward Phil Clarke at stand off typified the fate of Great Britain in this deciding John Smith's Test at a sell-out Elland Road stadium in Leeds.

Coach Ellery Hanley's game-plan was for the Wigan packman to block the middle of the field as he had done in an emergency role at Wembley in the first Test a month earlier. With three backs on the substitute bench, Clarke could then be drafted into the forwards later in the game when tactics or fatigue dictated.

Either way, the Lions' vice-captain was the one player they could not afford to lose during the early stages. The percentages did not work out as Britain were hit by a double injury blow.

The first problem came in the 14th minute when Alan Hunte was forced to retire with a knee ligament injury. Within 10 minutes, Clarke, a controversial choice at stand off, left the fray with damaged ankle ligaments sustained after an opponent accidentally fell on his leg in a tackle.

Despite Australia showing an obvious edge in class, Britain battled against the odds for an hour to trail only 7-2 to a fortunate Laurie Daley try. But once the elusive Daley set up a 57th minute try for Rod Wishart, British hopes virtually evaporated.

In the final 10 minutes, Australia crossed twice more as the British forwards visibly tired, three of the four substitutions having had to be made in the first half hour, scrum Bobby Goulding being held back until the 71st minute.

For the third successive Test, Britain had opened the scoring with a penalty goal, this time from the boot of Andrew Farrell in the fourth minute after skipper Shaun Edwards, back after suspension, was flattened by a wicked-looking high tackle from Dean Pay after the ball had been passed. Australian referee Bill Harrigan took no action.

Australia opened their try account in the 20th minute when Daley chipped over the British defence, the ball looking to be destined for safety before Bradford Northern centre Paul Newlove, in an effort to try to catch the ball, succeeded only in deflecting it. The astute Daley anticipated the blunder and gathered his own kick to touch down easily for Wishart to add the goal.

Scrum half Ricky Stuart, a rival to Steve Walters for the John Smith's Man of the Match award, completed his ball handling skills by dropping a goal seconds before the half-time whistle to give the Australians a hard earned 7-2 interval lead.

Rather than wilt as they had done in the second John Smith's Test at Old Trafford two weeks earlier, Britain re-emerged to set up their best chance of glory. The Lions showed all the grit and determination associated with a side searching for their first Ashes series success in 24 years and laid siege on the Kangaroo rearguard.

Australia were stretched and battered, matching their reputation as an attacking force with resilient rearguard action, Britain being denied the score which would have drastically changed the course of the game.

The catalogue of near misses mounted as loose forward Chris Joynt chose the wrong option near the Australians' line and surrendered possession, while Wishart prevented a try by kicking the ball away from Gary Connolly's grasp as he followed up Farrell's low kick.

The British pressure proved, literally, pointless. Hooker Steve Walters then made the hosts pay the ultimate price, helping create a try for Wishart before breaking free in the 70th minute to score himself. With six minutes left a touch of arrogant confidence by Stuart set up a try for Pay and Wishart's third goal signalled it was all over with the Ashes returning Down Under for at least another two years.

THIRD JOHN SMITH'S TEST

20 November 1994   **Elland Road, Leeds**

GREAT BRITAIN   4   AUSTRALIA   23

Gary Connolly (Wigan)	1.	Brett Mullins
Jason Robinson (Wigan)	2.	Andrew Ettingshausen
Alan Hunte (St. Helens)	3.	Mal Meninga, Capt.
Paul Newlove (Bradford N.)	4.	Steve Renouf
Martin Offiah (Wigan)	5.	Rod Wishart
Phil Clarke (Wigan)	6.	Laurie Daley
Shaun Edwards (Wigan), Capt.	7.	Ricky Stuart
Karl Harrison (Halifax)	8.	Glenn Lazarus
Lee Jackson (Sheffield E.)	9.	Steve Walters
Barrie McDermott (Wigan)	10.	Ian Roberts
Denis Betts (Wigan)	11.	Dean Pay
Andrew Farrell (Wigan)	12.	Bradley Clyde
Chris Joynt (St. Helens)	13.	Brad Fittler
Bobby Goulding (St. Helens)	14.	Allan Langer
Daryl Powell (Sheffield E.)	15.	Tim Brasher
Garry Schofield (Leeds)	16.	Greg Florimo
Sonny Nickle (St. Helens)	17.	David Farleigh

G: Farrell (2)

T: Daley, Pay, S. Walters, Wishart
G: Wishart (3), Stuart (dg)

Substitutions:
Powell for Hunte (11 min.)
Schofield for Clarke (23 min.)
Nickle for McDermott (32 min.)
Goulding for Joynt (71 min.)
Half-time: 2-7
Attendance: 39,468
Receipts: £584,264

Substitutions:
Florimo for Roberts (12 min.)
Brasher for Ettingshausen (61 min.)
Langer for S. Walters (75 min.)
Fairleigh for Lazarus (75 min.)
Referee: Bill Harrigan (Australia)

Scorechart

Minute	Score	GB	Aus
4:	Farrell (P)	2	0
20:	Daley (T)		
	Wishart (G)	2	6
39:	Stuart (DG)	2	7
57:	Wishart (T)	2	11
62:	Farrell (P)	4	11
70:	Walters (T)		
	Wishart (G)	4	17
74:	Pay (T)		
	Wishart (G)	4	23
	Scrums	8	3
	Penalties	9	3

Australia winger Rod Wishart, scorer of a try and three goals at Elland Road.

359

Kangaroo loose forward Brad Fittler, one of the successes of the 1994 John Smith's tour, squares up to Wigan's Henry Paul, with Ian Roberts looking on.

DOWN UNDER

WINFIELD CUP
1994 Premiership Grand Final

Canberra Raiders gave their captain Mal Meninga the perfect end to his Australian club career with a 36-12 trouncing of Canterbury-Bankstown at the Sydney Football Stadium. And Meninga brought down the curtain in style as he charged in for the last try after intercepting a pass 40 metres out.

But he could not overshadow Canberra second row David Furner, who won the Clive Churchill Medal as Man of the Match after scoring four goals and a try.

Furner also produced the clever midfield pass which sent Laurie Daley on a 50-metre tryscoring run and popped out another for Jason Croker to score.

Furner's display clinched him a place in the Kangaroos' squad named after the match and quashed any suggestions of favouritism by his father, Don, who was the chairman of selectors.

There was also an outstanding contribution to victory by Paul Osborne although he was substituted after only 25 minutes. But before he departed, Osborne had sent in Furner and Ken Nagas for the opening tries.

It was a remarkable change of fortune for the prop, who had planned to have a trial spell with Featherstone Rovers after appearing to be left out of Canberra's Grand Final plans.

He had not played in the first team for eight weeks but when John Lomax was suspended after being sent off in the semi-final coach Tim Sheens gave Osborne his chance.

Canterbury, who finished at the top of the league, had begun as slight favourites but they were struggling from the moment Martin Bella knocked on behind his own line straight from the kick-off.

It was the fifth successive final in which no British player was involved.

1994 WINFIELD CUP

	P.	W.	D.	L.	F.	A.	Pts
Canterbury-Bankstown	22	18	0	4	537	340	36
North Sydney	22	17	1	4	517	291	35
Canberra	22	17	0	5	677	298	34
Manly-Warringah	22	16	1	5	605	311	33
Brisbane Broncos	22	13	1	8	544	316	27
Illawarra	22	11	3	8	484	387	25
Cronulla-Sutherland	22	12	0	10	432	401	24
Penrith	22	10	2	10	404	448	22
South Sydney	22	9	1	12	401	569	19
Newcastle	22	9	0	13	427	458	18
St. George	22	9	0	13	386	497	18
Parramatta	22	7	1	14	350	474	15
Western Suburbs	22	6	2	14	439	650	14
Eastern Suburbs	22	6	1	15	344	513	13
Gold Coast	22	5	1	16	363	618	11
Balmain	22	4	0	18	303	642	8

WINFIELD CUP GRAND FINAL

25 September 1994   **Sydney Football Stadium**

CANBERRA 36   CANTERBURY-BANKSTOWN 12

Brett Mullins	1.	Scott Wilson
Ken Nagas	2.	Jason Williams
Mal Meninga, Capt.	3.	Steve Hughes
Ruben Wiki	4.	Jarrod McCracken
Noa Nadruku	5.	Daryl Halligan
Laurie Daley	6.	Terry Lamb, Capt.
Ricky Stuart	7.	Craig Polla-Mounter
Quentin Pongia	8.	Darren Britt
Steve Walters	9.	Jason Hetherington
Paul Osborne	10.	Martin Bella
Jason Croker	11.	Jason Smith
David Furner	12.	Dean Pay
Bradley Clyde	13.	Jim Dymock

T: Nagas (2), Furner, Daley
Nadruku, Croker, Meninga
G: Furner (4)
Substitutions:
Brett Hetherington for Osborne
David Westley for Pongia
Coach: Tim Sheens
Half-time: 19-6
Referee: Greg McCallum
Attendance: 42,234

T: Williams, Hetherington
G: Halligan (2)
Substitutions:
Matt Ryan for Wilson
Simon Gillies for Smith
Mark Brokenshire for Bella
Steve Price for Gillies
Coach: Chris Anderson
Clive Churchill Medal for Man of the
Match: David Furner (Canberra)

WINFIELD CUP PLAY-OFF

Major preliminary semi-final
Canberra 26 v. North Sydney 12
Minor preliminary semi-final
Brisbane Broncos 16 v. Manly-Warringah 4
Minor semi-final
North Sydney 15 v. Brisbane Broncos 14
Major semi-final
Canterbury-Bankstown 19 v. Canberra 18
Preliminary final
Canberra 22 v. North Sydney 9
Grand Final
Canberra 36 v. Canterbury-Bankstown 12

• All matches played at the Sydney Football
Stadium.

LEADING SCORERS

• Not including play-offs.

Tries
22 Steve Renouf (Brisbane Broncos)
Goals (inc. drop goals)
108 Matthew Ridge (Manly-Warringah)
Points
259 Daryl Halligan (Canterbury-Bankstown)

BRITISH PLAYERS IN 1994 WINFIELD CUP
John Bentley of Halifax was the only British
player to appear in the Winfield Cup during the
1994 season. The Halifax and Great Britain
winger made 10 appearances for Balmain,
including one as a substitute, and scored one try.
   Although Bentley made a fair impression,
Balmain did not win one match while he
played for them and finished bottom of the
Winfield Cup table.
   Five British players had appeared in the
Winfield Cup the previous year.

BRITISH PLAYERS IN GRAND FINALS

British players who have appeared in the Sydney Grand Final are:

Dick Huddart (St. George) 1966 winners, 1 try

Dave Bolton (Balmain) 1966 losers; 1969 winners, 2 drop goals

Mervyn Hicks (Canterbury) 1967 losers

Ken Batty (St. George) 1971 losers

Malcolm Reilly (Manly) 1972 winners; 1973 winners

Tommy Bishop (Cronulla) 1973 losers

Bob Wear (Cronulla) 1973 losers

Cliff Watson (Cronulla) 1973 losers

Brian Lockwood (Canterbury) 1974 losers

Gary Stephens (Manly) 1976 winners

Steve Norton (Manly) 1976 winners

Phil Lowe (Manly) 1976 winners, 1 try

Kevin Ward (Manly) 1987 winners

Ellery Hanley (Balmain) 1988 losers

Andy Currier (Balmain) 1989 losers, 3 goals

Shaun Edwards (Balmain) 1989 losers, sub

Apart from Hicks, all the above also appeared in a Challenge Cup final at Wembley. In addition, Len Killeen, the South African winger who began his League career with St. Helens, also played at Wembley and got a Grand Final winners' medal with Balmain in 1969 when he kicked two goals.

Australians who have achieved the big double since the Grand Final became mandatory in 1954 are: Chris Anderson, Harry Bath, Graham Eadie, Andrew Farrar, John Ferguson, Kerry Hemsley, Brett Kenny, John Muggleton, Michael O'Connor, Julian O'Neill, Peter Sterling and Paul Vautin.

There were a record four British players in the 1973 Grand Final. Reilly got a winners' medal with Manly, while Bishop, Watson and Wear were in the beaten Cronulla side.

Three British players — Stephens, Norton and Lowe — were also in the Manly side which won the final in 1976.

Ellery Hanley was the first player to appear in both major finals in the same year. In 1988 he led Wigan to success at Wembley and four months later was in Balmain's beaten Grand Final team.

Shaun Edwards is the only other British player to play in both finals in the same year. He was stand off when Wigan beat St. Helens at Wembley in 1989 and made a late substitute appearance for Balmain when they were beaten by Canberra at Sydney.

Julian O'Neill is the only Australian to have played in the Challenge Cup final at Wembley and the Grand Final in the same year. He made a substitute appearance for Widnes when they were beaten by Wigan in 1993 and was full back in the Brisbane Broncos side that beat St. George later that year.

Great Britain prop Cliff Watson, a Sydney Grand Finalist with Cronulla in 1973.

British forward Phil Lowe, a tryscorer for Manly in their 1976 Sydney Grand Final victory.

STATE OF ORIGIN

The State of Origin matches between New South Wales and Queensland began in 1980 and are now established as a major part of the Australian Rugby League scene.

Their introduction revived interest in the inter-state matches which had been dominated by New South Wales, who had won the last 15 matches by mainly wide margins.

Under the old system, players appeared for the state in which they were playing club rugby at the time, and this gave a big advantage to New South Wales because many of Queensland's best players were with Sydney clubs.

But in State of Origin matches players appear for the state in which they first played senior rugby, and this has resulted in the matches becoming more fiercely and evenly fought before increased attendances.

NEW SOUTH WALES v. QUEENSLAND RESULTS State of Origin only. *Not part of 1987 series.

Date	Winner	Score	Venue	Attendance
8 July 1980	Queensland	20-10	Brisbane	31,000
28 July 1981	Queensland	22-15	Brisbane	25,613
1 June 1982	New South Wales	20-16	Brisbane	27,326
8 June 1982	Queensland	11-7	Brisbane	19,435
22 June 1982	Queensland	10-5	Sydney	20,242
7 June 1983	Queensland	24-12	Brisbane	29,412
21 June 1983	New South Wales	10-6	Sydney	21,620
28 June 1983	Queensland	43-22	Brisbane	26,084
29 May 1984	Queensland	29-12	Brisbane	33,662
19 June 1984	Queensland	14-2	Sydney	29,088
17 July 1984	New South Wales	22-12	Brisbane	16,599
28 May 1985	New South Wales	18-2	Brisbane	33,011
11 June 1985	New South Wales	21-14	Sydney	39,068
23 July 1985	Queensland	20-6	Brisbane	18,825
27 May 1986	New South Wales	22-16	Brisbane	33,000
10 June 1986	New South Wales	24-20	Sydney	40,707
1 July 1986	New South Wales	18-16	Brisbane	21,097
2 June 1987	New South Wales	20-16	Brisbane	33,411
16 June 1987	Queensland	12-6	Sydney	42,048
15 July 1987	Queensland	10-8	Brisbane	33,000
*6 Aug. 1987	New South Wales	30-18	California	12,349
17 May 1988	Queensland	26-18	Sydney	26,441
31 May 1988	Queensland	16-6	Brisbane	31,817
21 June 1988	Queensland	38-22	Sydney	16,910
23 May 1989	Queensland	36-6	Brisbane	33,000
14 June 1989	Queensland	16-12	Sydney	40,000
28 June 1989	Queensland	36-16	Brisbane	33,000
9 May 1990	New South Wales	8-0	Sydney	41,235
30 May 1990	New South Wales	12-6	Melbourne	25,800
13 June 1990	Queensland	14-10	Brisbane	31,000
8 May 1991	Queensland	6-4	Brisbane	31,500
29 May 1991	New South Wales	14-12	Sydney	41,520
12 June 1991	Queensland	14-12	Brisbane	32,500
6 May 1992	New South Wales	14-6	Sydney	40,039
20 May 1992	Queensland	5-4	Brisbane	32,000
3 June 1992	New South Wales	16-4	Sydney	41,878
3 May 1993	New South Wales	14-10	Brisbane	33,000
17 May 1993	New South Wales	16-12	Sydney	41,895
31 May 1993	Queensland	24-12	Brisbane	31,500
23 May 1994	Queensland	16-12	Sydney	41,859
8 June 1994	New South Wales	14-0	Melbourne	87,161
20 June 1994	New South Wales	27-12	Brisbane	42,000

SUMMARY New South Wales won 19; Queensland won 23. Since it became a three-match series in 1982, Queensland have won seven series to New South Wales's six.

ENGLISH REFEREES English referees who have taken charge of State of Origin matches are: Billy Thompson on 8 July 1980 and Robin Whitfield on 28 June 1983.

1994 STATE OF ORIGIN MATCHES *Denotes captain

23 May
Sydney
New South Wales 12

Brasher (Balmain)
Wishart (Illawarra) 1g
Fittler (Penrith)
McGregor (Illawarra)
G. Mackay (Penrith) 1g
*Daley (Canberra)
Stuart (Canberra)
Roberts (Manly)
Elias (Balmain)
Lazarus (Brisbane B.)
Sironen (Balmain)
Harragon (Newcastle) 1t
B. Mackay (St. George) 1t

Subs: Ettingshausen (Cronulla)
Barnhill (St. George)
Gillespie (Manly)
Johns (Brisbane B.)

8 June
Melbourne
New South Wales 14

Brasher (Balmain) 3g
Ettingshausen (Cronulla)
Fittler (Penrith)
McGregor (Illawarra) 1t
Mullins (Canberra)
*Daley (Canberra)
Stuart (Canberra)
Harragon (Newcastle)
Elias (Balmain)
Lazarus (Brisbane B.) 1t
Sironen (Balmain)
Pay (Canterbury)
Clyde (Canberra)

Subs: B. Mackay (St. George)
Barnhill (St. George)
Nagas (Canberra)

20 June
Brisbane
New South Wales 27

Brasher (Balmain) 4g
Ettingshausen (Cronulla)
Fittler (Penrith) 1t, 1dg
McGregor (Illawarra)
Mullins (Canberra) 1t
*Daley (Canberra) 1t
Stuart (Canberra)
Harragon (Newcastle)
Elias (Balmain) 2dg
Roberts (Manly)
Sironen (Balmain)
Pay (Canterbury)
Clyde (Canberra) 1t

Subs: B. Mackay (St. George)
Barnhill (St. George)
Johns (Brisbane B.)
Nagas (Canberra)

Queensland 16

O'Neill (Brisbane B.) 1t
Hancock (Brisbane B.)
*Meninga (Canberra) 2g
Renouf (Brisbane B.)
Carne (Brisbane B.) 1t
Kevin Walters (Brisbane B.)
Langer (Brisbane B.)
Gee (Brisbane B.)
S. Walters (Canberra)
Bella (Canterbury)
Gillmeister (Penrith)
Larson (Norths)
Moore (Norths)

Subs: Hohn (Brisbane B.)
D. Smith (Canterbury)
Fritz (Illawarra)
M. Coyne (St. George) 1t

Referee: Bill Harrigan
Man of the Match: Carne

Queensland 0

O'Neill (Brisbane B.)
Hancock (Brisbane B.)
*Meninga (Canberra)
M. Coyne (St. George)
Carne (Brisbane B.)
Kevin Walters (Brisbane B.)
Langer (Brisbane B.)
Gee (Brisbane B.)
Kerrod Walters (Brisbane B.)
Fritz (Illawarra)
Gillmeister (Penrith)
Larson (Norths)
Moore (Norths)

Subs: Hohn (Brisbane B.)
D. Smith (Canterbury)
Tallis (St. George)
Vowles (Gold Coast)

Referee: Graham Annesley
Man of the Match: Harragon

Queensland 12

O'Neill (Brisbane B.) 2g
Hancock (Brisbane B.)
*Meninga (Canberra)
Renouf (Brisbane B.) 1t
Carne (Brisbane B.)
Kevin Walters (Brisbane B.)
Langer (Brisbane B.)
Hohn (Brisbane B.)
S. Walters (Canberra)
Fritz (Illawarra)
Larson (Norths)
Moore (Norths)
J. Smith (Canterbury)

Subs: D. Smith (Canterbury)
Gee (Brisbane B.) 1t
Tallis (St. George)
M. Coyne (St. George)

Referee: Bill Harrigan
Man of the Match: Elias

NEW SOUTH WALES v. QUEENSLAND RECORDS
State of Origin only.

NEW SOUTH WALES
Highest score:	30-18 at California, 6 August 1987
Widest margin:	18-2 at Brisbane, 28 May 1985
Most full appearances:	19 by Michael O'Connor (St. George, Manly)
Most tries in a match:	3 by Chris Anderson (Canterbury), 28 June 1983
Most goals in a match:	No player has kicked more than five
Most points in a match:	18 (2t,5g) Michael O'Connor (Manly), 28 May 1985
★Biggest home attendance:	42,048 at Sydney Cricket Ground, 16 June 1987

QUEENSLAND

Highest score:	43-22 at Brisbane, 28 June 1983
Widest margin:	36-6 at Brisbane, 23 May 1989
Most full appearances:	32 by Mal Meninga (Souths, B & Canberra)
Most tries in a match:	3 by Kerry Boustead (Manly), 29 May 1984
Most goals in a match:	7 by Mal Meninga (Souths, B), 8 July 1980
Most points in a match:	16 (2t,4g) by Mal Meninga (Canberra), 23 May 1989 and Dale Shearer (Manly), 28 June 1989
★Biggest home attendance:	42,000 at Lang Park, Brisbane, 20 June 1994

Coaches:

New South Wales:	Ted Glossop (1980, 1981, 1983); Frank Stanton (1982, 1984); Terry Fearnley (1985); Ron Willey (1986, 1987); John Peard (1988); Jack Gibson (1989, 1990); Tim Sheens (1991); Phil Gould (1992, 1993, 1994)
Queensland:	John McDonald (1980); Arthur Beetson (1981, 1982, 1983, 1984, 1989, 1990); Des Morris (1985); Wayne Bennett (1986, 1987, 1988); Graham Lowe (1991, 1992); Wally Lewis (1993, 1994)

★Biggest attendance of all is 87,161 at Melbourne Cricket Ground on 8 June 1994.

NEW SOUTH WALES REGISTER

The following is a register of players who have appeared for New South Wales in the State of Origin series plus the match against Queensland in the United States of America, up to and including 1994.
+ indicates number of matches played as a substitute. B-Brisbane, S-Sydney.

ALEXANDER, Greg (4+2) Penrith
ANDERSON, Chris (4) Canterbury
AYLIFFE, Royce (1+2) Easts, S
BARNHILL, David (+3) St. George

BLAKE, Phil (+1) Souths, S
BOWDEN, Steve (1) Newtown
BOYD, Les (3) Manly
BOYLE, David (2+2) Souths, S
BRASHER, Tim (6+1) Balmain
BRENTNALL, Greg (4) Canterbury
BROOKS, David (1) Balmain
BROWN, Ray (1+2) Manly
BUGDEN, Geoff (2) Parramatta

CARTER, Steve (+1) Penrith
CARTWRIGHT, John (5+3) Penrith
CLEAL, Noel (11+1) Manly
CLYDE, Bradley (12) Canberra
CONLON, Ross (3) Canterbury
COOPER, Bob (1) Wests, S
COVENEY, John (2) Canterbury
CROKER, Jason (+1) Canberra
CRONIN, Mick (6) Parramatta

DALEY, Laurie (14) Canberra
DALEY, Phil (3) Manly
DAVIDSON, Les (5) Souths, S
DOCKING, Jonathan (2) Cronulla
DOWLING, Gary (+1) Parramatta
DUKE, Phillip (1) Moree
DUNN, Paul (2+1) Canterbury

EADIE, Graham (1) Manly
EDGE, Steve (1) Parramatta
ELIAS, Ben (19) Balmain
ELLA, Steve (3+4) Parramatta
ETTINGSHAUSEN, Andrew (20+2) Cronulla

FAHEY, Terry (2) Easts, S
FAIRLEIGH, David (1+3) Norths, S
FARRAR, Andrew (5+2) Canterbury
FENECH, Mario (2) Souths, S
FERGUSON, John (8) Easts, S 3; Canberra 5

FIELD, Paul (2) Cootamundra
FITTLER, Brad (10+2) Penrith
FLORIMO, Greg (+1) Norths, S
FOLKES, Steve (8+1) Canterbury

GERARD, Geoff (2) Manly
GEYER, Mark (3) Penrith
GILLESPIE, David (5+10) Canterbury 3+3; Wests 2+6; Manly (+1)
GOURLEY, Scott (+1) St. George
GROTHE, Eric (9) Parramatta
GURR, Marty (2) Easts, S

HAMBLY, Gary (1) Souths, S
HANSON, Steve (1) Norths, S
HARRAGON, Paul (9) Newcastle
HASLER, Des (6+6) Manly
HASTINGS, Kevin (+1) Easts, S
HETHERINGTON, Brian (1+1) Illawarra
HILDITCH, Ron (1) Parramatta
HILL, Terry (+1) Wests, S
HUNT, Neil (2) Parramatta

IZZARD, Brad (2+2) Penrith

JACK, Garry (17) Balmain
JARVIS, Pat (6+2) St. George 4+2; Canterbury 2
JENSEN, Barry (1) Newtown
JOHNS, Chris (7+2) Brisbane Broncos
JOHNSTON, Brian (8) St. George
JOHNSTON, Lindsay (2) Norths, S
JURD, Stan (1+1) Parramatta

KELLY, Peter (2) Penrith
KENNY, Brett (16+1) Parramatta
KRILICH, Max (5) Manly

LAMB, Terry (4+3) Canterbury 3+3; Wests, S 1
LANGMACK, Paul (3+1) Canterbury
LAZARUS, Glenn (9+4) Canberra 1+4; Brisbane Broncos 8
LEIS, Jim (1) Wests, S
LYONS, Cliff (6) Manly
LYONS, Graham (2+1) Souths, S

McCORMACK, Robbie (1+1) Newcastle
McGAW, Mark (10+3) Cronulla
McGREGOR, Paul (8) Illawarra
McGUIRE, Bruce (5) Balmain
MACKAY, Brad (8+6) St. George
MACKAY, Graham (4) Penrith
McKINNON, Don (1) Norths, S
MARTIN, Steve (+1) Manly
MATTERSON, Terry, (+1) Brisbane Broncos
MELROSE, Tony (1) Souths, S
MERLO, Paul (1) Wests, S
MILLER, Gavin (5) Cronulla
MORRIS, Steve (2) St. George
MORTIMER, Chris (8+1) Canterbury 7; Penrith 1+1
MORTIMER, Steve (8+1) Canterbury
MUGGLETON, John (2) Parramatta
MULLINS, Brett (2) Canberra

NAGAS, Ken (+2) Canberra
NISZCZOT, Ziggy (2) Souths, S

O'CONNOR, Michael (19) St. George 6; Manly 13

PAY, Dean (2) Canterbury
PEARCE, Wayne (15) Balmain
POTTER, Michael (+1) Canterbury
PRICE, Ray (8) Parramatta

RAMPLING, Tony (2+1) Souths, S
RAUDONIKIS, Tom (1) Newtown

ROACH, Steve (17) Balmain
ROBERTS, Ian (9) Manly
ROGERS, Steve (4) Cronulla

SALVATORI, Craig (+5) Easts, S
SARGENT, Mark (+1) Newcastle
SIGSWORTH, Phil (3) Newtown 2; Manly 1
SIMMONS, Royce (10) Penrith
SIMON, John (1) Illawarra
SIRONEN, Paul (11+3) Balmain
STERLING, Peter (13) Parramatta
STONE, Robert (+1) St. George
STUART, Ricky (14) Canberra

TAYLOR, Jason (+2) Wests, S
THOMPSON, Alan (5+1) Manly
TOOVEY, Geoff (+1) Manly
TREWHELLA, David (1+1) Easts, S
TUNKS, Peter (7+2), Souths 1; Canterbury 6+2

WALFORD, Ricky (1) St. George
WALSH, Chris (1) St. George
WILSON, Alan (+2) Cronulla
WISHART, Rod (12) Illawarra
WRIGHT, Rex (1) N. Newcastle
WYNN, Graeme (1) St. George
WYNN, Peter (4) Parramatta

YOUNG, Craig (4+1) St. George

QUEENSLAND REGISTER

The following is a register of players who have appeared for Queensland in the State of Origin series plus the match against New South Wales in the United States of America, up to and including 1994.
+ indicates number of matches played as a substitute. B-Brisbane, S-Sydney.

ALLEN, Gavin (2+3) Brisbane Broncos
ASTILL, Bruce (+1) Souths, B

BACKER, Brad (3) Easts, B
BACKO, Sam (7) Canberra 3; Brisbane Broncos 4
BEETSON, Arthur (1) Parramatta
BELCHER, Gary (16) Canberra
BELLA, Martin (21) Norths, S 8; Manly 9;
    Canterbury 4
BOUSTEAD, Kerry (6) Easts, S 3; Manly 3
BRENNAN, Mitch (4) Souths, S 3; Redcliffe 1
BROHMAN, Darryl (2) Penrith
BROWN, Dave (9+1) Manly 5+1; Easts, S 4
BRUNKER, Adrian (3) Newcastle
BUTLER, Terry (1) Wynnum Manly

CARNE, Willie (11) Brisbane Broncos
CARR, Norm (2) Wests, B
CLOSE, Chris (9) Manly 7; Redcliffe 2
CONESCU, Greg (20) Norths, B 4; Redcliffe 10;
    Gladstone Brothers 3; Brisbane Broncos 3
COYNE, Gary (2+9) Canberra
COYNE, Mark (5+6) St. George
CURRIE, Tony (8+5) Wests, B +2; Redcliffe +2;
    Canterbury 5+1; Brisbane Broncos 3

DALLAS, Brett (1) Canterbury
DOWLING, Greg (11) Wynnum Manly 7; Norths, B 4
DOWLING, John (3) St. George

FRENCH, Brett (1+4) Wynnum Manly 1+1;
    Norths, S +3
FRENCH, Ian (3+6) Wynnum Manly 2+3;
    Norths, S 1+3
FRITZ, Darren (2+1) Illawarra
FULLERTON-SMITH, Wally (12) Redcliffe 8;
    St. George 4

GEE, Andrew (5+3) Brisbane Broncos
GILLMEISTER, Trevor (10+6) Easts, S 5+5;
    Brisbane Broncos 3+1; Penrith 2

HAGAN, Michael (2+3) Newcastle
HANCOCK, Michael (13) Brisbane Broncos
HANCOCK, Rohan (5) Easts, B 1; Toowoomba
    Wattles 4
HAUFF, Paul (3) Brisbane Broncos
HENRICK, Ross (2+1) Norths, B 1; Fortitude Valley 1+1
HEUGH, Cavill (2+1) Easts, B
HOHN, Mark (3+3) Brisbane Broncos

JACKSON, Peter (14+2) Canberra 7; Souths, B +1;
    Brisbane Broncos 1+1; Norths, S 6
JACKSON, Steve (5+4) Wests, S 3+1; Gold Coast 2+3
JONES, Gavin (3+1) Norths, S 3; Easts, B +1

KELLAWAY, Bob (+2) Souths, B+1; Brothers +2
KHAN, Paul (4) Easts, B 3; Cronulla 1
KILROY, Joe (2) Brisbane Broncos
KISS, Les (4) Norths, S

LANG, John (1) Easts, S
LANGER, Allan (24) Ipswich 4; Brisbane Broncos 20
LARSON, Gary (12) Norths, S
LEWIS, Wally (31) Wynnum Manly 13;
    Fortitude Valley 8; Brisbane Broncos 7;
    Gold Coast 3
LINDNER, Bob (22+3) Souths, B 1; Wynnum
    Manly 5; Parramatta 6; Gold Coast 2; Wests, S 5+1;
    Illawarra 3

McCABE, Paul (5) Easts, S 1; Manly 4
McINDOE, Alan (9) Illawarra 3; Penrith 6
McLEAN, Mike (4+1) Newcastle 3; Gold Coast 1+1
MENINGA, Mal (32) Souths, B 13; Canberra 19
MILES, Gene (19) Wynnum Manly 14;
    Brisbane Broncos 5
MOORE, Billy (6+2) Norths, S
MORRIS, Rod (4) Balmain 2; Wynnum Manly 2
MURRAY, Mark (14+1) Fortitude Valley 3; Redcliffe 11;
    Norths +1

NIEBLING, Bryan (9) Fortitude Valley 3; Redcliffe 6

OLIPHANT, Greg (1) Balmain
O'NEILL, Julian (4+1) Brisbane Broncos

PHELAN, Chris (2) Souths, B 1; Parramatta 1

QUINN, Graham (1) St. George

REDDY, Rod (1) St. George
RENOUF, Steve (3+2) Brisbane Broncos
RIBOT, John (8) Manly 5; Redcliffe 3

SCOTT, Colin (16+1) Wynnum Manly 15+1;
    Easts, B 1
SHEARER, Dale (19+5) Manly 11+2;
    Brisbane Broncos 3+2; Gold Coast 5+1
SMITH, Allan (1) Norths, S
SMITH, Darren (+7) Canterbury
SMITH, Gary (+1) Brothers
SMITH, Jason (1) Canterbury
STACEY, Steve (2) Easts, B
STAINS, Danny (4) Cronulla

TALLIS, Gorden (+2) St. George
TESSMAN, Brad (4+1) Souths, B 3; Easts, S 1+1
TRONC, Scott (+1) Wests, S

VAUTIN, Paul (20+2) Manly 19+2; Easts, S 1
VOWLES, Adrian (+1) Gold Coast

WALKER, Bruce (1) Manly
WALTERS, Kerrod (6) Brisbane Broncos
WALTERS, Kevin (6+8) Canberra +1;
    Brisbane Broncos 6+7
WALTERS, Steve (12) Canberra

FRANCE TOUR OF PAPUA NEW GUINEA, AUSTRALIA AND FIJI 1994

Date	Result	Score	Opposition	Venue	Attendance
IN PAPUA NEW GUINEA					
14 June	Won	16-14	**Highlands Zone** T: Chamorin, Entat G: Torreilles (4)	Minj	5,000
19 June	Lost	8-17	**PNG Colts** T: Garcia, Sirvent	Madang	6,000
22 June	Lost	20-22	**Selection du Morobe** T: Fraisse (2), Accroue, Garcia G: Loukili (2)	Lae	4,000
26 June	Lost	22-29	**PAPUA NEW GUINEA**	Port Moresby	8,000

Papua New Guinea:
David Buko; Ric Emanuel (1g, 1dg), Philip Boge (Capt),
David Gomia (1t), James Miviri (1t); Tuksy Karu (3g), Adrian Lam;
James Sikai, James Naipo (1t), Max Tiri, Ben Biri, Ronald Vue,
Tuiyo Evei (1t).
Subs: Luke Waldiat, Nander Yer, Mathew Midi, Stanley Gene (1t).
France:
Jean Frison; Jean-Marc Garcia (1t), David Despin, David Fraisse (1t),
Frantza Martial; Pierre Chamorin, Patrick Entat (Capt); Bernard Llong
(1t), Patrick Torreilles (3g), Theo Anast, Ezzedine Attia,
Franck Esponda, Thierry Valero.
Subs: Stephane Tena, Christophe Grandjean, Christophe Martinez (1t).
Referee: Denis Hale (New Zealand).

Date	Result	Score	Opposition	Venue	Attendance

IN AUSTRALIA

Date	Result	Score	Opposition	Venue	Attendance
2 July	Lost	12-19	**Cairns Connection**	Cairns	4,000

T: Baudomin, Brioux.
G: Loukili (2)

| 6 July | Lost | 0-58 | **AUSTRALIA** | Parramatta | 27,318 |

Australia:
Brett Mullins (1t); Michael Hancock, Mal Meninga (Capt, 1t,5g),
Steve Renouf (3t), Andrew Ettingshausen (1t); Laurie Daley (2t),
Allan Langer; Ian Roberts (2t), Steve Walters, Paul Harragon,
Paul Sironen, David Fairleigh, Brad Fittler (1t).
Subs: Tim Brasher, Brad Mackay, Paul McGregor (1t),
Mark Hohn (all played).
France:
Jean Frison; Jean-Marc Garcia, David Despin, David Fraisse,
Claude Sirvent; Pierre Chamorin, Patrick Entat (Capt);
Bernard Llong, Patrick Torreilles, Theo Anast, Ezzedine Attia,
Patrick Accroue, Stephane Tena.
Subs: Cyril Baudouin, Jean-Charles Giorgi, Jean-Marc Vincent,
Christophe Martinez (all played).
Referee: Denis Hale (New Zealand).

IN FIJI

Date	Result	Score	Opposition	Venue	Attendance
9 July	Lost	12-20	**FIJI** (Not a full Test)	Suva	4,800

Fiji:
Veramua Dikidikalati; Ratu Risi Cavuilati (1t), Philimoni Seru,
Lee Nalagilagi, Noa Nadruku; Noa Nayacakalou (1g),
Ropate Senikuratiri (1t, 1g); Voate Vasekava, Mesake Seavula,
James Pickering (Capt), Ylaiyasi Wainidroa (1t), Pio Kubuai,
Samuela Marayawa.
Subs: Illy Toga (1t), Joji Vatubua, Iliesa Nakailagi, Kalaveti Naisoro.
France:
Jean Frison; Pascal Bomati, Frantza Martial, David Fraisse,
Claude Sirvent (1t); David Despin, Patrick Entat (Capt);
Cyril Baudouin, Patrick Torreilles (1g), Theo Anast, Ezzedine Attia,
Patrick Accroue, Pierre Chamorin (1g). Subs: Moussa Loukili, Regis
Brioux, Christophe Grandjean (1t), Jean-Marc Vincent.
Referee: Graham Annesley (Australia).

TOUR SUMMARY

P	W	L	F	A
7	1	6	90	179

TOUR REGISTER
Manager: Charles Zalduendo
Coach: Jean-Christophe Vergeynst

Player	Club	App*	T	G	Pts
ACCROUE, Patrick	Avignon	3	1	–	4
ANAST, Theo	St. Gaudens	5	–	–	–
ATTIA, Ezzedine	Carpentras	5	–	–	–
BAUDOUIN, Cyril	Carpentras	6	1	–	4
BOMATI, Pascal	XIII Catalan	4	–	–	–
BRIOUX, Regis	Villeneuve	4	1	–	4
CHAMORIN, Pierre	St. Esteve	5	1	1	6
COUTTET, Alexandre	Carcassonne	3	–	–	–
DESPIN, David	Villeneuve	6	–	–	–
ENTAT, Patrick	Avignon	5	1	–	4
ESPONDA, Franck	St. Esteve	2	–	–	–
FRAISSE, David	Sheffield E.	5	3	–	12
FRISON, Jean	Villefranche-R	6	–	–	–
GARCIA, Jean-Marc	St. Esteve	6	3	–	12
GIORGI, Jean-Charles	Cannes	4	–	–	–
GRANDJEAN, Christophe	Lezignan	6	1	–	4
LLONG, Bernard	XIII Catalan	3	1	–	4
LOUKILI, Moussa	Lezignan	4	–	4	8
MARTIAL, Frantza	St. Esteve	4	–	–	–
MARTINEZ, Christophe	St. Gaudens	5	1	–	4
SIRVENT, Claude	St. Gaudens	5	2	–	8
TENA, Stephane	XIII Catalan	4	–	–	–
TORREILLES, Patrick	Pia	5	–	8	16
VALERO, Thierry	Lezignan	4	–	–	–
VINCENT, Jean-Marc	St. Gaudens	5	–	–	–

*Include substitute appearances

NEW ZEALAND TOUR OF PAPUA NEW GUINEA 1994
(Including one match in Australia)

Date	Result	Score	Opposition	Venue	Attendance
IN AUSTRALIA					
9 October	Won	44-16	**Cairns Connection**	Cairns	3,000
			T: Freeman, Tatupu, Taewa, Williams, Wiki, McCracken, Kearney		
			G: Halligan (5), Ridge (3)		
IN PAPUA NEW GUINEA					
11 October	Won	40-4	**Port Moresby Vipers**	Port Moresby	9,000
			T: Freeman, Smith, Halligan, Whittaker, Lowrie, Lomax		
			G: Halligan (6), Ngamu (2)		

| 16 October | Won | 28-12 | **PAPUA NEW GUINEA** | Goroka | 12,000 |

Papua New Guinea:
David Buko (2g); James Miviri (1t), David Gomia, Philip Boge,
Ric Emmanuel; Aquila Emil (1t), Adrian Lam; Ben Biri, Daroa Ben
Moide (Capt), Tuiyo Evei, Max Tiri, Nande Yer, James Naipo.
Subs: Stanley Gene, Kera Ngaffin.
New Zealand:
Matthew Ridge; Daryl Halligan (6g), Jarrod McCracken,
Ruben Wiki (1t), Sean Hoppe; Gene Ngamu (2t), Gary Freeman;
John Lomax, Duane Mann (Capt), Jason Lowrie, Stephen Kearney,
Tawera Nikau (1t), Brendon Tuuta.
Subs: Hitro Okesene, Jason Williams, Aaron Whittaker,
Tony Tatupu.
Referee: Jim Stokes (New Zealand).

| 19 October | Won | 34-2 | **Northern Zone** | Lae | 3,500 |

T: Hoppe (3), Tawea (2),
Wiki, Stuart
G: Whittaker (3)

| 23 October | Won | 30-16 | **PAPUA NEW GUINEA** | Port Moresby | 14,000 |

Papua New Guinea:
David Buko (1t); James Miviri, David Gomia, John Okul (1t),
Ric Emanuel (2g); Aquila Emil, Adrian Lam; Tuiyo Evei,
Ronald Vue, Kera Ngaffin, Max Tiri, Daroa Ben Moide (Capt),
James Naipo.
Subs: Stanley Gene (1t), Ben Biri, Joshua Kouoru, Nande Yer.
New Zealand:
Matthew Ridge (1t); Daryl Halligan (1t,7g), Jarrod McCracken,
Ruben Wiki, Sean Hoppe; Gene Ngamu (1t), Gary Freeman;
John Lomax, Duane Mann (Capt), Terry Hermannson,
Stephen Kearney, Tawera Nikau, Brendon Tuuta (1t).
Subs: Hitro Okesene, Jason Williams, Brent Stuart.
Referee: Jim Stokes (New Zealand).

TOUR SUMMARY

P	W	L	F	A
5	5	0	176	50

TOUR REGISTER
Captain: Duane Mann
Coach: Frank Endacott
Managers: Bevan Olsen and Ray Haffenden

Player	Club	App*	T	G	Pts
DORREEN, Mike	Hawkes Bay	2	0	0	0
FREEMAN, Gary	Penrith (A)	5	2	0	8
HALLIGAN, Daryl	Canterbury-Bankstown(A)	4	2	24	56
HERMANSSON, Terry	South Sydney (A)	3	0	0	0
HOPPE, Sean	North Sydney (A)	5	3	0	12
KEARNEY, Stephen	Western Suburbs (A)	5	1	0	4
LOMAX, John	Canberra (A)	5	1	0	4
LOWRIE, Jason	Eastern Suburbs (A)	5	1	0	4
McCRACKEN, Jarrod	Canterbury-Bankstown(A)	4	1	0	4
MANN, Duane	North Harbour	4	0	0	0
NGAMU, Gene	South Sydney (A)	4	3	2	16
NIKAU, Tawera	Castleford (GB)	4	1	0	4
O'KESENE, Hitro	Counties-Manukau	5	0	0	0
PONGIA, Quentin	Canberra (A)	1	0	0	0
RIDGE, Matthew	Manly-Warrington (A)	4	1	3	10
SMITH, Tyran	South Sydney (A)	3	1	0	4
†STUART, Brent	Western Suburbs (A)	3	1	0	4
TAEWA, Whetu	Counties-Manukau	3	3	0	12
TATUPU, Tony	North Harbour	4	1	0	4
TUUTA, Brendon	Featherstone R. (GB)	2	1	0	4
WHITTAKER, Aaron	Wakefield T. (GB)	4	1	3	10
WIKI, Ruben	Canberra (A)	5	3	0	12
WILLIAMS, Jason	Canterbury-Bankstown(A)	5	1	0	4
TOTALS			**28**	**32**	**176**

*Including substitute appearances
(A) indicates Australia
(GB) indicates Great Britain
†replacement for injured Quentin Pongia.

Great Britain winger Jason Robinson, an ever-present in the 1994 John Smith's Test series against Australia.

GREAT BRITAIN

Great Britain, with new coach Ellery Hanley at the helm, pulled off a memorable victory in the opening encounter of the three-match John Smith's Test series but could not wrest the Ashes from world champions Australia.

The Kangaroos bounced back to take the second Test 38-8 at Manchester United's Old Trafford and clinch the series with a 23-4 success at Elland Road, Leeds.

The triple meeting with the Australians was Great Britain's total workload for 1994-95, their spring clash with the French being replaced by the re-introduction of the John Smith's European Championship involving England, France and Wales in preparation for the autumn's Centenary World Cup.

The 1994 Ashes series attracted record attendances and receipts and marked the equalling of Mick Sullivan's record haul of 46 Test appearances by Garry Schofield.

The build up to the John Smith's Tests included the shock decision by Great Britain coach Malcolm Reilly to take up the post of coach at Australian club Newcastle Knights following the three-match series. Reilly's announcement of the appointment was followed days later by his resignation from the national position.

Shaun Edwards was named as captain for the series, vice-captain Phil Clarke deputising in the second Test when Edwards was suspended following his dismissal at Wembley.

Great Britain debutants during the Ashes encounters were Wigan forwards Mick Cassidy and Barrie McDermott.

Wigan provided a record-equalling eight players for the third Test . . . Gary Connolly, Jason Robinson, Martin Offiah, Phil Clarke, Shaun Edwards, Barrie McDermott, Denis Betts and Andrew Farrell. The Ashes series is fully chronicled in the chapter 1994 KANGAROOS.

Handshakes from the fans for Great Britain's Ellery Hanley after a victorious debut as national coach in the 8-4 victory over Australia in October 1994.

TESTS

● Although early Tests were played under the titles of Northern Union or England, it is acceptable to regard them as Great Britain.
W-Won, D-Drawn, L-Lost refer to Great Britain.

GREAT BRITAIN v. AUSTRALIA

12 Dec. 1908	D	22-22	QPR, London	2,000
23 Jan. 1909	W	15-5	Newcastle	22,000
15 Feb. 1909	W	6-5	Birmingham	9,000
18 Jun. 1910	W	27-20	Sydney	42,000
2 Jul. 1910	W	22-17	Brisbane	18,000
8 Nov. 1911	L	10-19	Newcastle	6,500
16 Dec. 1911	D	11-11	Edinburgh	6,000
1 Jan. 1912	L	8-33	Birmingham	4,000
27 Jun. 1914	W	23-5	Sydney	40,000
29 Jun. 1914	L	7-12	Sydney	55,000
4 Jul. 1914	W	14-6	Sydney	34,420
26 Jun. 1920	L	4-8	Brisbane	28,000
3 Jul. 1920	L	8-21	Sydney	40,000
10 Jul. 1920	W	23-13	Sydney	32,000
1 Oct. 1921	W	6-5	Leeds	32,000
5 Nov. 1921	L	2-16	Hull	21,504
14 Jan. 1922	W	6-0	Salford	21,000
23 Jun. 1924	W	22-3	Sydney	50,000
28 Jun. 1924	W	5-3	Sydney	33,842
12 Jul. 1924	L	11-21	Brisbane	36,000
23 Jun. 1928	W	15-12	Brisbane	39,200
14 Jul. 1928	W	8-0	Sydney	44,548
21 Jul. 1928	L	14-21	Sydney	37,000
5 Oct. 1929	L	8-31	Hull K.R.	20,000
9 Nov. 1929	W	9-3	Leeds	31,402
4 Jan. 1930	D	0-0	Swinton	34,709
15 Jan. 1930	W	3-0	Rochdale	16,743
6 Jun. 1932	W	8-6	Sydney	70,204
18 Jun. 1932	L	6-15	Brisbane	26,500
16 Jul. 1932	W	18-13	Sydney	50,053
7 Oct. 1933	W	4-0	Belle Vue, Manchester	34,000
11 Nov. 1933	W	7-5	Leeds	29,618
16 Dec. 1933	W	19-16	Swinton	10,990
29 Jun. 1936	L	8-24	Sydney	63,920
4 Jul. 1936	W	12-7	Brisbane	29,486
18 Jul. 1936	W	12-7	Sydney	53,546
16 Oct. 1937	W	5-4	Leeds	31,949
13 Nov. 1937	W	13-3	Swinton	31,724
18 Dec. 1937	L	3-13	Huddersfield	9,093
17 Jun. 1946	D	8-8	Sydney	64,527
6 Jul. 1946	W	14-5	Brisbane	40,500
20 Jul. 1946	W	20-7	Sydney	35,294
9 Oct. 1948	W	23-21	Leeds	36,529
6 Nov. 1948	W	16-7	Swinton	36,354
29 Jan. 1949	W	23-9	Bradford	42,000
12 Jun. 1950	W	6-4	Sydney	47,215
1 Jul. 1950	L	3-15	Brisbane	35,000
22 Jul. 1950	L	2-5	Sydney	47,178
4 Oct. 1952	W	19-6	Leeds	34,505
8 Nov. 1952	W	21-5	Swinton	32,421
13 Dec. 1952	L	7-27	Bradford	30,509
12 Jun. 1954	L	12-37	Sydney	65,884
3 Jul. 1954	W	38-21	Brisbane	46,355
17 Jul. 1954	L	16-20	Sydney	67,577
17 Nov. 1956	W	21-10	Wigan	22,473
1 Dec. 1956	L	9-22	Bradford	23,634
15 Dec. 1956	W	19-0	Swinton	17,542
14 Jun. 1958	L	8-25	Sydney	68,777
5 Jul. 1958	W	25-18	Brisbane	32,965
19 Jul. 1958	W	40-17	Sydney	68,720
17 Oct. 1959	L	14-22	Swinton	35,224
21 Nov. 1959	W	11-10	Leeds	30,184
12 Dec. 1959	W	18-12	Wigan	26,089
9 Jun. 1962	W	31-12	Sydney	70,174
30 Jun. 1962	W	17-10	Brisbane	34,766
14 Jul. 1962	L	17-18	Sydney	42,104
16 Oct. 1963	L	2-28	Wembley	13,946
9 Nov. 1963	L	12-50	Swinton	30,833
30 Nov. 1963	W	16-5	Leeds	20,497
25 Jun. 1966	W	17-13	Sydney	57,962
16 Jul. 1966	L	4-6	Brisbane	45,057
23 Jul. 1966	L	14-19	Sydney	63,503
21 Oct. 1967	W	16-11	Leeds	22,293
3 Nov. 1967	L	11-17	White City, London	17,445
9 Dec. 1967	L	3-11	Swinton	13,615
6 Jun. 1970	L	15-37	Brisbane	42,807
20 Jun. 1970	W	28-7	Sydney	60,962
4 Jul. 1970	W	21-17	Sydney	61,258
3 Nov. 1973	W	21-12	Wembley	9,874
24 Nov. 1973	L	6-14	Leeds	16,674
1 Dec. 1973	L	5-15	Warrington	10,019
15 Jun. 1974	L	6-12	Brisbane	30,280
6 Jul. 1974	W	16-11	Sydney	48,006
20 Jul. 1974	L	18-22	Sydney	55,505
21 Oct. 1978	L	9-15	Wigan	17,644
5 Nov. 1978	W	18-14	Bradford	26,447
18 Nov. 1978	L	6-23	Leeds	29,627
16 Jun. 1979	L	0-35	Brisbane	23,051
30 Jun. 1979	L	16-24	Sydney	26,837
14 Jul. 1979	L	2-28	Sydney	16,844
30 Oct. 1982	L	4-40	Hull C. FC	26,771
20 Nov. 1982	L	6-27	Wigan	23,216

28 Nov. 1982	L	8-32	Leeds	17,318
9 Jun. 1984	L	8-25	Sydney	30,190
26 Jun. 1984	L	6-18	Brisbane	26,534
7 Jul. 1984	L	7-20	Sydney	18,756
25 Oct. 1986	L	16-38	Man U. FC	50,583
8 Nov. 1986	L	4-34	Elland Rd, Leeds	30,808
* 22 Nov. 1986	L	15-24	Wigan	20,169
11 Jun. 1988	L	6-17	Sydney	24,202
28 Jun. 1988	L	14-34	Brisbane	27,103
* 9 Jul. 1988	W	26-12	Sydney	15,994
27 Oct. 1990	W	19-12	Wembley	54,569
10 Nov. 1990	L	10-14	Man U. FC	46,615
* 24 Nov. 1990	L	0-14	Elland Rd, Leeds	32,500
12 Jun. 1992	L	6-22	Sydney	40,141
26 Jun. 1992	W	33-10	Melbourne	30,257
* 3 Jul. 1992	L	10-16	Brisbane	32,313
22 Oct. 1994	W	8-4	Wembley	57,034
5 Nov. 1994	L	8-38	Man U. FC	43,930
20 Nov. 1994	L	4-23	Elland Rd, Leeds	39,468

* Also World Cup match.

	Played	Won	Drawn	Lost	Tries	Goals	Dr	Pts for
Great Britain	111	53	4	54	264	276	7	1382
Australia	111	54	4	53	320	343	7	1718

GREAT BRITAIN-AUSTRALIA TEST MATCH RECORDS

Britain

Highest score:	40-17 Third Test at Sydney, 19 July 1958
Widest margin win:	As above and
	33-10 Second Test at Melbourne, 26 June 1992
Most tries in a match:	4 by Jim Leytham (Wigan) Second Test at Brisbane, 2 July 1910
Most goals in a match:	10 by Lewis Jones (Leeds) Second Test at Brisbane, 3 July 1954
Most points in a match:	20 by Lewis Jones (as above)
	20 (2t, 7g) by Roger Millward (Hull K.R.) Second Test at Sydney, 20 June 1970
Biggest attendance:	57,034 First Test at Wembley, London, 22 October 1994

● For the World Cup final at Wembley on 24 October 1992, there was an attendance of 73,631

Australia

Highest score:	50-12 Second Test at Swinton, 9 Nov 1963 (Also widest margin win)
Most tries in a match:	3 by Jimmy Devereux, First Test at QPR, London, 12 December 1908
	3 by Reg Gasnier, First Test at Swinton, 17 October 1959
	3 by Reg Gasnier, First Test at Wembley, 16 October 1963
	3 by Ken Irvine, Second Test at Swinton, 9 November 1963
	3 by Ken Irvine, Third Test at Sydney, 23 July 1966
	3 by Gene Miles, First Test at Old Trafford, Manchester, 25 October 1986
	3 by Michael O'Connor, First Test at Old Trafford, Manchester, 25 October 1986
Most goals in a match:	10 by Mick Cronin, First Test at Brisbane, 16 June 1979
Most points in a match:	22 (3t, 5g) by Michael O'Connor, First Test at Old Trafford, Manchester, 25 October 1986
Biggest attendance:	70,204 First Test at Sydney, 6 June 1932

● In a World Cup match at Perpignan, France, on 29 October 1972, Bobby Fulton scored 3 tries

GREAT BRITAIN v. NEW ZEALAND

25 Jan. 1908	W	14-6	Leeds	8,182
8 Feb. 1908	L	6-18	Chelsea	14,000
15 Feb. 1908	L	5-8	Cheltenham	4,000
30 Jul. 1910	W	52-20	Auckland	16,000
1 Aug. 1914	W	16-13	Auckland	15,000
31 Jul. 1920	W	31-7	Auckland	34,000
7 Aug. 1920	W	19-3	Christchurch	10,000
14 Aug. 1920	W	11-10	Wellington	4,000
2 Aug. 1924	L	8-16	Auckland	22,000
6 Aug. 1924	L	11-13	Wellington	6,000
9 Aug. 1924	W	31-18	Dunedin	14,000
2 Oct. 1926	W	28-20	Wigan	14,500
13 Nov. 1926	W	21-11	Hull	7,000
15 Jan. 1927	W	32-17	Leeds	6,000
4 Aug. 1928	L	13-17	Auckland	28,000
18 Aug. 1928	W	13-5	Dunedin	12,000
25 Aug. 1928	W	6-5	Christchurch	21,000
30 Jul. 1932	W	24-9	Auckland	25,000
13 Aug. 1932	W	25-14	Christchurch	5,000
20 Aug. 1932	W	20-18	Auckland	6,500
8 Aug. 1936	W	10-8	Auckland	25,000
15 Aug. 1936	W	23-11	Auckland	17,000
10 Aug. 1946	L	8-13	Auckland	10,000
4 Oct. 1947	W	11-10	Leeds	28,445
8 Nov. 1947	L	7-10	Swinton	29,031
20 Dec. 1947	W	25-9	Bradford	42,680
29 Jul. 1950	L	10-16	Christchurch	10,000
12 Aug. 1950	L	13-20	Auckland	20,000
6 Oct. 1951	W	21-15	Bradford	37,475
10 Nov. 1951	W	20-19	Swinton	29,938
15 Dec. 1951	W	16-12	Leeds	18,649
24 Jul. 1954	W	27-7	Auckland	22,097
31 Jul. 1954	L	14-20	Greymouth	4,240
14 Aug. 1954	W	12-6	Auckland	6,186
8 Oct. 1955	W	25-6	Swinton	21,937
12 Nov. 1955	W	27-12	Bradford	24,443
17 Dec. 1955	L	13-28	Leeds	10,438
26 Jul. 1958	L	10-15	Auckland	25,000
9 Aug. 1958	W	32-15	Auckland	25,000
30 Sep. 1961	L	11-29	Leeds	16,540
21 Oct. 1961	W	23-10	Bradford	19,980
4 Nov. 1961	W	35-19	Swinton	22,536

28 Jul. 1962	L	0-19	Auckland	14,976
11 Aug. 1962	L	8-27	Auckland	16,411
25 Sep. 1965	W	7-2	Swinton	8,541
23 Oct. 1965	W	15-9	Bradford	15,740
6 Nov. 1965	D	9-9	Wigan	7,919
6 Aug. 1966	W	25-8	Auckland	14,494
20 Aug. 1966	W	22-14	Auckland	10,657
11 Jul. 1970	W	19-15	Auckland	15,948
19 Jul. 1970	W	23-9	Christchurch	8,600
25 Jul. 1970	W	33-16	Auckland	13,137
25 Sep. 1971	L	13-18	Salford	3,764
16 Oct. 1971	L	14-17	Castleford	4,108
6 Nov. 1971	W	12-3	Leeds	5,479
27 Jul. 1974	L	8-13	Auckland	10,466
4 Aug. 1974	W	17-8	Christchurch	6,316
10 Aug. 1974	W	20-0	Auckland	11,574
21 Jul. 1979	W	16-8	Auckland	9,000
5 Aug. 1979	W	22-7	Christchurch	8,500
11 Aug. 1979	L	11-18	Auckland	7,000
18 Oct. 1980	D	14-14	Wigan	7,031
2 Nov. 1980	L	8-12	Bradford	10,946
15 Nov. 1980	W	10-2	Leeds	8,210
14 Jul. 1984	L	0-12	Auckland	10,238
22 Jul. 1984	L	12-28	Christchurch	3,824
28 Jul. 1984	L	16-32	Auckland	7,967
19 Oct. 1985	L	22-24	Leeds	12,591
2 Nov. 1985	W	25-8	Wigan	15,506
★ 9 Nov. 1985	D	6-6	Elland Rd,	
			Leeds	22,209
★ 17 Jul. 1988	L	10-12	Christchurch	8,525
21 Oct. 1989	L	16-24	Man U. FC	18,273
28 Oct. 1989	W	26-6	Elland Rd,	
			Leeds	13,073
★ 11 Nov. 1989	W	10-6	Wigan	20,346
24 Jun. 1990	W	11-10	Palmerston N.	8,073
8 Jul. 1990	W	16-14	Auckland	7,843
★ 15 Jul. 1990	L	18-21	Christchurch	3,133
12 Jul. 1992	L	14-15	Palmerston N.	11,548
19 Jul. 1992	W	19-16	Auckland	10,223
16 Oct. 1993	W	17-0	Wembley	36,131
30 Oct. 1993	W	29-12	Wigan	16,502
6 Nov. 1993	W	29-10	Leeds	15,139

★ Also World Cup match.

	Played	Won	Drawn	Lost	Tries	Goals	Dr	Pts for
Great Britain	82	51	3	28	291	236	8	1401
New Zealand	82	28	3	51	185	232	2	1062

GREAT BRITAIN-NEW ZEALAND TEST MATCH RECORDS

Britain

Highest score:	52-20 First Test at Auckland, 30 July 1910 (Also widest margin win)
Most tries in a match:	4 by Billy Boston (Wigan) First Test at Auckland, 24 July 1954
	4 by Garry Schofield (Hull) Second Test at Wigan, 2 November 1985
Most goals in a match:	7 by Eric Fraser (Warrington) Second Test at Auckland, 9 August 1958
	7 by Neil Fox (Wakefield T.) Third Test at Swinton, 4 November 1961
Most points in a match:	16 (4t) by Garry Schofield (Hull) Second Test at Wigan, 2 November 1985
Biggest attendance:	42,680 Third Test at Bradford, 20 December 1947

● In a World Cup match at Pau, France, on 4 November 1972, Britain won 53-19 with John Holmes (Leeds) scoring 26 points from 10 goals and two tries.
In a World Cup match at Sydney on 8 June 1968, Bev Risman scored 7 goals.

New Zealand

Highest score:	32-16 Third Test at Auckland, 28 July 1984
Widest margin win:	19-0 First Test at Auckland, 28 July 1962
	27-8 Second Test at Auckland, 11 August 1962

No player has scored three tries or more in a Test.

Most goals and points:	7g-14pts by Des White, Second Test at Greymouth, 31 July 1954
	Jack Fagan, First Test at Headingley, 30 September 1961
	Ernie Wiggs, Second Test at Auckland, 20 August 1966
Biggest attendance:	34,000 First Test at Auckland, 31 July 1920

● In a World Cup match at Sydney, Australia, on 25 June 1957, Bill Sorensen also scored 7 goals, 14 points.

GREAT BRITAIN v. FRANCE

● **Results since France were given Test match status.**

26 Jan. 1957	W	45-12	Leeds	20,221	8 Mar. 1964	W	11-5	Perpignan	4,326
3 Mar. 1957	D	19-19	Toulouse	16,000	18 Mar. 1964	W	39-0	Leigh	4,750
10 Apr. 1957	W	29-14	St. Helens	23,250	6 Dec. 1964	L	8-18	Perpignan	15,000
3 Nov. 1957	W	25-14	Toulouse	15,000	23 Jan. 1965	W	17-7	Swinton	9,959
23 Nov. 1957	W	44-15	Wigan	19,152	16 Jan. 1966	L	13-18	Perpignan	6,000
2 Mar. 1958	W	23-9	Grenoble	20,000	5 Mar. 1966	L	4-8	Wigan	14,004
14 Mar. 1959	W	50-15	Leeds	22,000	22 Jan. 1967	W	16-13	Carcassonne	10,650
5 Apr. 1959	L	15-24	Grenoble	8,500	4 Mar. 1967	L	13-23	Wigan	7,448
6 Mar. 1960	L	18-20	Toulouse	15,308	11 Feb. 1968	W	22-13	Paris	8,000
26 Mar. 1960	D	17-17	St. Helens	14,000	2 Mar. 1968	W	19-8	Bradford	14,196
11 Dec. 1960	W	21-10	Bordeaux	8,000	30 Nov. 1968	W	34-10	St. Helens	6,080
28 Jan. 1961	W	27-8	St. Helens	18,000	2 Feb. 1969	L	9-13	Toulouse	10,000
17 Feb. 1962	L	15-20	Wigan	17,277	7 Feb. 1971	L	8-16	Toulouse	14,960
11 Mar. 1962	L	13-23	Perpignan	14,000	17 Mar. 1971	W	24-2	St. Helens	7,783
2 Dec. 1962	L	12-17	Perpignan	5,000	6 Feb. 1972	W	10-9	Toulouse	11,508
3 Apr. 1963	W	42-4	Wigan	19,487	12 Mar. 1972	W	45-10	Bradford	7,313
					20 Jan. 1974	W	24-5	Grenoble	5,500
					17 Feb. 1974	W	29-0	Wigan	10,105
					6 Dec. 1981	W	37-0	Hull	13,173

20 Dec. 1981	L	2-19	Marseilles	6,500		21 Jan. 1989	W	26-10	Wigan	8,266
20 Feb. 1983	W	20-5	Carcassonne	3,826		5 Feb. 1989	W	30-8	Avignon	6,500
6 Mar. 1983	W	17-5	Hull	6,055		18 Mar. 1990	W	8-4	Perpignan	6,000
29 Jan. 1984	W	12-0	Avignon	4,000		7 Apr. 1990	L	18-25	Leeds	6,554
17 Feb. 1984	W	10-0	Leeds	7,646		* 27 Jan. 1991	W	45-10	Perpignan	3,965
1 Mar. 1985	W	50-4	Leeds	6,491		16 Feb. 1991	W	60-4	Leeds	5,284
17 Mar. 1985	L	16-24	Perpignan	5,000		16 Feb. 1992	W	30-12	Perpignan	5,688
* 16 Feb. 1986	D	10-10	Avignon	4,000		* 7 Mar. 1992	W	36-0	Hull	5,250
1 Mar. 1986	W	24-10	Wigan	8,112		7 Mar. 1993	W	48-6	Carcassonne	5,500
* 24 Jan. 1987	W	52-4	Leeds	6,567		2 Apr. 1993	W	72-6	Leeds	8,196
8 Feb. 1987	W	20-10	Carcassonne	2,000		20 Mar. 1994	W	12-4	Carcassonne	7,000
24 Jan. 1988	W	28-14	Avignon	6,500		*Also World Cup match.				
6 Feb. 1988	W	30-12	Leeds	7,007						

	Played	Won	Drawn	Lost	Tries	Goals	Dr	Pts for
Great Britain	59	42	3	14	282	258	1	1473
France	59	14	3	42	106	137	4	625

GREAT BRITAIN-FRANCE TEST MATCH RECORDS

Britain

Highest score:	72-6 at Leeds, 2 April 1993 (Also widest margin win)
Most tries in a match:	5 by Martin Offiah (Widnes) at Leeds, 16 February 1991
Most goals in a match:	10 by Bernard Ganley (Oldham) at Wigan, 23 November 1957
	10 by Jonathan Davies (Widnes) at Leeds, 2 April 1993
Most points in a match:	21 (1t, 9g) by Lewis Jones (Leeds) at Leeds, 26 January 1957
	21 (1t, 9g) by Neil Fox (Wakefield T.) at Wigan, 3 April 1963
	21 (1t, 9g) by Neil Fox (Wakefield T.) at Leigh, 18 March 1964
Biggest attendance:	23,250 at St. Helens, 10 April 1957

France

Highest score:	25-18 at Leeds, 7 April 1990
Widest margin win:	19-2 at Marseilles, 20 December 1981
Most tries in a match:	3 by Didier Couston at Perpignan, 17 March 1985
Most goals in a match:	7 by Pierre Lacaze at Wigan, 4 March 1967
Most points in a match:	14 by Pierre Lacaze (as above)
	14 (2t, 4g) by Gilbert Benausse at Wigan, 17 February 1962
Biggest attendance:	20,000 at Grenoble, 2 March 1958

● In a World Cup match at Toulouse on 7 November 1954, there were 37,471

Additional Great Britain v. France

Pre-Test status

22 May 1952	L	12-22	Paris	16,466
24 May 1953	L	17-28	Lyons	
27 Apr. 1954	W	17-8	Bradford	14,153
11 Dec. 1955	L	5-17	Paris	18,000
11 Apr. 1956	W	18-10	Bradford	10,453

Other match

31 July 1982	L	7-8	Venice	1,500

GREAT BRITAIN v. PAPUA NEW GUINEA

5 Aug. 1984	W	38-20	Mt. Hagen	7,510
* 24 Oct. 1987	W	42-0	Wigan	9,121
* 22 May 1988	W	42-22	Port Moresby	12,107
27 May 1990	L	18-20	Goroka	11,598
* 2 Jun. 1990	W	40-8	Port Moresby	5,969
* 9 Nov. 1991	W	56-4	Wigan	4,193
31 May 1992	W	20-14	Port Moresby	7,294

*Also World Cup match.

	Played	Won	Lost	Tries	Goals	Dr	Pts for
Great Britain	7	6	1	45	38	0	256
Papua New Guinea	7	1	6	14	15	2	88

GREAT BRITAIN-PAPUA NEW GUINEA TEST MATCH RECORDS

Britain
Highest score:	56-4 at Wigan, 9 November 1991 (Also widest margin win)
Most tries in a match:	No player has scored 3 or more
Most goals in a match:	8 by Jonathan Davies (Widnes) at Wigan, 9 November 1991
Most points in a match:	16 by Jonathan Davies (Widnes) as above
Biggest attendance:	9,121 at Wigan, 24 October 1987

Papua New Guinea
Highest score:	22-42 at Port Moresby, 22 May 1988
Only win:	20-18 at Goroka, 27 May 1990
Most tries in a match:	No player has scored 3 or more
Most goals in a match:	6 by Bal Numapo at Goroka, 27 May 1990
Most points in a match:	11 (5g, 1dg) by Bal Numapo as above
Biggest attendance:	12,107 at Port Moresby, 22 May 1988

CLUB REPRESENTATION

Wigan hold the record for most players supplied by one club for a Test or World Cup match. They have had eight in Great Britain's starting line-up on four occasions as follows:

v. Papua New Guinea at Wigan on 24 October 1987. Won 42-0: Steve Hampson, David Stephenson, Joe Lydon, Shaun Edwards, Andy Gregory, Brian Case, Andy Goodway and Ellery Hanley (capt).

v. Australia at Melbourne on 26 June 1992. Won 33-10: Martin Offiah, Shaun Edwards, Kelvin Skerrett, Martin Dermott, Andy Platt, Denis Betts, Billy McGinty and Phil Clarke.

v. Australia at Brisbane on 3 July 1992. Lost 10-16: As above.

v. Australia at Elland Road, Leeds, on 20 November 1994. Lost 4-23: Gary Connolly, Jason Robinson, Martin Offiah, Phil Clarke, Shaun Edwards (capt.), Barrie McDermott, Denis Betts and Andrew Farrell.

In the second and third Tests of 1992 Wigan became the only club to provide all six forwards.

Wigan had a record 10 players on duty for the first 1992 Test against Australia, seven in the starting line-up plus three substitutes, all of whom played. For a brief period, there were a record nine Wigan players in action.

Wigan also hold the record for the total of players selected from one club over the years with 88.

Only three of last season's clubs have not had a player selected for Great Britain — Bramley, Carlisle and Doncaster.

Of the extinct clubs only Broughton Rangers (later Belle Vue Rangers), Merthyr Tydfil, St. Helens Recs and Runcorn had players selected for Britain.

*A register of each club's representation for Great Britain is featured in the CLUBS section.

GREAT BRITAIN TEAMS
...A 20-year review

The following is a compendium of Great Britain Test and World Cup teams since the start of the 1975-76 season.

Initials are included where more than one celebrated player shared a surname in the same era. Only playing substitutes are included on the teamsheet.

(WC): World Cup t: try g: goal dg: drop goal * captain

Wingman Stuart Wright, capped seven times for Great Britain in 1977 and 1978.

1977 France (WC)
Auckland: 5 June
Won 23-4
Fairbairn (Wigan) 7g
Fielding (Salford)
Holmes (Leeds)
Dyl (Leeds) 1t
Wright, S. (Widnes) 1t
*Millward (Hull K.R.) 1t
Nash (Salford)
Thompson, J. (Featherstone R.)
Ward, D. (Leeds)
Pitchford, S. (Leeds)
Bowman, E. (Workington T.)
Nicholls (St. Helens)
Hogan (Barrow)
Sub: Gill, K. (Salford)
    Casey (Hull K.R.)

1977 New Zealand (WC)
Christchurch: 12 June
Won 30-12
Fairbairn (Wigan) 6g
Wright, S. (Widnes) 2t
Holmes (Leeds)
Dyl (Leeds)
Francis, W. (Wigan)
*Millward (Hull K.R.) 1t
Nash (Salford)
Thompson, J. (Featherstone R.)
Ward, D. (Leeds)
Pitchford, S. (Leeds)
Bowman, E. (Workington T.) 1t
Nicholls (St. Helens) 1t
Hogan (Barrow) 1t
Sub: Casey (Hull K.R.)

1977 Australia (WC)
Brisbane: 18 June
Lost 5-19
Fairbairn (Wigan) 1g
Wright, S. (Widnes)
Francis, W. (Wigan)
Dyl (Leeds)
Fielding (Salford)
*Millward (Hull K.R.) 1t
Nash (Salford)
Thompson, J. (Featherstone R.)
Ward, D. (Leeds)
Pitchford, S. (Leeds)
Bowman, E. (Workington T.)
Nicholls (St. Helens)
Hogan (Barrow)
Sub: Holmes (Leeds)
    Smith, P. (Featherstone R.)

1977 Australia (WC)
Sydney: 25 June
Lost 12-13
Fairbairn (Wigan) 3g
Wright, S. (Widnes)
Holmes (Leeds)
Dyl (Leeds)
Francis, W. (Wigan)
*Millward (Hull K.R.)
Nash (Salford)
Thompson, J. (Featherstone R.)
Elwell (Widnes)
Pitchford, S. (Leeds) 1t
Bowman, E. (Workington T.)
Casey (Hull K.R.)
Hogan (Barrow)
Sub: Gill, K. (Salford) 1t
    Smith, P. (Featherstone R.)

1978 Australia
Wigan: 21 Oct.
Lost 9-15
Fairbairn (Wigan) 3g
Wright, S. (Widnes)
Hughes (Widnes)
Cunningham (St. Helens)
Bevan, J. (Warrington) 1t
*Millward (Hull K.R.)
Nash (Salford)
Thompson, J. (Featherstone R.)
Ward, D. (Leeds)
Rose, P. (Hull K.R.)
Nicholls (St. Helens)
Casey (Hull K.R.)
Norton (Hull)
Sub: Holmes (Leeds)
    Hogan (Barrow)

1978 Australia
Bradford: 5 Nov.
Won 18-14
Fairbairn (Wigan) 6g
Wright, S. (Widnes) 2t
Joyner (Castleford)
Dyl (Leeds)
Atkinson, J. (Leeds)
*Millward (Hull K.R.)
Nash (Salford)
Mills (Widnes)
Fisher (Bradford N.)
Lockwood (Hull K.R.)
Nicholls (St. Helens)
Lowe, P. (Hull K.R.)
Norton (Hull)
Sub: Holmes (Leeds)
    Rose, P. (Hull K.R.)

1978 Australia
Leeds: 18 Nov.
Lost 6-23
Fairbairn (Wigan)
Wright, S. (Widnes)
Joyner (Castleford)
Bevan, J. (Warrington) 1t
Atkinson, J. (Leeds)
*Millward (Hull K.R.) 1t
Nash (Salford)
Mills (Widnes)
Fisher (Bradford N.)
Farrar (Hull)
Nicholls (St. Helens)
Lowe, P. (Hull K.R.)
Norton (Hull)
Sub: Holmes (Leeds)
    Rose, P. (Hull K.R.)

1979 Australia
Brisbane: 16 June
Lost 0-35
Woods, J. (Leigh)
Barends (Bradford N.)
Joyner (Castleford)
Hughes (Widnes)
Mathias (St. Helens)
Holmes (Leeds)
Stephens (Castleford)
Mills (Widnes)
Ward, D. (Leeds)
Skerrett, T. (Wakefield T.)
Nicholls (St. Helens)
*Laughton (Widnes)
Norton (Hull)
Sub: Evans, S. (Featherstone R.)
    Hogan (Hull K.R.)

1979 Australia
Sydney: 30 June
Lost 16-24
Fairbairn (Wigan)
Barends (Bradford N.)
Joyner (Castleford) 1t
Woods, J. (Leigh) 5g
Hughes (Widnes) 1t
Holmes (Leeds)
Stephens (Castleford)
*Nicholls (St. Helens)
Ward, D. (Leeds)
Skerrett, T. (Wakefield T.)
Casey (Bradford N.)
Grayshon (Bradford N.)
Adams, M. (Widnes)
Sub: Evans, S. (Featherstone R.)
    Watkinson (Hull K.R.)

1979 Australia
Sydney: 14 July
Lost 2-28
Fairbairn (Wigan) 1g
Evans, S. (Featherstone R.)
Joyner (Castleford)
Woods, J. (Leigh)
Hughes (Widnes)
Topliss (Wakefield T.)
Redfearn, A. (Bradford N.)
*Nicholls (St. Helens)
Ward, D. (Leeds)
Casey (Bradford N.)
Hogan (Hull K.R.)
Grayshon (Bradford N.)
Norton (Hull)
Sub: Holmes (Leeds)
    Adams, M. (Widnes)

1979 New Zealand
Auckland: 21 July
Won 16-8
Fairbairn (Wigan) 1t, 2g
Evans, S. (Featherstone R.) 1t
Joyner (Castleford)
Smith, M. (Hull K.R.) 1t
Hughes (Widnes) 1t
Holmes (Leeds)
Stephens (Castleford)
Casey (Bradford N.)
Ward, D. (Leeds)
*Nicholls (St. Helens)
Hogan (Hull K.R.)
Grayshon (Bradford N.)
Adams, M. (Widnes)
Sub: Lockwood (Hull K.R.)

1979 New Zealand
Christchurch: 5 Aug.
Won 22-7
Fairbairn (Wigan) 5g
Evans, S. (Featherstone R.) 1t
Joyner (Castleford)
Smith, M. (Hull K.R.)
Hughes (Widnes) 1t
Holmes (Leeds)
Stephens (Castleford)
*Nicholls (St. Helens)
Ward, D. (Leeds)
Skerrett, T. (Wakefield T.)
Casey (Bradford N.) 1t
Grayshon (Bradford N.) 1t
Adams, M. (Widnes)

1979 New Zealand
Auckland: 11 Aug.
Lost 11-18
Fairbairn (Wigan) 1g
Evans, S. (Featherstone R.)
Joyner (Castleford)
Smith, M. (Hull K.R.) 1t
Hughes (Widnes) 1t
Holmes (Leeds)
Stephens (Castleford) 1t
Skerrett, T. (Wakefield T.)
Ward, D. (Leeds)
*Nicholls (St. Helens)
Casey (Bradford N.)
Grayshon (Bradford N.)
Adams, M. (Widnes)
Sub: Woods, J. (Leigh)
    Hogan (Hull K.R.)

1980 New Zealand
Wigan: 18 Oct.
Drew 14-14
*Fairbairn (Wigan) 4g
Camilleri (Barrow) 1t
Joyner (Castleford)
Smith, M. (Hull K.R.) 1t
Bentley, K. (Widnes)
Hartley, S. (Hull K.R.)
Dick (Leeds)
Holdstock (Hull K.R.)
Watkinson (Hull K.R.)
Skerrett, T. (Hull)
Gorley, L. (Widnes)
Grayshon (Bradford N.)
Casey (Hull K.R.)
Sub: Pinner (St. Helens)

1980 New Zealand
Bradford: 2 Nov.
Lost 8-13
*Fairbairn (Wigan) 4g
Drummond (Leigh)
Joyner (Castleford)
Smith, M. (Hull K.R.)
Camilleri (Barrow)
Kelly, K. (Warrington)
Dick (Leeds)
Holdstock (Hull K.R.)
Elwell (Widnes)
Shaw, G. (Widnes)
Casey (Hull K.R.)
Grayshon (Bradford N.)
Pinner (St. Helens)
Sub: Evans, S. (Featherstone R.)
    Gorley, L. (Widnes)

1980 New Zealand
Leeds: 15 Nov.
Won 10-2
Burke (Widnes) 2g
Drummond (Leigh) 2t
Joyner (Castleford)
Evans, S. (Featherstone R.)
Atkinson, J. (Leeds)
Woods, J. (Leigh)
Walker (Whitehaven)
Skerrett, T. (Hull)
Elwell (Widnes)
*Casey (Hull K.R.)
Gorley, P. (St. Helens)
Adams, M. (Widnes)
Norton (Hull)

1981 France
Hull: 6 Dec.
Won 37-0
Fairbairn (Hull K.R.) 1g
Drummond (Leigh) 2t
Smith, M. (Hull K.R.)
Woods, J. (Leigh) 1t, 7g
Gill, H. (Wigan) 3t
Hartley, S. (Hull K.R.) 1t
Gregory, A. (Widnes)
Grayshon (Bradford N.)
*Ward, D. (Leeds)
Skerrett, T. (Hull)
Gorley, L. (Widnes)
Gorley, P. (St. Helens)
Norton (Hull)
Sub: Burke (Widnes)
    Szymala (Barrow)

1981 France
Marseilles: 20 Dec.
Lost 2-19
Burke (Widnes)
Drummond (Leigh)
Smith, M. (Hull K.R.)
Woods, J. (Leigh) 1g
Gill, H. (Wigan)
Hartley, S. (Hull K.R.)
Gregory, A. (Widnes)
*Grayshon (Bradford N.)
Watkinson (Hull K.R.)
Skerrett, T. (Hull)
Gorley, L. (Widnes)
Szymala (Barrow)
Norton (Hull)
Sub: Gorley, P. (St. Helens)

1982 Australia
Hull City FC: 30 Oct.
Lost 4-40
Fairbairn (Hull K.R.)
Drummond (Leigh)
Hughes (Widnes)
Dyl (Leeds)
Evans, S. (Hull)
Woods, J. (Leigh)
*Nash (Salford)
Grayshon (Bradford N.)
Ward, D. (Leeds)
Skerrett, T. (Hull)
Gorley, L. (Widnes)
Crooks, L. (Hull) 2g
Norton (Hull)
Sub: Heron, D. (Leeds)

1982 Australia
Wigan: 20 Nov.
Lost 6-27
Mumby (Bradford N.) 3g
Drummond (Leigh)
Smith, M. (Hull K.R.)
Stephenson (Wigan)
Gill, H. (Wigan)
Holmes (Leeds)
Kelly, K. (Warrington)
*Grayshon (Bradford N.)
Dalgreen (Fulham)
Skerrett, T. (Hull)
Eccles (Warrington)
Burton (Hull K.R.)
Heron, D. (Leeds)
Sub: Woods, J. (Leigh)
       Rathbone (Bradford N.)

1982 Australia
Leeds: 28 Nov.
Lost 8-32
Fairbairn (Hull K.R.)
Drummond (Leigh)
Stephenson (Wigan)
Smith, M. (Hull K.R.)
Evans, S. (Hull) 1t
*Topliss (Hull)
Gregory, A. (Widnes)
O'Neill, M. (Widnes)
Noble (Bradford N.)
Rose, P. (Hull)
Smith, P. (Featherstone R.)
Crooks, L. (Hull) 2g, 1dg
Crane (Hull)
Sub: Courtney (Warrington)

1983 France
Carcassonne: 20 Feb.
Won 20-5
Burke (Widnes) 1g
Drummond (Leigh)
Joyner (Castleford) 1t
Duane, R. (Warrington)
Lydon (Widnes) 1t, 3g
Myler, A. (Widnes)
Gregory, A. (Widnes)
O'Neill, M. (Widnes)
Noble (Bradford N.) 1t
Goodway (Oldham) 1t
*Casey (Hull K.R.)
Rathbone (Bradford N.)
Flanagan (Oldham)
Sub: Woods, J. (Leigh)
       Smith, P. (Featherstone R.)

1983 France
Hull: 6 Mar.
Won 17-5
Mumby (Bradford N.) 4g
Drummond (Leigh)
Joyner (Castleford)
Duane, R. (Warrington) 1t
Lydon (Widnes)
Myler, A. (Widnes)
Gregory, A. (Widnes) 1t
O'Neill, M. (Widnes)
Noble (Bradford N.)
Goodway (Oldham)
*Casey (Hull K.R.)
Rathbone (Bradford N.)
Flanagan (Oldham)
Sub: Smith, P. (Featherstone R.) 1t

1984 France
Avignon: 29 Jan.
Won 12-0
*Mumby (Bradford N.)
Drummond (Leigh)
Duane, R. (Warrington)
Foy, D. (Oldham) 1t
Clark (Hull K.R.)
Lydon (Widnes)
Cairns (Barrow)
Rayne, Keith (Leeds)
Watkinson (Hull K.R.)
Goodway (Oldham) 1t
Worrall, M. (Oldham)
Hobbs, D. (Featherstone R.)
Hall (Hull K.R.)
Sub: Hanley (Bradford N.)
       Crooks, L. (Hull) 2g

1984 France
Leeds: 17 Feb.
Won 10-0
Mumby (Bradford N.)
Clark (Hull K.R.)
Joyner (Castleford)
Schofield (Hull)
Basnett (Widnes)
Hanley (Bradford N.)
Cairns (Barrow)
Rayne, Keith (Leeds)
*Noble (Bradford N.)
Ward, K. (Castleford)
Jasiewicz (Bradford N.)
Hobbs, D. (Featherstone R.) 5g
Hall (Hull K.R.)
Sub: Smith, M. (Hull K.R.)
       Smith, P. (Featherstone R.)

1984 Australia
Sydney: 9 June
Lost 8-25
Burke (Widnes) 2g
Drummond (Leigh)
Schofield (Hull) 1t
Mumby (Bradford N.)
Hanley (Bradford N.)
Foy, D. (Oldham)
Holding (St. Helens)
Crooks, L. (Hull)
*Noble (Bradford N.)
Goodway (Oldham)
Burton (Hull K.R.)
Worrall, M. (Oldham)
Adams, M. (Widnes)
Sub: Lydon (Widnes)
       Hobbs, D. (Featherstone R.)

1984 Australia
Brisbane: 26 June
Lost 6-18
Burke (Widnes) 1g
Drummond (Leigh)
Schofield (Hull) 1t
Mumby (Bradford N.)
Hanley (Bradford N.)
Myler, A. (Widnes)
Holding (St. Helens)
Rayne, Keith (Leeds)
*Noble (Bradford N.)
Crooks, L. (Hull)
Burton (Hull K.R.)
Goodway (Oldham)
Worrall, M. (Oldham)
Sub: Gregory, A. (Widnes)
       Adams, M. (Widnes)

1984 Australia
Sydney: 7 July
Lost 7-20
Burke (Widnes) 1g
Drummond (Leigh)
Schofield (Hull)
Mumby (Bradford N.)
Hanley (Bradford N.) 1t
Myler, A. (Widnes)
Holding (St. Helens) 1dg
Hobbs, D. (Featherstone R.)
*Noble (Bradford N.)
Case (Wigan)
Burton (Hull K.R.)
Goodway (Oldham)
Adams, M. (Widnes)

1984 New Zealand
Auckland: 14 July
Lost 0-12
Burke (Widnes)
Drummond (Leigh)
Schofield (Hull)
Mumby (Bradford N.)
Hanley (Bradford N.)
Smith, M. (Hull K.R.)
Holding (St. Helens)
Hobbs, D. (Featherstone R.)
*Noble (Bradford N.)
Case (Wigan)
Burton (Hull K.R.)
Goodway (Oldham)
Adams, M. (Widnes)

1984 New Zealand
Christchurch: 22 July
Lost 12-28
Burke (Widnes) 2g
Drummond (Leigh)
Hanley (Bradford N.) 1t
Mumby (Bradford N.)
Lydon (Widnes)
Myler, A. (Widnes) 1t
Gregory, A. (Widnes)
Hobbs, D. (Featherstone R.)
*Noble (Bradford N.)
Case (Wigan)
Burton (Hull K.R.)
Goodway (Oldham)
Adams, M. (Widnes)
Sub: Joyner (Castleford)
Beardmore, K. (Castleford)

1984 New Zealand
Auckland: 28 July
Lost 16-32
Burke (Widnes) 4g
Drummond (Leigh)
Hanley (Bradford N.) 1t
Mumby (Bradford N.) 1t
Lydon (Widnes)
Myler, A. (Widnes)
Gregory, A. (Widnes)
Hobbs, D. (Featherstone R.)
*Noble (Bradford N.)
Case (Wigan)
Adams, M. (Widnes)
Goodway (Oldham)
Flanagan (Oldham)
Sub: Donlan (Leigh)
Joyner (Castleford)

1984 Papua New Guinea
Mount Hagen: 5 Aug.
Won 38-20
Burke (Widnes) 1t, 5g
Drummond (Leigh) 2t
Hanley (Bradford N.) 1t
Mumby (Bradford N.) 1t
Lydon (Widnes)
Myler, A. (Widnes)
Gregory, A. (Widnes)
Rayne, Keith (Leeds) 1t
*Noble (Bradford N.)
Goodway (Oldham)
Flanagan (Oldham)
Hobbs, D. (Featherstone R.) 1t
Adams, M. (Widnes)
Sub: Donlan (Leigh)
Proctor (Hull)

1985 France
Leeds: 1 Mar.
Won 50-4
Edwards (Wigan)
Ledger (St. Helens)
Creasser (Leeds) 8g
Gribbin (Whitehaven) 1t
Gill, H. (Wigan) 1t
Hanley (Bradford N.) 2t
Fox (Featherstone R.) 2t, 1g
Dickinson (Leeds)
Watkinson (Hull K.R.) 1t
Dannatt (Hull)
*Goodway (Oldham)
Rathbone (Bradford N.)
Divorty (Hull) 1t
Sub: Gibson (Batley)
Platt (St. Helens)

1985 France
Perpignan: 17 Mar.
Lost 16-24
Johnson, C. (Leigh)
Clark (Hull K.R.)
Creasser (Leeds) 1g
Foy, D. (Oldham) 1t
Ford, P. (Wigan) 2t
*Hanley (Bradford N.)
Fox (Featherstone R.)
Dickinson (Leeds)
Kiss (Wigan)
Wane (Wigan)
Dannatt (Hull)
Rathbone (Bradford N.)
Divorty (Hull) 1g
Sub: Harkin, P. (Hull K.R.)
Powell, R. (Leeds)

1985 New Zealand
Leeds: 19 Oct.
Lost 22-24
Burke (Widnes) 3g
Drummond (Leigh)
Schofield (Hull)
Hanley (Wigan) 1t
Lydon (Widnes) 1t, 2g
Myler, A. (Widnes)
Fox (Featherstone R.)
Crooks, L. (Hull)
Watkinson (Hull K.R.)
Fieldhouse (Widnes)
Goodway (Wigan) 1t
Potter (Wigan)
*Pinner (St. Helens)
Sub: Arkwright (St. Helens)

1985 New Zealand
Wigan: 2 Nov.
Won 25-8
Burke (Widnes)
Drummond (Leigh)
Schofield (Hull) 4t
Hanley (Wigan)
Lydon (Widnes) 4g
Myler, A. (Widnes)
Fox (Featherstone R.)
Grayshon (Leeds)
Watkinson (Hull K.R.)
Fieldhouse (Widnes)
Goodway (Wigan)
Potter (Wigan)
*Pinner (St. Helens) 1dg
Sub: Edwards (Wigan)
Burton (Hull K.R.)

1985 New Zealand (Also WC)
Elland Rd, Leeds: 9 Nov.
Drew 6-6
Burke (Widnes)
Drummond (Leigh)
Schofield (Hull)
Edwards (Wigan)
Lydon (Widnes)
Hanley (Wigan)
Fox (Featherstone R.)
Grayshon (Leeds)
Watkinson (Hull K.R.)
Fieldhouse (Widnes)
Goodway (Wigan)
Potter (Wigan)
*Pinner (St. Helens)
Sub: Arkwright (St. Helens)
　　　Crooks, L. (Hull) 3g

1986 France (Also WC)
Avignon: 16 Feb.
Drew 10-10
Burke (Widnes)
Drummond (Leigh)
Schofield (Hull)
Hanley (Wigan) 1t
Gill, H. (Wigan)
Myler, A. (Widnes)
Fox (Featherstone R.)
Crooks, L. (Hull) 3g
Watkinson (Hull K.R.)
Wane (Wigan)
Potter (Wigan)
Fieldhouse (Widnes)
*Pinner (St. Helens)

1986 France
Wigan: 1 Mar.
Won 24-10
Lydon (Wigan)
Drummond (Leigh) 1t
Schofield (Hull) 1t, 2g
Marchant (Castleford) 1t
Laws (Hull K.R.)
Myler, A. (Widnes)
Fox (Featherstone R.)
Crooks, L. (Hull) 2g
*Watkinson (Hull K.R.)
Fieldhouse (Widnes)
Rayne, Kevin (Leeds)
James (Halifax) 1t
Potter (Wigan)
Sub: Platt (St. Helens)

1986 Australia
Man U. FC: 25 Oct.
Lost 16-38
Lydon (Wigan) 1t
Marchant (Castleford)
Schofield (Hull) 2t
Hanley (Wigan)
Gill, H. (Wigan) 1g
Myler, A. (Widnes)
Fox (Featherstone R.)
Ward, K. (Castleford)
*Watkinson (Hull K.R.)
Fieldhouse (Widnes)
Crooks, L. (Hull) 1g
Potter (Wigan)
Goodway (Wigan)

1986 Australia
Elland Rd, Leeds: 8 Nov.
Lost 4-34
Lydon (Wigan)
Ledger (St. Helens)
Schofield (Hull) 1t
Marchant (Castleford)
Gill, H. (Wigan)
Myler, A. (Widnes)
Fox (Featherstone R.)
Ward, K. (Castleford)
*Watkinson (Hull K.R.)
Fieldhouse (St. Helens)
Crooks, L. (Hull)
Potter (Wigan)
Goodway (Wigan)
Sub: Edwards (Wigan)
　　　Platt (St. Helens)

1986 Australia (Also WC)
Wigan: 22 Nov.
Lost 15-24
Lydon (Wigan) 2g
Gill, H. (Wigan) 1g
Schofield (Hull) 2t, 1dg
Stephenson (Wigan)
Basnett (Widnes)
Myler, A. (Widnes)
Gregory, A. (Warrington)
Ward, K. (Castleford)
*Watkinson (Hull K.R.)
Crooks, L. (Hull)
Burton (Hull K.R.)
Goodway (Wigan)
Pinner (Widnes)
Sub: Potter (Wigan)

1987 France (Also WC)
Leeds: 24 Jan.
Won 52-4
Lydon (Wigan) 1t, 8g
Forster (Warrington) 1t
Schofield (Hull)
Stephenson (Wigan)
Gill, H. (Wigan)
*Hanley (Wigan) 2t
Edwards (Wigan) 2t
Hobbs, D. (Oldham)
Beardmore, K. (Castleford)
Crooks, L. (Hull)
Goodway (Wigan) 1t
Haggerty (St. Helens)
Gregory, M. (Warrington) 2t
Sub: Creasser (Leeds)
　　　England (Castleford)

1987 France
Carcassonne: 8 Feb.
Won 20-10
Lydon (Wigan) 4g
Forster (Warrington)
Schofield (Hull)
*Hanley (Wigan) 1t
Gill, H. (Wigan) 1t
Edwards (Wigan)
Gregory, A. (Wigan)
Hobbs, D. (Oldham)
Beardmore, K. (Castleford) 1t
England (Castleford)
Burton (Hull K.R.)
Haggerty (St. Helens)
Gregory, M. (Warrington)
Sub: Dixon (Halifax)

1987 Papua New Guinea (Also WC)
Wigan: 24 Oct.
Won 42-0
Hampson (Wigan)
Drummond (Warrington)
Stephenson (Wigan) 7g
Lydon (Wigan) 1t
Ford, P. (Bradford N.) 1t
Edwards (Wigan) 2t
Gregory, A. (Wigan) 1t
Ward, K. (Castleford)
Groves (St. Helens)
Case (Wigan)
Medley (Leeds) 1t
Goodway (Wigan)
*Hanley (Wigan) 1t
Sub: Woods, J. (Warrington)
　　　Fairbank (Bradford N.)

1988 France
Avignon: 24 Jan.
Won 28-14
Hampson (Wigan)
Drummond (Warrington) 1t
Schofield (Leeds) 2t
Loughlin (St. Helens) 3g
Offiah (Widnes) 1t
*Hanley (Wigan) 1t
Edwards (Wigan)
Ward, K. (Castleford)
Beardmore, K. (Castleford)
Waddell (Oldham)
Powell, R. (Leeds)
Medley (Leeds)
Platt (St. Helens)
Sub: Creasser (Leeds) 1g
   Dixon (Halifax)

1988 France
Leeds: 6 Feb.
Won 30-12
Hampson (Wigan)
Plange (Castleford) 1t
Schofield (Leeds) 1t, 5g
*Hanley (Wigan) 2t
Ford, P. (Bradford N.)
Edwards (Wigan)
Gregory, A. (Wigan) 1t
Ward, K. (Castleford)
Beardmore, K. (Castleford)
Waddell (Oldham)
Powell, R. (Leeds)
Dixon (Halifax)
Platt (St. Helens)
Sub: Stephenson (Leeds)
   Medley (Leeds)

1988 Papua New Guinea (Also WC)
Port Moresby: 22 May
Won 42-22
Loughlin (St. Helens) 7g
Ford, P. (Bradford N.)
Schofield (Leeds) 2t
Stephenson (Leeds) 1t
Gill, H. (Wigan) 2t
Edwards (Wigan)
Gregory, A. (Wigan)
Ward, K. (Castleford)
Beardmore, K. (Castleford)
Case (Wigan)
Medley (Leeds) 1t
Gregory, M. (Warrington) 1t
*Hanley (Wigan)
Sub: Hulme, D. (Widnes)
   Dixon (Halifax)

1988 Australia
Sydney: 11 June
Lost 6-17
Loughlin (St. Helens) 1g
Ford, P. (Bradford N.)
Schofield (Leeds)
Stephenson (Leeds)
Offiah (Widnes)
Hulme, D. (Widnes)
Gregory, A. (Wigan)
Ward, K. (Castleford)
Beardmore, K. (Castleford)
Dixon (Halifax)
Gregory, M. (Warrington)
Platt (St. Helens)
*Hanley (Wigan) 1t
Sub: Gill, H. (Wigan)
   Powell, R. (Leeds)

1988 Australia
Brisbane: 28 June
Lost 14-34
Loughlin (St. Helens) 3g
Gill, H. (Wigan)
Ford, P. (Bradford N.) 1t
*Hanley (Wigan)
Offiah (Widnes) 1t
Hulme, D. (Widnes)
Gregory, A. (Wigan)
Ward, K. (Castleford)
Beardmore, K. (Castleford)
Powell, R. (Leeds)
Dixon (Halifax)
Platt (St. Helens)
Gregory, M. (Warrington)
Sub: Wright, D. (Widnes)
   Hulme, P. (Widnes)

1988 Australia (Also WC)
Sydney: 9 July
Won 26-12
Ford, P. (Bradford N.) 1t
Gill, H. (Wigan) 2t
Stephenson (Leeds)
Loughlin (St. Helens) 3g
Offiah (Widnes) 1t
Hulme, D. (Widnes)
Gregory, A. (Wigan)
Ward, K. (Castleford)
Hulme, P. (Widnes)
Waddell (Oldham)
Gregory, M. (Warrington) 1t
Powell, R. (Leeds)
*Hanley (Wigan)
Sub: Case (Wigan)

1988 New Zealand (Also WC)
Christchurch: 17 July
Lost 10-12
Ford, P. (Bradford N.)
Gill, H. (Wigan)
Stephenson (Leeds)
Loughlin (St. Helens) 1t, 1g
Offiah (Widnes)
Hulme, D. (Widnes) 1t
Gregory, A. (Wigan)
Ward, K. (Castleford)
Beardmore, K. (Castleford)
Waddell (Oldham)
Gregory, M. (Warrington)
Powell, R. (Leeds)
*Hanley (Wigan)
Sub: Hulme, P. (Widnes)

1989 France
Wigan: 21 Jan.
Won 26-10
Tait (Widnes)
Ford, P. (Leeds) 1t
Loughlin (St. Helens) 3g
Lydon (Wigan) 1t
Offiah (Widnes) 1t
Edwards (Wigan) 1t
Gregory, A. (Wigan)
Ward, K. (Castleford)
Beardmore, K. (Castleford)
Waddell (Leeds)
Gregory, M. (Warrington)
Powell, R. (Leeds)
*Hanley (Wigan) 1t
Sub: Williams, P. (Salford)
   Eyres (Widnes)

1989 France
Avignon: 5 Feb.
Won 30-8
Tait (Widnes) 1t
Ford, P. (Leeds) 2t
Williams, P. (Salford) 1t
Lydon (Wigan) 3g
Offiah (Widnes)
Edwards (Wigan) 1t
Gregory, A. (Wigan)
Ward, K. (Castleford)
Beardmore, K. (Castleford)
Crooks, L. (Leeds)
Gregory, M. (Warrington)
Powell, R. (Leeds)
*Hanley (Wigan) 1t
Sub: Hampson (Wigan)
   England (Castleford)

1989 New Zealand
Man U. FC: 21 Oct.
Lost 16-24
Tait (Widnes) 1t
Ford, P. (Leeds) 1t
Currier (Widnes)
Loughlin (St. Helens) 2g
Offiah (Widnes) 1t
Hulme, D. (Widnes)
Gregory, A. (Wigan)
Skerrett, K. (Bradford N.)
Beardmore, K. (Castleford)
Hobbs, D. (Bradford N.)
Goodway (Wigan)
Platt (Wigan)
*Gregory, M. (Warrington)
Sub: Edwards (Wigan)
    Newlove (Featherstone R.)

1989 New Zealand
Elland Rd, Leeds: 28 Oct.
Won 26-6
Hampson (Wigan)
Ford, P. (Leeds)
Newlove (Featherstone R.)
Loughlin (St. Helens) 5g
Offiah (Widnes) 1t
Edwards (Wigan) 1t
Hulme, D. (Widnes)
Skerrett, K. (Bradford N.)
Hulme, P. (Widnes)
Platt (Wigan)
Goodway (Wigan) 2t
Powell, R. (Leeds)
*Gregory, M. (Warrington)
Sub: Hobbs, D. (Bradford N.)
    Fox (Featherstone R.)

1989 New Zealand (Also WC)
Wigan: 11 Nov.
Won 10-6
Tait (Widnes) 1t
Ford, P. (Leeds)
Newlove (Featherstone R.)
Loughlin (St. Helens) 1g
Offiah (Widnes) 1t
Edwards (Wigan)
Hulme, D. (Widnes)
Skerrett, K. (Bradford N.)
Hulme, P. (Widnes)
Platt (Wigan)
Goodway (Wigan)
Powell, R. (Leeds)
*Gregory, M. (Warrington)
Sub: Lydon (Wigan)
    England (Castleford)

1990 France
Perpignan: 18 Mar.
Won 8-4
Tait (Widnes)
Lydon (Wigan)
Schofield (Leeds) 2g
Loughlin (St. Helens)
Offiah (Widnes) 1t
Edwards (Wigan)
Gregory, A. (Wigan)
Skerrett, K. (Bradford N.)
Beardmore, K. (Castleford)
Platt (Wigan)
Gregory, M. (Warrington)
Goodway (Wigan)
*Hanley (Wigan)
Sub: Powell, D. (Sheffield E.)
    Betts (Wigan)

1990 France
Leeds: 7 Apr.
Lost 18-25
Tait (Widnes) 1t
Cordle (Bradford N.) 1t
Schofield (Leeds)
Gibson (Leeds)
Offiah (Widnes) 1t
Steadman (Castleford) 3g
*Edwards (Wigan)
Skerrett, K. (Bradford N.)
Beardmore, K. (Castleford)
England (Castleford)
Betts (Wigan)
Fairbank (Bradford N.)
Gregory, M. (Warrington)
Sub: Irwin (Castleford)
    Bishop (Hull K.R.)

1990 Papua New Guinea
Goroka: 27 May
Lost 18-20
Tait (Widnes)
Eastwood (Hull) 1t
Powell, D. (Sheffield E.)
Davies (Widnes) 1t, 3g
Gibson (Leeds)
Schofield (Leeds)
Goulding (Wigan) 1t
Powell, R. (Leeds)
Jackson, L. (Hull)
Dixon (Leeds)
Betts (Wigan)
Fairbank (Bradford N.)
*Gregory, M. (Warrington)
Sub: Irwin (Castleford)
    England (Castleford)

1990 Papua New Guinea (Also WC)
Port Moresby: 2 June
Won 40-8
Tait (Widnes)
Eastwood (Hull) 1t
Davies (Widnes) 6g
Powell, D. (Sheffield E.) 1t
Gibson (Leeds) 2t
Schofield (Leeds) 1t
Goulding (Wigan) 1t
Powell, R. (Leeds)
Jackson, L. (Hull)
England (Castleford)
Betts (Wigan)
Dixon (Leeds) 1t
*Gregory, M. (Warrington)
Sub: Fox (Featherstone R.)
    Clarke (Wigan)

1990 New Zealand
Palmerston North: 24 June
Won 11-10
Bibb (Featherstone R.)
Davies (Widnes) 1t, 1g
Lydon (Wigan)
Gibson (Leeds) 1t
Offiah (Widnes)
Schofield (Leeds) 1dg
Goulding (Wigan)
Skerrett, K. (Bradford N.)
Dermott (Wigan)
England (Castleford)
Betts (Wigan)
Dixon (Leeds)
*Gregory, M. (Warrington)
Sub: Powell, D. (Sheffield E.)
    Powell, R. (Leeds)

1990 New Zealand
Auckland: 8 July
Won 16-14
Lydon (Wigan)
Davies (Widnes) 2g
Powell, D. (Sheffield E.)
Gibson (Leeds)
Offiah (Widnes) 1t
Schofield (Leeds) 1t
Goulding (Wigan)
Skerrett, K. (Bradford N.)
Jackson, L. (Hull)
England (Castleford)
Betts (Wigan) 1t
Dixon (Leeds)
*Gregory, M. (Warrington)
Sub: Irwin (Castleford)
    Powell, R (Leeds)

1990 New Zealand (Also WC)
Christchurch: 15 July
Lost 18-21
Lydon (Wigan)
Davies (Widnes) 3g
Gibson (Leeds)
Powell, D. (Sheffield E.)
Offiah (Widnes) 1t
Schofield (Leeds) 1t
Goulding (Wigan)
Skerrett, K. (Bradford N.)
Dermott (Wigan)
England (Castleford)
Betts (Wigan)
Powell, R. (Leeds) 1t
*Gregory, M. (Warrington)
Sub: Irwin (Castleford)
     Dixon (Leeds)

1990 Australia (Also WC)
Elland Rd, Leeds: 24 Nov.
Lost 0-14
Hampson (Wigan)
Eastwood (Hull)
Powell, D. (Sheffield E.)
Gibson (Leeds)
Offiah (Widnes)
Schofield (Leeds)
Gregory, A. (Wigan)
Harrison (Hull)
Jackson, L. (Hull)
Platt (Wigan)
Betts (Wigan)
Dixon (Leeds)
*Hanley (Wigan)
Sub: Davies (Widnes)
     Gregory, M. (Warrington)
     Powell, R. (Leeds)

1991 Papua New Guinea (Also WC)
Wigan: 9 Nov.
Won 56-4
Hampson (Wigan)
Newlove (Featherstone R.) 1t
Powell, D. (Sheffield E.) 1t
Davies (Widnes) 8g
Sullivan, A. (St. Helens) 1t
*Schofield (Leeds) 1t
Edwards (Wigan)
Harrison (Halifax)
Dermott (Wigan)
Platt (Wigan)
Betts (Wigan) 1t
Moriarty (Widnes) 2t
Jackson, M. (Wakefield T.) 2t
Sub: Connolly (St. Helens)
     Fox (Featherstone R.)
     Fairbank (Bradford N.) 1t
     Price, G. H. (Wakefield T.)

1990 Australia
Wembley: 27 Oct.
Won 19-12
Hampson (Wigan)
Eastwood (Hull) 2t, 3g
Powell, D. (Sheffield E.)
Gibson (Leeds)
Offiah (Widnes) 1t
Schofield (Leeds) 1dg
Gregory, A. (Wigan)
Harrison (Hull)
Jackson, L. (Hull)
Dixon (Leeds)
Betts (Wigan)
Powell, R. (Leeds)
*Hanley (Wigan)
Sub: Fairbank (Bradford N.)
     Ward, K. (St. Helens)

1991 France (Also WC)
Perpignan: 27 Jan.
Won 45-10
Hampson (Wigan)
Eastwood (Hull) 6g
Powell, D. (Sheffield E.)
Gibson (Leeds)
Offiah (Widnes) 2t
Schofield (Leeds) 2t, 1dg
Edwards (Wigan) 2t
Lucas (Wigan)
Jackson, L. (Hull)
Platt (Wigan) 1t
Betts (Wigan) 1t
Holliday (Widnes)
*Hanley (Wigan)
Sub: Aston (Sheffield E.)
     Ellis, S. (Castleford)
     Fairbank (Bradford N.)

1992 France
Perpignan: 16 Feb.
Won 30-12
Tait (Widnes)
Devereux (Widnes) 1t
Connolly (St. Helens)
*Davies (Widnes) 3g
Bentley, J. (Leeds) 1t
Griffiths (St. Helens) 1t
Goulding (Leeds)
Crooks, L. (Castleford)
Jackson, L. (Hull)
Dixon (Leeds)
Fairbank (Bradford N.)
Jackson, M. (Wakefield T.)
Holliday (Widnes)
Sub: Powell, D. (Sheffield E.)
     Steadman (Castleford) 2t
     Jones, M. (Hull)
     Eyres (Widnes) 1t

1990 Australia
Man U. FC: 10 Nov.
Lost 10-14
Hampson (Wigan)
Eastwood (Hull) 1g
Powell, D. (Sheffield E.)
Gibson (Leeds)
Offiah (Widnes)
Schofield (Leeds)
Gregory, A. (Wigan)
Harrison (Hull)
Jackson, L. (Hull)
Platt (Wigan)
Betts (Wigan)
Dixon (Leeds) 1t
*Hanley (Wigan)
Sub: Loughlin (St. Helens) 1t
     Ward, K. (St. Helens)

1991 France
Leeds: 16 Feb.
Won 60-4
Hampson (Wigan) 1t
Eastwood (Hull) 1t, 8g
Powell, D. (Sheffield E.)
Loughlin (St. Helens)
Offiah (Widnes) 5t
Schofield (Leeds) 3t
Edwards (Wigan) 1t
Dannatt (Hull)
Jackson, L. (Hull)
Platt (Wigan)
Eyres (Widnes)
Fairbank (Bradford N.)
*Hanley (Wigan)
Sub: Ellis, K. (Warrington)
     Ellis, S. (Castleford)
     England (Castleford)
     Powell, R. (Leeds)

1992 France (Also WC)
Hull: 7 Mar.
Won 36-0
Steadman (Castleford)
Eastwood (Hull) 1t, 6g
Connolly (St. Helens)
Bateman (Warrington)
Hunte (St. Helens) 1t
Powell, D. (Sheffield E.)
*Edwards (Wigan)
Crooks, L. (Castleford)
Dermott (Wigan) 1t
Skerrett, K. (Wigan)
Betts (Wigan)
Fairbank (Bradford N.)
Holliday (Widnes) 1t
Sub: Fox (Featherstone R.) 1t
     Platt (Wigan) 1t
     McNamara (Hull)

1992 Papua New Guinea
Port Moresby: 31 May
Won 20-14
Hampson (Wigan)
Eastwood (Hull) 1t
*Schofield (Leeds)
Loughlin (St. Helens) 2g
Offiah (Wigan) 2t
Powell, D. (Sheffield E.)
Edwards (Wigan)
Crooks, L. (Castleford)
Dermott (Wigan)
Platt (Wigan)
Betts (Wigan)
Fairbank (Bradford N.)
Clarke (Wigan) 1t
Sub: Lydon (Wigan)
    Skerrett, K. (Wigan)
    Newlove (Featherstone R.)
    Nickle (St. Helens)

1992 Australia
Brisbane: 3 July
Lost 10-16
Steadman (Castleford)
Eastwood (Hull) 3g
Powell, D. (Sheffield E.)
Newlove (Featherstone R.)
Offiah (Wigan) 1t
*Schofield (Leeds)
Edwards (Wigan)
Skerrett, K. (Wigan)
Dermott (Wigan)
Platt (Wigan)
Betts (Wigan)
McGinty (Wigan)
Clarke (Wigan)
Sub: Connolly (St. Helens)
    Hulme, P. (Widnes)
    Lydon (Wigan)
    Harrison (Halifax)

1992 Australia (WC Final)
Wembley: 24 Oct.
Lost 6-10
Lydon (Wigan)
Hunte (St. Helens)
Connolly (St. Helens)
*Schofield (Leeds)
Offiah (Wigan)
Edwards (Wigan)
Fox (Bradford N.) 3g
Ward, K. (St. Helens)
Dermott (Wigan)
Platt (Wigan)
Betts (Wigan)
Clarke (Wigan)
Hanley (Leeds)
Sub: Devereux (Widnes)
    Tait (Leeds)
    Skerrett, K. (Wigan)
    Eyres (Widnes)

1992 Australia
Sydney: 12 June
Lost 6-22
Steadman (Castleford)
Newlove (Featherstone R.)
Powell, D. (Sheffield E.)
Loughlin (St. Helens)
Offiah (Wigan)
*Schofield (Leeds)
Gregory, A. (Wigan)
Skerrett, K. (Wigan)
Dermott (Wigan)
Crooks, L. (Castleford) 1g
Betts (Wigan)
Platt (Wigan)
Clarke (Wigan)
Sub: Edwards (Wigan)
    Jackson, M. (Wakefield T.)
    Lydon (Wigan) 1t
    Lucas (Wigan)

1992 New Zealand
Palmerston North: 12 July
Lost 14-15
Steadman (Castleford)
Eastwood (Hull) 3g
Powell, D. (Sheffield E.)
Connolly (St. Helens)
Offiah (Wigan)
*Schofield (Leeds)
Edwards (Wigan) 1t
Skerrett, K. (Wigan)
Jackson, L. (Hull)
Platt (Wigan)
Betts (Wigan)
McGinty (Wigan)
Clarke (Wigan) 1t
Sub: Lydon (Wigan)
    Hulme, P. (Widnes)
    Harrison (Halifax)

1993 France
Carcassonne: 7 Mar.
Won 48-6
Spruce (Widnes)
Devereux (Widnes) 1t
Currier (Widnes) 6g
Connolly (St. Helens)
Hunte (St. Helens)
*Schofield (Leeds) 3t
Edwards (Wigan) 1t
Cowie (Wigan)
McCurrie (Widnes)
Molloy (Leeds)
Eyres (Widnes) 1t
Clarke (Wigan)
Hanley (Leeds) 2t
Sub: Ford, M. (Castleford) 1t
    Joynt (St. Helens)
    Bateman (Warrington)
    McNamara (Hull)

1992 Australia
Melbourne: 26 June
Won 33-10
Steadman (Castleford) 1t
Eastwood (Hull) 6g
Newlove (Featherstone R.) 1t
Powell, D. (Sheffield E.)
Offiah (Wigan) 1t
*Schofield (Leeds) 1t, 1dg
Edwards (Wigan)
Skerrett, K. (Wigan)
Dermott (Wigan)
Platt (Wigan)
Betts (Wigan)
McGinty (Wigan)
Clarke (Wigan) 1t
Sub: Connolly (St. Helens)
    Hulme, P. (Widnes)
    Lydon (Wigan)
    Harrison (Halifax)

1992 New Zealand
Auckland: 19 July
Won 19-16
Steadman (Castleford)
Eastwood (Hull) 3g
Powell, D. (Sheffield E.)
Connolly (St. Helens)
Offiah (Wigan) 1t
*Schofield (Leeds) 1dg
Edwards (Wigan)
Harrison (Halifax)
Jackson, L. (Hull) 1t
Platt (Wigan)
Betts (Wigan) 1t
McGinty (Wigan)
Clarke (Wigan)
Sub: Newlove (Featherstone R.)
    Jackson, M. (Wakefield T.)
    Devereux (Widnes)
    Fairbank (Bradford N.)

1993 France
Leeds: 2 Apr.
Won 72-6
Tait (Leeds) 2t
Devereux (Widnes) 1t
Newlove (Featherstone R.) 3t
Connolly (St. Helens)
Hunte (St. Helens) 2t
Davies (Widnes) 10g
Edwards (Wigan) 2t
Harrison (Halifax)
Dermott (Wigan)
*Platt (Wigan)
Betts (Wigan) 1t
Eyres (Widnes)
Clarke (Wigan)
Sub: Ford, M. (Castleford) 1t
    Fairbank (Bradford N.)
    Powell, D. (Sheffield E.) 1t
    Nickle (St. Helens)

1993 New Zealand
Wembley: 16 Oct.
Won 17-0
Davies (Warrington) 2g, 1dg
Robinson (Wigan) 2t
Newlove (Bradford N.)
Connolly (Wigan)
Devereux (Widnes) 1t
*Schofield (Leeds)
Edwards (Wigan)
Harrison (Halifax)
Dermott (Wigan)
Fairbank (Bradford N.)
Betts (Wigan)
Joynt (St. Helens)
Clarke (Wigan)
Sub: Powell, D. (Sheffield E.)
　　　Eyres (Leeds)
　　　Tait (Leeds)
　　　Nickle (St. Helens)

1994 France
Carcassonne: 20 Mar.
Won 12-4
Steadman (Castleford)
Bentley, J. (Halifax)
Connolly (Wigan)
Newlove (Bradford N.) 1t
Offiah (Wigan)
*Schofield (Leeds)
Edwards (Wigan) 1t
Crooks, L. (Castleford) 1g
Jackson, L. (Sheffield E.)
Molloy (Featherstone R.)
Farrell (Wigan) 1g
Fairbank (Bradford N.)
Joynt (St. Helens)
Sub: Ellis, S. (Castleford)
　　　Moriarty (Widnes)
　　　Powell, D. (Sheffield E.)
　　　Mather (Wigan)

1994 Australia
Elland Rd, Leeds: 20 Nov.
Lost 4-23
Connolly (Wigan)
Robinson (Wigan)
Hunte (St. Helens)
Newlove (Bradford N.)
Offiah (Wigan)
Clarke (Wigan)
*Edwards (Wigan)
Harrison (Halifax)
Jackson, L. (Sheffield E.)
McDermott (Wigan)
Betts (Wigan)
Farrell (Wigan) 2g
Joynt (St. Helens)
Sub: Goulding (St. Helens)
　　　Powell, D. (Sheffield E.)
　　　Schofield (Leeds)
　　　Nickle (St. Helens)

1993 New Zealand
Wigan: 30 Oct.
Won 29-12
Davies (Warrington) 4g
Devereux (Widnes) 2t
Connolly (Wigan)
Newlove (Bradford N.) 1t
Offiah (Wigan) 1t
*Schofield (Leeds) 1t, 1dg
Edwards (Wigan)
Harrison (Halifax)
Jackson, L. (Sheffield E.)
Fairbank (Bradford N.)
Nickle (St. Helens)
Joynt (St. Helens)
Clarke (Wigan)
Sub: Powell, D. (Sheffield E.)
　　　Eyres (Leeds)
　　　Tait (Leeds)
　　　Jackson, M. (Halifax)

1994 Australia
Wembley: 22 Oct.
Won 8-4
Davies (Warrington) 1t, 1g
Robinson (Wigan)
Connolly (Wigan)
Hunte (St. Helens)
Offiah (Wigan)
Powell, D. (Sheffield E.)
*Edwards (Wigan)
Harrison (Halifax)
Jackson, L. (Sheffield E.)
Joynt (St. Helens)
Betts (Wigan)
Farrell (Wigan)
Clarke (Wigan)
Sub: Goulding (St. Helens) 1g
　　　McDermott (Wigan)
　　　Bateman (Warrington)
　　　Cassidy (Wigan)

1993 New Zealand
Leeds: 6 Nov.
Won 29-10
Davies (Warrington) 1t, 4g, 1dg
Devereux (Widnes)
Connolly (Wigan)
Newlove (Bradford N.)
Offiah (Wigan) 1t
*Schofield (Leeds)
Edwards (Wigan)
Skerrett, K. (Wigan)
Jackson, L. (Sheffield E.)
Fairbank (Bradford N.) 1t
Farrell (Wigan) 1t
Joynt (St. Helens)
Clarke (Wigan) 1t
Sub: Powell, D. (Sheffield E.)
　　　Nickle (St. Helens)
　　　Tait (Leeds)
　　　Jackson, M. (Halifax)

1994 Australia
Man. U. FC: 5 Nov.
Lost 8-38
Steadman (Castleford)
Robinson (Wigan)
Connolly (Wigan)
Hunte (St. Helens)
Offiah (Wigan)
Powell, D. (Sheffield E.)
Goulding (St. Helens) 2g
Harrison (Halifax)
Jackson, L. (Sheffield E.)
Joynt (St. Helens)
Betts (Wigan)
Farrell (Wigan)
*Clarke (Wigan)
Sub: Schofield (Leeds)
　　　McDermott (Wigan)
　　　Newlove (Bradford N.) 1t
　　　Cassidy (Wigan)

GREAT BRITAIN REGISTER

The following is a record of the 617 players who have appeared for Great Britain in 285 Test and World Cup matches.

It does not include matches against France before 1957, the year they were given official Test match status.

Figures in brackets are the total of appearances, with the plus sign indicating substitute appearances, e.g. (7+3).

For matches against touring teams, the year given is for the first half of the season.

World Cup matches are in bold letters except when also classified as Test matches. Substitute appearances are in lower case letters.

A - Australia, F - France, NZ - New Zealand, P - Papua New Guinea.

ACKERLEY, Alvin (2) Halifax: 1952 A; 1958 NZ
ADAMS, Les (1) Leeds: 1932 A
ADAMS, Mick (11+2) Widnes: 1979 Aa,NZ3;
1980 NZ; 1984 A2a,NZ3,P
ARKWRIGHT, Chris (+2) St. Helens: 1985 nz2
ARKWRIGHT, Jack (6) Warrington: 1936 A2,NZ;
1937 A3
ARMITT, Tom (8) Swinton: 1933 A; 1936 A2,NZ2;
1937 A3
ASHBY, Ray (2) Liverpool: 1964 F; Wigan: 1965 F
ASHCROFT, Ernest (11) Wigan: 1947 NZ2; 1950
A3,NZ; 1954 A3,NZ2
ASHCROFT, Kevin (5+1) Leigh: **1968 A**; 1968 F;
1969 F; **1970 F,NZ**; Warrington: 1974 nz
ASHTON, Eric (26) Wigan: **1957 A,NZ**; 1958
A2,NZ2; 1959 F, A3; 1960 F2; **1960 NZ,A**;
1961 NZ3; 1962 F3,A3; 1963 F,A2
ASHURST, Bill (3) Wigan: 1971 NZ; 1972 F2
ASKIN, Tom (6) Featherstone R: 1928 A3,NZ3
ASPINALL, Willie (1) Warrington: 1966 NZ
ASTON, Len (3) St. Helens: 1947 NZ3
ASTON, Mark (+1) Sheffield E: 1991 f
ATKINSON, Arthur (11) Castleford: 1929 A3; 1932
A3,NZ3; 1933 A; 1936 A
ATKINSON, John (26) Leeds: **1968 F,NZ**; 1970
A3,NZ3; **1970 A2,F,NZ**; 1971 F2,NZ; 1972
F2; **1972 A2,F,NZ**; 1973 A2; 1978 A2; 1980 NZ
AVERY, Albert (4) Oldham: 1910 A,NZ; 1911 A2

BACON, Jim (11) Leeds: 1920 A3,NZ3; 1921 A3;
1924 A; 1926 NZ
BARENDS, David (2) Bradford N: 1979 A2
BARTON, Frank (1) Wigan: 1951 NZ
BARTON, John (2) Wigan: 1960 F; 1961 NZ
BASNETT, John (2) Widnes: 1984 F; 1986 A
BASSETT, Arthur (2) Halifax: 1946 A2
BATEMAN, Allan (1+2) Warrington: 1992 F;
1993 f; 1994 a
BATES, Alan (2+2) Dewsbury: 1974 F2,nz2
BATTEN, Billy (10) Hunslet: 1907 NZ; 1908 A3;
1910 A2,NZ; 1911 A2; Hull: 1921 A
BATTEN, Eric (4) Bradford N: 1946 A2,NZ; 1947 NZ
BATTEN, Ray (3) Leeds: 1969 F; 1973 A2
BAXTER, Johnnie (1) Rochdale H: 1907 NZ
BEAMES, Jack (2) Halifax: 1921 A2
BEARDMORE, Kevin (13+1) Castleford: 1984 nz;
1987 F2; 1988 F2,P,A2,NZ; 1989 F2,NZ;
1990 F2
BELSHAW, Billy (8) Liverpool S: 1936 A3,NZ2;
1937 A; Warrington: 1937 A2
BENNETT, Jack (7) Rochdale H: 1924 A3,NZ3;
Wigan: 1926 NZ
BENTHAM, Billy (2) Broughton R: 1924 NZ2
BENTHAM, Nat (10) Wigan H: 1928 A3,NZ3;
Halifax: 1929 A2; Warrington: 1929 A2
BENTLEY, John (2) Leeds: 1992 F; Halifax: 1994 F
BENTLEY, Keith (1) Widnes: 1980 NZ

BENYON, Billy (5+1) St. Helens: 1971 F2,NZnz;
1972 F2
BETTS, Denis (24+1) Wigan: 1990 fF,P2,NZ3,A3;
1991 F,P; 1992 F,P,A3,NZ2, **A**; 1993F,NZ;
1994 A3
BEVAN, Dai (1) Wigan: 1952 A
BEVAN, John (6) Warrington: 1974 A2,NZ2;
1978 A2
BEVERLEY, Harry (6) Hunslet: 1936 A3; 1937 A;
Halifax: 1937 A2
BIBB, Chris (1) Featherstone R: 1990 NZ
BIRCH, Jim (1) Leeds: 1907 NZ
BISHOP, David (+1) Hull KR: 1990 f .
BISHOP, Tommy (15) St. Helens: 1966 A3,NZ2;
1967 A3; 1968 F3; **1968 A,F,NZ**; 1969 F
BLAN, Billy (3) Wigan: 1951 NZ3
BLINKHORN, Tom (1) Warrington: 1929 A
BOLTON, Dave (23) Wigan: 1957 F3; 1958 F,A2;
1959 F,A3; 1960 F2; 1961 NZ3; 1962 F2,A,NZ2;
1963 F,A2
BOSTON, Billy (31) Wigan: 1954 A2,NZ3; 1955
NZ; 1956 A3; 1957 F5; **1957 F,A**; 1958 F; 1959
A; 1960 F; **1960 A**; 1961 F,NZ3; 1962
F2,A3,NZ; 1963 F
BOTT, Charlie (1) Oldham: 1966 F
BOWDEN, Jim (3) Huddersfield: 1954 A2,NZ
BOWEN, Frank (3) St. Helens Recs: 1928 NZ3
BOWERS, Joe (1) Rochdale H: 1920 NZ
BOWMAN, Eddie (4) Workington T: **1977 F,NZ,A2**
BOWMAN, Harold (8) Hull: 1924 NZ2; 1926 NZ2;
1928 A2,NZ; 1929 A
BOWMAN, Ken (3) Huddersfield: 1962 F;
1963 F,A
BOYLEN, Frank (1) Hull: 1908 A
BRADSHAW, Tommy (6) Wigan: 1947 NZ2;
1950 A3,NZ
BRIDGES, John "Keith" (3) Featherstone R:
1974 F2,A
BRIGGS, Brian (1) Huddersfield: 1954 NZ
BROGDEN, Stan (16) Huddersfield: 1929 A;
1932 A3,NZ3; 1933 A2; Leeds: 1936 A3,NZ2;
1937 A2
BROOKE, Ian (13) Bradford N: 1966 A3,NZ2;
Wakefield T: 1967 A3; 1968 F2; **1968 A,F,NZ**
BROOKS, Ernie (3) Warrington: 1908 A3
BROUGH, Albert (2) Oldham: 1924 A,NZ
BROUGH, Jim (5) Leeds: 1928 A2,NZ2; 1936 A
BROWN, Gordon (6) Leeds: **1954 F2,NZ,A**;
1955 NZ2
BRYANT, Bill (4+1) Castleford: 1964 F2; 1966 Aa;
1967 F
BUCKLEY, Alan (7) Swinton: 1963 A; 1964 F;
1965 NZ; 1966 F,A2,NZ
BURGESS, Bill (16) Barrow: 1924 A3,NZ3;
1926 NZ3; 1928 A3,NZ2; 1929 A2
BURGESS, Bill (14) Barrow: 1962 F; 1963 A; 1965
NZ; 1966 F,A3,NZ2; 1967 F,A; 1968 F; Salford:
1969 F

BURGHAM, Oliver (1) Halifax: 1911 A
BURKE, Mick (14+1) Widnes: 1980 NZ; 1981 fF;
1983 F; 1984 A3,NZ3,P; 1985 NZ3; 1986 F
BURNELL, Alf (3) Hunslet: 1951 NZ2; 1954 NZ
BURTON, Chris (8+1) Hull KR: 1982 A; 1984
A3,NZ2; 1985 nz; 1986 A; 1987 F
BURWELL, Alan (7+1) Hull KR: 1967 a; 1968 F3;
1968 A,F,NZ; 1969 F
BUTTERS, Fred (2) Swinton: 1929 A2

CAIRNS, David (2) Barrow: 1984 F2
CAMILLERI, Chris (2) Barrow: 1980 NZ2
CARLTON, Frank (2) St. Helens: 1958 NZ; Wigan:
1962 NZ
CARR, Charlie (7) Barrow: 1924 A2,NZ2;
1926 NZ3
CARTWRIGHT, Joe (7) Leigh: 1920 A,NZ3;
1921 A3
CASE, Brian (6+1) Wigan: 1984 A,NZ3; 1987 P;
1988 P,a
CASEY, Len (12+2) Hull KR: **1977 f,nz,A**; 1978 A;
Bradford N: 1979 A2,NZ3; Hull KR: 1980 NZ3;
1983 F2
CASSIDY, Mick (+2) Wigan: 1994 a2
CASTLE, Frank (4) Barrow: 1952 A3; 1954 A
CHALLINOR, Jim (3) Warrington: 1958 A,NZ;
1960 F
CHARLTON, Paul (18+1) Workington T: 1965
NZ; Salford: **1970 nz**; 1972 F2; **1972 A2,F,NZ**;
1973 A3; 1974 F2,A3,NZ3
CHERRINGTON, Norman (1) Wigan: 1960 F
CHILCOTT, Jack (3) Huddersfield: 1914 A3
CHISNALL, Dave (2) Leigh: 1970 A; **1970 NZ**
CHISNALL, Eric (4) St. Helens: 1974 A2,NZ2
CLAMPITT, Jim (3) Broughton R: 1907 NZ;
1911 A; 1914 NZ
CLARK, Doug (11) Huddersfield: 1911 A2; 1914
A3; 1920 A3,NZ3
CLARK, Garry (3) Hull KR: 1984 F2; 1985 F
CLARK, Mick (5) Leeds: 1968 F2; **1968 A,F,NZ**
CLARKE, Colin (7) Wigan: 1965 NZ; 1966 F,NZ;
1967 F; 1973 A3
CLARKE, Phil (15+1) Wigan: 1990 p; 1992
P,A3,NZ2, **A**; 1993 F2,NZ3; 1994 A3
CLAWSON, Terry (14) Featherstone R: 1962 F2;
Leeds: **1972 A2,F**; Oldham: 1973 A3; 1974
F2,A2,NZ2
CLOSE, Don (1) Huddersfield: 1967 F
COLDRICK, Percy (4) Wigan: 1914 A3,NZ
COLLIER, Frank (2) Wigan: 1963 A; Widnes: 1964 F
CONNOLLY, Gary (14+3) St. Helens: 1991 p; 1992
F2,a2,NZ2,**A**; 1993 F2; Wigan: 1993 NZ3;
1994 F, A3
CORDLE, Gerald (1) Bradford N: 1990 F
COULMAN, Mike (2+1) Salford: 1971 f,NZ2
COURTNEY, Neil (+1) Warrington: 1982 a
COVERDALE, Bob (4) Hull: **1954 F2,NZ,A**
COWIE, Neil (1) Wigan: 1993 F

CRACKNELL, Dick (2) Huddersfield: 1951 NZ2
CRANE, Mick (1) Hull: 1982 A
CREASSER, David (2+2) Leeds: 1985 F2; 1987 f;
1988 f
CROOKS, Lee (17+2) Hull: 1982 A2; 1984 f,A2;
1985 NZnz; 1986 F2,A3; 1987 F; Leeds: 1989 F;
Castleford: 1992 F2,P,A; 1994 F
CROSTON, Jim (1) Castleford: 1937 A
CROWTHER, Hector (1) Hunslet: 1929 A
CUNLIFFE, Billy (11) Warrington: 1920 A,NZ2;
1921 A3; 1924 A3,NZ; 1926 NZ
CUNLIFFE, Jack (4) Wigan: 1950 A,NZ; 1951
NZ; 1954 A
CUNNIFFE, Bernard (1) Castleford: 1937 A
CUNNINGHAM, Eddie (1) St. Helens: 1978 A
CURRAN, George (6) Salford: 1946 A,NZ; 1947
NZ; 1948 A3
CURRIER, Andy (2) Widnes: 1989 NZ; 1993 F
CURZON, Ephraim (1) Salford: 1910 A

DAGNALL, Bob (4) St. Helens: 1961 NZ2; 1964 F;
1965 F
DALGREEN, John (1) Fulham: 1982 A
DANBY, Tom (3) Salford: 1950 A2,NZ
DANIELS, Arthur (3) Halifax: 1952 A2; 1955 NZ
DANNATT, Andy (3) Hull: 1985 F2; 1991 F
DARWELL, Joe (5) Leigh: 1924 A3,NZ2
DAVIES, Alan (20) Oldham: 1955 NZ; 1956 A3;
1957 F,A; 1957 F2; 1958 F,A2,NZ2; 1959 F2,A;
1960 NZ,F,A; 1960 F
DAVIES, Billy (1) Swinton: 1968 F
DAVIES, Billy J (1) Castleford: 1933 A
DAVIES, Evan (3) Oldham: 1920 NZ3
DAVIES, Jim (2) Huddersfield: 1911 A2
DAVIES, Jonathan (12+1) Widnes: 1990 P2,NZ3,a;
1991 P; 1992 F; 1993 F; Warrington: 1993 NZ3;
1994 A
DAVIES, Will T (1) Halifax: 1911 A
DAVIES, Willie A (2) Leeds: 1914 A,NZ
DAVIES, Willie T.H (3) Bradford N: 1946 NZ;
1947 NZ2
DAWSON, Edgar (1) York: 1956 A
DERMOTT, Martin (11) Wigan: 1990 NZ2; 1991 P;
1992 F,P,A3,**A**; 1993 F,NZ
DEVEREUX, John (6+2) Widnes: 1992 F,nz,**a**;
1993 F2,NZ3
DICK, Kevin (2) Leeds: 1980 NZ2
DICKENSON, George (1) Warrington: 1908 A
DICKINSON, Roy (2) Leeds: 1985 F2
DINGSDALE, Billy (3) Warrington: 1929 A2;
1933 A
DIVORTY, Gary (2) Hull: 1985 F2
DIXON, Colin (12+2) Halifax: 1968 F; Salford:
1969 F; 1971 NZ; **1972 F**; 1973 a2; 1974
F2,A3,NZ3
DIXON, Malcolm (2) Featherstone R: 1962 F;
1964 F

DIXON, Paul (11+4) Halifax: 1987 f; 1988
fF,p,A2; Leeds: 1990 P2,NZ2nz,A3; 1992 F
DOCKAR, Alec (1) Hull KR: 1947 NZ
DONLAN, Steve (+2) Leigh: 1984 nz,p
DRAKE, Bill (1) Hull: 1962 F
DRAKE, Jim (1) Hull: 1960 F
DRUMMOND, Des (24) Leigh: 1980 NZ2; 1981
F2; 1982 A3; 1983 F2; 1984 F,A3,NZ3,P; 1985
NZ3; 1986 F2; Warrington: 1987 P; 1988 F
DUANE, Ronnie (3) Warrington: 1983 F2; 1984 F
DUTTON, Ray (6) Widnes: 1970 NZ2; **1970
A2,F,NZ**
DYL, Les (11) Leeds: 1974 A2,NZ3; **1977 F,NZ,A2**;
1978 A; 1982 A
DYSON, Frank (1) Huddersfield: 1959 A

EASTWOOD, Paul (13) Hull: 1990 P2,A3; 1991
F2; 1992 F,P,A2,NZ2
ECCLES, Bob (1) Warrington: 1982 A
ECCLES, Percy (1) Halifax: 1907 NZ
ECKERSLEY, David (2+2) St. Helens: 1973 Aa;
1974 Aa
EDGAR, Brian (11) Workington T: 1958 A,NZ;
1961 NZ; 1962 A3,NZ; 1965 NZ; 1966 A3
EDWARDS, Alan (7) Salford: 1936 A3,NZ2;
1937 A2
EDWARDS, Derek (3+2) Castleford: 1968 f; 1970
A; 1971 NZ2nz
EDWARDS, Shaun (32+4) Wigan: 1985 F,nzNZ;
1986 a; 1987 F2,P; 1988 F2,P; 1989 F2,nzNZ2;
1990 F2; 1991 F2,P; 1992 F,P,aA2,NZ2,**A**;
1993 F2,NZ3; 1994 F,A2
EGAN, Joe (14) Wigan: 1946 A3; 1947 NZ3; 1948
A3; 1950 A3,NZ2
ELLABY, Alf (13) St. Helens: 1928 A3,NZ2; 1929
A2; 1932 A3,NZ2; 1933 A
ELLIS, Kevin (+1) Warrington: 1991 f
ELLIS, St. John (+3) Castleford: 1991 f2; 1994 f
ELWELL, Keith (3) Widnes: **1977 A**; 1980 NZ2
ENGLAND, Keith (6+5) Castleford: 1987 fF; 1989
f,nz; 1990 F,pP,NZ3; 1991 f
EVANS, Bryn (10) Swinton: 1926 NZ; 1928 NZ;
1929 A; 1932 A2,NZ3; 1933 A2
EVANS, Frank (4) Swinton: 1924 A2,NZ2
EVANS, Jack (4) Hunslet: 1951 NZ; 1952 A3
EVANS, Jack (3) Swinton: 1926 NZ3
EVANS, Roy (4) Wigan: 1961 NZ2; 1962 F,NZ
EVANS, Steve (7+3) Featherstone R: 1979 Aa2,NZ3;
1980 NZnz; Hull: 1982 A2
EYRE, Ken (1) Hunslet: 1965 NZ
EYRES, Richard (3+6) Widnes: 1989 f; 1991 fF;
1992 f,a; 1993 F2; Leeds: 1993 nz2

FAIRBAIRN, George (17) Wigan: **1977 F,NZ,A2**;
1978 A3; 1979 A2,NZ3; 1980 NZ2; Hull KR:
1981 F; 1982 A2
FAIRBANK, Karl (10+6) Bradford N: 1987 p; 1990
F,P,a; 1991 fF,p; 1992 F2,P,nz; 1993 f,NZ3; 1994 F

FAIRCLOUGH, Les (6) St. Helens: 1926 NZ; 1928
A2,NZ2; 1929 A
FARRAR, Vince (1) Hull: 1978 A
FARRELL, Andrew (5) Wigan: 1993 NZ; 1994 F, A3
FEATHERSTONE, Jim (6) Warrington: 1948 A;
1950 NZ2; 1952 A3
FEETHAM, Jack (8) Hull KR: 1929 A; Salford:
1932 A2,NZ2; 1933 A3
FIELD, Harry (3) York: 1936 A,NZ2
FIELD, Norman (1) Batley: 1963 A
FIELDHOUSE, John (7) Widnes: 1985 NZ3; 1986
F2,A; St. Helens: 1986 A
FIELDING, Keith (3) Salford: 1974 F2; **1977 F**
FILDES, Alec (15) St. Helens Recs: 1926 NZ2;
1928 A3,NZ3; 1929 A3; St. Helens: 1932 A,NZ3
FISHER, Tony (11) Bradford N: 1970 A2,NZ3;
1970 A; Leeds: **1970 A**; 1971 F2; Bradford N:
1978 A2
FLANAGAN, Peter (14) Hull KR: 1962 F; 1963 F;
1966 A3,NZ; 1967 A3; 1968 F2; **1968 F,NZ**;
1970 A
FLANAGAN, Terry (4) Oldham: 1983 F2; 1984 NZ,P
FOGERTY, Terry (2+1) Halifax: 1966 nz; Wigan:
1967 F; Rochdale H: 1974 F
FORD, Mike (+2) Castleford: 1993 f2
FORD, Phil (13) Wigan: 1985 F; Bradford N: 1987
P; 1988 F,P,A3,NZ; Leeds: 1989 F2,NZ3
FORSTER, Mark (2) Warrington: 1987 F2
FOSTER, Frank (1) Hull KR: 1967 A
FOSTER, Peter (3) Leigh: 1955 NZ3
FOSTER, Trevor (3) Bradford N: 1946 NZ;
1948 A2
FOX, Deryck (10+4) Featherstone R: 1985 F2,
NZ3; 1986 F2,A2; 1989 nz; 1990 p; 1991 p;
1992 f; Bradford N: 1992 **A**
FOX, Don (1) Featherstone R: 1963 A
FOX, Neil (29) Wakefield T: 1959 F,A2; 1960 F3;
1961 NZ2; 1962 F3,A3,NZ2; 1963 A2,F; 1964
F; 1965 F; 1966 F; 1967 F2,A; 1968 F3; 1969 F
FOY, Des (3) Oldham: 1984 F,A; 1985 F
FRANCIS, Bill (4) Wigan: 1967 A; **1977 NZ,A2**
FRANCIS, Roy (1) Barrow: 1947 NZ
FRASER, Eric (16) Warrington: 1958 A3,NZ2;
1959 F2,A; 1960 F3; **1960 F,NZ**; 1961 F,NZ2
FRENCH, Ray (4) Widnes: 1961 F; **1968 A,NZ**
FRODSHAM, Alf (3) St. Helens: 1928 NZ2; 1929 A

GABBITAS, Brian (1) Hunslet: 1959 F
GALLAGHER, Frank (12) Dewsbury: 1920 A3;
1921 A; Batley: 1924 A3,NZ3; 1926 NZ2
GANLEY, Bernard (3) Oldham: 1957 F2; 1958 F
GARDINER, Danny (1) Wigan: 1965 NZ
GEE, Ken (17) Wigan: 1946 A3,NZ; 1947 NZ3;
1948 A3; 1950 A3,NZ2; 1951 NZ2
GEMMELL, Dick (3) Leeds: 1964 F; Hull: 1968 F;
1969 F
GIBSON, Carl (10+1) Batley: 1985 f; Leeds: 1990
F,P2,NZ3,A3; 1991 F

GIFFORD, Harry (2) Barrow: 1908 A2
GILFEDDER, Laurie (5) Warrington: 1962 A,NZ2,F;
1963 F
GILL, Henderson (14+1) Wigan: 1981 F2; 1982 A;
1985 F; 1986 F,A3; 1987 F2; 1988 P,A2a,NZ
GILL, Ken (5+2) Salford: 1974 F2,A2,NZ; **1977 f,a**
GOODWAY, Andy (23) Oldham: 1983 F2; 1984
F,A3,NZ3,P; 1985 F; Wigan: 1985 NZ3; 1986
A3; 1987 F,P; 1989 NZ3; 1990 F
GOODWIN, Dennis (5) Barrow: 1957 F2; 1958
F,NZ2
GORE, Jack (1) Salford: 1926 NZ
GORLEY, Les (4+1) Widnes: 1980 NZnz; 1981
F2; 1982 A
GORLEY, Peter (2+1) St. Helens: 1980 NZ;
1981 Ff
GOULDING, Bobby (7+2) Wigan: 1990 P2,NZ3;
Leeds: 1992 F; St. Helens: 1994 Aa2
GOWERS, Ken (14) Swinton: 1962 F; 1963 F,A3;
1964 F2; 1965 NZ2; 1966 F2,A,NZ2
GRAY, John (5+3) Wigan: 1974 f2,A2a,NZ3
GRAYSHON, Jeff (13) Bradford N: 1979 A2,NZ3;
1980 NZ2; 1981 F2; 1982 A2; Leeds: 1985 NZ2
GREENALL, Doug (6) St. Helens: 1951 NZ3; 1952
A2; 1954 NZ
GREENALL, Johnny (1) St. Helens Recs: 1921 A
GREENOUGH, Bobby (1) Warrington: **1960 NZ**
GREGORY, Andy (25+1) Widnes: 1981 F2; 1982
A; 1983 F2; 1984 a,NZ2,P; Warrington: 1986
A; Wigan: 1987 F,P; 1988 F,P,A3,NZ; 1989
F2,NZ; 1990 F,A3; 1992 A
GREGORY, Mike (19+1) Warrington: 1987 F2;
1988 P,A3,NZ; 1989 F2,NZ3; 1990 F2,P2,NZ3,a
GRIBBIN, Vince (1) Whitehaven: 1985 F
GRIFFITHS, Jonathan (1) St. Helens: 1992 F
GRONOW, Ben (7) Huddersfield: 1911 A2; 1920 A2,NZ3
GROVES, Paul (1) St. Helens: 1987 P
GRUNDY, Jack (12) Barrow: 1955 NZ3; 1956 A3;
1957 F3; **1957 F,A,NZ**
GUNNEY, Geoff (11) Hunslet: 1954 NZ3; 1956 A;
1957 F3; **1957 F,NZ**; 1964 F; 1965 F
GWYNNE, Emlyn (3) Hull: 1928 A,NZ; 1929 A
GWYTHER, Elwyn (6) Belle Vue R: 1947 NZ2;
1950 A3; 1951 NZ

HAGGERTY, Roy (2) St. Helens: 1987 F2
HAIGH, Bob (5+1) Wakefield T: **1968 A,F**; Leeds:
1970 NZ,a; 1971 F,NZ
HALL, Billy (4) Oldham: 1914 A3,NZ
HALL, Dave (2) Hull KR: 1984 F2
HALLAS, Derek (2) Leeds: 1961 F,NZ
HALMSHAW, Tony (1) Halifax: 1971 NZ
HALSALL, Hector (1) Swinton: 1929 A
HAMPSON, Steve (11+1) Wigan: 1987 P; 1988
F2; 1989 f,NZ; 1990 A3; 1991 F2,P; 1992 P
HANLEY, Ellery (35+1) Bradford N: 1984
fF,A3,NZ3,P; 1985 F2; Wigan: 1985 NZ3;
1986 F,A; 1987 F2,P; 1988 F2,P,A3,NZ; 1989
F2; 1990 F,A3; 1991 F2; Leeds: 1992 **A**; 1993 F

HARDISTY, Alan (12) Castleford: 1964 F3; 1965
F,NZ; 1966 A3,NZ; 1967 F2; 1970 A
HARE, Ian (1) Widnes: 1967 F
HARKIN, Paul (+1) Hull KR: 1985 f
HARRIS, Tommy (25) Hull: 1954 NZ2; 1956 A3;
1957 F5; **1957 F,A**; 1958 A3,NZ,F; 1959
F2,A3; 1960 F2; **1960 NZ**
HARRISON, Fred (3) Leeds: 1911 A3
HARRISON, Karl (11+3) Hull: 1990 A3; Halifax:
1991 P; 1992 a2,nzNZ; 1993 F,NZ2; 1994 A3
HARRISON, Mick (7) Hull: 1967 F2; 1971 NZ2;
1972 F2; 1973 A
HARTLEY, Dennis (11) Hunslet: 1964 F2; Castleford:
1968 F; 1969 F; 1970 A2,NZ2; **1970 A2,F**
HARTLEY, Steve (3) Hull KR: 1980 NZ; 1981 F2
HELME, Gerry (12) Warrington: 1948 A3; 1954
A3,NZ2; **1954 F2,A,NZ**
HEPWORTH, Keith (11) Castleford: 1967 F2; 1970
A3,NZ2; **1970 A2,F,NZ**
HERBERT, Norman (6) Workington T: 1961 NZ;
1962 F,A3,NZ
HERON, David (1+1) Leeds: 1982 aA
HESKETH, Chris (21+2) Salford: 1970 NZ; **1970
NZ,a**; 1971 Ff,NZ3; **1972 A2,F,NZ**; 1973 A3;
1974 F2,A3,NZ3
HICKS, Mervyn (1) St. Helens: 1965 NZ
HIGGINS, Fred (6) Widnes: 1950 A3,NZ2;
1951 NZ
HIGGINS, Harold (2) Widnes: 1937 A2
HIGSON, John (2) Hunslet: 1908 A2
HILL, Cliff (1) Wigan: 1966 F
HILL, David (1) Wigan: 1971 F
HILTON, Herman (7) Oldham: 1920 A3,NZ3;
1921 A
HILTON, Jack (4) Wigan: 1950 A2,NZ2
HOBBS, David (10+2) Featherstone R: 1984
F2,Aa,NZ3,P; Oldham: 1987 F2; Bradford N:
1989 NZnz
HODGSON, Martin (16) Swinton: 1929 A2; 1932
A3,NZ3; 1933 A3; 1936 A3,NZ; 1937 A
HOGAN, Phil (6+3) Barrow: **1977 F,NZ,A2**; 1978
a; Hull KR: 1979 Aa,NZnz
HOGG, Andrew (1) Broughton R: 1907 NZ
HOLDEN, Keith (1) Warrington: 1963 A
HOLDER, Billy (1) Hull: 1907 NZ
HOLDING, Neil (4) St. Helens: 1984 A3,NZ
HOLDSTOCK, Roy (2) Hull KR: 1980 NZ2
HOLLAND, Dave (4) Oldham: 1914 A3,NZ
HOLLIDAY, Bill (9+1) Whitehaven: 1964 F; Hull
KR: 1965 F,NZ3; 1966 Ff; 1967 A3
HOLLIDAY, Les (3) Widnes: 1991 F; 1992 F2
HOLLINDRAKE, Terry (1) Keighley: 1955 NZ
HOLMES, John (14+6) Leeds: 1971 NZ; 1972 F2;
1972 Aa,NZ; **1977 F,NZ,Aa**; 1978 a3; 1979
A2a,NZ3; 1982 A
HORNE, Willie (8) Barrow: 1946 A3; 1947 NZ;
1948 A; 1952 A3
HORTON, Bill (14) Wakefield T: 1928 A3,NZ3;
1929 A; 1932 A3,NZ; 1933 A3

HOWLEY, Tommy (6) Wigan: 1924 A3,NZ3
HUDDART, Dick (16) Whitehaven: 1958 A2,NZ2;
St. Helens: 1959 A; 1961 NZ3; 1962 F2,A3,NZ2;
1963 A
HUDSON, Barney (8) Salford: 1932 NZ; 1933 A2;
1936 A,NZ2; 1937 A2
HUDSON, Bill (1) Wigan: 1948 A
HUGHES, Eric (8) Widnes: 1978 A; 1979 A3,NZ3;
1982 A
HULME, David (7+1) Widnes: 1988 p,A3,NZ;
1989 NZ3
HULME, Paul (3+5) Widnes: 1988 aA,nz; 1989
NZ2; 1992 a2,nz
HUNTE, Alan (7) St. Helens: 1992 F,A; 1993 F2;
1994 A3
HURCOMBE, Danny (8) Wigan: 1920 A2,NZ;
1921 A; 1924 A2,NZ2
HYNES, Syd (12+1) Leeds: 1970 A2,NZ2nz; **1970
A2,F,NZ**; 1971 F; 1973 A3

IRVING, Bob (8+3) Oldham: 1967 F2,A3; 1970
a,NZ; 1971 NZ; 1972 f; **1972 NZ,a**
IRWIN, Shaun (+4) Castleford: 1990 f,p,nz2

JACKSON, Ken (2) Oldham: 1957 F2
JACKSON, Lee (17) Hull: 1990 P2,NZ,A3; 1991
F2; 1992 F,NZ2; Sheffield E: 1993 NZ2; 1994 F, A3
JACKSON, Michael (2+4) Wakefield T: 1991 P;
1992 F,a,nz; Halifax: 1993 nz2
JACKSON, Phil (27) Barrow: 1954 A3,NZ3; **1954
F2,A,NZ**; 1955 NZ3; 1956 A3; **1957 F,NZ**;
1957 F5; 1958 F,A2,NZ
JAMES, Neil (1) Halifax: 1986 F
JARMAN, Billy (2) Leeds: 1914 A2
JASIEWICZ, Dick (1) Bradford N: 1984 F
JEANES, David (8) Wakefield T: 1971 F,NZ2; 1972
F2; Leeds: **1972 A2,NZ**
JENKINS, Bert (12) Wigan: 1907 NZ3; 1908 A3;
1910 A,NZ; 1911 A2; 1914 A,NZ
JENKINS, Dai (1) Hunslet: 1929 A
JENKINS, Dai (1) Leeds: 1947 NZ
JENKINS, Emlyn (9) Salford: 1933 A; 1936
A3,NZ2; 1937 A3
JENKINSON, Albert (2) Hunslet: 1911 A2
JOHNSON, Albert (4) Widnes: 1914 A,NZ;
1920 A2
JOHNSON, Albert (6) Warrington: 1946 A2,NZ;
1947 NZ3
JOHNSON, Chris (1) Leigh: 1985 F
JOLLEY, Jim (3) Runcorn: 1907 NZ3
JONES, Berwyn (3) Wakefield T: 1964 F; 1965 F;
1966 F
JONES, Dai (2) Merthyr: 1907 NZ2
JONES, Ernest (4) Rochdale H: 1920 A,NZ3
JONES, Joe (1) Barrow: 1946 NZ
JONES, Keri (2) Wigan: **1970 F,NZ**
JONES, Les (1) St. Helens: 1971 NZ
JONES, Lewis (15) Leeds: 1954 A3,NZ3; 1955
NZ3; 1957 F3; **1957 F,A,NZ**

JONES, Mark (+1) Hull: 1992 f
JORDAN, Gary (2) Featherstone R: 1964 F; 1967 A
JOYNER, John (14+2) Castleford: 1978 A2; 1979
A3,NZ3; 1980 NZ3; 1983 F2; 1984 F,nz2
JOYNT, Chris (7+1) St. Helens: 1993 f,NZ3;
1994 F,A3
JUBB, Ken (2) Leeds: 1937 A2
JUKES, Bill (6) Hunslet: 1908 A3; 1910 A2,NZ

KARALIUS, Tony (4+1) St. Helens: 1971 NZ3;
1972 F; **1972 nz**
KARALIUS, Vince (12) St. Helens: 1958 A2,NZ2;
1959 F; **1960 NZ,F,A**; 1960 F; 1961 F;
Widnes: 1963 A2
KEEGAN, Arthur (9) Hull: 1966 A2; 1967 F2,A3;
1968 F; 1969 F
KELLY, Ken (4) St. Helens: 1972 F2; Warrington:
1980 NZ; 1982 A
KEMEL, George (2) Widnes: 1965 NZ2
KERSHAW, Herbert (2) Wakefield T: 1910 A,NZ
KINNEAR, Roy (1) Wigan: 1929 A
KISS, Nicky (1) Wigan: 1985 F
KITCHEN, Frank (2) Leigh: **1954 A,NZ**
KITCHIN, Phil (1) Whitehaven: 1965 NZ
KITCHING, Jack (1) Bradford N: 1946 A
KNAPMAN, Ernest (1) Oldham: 1924 NZ
KNOWELDEN, Bryn (1) Barrow: 1946 NZ

LAUGHTON, Doug (15) Wigan: 1970 A3,NZ2;
1970 A2,F,NZ; 1971 F2; Widnes: 1973 A; 1974
F2; 1979 A
LAWRENSON, John (3) Wigan: 1948 A3
LAWS, David (1) Hull KR: 1986 F
LEDGARD, Jim (11) Dewsbury: 1947 NZ2; Leigh:
1948 A; 1950 A2,NZ; 1951 NZ; **1954 F2,A,NZ**
LEDGER, Barry (2) St. Helens: 1985 F; 1986 A
LEWIS, Gordon (1) Leigh: 1965 NZ
LEYTHAM, Jim (5) Wigan: 1907 NZ2; 1910
A2,NZ
LITTLE, Syd (10) Oldham: 1956 A; 1957 F5; **1957
F,A,NZ**; 1958 F
LLEWELLYN, Tom (2) Oldham: 1907 NZ2
LLOYD, Robbie (1) Halifax: 1920 A
LOCKWOOD, Brian (8+1) Castleford: **1972
A2,F,NZ**; 1973 A2; 1974 F; Hull KR: 1978 A;
1979 nz
LOMAS, Jim (7) Salford: 1908 A2; 1910 A2,NZ;
Oldham: 1911 A2
LONGSTAFF, Fred (2) Huddersfield: 1914 A,NZ
LONGWORTH, Bill (3) Oldham: 1908 A3
LOUGHLIN, Paul (14+1) St. Helens: 1988
F,P,A3,NZ; 1989 F,NZ3; 1990 F,a; 1991 F;
1992 P,A
LOWE, John (1) Leeds: 1932 NZ
LOWE, Phil (12) Hull KR: 1970 NZ; 1972 F2; **1972
A2,F,NZ**; 1973 A3; 1978 A2
LOXTON, Ken (1) Huddersfield: 1971 NZ
LUCAS, Ian (1+1) Wigan: 1991 F; 1992 a

LYDON, Joe (23+7) Widnes: 1983 F2; 1984
F,a,NZ2,P; 1985 NZ3; Wigan: 1986 F,A3; 1987
F2,P; 1989 F2,nz; 1990 F,NZ3; 1992 p,a3,nz,**A**
McCORMICK, Stan (3) Belle Vue R: 1948 A2; St.
Helens: 1948 A
McCUE, Tommy (6) Widnes: 1936 A; 1937 A; 1946
A3,NZ
McCURRIE, Steve (1) Widnes: 1993 F
McDERMOTT, Barrie (1+2) Wigan: 1994 Aa2
McGINTY, Billy (4) Wigan: 1992 A2,NZ2
McINTYRE, Len (1) Oldham: 1963 A
McKEATING, Vince (2) Workington T: 1951 NZ2
McKINNEY, Tom (11) Salford: 1951 NZ; 1952 A2;
1954 A3,NZ; Warrington: 1955 NZ3; St.
Helens: **1957 NZ**
McNAMARA, Steve (+2) Hull: 1992 f; 1993 f
McTIGUE, Brian (25) Wigan: 1958 A2,NZ2; 1959
F2,A3; 1960 F2; **1960 NZ,F,A**; 1961 F,NZ3;
1962 F,A3,NZ2; 1963 F
MANN, Arthur (2) Bradford N: 1908 A2
MANTLE, John (13) St. Helens: 1966 F2,A3; 1967
A2; 1969 F; 1971 F2,NZ2; 1973 A
MARCHANT, Tony (3) Castleford: 1986 F,A2
MARTIN, Billy (1) Workington T: 1962 F
MARTYN, Mick (2) Leigh: 1958 A; 1959 A
MATHER, Barrie-Jon (+1) Wigan: 1994 f
MATHIAS, Roy (1) St. Helens: 1979 A
MEASURES, Jim (2) Widnes: 1963 A2
MEDLEY, Paul (3+1) Leeds: 1987 P; 1988 Ff,P
MIDDLETON, Alf (1) Salford: 1929 A
MILLER, Joe (1) Wigan: 1911 A
MILLER, Joe "Jack" (6) Warrington: 1933 A3; 1936
A,NZ2
MILLS, Jim (6) Widnes: 1974 A2,NZ; 1978 A2;
1979 A
MILLWARD, Roger (28+1) Castleford: 1966 F;
Hull KR: 1967 A3; 1968 F2; **1968 A,F,NZ**;
1970 A2,NZ3; 1971 F,NZ3; 1973 A; 1974 A2a;
1977 F,NZ,A2; 1978 A3
MILNES, Alf (2) Halifax: 1920 A2
MOLLOY, Steve (1) Leeds: 1993 F; Featherstone R: 1994 F
MOONEY, Walter (2) Leigh: 1924 NZ2
MOORHOUSE, Stan (2) Huddersfield: 1914 A,NZ
MORGAN, Arnold (4) Featherstone R: 1968 F2;
1968 F,NZ
MORGAN, Edgar (2) Hull: 1921 A2
MORGAN, Ron (2) Swinton: 1963 F,A
MORIARTY, Paul (1+1) Widnes: 1991 P; 1994 f
MORLEY, Jack (2) Wigan: 1936 A; 1937 A
MORTIMER, Frank (2) Wakefield T: 1956 A2
MOSES, Glyn (9) St. Helens: 1955 NZ2; 1956 A;
1957 F3; **1957 F,A,NZ**
MUMBY, Keith (11) Bradford N: 1982 A; 1983 F;
1984 F2,A3,NZ3,P
MURPHY, Alex (27) St. Helens: 1958 A3,NZ; 1959
F2,A; **1960 NZ,F,A**; 1960 F; 1961 F,NZ3;
1962 F,A3; 1963 A2; 1964 F; 1965 F,NZ; 1966
F2; Warrington: 1971 NZ

MURPHY, Harry (1) Wakefield T: 1950 A
MYLER, Frank (23+1) Widnes: **1960 NZ,F,A;**
1960 F; 1961 F; 1962 F; 1963 A; 1964 F; 1965
F,NZ; 1966 A,NZnz; 1967 F2; St. Helens:
1970 A3,NZ3; **1970 A2,F**
MYLER, Tony (14) Widnes: 1983 F2; 1984 A2,NZ2,P;
1985 NZ2; 1986 F2,A3

NASH, Steve (24) Featherstone R: 1971 F,NZ; 1972
F2; **1972 A2,F,NZ**; 1973 A2; 1974 A3,NZ3;
Salford: **1977 F,NZ,A2**; 1978 A3; 1982 A
NAUGHTON, Albert (2) Warrington: **1954 F2**
NEWBOULD, Tommy (1) Wakefield T: 1910 A
NEWLOVE, Paul (12+4) Featherstone R: 1989
nzNZ2; 1991 P; 1992 p,A3,nz; 1993 F; Bradford N:
1993 NZ3; 1994 F,Aa
NICHOLLS, George (29) Widnes: 1971 NZ; 1972
F2; **1972 A2,F,NZ**; St. Helens: 1973 A2; 1974
F2,A3,NZ3; **1977 F,NZ,A**; 1978 A3; 1979
A3,NZ3
NICHOLSON, Bob (3) Huddersfield: 1946 NZ
1948 A2
NICKLE, Sonny (1+5) St. Helens: 1992 p; 1993
f,NZnz2; 1994 a
NOBLE, Brian (11) Bradford N: 1982 A; 1983 F2;
1984 F,A3,NZ3,P
NORTON, Steve (11+1) Castleford: 1974 a,NZ2;
Hull: 1978 A3; 1979 A2; 1980 NZ; 1981 F2;
1982 A

OFFIAH, Martin (33) Widnes: 1988 F,A3,NZ; 1989
F2,NZ3; 1990 F2,NZ3,A3; 1991 F2; Wigan:
1992 P,A3,NZ2,**A**; 1993 NZ2; 1994 F,A3
O'GRADY, Terry (6) Oldham: 1954 A2,NZ3;
Warrington: 1961 NZ
OLIVER, Joe (4) Batley: 1928 A3,NZ
O'NEILL, Dennis (2+1) Widnes: 1971 nz; **1972 A,F**
O'NEILL, Mike (3) Widnes: 1982 A; 1983 F2
OSTER, Jack (1) Oldham: 1929 A
OWEN, Jim (1) St. Helens Recs: 1921 A
OWEN, Stan (1) Leigh: 1958 F
OWENS, Ike (4) Leeds: 1946 A3,NZ

PADBURY, Dick (1) Runcorn: 1908 A
PALIN, Harold (2) Warrington: 1947 NZ2
PARKER, Dave (2) Oldham: 1964 F2
PARKIN, Jonty (17) Wakefield T: 1920 A2,NZ3;
1921 A2; 1924 A3,NZ; 1926 NZ2; 1928 A,NZ;
1929 A2
PARR, Ken (1) Warrington: 1968 F
PAWSEY, Charlie (7) Leigh: 1952 A3; 1954 A2,NZ2
PEPPERELL, Albert (2) Workington T: 1950 NZ;
1951 NZ
PHILLIPS, Doug (4) Oldham: 1946 A3; Belle Vue
R: 1950 A
PIMBLETT, Albert (3) Warrington: 1948 A3
PINNER, Harry (6+1) St. Helens: 1980 nzNZ;
1985 NZ3; 1986 F; Widnes: 1986 A
PITCHFORD, Frank (2) Oldham: 1958 NZ;
1962 F

PITCHFORD, Steve (4) Leeds: **1977 F,NZ,A2**
PLANGE, David (1) Castleford: 1988 F
PLATT, Andy (21+4) St. Helens: 1985 f; 1986 f,a;
1988 F2,A2; Wigan: 1989 NZ3; 1990 F,A2;
1991 F2,P; 1992 f,P,A3,NZ2,**A**; 1993 F
POLLARD, Charlie (1) Wakefield T: 1924 NZ
POLLARD, Ernest (2) Wakefield T: 1932 A2
POLLARD, Roy (1) Dewsbury: 1950 NZ
POOLE, Harry (3) Hull KR: 1964 F; Leeds: 1966 NZ2
POTTER, Ian (7+1) Wigan: 1985 NZ3;
1986 F2,A2a
POWELL, Daryl (19+9) Sheffield E: 1990
f,P2,nzNZ2,A3; 1991 F2,P; 1992 fF,P,A3,NZ2;
1993 f,nz3; 1994 f,A2a
POWELL, Roy (13+6) Leeds: 1985 f; 1988
F2,A2a,NZ; 1989 F2,NZ2; 1990 P2,nz2NZ,Aa;
1991 f
POYNTON, Harold (3) Wakefield T: 1962 A2,NZ
PRESCOTT, Alan (28) St. Helens: 1951 NZ2; 1952
A3; 1954 A3,NZ3; 1955 NZ3; 1956 A3; 1957
F5; **1957 F,A,NZ**; 1958 F,A2
PRICE, Gary H (+1) Wakefield T: 1991 p
PRICE, Jack (6) Broughton R: 1921 A2; Wigan:
1924 A2,NZ2
PRICE, Malcolm (2) Rochdale H: 1967 A2
PRICE, Ray (9) Warrington: 1954 A,NZ2; 1955
NZ; 1956 A3; 1957 F2
PRICE, Terry (1) Bradford N: 1970 A
PRIOR, Bernard (1) Hunslet: 1966 F
PROCTOR, Wayne (+1) Hull: 1984 p
PROSSER, Dai (1) Leeds: 1937 A
PROSSER, Stuart (1) Halifax: 1914 A

RAE, Johnny (1) Bradford N: 1965 NZ
RAMSDALE, Dick (8) Wigan: 1910 A2; 1911 A2;
1914 A3,NZ
RAMSEY, Bill (7+1) Hunslet: 1965 NZ2; 1966
F,A2,NZ2; Bradford N; 1974 nz
RATCLIFFE, Gordon (3) Wigan: 1947 NZ;
1950 A2
RATHBONE, Alan (4+1) Bradford N: 1982 a;
1983 F2; 1985 F2
RAYNE, Keith (4) Leeds: 1984 F2,A,P
RAYNE, Kevin (1) Leeds: 1986 F
REDFEARN, Alan (1) Bradford N: 1979 A
REDFEARN, David (6+1) Bradford N: **1972 nz**;
1974 F2,A,NZ3
REES, Billo (11) Swinton: 1926 NZ2; 1928
A3,NZ3; 1929 A3
REES, Dai (1) Halifax: 1926 NZ
REES, Tom (1) Oldham: 1929 A
REILLY, Malcolm (9) Castleford: 1970 A3,NZ3;
1970 A2,F
RENILSON, Charlie (7+1) Halifax: 1965 NZ; 1967
a; 1968 F3; **1968 A,F,NZ**
RHODES, Austin (4) St. Helens: **1957 NZ; 1960
F,A**; 1961 NZ
RICHARDS, Maurice (2) Salford: 1974 A,NZ

RILEY, Joe (1) Halifax: 1910 A
RING, Johnny (2) Wigan: 1924 A; 1926 NZ
RISMAN, Gus (17) Salford: 1932 A,NZ3; 1933 A3;
1936 A2,NZ2; 1937 A3; 1946 A3
RISMAN, Bev (5) Leeds: 1968 F2; **1968 A,F,NZ**
RIX, Sid (9) Oldham: 1924 A3,NZ3; 1926 NZ3
ROBERTS, Ken (10) Halifax: 1963 A; 1964 F2;
1965 F,NZ3; 1966 F,NZ2
ROBINSON, Asa (3) Halifax: 1907 NZ; 1908 A2
ROBINSON, Bill (2) Leigh: 1963 F,A
ROBINSON, Dave (13) Swinton: 1965 NZ; 1966
F2,A3,NZ2; 1967 F2,A2; Wigan: 1970 A
ROBINSON, Don (10) Wakefield T: **1954 F2,NZ,A**;
1955 NZ; Leeds: 1956 A2; 1959 A2; 1960 F
ROBINSON, Jack (2) Rochdale H: 1914 A2
ROBINSON, Jason (4) Wigan: 1993 NZ; 1994 A3
ROGERS, Johnny (7) Huddersfield: 1914 A; 1920
A3; 1921 A3
ROSE, David (4) Leeds: **1954 F2,A,NZ**
ROSE, Paul (2+3) Hull KR: 1974 a; 1978 Aa2;
Hull: 1982 A
ROUND, Gerry (8) Wakefield T: 1959 A; 1962
F2,A3,NZ2
RUDDICK, George (3) Broughton R: 1907 NZ2;
1910 A
RYAN, Bob (5) Warrington: 1950 A,NZ2; 1951 NZ;
1952 A
RYAN, Martin (4) Wigan: 1947 NZ; 1948 A2;
1950 A
RYDER, Ron (1) Warrington: 1952 A

SAYER, Bill (7) Wigan: 1961 NZ; 1962 F,A3,NZ;
1963 A
SCHOFIELD, Derrick (1) Halifax: 1955 NZ
SCHOFIELD, Garry (44+2) Hull: 1984 F,A3,NZ;
1985 NZ3; 1986 F2,A3; 1987 F2; Leeds: 1988
F2,P,A; 1990 F2,P2,NZ3,A3; 1991 F2,P; 1992
P,A3,NZ2,**A**; 1993 F,NZ3; 1994 F,a2
SEABOURNE, Barry (1) Leeds: 1970 NZ
SENIOR, Ken (2) Huddersfield: 1965 NZ; 1967 F
SHARROCK, Jim (4) Wigan: 1910 A2,NZ; 1911 A
SHAW, Brian (6) Hunslet: 1956 A2; **1960 F,A**; 1960
F; Leeds: 1961 F
SHAW, Glyn (1) Widnes: 1980 NZ
SHAW, John (5) Halifax: **1960 F,A**; 1960 F; 1961 F;
1962 NZ
SHELTON, Geoff (7) Hunslet: 1964 F2; 1965 NZ3;
1966 F2
SHOEBOTTOM, Mick (10+2) Leeds: **1968 A,nz**;
1969 F; 1970 A2a,NZ; **1970 A2,F,NZ**; 1971 F
SHUGARS, Frank (1) Warrington: 1910 NZ
SILCOCK, Dick (1) Wigan: 1908 A
SILCOCK, Nat (12) Widnes: 1932 A2,NZ2; 1933
A3; 1936 A3; 1937 A2
SILCOCK, Nat (3) Wigan: 1954 A3
SIMMS, Barry (1) Leeds: 1962 F
SKELHORNE, George "Jack" (7) Warrington:
1920 A,NZ3; 1921 A3

SKERRETT, Kelvin (14+2) Bradford N: 1989
NZ3; 1990 F2,NZ3; Wigan: 1992 F,p,A3,NZ,a;
1993 NZ
SKERRETT, Trevor (10) Wakefield T: 1979 A2,NZ2;
Hull: 1980 NZ2; 1981 F2; 1982 A2
SLOMAN, Bob (5) Oldham: 1928 A3,NZ2
SMALES, Tommy (8) Huddersfield: 1962 F; 1963
F,A; 1964 F2; Bradford N: 1965 NZ3
SMALL, Peter (1) Castleford: 1962 NZ
SMITH, Alan (10) Leeds: 1970 A2,NZ3; **1970 A2;**
1971 F2; 1973 A
SMITH, Arthur (6) Oldham: 1907 NZ3; 1908 A3
SMITH, Bert (2) Bradford N: 1926 NZ2
SMITH, Fred (9) Hunslet: 1910 A,NZ; 1911 A3;
1914 A3,NZ
SMITH, Geoff (3) York: 1963 A; 1964 F2
SMITH, Mike (10+1) Hull KR: 1979 NZ3; 1980
NZ2; 1981 F2; 1982 A2; 1984 f,NZ
SMITH, Peter (1+5) Featherstone R: **1977 a2;** 1982
A; 1983 f2; 1984 f
SMITH, Sam (4) Hunslet: **1954 A,NZ,F2**
SMITH, Stanley (11) Wakefield T: 1929 A; Leeds:
1929 A2; 1932 A3,NZ3; 1933 A2
SOUTHWARD, Ike (11) Workington T: 1958
A3,NZ; Oldham: 1959 F2,A2; 1960 F2;
1962 NZ
SPENCER, Jack (1) Salford: 1907 NZ
SPRUCE, Stuart (1) Widnes: 1993 F
STACEY, Cyril (1) Halifax: 1920 NZ
STEADMAN, Graham (9+1) Castleford: 1990 F;
1992 fF,A3,NZ2; 1994 F,A
STEPHENS, Gary (5) Castleford: 1979 A2,NZ3
STEPHENSON, David (9+1) Wigan: 1982 A2;
1986 A; 1987 F,P; Leeds: 1988 f,P,A2,NZ
STEPHENSON, Mick (5+1) Dewsbury: 1971 nz;
1972 F; **1972 A2,F,NZ**
STEVENSON, Jeff (19) Leeds: 1955 NZ3; 1956
A3; 1957 F5; **1957 F,A,NZ;** 1958 F; York: 1959
A2; 1960 F2
STOCKWELL, Squire (3) Leeds: 1920 A; 1921 A2
STONE, Billy (8) Hull: 1920 A3,NZ3; 1921 A2
STOPFORD, John (12) Swinton: 1961 F; 1963
F,A2; 1964 F2; 1965 F,NZ2; 1966 F2,A
STOTT, Jim (1) St. Helens: 1947 NZ
STREET, Harry (4) Dewsbury: 1950 A3,NZ
SULLIVAN, Anthony (1) St. Helens: 1991 P
SULLIVAN, Clive (17) Hull: 1967 F; **1968 A,F,NZ;**
1970 A; 1971 NZ3; 1972 F2; **1972 A2,F,NZ;**
1973 A3
SULLIVAN, Jim (25) Wigan: 1924 A3,NZ; 1926
NZ3; 1928 A3,NZ3; 1929 A3; 1932 A3,NZ3;
1933 A3
SULLIVAN, Mick (46) Huddersfield: **1954 F2,NZ,A;**
1955 NZ3; 1956 A3; 1957 F3; **1957 F,A,NZ;**
Wigan: 1957 F2; 1958 F,A3,NZ2; 1959 F2,A3;
1960 F3; **1960 F,NZ,A;** St. Helens: 1961
F,NZ2; 1962 F3,A3,NZ; York: 1963 A
SZYMALA, Eddie (1+1) Barrow: 1981 fF

TAIT, Alan (10+4) Widnes: 1989 F2,NZ2; 1990
F2,P2; 1992 F; Leeds: 1992 **a;** 1993 F,nz3
TAYLOR, Bob (2) Hull: 1921 A; 1926 NZ
TAYLOR, Harry (3) Hull: 1907 NZ3
TEMBEY, John (2) St. Helens: 1963 A; 1964 F
TERRY, Abe (11) St. Helens: 1958 A2; 1959 F2,A3;
1960 F; 1961 F,NZ; Leeds: 1962 F
THOMAS, Arthur "Ginger" (4) Leeds: 1926 NZ2;
1929 A2
THOMAS, George (1) Warrington: 1907 NZ
THOMAS, Gwyn (9) Wigan: 1914 A; Huddersfield:
1920 A3,NZ2; 1921 A3
THOMAS, Johnny (8) Wigan: 1907 NZ; 1908 A3;
1910 A2,NZ; 1911 A
THOMAS, Les (1) Oldham: 1947 NZ
THOMAS, Phil (1) Leeds: 1907 NZ
THOMPSON, Cecil (2) Hunslet: 1951 NZ2
THOMPSON, Jim (20+1) Featherstone R: 1970
A2,NZ2; **1970 A2,F,NZ;** 1971 Ff; 1974 A3,NZ3;
1977 F,NZ,A2; Bradford N: 1978 A
THOMPSON, Joe (12) Leeds: 1924 A,NZ2; 1928
A,NZ; 1929 A; 1932 A3,NZ3
THORLEY, John (4) Halifax: **1954 F2,NZ,A**
TOOHEY, Ted (3) Barrow: 1952 A3
TOPLISS, David (4) Wakefield T: 1973 A2; 1979 A;
Hull: 1982 A
TRAILL, Ken (8) Bradford N: 1950 NZ2; 1951
NZ; 1952 A3; 1954 A,NZ
TROUP, Alec (2) Barrow: 1936 NZ2
TURNBULL, Andrew (1) Leeds: 1951 NZ
TURNER, Derek (24) Oldham: 1956 A2; 1957 F5;
1957 F,A,NZ; 1958 F; Wakefield T: 1959 A;
1960 F3; **1960 NZ,A;** 1961 F,NZ; 1962
A2,NZ2,F
TYSON, Brian (3) Hull KR: 1963 A; 1965 F;
1967 F
TYSON, George (4) Oldham: 1907 NZ; 1908 A3

VALENTINE, Bob (1) Huddersfield: 1967 A
VALENTINE, Dave (15) Huddersfield: 1948 A3;
1951 NZ; 1952 A2; 1954 A3,NZ2; **1954
F2,NZ,A**
VINES, Don (3) Wakefield T: 1959 F2,A

WADDELL, Hugh (5) Oldham: 1988 F2,A,NZ;
Leeds: 1989 F
WAGSTAFF, Harold (12) Huddersfield: 1911 A2;
1914 A3,NZ; 1920 A2,NZ2; 1921 A2
WALKER, Arnold (1) Whitehaven: 1980 NZ
WALLACE, Jim (1) St. Helens Recs: 1926 NZ
WALSH, Joe (1) Leigh: 1971 NZ
WALSH, John (4+1) St. Helens: 1972 f; **1972
A2,F,NZ**
WALTON, Doug (1) Castleford: 1965 F
WANE, Shaun (2) Wigan: 1985 F; 1986 F
WARD, Billy (1) Leeds: 1910 A
WARD, David (12) Leeds: **1977 F,NZ,A;** 1978 A;
1979 A3,NZ3; 1981 F; 1982 A
WARD, Edward (3) Wigan: 1946 A2; 1947 NZ

WARD, Ernest (20) Bradford N: 1946 A3,NZ; 1947 NZ2; 1948 A3; 1950 A3,NZ2; 1951 NZ3; 1952 A3
WARD, Johnny (4) Castleford: 1963 A; 1964 F2; Salford: 1970 NZ
WARD, Kevin (15+2) Castleford: 1984 F; 1986 A3; 1987 P; 1988 F2,P,A3,NZ; 1989 F2; St. Helens: 1990 a2; 1992 **A**
WARLOW, John (6+1) St. Helens: 1964 F; **1968 f,NZ**; 1968 F; Widnes: 1971 F2,NZ
WARWICK, Silas (2) Salford: 1907 NZ2
WATKINS, Billy (7) Salford: 1933 A; 1936 A2,NZ2; 1937 A2
WATKINS, David (2+4) Salford: 1971 f,NZ; 1973 a; 1974 f2,A
WATKINSON, David (12+1) Hull KR: 1979 a; 1980 NZ; 1981 F; 1984 F; 1985 F,NZ3; 1986 F2,A3
WATSON, Cliff (29+1) St. Helens: 1963 A2; 1966 F2,A3,NZ2; 1967 F,A3; 1968 F2; **1968 A,F,nz**; 1969 F; 1970 A3,NZ3; **1970 A2,F,NZ**; 1971 F
WATTS, Basil (5) York: **1954 F2,NZ,A**; 1955 NZ
WEBSTER, Fred (3) Leeds: 1910 A2,NZ
WHITCOMBE, Frank (2) Bradford N: 1946 A2
WHITE, Les (7) Hunslet: 1932 A3,NZ2; 1933 A2
WHITE, Les (6) York: 1946 A3,NZ; Wigan: 1947 NZ2
WHITE, Tommy (1) Oldham: 1907 NZ
WHITEHEAD, Derek (3) Warrington: 1971 F2,NZ
WHITELEY, Johnny (15) Hull: **1957 A**; 1958 A3,NZ; 1959 F2,A2; 1960 F; **1960 NZ,F**; 1961 NZ2; 1962 F
WILKINSON, Jack (13) Halifax: 1954 A,NZ2; 1955 NZ3; Wakefield T: 1959 A; 1960 F2; **1960 NZ,F,A**; 1962 NZ
WILLIAMS, Billy (2) Salford: 1929 A; 1932 A
WILLIAMS, Dickie (12) Leeds: 1948 A2; 1950 A2,NZ2; 1951 NZ3; Hunslet: 1954 A2,NZ
WILLIAMS, Frank (2) Halifax: 1914 A2
WILLIAMS, Peter (1+1) Salford: 1989 fF
WILLICOMBE, David (3) Halifax: 1974 F; Wigan: 1974 F,NZ
WILSON, George (3) Workington T: 1951 NZ3
WILSON, Harry (3) Hunslet: 1907 NZ3
WINSLADE, Charlie (1) Oldham: 1959 F
WINSTANLEY, Billy (5) Leigh: 1910 A,NZ; Wigan: 1911 A3
WOOD, Alf (4) Oldham: 1911 A2; 1914 A,NZ
WOODS, Harry (6) Liverpool S: 1936 A3,NZ2; Leeds: 1937 A
WOODS, Jack (1) Barrow: 1933 A
WOODS, John (7+4) Leigh: 1979 A3,nz; 1980 NZ; 1981 F2; 1982 Aa; 1983 f; Warrington: 1987 p
WOODS, Tommy (2) Rochdale H: 1911 A2
WORRALL, Mick (3) Oldham: 1984 F,A2
WRIGHT, Darren (+1) Widnes: 1988 a
WRIGHT, Joe (1) Swinton: 1932 NZ
WRIGHT, Stuart (7) Widnes: **1977 F,NZ,A2**; 1978 A3
WRIGLESWORTH, Geoff (5) Leeds: 1965 NZ; 1966 A2,NZ2

YOUNG, Chris (5) Hull KR: 1967 A3; 1968 F2
YOUNG, Frank (1) Leeds: 1908 A
YOUNG, Harold (1) Huddersfield: 1929 A

Utility man Daryl Powell, whose three appearances against Australia in 1994 took his tally of caps to 28.

Phil Clarke, captain of Great Britain in the second John Smith's Test against Australia in November 1994.

GREAT BRITAIN TOUR SUMMARIES

1910	P	W	D	L	T	G	For Pts	T	G	Against Pts
In Australia	14	9	1	4	76	56	340	51	47	247
In New Zealand	4	4	0	0	43	29	187	11	7	47
TOTAL	18	13	1	4	119	85	527	62	54	294
1914	P	W	D	L	T	G	Pts	T	G	Pts
In Australia	12	9	0	3	77	55	341	24	31	134
In New Zealand	6	6	0	0	46	28	194	12	13	62
TOTAL	18	15	0	3	123	83	535	36	44	196
1920	P	W	D	L	T	G	Pts	T	G	Pts
In Australia	15	12	0	3	83	64	377	48	42	228
In New Zealand	10	9	0	1	89	47	361	24	16	104
TOTAL	25	21	0	4	172	111	738	72	58	332
1924	P	W	D	L	T	G	Pts	T	G	Pts
In Australia	18	14	0	4	104	77	466	56	45	258
In New Zealand	9	7	0	2	64	40	272	25	21	117
TOTAL	27	21	0	6	168	117	738	81	66	375
1928	P	W	D	L	T	G	Pts	T	G	Pts
In Australia	16	11	1	4	67	60	321	43	45	219
In New Zealand	8	7	0	1	55	36	237	16	12	72
TOTAL	24	18	1	5	122	96	558	59	57	291
1932	P	W	D	L	T	G	Pts	T	G	Pts
In Australia	18	15	1	2	105	84	483	32	38	172
In New Zealand	8	8	0	0	65	52	299	17	18	87
TOTAL	26	23	1	2	170	136	782	49	56	259
1936	P	W	D	L	T	G	Pts	T	G	Pts
In Australia	17	14	0	3	79	82	401	38	45	204
In New Zealand	8	8	0	0	52	27	210	8	16	56
TOTAL	25	22	0	3	131	109	611	46	61	260
1946	P	W	D	L	T	G	Pts	T	G	Pts
In Australia	20	16	1	3	146	100	638	36	45	198
In New Zealand	7	5	0	2	35	20	145	12	21	78
TOTAL	27	21	1	5	181	120	783	48	66	276
1950	P	W	D	L	T	G	Pts	T	G	Pts
In Australia	19	15	0	4	133	102	603	22	56	178
In New Zealand	6	4	0	2	37	25	161	16	20	88
TOTAL	25	19	0	6	170	127	764	38	76	266

	P	W	D	L	T	G	**For** Pts	T	G	**Against** Pts
1954										
In Australia	★22	13	1	7	133	114	627	78	96	426
In New Zealand	10	8	0	2	60	56	292	14	32	106
TOTAL	★32	21	1	9	193	170	919	92	128	532

★One match abandoned. Scores included in points total.

	P	W	D	L	T	G	Pts	T	G	Pts
1958										
In Australia	21	19	1	1	184	129	810	64	93	378
In New Zealand	9	8	0	1	88	61	386	18	27	108
TOTAL	30	27	1	2	272	190	1,196	82	120	486

	P	W	D	L	T	G	Pts	T	G	Pts
1962										
In Australia	21	18	0	3	151	113	679	61	60	303
In New Zealand	9	6	0	3	73	50	319	35	28	161
TOTAL	30	24	0	6	224	163	998	96	88	464

	P	W	D	L	T	G	Pts	T	G	Pts
1966										
In Australia	22	13	0	9	112	85	506	47	83	307
In New Zealand	8	8	0	0	57	47	265	10	24	78
TOTAL	30	21	0	9	169	132	771	57	107	385

	P	W	D	L	T	G	Pts	T	G	Pts
1970										
In Australia	17	15	1	1	104	92	496	27	66	213
In New Zealand	7	7	0	0	61	37	257	9	24	75
TOTAL	24	22	1	1	165	129	753	36	90	288

	P	W	D	L	T	G	DG	Pts	T	G	DG	Pts
1974												
In Australia	20	15	0	5	104	93	2	500	38	59	3	235
In New Zealand	8	6	0	2	37	32	0	175	8	27	0	78
TOTAL	28	21	0	7	141	125	2	675	46	86	3	313

	P	W	D	L	T	G	DG	Pts	T	G	Pts
1979											
In Australia	18	13	1	4	66	73	3	347	39	68	253
In New Zealand	9	8	0	1	48	34	0	212	15	12	69
TOTAL	27	21	1	5	114	107	3	559	54	80	332

	P	W	D	L	T	G	DG	Pts	T	G	DG	Pts
1984												
In Australia	15	11	0	4	70	59	1	399	40	46	2	254
In New Zealand	8	4	0	4	32	25	1	179	21	21	0	126
In Papua New Guinea	1	1	0	0	7	5	0	38	4	2	0	20
TOTAL	24	16	0	8	109	89	2	616	65	69	2	400

	P	W	D	L	T	G	DG	Pts	T	G	DG	Pts
1988												
In Papua New Guinea	2	2	0	0	13	13	0	78	7	6	0	40
In Australia	13	8	0	5	59	47	0	330	42	36	1	241
In New Zealand	3	1	0	2	8	8	0	48	10	10	0	60
TOTAL	18	11	0	7	80	68	0	456	59	52	1	341

1990	P	W	D	L	T	G	DG	**For** Pts	T	G	DG	**Against** Pts
In Papua New Guinea	5	4	0	1	31	24	0	172	7	15	2	60
In New Zealand	10	6	0	4	30	28	3	179	24	32	1	161
TOTAL	15	10	0	5	61	52	3	351	31	47	3	221
1992	P	W	D	L	T	G	DG	Pts	T	G	DG	Pts
In Papua New Guinea	3	3	0	0	15	11	0	82	8	8	1	49
In Australia	10	7	0	3	32	29	2	188	20	19	0	118
In New Zealand	4	3	0	1	10	11	2	64	7	8	1	45
TOTAL	17	13	0	4	57	51	4	334	35	35	2	212

GREAT BRITAIN TOUR SQUADS TO AUSTRALIA AND NEW ZEALAND

Captains in bold

1910 Tour

J. Lomas (Salford)
A. Avery (Oldham)
J. Bartholomew (Huddersfield)
W. Batten (Hunslet)
F. Boylen (Hull)
E. Curzon (Salford)
J. Davies (Huddersfield)
F. Farrar (Hunslet)
T. Helm (Oldham)
B. Jenkins (Wigan)
T. Jenkins (Ebbw Vale)
W. Jukes (Hunslet)
H. Kershaw (Wakefield T.)
J. Leytham (Wigan)
T. Newbould (Wakefield T.)
R. Ramsdale (Wigan)
J. Riley (Halifax)
G. Ruddick (Broughton R.)
J. Sharrock (Wigan)
F. Shugars (Warrington)
F. Smith (Hunslet)
J. Thomas (Wigan)
W. Ward (Leeds)
F. Webster (Leeds)
W. Winstanley (Leigh)
F. Young (Leeds)

Managers: J. Clifford
(Huddersfield) and J.
Houghton (St. Helens)

1914 Tour

H. Wagstaff (Huddersfield)
J. Chilcott (Huddersfield)
J. Clampitt (Broughton R.)
D. Clark (Huddersfield)
A. Coldrick (Wigan)
W. A. Davies (Leeds)
A. Francis (Hull)
J. Guerin (Hunslet)
W. Hall (Oldham)
D. Holland (Oldham)
J. Jarman (Leeds)
B. Jenkins (Wigan)
A. Johnson (Widnes)
F. Longstaff (Huddersfield)
S. Moorhouse (Huddersfield)
J. O'Garra (Widnes)
W. Prosser (Halifax)
R. Ramsdale (Wigan)
J. Robinson (Rochdale H.)
J. Rogers (Huddersfield)
W. Roman (Rochdale H.)
J. Smales (Hunslet)
F. Smith (Hunslet)
G. Thomas (Wigan)
F. Williams (Halifax)
A. Wood (Oldham)

Managers: J. Clifford
(Huddersfield) and J.
Houghton (St. Helens)

1920 Tour

H. Wagstaff (Huddersfield)
J. Bacon (Leeds)
J. Bowers (Rochdale H.)
J. Cartwright (Leigh)
D. Clark (Huddersfield)
W. Cunliffe (Warrington)
E. Davies (Oldham)
J. Doyle (Barrow)
F. Gallagher (Dewsbury)
B. Gronow (Huddersfield)
H. Hilton (Oldham)
D. Hurcombe (Wigan)
A. Johnson (Widnes)
E. Jones (Rochdale H.)
R. Lloyd (Halifax)
A. Milnes (Halifax)
J. Parkin (Wakefield T.)
G. Rees (Leeds)
W. Reid (Widnes)
J. Rogers (Huddersfield)
G. Skelhorne (Warrington)
J. Stacey (Halifax)
S. Stockwell (Leeds)
W. Stone (Hull)
G. Thomas (Huddersfield)
A. Wood (Oldham)

Managers: S. Foster (Halifax)
and J. Wilson (Hull K.R.)

1924 Tour

J. Parkin (Wakefield T.)
J. Bacon (Leeds)
J. Bennett (Rochdale H.)
W. Bentham (Broughton R.)
H. Bowman (Hull)
A. Brough (Oldham)
W. Burgess (Barrow)
C. Carr (Barrow)
W. Cunliffe (Warrington)
J. Darwell (Leigh)
F. Evans (Swinton)
F. Gallagher (Batley)
B. Gronow (Huddersfield)
T. Howley (Wigan)
D. Hurcombe (Wigan)
E. Knapman (Oldham)
W. Mooney (Leigh)
C. Pollard (Wakefield T.)
J. Price (Wigan)
D. Rees (Halifax)
J. Ring (Wigan)
S. Rix (Oldham)
R. Sloman (Oldham)
J. Sullivan (Wigan)
J. Thompson (Leeds)
S. Whitty (Hull)

Managers: J.H. Dannatt
(Hull) and E. Osborne
(Warrington)

1928 Tour

J. Parkin (Wakefield T.)
T. Askin (Featherstone R.)
N. Bentham (Wigan Highfield)
F. Bowen (St. Helens Recs)
H. Bowman (Hull)
J. Brough (Leeds)
W. Burgess (Barrow)
O. Dolan (St. Helens Recs)
A. Ellaby (St. Helens)
B. Evans (Swinton)
J. Evans (Swinton)
L. Fairclough (St. Helens)
A. Fildes (St. Helens Recs)
A. Frodsham (St. Helens)
W. Gowers (Rochdale H.)
E. Gwynne (Hull)
B. Halfpenny (St. Helens)
W. Horton (Wakefield T.)
J. Oliver (Batley)
W. Rees (Swinton)
M. Rosser (Leeds)
R. Sloman (Oldham)
J. Sullivan (Wigan)
J. Thompson (Leeds)
W. Williams (Salford)
H. Young (Bradford N.)

Managers: G. Hutchins
(Oldham) and E. Osborne
(Warrington)

1932 Tour

J. Sullivan (Wigan)
L. Adams (Leeds)
A. Atkinson (Castleford)
S. Brogden (Huddersfield)
F. Butters (Swinton)
I. Davies (Halifax)
W. Dingsdale (Warrington)
A. Ellaby (St. Helens)
B. Evans (Swinton)
J. Feetham (Salford)
N. Fender (York)
A. Fildes (St. Helens)
M. Hodgson (Swinton)
W. Horton (Wakefield T.)
B. Hudson (Salford)
J. Lowe (Leeds)
E. Pollard (Wakefield T.)
A. Risman (Salford)
G. Robinson (Wakefield T.)
N. Silcock (Widnes)
S. Smith (Leeds)
J. Thompson (Leeds)
L. White (Hunslet)
W. Williams (Salford)
J. Woods (Barrow)
J. Wright (Swinton)

Managers: R. Anderton
(Warrington) and G. Hutchins
(Oldham)

1936 Tour

J. Brough (Leeds)
J. Arkwright (Warrington)
T. Armitt (Swinton)
A. Atkinson (Castleford)
W. Belshaw (Liverpool S.)
H. Beverley (Hunslet)
S. Brogden (Leeds)
E. Davies (Wigan)
A. Edwards (Salford)
H. Ellerington (Hull)
G. Exley (Wakefield T.)
H. Field (York)
F. Harris (Leeds)
M. Hodgson (Swinton)

B. Hudson (Salford)
E. Jenkins (Salford)
H. Jones (Keighley)
T. McCue (Widnes)
J. Miller (Warrington)
J. Morley (Wigan)
A. Risman (Salford)
N. Silcock (Widnes)
S. Smith (Leeds)
L. Troup (Barrow)
W. Watkins (Salford)
H. Woods (Liverpool S.)

Managers: R. Anderton
(Warrington) and
W. Popplewell (Bramley)

1946 Tour

A. Risman (Salford)
A. Bassett (Halifax)
E. Batten (Bradford N.)
G. Curran (Salford)
W.T.H. Davies (Bradford N.)
J. Egan (Wigan)
T. Foster (Bradford N.)
K. Gee (Wigan)
W. Horne (Barrow)
F. Hughes (Workington T.)
D. Jenkins (Leeds)
A. Johnson (Warrington)

J. Jones (Barrow)
J. Kitching (Bradford N.)
B. Knowelden (Barrow)
J. Lewthwaite (Barrow)
T. McCue (Widnes)
H. Murphy (Wakefield T.)
R. Nicholson (Huddersfield)
I. Owens (Leeds)
D. Phillips (Oldham)
M. Ryan (Wigan)
Edward Ward (Wigan)
Ernest Ward (Bradford N.)
F. Whitcombe (Bradford N.)
L. White (York)

Managers: W. Popplewell
(Bramley) and W. Gabbatt
(Barrow)

1950 Tour

E. Ward (Bradford N.)
E. Ashcroft (Wigan)
T. Bradshaw (Wigan)
J. Cunliffe (Wigan)
T. Danby (Salford)
A. Daniels (Halifax)
J. Egan (Wigan)
J. Featherstone (Warrington)
K. Gee (Wigan)
E. Gwyther (Belle Vue R.)
F. Higgins (Widnes)
J. Hilton (Wigan)
W. Horne (Barrow)
J. Ledgard (Leigh)
H. Murphy (Wakefield T.)
D. Naughton (Widnes)
F. Osmond (Swinton)
A. Pepperell (Workington T.)
D. Phillips (Belle Vue R.)
R. Pollard (Dewsbury)
G. Ratcliffe (Wigan)
M. Ryan (Wigan)
R. Ryan (Warrington)
H. Street (Dewsbury)
K. Traill (Bradford N.)
R. Williams (Leeds)

Managers: G. Oldroyd
(Dewsbury) and T. Spedding
(Belle Vue R.)

1954 Tour

R. Williams (Hunslet)
E. Ashcroft (Wigan)
W. Boston (Wigan)
J. Bowden (Huddersfield)
B. Briggs (Huddersfield)
A. Burnell (Hunslet)
E. Cahill (Rochdale H.)
F. Castle (Barrow)
J. Cunliffe (Wigan)
D. Greenall (St. Helens)
G. Gunney (Hunslet)
T. Harris (Hull)
G. Helme (Warrington)
J. Henderson (Workington T.)
P. Jackson (Barrow)
B. L. Jones (Leeds)
T. McKinney (Salford)
T. O'Grady (Oldham)
C. Pawsey (Leigh)
A. Prescott (St. Helens)
R. Price (Warrington)
N. Silcock (Wigan)
K. Traill (Bradford N.)
A. Turnbull (Leeds)
D. Valentine (Huddersfield)
J. Wilkinson (Halifax)

Managers: T. Hesketh
(Wigan) and H. Rawson
(Hunslet)

1958 Tour

A. Prescott (St. Helens)
A. Ackerley (Halifax)
H. Archer (Workington T.)
E. Ashton (Wigan)
D. Bolton (Wigan)
F. Carlton (St. Helens)
J. Challinor (Warrington)
A. Davies (Oldham)
B. Edgar (Workington T.)
E. Fraser (Warrington)
D. Goodwin (Barrow)
T. Harris (Hull)
R. Huddart (Whitehaven)
K. Jackson (Oldham)
P. Jackson (Barrow)
V. Karalius (St. Helens)

B. McTigue (Wigan)
M. Martyn (Leigh)
G. Moses (St. Helens)
A. Murphy (St. Helens)
F. Pitchford (Oldham)
I. Southward (Workington T.)
M. Sullivan (Wigan)
A. Terry (St. Helens)
J. Whiteley (Hull)
W. Wookey (Workington T.)

Managers: B. Manson
(Swinton) and T. Mitchell
(Workington T.)
Coach: J. Brough
(Workington T.)

1962 Tour

E. Ashton (Wigan)
D. Bolton (Wigan)
W. Boston (Wigan)
F. Carlton (Wigan)
G. Cooper (Featherstone R.)
B. Edgar (Workington T.)
R. Evans (Wigan)
D. Fox (Featherstone R.)
N. Fox (Wakefield T.)
E. Fraser (Warrington)
L. Gilfedder (Warrington)
N. Herbert (Workington T.)
R. Huddart (St. Helens)
B. McTigue (Wigan)
A. Murphy (St. Helens)
K. Noble (Huddersfield)
H. Poynton (Wakefield T.)
G. Round (Wakefield T.)
W. Sayer (Wigan)
J. Shaw (Halifax)
P. Small (Castleford)
I. Southward (Workington T.)
M. Sullivan (St. Helens)
J. Taylor (Hull K.R.)
D. Turner (Wakefield T.)
J. Wilkinson (Wakefield T.)

Managers: S. Hadfield
(Wakefield T.) and A. Walker
(Rochdale H.)
Coach: C. Hutton (Hull K.R.)

1966 Tour

H. Poole (Leeds)
W. Aspinall (Warrington)
T. Bishop (St. Helens)
I. Brooke (Bradford N.)
W. Bryant (Castleford)
A. Buckley (Swinton)
W. Burgess (Barrow)
C. Clarke (Wigan)
G. Crewdson (Keighley)
C. Dooler (Featherstone R.)
B. Edgar (Workington T.)
P. Flanagan (Hull K.R.)
T. Fogerty (Halifax)
K. Gowers (Swinton)
A. Hardisty (Castleford)
B. Jones (Wakefield T.)
A. Keegan (Hull)
J. Mantle (St. Helens)
F. Myler (Widnes)
W. Ramsey (Hunslet)
K. Roberts (Halifax)
D. Robinson (Swinton)
G. Shelton (Hunslet)
J. Stopford (Swinton)
C. Watson (St. Helens)
G. Wriglesworth (Leeds)

Managers: W. Spaven (Hull
K.R.) and J. Errock (Oldham)

1970 Tour

F. Myler (St. Helens)
J. Atkinson (Leeds)
D. Chisnall (Leigh)
R. Dutton (Widnes)
D. Edwards (Castleford)
A. Fisher (Bradford N.)
P. Flanagan (Hull K.R.)
A. Hardisty (Castleford)
D. Hartley (Castleford)
K. Hepworth (Castleford)
C. Hesketh (Salford)
S. Hynes (Leeds)
R. Irving (Oldham)
D. Laughton (Wigan)
P. Lowe (Hull K.R.)
R. Millward (Hull K.R.)
T. Price (Bradford N.)

M. Reilly (Castleford)
D. Robinson (Wigan)
B. Seabourne (Leeds)
M. Shoebottom (Leeds)
A. Smith (Leeds)
C. Sullivan (Hull)
J. Thompson (Featherstone R.)
J. Ward (Salford)
C. Watson (St. Helens)

Manager: J. Harding (Leigh)
Coach: J. Whiteley (Hull)

1974 Tour

C. Hesketh (Salford)
K. Ashcroft (Warrington)
J. Atkinson (Leeds)
A. Bates (Dewsbury)
J. Bates (Dewsbury)
J. Bevan (Warrington)
J. Bridges (Featherstone R.)
J. Butler (Rochdale H.)
P. Charlton (Salford)
E. Chisnall (St. Helens)
T. Clawson (Oldham)
C. Dixon (Salford)
L. Dyl (Leeds)
D. Eckersley (St. Helens)
K. Gill (Salford)
J. Gray (Wigan)
J. Mills (Widnes)
R. Millward (Hull K.R.)
S. Nash (Featherstone R.)
G. Nicholls (St. Helens)
S. Norton (Castleford)
D. Redfearn (Bradford N.)
P. Rose (Hull K.R.)
J. Thompson (Featherstone R.)
D. Watkins (Salford)
D. Willicombe (Wigan)

Replacements during tour
W. Ramsey (Bradford N.) for
J. Bates; M. Richards
(Salford) for Atkinson

Manager: R. Parker
(Blackpool B.)
Coach: J. Challinor
(St. Helens)

1979 Tour

D. Laughton (Widnes)
M. Adams (Widnes)
D. Barends (Bradford N.)
L. Casey (Bradford N.)
S. Evans (Featherstone R.)
P. Glynn (St. Helens)
J. Grayshon (Bradford N.)
P. Hogan (Hull K.R.)
J. Holmes (Leeds)
E. Hughes (Widnes)
M. James (St. Helens)
J. Joyner (Castleford)
G. Liptrot (St. Helens)
B. Lockwood (Hull K.R.)
T. Martyn (Warrington)
R. Mathias (St. Helens)
J. Mills (Widnes)
R. Millward (Hull K.R.)
K. Mumby (Bradford N.)
S. Nash (Salford)
G. Nicholls (St. Helens)
S. Norton (Hull)
A. Redfearn (Bradford N.)
T. Skerrett (Wakefield T.)
M. Smith (Hull K.R.)
G. Stephens (Castleford)
C. Stone (Hull)
D. Ward (Leeds)
D. Watkinson (Hull K.R.)
J. Woods (Leigh)

Replacements during tour
J. Burke (Wakefield T.) for
Mills; G. Fairbairn (Wigan)
for Martyn; D. Topliss
(Wakefield T.) for Millward

Managers: H. Womersley
(Bradford N.) and
R. Gemmell (Hull)
Coach: E. Ashton (St. Helens)

1984 Tour*

B. Noble (Bradford N.)
M. Adams (Widnes)
R. Ashton (Oldham)
K. Beardmore (Castleford)
M. Burke (Widnes)
C. Burton (Hull K.R.)
B. Case (Wigan)
G. Clark (Hull K.R.)
L. Crooks (Hull)
S. Donlan (Leigh)
D. Drummond (Leigh)
R. Duane (Warrington)
T. Flanagan (Oldham)
D. Foy (Oldham)
A. Goodway (Oldham)
A. Gregory (Widnes)
E. Hanley (Bradford N.)
D. Hobbs (Featherstone R.)
N. Holding (St. Helens)
J. Joyner (Castleford)
J. Lydon (Widnes)
K. Mumby (Bradford N.)
A. Myler (Widnes)
M. O'Neill (Widnes)
H. Pinner (St. Helens)
W. Proctor (Hull)
Keith Rayne (Leeds)
G. Schofield (Hull)
M. Smith (Hull K.R.)
M. Worrall (Oldham)

Replacement during tour
J. Basnett (Widnes) for Duane

Managers: R. Gemmell (Hull)
and R. Davis (RLHQ)
Coach: Frank Myler (Oldham)

*One match in Papua New
Guinea

1988 Tour*

E. Hanley (Wigan)
K. Beardmore (Castleford)
B. Case (Wigan)
L. Crooks (Leeds)
P. Dixon (Halifax)
S. Edwards (Wigan)
K. Fairbank (Bradford N.)
M. Ford (Oldham)
P. Ford (Bradford N.)
C. Gibson (Leeds)
H. Gill (Wigan)
A. Gregory (Wigan)
M. Gregory (Warrington)
P. Groves (St. Helens)
R. Haggerty (St. Helens)
D. Hulme (Widnes)
P. Loughlin (St. Helens)
P. Medley (Leeds)
M. Offiah (Widnes)
A. Platt (St. Helens)
R. Powell (Leeds)
G. Schofield (Leeds)
D. Stephenson (Leeds)
H. Waddell (Oldham)
K. Ward (Castleford)
I. Wilkinson (Halifax)

Replacements during tour
D. Wright (Widnes) for
Edwards; A. Currier (Widnes)
and P. Hulme (Widnes) for
Schofield and Medley; R. Eyres
(Widnes) and J. Joyner
(Castleford) for Crooks, Dixon
and Platt

Managers: L. Bettinson
(Salford) and D. Howes
(RLHQ)
Coach: M. Reilly

*Including Papua New Guinea

1990 Tour*

M. Gregory (Warrington)
D. Betts (Wigan)
C. Bibb (Featherstone R.)
D. Bishop (Hull K.R.)
P. Clarke (Wigan)
J. Davies (Widnes)
M. Dermott (Wigan)
P. Dixon (Leeds)
P. Eastwood (Hull)
K. England (Castleford)
K. Fairbank (Bradford N.)
D. Fox (Featherstone R.)
C. Gibson (Leeds)
R. Goulding (Wigan)
S. Irwin (Castleford)
L. Jackson (Hull)
I. Lucas (Wigan)
J. Lydon (Wigan)
M. Offiah (Widnes)
D. Powell (Sheffield E.)
R. Powell (Leeds)
G. H. Price (Wakefield T.)
G. Schofield (Leeds)
R. Simpson (Bradford N.)
K. Skerrett (Bradford N.)
I. Smales (Featherstone R.)
G. Steadman (Castleford)
A. Sullivan (Hull K.R.)
A. Tait (Widnes)

Replacements during tour
J. Devereux (Widnes) for
Sullivan; D. Lyon
(Warrington) for Tait

Manager: M. Lindsay (Wigan)
Coach: M. Reilly

*Papua New Guinea and
New Zealand only

1992 Tour*

E. Hanley (Leeds)
D. Betts (Wigan)
P. Clarke (Wigan)
G. Connolly (St. Helens)
N. Cowie (Wigan)
L. Crooks (Castleford)
M. Dermott (Wigan)
J. Devereux (Widnes)
P. Eastwood (Hull)
S. Edwards (Wigan)
K. Ellis (Warrington)
K. Fairbank (Bradford N.)
D. Fox (Featherstone R.)
A. Gregory (Wigan)
G. Hallas (Hull K.R.)

S. Hampson (Wigan)
L. Holliday (Widnes)
A. Hunte (St. Helens)
L. Jackson (Hull)
M. Jackson (Wakefield T.)
P. Loughlin (St. Helens)
I. Lucas (Wigan)
J. Lydon (Wigan)
W. McGinty (Wigan)
P. Newlove (Featherstone R.)
S. Nickle (St. Helens)
M. Offiah (Wigan)
A. Platt (Wigan)
D. Powell (Sheffield E.)
G. Schofield (Leeds)

K. Skerrett (Wigan)
G. Steadman (Castleford)

Replacements during tour
P. Hulme (Widnes) for Nickle
K. Harrison (Halifax),
S. McNamara (Hull), D. Myers
(Wigan), M. Aston (Sheffield E.)
and P. Broadbent (Sheffield E.)
for Gregory, Holliday, Loughlin,
Hanley and Lucas; D. Sampson
(Castlford) for Cowie

Manager: M. Lindsay (Wigan)
Coach: M. Reilly

*Including Papua New Guinea

ALL TIME TOUR RECORDS

IN AUSTRALIA
Highest score: 101-0 v. South Australia in 1914

Biggest defeat: 42-6 v. New South Wales in 1920
(Also *widest margin*)

Fewest defeats: 1 (and 1 draw) from 21 matches in 1958 and
from 17 matches in 1970

Most defeats: 9 from 22 matches in 1966

Biggest attendances: 70,419 v. New South Wales (Sydney) in
1950

IN NEW ZEALAND
Highest score: 81-14 v. Bay of Plenty in 1962

Widest margin win: 72-3 v. Buller in 1928
72-3 v. North Island in 1958

Biggest defeat: 46-13 v. Auckland in 1962 (Also *widest margin*)

Fewest defeats: The tourists have won all their matches in the
following years: 1910 (4 matches), 1914 (6), 1932 (8), 1936
(8), 1966 (8), 1970 (7).

Most defeats: 4 from 8 matches in 1984

Biggest attendance: 35,000 v. Auckland in 1920

PLAYERS' FULL TOUR RECORDS
Most full appearances: 24 by Dick Huddart in 1958

Most tries: 38 by Mick Sullivan in 1958

Most goals and points: 127g, 278 pts by Lewis Jones in 1954

Most tours: 4 by Garry Schofield (1984, 1988, 1990, 1992)

Biggest club representation: 13+1 replacement by Wigan in
1992 — Denis Betts, Phil Clarke, Neil Cowie, Martin
Dermott, Shaun Edwards, Andy Gregory, Steve Hampson,
Ian Lucas, Joe Lydon, Billy McGinty, Martin Offiah, Andy
Platt, Kelvin Skerrett, plus David Myers as a replacement

Brothers touring together: Bryn and Jack Evans (1928), Don
and Neil Fox (1962), Alan and John Bates (1974), David and
Paul Hulme (1988, Paul as replacement)

Great Britain tour squad 1950, left to right.
Back row: Danby, Ashcroft, Naughton, Phillips, Street, Osmond, Pollard, Traill.
Middle row: Daniels, Ryan, Featherstone, Gee, Higgins, Ward (Capt.), Egan, Gwyther, Ryan, Horne, Hilton, Cunliffe.
Front row: Bradshaw, Ledgard, Williams, Murphy, Pepperell, Ratcliffe.

Great Britain Test squad 1978, left to right.
Back row: Cunningham, Thompson, Norton, Fairbairn, Nicholls, Hogan.
Middle row: Barrett (Physio), Rose, Wright, Hughes, Casey, Lockwood, Bevan, Holmes, Robinson (Equipment).
Front row: Nash, Womersley (Manager), Millward (Capt.), Fox (Coach), Ward.

GREAT BRITAIN IN THE WORLD CUP

A — Australia, Fr — France, GB — Great Britain, NZ — New Zealand, PNG — Papua New Guinea

1954 in France   *Winners:* Great Britain

30 Oct.	Fr	22	NZ	13	Paris	13,240
31 Oct.	GB	28	A	13	Lyons	10,250
7 Nov.	GB	13	Fr	13	Toulouse	37,471
7 Nov.	A	34	NZ	15	Marseilles	20,000
11 Nov.	GB	26	NZ	6	Bordeaux	14,000
11 Nov.	A	5	Fr	15	Nantes	13,000

Play-off

13 Nov.	GB	16	Fr	12	Paris	30,368

Final Table

	P.	W.	D.	L.	F.	A.	Pts.
Great Britain	3	2	1	0	67	32	5
France	3	2	1	0	50	31	5
Australia	3	1	0	2	52	58	2
New Zealand	3	0	0	3	34	82	0

1957 in Australia   *Winners:* Australia

15 June	GB	23	Fr	5	Sydney	50,007
15 June	A	25	NZ	5	Brisbane	29,636
17 June	GB	6	A	31	Sydney	57,955
17 June	NZ	10	Fr	14	Brisbane	28,000
22 June	A	26	Fr	9	Sydney	35,158
25 June	GB	21	NZ	29	Sydney	14,263

Final Table

	P.	W.	D.	L.	F.	A.	Pts.
Australia	3	3	0	0	82	20	6
Great Britain	3	1	0	2	50	65	2
New Zealand	3	1	0	2	44	60	2
France	3	1	0	2	28	59	2

1960 in England   *Winners:* Great Britain

24 Sep.	GB	23	NZ	8	Bradford	20,577
24 Sep.	A	13	Fr	12	Wigan	20,278
1 Oct.	A	21	NZ	15	Leeds	10,773
1 Oct.	GB	33	Fr	7	Swinton	22,923
8 Oct.	A	3	GB	10	Bradford	32,773
8 Oct.	NZ	9	Fr	0	Wigan	2,876

Final Table

	P.	W.	D.	L.	F.	A.	Pts.
Great Britain	3	3	0	0	66	18	6
Australia	3	2	0	1	37	37	4
New Zealand	3	1	0	2	32	44	2
France	3	0	0	3	19	55	0

1968 in Australia   *Winners:* Australia
and New Zealand

25 May	A	25	GB	10	Sydney	62,256
25 May	Fr	15	NZ	10	Auckland	18,000
1 June	A	31	NZ	12	Brisbane	23,608
2 June	Fr	7	GB	2	Auckland	15,760
8 June	A	37	Fr	4	Brisbane	32,600
8 June	GB	38	NZ	14	Sydney	14,105

Final Table

	P.	W.	D.	L.	F.	A.	Pts.
Australia	3	3	0	0	93	26	6
France	3	2	0	1	26	49	4
Great Britain	3	1	0	2	50	46	2
New Zealand	3	0	0	3	36	84	0

Play-off final

10 June	A	20	Fr	2	Sydney	54,290

1970 in England   *Winners:* Australia

21 Oct.	A	47	NZ	11	Wigan	9,586
24 Oct.	GB	11	A	4	Leeds	15,084
25 Oct.	NZ	16	Fr	15	Hull	3,824
28 Oct.	GB	6	Fr	0	Castleford	8,958
31 Oct.	GB	27	NZ	17	Swinton	5,609
1 Nov.	Fr	17	A	15	Bradford	6,215

Final Table

	P.	W.	D.	L.	F.	A.	Pts.
Great Britain	3	3	0	0	44	21	6
Australia	3	1	0	2	66	39	2
France	3	1	0	2	32	37	2
New Zealand	3	1	0	2	44	89	2

Play-off final

7 Nov.	A	12	GB	7	Leeds	18,776

1972 in France   *Winners:* Great Britain

28 Oct.	Fr	20	NZ	9	Marseilles	20,748
29 Oct.	GB	27	A	21	Perpignan	6,324
1 Nov.	A	9	NZ	5	Paris	8,000
1 Nov.	GB	13	Fr	4	Grenoble	5,321
4 Nov.	GB	53	NZ	19	Pau	7,500
5 Nov.	A	31	Fr	9	Toulouse	10,332

Final Table

	P.	W.	D.	L.	F.	A.	Pts.
Great Britain	3	3	0	0	93	44	6
Australia	3	2	0	1	61	41	4
France	3	1	0	2	33	53	2
New Zealand	3	0	0	3	33	82	0

Play-off final

| 11 Nov. | GB | 10 | A | 10 | Lyons | 4,231 |

No further score after extra-time so Great Britain took the championship because they had scored the greatest number of points in the qualifying League table.

1977 in Australia   *Winners:* Australia
and New Zealand

29 May	A	27	NZ	12	Auckland	18,000
5 June	GB	23	Fr	4	Auckland	10,000
11 June	A	21	Fr	9	Sydney	13,231
12 June	GB	30	NZ	12	C'church	7,000
18 June	A	19	GB	5	Brisbane	27,000
19 June	NZ	28	Fr	20	Auckland	8,000

Final Table

	P.	W.	D.	L.	F.	A.	Pts.
Australia	3	3	0	0	67	26	6
Great Britain	3	2	0	1	58	35	4
New Zealand	3	1	0	2	52	77	2
France	3	0	0	3	33	72	0

Play-off final

| 25 June | A | 13 | GB | 12 | Sydney | 24,457 |

1985-88 Series   *Winners:* Australia

1985

7 July	NZ	18	A	0	Auckland	19,000
9 Nov.	GB	6	NZ	6	Leeds	22,209
7 Dec.	Fr	0	NZ	22	Perpignan	5,000

1986

16 Feb.	Fr	10	GB	10	Avignon	4,000
29 July	A	32	NZ	12	Brisbane	22,811
17 Aug.	PNG	24	NZ	22	Port Moresby	15,000
4 Oct.	PNG	12	A	62	Port Moresby	17,000
22 Nov.	GB	15	A	24	Wigan	20,169
13 Dec.	Fr	0	A	52	Carcassonne	3,000

1987

24 Jan.	GB	52	Fr	4	Leeds	6,567
24 Oct.	GB	42	PNG	0	Wigan	9,121
15 Nov.	Fr	21	PNG	4	Carcassonne	5,000

1988

22 May	PNG	22	GB	42	Port Moresby	12,077
9 July	A	12	GB	26	Sydney	15,994
10 July	NZ	66	PNG	14	Auckland	8,392
17 July	NZ	12	GB	10	Christchurch	8,525
20 July	A	70	PNG	8	Wagga Wagga	11,685

Final Table

	P.	W.	D.	L.	F.	A.	Pts.
Australia	7	5	0	2	252	91	12★
New Zealand	7	4	1	2	158	86	11★
Great Britain	8	4	2	2	203	90	10
P. N. Guinea	7	1	0	6	84	325	4★
France	5	1	1	3	35	140	3

★Awarded two points in lieu of France's non-fulfilment of fixtures Down Under.

Play-off final

1988
| 9 Oct. | A | 25 | NZ | 12 | Auckland | 47,363 |

1989

23 July	NZ	14	A	22	Auckland	15,000
11 Nov.	GB	10	NZ	6	Wigan	20,345
3 Dec.	Fr	0	NZ	34	Carcassonne	4,208

1990

2 June	PNG	8	GB	40	PortMoresby	5,969
27 June	A	34	Fr	2	Parkes	12,384
15 July	NZ	21	GB	18	Christchurch	3,133
11 Aug.	PNG	10	NZ	18	PortMoresby	10,000
24 Nov.	GB	0	A	14	Leeds	32,500
9 Dec.	Fr	10	A	34	Perpignan	3,428

1991

27 Jan.	Fr	10	GB	45	Perpignan	3,965
23 June	NZ	32	FR	10	Christchurch	2,000
1 July	PNG	18	Fr	20	Goroka	11,485
31 July	NZ	12	A	40	Brisbane	29,139
13 Oct.	PNG	6	A	40	PortMoresby	14,500
9 Nov.	GB	56	PNG	4	Wigan	4,193
24 Nov.	Fr	28	PNG	14	Carcassonne	1,440

1992

1 Mar.	GB	36	Fr	0	Hull	5,250
3 July	A	16	GB	10	Brisbane	32,313
5 July	NZ	66	PNG	10	Auckland	3,000
15 July	A	36	PNG	14	Townsville	12,470

Final Table

	P.	W.	D.	L.	F.	A.	Pts.
Australia	8	8	0	0	236	68	16
Great Britain	8	5	0	3	215	79	10
New Zealand	8	5	0	3	203	120	10
France	8	2	0	6	80	247	4
P. N. Guinea	8	0	0	8	84	304	0

Play-off final

1992
| 24 Oct. | A | 10 | GB | 6 | Wembley | 73,361 |

GREAT BRITAIN WORLD CUP SQUADS

Captains in bold

1954 IN FRANCE

D. Valentine (Huddersfield)
W. Banks (Huddersfield)
H. Bradshaw (Huddersfield)
G. Brown (Leeds)
R. Coverdale (Hull)
G. Helme (Warrington)
P. Jackson (Barrow)
F. Kitchen (Leigh)
J. Ledgard (Leigh)

A. Naughton (Warrington)
D. Robinson (Wakefield T.)
D. Rose (Leeds)
R. Rylance (Huddersfield)
S. Smith (Hunslet)
M. Sullivan (Huddersfield)
J. Thorley (Halifax)
B. Watts (York)
J. Whiteley (Hull)

Manager: G. Shaw (Castleford)

1957 IN AUSTRALIA

A. Prescott (St. Helens)
E. Ashton (Wigan)
W. Boston (Wigan)
A. Davies (Oldham)
J. Grundy (Barrow)
G. Gunney (Hunslet)
T. Harris (Hull)
P. Jackson (Barrow)
B.L. Jones (Leeds)

S. Little (Oldham)
T. McKinney (St. Helens)
G. Moses (St. Helens)
R. Price (Warrington)
A. Rhodes (St. Helens)
J. Stevenson (Leeds)
M. Sullivan (Huddersfield)
D. Turner (Oldham)
J. Whiteley (Hull)

Managers: W. Fallowfield (RL Secretary) and H. Rawson (Hunslet)

1960 IN ENGLAND

E. Ashton (Wigan)
W. Boston (Wigan)
J. Challinor (Warrington)
A. Davies (Oldham)
E. Fraser (Warrington)
R. Greenough (Warrington)
T. Harris (Hull)
V. Karalius (St. Helens)
B. McTigue (Wigan)

A. Murphy (St. Helens)
F. Myler (Widnes)
A. Rhodes (St. Helens)
B. Shaw (Hunslet)
J. Shaw (Halifax)
M. Sullivan (Wigan)
D. Turner (Wakefield T.)
J. Whiteley (Hull)
J. Wilkinson (Wakefield T.)

Manager: W. Fallowfield (RL Secretary)

1968 IN AUSTRALIA AND NEW ZEALAND

B. Risman (Leeds)
K. Ashcroft (Leigh)
J. Atkinson (Leeds)
T. Bishop (St. Helens)
I. Brooke (Wakefield T.)
A. Burwell (Hull K.R.)
M. Clark (Leeds)

D. Edwards (Castleford)
P. Flanagan (Hull K.R.)
R. French (Widnes)
R. Haigh (Wakefield T.)
R. Millward (Hull K.R.)
A. Morgan (Featherstone R.)
C. Renilson (Halifax)

M. Shoebottom (Leeds)
C. Sullivan (Hull)
J. Warlow (St. Helens)
C. Watson (St. Helens)
C. Young (Hull K.R.)

Manager: W. Fallowfield (RL Secretary)   Coach: C. Hutton (Hull K.R.)

412

1970 IN ENGLAND

F. Myler (St. Helens)
K. Ashcroft (Leigh)
J. Atkinson (Leeds)
P. Charlton (Salford)
D. Chisnall (Leigh)
R. Dutton (Widnes)
A. Fisher (Bradford N. & Leeds)

R. Haigh (Leeds)
D. Hartley (Castleford)
K. Hepworth (Castleford)
C. Hesketh (Salford)
S. Hynes (Leeds)
K. Jones (Wigan)
D. Laughton (Wigan)

M. Reilly (Castleford)
M. Shoebottom (Leeds)
A. Smith (Leeds)
J. Thompson (Featherstone R.)
C. Watson (St. Helens)

Manager: J. Harding (Leigh)   Coach: J. Whiteley (Hull K.R.)

1972 IN FRANCE

C. Sullivan (Hull)
J. Atkinson (Leeds)
P. Charlton (Salford)
T. Clawson (Leeds)
C. Dixon (Salford)
C. Hesketh (Salford)
J. Holmes (Leeds)

R. Irving (Oldham)
D. Jeanes (Leeds)
A. Karalius (St. Helens)
B. Lockwood (Castleford)
P. Lowe (Hull K.R.)
S. Nash (Featherstone R.)
G. Nicholls (Widnes)

D. O'Neill (Widnes)
D. Redfearn (Bradford N.)
M. Stephenson (Dewsbury)
D. Topliss (Wakefield T.)
John Walsh (St. Helens)

Manager: W. Spaven (Hull K.R.)   Coach: J. Challinor (St. Helens)

1977 IN AUSTRALIA AND NEW ZEALAND

R. Millward (Hull K.R.)
E. Bowman (Workington T.)
L. Casey (Hull K.R.)
L. Dyl (Leeds)
K. Elwell (Widnes)
G. Fairbairn (Wigan)
K. Fielding (Salford)

W. Francis (Wigan)
K. Gill (Salford)
A. Hodkinson (Rochdale H.)
P. Hogan (Barrow)
J. Holmes (Leeds)
G. Lloyd (Castleford)
S. Nash (Salford)

G. Nicholls (St. Helens)
S. Pitchford (Leeds)
P. Smith (Featherstone R.)
J. Thompson (Featherstone R.)
D. Ward (Leeds)
S. Wright (Widnes)

Manager: R. Parker (Blackpool B.)   Coach: D. Watkins (Salford)

St. Helens prop Alan Prescott, skipper of the 1957 Great Britain World Cup squad.

1960 World Cup duty for Halifax hooker John "Joby" Shaw.

413

GREAT BRITAIN RECORDS

● In Test and World Cup matches.

MOST TRIES IN CAREER

*41 Mick Sullivan (Huddersfield, Wigan,
    St. Helens, York)................................. 1954-63
31 Garry Schofield (Hull, Leeds) 1984-
26 Martin Offiah (Widnes, Wigan) 1988-
24 Billy Boston (Wigan) 1954-63
20 Ellery Hanley (Bradford N., Wigan, Leeds). 1984-
17 Roger Millward (Cas'd, Hull K.R.) 1966-78
16 Alex Murphy (St. Helens, Warrington)...... 1958-71
15 Shaun Edwards (Wigan) 1985-
14 Eric Ashton (Wigan)............................. 1957-63
14 Neil Fox (Wakefield T.).......................... 1959-69
13 Clive Sullivan (Hull)............................ 1967-73
12 John Atkinson (Leeds).......................... 1968-80
10 Jim Leytham (Wigan).......................... 1907-10

*Mick Sullivan also scored two tries for Great Britain against France before the matches were given Test status.

●Most tries by a forward is eight by Derek Turner (Oldham, Wakefield T.) 1956-62; and Phil Lowe (Hull K.R.) 1970-78.

MOST GOALS IN CAREER

93 Neil Fox (Wakefield T.) 1959-69
66 Lewis Jones (Leeds)............................... 1954-57
64 Jim Sullivan (Wigan)............................ 1924-33
53 Eric Fraser (Warrington) 1958-61
49 Jonathan Davies (Widnes, Warrington) 1990-
44 George Fairbairn (Wigan, Hull K.R.) 1977-82
39 Paul Eastwood (Hull) 1990-
31 Paul Loughlin (St. Helens) 1988-
26 Joe Lydon (Widnes, Wigan).................... 1983-
25 Terry Clawson
    (Featherstone R., Leeds, Oldham) 1962-74
22 Ray Dutton (Widnes)............................ 1970
22 John Holmes (Leeds) 1971-82
22 Ernest Ward (Bradford N.)...................... 1946-52
21 Mick Burke (Widnes)............................ 1980-86
21 Ken Gowers (Swinton)........................... 1962-66

MOST POINTS IN CAREER

228 Neil Fox (Wakefield T.)......................... 1959-69
149 Garry Schofield (Hull, Leeds) 1984-
147 Lewis Jones (Leeds) 1954-57
128 Jim Sullivan (Wigan) 1924-33
123 Mick Sullivan (Huddersfield, Wigan,
     St. Helens, York)................................. 1954-63
112 Jonathan Davies (Widnes, Warrington) 1990-
109 Eric Fraser (Warrington)...................... 1958-61
106 Paul Eastwood (Hull)........................... 1990-
104 Martin Offiah (Widnes, Wigan) 1988-
91 George Fairbairn (Wigan, Hull K.R.) 1977-82
81 Roger Millward (Castleford, Hull K.R.) 1966-78
80 Ellery Hanley (Bradford N., Wigan, Leeds)... 1984-
79 Joe Lydon (Widnes, Wigan) 1983-

MOST TRIES IN A MATCH

5 by Martin Offiah (Widnes) v. France at Leeds
    16 February, 1991
4 by Jim Leytham (Wigan) v. Australia at Brisbane
    2 July, 1910
    Billy Boston (Wigan) v. New Zealand at Auckland
    24 July, 1954
    Alex Murphy (St. Helens) v. France at Leeds
    14 March, 1959
    Garry Schofield (Hull) v. New Zealand at Wigan
    2 November, 1985
3 by Bill Jukes (Hunslet) v. Australia at Sydney
    18 June, 1910
    Bert Avery (Oldham) v. New Zealand at Auckland
    30 July, 1910
    Billy Stone (Hull) v. New Zealand at Auckland
    31 July, 1920
    Jonty Parkin (Wakefield T.) v. New Zealand at
    Auckland 31 July, 1920
    Charlie Carr (Barrow) v. New Zealand at Leeds
    15 January, 1927
    Stan Smith (Leeds) v. Australia at Sydney
    16 July, 1932
    Arthur Bassett (Halifax) v. Australia at Brisbane
    6 July, 1946
    George Wilson (Workington T.) v. New Zealand at
    Bradford 6 October, 1951
    Mick Sullivan (Huddersfield) v. New Zealand at
    Bradford 12 November, 1955
    Dave Bolton (Wigan) v. France at Wigan
    23 November, 1957
    Mick Sullivan (Wigan) v. Australia at Sydney
    19 July, 1958
    Mick Sullivan (Wigan) v. New Zealand at
    Auckland 9 August, 1958
    Mick Sullivan (Wigan) v. France at Leeds
    14 March, 1959
    Clive Sullivan (Hull) v. New Zealand at Sydney
    (World Cup) 8 June, 1968
    Bill Burgess (Barrow) v. France at St. Helens
    30 November, 1968
    Keith Fielding (Salford) v. France at Grenoble
    20 January, 1974
    Henderson Gill (Wigan) v. France at Hull
    6 December, 1981
    Garry Schofield (Leeds) v. France at Leeds
    16 February, 1991
    Garry Schofield (Leeds) v. France at Carcassonne
    7 March, 1993
    Paul Newlove (Featherstone R.) v. France at Leeds
    2 April, 1993

●Bill Jukes and Bert Avery are the only forwards to have scored hat-tricks for Great Britain, both on tour in 1910.

MOST GOALS IN A MATCH

10 by Lewis Jones (Leeds) v. Australia at Brisbane
3 July, 1954
Bernard Ganley (Oldham) v. France at Wigan
23 November, 1957
John Holmes (Leeds) v. New Zealand at Pau
(World Cup) 4 November, 1972
Jonathan Davies (Widnes) v. France at Leeds
2 April, 1993

9 by Lewis Jones (Leeds) v. France at Leeds
26 January, 1957
Neil Fox (Wakefield T.) v. France at Wigan
3 April, 1963
Neil Fox (Wakefield T.) v. France at Leigh
18 March, 1964

8 by Eric Fraser (Warrington) v. Australia at Sydney
19 July, 1958
David Creasser (Leeds) v. France at Leeds
1 March, 1985
Joe Lydon (Wigan) v. France at Leeds
24 January, 1987
Paul Eastwood (Hull) v. France at Leeds
16 February, 1991
Jonathan Davies (Widnes) v. Papua New Guinea
at Wigan 9 November, 1991

7 by Lewis Jones (Leeds) v. France at St. Helens
10 April, 1957
Eric Fraser (Warrington) v. New Zealand at
Auckland 9 August, 1958
Eric Fraser (Warrington) v. France at Leeds
14 March, 1959
Neil Fox (Wakefield T.) v. New Zealand at
Swinton 4 November, 1961
Neil Fox (Wakefield T.) v. France at Swinton
23 January, 1965
Bev Risman (Leeds) v. New Zealand at Sydney
(World Cup) 8 June, 1968
Roger Millward (Hull K.R.) v. Australia at
Sydney 20 June, 1970
George Fairbairn (Wigan) v. France at Auckland
(World Cup) 5 June, 1977
John Woods (Leigh) v. France at Hull
6 December, 1981
David Stephenson (Wigan) v. Papua New Guinea
at Wigan 24 October, 1987
Paul Loughlin (St. Helens) v. Papua New Guinea
at Port Moresby 22 May, 1988

MOST POINTS IN A MATCH

26 (2t, 10g) by John Holmes (Leeds) v. New Zealand
at Pau (World Cup)
4 November, 1972
21 (1t, 9g) by Lewis Jones (Leeds) v. France at
Leeds 26 January, 1957
Neil Fox (Wakefield T.) v. France at
Wigan 3 April, 1963
Neil Fox (Wakefield T.) v. France at
Leigh 18 March, 1964

20 (10g) by Lewis Jones (Leeds) v. Australia at
Brisbane 3 July, 1954
(10g) Bernard Ganley (Oldham) v. France at
Wigan 23 November, 1957
(2t, 7g) Roger Millward (Hull K.R.) v.
Australia at Sydney 20 June, 1970
(1t, 8g) Joe Lydon (Wigan) v. France at Leeds
24 February, 1987
(5t) Martin Offiah (Widnes) v. France at
Leeds 16 February, 1991
(1t, 8g) Paul Eastwood (Hull) v. France at
Leeds 16 February, 1991
(10g) Jonathan Davies (Widnes) v. France at
Leeds 2 April, 1993

MOST APPEARANCES

46	Mick Sullivan*
46(2)	Garry Schofield
36(1)	Ellery Hanley
36(4)	Shaun Edwards
33	Martin Offiah
31	Billy Boston
30(1)	Cliff Watson
30(7)	Joe Lydon
29	George Nicholls
29	Neil Fox
29(1)	Roger Millward
28	Alan Prescott
28(9)	Daryl Powell
27	Phil Jackson
27	Alex Murphy
26	Eric Ashton
26	John Atkinson
26(1)	Andy Gregory
25	Brian McTigue
25	Jim Sullivan
25	Tommy Harris
25(1)	Denis Betts
25(4)	Andy Platt

( ) Indicates substitute appearance
included in total

* Mick Sullivan's joint record number of
appearances includes a record run of 36
successive matches. In addition he played in
two matches against France before they were
given Test status.

LONGEST TEST CAREERS

14 years — Gus Risman
1932 to 1946 (17 appearances)
13 years 9 months — Billy Batten
1908 to 1921 (10 appearances)
13 years 6 months — Alex Murphy
1958 to 1971 (27 appearances)
12 years 9 months — Roger Millward
1966 to 1978 (28 + 1 appearances)
12 years 6 months — John Atkinson
1968 to 1980 (26 appearances)
12 years 6 months — Terry Clawson
1962 to 1974 (14 appearances)

YOUNGEST TEST PLAYER

Paul Newlove was 18 years 72 days old when he made his Great Britain Test debut as a 76th-minute substitute in the first Test against New Zealand at Old Trafford, Manchester, on 21 October 1989, making his full debut a week later. Born on 10 August 1971, he beat the previous record held by Shaun Edwards (born 17 October 1966) who was 18 years 135 days old when capped against France at Leeds on 1 March 1985.

Roger Millward (born 16 September 1947) was 18 years 37 days old when he was a non-playing substitute for the second Test against New Zealand at Bradford on 23 October 1965.

OLDEST TEST PLAYER

Jeff Grayshon (born 4 March 1949) was 36 years 8 months when he played in his last Test for Britain, against New Zealand at Elland Road, Leeds, on 9 November 1985.

RECORD TEAM CHANGES

The record number of team changes made by the Great Britain selectors is 10, on three occasions, all against Australia.

In 1929, Britain crashed 31-8 to Australia in the first Test at Hull KR and retained only three players for the second Test at Leeds, where they won 9-3.

After their biggest ever defeat of 50-12 in the 1963 second Test at Swinton, Britain dropped nine players and were forced to make another change when Vince Karalius was injured and replaced by Don Fox. Britain stopped Australia making a clean sweep of the series by winning 16-5 at Leeds in the last Test.

Following the 40-4 first Test defeat at Hull City's soccer ground in 1982, the selectors again made 10 changes, not including substitutes, Britain going down 27-6 in the second Test at Wigan.

Britain have never fielded the same team for three or more successive Tests.

Wales skipper Jonathan Davies shows off the John Smith's Trophy after the Welsh lifted the European Championship for the first time in 57 years with a 1995 double over England and France.

ENGLAND AND WALES

1994-95 REVIEW

A reversion to the policy of selection qualification by grandparentage provided Wales with the springboard to lift the European Championship title for the first time in 57 years.

Since re-formation in October 1991, the Dragons had relied on Welsh-born players and those one generation removed. But with the Halifax Centenary World Cup on the horizon, the Welsh management successfully applied for the qualification extension to be re-introduced to boost the size and quality of their limited squad.

Fielding five Anglo-Welsh debutants – Wigan quartet Paul Atcheson, Kelvin Skerrett, Martin Hall and Neil Cowie, plus Richard Eyres of Leeds – the Welsh beat a weakened England 18-16 at Cardiff before securing the John Smith's European Championship with a 22-10 success over France in the mud at Carcassonne. Only six of the Welsh starting line-up were former Welsh Rugby Union players.

In between the two Welsh triumphs, a virtual second string England snatched a 19-16 victory over France at Gateshead to take second place in the three-nation tournament, re-introduced for the first time since 1981 as preparation for England and Wales' participation in the autumn's 10-nation World Cup.

The Championship was more eventful off the field than on it as the three-match itinerary became embroiled in controversy and incident.

Wales had taken stock of their 46-4 hammering by Australia in their John Smith's tour encounter in Cardiff at the end of October – as detailed in the section 1994 KANGAROOS – and decided that strength-ening was needed despite being number four seed for the Centenary World Cup.

The League sanctioned their request to revert to the grandparent qualification which prevailed during the previous fielding of a Welsh team from 1975 to 1984. Skerrett's

desire to serve Wales in preference to an almost guaranteed England place caused most surprise when he elected to emulate his uncle, Trevor, who gained seven Welsh caps, including captaincy against England at Ebbw Vale in 1984.

Eyres was admitted into the Welsh ranks at the second attempt. The League originally ruled that his appearance for England – against Wales – in November 1992 made him ineligible. After an appeal was upheld on the grounds that there was no choice at the time, the Leeds forward was given the go-ahead to become a double international.

England's selection plans for Cardiff were hampered by the League's decision to send a handful of capped players in the Great Britain squad to take part in the Coca-Cola World Sevens in Sydney, the outward journey coinciding with the Wales encounter. The 10-man sevens party included international regulars Denis Betts, Lee Jackson, Chris Joynt and Martin Offiah, who withdrew through injury prior to departure.

The England selection of Featherstone Rovers winger Ikram Butt, the Leeds-born son of Pakistani parents, heralded the first Asian player to be capped.

For England's mid-week meeting with France in the North-East two weeks later, coach Ellery Hanley selected a full strength line-up including a total of nine players from Wigan and St. Helens. Five days before the international, the two sides met in the Silk Cut Challenge Cup and drew 16-16 at Central Park.

The League ruled that due to fixture congestion and television obligations the Cup replay would take place on the same night as the John Smith's international, forcing Hanley to draft in 11 new faces two days before the game to replace the Cup-tied nine players, plus injured Harvey Howard and Anthony Farrell.

On the field, Wales opened the European tournament with a dramatic two-point home victory over England to end a seven-match losing run against their arch rivals, their last

Sheffield Eagles prop Paul Broadbent scores England's opening try against France on his international debut.

success being at Leeds in January 1977.

The famous Welsh success was based on the new-found pack power boosted by the inclusion of the Anglo-Welsh newcomers, plus the inspiration of skipper Jonathan Davies, whose boot contributed four goals and the two deciding drop goals inside the last 10 minutes.

England had valid excuses with a line-up weakened by the Sydney Sevens duty and injuries, including would-be skipper Shaun Edwards, and even the withdrawal of Leeds full back Alan Tait, who preferred not to play for England having represented Scotland at Rugby Union. The Lions were further depleted by the late absence of centre Gary Connolly with an ankle injury and the withdrawal during the game of injured trio Paul Newlove, Jason Robinson and debutant hooker Richard Russell.

But England's problems could not take the gloss off the Welsh victory. Wales made a superb start with scrum half Kevin Ellis scoring the first of his two tries in the 19th minute by taking a pass from Hall before

darting through to score unchallenged under the posts. They only lost their way early in the second half when England scored two of their three tries.

Full back Richard Gay, one of five senior international newcomers in the English ranks, equalised from a superb pass from Garry Schofield. Two goals from Davies to one from Deryck Fox gave Wales an 8-6 interval lead.

England rallied and took the lead after a long break by Newlove in the 48th minute. Fox's towering kick was fumbled by Atcheson, under pressure from Sonny Nickle, and Fox collected to score.

Four minutes later, substitute Steve McCurrie sent out a well-timed pass for Wigan winger Jason Robinson to score in the corner.

But Wales refused to buckle despite being 16-8 in arrears, their outstanding spirit being allied to a co-ordinated gameplan and brave defence. A magnificent second touchdown by Ellis, who was named John Smith's Man of the Match, came in the 67th minute after a fine move involving Atcheson and Allan Bateman.

Two goals from Davies brought the scores level.

Experienced Davies kept his cool to send over vital drop goals in the 71st and 78th minutes to clinch the win, achieved in the absence of the likes of the injured John Devereux, Scott Gibbs and Gerald Cordle.

England's 17-man squad for the second John Smith's International a fortnight later included nine new senior caps following the withdrawal of 11 original selections due to the Challenge Cup replay at St. Helens, injuries and illness, including winger Butt being a flu victim on the day of the match.

Sheffield Eagles' Daryl Powell, a veteran of 28 Great Britain appearances, was appointed to lead an international side for the first time, starting at loose forward for the first time in his international career. Powell responded to the dual responsibility by claiming the John Smith's Man of the Match award.

Club colleague Paul Broadbent marked a solid front row debut by scoring England's first try in the 15th minute, while centre Nick Pinkney celebrated being Keighley's first England international for 26 years by sprinting 40 metres for his 34th try of the season.

Wakefield Trinity stand off Nigel Wright continued his rehabilitation programme by producing some neat touches in difficult conditions on his senior international debut, popping over a 42nd minute drop goal to edge England 15-8 ahead.

Full back Gay followed up his impressive debut against Wales with another splendid all-round game which included one of the best solo runs of the night when he slipped past three defenders on a 40-metre break.

France had the encouragement of a seventh minute try by Jean-Marc Garcia to take the lead after good approach work by three of their four English-based players – Featherstone Rovers' duo Daniel Divet and Frederic Banquet plus Patrick Entat of Leeds.

Entat, who had lost his first team place,

continued to be a threat to England and his well-placed kick enabled Banquet to dive over for a first half touchdown in the corner, the pair repeating the move for Banquet to go in for France's third try to which Stephane Millet added his second goal.

Wales travelled to Carcassonne needing at least a draw to clinch the title. Despite atrocious conditions following 48 hours of incessant rain, the determined Dragons battled in style to record only their fourth victory on French soil in 20 matches and take the European Championship for the first time since 1938.

Their fourth success in 23 Championships was achieved with a change of gameplan from the expected expansive approach due to the Carcassonne mud, made worse by the staging of an Academy under-19 international curtain-raiser.

Warrington centre Bateman scored two of Wales' four tries, while a courageous example was set by packmen Eyres, Mark Perrett and Paul Moriarty, who was named John Smith's Man of the Match and the series. Skipper Davies again played an inspirational role, setting up two of the tries as well as kicking three goals.

The title success, which complemented his Union triumph in 1988, rounded off a memorable week for Davies, who became a father for the third time earlier in the week, the impending birth at one time threatening his participation in the decider.

France, who were the last European Champions in 1981, took the lead with a Millet penalty goal in the third minute, prop Bernard Llong adding a try shortly afterwards. Wales roared back with a touchdown from teenage winger Iestyn Harris before going in front in the 28th minute when Hall sent in Bateman, who had experienced some difficulty getting time off work to travel to France.

Five minutes before half-time, France regained the lead when Garcia touched down following Patrick Torreilles' kick for the corner to make it 10-8.

The Welsh struck a crucial blow within a minute of the re-start when Davies's superb sidestep and run ended with full back Atcheson scoring. In the 61st minute Davies sent up one of his specialist towering kicks which was fumbled by winger Sirvent for Bateman to race in for his second try.

Davies rounded off the comfortable Welsh victory with two further goals for a 22-10 scoreline; the launch of title celebrations; and the shortening of Wales' odds in the betting for the Centenary World Cup.

FINAL TABLE

	P.	W.	D.	L.	F.	A.	Pts
Wales	2	2	0	0	40	26	4
England	2	1	0	1	35	34	2
France	2	0	0	2	26	41	0

JOHN SMITH'S EUROPEAN CHAMPIONSHIP

1 February 1995   **Ninian Park, Cardiff**

WALES 18		**ENGLAND 16**
Phil Atcheson (Wigan)	1.	Richard Gay (Hull)
Phil Ford (Salford)	2.	Jason Robinson (Wigan)
Allan Bateman (Warrington)	3.	Daryl Powell (Sheffield E.)
Iestyn Harris (Warrington)	4.	Paul Newlove (Bradford N.)
Anthony Sullivan (St. Helens)	5.	Ikram Butt (Featherstone R.)
Jonathan Davies (Warrington), Capt.	6.	Garry Schofield (Leeds)
Kevin Ellis (Workington T.)	7.	Deryck Fox (Bradford N.)
Kelvin Skerrett (Wigan)	8.	Karl Harrison (Halifax)
Martin Hall (Wigan)	9.	Richard Russell (Castleford)
David Young (Salford)	10.	Harvey Howard (Leeds)
Paul Moriarty (Halifax)	11.	Anthony Farrell (Sheffield E.)
Mark Perrett (Halifax)	12.	Sonny Nickle (St. Helens)
Richard Eyres (Leeds)	13.	Phil Clarke (Wigan), Capt.
Adrian Hadley (Widnes)	14.	Simon Baldwin (Halifax)
Daio Powell (Wakefield T.)	15.	Mick Cassidy (Wigan)
Neil Cowie (Wigan)	16.	Steve McNamara (Hull)
Rowland Phillips (Workington T.)	17.	Steve McCurrie (Widnes)

T: Ellis (2)
G: Davies (4, 2dg)
Substitutions:
Cowie for Young (46 min.)
Phillips for Perrett (53 min.)
Half-time: 8-6
Referee: Russell Smith (Castleford)
Attendance: 6,232

T: Gay, Fox, Robinson
G: Fox (2)
Substitutions:
McCurrie for Russell (21 min.)
Cassidy for Schofield (43 min.)
Baldwin for Newlove (66 min.)
McNamara for Howard (67 min.)

15 February 1995 Gateshead

ENGLAND 19 FRANCE 16

Richard Gay (Hull)	1.	Laurent Lucchese (Sheffield E.)
John Bentley (Halifax)	2.	Pascal Bomati (XIII Catalan)
Nick Pinkney (Keighley C.)	3.	Frederic Banquet (Featherstone R.)
Richard Goddard (Castleford)	4.	Stephane Millet (St. Gaudens)
Francis Cummins (Leeds)	5.	Jean-Marc Garcia (St. Esteve)
Nigel Wright (Wakefield T.)	6.	David Despin (Limoux)
Deryck Fox (Bradford N.)	7.	Patrick Entat (Leeds)
Paul Broadbent (Sheffield E.)	8.	Carl Jaavuo (Pia)
Lee Jackson (Sheffield E.)	9.	Stephane Tena (XIII Catalan)
Steve McNamara (Hull)	10.	Frederic Teixido (Limoux)
Simon Baldwin (Halifax)	11.	Daniel Divet (Featherstone R.)
Stephen Holgate (Workington T.)	12.	Didier Cabestany (XIII Catalan), Capt.
Daryl Powell (Sheffield E.), Capt.	13.	Jacques Pech (Pia)
Tony Smith (Castleford)	14.	Ezzedine Attia (Cannes)
Steve McCurrie (Widnes)	15.	Claude Sirvent (St. Gaudens)
Roger Simpson (Bradford N.)	16.	Lillian Hebert (Pia)
Mark Hilton (Warrington)	17.	Jean Luc Ramondou (Pamiers)

T: Broadbent, Pinkney, Cummins
G: Fox (3), Wright (dg)
Substitutions:
McCurrie for Jackson (51 min.)
Simpson for Goddard (58 min.)
Hilton for McNamara (66 min.)
Smith for Wright (67 min.)
Referee: Jean-Louis Aribaud (France)

T: Banquet (2), Garcia
G: Millet (2)
Substitutions:
Attia for Jaavuo (48 min.)
Hebert for Pech (65 min.)
Sirvent for Teixido (72 min.)
Half-time: 14-8
Attendance: 6,103

England's makeshift squad are all smiles after the 19-16 win over France at Gateshead.

5 March 1995   Carcassonne

WALES 22   FRANCE 10

Paul Atcheson (Wigan)	1.	Laurent Lucchese (Sheffield E.)
Anthony Sullivan (St. Helens)	2.	Claude Sirvent (St. Gaudens)
John Devereux (Widnes)	3.	Stephane Millet (St. Gaudens)
Allan Bateman (Warrington)	4.	Pierre Chamorin (St. Esteve)
Iestyn Harris (Warrington)	5.	Jean-Marc Garcia (St. Esteve)
Jonathan Davies (Warrington), Capt.	6.	David Despin (Limoux)
Kevin Ellis (Workington T.)	7.	Patrick Entat (Leeds), Capt.
Kelvin Skerrett (Wigan)	8.	Bernard Llong (XIII Catalan)
Martin Hall (Wigan)	9.	Patrick Torreilles (Pia)
David Young (Salford)	10.	Frederic Teixido (Limoux)
Paul Moriarty (Halifax)	11.	Daniel Divet (Featherstone R.)
Mark Perrett (Halifax)	12.	Ezzedine Attia (Cannes)
Richard Eyres (Leeds)	13.	Thierry Valero (Lezignan)
Phil Ford (Salford)	14.	Frederic Banquet (Featherstone R.)
Neil Cowie (Wigan)	15.	Jacques Pech (Pia)
Adrian Hadley (Widnes)	16.	Lillian Hebert (Pia)
Rowland Phillips (Workington T.)	17.	Brian Coles (XIII Catalan)

T: Bateman (2), Harris, Atcheson
G: Davies (3)
Substitutions:
Cowie for Young (48 min.)
Phillips for Perrett (57 min.)
Hadley for Devereux (65 min.)
Ford for Sullivan (77 min.)
Half-time: 8-10
Referee: John Connolly (Wigan)

T: Llong, Garcia
G: Millet
Substitutions:
Pech for Attia (48 min.)
Coles for Llong (56 min.)
Banquet for Millet (68 min.)
Hebert for Valero (74 min.)
Attendance: 6,000

The jubilant Wigan trio of, left to right, Paul Atcheson, Martin Hall and Kelvin Skerrett, part of the Anglo-Welsh connection which helped Wales lift the John Smith's European Championship title.

EUROPEAN CHAMPIONSHIP

● The following is a list of European Championship matches since the tournament was introduced in 1935, the year that France emerged as an international competitor.

E — England, Fr — France, ON — Other Nationalities, W — Wales

1934-35   *Winners:* England on points average

1 Jan.	Fr	18	W	11	Bordeaux
28 Mar.	Fr	15	E	15	Paris
10 Apr.	E	24	W	11	Liverpool

1935-36   *Winners:* Wales

23 Nov.	W	41	Fr	7	Llanelli
1 Feb.	E	14	W	17	Hull K.R.
16 Feb.	Fr	7	E	25	Paris

1936-37   *Winners:* Wales

7 Nov.	W	3	E	2	Pontypridd
6 Dec.	Fr	3	W	9	Paris
10 Apr.	E	23	Fr	9	Halifax

1937-38   *Winners:* Wales

29 Jan.	E	6	W	7	Bradford
20 Mar.	Fr	15	E	17	Paris
2 Apr.	W	18	Fr	2	Llanelli

1938-39   *Winners:* France

5 Nov.	W	17	E	9	Llanelli
25 Feb.	E	9	Fr	12	St. Helens
16 Apr.	Fr	16	W	10	Bordeaux

1945-46   *Winners:* England on points average

24 Nov.	W	11	E	3	Swansea
23 Feb.	E	16	Fr	6	Swinton
24 Mar.	Fr	19	W	7	Bordeaux

1946-47   *Winners:* England

12 Oct.	E	10	W	13	Swinton
16 Nov.	W	5	E	19	Swansea
8 Dec.	Fr	0	E	3	Bordeaux
18 Jan.	Fr	14	W	5	Marseilles
12 Apr.	W	17	Fr	15	Swansea
17 May	E	5	Fr	2	Leeds

1947-48   *Winners:* England

20 Sep.	E	8	W	10	Wigan
25 Oct.	E	20	Fr	15	Huddersfield
23 Nov.	Fr	29	W	21	Bordeaux
6 Dec.	W	7	E	18	Swansea
20 Mar.	W	12	Fr	20	Swansea
11 Apr.	Fr	10	E	25	Marseilles

1948-49   *Winners:* France

22 Sep.	E	11	W	5	Wigan
23 Oct.	W	9	Fr	12	Swansea
28 Nov.	Fr	5	E	12	Bordeaux
5 Feb.	W	14	E	10	Swansea
12 Mar.	E	5	Fr	12	Wembley
10 Apr.	Fr	11	W	0	Marseilles

1949-50   *Winners:* England on points average

19 Sep.	E	7	ON	13	Workington
22 Oct.	W	5	ON	6	Abertillery
12 Nov.	W	16	Fr	8	Swansea
4 Dec.	Fr	5	E	13	Bordeaux
15 Jan.	Fr	8	ON	3	Marseilles
1 Mar.	E	11	W	6	Wigan

1950-51   *Winners:* France on points average

14 Oct.	W	4	E	22	Abertillery
11 Nov.	E	14	Fr	9	Leeds
10 Dec.	Fr	16	ON	3	Bordeaux
31 Mar.	W	21	ON	27	Swansea
11 Apr.	E	10	ON	35	Wigan
15 Apr.	Fr	28	W	13	Marseilles

1951-52   *Winners:* France on points average

19 Sep.	E	35	W	11	St. Helens
3 Nov.	ON	17	Fr	14	Hull
25 Nov.	Fr	42	E	13	Marseilles
1 Dec.	W	11	ON	22	Abertillery
6 Apr.	Fr	20	W	12	Bordeaux
23 Apr.	E	31	ON	18	Wigan

1952-53   *Winners:* Other Nats on points average

17 Sep.	E	19	W	8	Wigan
18 Oct.	E	12	ON	31	Huddersfield
25 Oct.	W	22	Fr	16	Leeds
23 Nov.	Fr	10	ON	29	Marseilles
11 Apr.	Fr	13	E	15	Paris
15 Apr.	W	18	ON	16	Warrington

1953-54   *Winners:* England

16 Sep.	E	24	W	5	St. Helens
7 Oct.	ON	30	W	5	Bradford
18 Oct.	Fr	10	ON	15	Bordeaux
7 Nov.	E	7	Fr	5	Bradford
28 Nov.	E	30	ON	22	Wigan
13 Dec.	Fr	23	W	22	Marseilles

● Championship suspended in 1954-55 because of World Cup

1955-56   *Winners:* Other Nationalities

12 Sep.	E	16	ON	33	Wigan
19 Oct.	ON	32	Fr	19	Leigh
10 May	Fr	23	E	9	Lyons

1969-70   *Winners:* England on points average

18 Oct.	E	40	W	23	Leeds
23 Oct.	W	2	Fr	8	Salford
25 Oct.	E	11	Fr	11	Wigan
25 Jan.	Fr	11	W	15	Perpignan
24 Feb.	E	26	W	7	Leeds
15 Mar.	Fr	14	E	9	Toulouse

1974-75   *Winners:* England

19 Jan.	Fr	9	E	11	Perpignan
16 Feb.	W	21	Fr	8	Swansea
25 Feb.	E	12	W	8	Salford

● Championship suspended in 1975-76 because of World Cup

1976-77   *Winners:* France

29 Jan.	E	2	W	6	Leeds
20 Feb.	Fr	13	W	2	Toulouse
20 Mar.	Fr	28	E	15	Carcassonne

1977-78   *Winners:* England

15 Jan.	W	29	Fr	7	Widnes
5 Mar.	Fr	11	E	13	Toulouse
28 May	E	60	W	13	St. Helens

1978-79   *Winners:* England

4 Feb.	Fr	15	W	8	Narbonne
16 Mar.	E	15	W	7	Widnes
24 Mar.	E	12	Fr	6	Warrington

1979-80   *Winners:* England

26 Jan.	W	7	Fr	21	Widnes
29 Feb.	E	26	W	9	Hull K.R.
16 Mar.	Fr	2	E	4	Narbonne

1980-81   *Winners:* France

31 Jan.	Fr	23	W	5	Narbonne
21 Feb.	E	1	Fr	5	Leeds
18 Mar.	E	17	W	4	Hull K.R.

1994-95   *Winners:* Wales

1 Feb.	W	18	E	16	Cardiff C. FC
15 Feb.	E	19	Fr	16	Gateshead
5 Mar.	Fr	10	W	22	Carcassone

1975 WORLD CHAMPIONSHIP

Winners: Australia (home and away basis)

Date	Match and Result				Venue	Attendance
2 Mar.	France	14	Wales	7	Toulouse	7,563
16 Mar.	England	20	France	2	Leeds	10,842
1 June	Australia	36	New Zealand	8	Brisbane	10,000
10 June	Wales	12	England	7	Brisbane	6,000
14 June	Australia	30	Wales	13	Sydney	25,386
15 June	New Zealand	27	France	0	Christchurch	2,500
21 June	New Zealand	17	England	17	Auckland	12,000
22 June	Australia	26	France	6	Brisbane	9,000
28 June	New Zealand	13	Wales	8	Auckland	18,000
28 June	Australia	10	England	10	Sydney	33,858
20 Sep.	England	22	Wales	16	Warrington	5,034
27 Sep.	New Zealand	8	Australia	24	Auckland	18,000
11 Oct.	France	2	England	48	Bordeaux	1,581
17 Oct.	France	12	New Zealand	12	Marseilles	18,000
19 Oct.	Wales	6	Australia	18	Swansea	11,112
25 Oct.	England	27	New Zealand	12	Bradford	5,507
26 Oct.	France	2	Australia	41	Perpignan	10,440
1 Nov.	England	16	Australia	13	Wigan	9,393
2 Nov.	Wales	25	New Zealand	24	Swansea	2,645
6 Nov.	Wales	23	France	2	Salford	2,247

	P.	W.	D.	L.	F.	A.	Pts
Australia	8	6	1	1	198	69	13
England	8	5	2	1	167	84	12
Wales	8	3	0	5	110	130	6
New Zealand	8	2	2	4	121	149	6
France	8	1	1	6	40	204	3

Final Table

1975 World Championship squads for Australasian section

ENGLAND
R. Millward (Hull K.R.)
J. Atkinson (Leeds)
J. Bridges (Featherstone R.)
D. Chisnall (Warrington)
E. Chisnall (St. Helens)
P. Cookson (Leeds)
M. Coulman (Salford)
G. Dunn (Hull K.R.)
L. Dyl (Leeds)
G. Fairbairn (Wigan)
K. Fielding (Salford)
K. Gill (Salford)
P. Gordon (Warrington)
T. Martyn (Warrington)
M. Morgan (Wakefield T.)
S. Nash (Featherstone R.)
G. Nicholls (St. Helens)
D. Noonan (Warrington)
S. Norton (Castleford)
J. Walsh (St. Helens)
Manager: W. Oxley (Barrow)
Coach: A.J. Murphy (Warrington)

WALES
D. Watkins (Salford)
P. Banner (Salford)
B. Butler (Swinton)
K. Coslett (St. Helens)
E. Cunningham (St. Helens)
C. Dixon (Salford)
R. Evans (Swinton)
T. Fisher (Leeds)
W. Francis (Wigan)
J. Mantle (St. Helens)
R. Mathias (St. Helens)
J. Mills (Widnes)
M. Nicholas (Warrington)
P. Rowe (Blackpool B.)
C. Sullivan (Hull K.R.)
D. Treasure (Oldham)
G. Turner (Hull K.R.)
R. Wanbon (Warrington)
D. Willicombe (Wigan)
F. Wilson (St. Helens)
Manager: R. Simpson (Castleford)
Coach: L. Pearce (Halifax)

ENGLAND – OTHER INTERNATIONAL MATCHES

● W-Won, D-Drawn, L-Lost refer to England.

v. AUSTRALIA
2 Jan. 1909	W	14-9	Huddersfield
3 Feb. 1909	D	17-17	Glasgow
3 Mar. 1909	W	14-7	Everton
18 Oct. 1911	L	6-11	Fulham
6 Dec. 1911	W	5-3	Nottingham
10 Oct. 1921	W	5-4	Arsenal
*31 Dec. 1933	L	13-63	Paris
*13 Jan. 1934	W	19-14	Gateshead
12 Nov. 1975	L	0-25	Leeds

*Included Welsh players.

v. FRANCE
*15 Apr. 1934	W	32-21	Paris
17 Nov. 1962	W	18-6	Leeds

*Included Welsh players.

v. NEW ZEALAND
11 Jan. 1908	W	18-16	Wigan

v. PAPUA NEW GUINEA
16 July 1975	W	40-12	Port Moresby

v. WALES

20 Apr. 1908	L	18-35	Tonypandy
28 Dec. 1908	W	31-7	Broughton
4 Dec. 1909	W	19-13	Wakefield
9 Apr. 1910	L	18-39	Ebbw Vale
10 Dec. 1910	W	39-13	Coventry
1 Apr. 1911	W	27-8	Ebbw Vale
20 Jan. 1912	W	31-5	Oldham
15 Feb. 1913	W	40-16	Plymouth
14 Feb. 1914	W	16-12	St. Helens
19 Jan. 1921	W	35-9	Leeds
11 Dec. 1922	W	12-7	London, Herne Hill
7 Feb. 1923	L	2-13	Wigan
1 Oct. 1923	W	18-11	Huddersfield
7 Feb. 1925	W	27-22	Workington
30 Sep. 1925	W	18-14	Wigan
12 Apr. 1926	W	30-22	Pontypridd
6 Apr. 1927	W	11-8	Broughton
11 Jan. 1928	W	20-12	Wigan
14 Nov. 1928	W	39-15	Cardiff
18 Mar. 1931	W	23-18	Huddersfield
27 Jan. 1932	W	19-2	Salford
30 Nov. 1932	W	14-13	Leeds
23 Dec. 1939	L	3-16	Bradford
9 Nov. 1940	W	8-5	Oldham
18 Oct. 1941	D	9-9	Bradford
27 Feb. 1943	W	15-9	Wigan
26 Feb. 1944	D	9-9	Wigan
10 Mar. 1945	W	18-8	Wigan
7 Nov. 1968	L	17-24	Salford
8 Nov. 1981	W	20-15	Cardiff
14 Oct. 1984	W	28-9	Ebbw Vale
27 Nov. 1992	W	36-11	Swansea C. FC

v. OTHER NATIONALITIES

5 Apr. 1904	L	3-9	Wigan
2 Jan. 1905	W	26-11	Bradford (Park Avenue)
1 Jan. 1906	D	3-3	Wigan
*5 Feb. 1921	W	33-16	Workington
15 Oct. 1924	L	17-23	Leeds
4 Feb. 1926	W	37-11	Whitehaven
20 Mar. 1929	W	27-20	Leeds
7 Apr. 1930	L	19-35	Halifax
1 Oct. 1930	W	31-18	St. Helens
30 Mar. 1933	W	34-27	Workington

*Other Nationalities side all-Welsh.

ENGLAND RECORDS

Highest score: 60-13 v. Wales at St. Helens, 28 May 1978 (Also widest margin win)

Highest score against: 63-13* v. Australia at Paris, 31 December 1933

*England included Welshmen. Highest score against All-England side 42-13 v. France at Marseilles, 25 November 1951 (Also widest margin defeat)

Most tries in a match: 4 by J. Leytham (Wigan) v. Other Nationalities at Bradford, 2 January 1905

4 by S. Moorhouse (Huddersfield) v. Wales at Plymouth, 15 February 1913

4 by P. Norburn (Swinton) v. Other Nationalities at Wigan, 28 November 1953

4 by K. Fielding (Salford) v. France at Bordeaux, 11 October 1975

4 by S. Wright (Widnes) v. Wales at St. Helens, 28 May 1978

Most goals and points in a match: 9g-21pts by G. Pimblett (St. Helens) v. Wales at St. Helens, 28 May 1978

Biggest home attendance: 27,500 v. Wales at Wigan, 1 March 1950

WALES — OTHER INTERNATIONAL MATCHES

● W-Won, D-Drawn, L-Lost refer to Wales.

v. FRANCE
*19 May 1955	L	11-24	Nantes
1 Mar. 1959	L	8-25	Toulouse
17 Feb. 1963	L	3-23	Toulouse
9 Mar. 1969	L	13-17	Paris
22 Mar. 1992	W	35-6	Swansea C. FC
13 Dec. 1992	W	19-18	Perpignan
4 Mar. 1994	W	13-12	Cardiff C. FC

*v. France 'B'

v. NEW ZEALAND
1 Jan. 1908	W	9-8	Aberdare
4 Dec. 1926	W	34-8	Pontypridd
18 Oct. 1947	L	20-28	Swansea
7 Dec. 1951	L	3-15	Bradford
3 Oct. 1993	L	19-24	Swansea C. FC

v. AUSTRALIA
7 Oct. 1911	L	20-28	Ebbw Vale
10 Dec. 1921	L	16-21	Pontypridd
18 Jan. 1930	L	10-26	Wembley
30 Dec. 1933	L	19-51	Wembley
20 Nov. 1948	L	5-12	Swansea
15 Oct. 1978	L	3-8	Swansea
24 Oct. 1982	L	7-37	Cardiff C. FC
30 Oct. 1994	L	4-46	Cardiff C. FC

A Welsh League XIII beat Australia 14-13 at Merthyr on 16 January 1909.

v. PAPUA NEW GUINEA
27 Oct. 1991	W	68-0	Swansea C. FC

v. NORTHERN RL
17 Apr. 1937	W	15-12	Newcastle

v. EMPIRE XIII
19 May 1951	L	16-29	Llanelli

Nine-cap Welsh international winger Anthony Sullivan, in action against the 1994 Australian tourists.

WALES RECORDS

Highest score:	68-0 v. Papua New Guinea at Swansea C. FC, 27 October 1991 (Also widest margin win)
Highest score against:	60-13 v. England at St. Helens, 28 May 1978 (Also widest margin defeat)
Most tries in a match:	4 by W. T. Davies (Halifax) v. Australia at Ebbw Vale, 7 October 1911
Most goals and points in a match:	8g-24pts by Jonathan Davies (Widnes) v. Papua New Guinea at Swansea C. FC, 27 October 1991
Biggest home attendance:	30,000 v. England at Swansea, 24 November 1945

ENGLAND TEAMS ● From 1975 to 1982, revived in 1984 for one game and reintroduced in 1992.

1975 France

Perpignan: 19 Jan.

Won 11-9

Murphy (Oldham) 1t
Fielding (Salford) 1t
Walsh (St. Helens)
Dyl (Leeds) 1t
Redfearn, D. (Bradford N.)
Topliss (Wakefield T.)
*Millward (Hull K.R.)
Coulman (Salford)
Gray (Wigan) 1g
Millington (Hull K.R.)
Cunningham (Barrow)
Chisnall, E. (St. Helens)
Nicholls (St. Helens)
Sub: Eckersley (St. Helens)
　　Morgan (Wakefield T.)

1975 Wales

Salford: 25 Feb.

Won 12-8

Sheard (Wakefield T.)
Dunn (Hull K.R.)
Noonan (Warrington) 1t
Dyl (Leeds)
Atkinson (Leeds) 1t
Gill, K. (Salford)
*Millward (Hull K.R.)
Coulman (Salford)
Gray (Wigan) 3g
Jackson, P. (Bradford N.)
Martyn (Warrington)
Cunningham (Barrow)
Morgan (Wakefield T.)
Sub: Chisnall, D. (Warrington)

1975 France (WC)

Leeds: 16 Mar.

Won 20-2

Charlton (Salford)
Fielding (Salford) 2t
Noonan (Warrington)
Dyl (Leeds)
Atkinson (Leeds)
Gill, K. (Salford)
*Millward (Hull K.R.) 1t
Chisnall, D. (Warrington)
Gray (Wigan) 4g
Jackson, P. (Bradford N.)
Martyn (Warrington)
Nicholls (St. Helens)
Philbin (Warrington)
Sub: Morgan (Wakefield T.) 1t

1975 Wales (WC)

Brisbane: 10 June

Lost 7-12

Fairbairn (Wigan) 2g
Fielding (Salford)
Noonan (Warrington)
Dyl (Leeds)
Atkinson (Leeds)
*Millward (Hull K.R.)
Nash (Featherstone R.)
Chisnall, D. (Warrington)
Morgan (Wakefield T.)
Coulman (Salford)
Chisnall, E. (St. Helens)
Nicholls (St. Helens)
Norton (Castleford)
Sub: Gill, K. (Salford)
　　Martyn (Warrington) 1t

1975 New Zealand (WC)

Auckland: 21 June

Drew 17-17

Fairbairn (Wigan) 2t,4g
Fielding (Salford)
Walsh (St. Helens)
Dyl (Leeds)
Atkinson (Leeds) 1t
Gill, K. (Salford)
Nash (Featherstone R.)
Chisnall, D. (Warrington)
Bridges (Featherstone R.)
Chisnall, E. (St. Helens)
*Nicholls (St. Helens)
Cookson (Leeds)
Norton (Castleford)
Sub: Morgan (Wakefield T.)

1975 Australia (WC)

Sydney: 28 June

Drew 10-10

Fairbairn (Wigan) 2g
Fielding (Salford)
Walsh (St. Helens)
Dyl (Leeds)
Dunn (Hull K.R.) 1t
*Millward (Hull K.R.)
Nash (Featherstone R.)
Coulman (Salford)
Bridges (Featherstone R.)
Morgan (Wakefield T.)
Nicholls (St. Helens)
Cookson (Leeds)
Norton (Castleford)
Sub: Gill, K. (Salford) 1t
　　Chisnall, E. (St. Helens)

1975 Wales (WC)

Warrington: 20 Sep.

Won 22-16

Fairbairn (Wigan) 6g
Fielding (Salford) 1t
Hughes (Widnes) 1t
Holmes (Leeds) 1t
Atkinson (Leeds)
Gill, K. (Salford)
*Millward (Hull K.R.)
Hogan, B. (Wigan)
Bridges (Featherstone R.) 1dg
Forsyth (Bradford N.)
Grayshon (Dewsbury)
Irving (Wigan)
Norton (Castleford)
Sub: Eckersley (St. Helens)
　　Nicholls (St. Helens)

1975 France (WC)

Bordeaux: 11 Oct.

Won 48-2

Fairbairn (Wigan) 4g
Fielding (Salford) 4t
Hughes (Widnes) 1t
Holmes (Leeds) 2t
Dunn (Hull K.R.) 2t
Gill, K. (Salford) 1t
*Millward (Hull K.R.) 2g
Hogan, B. (Wigan) 1t
Bridges (Featherstone R.)
Forsyth (Bradford N.) 1t
Grayshon (Dewsbury)
Irving (Wigan)
Norton (Castleford)
Sub: Eckersley (St. Helens)
　　Nicholls (St. Helens)

1975 New Zealand (WC)

Bradford: 25 Oct.

Won 27-12

Fairbairn (Wigan) 3g
Wright (Wigan) 1t
Hughes (Widnes) 1t
Holmes (Leeds)
Dunn (Hull K.R.) 1t
Gill, K. (Salford) 3t
*Millward (Hull K.R.)
Hogan, B. (Wigan)
Bridges (Featherstone R.)
Forsyth (Bradford N.)
Grayshon (Dewsbury)
Adams (Widnes)
Norton (Castleford) 1t
Sub: Dyl (Leeds)
　　Nicholls (St. Helens)

1975 Australia (WC)
Wigan: 1 Nov.
Won 16-13
Fairbairn (Wigan) 5g
Dunn (Hull K.R.)
Holmes (Leeds) 1t
Dyl (Leeds)
Redfearn, D. (Bradford N.)
Gill, K. (Salford)
*Millward (Hull K.R.)
Hogan, B. (Wigan)
Bridges (Featherstone R.)
Thompson (Featherstone R.)
Grayshon (Dewsbury) 1t
Irving (Wigan)
Norton (Castleford)
Sub: Hughes (Widnes)
    Adams (Widnes)

1977 Wales
Leeds: 29 Jan.
Lost 2-6
Fairbairn (Wigan) 1g
Wright (Widnes)
Holmes (Leeds)
Dyl (Leeds)
Jones (St. Helens)
Gill, K. (Salford)
*Millward (Hull K.R.)
Hogan, B. (Wigan)
Bridges (Featherstone R.)
Thompson (Featherstone R.)
Grayshon (Dewsbury)
Gorley, L. (Workington T.)
Laughton (Widnes)
Sub: Eckersley (St. Helens)
    Reilly (Castleford)

1977 France
Carcassonne: 20 Mar.
Lost 15-28
Fairbairn (Wigan) 3g
Dunn (Hull K.R.)
Hughes (Widnes)
Dyl (Leeds)
Smith, D. (Leeds) 1t
Gill, K. (Salford)
*Millward (Hull K.R.)
Coulman (Salford)
Ward (Leeds)
Farrar (Featherstone R.)
Lowe (Hull K.R.) 1t
Rose (Hull K.R.)
Norton (Castleford)
Sub: Holmes (Leeds)
    Nicholls (St. Helens) 1t

1978 France
Toulouse: 5 Mar.
Won 13-11
Fairbairn (Wigan) 2g
Wright (Widnes)
Hughes (Widnes) 2t
Dyl (Leeds)
Atkinson (Leeds)
*Millward (Hull K.R.)
Nash (Salford)
Harrison (Leeds)
Elwell (Widnes)
Nicholls (St. Helens)
Lowe (Hull K.R.)
Adams (Widnes)
Casey (Hull K.R.)
Sub: Holmes (Leeds) 1t
    Thompson (Bradford N.)

1978 Wales
St. Helens: 28 May
Won 60-13
Pimblett (St. Helens) 1t,9g
Wright (Widnes) 4t
Hughes (Widnes) 2t
Dyl (Leeds) 1t
Atkinson (Leeds) 2t
*Millward (Hull K.R.) 1t
Nash (Salford) 1t
Harrison (Leeds)
Elwell (Widnes)
Nicholls (St. Helens)
Rose (Hull K.R.)
Casey (Hull K.R.) 1t
Norton (Hull) 1t
Sub: Eckersley (St. Helens)
    Thompson (Bradford N.)

1979 Wales
Widnes: 16 Mar.
Won 15-7
Mumby (Bradford N.) 1t,1g
Wright (Widnes)
Glynn (St. Helens)
Smith, K. (Wakefield T.) 1t
Hughes (Widnes)
Kelly, K. (Warrington)
Stephens (Castleford)
Beverley (Workington T.)
Liptrot (St. Helens)
*Lockwood (Hull K.R.)
Martyn (Warrington)
Grayshon (Bradford N.)
Adams (Widnes)
Sub: Woods (Leigh) 1t,2g
    Watkinson (Hull K.R.)

1979 France
Warrington: 24 Mar.
Won 12-6
Mumby (Bradford N.)
Wright (Widnes)
Glynn (St. Helens)
Woods (Leigh) 3g
Hughes (Widnes) 1t
Evans (Featherstone R.)
Redfearn, A. (Bradford N.)
Tindall (Hull)
Liptrot (St. Helens)
*Lockwood (Hull K.R.)
Martyn (Warrington) 1t
Grayshon (Bradford N.)
Hogan, P. (Hull K.R.)
Sub: Banks (York)
    Szymala (Barrow)

1980 Wales
Hull K.R.: 29 Feb.
Won 26-9
Fairbairn (Wigan) 1t,6g
Wright (Widnes)
Joyner (Castleford) 1t
Smith, M. (Hull K.R.)
Drummond (Leigh)
Evans (Featherstone R.)
Holding (St. Helens)
Holdstock (Hull K.R.) 1t
*Ward (Leeds)
Rayne, Keith (Wakefield T.) 1t
Casey (Hull K.R.)
Gorley, P. (St. Helens)
Pinner (St. Helens) 2dg
Sub: Woods (Leigh)
    Grayshon (Bradford N.)

1980 France
Narbonne: 16 Mar.
Won 4-2
Fairbairn (Wigan)
Drummond (Leigh)
Smith, M. (Hull K.R.)
Joyner (Castleford)
Evans (Featherstone R.) 1t
Woods (Leigh)
Redfearn, A. (Bradford N.) 1dg
Holdstock (Hull K.R.)
*Ward (Leeds)
Rayne, Keith (Wakefield T.)
Grayshon (Bradford N.)
Smith, P. (Featherstone R.)
Pinner (St. Helens)
Sub: Gorley, P. (St. Helens)

1981 France

Leeds: 21 Feb.

Lost 1-5

*Fairbairn (Wigan) 1dg
Drummond (Leigh)
Joyner (Castleford)
Smith, M. (Hull K.R.)
Fenton (Castleford)
Kelly, K. (Warrington)
Walker (Whitehaven)
O'Neill (Wigan)
Ward (Leeds)
Case (Warrington)
Casey (Hull K.R.)
Potter (Warrington)
Pinner (St. Helens)
Sub: Woods (Leigh)
    Pattinson (Workington T.)

1984 Wales

Ebbw Vale: 14 Oct.

Won 28-9

Burke (Widnes) 1t,4g
Drummond (Leigh)
Schofield (Hull)
Hanley (Bradford N.) 1t
Clark (Hull K.R.) 3t
*Donlan (Leigh)
Cairns (Barrow)
Hobbs (Featherstone R.)
Beardmore, K. (Castleford)
Waddell (Blackpool B.)
Kelly, A. (Hull K.R.)
Goodway (Oldham)
Huddart (Whitehaven)
Sub: Ledger (St. Helens)
    Arkwright (St. Helens)

1995 France

Gateshead: 15 Feb.

Won 19-16

Gay (Hull)
Bentley (Halifax)
Pinkney (Keighley C.) 1t
Goddard (Castleford)
Cummins (Leeds) 1t
Wright (Wakefield T.) 1dg
Fox (Bradford N.) 3g
Broadbent (Sheffield E.) 1t
Jackson, L. (Sheffield E.)
McNamara (Hull)
Baldwin (Halifax)
Holgate (Workington T.)
*Powell, D. (Sheffield E.)
Sub: Smith, T. (Castleford)
    McCurrie (Widnes)
    Simpson (Bradford N.)
    Hilton (Warrington)

1981 Wales

Hull K.R.: 18 Mar.

Won 17-4

*Fairbairn (Wigan) 4g
Richardson (Castleford)
Joyner (Castleford) 1t
Smith, M. (Hull K.R.)
Fenton (Castleford)
Kelly, K. (Warrington) 1t
Nash (Salford)
Holdstock (Hull K.R.)
Ward (Leeds)
Casey (Hull K.R.)
Potter (Warrington)
Pattinson (Workington T.)
Norton (Hull)
Sub: Woods (Leigh) 1t
    Adams (Widnes)

1992 Wales

Swansea C. FC: 27 Nov.

Won 36-11

Spruce (Widnes) 1t
Hunte (St. Helens)
Connolly (St. Helens)
Newlove (Featherstone R.) 1t
Offiah (Wigan) 2t
*Schofield (Leeds) 1t
Ford (Castleford)
Crooks (Castleford) 1t,4g
Jackson, L. (Hull)
Molloy (Leeds)
Eyres (Widnes)
Clarke (Wigan)
Hanley (Leeds) 1t
Sub: Powell, D. (Sheffield E.)
    Joynt (St. Helens)
    Critchley (Salford)
    Busby (Hull)

1981 Wales

Cardiff C. FC: 8 Nov.

Won 20-15

Fairbairn (Hull K.R.) 1g
Drummond (Leigh) 1t
Smith, M. (Hull K.R.)
Dyl (Leeds)
Gill, H. (Wigan) 1t
Woods (Leigh) 3g
Nash (Salford)
Grayshon (Bradford N.) 1t
*Ward (Leeds)
Millington (Hull K.R.)
Lowe (Hull K.R.)
Gorley, P. (St. Helens) 1t
Norton (Hull)
Sub: Gorley, L. (Widnes)

1995 Wales

Cardiff C. FC: 1 Feb.

Lost 16-18

Gay (Hull) 1t
Robinson (Wigan) 1t
Powell, D. (Sheffield E.)
Newlove (Bradford N.)
Butt (Featherstone R.)
Schofield (Leeds)
Fox (Bradford N.) 1t,2g
Harrison (Halifax)
Russell (Castleford)
Howard (Leeds)
Farrell, Ant. (Sheffield E.)
Nickle (St. Helens)
*Clarke (Wigan)
Sub: Baldwin (Halifax)
    Cassidy (Wigan)
    McNamara (Hull)
    McCurrie (Widnes)

Hull's Dean Busby, a 1992 substitute against Wales.

Richard Eyres, a 1992 England debutant before switching to Wales in 1995.

ENGLAND REGISTER
● Since reintroduction in 1975

The following is a register of England appearances since the reintroduction of European and World Championship matches in 1975, but does not include the challenge match against Australia played after the 1975 World Championship.

Figures in brackets are the total appearances for England since 1975, with the plus sign indicating substitute appearances, e.g. (7+3).

A few players also played in the 1969-70 European Championship and this is shown as an additional total outside bracket, e.g. (11)2.

World Championship matches are in bold letters. Substitute appearances are in lower case letters.

A - Australia, F - France,
NZ - New Zealand, W - Wales.

ADAMS, Mick (3+2) Widnes: 1975 **NZ, a**; 1978 F; 1979 W; 1981 w
ARKWRIGHT, Chris (+1) St. Helens: 1984 w
ATKINSON, John (7)4 Leeds: 1975 W, **F, W, NZ, W**; 1978 F, W

BALDWIN, Simon (1+1) Halifax: 1995 w, F
BANKS, Barry (+1) York: 1979 f
BEARDMORE, Kevin (1) Castleford: 1984 W
BENTLEY, John (1) Halifax: 1995 F
BEVERLEY, Harry (1) Workington T: 1979 W
BRIDGES, John "Keith" (7) Featherstone R: 1975 **NZ, A, W, F, NZ, A**; 1977 W
BROADBENT, Paul (1) Sheffield E.: 1995 F
BURKE, Mick (1) Widnes: 1984 W
BUSBY, Dean (+1) Hull: 1992 w
BUTT, IKRAM (1) Featherstone R.: 1995 W

CAIRNS, David (1) Barrow: 1984 W
CASE, Brian (1) Warrington: 1981 F
CASEY, Len (5) Hull KR: 1978 F, W; 1980 W; 1981 F, W
CASSIDY, Mick (+1) Wigan: 1995w
CHARLTON, Paul (1) Salford: 1975 **F**
CHISNALL, Dave (3+1) Warrington: 1975 w, **F, W, NZ**
CHISNALL, Eric (3+1) St. Helens: 1975 F, **W, NZ, a**
CLARK, Garry (1) Hull KR: 1984 W
CLARKE, Phil (2) Wigan: 1992 W; 1995 W
CONNOLLY, Gary (1) St. Helens: 1992 W
COOKSON, Phil (2) Leeds: 1975 **NZ, A**
COULMAN, Mike (5) Salford: 1975 F, W, **W, A**; 1977 F
CRITCHLEY, Jason (+1) Salford: 1992 w
CROOKS, Lee (1) Castleford: 1992 W
CUMMINS, Francis (1) Leeds: 1995 F
CUNNINGHAM, John (2) Barrow: 1975 F, W

DONLAN, Steve (1) Leigh: 1984 W
DRUMMOND, Des (5) Leigh: 1980 W, F; 1981 F, W; 1984 W

DUNN, Ged (6) Hull KR: 1975 W, **A, F, NZ, A**; 1977 F
DYL, Les (12+1) Leeds: 1975 F, W, **F, W, NZ, A, nz, A**; 1977 W, F; 1978 F, W; 1981 W

ECKERSLEY, Dave (+5) St. Helens: 1975 f, **w, f**; Widnes: 1977 w; 1978 w
ELWELL, Keith (2) Widnes: 1978 F, W
EVANS, Steve (3) Featherstone R: 1979 F; 1980 W, F
EYRES, Richard (1) Widnes: 1992 W

FAIRBAIRN, George (15) Wigan: 1975 **W, NZ, A, W, F, NZ, A**; 1977 W, F; 1978 F; 1980 W, F; 1981 F, W; Hull KR: 1981 W
FARRAR, Vince (1) Featherstone R: 1977 F
FARRELL, Anthony (1) Sheffield E.: 1995 W
FENTON, Steve (2) Castleford: 1981 F, W
FIELDING, Keith (7) Salford: 1975 F, **F, W, NZ, A, W, F**
FORD, Mike (1) Castleford: 1992 W
FORSYTH, Colin (3) Bradford N: 1975 **W, F, NZ**
FOX, Deryck (2) Bradford N.: 1995 W, F

GAY, Richard (2) Hull: 1995 W, F
GILL, Henderson (1) Wigan: 1981 W
GILL, Ken (9+2) Salford: 1975 W, **F, w, NZ, a, W, F, NZ, A**; 1977 W, F
GLYNN, Peter (2) St. Helens: 1979 W, F
GODDARD, Richard (1) Castleford: 1995 F
GOODWAY, Andy (1) Oldham: 1984 W
GORLEY, Les (1+1) Workington T: 1977 W; Widnes: 1981 w
GORLEY, Peter (2+1) St. Helens: 1980 W, f; 1981 W
GRAY, John (3) Wigan: 1975 F, W, **F**
GRAYSHON, Jeff (9+1) Dewsbury: 1975 **W, F, NZ, A**; 1977 W; Bradford N: 1979 W, F; 1980 w, F; 1981 W

HANLEY, Ellery (2) Bradford N: 1984 W; Leeds: 1992 W
HARRISON, Karl (1) Halifax: 1995 W
HARRISON, Mick (2) Leeds: 1978 F, W
HILTON, Mark (+1) Warrington, 1995 f
HOBBS, David (1) Featherstone R: 1984 W
HOGAN, Brian (5) Wigan: 1975 **W, F, NZ, A**; 1977 W
HOGAN, Phil (1) Hull KR: 1979 F
HOLDING, Neil (1) St. Helens: 1980 W
HOLDSTOCK, Roy (3) Hull KR: 1980 W, F; 1981 W
HOLGATE, Stephen (1) Workington T.: 1995 F
HOLMES, John (5+2) Leeds: 1975 **W, F, NZ, A**;
    1977 W, f; 1978 f
HOWARD, Harvey (1) Leeds: 1995 W
HUDDART, Milton (1) Whitehaven: 1984 W
HUGHES, Eric (8+1) Widnes: 1975 **W, F, NZ, a**;
    1977 F; 1978 F, W; 1979 W, F
HUNTE, Alan (1) St. Helens: 1992 W

IRVING, Bob (3) Wigan: 1975 **W, F, A**

JACKSON, Lee (2) Hull: 1992 W; Sheffield E.: 1995 F
JACKSON, Phil (2) Bradford N: 1975 W, **F**
JONES, Les (1) St. Helens: 1977 W
JOYNER, John (4) Castleford: 1980 W, F; 1981 F, W
JOYNT, Chris (+1) St. Helens: 1992 w

KELLY, Andy (1) Hull KR: 1984 W
KELLY, Ken (3) Warrington: 1979 W; 1981 F, W

LAUGHTON, Doug (1) Widnes: 1977 W
LEDGER, Barry (+1) St. Helens: 1984 w
LIPTROT, Graham (2) St. Helens: 1979 W, F
LOCKWOOD, Brian (2)+1 Hull KR: 1979 W, F
LOWE, Phil (3)2 Hull KR: 1977 F; 1978 F; 1981 W

McCURRIE, Steve (+2) Widnes: 1995 w, f
McNAMARA Steve (1+1) Hull: 1995, w, F
MARTYN, Tommy (4+1) Warrington: 1975 W, **F**, w;
    1979 W, F
MILLINGTON, John (2) Hull KR: 1975 F; 1981 W
MILLWARD, Roger (13)3+1 Hull KR: 1975 F, W,
    F, W, A, W, F, NZ, A; 1977 W, F; 1978 F, W
MOLLOY, Steve (1) Leeds: 1992 W
MORGAN, Mick (3+3) Wakefield T: 1975 f, W, f, **W,
    nz, A**
MUMBY, Keith (2) Bradford N: 1979 W, F
MURPHY, Martin (1) Oldham: 1975 F

NASH, Steve (7) Featherstone R: 1975 **W, NZ, A**;
    Salford: 1978 F, W; 1981 W, W
NEWLOVE, Paul (2) Featherstone R: 1992 W;
    Bradford N.: 1995 W
NICHOLLS, George (7+4) St. Helens: 1975 F, **F, W,
    NZ, A, w, nz, f**; 1977 f; 1978 F, W

NICKLE, Sonny (1) St. Helens: 1995 W
NOONAN, Derek (3) Warrington: 1975 W, **F, W**
NORTON, Steve (11) Castleford: 1975 **W, NZ, A, W, F,
    NZ, A**; 1977 F; Hull: 1978 W; 1981 W, W

OFFIAH, Martin (1) Wigan: 1992 W
O'NEILL, Steve (1) Wigan: 1981 F

PATTINSON, Bill (1+1) Workington T: 1981 f, W
PHILBIN, Barry (1) Warrington: 1975 **F**
PIMBLETT, Geoff (1) St. Helens: 1978 W
PINKNEY, Nick (1) Keighley C.: 1995 F
PINNER, Harry (3) St. Helens: 1980 W, F; 1981 F
POTTER, Ian (2) Warrington: 1981 F, W
POWELL, Daryl (2+1) Sheffield E: 1992 w; 1995 W, F

RAYNE, Keith (2) Wakefield T: 1980 W, F
REDFEARN, Alan (2) Bradford N: 1979 F; 1980 F
REDFEARN, Dave (2) Bradford N: 1975 F, **A**
REILLY, Malcolm (+1)2 Castleford: 1977 w
RICHARDSON, Terry (1) Castleford: 1981 W
ROBINSON, Jason (1) Wigan: 1995 W
ROSE, Paul (2) Hull KR: 1977 F; 1978 W
RUSSELL, Richard (1) Castleford: 1995 W

SCHOFIELD, Garry (3) Hull: 1984 W; Leeds: 1992 W;
    1995 W
SHEARD, Les (1) Wakefield T: 1975 W
SIMPSON, Roger (+1) Bradford N.: 1995 f
SMITH, David (1) Leeds: 1977 F
SMITH, Keith (1) Wakefield T: 1979 W
SMITH, Mike (5) Hull KR: 1980 W, F; 1981 F, W, W
SMITH, Peter (1) Featherstone R: 1980 F
SMITH, Tony (+1) Castleford: 1995 f
SPRUCE, Stuart (1) Widnes: 1992 W
STEPHENS, Gary (1) Castleford: 1979 W
SZYMALA, Eddie (+1) Barrow: 1979 f

THOMPSON, Jimmy (2+1)1 Featherstone R: 1975 **A**;
    1977 W; Bradford N: 1978 w
TINDALL, Keith (1) Hull: 1979 F
TOPLISS, David (1) Wakefield T: 1975 F

WADDELL, Hugh (1) Blackpool B: 1984 W
WALKER, Arnold (1) Whitehaven: 1981 F
WALSH, John (3) St. Helens: 1975 F, **NZ, A**
WARD, David (6) Leeds: 1977 F; 1980 W, F;
    1981 F, W, W
WATKINSON, David (+1) Hull KR: 1977 w
WOODS, John (3+4) Leigh: 1979 w, F; 1980 w, F;
    1981 f, w, W
WRIGHT, Nigel (1) Wakefield T.: 1995 F
WRIGHT, Stuart (7) Wigan: 1975 **NZ**; Widnes: 1977 W;
    1978 F, W; 1979 W, F; 1980 W

WALES TEAMS ● From 1975, when it revived after a gap of five years and continued until 1984, before folding again. Revived in 1991.

1975 France
Swansea: 16 Feb.
Won 21-8
Francis (Wigan)
Mathias (St. Helens) 1t
Willicombe (Wigan)
Wilson, F. (St. Helens)
Bevan (Warrington) 2t
*Watkins (Salford) 1dg
Banner (Salford)
Mills (Widnes) 1t
Fisher (Leeds)
Mantle (St. Helens)
Nicholas (Warrington)
Dixon (Salford)
Coslett (St. Helens) 4g
Sub: Gallacher (Keighley)

1975 England
Salford: 25 Feb.
Lost 8-12
Francis (Wigan)
Mathias (St. Helens)
Willicombe (Wigan)
Wilson, F. (St. Helens)
Bevan (Warrington)
*Watkins (Salford) 1t,1g,1dg
Banner (Salford)
Mills (Widnes)
Evans (Swinton)
Mantle (St. Helens)
Dixon (Salford)
Gallacher (Keighley)
Coslett (St. Helens) 1g
Sub: Turner (Hull K.R.)
    Nicholas (Warrington)

1975 France (WC)
Toulouse: 2 Mar.
Lost 7-14
Francis (Wigan)
Mathias (St. Helens)
Willicombe (Wigan)
Wilson, F. (St. Helens) 1t
Richards (Salford)
*Watkins (Salford)
Banner (Salford)
Murphy (Bradford N.)
Evans (Swinton)
Butler (Swinton)
Dixon (Salford)
Mantle (St. Helens)
Coslett (St. Helens) 2g
Sub: Wallace (York)

1975 England (WC)
Brisbane: 10 June
Won 12-7
Francis (Wigan)
Sullivan, C. (Hull K.R.) 1t
*Watkins (Salford) 3g
Willicombe (Wigan)
Mathias (St. Helens)
Treasure (Oldham) 1t
Banner (Salford)
Mills (Widnes)
Fisher (Leeds)
Wanbon (Warrington)
Dixon (Salford)
Cunningham, E. (St. Helens)
Coslett (St. Helens)
Sub: Wilson, F. (St. Helens)
    Mantle (St. Helens)

1975 Australia (WC)
Sydney: 14 June
Lost 13-30
Francis (Wigan)
Sullivan, C. (Hull K.R.)
*Watkins (Salford) 5g
Willicombe (Wigan)
Mathias (St. Helens)
Turner (Hull K.R.)
Treasure (Oldham)
Mills (Widnes)
Fisher (Leeds) 1t
Wanbon (Warrington)
Mantle (St. Helens)
Cunningham, E. (St. Helens)
Coslett (St. Helens)
Sub: Wilson, F. (St. Helens)
    Rowe (Blackpool B.)

1975 New Zealand (WC)
Auckland: 28 June
Lost 8-13
Francis (Wigan) 1t
Sullivan, C. (Hull K.R.)
*Watkins (Salford) 1g
Willicombe (Wigan)
Mathias (St. Helens)
Treasure (Oldham)
Banner (Salford)
Mills (Widnes) 1t
Fisher (Leeds)
Wanbon (Warrington)
Mantle (St. Helens)
Dixon (Salford)
Coslett (St. Helens)
Sub: Butler (Swinton)

1975 England (WC)
Warrington: 20 Sep.
Lost 16-22
Francis (Wigan)
Sullivan, C. (Hull K.R.)
*Watkins (Salford) 5g
Wilson, F. (St. Helens)
Bevan (Warrington)
Treasure (Oldham)
Banner (Salford) 1t
Mantle (St. Helens)
Fisher (Castleford)
James (St. Helens)
Cunningham, E. (St. Helens)
Gregory (Wigan)
Coslett (St. Helens) 1t
Sub: Turner (Hull K.R.)
    Rowe (Blackpool B.)

1975 Australia (WC)
Swansea: 19 Oct.
Lost 6-18
*Watkins (Salford) 3g
Mathias (St. Helens)
Francis (Wigan)
Wilson, F. (St. Helens)
Bevan (Warrington)
Turner (Hull K.R.)
Banner (Featherstone R.)
Mills (Widnes)
Fisher (Castleford)
Mantle (St. Helens)
Cunningham, E. (St. Helens)
Dixon (Salford)
Coslett (St. Helens)
Sub: Rowe (Blackpool B.)

1975 New Zealand (WC)
Swansea: 2 Nov.
Won 25-24
*Watkins (Salford) 5g
Mathias (St. Helens)
Wilson, F. (St. Helens)
Willicombe (Wigan) 1t
Bevan (Warrington) 1t
Francis (Wigan) 2t
Banner (Featherstone R.)
Mills (Widnes)
Fisher (Castleford)
Murphy (Bradford N.)
Mantle (St. Helens) 1t
Gallacher (Keighley)
Gregory (Wigan)
Sub: Jones, C. (Leigh)

1975 France (WC)

Salford: 6 Nov.

Won 23-2

*Watkins (Salford) 4g
Mathias (St. Helens)
Wilson, F. (St. Helens)
Willicombe (Wigan) 1t
Bevan (Warrington) 1t
Francis (Wigan) 1t
Banner (Featherstone R.) 1t
Mantle (St. Helens)
Evans (Swinton)
Murphy (Bradford N.)
Gregory (Wigan) 1t
Gallacher (Keighley)
Jones, C. (Leigh)
Sub: Turner (Hull K.R.)
     Butler (Warrington)

1978 France

Widnes: 15 Jan.

Won 29-7

Risman (Workington T.)
Mathias (St. Helens) 1t
Willicombe (Wigan)
Cunningham, E. (St. Helens) 1t
Sullivan, C. (Hull K.R.) 1t
*Francis (St. Helens) 1t
Woods (Widnes) 7g
Mills (Widnes) 1t
Evans (Salford)
James (St. Helens)
Nicholas (Warrington)
Shaw (Widnes)
Dixon (Salford)
Sub: Pritchard (Barrow)
     Jones, C. (Leigh)

1979 France

Narbonne: 4 Feb.

Lost 8-15

Box (Featherstone R.)
Sullivan, C. (Hull K.R.)
*Watkins (Salford) 2g,1dg
Bevan (Warrington)
Juliff (Wakefield T.)
Francis (St. Helens)
Woods (Rochdale H.)
Murphy (St. Jacques)
Cunningham, T. (Warrington)
James (St. Helens)
Skerrett (Wakefield T.)
Rowe (Huddersfield) 1t
Mathias (St. Helens)
Sub: Johns (Salford)
     Risman (Workington T.)

1977 England

Leeds: 29 Jan.

Won 6-2

*Watkins (Salford)
Mathias (St. Helens)
Bevan (Warrington)
Cunningham, E. (St. Helens) 1t
Richards (Salford)
Francis (Wigan)
Woods (Widnes) 1g
Mills (Workington T.)
Fisher (Castleford)
Mantle (Salford)
Nicholas (Warrington)
Dixon (Salford)
Rowe (Huddersfield) 1dg
Sub: Wilkins (Workington T.)

1978 England

St. Helens: 28 May

Lost 13-60

Watkins (Salford) 1g
Mathias (St. Helens)
Turner (Hull)
Willicombe (Wigan) 1t
Sullivan, C. (Hull K.R.) 1t
*Francis (St. Helens)
Woods (Widnes) 1g
Mills (Widnes)
Evans (Salford)
James (St. Helens) 1t
Davies, F. (New Hunslet)
Mantle (Leigh)
Cunningham, E. (St. Helens)
Sub: Pritchard (Barrow)
     Jones, C. (Leigh)

1979 England

Widnes: 16 Mar.

Lost 7-15

Box (Featherstone R.) 1t,2g
Sullivan, C. (Hull K.R.)
Risman (Workington T.)
Bevan (Warrington)
Juliff (Wakefield T.)
*Francis (St. Helens)
Woods (Rochdale H.)
Mills (Widnes)
Cunningham, T. (Warrington)
James (St. Helens)
Skerrett (Wakefield T.)
Rowe (Huddersfield)
Mathias (St. Helens)
Sub: Prendiville (Hull)
     Nicholas (Warrington)

1977 France

Toulouse: 20 Feb.

Lost 2-13

Wilkins (Workington T.)
Mathias (St. Helens)
Bevan (Warrington)
Treasure (Oldham)
Sullivan, C. (Hull K.R.)
*Francis (Wigan)
Woods (Widnes) 1g
Mills (Widnes)
Fisher (Castleford)
Butler (Warrington)
Nicholas (Warrington)
Dixon (Salford)
Rowe (Huddersfield)
Sub: Curling (Warrington)
     Murphy (Bradford N.)

1978 Australia

Swansea: 15 Oct.

Lost 3-8

*Watkins (Salford) 1g,1dg
Sullivan, C. (Hull K.R.)
Willicombe (Wigan)
Cunningham, E. (St. Helens)
Bevan (Warrington)
Francis (St. Helens)
Woods (Widnes)
Mills (Widnes)
Fisher (Bradford N.)
James (St. Helens)
Shaw (Widnes)
Skerrett (Wakefield T.)
Mathias (St. Helens)

1980 France

Widnes: 26 Jan.

Lost 7-21

Box (Featherstone R.)
Juliff (Wakefield T.)
Diamond (Wakefield T.) 2g
Bevan (Warrington) 1t
Camilleri (Barrow)
*Francis (Oldham)
Flowers (Wigan)
James (St. Helens)
Parry (Blackpool B.)
Shaw (Widnes)
McJennett (Barrow)
Skerrett (Wakefield T.)
Mathias (St. Helens)
Sub: Griffiths, C. (St. Helens)
     Seldon (St. Helens)

1980 England
Hull K.R.: 29 Feb.
Lost 9-26
Box (Featherstone R.)
Prendiville (Hull)
Walters (Hull)
*Francis (Oldham)
Juliff (Wakefield T.) 1t
Woods (Hull) 3g
Flowers (Wigan)
James (St. Helens)
Parry (Blackpool B.)
Shaw (Widnes)
Seldon (St. Helens)
Bevan (Warrington)
Mathias (St. Helens)
Sub: Diamond (Wakefield T.)

1981 England
Cardiff C. FC: 8 Nov.
Lost 15-20
Pritchard (Cardiff C.)
Cambriani (Fulham)
Bayliss (St. Helens)
Fenwick (Cardiff C.) 4g
*Bevan (Warrington)
Wilson, D. (Swinton) 1dg
Flowers (Wigan) 1t
James (St. Helens)
Parry (Blackpool B.)
David (Cardiff C.)
Shaw (Widnes)
Herdman (Fulham)
Ringer (Cardiff C.)
Sub: Prendiville (Hull) 1t
        Owen, R. (St. Helens)

1991 Papua New Guinea
Swansea C. FC: 27 Oct.
Won 68-0
Ford (Leeds) 3t
Devereux (Widnes)
Bateman (Warrington) 1t
*Davies, J. (Widnes) 2t,8g
Sullivan, A. (St. Helens) 2t
Griffiths, J. (St. Helens) 1t
Ellis (Warrington) 1t
Jones, M. (Hull)
Williams, Barry (Carlisle)
Young (Salford)
Ackerman (Carlisle) 1t
Moriarty (Widnes)
Bishop (Hull K.R.) 1t
Sub: Hadley (Salford) 1t
        Phillips (Warrington)
        Silva (Halifax)
        Pearce (Scarborough P.)

1981 France
Narbonne: 31 Jan.
Lost 5-23
Box (Wakefield T.)
Cambriani (Fulham)
Diamond (Wakefield T.)
*Bevan (Warrington)
Prendiville (Hull)
Wilson, D. (Swinton) 1g
Woods (Hull)
James (St. Helens)
Parry (Blackpool B.) 1t
Owen, G. (Oldham)
Skerrett (Hull)
Juliff (Wakefield T.)
Mathias (St. Helens)
Sub: Griffiths, C. (St. Helens)
        Owen, R. (St. Helens)

1982 Australia
Cardiff C. FC: 24 Oct.
Lost 7-37
Hopkins (Workington T.) 1g
Camilleri (Widnes)
Fenwick (Cardiff C.) 1g
*Bevan (Warrington)
Prendiville (Hull)
Hallett (Cardiff C.)
Williams, Brynmor (Cardiff C.) 1t
Shaw (Wigan)
Parry (Blackpool B.)
David (Cardiff C.)
Herdman (Fulham)
Juliff (Wigan)
Ringer (Cardiff C.)
Sub: McJennett (Barrow)

1992 France
Swansea C. FC: 22 Mar.
Won 35-6
Ford (Leeds) 1t
Devereux (Widnes) 1t
Bateman (Warrington) 1t
*Davies, J. (Widnes) 1t,5g,1dg
Sullivan, A. (St. Helens)
Griffiths, J. (St. Helens)
Ellis (Warrington)
Jones, M. (Hull)
Williams, Barry (Carlisle) 1t
Young (Salford)
Ackerman (Carlisle)
Marlow (Hull)
Bishop (Hull K.R.)
Sub: Hadley (Salford)
        Phillips (Warrington) 1t
        Cordle (Bradford N.)
        Pearce (Ryedale-York)

1981 England
Hull K.R.: 18 Mar.
Lost 4-17
Rule (Salford) 2g
Cambriani (Fulham)
Walters (Hull)
*Bevan (Warrington)
Juliff (Wakefield T.)
Wilson, D. (Swinton)
Woods (Hull)
James (St. Helens)
Parry (Blackpool B.)
Owen, G. (Oldham)
Skerrett (Hull)
Dixon (Hull K.R.)
Mathias (St. Helens)
Sub: Herdman (Fulham)

1984 England
Ebbw Vale: 14 Oct.
Lost 9-28
Hallett (Bridgend) 2g
Camilleri (Bridgend)
Prendiville (Hull)
Davies, M. (Bridgend)
Ford (Warrington)
Wilson, D. (Swinton) 1t,1dg
Flowers (Bridgend)
*Skerrett (Hull)
Preece (Bradford N.)
Shaw (Wigan)
McJennett (Barrow)
O'Brien (Bridgend)
Juliff (Wigan)
Sub: Johns (Blackpool B.)
        Walters (Bridgend)

1992 England
Swansea C. FC: 27 Nov.
Lost 11-36
Ford (Salford)
Cordle (Bradford N.)
Bateman (Warrington)
Devereux (Widnes) 1g
Sullivan, A. (St. Helens)
Griffiths, J. (St. Helens) 1t
Ellis (Warrington) 1dg
Jones, M. (Hull) 1t
Bishop (London C.)
*Young (Salford)
Moriarty (Widnes)
Marlow (Hull)
Ackerman (Salford)
Sub: Hadley (Widnes)
        Phillips (Warrington)
        Pearce (Ryedale-York)
        Moran (Leigh)

1992 France
Perpignan: 13 Dec.
Won 19-18
Ford (Salford)
Hadley (Widnes)
Bateman (Warrington) 1t
Devereux (Widnes) 1t
Sullivan, A. (St. Helens)
Pearce (Ryedale-York) 3g, 1dg
Ellis (Warrington)
Marlow (Hull)
Bishop (London C.)
*Young (Salford)
Moriarty (Widnes)
Phillips (Warrington)
Ackerman (Salford) 1t
Sub: Stevens (Hull)
    Moran (Leigh)
    Kennett (Swinton)
    Williams, P. (Salford)

1993 New Zealand
Swansea C. FC: 3 Oct.
Lost 19-24
Ford (Salford)
Cordle (Bradford N.) 2t
Bateman (Warrington)
Devereux (Widnes)
Sullivan, A. (St. Helens)
*Davies, J. (Warrington) 5g
Ellis (Warrington)
Jones, M. (Hull)
Williams, Barry (Carlisle)
Young (Salford)
Marlow (Wakefield T.)
Phillips (Warrington)
Griffiths, J. (St. Helens) 1dg
Sub: Hadley (Widnes)
    Ackerman (Cardiff I. ARL)

1994 France
Cardiff C. FC: 4 Mar.
Won 13-12
Ford (Salford)
Cordle (Bradford N.)
Bateman (Warrington)
*Davies, J. (Warrington) 4g, 1dg
Sullivan, A. (St. Helens)
Griffiths, J. (St. Helens)
Ellis (Warrington)
Jones, M. (Hull)
Williams, Barry (Carlisle)
Young (Salford)
Moriarty (Widnes)
Phillips (Warrington)
Perrett (Halifax)
Sub: Powell, D. (Bradford N.)
    Marlow (Wakefield T.)
    Webster (Salford) 1t

1994 Australia
Cardiff C. FC: 30 Oct.
Lost 4-46
Ford (Salford)
Sullivan, A. (St. Helens)
Gibbs, (St. Helens)
Devereux (Widnes)
Hadley (Widnes)
Harris (Warrington)
Ellis (Warrington)
*Young (Salford)
Griffiths (St. Helens)
Marlow (Wakefield T.)
Moriarty (Halifax)
Phillips (Warrington)
Perrett (Halifax)
Sub: Cordle (Bradford N.)
    Lee (Warrington)
    Webster (Salford)
    Powell, D. (Bradford N.) 1t

1995 England
Cardiff C. FC: 1 Feb.
Won 18-16
Atcheson (Wigan)
Ford (Salford)
Bateman (Warrington)
Harris (Warrington)
Sullivan (St. Helens)
*Davies (Warrington) 4g, 2dg
Ellis (Workington T.) 2t
Skerrett, K. (Wigan)
Hall (Wigan)
Young (Salford)
Moriarty (Halifax)
Perrett (Halifax)
Eyres (Leeds)
Sub: Cowie (Wigan)
    Phillips (Workington T.)

1995 France
Carcassonne: 5 Mar.
Won 22-10
Atcheson (Wigan) 1t
Sullivan, A. (St. Helens)
Devereux (Widnes)
Bateman (Warrington) 2t
Harris (Warrington) 1t
*Davies (Warrington) 3g
Ellis (Workington T.)
Skerrett, K. (Wigan)
Hall (Wigan)
Young (Salford)
Moriarty (Halifax)
Perrett (Halifax)
Eyres (Leeds)
Sub: Ford (Salford)
    Cowie (Wigan)
    Hadley (Widnes)
    Phillips (Workington T.)

Skipper Jonathan Davies, third from the left, leads the Welsh celebrations after their John Smith's triumph over England.

WALES REGISTER
● Since 1975

Figures in brackets are the total appearances for Wales since 1975, with the plus sign indicating substitute appearances, e.g. (7+3).

A few players also played in the 1969-70 European Championship and this is shown as an additional total outside bracket, e.g. (11)2.

World Championship matches are in bold letters. Substitute appearances are in lower case letters. A - Australia, E - England, F - France, NZ - New Zealand, P - Papua New Guinea.

ACKERMAN, Rob (4+1) Carlisle: 1991 P; 1992 F; Salford: 1992 E, F; Cardiff I. ARL: 1993 nz

ATCHESON, Paul (2) Wigan: 1995 E, F

BANNER, Peter (9) Salford: 1975 F, E, **F, E, NZ**; Featherstone R: 1975 **E, A, NZ, F**

BATEMAN, Allan (8) Warrington: 1991 P; 1992 F, E, F; 1993 NZ; 1994 F; 1995 E, F

BAYLISS, Steve (1) St. Helens: 1981 E

BEVAN, John (17) Warrington: 1975 F, E, **E, A, NZ, F**; 1977 E, F; 1978 A; 1979 F, E; 1980 F, E; 1981 F, E, E; 1982 A

BISHOP, David (4) Hull KR: 1991 P; 1992 F; London C: 1992 E, F

BOX, Harold (5) Featherstone R: 1979 F, E; 1980 F, E; Wakefield T: 1981 F

BUTLER, Brian (2+2) Swinton: 1975 **F, nz**; Warrington: 1975 f; 1977 F

CAMBRIANI, Adrian (3) Fulham: 1981 F, E, E

CAMILLERI, Chris (3) Barrow: 1980 F; Widnes: 1982 A; Bridgend: 1984 E

CORDLE, Gerald (3+2) Bradford N: 1991 p; 1992 E; 1993 NZ; 1994 F, a

COSLETT, Kel (8)2 St. Helens: 1975 F, E, **F, E, A, NZ, E, A**

COWIE, Neil (+2) Wigan: 1995 e, f

CUNNINGHAM, Eddie (8) St. Helens: 1975 **E, A, E, A**; 1977 E; 1978 F, E, A

CUNNINGHAM, Tommy (2) Warrington: 1979 F, E

CURLING, Dennis (+1) Warrington: 1977 f

DAVID, Tommy (2) Cardiff C: 1981 E; 1982 A

DAVIES, Frank (1) New Hunslet: 1978 E

DAVIES, Jonathan (6) Widnes: 1991 P; 1992 F; Warrington: 1993 NZ; 1994 F; 1995 E, F

DAVIES, Mike (1) Bridgend: 1984 E

DEVEREUX, John (7) Widnes: 1991 P; 1992 F, E, F; 1993 NZ; 1994 A; 1995 F

DIAMOND, Steve (2+1) Wakefield T: 1980 F, e; 1981 F

DIXON, Colin (10)3 Salford: 1975 F, E, **F, E, NZ, A**; 1977 E, F; 1978 F; Hull KR: 1981 E

ELLIS, Kevin (9) Warrington: 1991 P; 1992 F, E, F; 1993 NZ; 1994 F; A; Workington T. 1995 E, F

EVANS, Richard (5) Swinton: 1975 E, **F, F**; 1978 F; Salford: 1978 E

EYRES, Richard (2) Leeds: 1995 E, F

FENWICK, Steve (2) Cardiff C: 1981 E; 1982 A

FISHER, Tony (10)4 Leeds: 1975 F, **E, A, NZ**; Castleford: 1975 **E, A, NZ**; 1977 E, F; Bradford N: 1978 A

FLOWERS, Ness (4) Wigan: 1980 F, E; 1981 E; Bridgend: 1984 E

FORD, Phil (9+1) Warrington: 1984 E; Leeds: 1991 P; 1992 F; Salford: 1992 E, F; 1993 NZ; 1994 F, A; 1995 E, f

FRANCIS, Bill (19) Wigan: 1975 F, E, **F, E, A, NZ, E, A, NZ, F**; 1977 E, F; St. Helens: 1978 F, E, A; 1979 F, E; Oldham: 1980 F, E

GALLACHER, Stuart (3+1) Keighley: 1975 f, E, **NZ, F**

GIBBS, Scott (1) St. Helens: 1994 A

GREGORY, Brian (3) Wigan: 1975 **E, NZ, F**

GRIFFITHS, Clive (+2) St. Helens: 1980 f; 1981 f

GRIFFITHS, Jonathan (6) St. Helens: 1991 P; 1992 F, E; 1993 NZ; 1994 F, A

HADLEY, Adrian (2+5) Salford: 1991 p; 1992 f; Widnes: 1992 e, F; 1993 nz; 1994 A; 1995 f

HALL, Martin (2) Wigan: 1995 E, F

HALLETT, Lynn (2) Cardiff C: 1982 A; Bridgend: 1984 E

HARRIS, Iestyn (3) Warrington: 1994 A, 1995 E, F

HERDMAN, Martin (2+1) Fulham: 1981 e, E; 1982 A

HOPKINS, Lyn (1) Workington T: 1982 A

JAMES, Mel (11) St. Helens: 1975 **E**; 1978 F, E, A; 1979 F, E; 1980 F, E; 1981 F, E, E

JOHNS, Graeme (+2) Salford: 1979 f; Blackpool B: 1984 e

JONES, Clive (1+3) Leigh: 1975 **nz, F**; 1978 f, e

JONES, Mark (5) Hull: 1991 P; 1992 F, E; 1993 NZ; 1994 F

JULIFF, Brian (8) Wakefield T: 1979 F, E; 1980 F, E; 1981 F, E; Wigan: 1982 A; 1984 E

KENNETT, Paul (+1) Swinton: 1992 f

LEE, Jason (+1) Warrington: 1994 a

McJENNETT, Mark (2+1) Barrow: 1980 F; 1982 a; 1984 E

MANTLE, John (11+1)3 St. Helens: 1975 F, E, **F, e, A, NZ, E, A, NZ, F**; 1977 E; 1978 E

MARLOW, Ian (5+1) Hull: 1992 F, E, F; Wakefield T: 1993 NZ; 1994 f, A

MATHIAS, Roy (20) St. Helens: 1975 F, E, **F, E, A, NZ, A, NZ, F**; 1977 E, F; 1978 F, E, A; 1979 F, E; 1980 F, E; 1981 F, E

MILLS, Jim (13)4 Widnes: 1975 F, E, **E, A, NZ, A, NZ**; 1977 E, F; 1978 F, E, A; 1979 E

MORAN, Mark (+2) Leigh: 1992 e, f

MORIARTY, Paul (7) Widnes: 1991 P; 1992 E, F; 1994 F; Halifax: 1994 A; 1995 E, F

MURPHY, Mick (4+1) Bradford N: 1975 **F, NZ, F**; 1977 f; St. Jacques, France: 1979 F

NICHOLAS, Mike (4+2) Warrington: 1975 F, e; 1977 E, F; 1978 F; 1979 e

O'BRIEN, Chris (1) Bridgend: 1984 E

OWEN, Gareth (2) Oldham: 1981 E, F

OWEN, Roger (+2) St. Helens: 1981 f, e

PARRY, Donald (6) Blackpool B: 1980 F, E; 1981 F, E, E; 1982 A

PEARCE, Gary (1+3) Scarborough P: 1991 p; Ryedale-York: 1992 f, e, F

PERRETT, Mark (4) Halifax: 1994 F, A; 1995 E, F

PHILLIPS, Rowland (4+5) Warrington: 1991 p; 1992 f, e, F; 1993 NZ; 1994 F, A; Workington T.: 1995 e, f

POWELL, Daio (+2) Bradford N: 1994 f, a

PREECE, Chris (1) Bradford N: 1984 E

PRENDIVILLE, Paul (4+2) Hull: 1979 e; 1980 E; 1981 F, e; 1982 A; 1984 E

PRITCHARD, Gordon (1+2) Barrow: 1978 f, e; Cardiff C: 1981 E

RICHARDS, Maurice (2)1 Salford: 1975 **F**; 1977 E

RINGER, Paul (2) Cardiff C: 1981 E; 1982 A

RISMAN, John (2+1) Workington T: 1978 F; 1979 f, E

ROWE, Peter (4+3)2 Blackpool B: 1975 a, e, a; Huddersfield: 1977 F, E; 1979 F, E

RULE, Steve (1) Salford: 1981 E

SELDON, Chris (1+1) St. Helens: 1980 f, E

SHAW, Glyn (7) Widnes: 1978 F, A; 1980 F, E; 1981 E; Wigan: 1982 A; 1984 E

SILVA, Matthew (+1) Halifax: 1991 p

SKERRETT, Kelvin (2) Wigan: 1995 E, F

SKERRETT, Trevor (7) Wakefield T: 1978 A; 1979 F, E; 1980 F; Hull: 1981 F, E; 1984 E

STEVENS, Ian (+1) Hull: 1992 f

SULLIVAN, Anthony (9) St. Helens: 1991 P; 1992 F, E, F; 1993 NZ; 1994 F, A: 1995 E, F

SULLIVAN, Clive (10)4 Hull KR: 1975 **E, A, NZ, E**; 1977 F; 1978 F, E, A; 1979 F, E

Iestyn Harris is subject to a double Australian tackle by Brad Fittler (upper) and Glenn Lazarus on his debut for Wales, at the age of 18, in the John Smith's International at Cardiff in October 1994.

TREASURE, David (5) Oldham: 1975 **E, A, NZ, E**; 1977 F

TURNER, Glyn (3+3) Hull KR: 1975 e, **A, e, A, f**; Hull: 1978 E

WALLACE, Richard (+1) York: 1975 f

WALTERS, Graham (2+1) Hull: 1980 E; 1981 E; Bridgend 1984 e

WANBON, Bobby (3)3+1 Warrington: 1975 **E, A, NZ**

WATKINS, David (14) Salford: 1975 F, E, **F, E, A, NZ, E, A, NZ, F**; 1977 E; 1978 E, A; 1979 F

WEBSTER, Richard (+2) Salford: 1994 f, a

WILKINS, Ray (1+1) Workington T: 1977 e, F

WILLIAMS, Barry (4) Carlisle: 1991 P; 1992 F; 1993 NZ; 1994 F

WILLIAMS, Brynmor (1) Cardiff C: 1982 A

WILLIAMS, Peter (+1) Salford: 1992 f

WILLICOMBE, David (11)+2 Wigan: 1975 F, E, **F, E, A, NZ, NZ, F**; 1978 F, E, A

WILSON, Danny (4) Swinton: 1981 F, E, E; 1984 E

WILSON, Frank (7+2)4 St. Helens: 1975 F, E, **F, e, a, E, A, NZ, F**

WOODS, Paul (10) Widnes: 1977 E, F; 1978 F, E, A; Rochdale H: 1979 F, E; Hull: 1980 E; 1981 F, E

YOUNG, David (9) Salford: 1991 P; 1992 F, E, F; 1993 NZ; 1994 F, A; 1995 E, F

ENGLAND SYNOPSIS

	P	W	D	L	F	A
v. FRANCE						
Euro'n Championship	27	18	2	7	341	307
World Cup	2	2	0	0	68	4
Other matches	1	1	0	0	18	6
Totals	30	21	2	7	427	317
v. WALES						
Euro'n Championship	26	16	0	10	459	249
World Championship	2	1	0	1	29	28
Other matches	32	25	2	5	670	429
Totals	60	42	2	16	1,158	706
v. AUSTRALIA						
World Championship	2	1	1	0	26	23
Other matches	9	5	1	3	93	153
Totals	11	6	2	3	119	176
v. NEW ZEALAND						
World Championship	2	1	1	0	44	29
Others	1	1	0	0	18	16
Totals	3	2	1	0	62	45
v. PAPUA NEW GUINEA						
Other matches	1	1	0	0	40	12
v. OTHER NATIONALITIES						
Euro'n Championship	6	2	0	4	106	152
Other matches	10	6	1	3	230	173
Totals	16	8	1	7	336	325
GRAND TOTALS	**121**	**80**	**8**	**33**	**2,142**	**1,581**

WALES SYNOPSIS

	P	W	D	L	F	A
v. ENGLAND						
Euro'n Championship	26	10	0	16	249	459
World Championship	2	1	0	1	28	29
Other matches	32	5	2	25	429	670
Totals	60	16	2	42	706	1,158
v. FRANCE						
Euro'n Championship	26	10	0	16	356	377
World Championship	2	1	0	1	30	16
Other matches	6	3	0	3	91	101
Totals	34	14	0	20	477	494
v. AUSTRALIA						
World Championship	2	0	0	2	19	48
Other matches	8	0	0	8	84	229
Totals	10	0	0	10	103	277
v. NEW ZEALAND						
World Championship	2	1	0	1	33	37
Other matches	5	2	0	3	85	83
Totals	7	3	0	4	118	120
v. PAPUA NEW GUINEA						
Other matches	1	1	0	0	68	0
v. OTHER NATIONALITIES						
Euro'n Championship	5	1	0	4	60	101
GRAND TOTALS	**117**	**35**	**2**	**80**	**1,532**	**2,150**

Great Britain Under-21 debutant Andy Hay, of Castleford, off-loads in the 1995 John Smith's International with France at Albi.

UNDER-21s

Great Britain Under-21s crashed to a double defeat in a first-ever encounter with Australia and to their French counterparts.

The young Lions confronted the 1994 Kangaroos in the penultimate fixture of their 14-match John Smith's Tour, going down 54-10 despite a spirited performance at Gateshead International Stadium.

Four months later, the Under-21s – in the charge of Great Britain assistant coach Gary Hetherington – travelled to Albi to suffer a sixth defeat in 19 meetings with the French, a late drop goal clinching a 17-16 Gallic victory.

Seven new Under-21 caps were included in the starting line-up for the Australian tour game, which attracted a North-East crowd of more than 4,000, the team details being featured in the chapter 1994 KANGAROOS.

Having lost only the first John Smith's Test at Wembley and in high-scoring form, the green-and-golds were expected to open the floodgates. True to form, the Kangaroos scored two tries in the opening nine minutes, both from centre Terry Hill.

But the young Lions rallied and kept the score to a respectable 18-4 at the interval, St. Helens full back Steve Prescott scoring a try on his way to taking the home Man-of-the-Match award.

Prescott added three goals in the second half as Australia confirmed their superiority, especially as the youngsters tired in the last quarter, to run in a total of nine tries. Second row forward David Furner added nine goals to take the Kangaroos through the 500-point barrier for the tour.

Debutants Ryan Sheridan, the Sheffield Eagles scrum half, and Oldham hooker John Clarke were also impressive in the hard working Under-21 side.

In the Albi encouter, the Under-21s were sent reeling to their first defeat against France since 1991 by former Workington Town player Vincent Banet. The scrum half had played two first team matches for the Derwent Park outfit earlier in the season.

Banet broke the 16-16 deadlock four minutes from time with a close-range drop goal, his second attempt in as many minutes.

The young Britons had looked on course for a 14th Anglo-French victory when they led 14-10 at half-time. Britain fielded five players who had performed in England's 19-16 defeat of France at Gateshead the previous month, while France had only two senior international on view, plus several aged under-23.

Leigh loose forward Scott Martin opened the scoring after five minutes with a try created by Castleford duo Chris Smith and Richard Goddard. France replied within seven minutes, against the run of play, when Catalan star Banet chipped ahead for Limoux centre Pierre Jammes to race in for the touchdown.

Hull scrum half Mark Hewitt added his third goal to give the visitors a 10-4 lead, which was short-lived when France scored the best try of the match. St. Gaudens centre Arnaud Dulec swept round out-of-position winger Smith and Jammes added the goal to level the scores at 10-10.

Two minutes before the break, Britain were back in front when Warrington prop Mark Hilton, Halifax hooker Paul Rowley and Hewitt combined to feed Wakefield Trinity centre Adrian Flynn, who burst through three tackles to score wide on the left. Hewitt stretched their lead with a 57th minute penalty before the French staged a match-winning revival.

Substitute second row forward Jerome Bisson scored within five minutes of coming on midway through the second half, Dulec's conversion levelling the scores with 13 minutes left. Britain still looked capable of victory with two 40-metre runs from Huddersfield substitute Simon Reynolds and a last ditch sweeping passing movement involving nearly every player, but Banet's drop goal sealed their fate.

JOHN SMITH'S INTERNATIONAL
4 March 1995   **Albi**

GREAT BRITAIN 16		FRANCE 17
Steve Prescott (St. Helens)	1.	Jerome Frayssinous (Lezignan)
Chris Smith (Castleford)	2.	Pascal Bomati (XIII Catalan)
Richard Goddard (Castleford)	3.	Arnaud Dulec (St. Gaudens)
Adrian Flynn (Wakefield T.)	4.	Pierre Jammes (Limoux)
Francis Cummins (Leeds)	5.	Luc Eychenne (Carcassonne)
Nigel Wright (Wakefield T.)	6.	Christophe Canal (Villeneuve)
Mark Hewitt (Hull)	7.	Vincent Banet (XIII Catalan), Capt.
Alex Thompson (Sheffield E.), Capt.	8.	Cyril Baudouin (Carpentras)
Paul Rowley (Halifax)	9.	Stephane Tena (XIII Catalan)
Mark Hilton (Warrington)	10.	Frederic Sane (St. Esteve)
Andy Hay (Castleford)	11.	Sebastian Berdu (St. Esteve)
Simon Baldwin (Halifax)	12.	David Sabatier (Carcassonne)
Scott Martin (Leigh)	13.	Phillippe Ricard (Albi)
Karle Hammond (Widnes)	14.	Emanuel Fauvel (Villeneuve)
Simon Reynolds (Huddersfield)	15.	Laurent Garnier (Cabestany)
Jim Leatham (Leeds)	16.	Rachid Hechiche (Lyon)
Gareth Cochrane (Keighley C.)	17.	Jerome Bisson (Villeneuve)

T: Martin, Flynn
G: Hewitt (4)
Substitutions:
Cochrane for Baldwin (23 min.)
Hammond for Martin (62 min.)
Leatham for Thompson (68 min.)
Reynolds for Smith (75 min.)
Referee: Alan Bates (Workington)

T: Jammes, Dulec, Bisson
G: Jammes, Dulec, Banet (dg)
Substitutions:
Garnier for Berdu (39 min.)
Bisson for Sabatier (62 min.)
Hechiche for Ricard (74 min.)
Half-time: 14-10
Attendance: 800

GREAT BRITAIN
UNDER-21s RESULTS

25 Nov.	1984	W 24-8	v. F	Castleford		26 Jan.	1991	W 48-2	v. F	Limoux
16 Dec.	1984	W 8-2	v. F	Albi		15 Feb.	1991	L 6-16	v. F	Wigan
9 Oct.	1985	L 12-16	v. NZ	Bradford		30 Oct.	1991	W 58-0	v. P	Leeds
19 Jan.	1986	L 6-19	v. F	St. Esteve		6 Mar.	1992	W 56-2	v. F	Halifax
2 Feb.	1986	W 6-2	v. F	Whitehaven		20 Mar.	1992	W 34-2	v. F	Albi
8 Mar.	1987	W 40-7	v. F	St. Jean de Luz		17 Feb.	1993	W 46-10	v. F	Rochdale
						26 Oct.	1993	L 24-37	v. NZ	Workington
21 Mar.	1987	W 54-6	v. F	St. Helens		2 Dec.	1993	W 28-16	v. F	Warrington
6 Mar.	1988	L 13-14	v. F	Ausillon		15 Nov.	1994	L 10-54	v. A	Gateshead
19 Mar.	1988	L 4-8	v. F	St. Helens		4 Mar.	1995	L 16-17	v. F	Albi
20 Jan.	1989	W 30-0	v. F	Leeds						
4 Feb.	1989	L 8-16	v. F	Carpentras		Key: A — Australia F — France				
20 Jan.	1990	W 22-0	v. F	Villeneuve		NZ — New Zealand P — Papua New Guinea				
16 Feb.	1990	W 20-6	v. F	Doncaster						

GREAT BRITAIN UNDER-21s REGISTER

The following is a register of appearances for Great Britain Under-21s since this classification of match was introduced in 1984.

Figures in brackets are the total appearances, with the plus sign indicating substitute appearances, e.g. (3+1).

Away matches are in bold letters. Substitute appearances are in lower case letters.

ALLEN, Shaun (1) St. Helens: 1984 F
ANDERSON, Grant (4) Castleford: 1989 F, **F**; 1990 **F**, F
ANDERSON, Paul (2) Leeds: 1992 **F**; 1993 F
ATCHESON, Paul (1) Wigan: 1993 F

BALDWIN, Simon (1) Halifax: 1995 **F**
BECKWITH, Mark (1+1) Whitehaven: 1986 f, F
BETTS, Denis (4) Wigan: 1989 F, **F**; 1990 **F**, F
BIBB, Chris (5) Featherstone R.: 1987 F, F; 1988 F; 1989 F, **F**
BISHOP, Paul (1+1) Warrington: 1987 **F**, f
BONSON, Paul (2) Featherstone R.: 1992 F, **F**
BOOTHROYD, Giles (1) Castleford: 1989 F
BURGESS, Andy (+1) Salford: 1991 f
BUSBY, Dean (2+1) Hull: 1991 P; 1992 F, f

CARBERT, Brian (3) Warrington: 1985 NZ; 1986 **F**, F
CASSIDY, Frank (1+1) Swinton: 1988 f, F
CASSIDY, Jez (+3) Hull: 1993 nz, f; 1994a
CASSIDY, Mick (2+1) Wigan: 1993 f, NZ, F
CHAMBERLAIN, Richard (1+1) Hull K.R.: 1993 f, F
CHAMBERS, Gary (2) Warrington: 1991 **F**, F
CHRISTIE, Gary (1) Oldham: 1993 F
CLARK, Garry (2) Hull K.R.: 1984 F, **F**
CLARKE, John (1) Oldham: 1994A
CLARKE, Phil (5) Wigan: 1990 **F**; 1991 **F**, F; 1992 F, **F**
COCHRANE, Gareth (+1) Keighley C.: 1995 f
CONNOLLY, Gary (4) St. Helens: 1990 F; 1991 F, P; 1992 **F**
CONWAY, Mark (1) Leeds: 1984 F
CREASSER, David (5) Leeds: 1984 F, **F**; 1985 NZ; 1986 **F**, F
CRITCHLEY, Jason (+1) Widnes: 1990 f
CROOKS, Lee (2) Hull: 1984 F, **F**
CUMMINS, Francis (2) Leeds: 1994 A, 1995 **F**
CURRIER, Andy (2) Widnes: 1984 F, **F**

DALTON, James (3) Whitehaven: 1985 NZ; 1986 **F**, F
DANBY, Rob (2) Hull: 1993 NZ, F
DANNATT, Andy (6) Hull: 1984 F, **F**; 1985 NZ; 1986 **F**; 1987 **F**, F

DARBYSHIRE, Paul (1+1) Warrington: 1991 f, F
DELANEY, Paul (+2) Leeds: 1990 f, f
DERMOTT, Martin (5) Wigan: 1987 **F**, F; 1988 **F**, F; 1989 F
DISLEY, Gary (+1) Salford: 1987 f
DIVORTY, Gary (6) Hull: 1984 F; 1985 NZ; 1986 **F**, F; 1987 **F**, F
DIXON, Mike (1) Hull: 1991 P
DONOHUE, Jason (+2) Leigh: 1992 f; 1993 f

EASTWOOD, Paul (2) Hull: 1987 **F**, F
EDWARDS, Shaun (4) Wigan: 1984 F; 1985 NZ; 1987 **F**, F

FARRELL, Andrew (1) Wigan: 1993 NZ
FARRELL, Anthony (1+1) Huddersfield: 1989 f, **F**
FAWCETT, Vince (3) Leeds: 1990 **F**, F; 1991 **F**
FLETCHER, Mike (2) Hull K.R.: 1988 **F**, F
FLYNN, Adrian (1) Wakefield T.: 1995 **F**
FORD, Mike (3+1) Wigan: 1985 NZ; 1986 **F**; Leigh: 1987 f, F
FORSHAW, Michael (+2) Wigan: 1991 f, f
FORSTER, Mark (3) Warrington: 1985 NZ; 1986 **F**, F
FOX, Deryck (1) Featherstone R.: 1984 F

GILDART, Ian (6) Wigan: 1988 **F**, F; 1989 F, **F**; 1990 **F**, F
GODDARD, Richard (4) Wakefield T.: 1993 NZ, F; Castleford: 1994A; 1995 **F**
GOULDING, Bobby (5) Wigan: 1990 **F**, F; 1991 **F**, F; Leeds: 1991 P
GREGORY, Mike (1) Warrington: 1984 **F**
GRIBBIN, Vince (1+1) Whitehaven: 1984 f, **F**
GROVES, Paul (3) Salford: 1984 F, **F**; 1985 NZ

HALLAS, Graeme (1+2) Hull K.R.: 1991 P; 1992 f, f
HAMMOND, Karle (1+1) Widnes: 1994 A; 1995 f
HARCOMBE, Kevin (1) Rochdale H.: 1986 F
HARLAND, Lee (2+1) Halifax: 1993 NZ, f; 1994 A
HARMON, Neil (1+3) Warrington: 1988 f, F; 1989 f, f
HARRIS, Iestyn (2) Warrington: 1993 NZ, F
HAY, Andy (1) Castleford: 1995 **F**
HEWITT, Mark (1+1) Hull: 1994 a; 1995 **F**
HILL, Brendan (+1) Leeds: 1986 f
HILL, Kenny (3) Castleford: 1988 **F**, F; 1989 **F**
HILTON, Mark (2) Warrington: 1994A; 1995 **F**
HOLROYD, Graham (+1) Leeds: 1993 f
HUGHES, Gary (1) Leigh: 1986 F
HUGHES, Ian (1) Sheffield E.: 1993 F
HULME, David (2+1) Widnes: 1985 nz; 1986 **F**, F
HUNTE, Alan (2) St. Helens: 1990 **F**; 1991 F

IRWIN, Shaun (4) Castleford: 1988 **F**; 1989 F, **F**; 1990 **F**

JACKSON, Michael (+1) Hunslet: 1991 f
JOHNSON, Errol (2) Leeds: 1988 **F**, F
JOYNT, Chris (4) Oldham: 1991 P; 1992 F, **F**; St. Helens: 1993 F

LAY, Steve (+1) Hunslet: 1989 f
LEATHAM, Jim (+1) Leeds: 1994 f
LORD, Gary (1) Castleford: 1988 **F**
LOUGHLIN, Paul (2) St. Helens: 1987 **F**, F
LUCAS, Ian (4) Wigan: 1988 **F**, F; 1989 F, **F**
LUMB, Tim (+1) Hunslet: 1991 f
LYMAN, Paul (3) Featherstone R.: 1985 NZ; 1986 **F**, F
LYON, David (2) Widnes: 1985 NZ; 1986 **F**

McAVOY, Nathan (+1) Salford: 1994 a
McCORMACK, Kevin (2) St. Helens: 1987 **F**, F
McCURRIE, Steve (4+1) Widnes: 1991 P; 1992 f; 1993 F,
  NZ, F
McNAMARA, Steve (5) Hull: 1991 **F**, F, P; 1992 **F**; 1993 F
MAKIN, Craig (+1) Widnes: 1993 nz
MALONEY, Francis (2) Featherstone R.: 1993 NZ, F
MARTIN, Scott (2+2) Leigh: 1993 nz,f, Sheffield E.:
  1994 A; Leigh: 1995 **F**
MARTYN, Tommy (1+3) Oldham: 1991 **F**, f, p; 1992 f
MATHER, Barrie-Jon (3+1) Wigan: 1992 f; 1993 F, NZ, F
MEDLEY, Paul (2) Leeds: 1987 **F**, F
MOLLOY, Steve (2) Warrington: 1990 **F**, F
MOSLEY, James (1) Wakefield T.: 1993 F
MOUNTAIN, Dean (+1) Castleford: 1987 f
MOXON, Darren (1) Bradford N.: 1991 **F**
MYCOE, David (4) Sheffield E.: 1990 **F**; 1991 P; 1992 F, **F**
MYERS, David (5) Wigan: 1991 **F**, F, P; 1992 F, **F**

NEWLOVE, Paul (8) Featherstone R.: 1989 F, **F**; 1990 **F**, F;
  1991 **F**, P; 1992 F, **F**
NICKLE, Sonny (1) Sheffield E.: 1990 **F**

O'DONNELL, Gus (2) Wigan: 1992 F, **F**

PARKER, Wayne (2) Hull K.R.: 1988 **F**, F
PARR, Chris (1) Huddersfield: 1991 P
PEARSON, Martin (4) Featherstone R.: 1991 P; 1992 F, **F**;
  1993 F
PENNY, Lee (3) Warrington: 1993 F, NZ, F
PERRETT, Mark (2) Halifax: 1993 F, 1994 A
PICKSLEY, Richard (1) Sheffield E.: 1992 F
PINKNEY, Nick (+1) Ryedale-York: 1991 p
POWELL, Daio (2) Bradford N.: 1993 NZ, F
POWELL, Roy (5) Leeds: 1984 F, **F**; 1985 NZ; 1986 **F**, F
PRATT, Richard (2) Leeds: 1988 **F**, F
PRECIOUS, Andy (+1) Hunslet: 1991 p
PRESCOTT, Steve (2) St. Helens: 1994 A; 1995 **F**
PRICE, Gary H. (5+1) Wakefield T.: 1988 f; 1989 F, **F**;
  1990 F; 1991 **F**, F
PRICE, Richard (2) Hull: 1989 F, **F**
PROCTOR, Wayne (+1) Hull: 1984 f
PUCKERING, Neil (4) Hull: 1986 **F**, F; 1987 **F**, F

REYNOLDS, Simon (+1) Huddersfield: 1995 f
RICHARDS, Craig (2) Bradford N.: 1991 **F**, F
RILEY, Mike (2) St. Helens: 1992 F, **F**
RIPPON, Andy (1) Swinton: 1984 **F**

*Martin Pearson, Great Britain Under-21 record holder for
most goals and points in a match.*

ROBINSON, Jason (1) Wigan: 1993 F
ROBINSON, Steve (1) Halifax: 1988 F
ROEBUCK, Neil (+1) Castleford: 1990 f
ROUND, Paul (1+1) St. Helens: 1984 F, f
ROWLEY, Paul (1) Halifax: 1995 **F**
RUDD, Chris (2) Warrington: 1991 **F**, F
RUSSELL, Richard (1+1) Wigan: 1987 F; 1988 f

SAMPSON, Dean (1) Castleford: 1988 **F**
SANDERSON, Gary (4) Warrington: 1987 **F**, F; 1988 **F**, F
SCHOFIELD, Garry (2) Hull: 1984 **F**, F
SHERIDAN, Ryan (1) Sheffield E.: 1994 A
SLATER, Richard (+1) Wakefield T.: 1992 f
SMITH, Chris (2) Castleford: 1994 A; 1995 **F**
SMITH, Tony (1) Castleford: 1991 **F**
SOUTHERNWOOD, Graham (6) Castleford: 1990 **F**, F;
  1991 **F**, F; 1992 F, **F**
SOUTHERNWOOD, Roy (2) Castleford: 1989 F, **F**
SPRUCE, Stuart (+1) Widnes: 1991 f
STEPHENS, Gareth (2+1) Leeds: 1993 f, NZ, F
STREET, Tim (2) Leigh: 1989 F, **F**
SULLIVAN, Anthony (1) Hull K.R.: 1990 F
SUMNER, Phil (3) Warrington: 1990 F; 1991 P; 1992 F
SYKES, Nathan (1+1) Castleford: 1993 F; 1994 a

THOMPSON, Alex (3) Sheffield E.: 1993 NZ; 1994 A;
  1995 **F**
TURNER, Robert (1) Warrington: 1990 F

WANE, Shaun (3) Wigan: 1984 F; 1985 NZ; 1986 **F**
WESTHEAD, John (1+2) Leigh: 1985 nz; 1986 f, F
WRIGHT, Darren (2) Widnes: 1987 **F**; 1988 **F**
WRIGHT, Nigel (3+1) Wakefield T.: 1993 F; Wigan 1993
  nz; Wakefield T.: 1994 A, 1995 **F**

UNDER-21s RECORDS

Highest score:	58-0 v. Papua New Guinea at Leeds, 30 October 1991
Highest against:	10-54 v. Australia at Gateshead 15 November 1994
Most tries in a match:	3 by Neil Puckering (Hull) v. France at St. Helens, 21 March 1987 David Myers (Wigan) v. PNG at Leeds, 30 October 1991 David Myers (Wigan) v. France at Halifax, 6 March 1992 Martin Pearson (Featherstone R.) v. France at Halifax, 6 March 1992 David Myers (Wigan) v. France at Albi, 20 March 1992
Most goals in a match:	8 by Chris Rudd (Warrington) v. France at Limoux, 26 January 1991 Martin Pearson (Featherstone R.) v. PNG at Leeds, 30 October 1991
Most points in a match:	24 (3t,6g) by Martin Pearson (Featherstone R.) v. France at Halifax, 6 March 1992
Biggest attendance:	4,596 v. France at Doncaster, 16 February 1990

UNDER-24s RESULTS

3 Apr.	1965	W 17-9	v. F	Toulouse
20 Oct.	1965	W 12-5	v. F	Oldham
26 Nov.	1966	L 4-7	v. F	Bayonne
17 Apr.	1969	W 42-2	v. F	Castleford
14 Nov.	1976	W 19-2	v. F	Hull K.R.
5 Dec.	1976	W 11-9	v. F	Albi
12 Nov.	1977	W 27-9	v. F	Hull
18 Dec.	1977	W 8-4	v. F	Tonneins
4 Oct.	1978	L 8-30	v. A	Hull K.R.
14 Jan.	1979	W 15-3	v. F	Limoux
24 Nov.	1979	W 14-2	v. F	Leigh
13 Jan.	1980	W 11-7	v. F	Carcassonne
5 Nov.	1980	L 14-18	v. NZ	Fulham
10 Jan.	1981	W 9-2	v. F	Villeneuve
16 Jan.	1982	W 19-16	v. F	Leeds
21 Feb.	1982	W 24-12	v. F	Tonneins
16 Jan.	1983	W 19-5	v. F	Carpentras
11 Nov.	1983	W 28-23	v. F	Villeneuve
4 Dec.	1983	W 48-1	v. F	Oldham

GREAT BRITAIN UNDER-24s REGISTER
Since reintroduction in 1976

The following is a register of appearances by current players, who played at least one club game in 1994-95, for Great Britain Under-24s since this classification of match was reintroduced in 1976, until it was replaced by the new Under-21 level in 1984.

Figures in brackets are the total appearances, with the plus sign indicating substitute appearances, e.g. (7+3).

Away matches are in bold letters. Substitute appearances are in lower case letters.

ASHTON, Ray (3) Oldham: 1983 **F**, **F**, F

CROOKS, Lee (1) Hull: 1983 F

DRUMMOND, Des (5) Leigh: 1979 F; 1980 **F**; 1981 **F**; 1982 F, **F**

ECCLES, Bob (2) Warrington: 1978 A; 1979 F
ENGLAND, Keith (+1) Castleford: 1983 f

FIELDHOUSE, John (1+1) Warrington: 1983 **F**, f
FORD, Phil (1) Warrington: 1982 **F**

GREGORY, Andy (1) Widnes: 1982 F

HANLEY, Ellery (2) Bradford N.: 1982 F; 1983 F

LEDGER, Barry (2) St. Helens: 1983 **F**, F
LYDON, Joe (3) Widnes: 1983 **F**, **F**, F

MASKILL, Colin (1) Wakefield T.: 1983 **F**
MUMBY, Keith (6) Bradford N.: 1976 F, **F**; 1977 F, **F**; 1978 A; 1981 **F**

NOBLE, Brian (4) Bradford N.: 1982 F, **F**; 1983 **F**, F

O'NEILL, Mike (3+2) Widnes: 1980 nz; 1982 F, f; 1983 **F**, **F**

POTTER, Ian (4) Warrington: 1979 **F**; 1981 **F**; Leigh: 1982 F, **F**

SCHOFIELD, Garry (+2) Hull: 1983 f, f

Scrum half Mark Aston whose July 1994 move from Sheffield Eagles to Featherstone Rovers was fixed at £100,000 by the League's Transfer Tribunal.

TONGA (6)

Liuaki "Lee" Hansen	(Widnes)
Sam Hansen	(Barrow)
*Emosi Koloto	(Widnes)
Tau Liku	(Leigh)
Hamoni Tuavao	(Leigh)
Tevita Vaikona	(Hull)

*New Zealand Test player

WESTERN SAMOA (4)

Vila Matuatia	(Doncaster, St. Helens)
Apollo Perelini	(St. Helens)
John Schuster	(Halifax)
Va'aiga Tuigamala	(Wigan)

RECORD TRANSFERS

The first £1,000 transfer came in 1921 when Harold Buck joined Leeds from Hunslet, although there were reports at the time that another player was involved in the deal to make up the four-figure transfer. Other claims for the first £1,000 transfer are attached to Stan Bogden's move from Bradford Northern to Huddersfield in 1929. The following list shows how transfer fees have grown this century in straight cash deals only:

Season	Player	Position	From	To	Fee
1901-02	Jim Lomas	Centre	Bramley	Salford	£100
1910-11	Jim Lomas	Centre	Salford	Oldham	£300
1912-13	Billy Batten	Centre	Hunslet	Hull	£600
1921-22	Harold Buck	Wing	Hunslet	Leeds	£1,000
1929-30	Stanley Smith	Wing	Wakefield T.	Leeds	£1,075
1933-34	Stanley Brogden	Wing/Centre	Huddersfield	Leeds	£1,200
1937-38	Billy Belshaw	Full back	Liverpool S.	Warrington	£1,450
1946-47	Bill Davies	Full back/Centre	Huddersfield	Dewsbury	£1,650
1947-48	Bill Hudson	Forward	Batley	Wigan	£2,000
1947-48	Jim Ledgard	Full back	Dewsbury	Leigh	£2,650
1948-49	Ike Owens	Forward	Leeds	Castleford	£2,750
1948-49	Ike Owens	Forward	Castleford	Huddersfield	£2,750
1948-49	Stan McCormick	Wing	Belle Vue R.	St. Helens	£4,000
1949-50	Albert Naughton	Centre	Widnes	Warrington	£4,600
1950-51	Bruce Ryan	Wing	Hull	Leeds	£4,750
1950-51	Joe Egan	Hooker	Wigan	Leigh	£5,000
1950-51	Harry Street	Forward	Dewsbury	Wigan	£5,000
1957-58	Mick Sullivan	Wing	Huddersfield	Wigan	£9,500
1958-59	Ike Southward	Wing	Workington T.	Oldham	£10,650
1960-61	Mick Sullivan	Wing	Wigan	St. Helens	£11,000
1960-61	Ike Southward	Wing	Oldham	WorkingtonT.	£11,002 10s
1968-69	Colin Dixon	Forward	Halifax	Salford	£12,000
1969-70	Paul Charlton	Full back	Workington T.	Salford	£12,500
1972-73	Eric Prescott	Forward	St. Helens	Salford	£13,000
1975-76	Steve Nash	Scrum half	Featherstone R.	Salford	£15,000
1977-78	Bill Ashurst	Forward	Wigan	Wakefield T.	£18,000
1978-79	Clive Pickerill	Scrum half	Castleford	Hull	£20,000

1978-79	Phil Hogan	Forward	Barrow	Hull K.R.	£35,000
1979-80	Len Casey	Forward	Bradford N.	Hull K.R.	£38,000
1980-81	Trevor Skerrett	Forward	Wakefield T.	Hull	£40,000
1980-81	George Fairbairn	Full back	Wigan	Hull K.R.	£72,500
1985-86	Ellery Hanley	Centre/stand off	Bradford N.	Wigan	£85,000
1985-86	Joe Lydon	Centre	Widnes	Wigan	£100,000
1986-87	Andy Gregory	Scrum half	Warrington	Wigan	£130,000
1987-88	Lee Crooks	Forward	Hull	Leeds	£150,000
1987-88	Garry Schofield	Centre	Hull	Leeds	£155,000
1989-90	Graham Steadman	Stand off	Featherstone R.	Castleford	£170,000
1991-92	Ellery Hanley	Forward	Wigan	Leeds	£250,000
1991-92	Martin Offiah	Winger	Widnes	Wigan	£440,000

MOST MOVES

Geoff Clarkson extended his record number of transfers to 12 when he left Leigh for Featherstone Rovers on 27 October 1983. He played for 10 different English clubs and had a brief spell in Australia.

Clarkson, born on 12 August 1943, was 40 years old when he finished playing regular first team rugby in 1983-84. He turned professional with Wakefield Trinity in 1966 after gaining Yorkshire County forward honours with Wakefield Rugby Union Club. Clarkson's club career in England was as follows:

1966 - Wakefield T.
1968 - Bradford N.
1970 - Leigh
1971 - Warrington
1972 - Leeds
1975 - York
1976 - Bramley
1978 - Wakefield T. and Hull K.R.
1980 - Bradford N. and Oldham
1981 - Leigh
1983 - Featherstone R.

Hooker Lee Jackson, a Great Britain ever-present in 1994, shows off the first-ever John Smith's International Player of the Year award, presented in December 1994.

AWARDS

THE 1995 MAN OF STEEL AWARDS

Launched in the 1976-77 season, the Rugby Football League's official awards are presented to the Man of Steel, the personality judged to have made the biggest impact on the season; the First and Second Division Players of the Year, decided by a ballot of the players; the Young Player of the Year, under-21 at the start of the season; the Coach of the Year and Referee of the Year, all chosen by a panel of judges. The official award scheme was sponsored by Trumanns Steel from inception in 1977 to 1983, brewers Greenall Whitley taking over in 1984 until 1989. Stones Bitter took over sponsorship in 1990.

Stones Bitter Man of Steel

Denis Betts marked his departure to Auckland Warriors after nine years of service at Wigan by being crowned Stones Bitter Man of Steel 1995. The second row man received a cheque for £4,000 in recognition of his outstanding contribution to the Riversiders' historic first-ever modern day Grand Slam of all four domestic trophies, scoring 20 tries in his 37 appearances. The former Leigh Rangers amateur also figured for Great Britain in all three 1994 John Smith's Tests against Australia, taking his tally of caps to 25. He was previously Young Player of the Year in 1991.

Stones Bitter First Division Player

St. Helens scrum half **Bobby Goulding** topped the ballot of fellow Stones Bitter Championship players in his first season at Knowsley Road, having previously served Wigan, Leeds and Widnes. He made 36 appearances for the Saints, amassing 347 points from 11 tries, 148 goals and seven drop goals. His impressive club form earned a recall for Great Britain in the Anglo-Aussie John Smith's Tests, scoring three goals in three appearances.

Stones Bitter Second Division Player

Keighley Cougars centre **Nick Pinkney** made it a double celebration for the 1994-95 season by adding the Second Division Player title to his first England cap. The former Ryedale-York threequarter, in his second season at Cougar Park, broke his own club record with 45 tries from 37 appearances. He also scored a try on his England debut against France at Gateshead in the John Smith's European Championship.

Stones Bitter Young Player

Wigan second row man **Andrew Farrell** collected the Young Player of the Year award for the second successive season. The presentation was made only days before his 20th birthday at the end of a season in which he made 37 appearances, contributing five tries, 59 goals and a drop goal, a tally of 139 points. He was also an ever-present for Great Britain in the three-match John Smith's Test series against Australia, kicking two goals.

Stones Bitter Coach of the Year

Wigan's **Graeme West** completed his first full season in charge at Central Park by being crowned Coach of the Year. The Riversiders achieved the first-ever modern day Grand Slam of all four domestic trophies to add to World Club Challenge Trophy won at the start of June 1994.

Stones Bitter Referee of the Year

Castleford-based **Russell Smith** was named top whistler in his fourth season of top class refereeing. The former Bradford Northern player took charge of the Silk Cut Challenge Cup final, the Stones Bitter Second Division Premiership final, and Wales' home clash with England in the John Smith's European Championship.

● Other than the Man of Steel, each of the above five category winners received £1,000 and an inscribed memento.

	Man of Steel	1st Division Player	2nd Division Player	Young Player	Coach	Referee
1977	David Ward (Leeds)	Malcolm Reilly (Castleford)	Ged Marsh (Blackpool B.)	David Ward (Leeds)	Eric Ashton (St. Helens)	Billy Thompson (Huddersfield)
1978	George Nicholls (St. Helens)	George Nicholls (St. Helens)	John Woods (Leigh)	John Woods (Leigh)	Frank Myler (Widnes)	Billy Thompson (Huddersfield)
1979	Doug Laughton (Widnes)	Mick Adams (Widnes)	Steve Norton (Hull)	Steve Evans (Featherstone R.)	Doug Laughton (Widnes)	Mick Naughton (Widnes)
1980	George Fairbairn (Wigan)	Mick Adams (Widnes)	Steve Quinn (Featherstone R.)	Roy Holdstock (Hull K.R.)	Peter Fox (Bradford N.)	Fred Lindop (Wakefield)
1981	Ken Kelly (Warrington)	Ken Kelly (Warrington)	John Crossley (York)	Des Drummond (Leigh)	Billy Benyon (Warrington)	John Holdsworth (Kippax)
1982	Mick Morgan (Carlisle)	Steve Norton (Hull)	Mick Morgan (Carlisle)	Des Drummond (Leigh)	Arthur Bunting (Hull)	Fred Lindop (Wakefield)
1983	Allan Agar (Featherstone R.)	Keith Mumby (Bradford N.)	Steve Nash (Salford)	Brian Noble (Bradford N.)	Arthur Bunting (Hull)	Robin Whitfield (Widnes)
1984	Joe Lydon (Widnes)	Joe Lydon (Widnes)	David Cairns (Barrow)	Joe Lydon (Widnes)	Tommy Dawes (Barrow)	Billy Thompson (Huddersfield)
1985	Ellery Hanley (Bradford N.)	Ellery Hanley (Bradford N.)	Graham Steadman (York)	Lee Crooks (Hull)	Roger Millward (Hull K.R.)	Ron Campbell (Widnes)
1986	Gavin Miller (Hull K.R.)	Gavin Miller (Hull K.R.)	Derek Pyke (Leigh)	Shaun Edwards (Wigan)	Chris Anderson (Halifax)	Fred Lindop (Wakefield)
1987	Ellery Hanley (Wigan)	Andy Gregory (Wigan)	John Cogger (Runcorn H.)	Shaun Edwards (Wigan)	Graham Lowe (Wigan)	John Holdsworth (Kippax)
1988	Martin Offiah (Widnes)	Steve Hampson (Wigan)	Peter Smith (Featherstone R.)	Shaun Edwards (Wigan)	Doug Laughton (Widnes)	Fred Lindop (Wakefield)
1989	Ellery Hanley (Wigan)	David Hulme (Widnes)	Daryl Powell (Sheffield E.)	Paul Newlove (Featherstone R.)	Graham Lowe (Wigan)	John Holdsworth (Kippax)
1990	Shaun Edwards (Wigan)	Andy Goodway (Wigan)	John Woods (Rochdale H.)	Bobby Goulding (Wigan)	John Monie (Wigan)	Robin Whitfield (Widnes)

	Man of Steel	1st Division Player	2nd Division Player	3rd Division Player	Young Player	Coach	Referee
1991	Garry Schofield (Leeds)	Jonathan Davies (Widnes)	Tawera Nikau (Ryedale-York)	—	Denis Betts (Wigan)	John Monie (Wigan)	John Holdsworth (Kippax)
1992	Dean Bell (Wigan)	Graham Steadman (Castleford)	Iva Ropati (Oldham)	Wally Gibson (Huddersfield)	Gary Connolly (St. Helens)	John Monie (Wigan)	Robin Whitfield (Widnes)
1993	Andy Platt (Wigan)	Tea Ropati (St. Helens)	Paul Newlove (Featherstone R.)	Martin Wood (Keighley C.)	Jason Robinson (Wigan)	John Monie (Wigan)	John Connolly (Wigan)
1994	Jonathan Davies (Warrington)	Jonathan Davies (Warrington)	Martin Oglanby (Workington T.)	—	Andrew Farrell (Wigan)	John Joyner (Castleford)	John Connolly (Wigan)
1995	Denis Betts (Wigan)	Bobby Goulding (St. Helens)	Nick Pinkney (Keighley C.)	—	Andrew Farrell (Wigan)	Graeme West (Wigan)	Russell Smith (Castleford)

NOMINEES:

1977 *1st Division Player:* Bruce Burton (Castleford), Vince Farrar (Featherstone R.). *2nd Division Player:* Jeff Grayshon (Dewsbury), Keith Hepworth (Hull). *Young Player:* Jimmy Crampton (Hull), Harry Pinner (St. Helens). *Coach:* Keith Cotton (Featherstone R.), Mal Reilly (Castleford). *Referee:* Joe Jackson (Pudsey), Mick Naughton (Widnes).

1978 *1st Division Player:* Roger Millward (Hull K.R.), Harry Pinner (St. Helens). *2nd Division Player:* Phil Hogan (Barrow), Mick Morgan (York). *Young Player:* Neil Hague (Leeds), Keith Mumby (Bradford N.). *Coach:* Eric Ashton MBE (St. Helens), John Mantle (Leigh). *Referee:* Ron Campbell (Widnes), Fred Lindop (Wakefield).

1979 *1st Division Player:* Brian Lockwood (Hull K.R.), Tommy Martyn (Warrington). *2nd Division Player:* Barry Banks (York), John Wolford (Dewsbury). *Young Player:* Mick Burke (Widnes), John Woods (Leigh). *Coach:* Billy Benyon (Warrington), Arthur Bunting (Hull). *Referee:* Fred Lindop (Wakefield), Billy Thompson (Huddersfield).

1980 *1st Division Player:* Len Casey (Hull K.R.), George Fairbairn (Wigan). *2nd Division Player:* Mick Blacker (Halifax), John Wolford (Dewsbury). *Young Player:* Steve Hubbard (Hull K.R.), Harry Pinner (St. Helens). *Coach:* Maurice Bamford (Halifax), Arthur Bunting (Hull). *Referee:* Ron Campbell (Widnes), Billy Thompson (Huddersfield).

1981 *1st Division Player:* Mick Adams (Widnes), Tommy Martyn (Warrington). *2nd Division Player:* Arnie Walker (Whitehaven), Danny Wilson (Swinton). *Young Player:* Paul Harkin (Hull K.R.), Keith Mumby (Bradford N.). *Coach:* Reg Bowden (Fulham), Peter Fox (Bradford N.). *Referee:* Ron Campbell (Widnes), Fred Lindop (Wakefield).

1982 *1st Division Player:* Jeff Grayshon (Bradford N.), Andy Gregory (Widnes). *2nd Division Player:* Denis Boyd (Carlisle), Alan Fairhurst (Swinton). *Young Player:* Lee Crooks (Hull), Andy Gregory (Widnes). *Coach:* Doug Laughton (Widnes), Alex Murphy/Colin Clarke (Leigh). *Referee:* Gerry Kershaw (York), Billy Thompson (Huddersfield).

1983 *1st Division Player:* Bob Eccles (Warrington), David Topliss (Hull). *2nd Division Player:* Tommy David (Cardiff C.), Mike Lampkowski (Wakefield T.). *Young Player:* Ronnie Duane (Warrington), Andy Goodway (Oldham). *Coach:* Alex Murphy (Wigan), Frank Myler (Oldham). *Referee:* John Holdsworth (Leeds), Fred Lindop (Wakefield).

1984 *1st Division Player:* Garry Schofield (Hull), John Woods (Leigh). *2nd Division Player:* Lyn Hopkins (Workington T.), John Wolford (Hunslet). *Young Player:* Gary Divorty (Hull), Garry Schofield (Hull). *Coach:* Arthur Bunting (Hull), Roger Millward (Hull K.R.). *Referee:* Derek Fox (Wakefield), Fred Lindop (Wakefield).

1985 *1st Division Player:* Harry Pinner (St. Helens), Gary Prohm (Hull K.R.). *2nd Division Player:* Terry Langton (Mansfield M.), Peter Wood (Runcorn H.). *Young Player:* Deryck Fox (Featherstone R.), Andy Platt (St. Helens). *Coach:* Arthur Bunting (Hull), Colin Clarke/Alan McInnes (Wigan). *Referee:* Fred Lindop (Wakefield), Stan Wall (Leigh).

1986 *1st Division Player:* Steve Ella (Wigan), John Fieldhouse (Widnes). *2nd Division Player:* John Henderson (Leigh), Graham King (Hunslet). *Young Player:* Paul Lyman (Featherstone R.), Roy Powell (Leeds). *Coach:* Roger Millward (Hull K.R.), John Sheridan (Doncaster). *Referee:* John Holdsworth (Kippax), Robin Whitfield (Widnes).

456

1987 *1st Division Player:* Lee Crooks (Hull), Ellery Hanley (Wigan). *2nd Division Player:* Andy Bateman (Hunslet), Les Holliday (Swinton). *Young Player:* Paul Loughlin (St. Helens), Kevin McCormack (St. Helens). *Coach:* Chris Anderson (Halifax), Alex Murphy (St. Helens). *Referee:* Kevin Allatt (Southport), Fred Lindop (Wakefield).

1988 *1st Division Player:* Martin Offiah (Widnes), Kurt Sorensen (Widnes). *2nd Division Player:* Deryck Fox (Featherstone R.), Hugh Waddell (Oldham). *Young Player:* Paul Medley (Leeds), Steve Robinson (Halifax). *Coach:* Alex Murphy (St. Helens), Barry Seabourne (Bradford N.). *Referee:* John Holdsworth (Kippax), Ray Tennant (Castleford).

1989 *1st Division Player:* Andy Gregory (Wigan), Kelvin Skerrett (Bradford N.). *2nd Division Player:* Cavill Heugh (Barrow), Chris Johnson (Leigh). *Young Player:* Grant Anderson (Castleford), Denis Betts (Wigan). *Coach:* Peter Fox (Featherstone R.), Brian Smith (Hull). *Referee:* Ray Tennant (Castleford), Robin Whitfield (Widnes).

1990 *1st Division Player:* Deryck Fox (Featherstone R.), Andy Platt (Wigan). *2nd Division Player:* David Bishop (Hull K.R.), John Cogger (Oldham). *Young Player:* Denis Betts (Wigan), Anthony Sullivan (Hull K.R.). *Coach:* Tony Barrow (Oldham), Brian Johnson (Warrington). *Referee:* John Holdsworth (Kippax), Colin Morris (Huddersfield).

1991 *1st Division Player:* Andy Gregory (Wigan), George Mann (St. Helens). *2nd Division Player:* Steve Kerry (Salford), Peter Ropati (Leigh). *Young Player:* Phil Clarke (Wigan), Craig Richards (Bradford N.). *Coach:* Ray Ashton (Workington T.), Doug Laughton (Widnes). *Referee:* Brian Galtress (Bradford), Jim Smith (Halifax).

1992 *1st Division Player:* Dean Bell (Wigan), John Devereux (Widnes). *2nd Division Player:* Clayton Friend (Carlisle), Paul Topping (Leigh). *3rd Division Player:* Steve Carroll (Bramley), Paul Delaney (Dewsbury). *Young Player:* Paul Newlove (Featherstone R.), David Myers (Wigan). *Coach:* Alex Murphy (Huddersfield), Darryl Van de Velde (Castleford). *Referee:* Stuart Cummings (Widnes), John Holdsworth (Kippax).

1993 *1st Division Player:* Phil Clarke (Wigan), Andy Platt (Wigan). *2nd Division Player:* Neil Flanagan (Huddersfield), Brendon Tuuta (Featherstone R.). *3rd Division Player:* Clayton Friend (Whitehaven), Brad Hepi (Workington T.). *Young Player:* Chris Joynt (St. Helens), Nigel Wright (Wakefield T.). *Coach:* Peter Fox (Bradford N.), Mike McClennan (St. Helens). *Referee:* John Holdsworth (Kippax), Russell Smith (Castleford).

1994 *1st Division Player:* Lee Crooks (Castleford). *2nd Division Player:* Glen Tomlinson (Batley).

1995 *1st Division Player:* Denis Betts (Wigan), Va'aiga Tuigamala (Wigan). *2nd Division Player:* Steve Hall (Keighley C.), Glen Tomlinson (Batley). *Young Player:* Keiron Cunningham (St. Helens), Iestyn Harris (Warrington). *Coach:* Andy Goodway (Oldham), Phil Larder (Keighley C.). *Referee:* David Campbell (St. Helens), Stuart Cummings (Widnes).

Great Britain and Wigan second row man Denis Betts, selected as Stones Bitter Man of Steel 1995 on the eve of his departure for Auckland Warriors. Betts, chosen as Young Player of the Year in 1991, was also a nominee for Stones Bitter First Division Player of the Year 1995.

457

JOHN SMITH'S INTERNATIONAL PLAYER OF THE YEAR 1994

Sheffield Eagles 17-cap hooker Lee Jackson was awarded the inaugural title of John Smith's International Player of the Year.

The Great Britain number nine, an ever-present in the Lions' four Test matches in 1994, received a cheque for £1,000 and an inscribed cut-glass decanter and glasses.

The first-ever John Smith's International Player of the Year award was introduced to reflect annual individual performance in John Smith's Internationals contested by Great Britain, Wales and Great Britain Under-21s.

Jackson, who was Sheffield Eagles' club record signing in September 1993, played in Great Britain's World Sevens squad in Sydney in February 1994 and the 12-4 success over France in Carcassonne in March 1994 before being selected in all three John Smith's Tests against world champions Australia in the autumn.

His quartet of Test appearances in 1994 took Jackson's haul of Great Britain caps to 17, including all three Tests against the 1990 Kangaroos and tours Down Under in 1990 and 1992.

STONES BITTER TEAM OF THE MONTH AWARDS 1994-95

Introduced in the 1979-80 season, the scheme acknowledged the adjudged Team of the Month in either division.

A panel of judges representing Stones Bitter and the Rugby League selected the two monthly winners, the First Division winners receiving £500 and the Second Division £350, plus a framed citation.

The awards were sponsored for the first four seasons by Shopacheck before Lada Cars took over in the 1983-84 season and introduced the first-ever Team of the Year title. Stones Bitter took over the sponsorship in 1987-88, the 1995 Team of the Year, **Wigan,** receiving £1,500.

	First Division	Second Division
Oct.	Wigan	Keighley C.
Nov.	Wigan	Keighley C.
Dec.	Leeds	Keighley C.
Jan.	Workington T.	Whitehaven
Feb.	Oldham	Huddersfield
Mar.	Warrington	Batley
Apr./May	Wigan	Keighley C.

Team of the Year

1983-84: Widnes		**1989-90:** Wigan	
1984-85: Hull K.R.		**1990-91:** Wigan	
1985-86: Halifax		**1991-92:** Wigan	
1986-87: Wigan		**1992-93:** Wigan	
1987-88: Widnes		**1993-94:** Wigan	
1988-89: Wigan		**1994-95:** Wigan	

WALLACE ARNOLD – SUNDAY MIRROR ENTERTAINER AWARDS 1994-95

Introduced in 1986-87, the scheme was spon sored by Wallace Arnold and promoted by th *Sunday Mirror.*

Each month a player was chosen as Enter tainer of the Month to receive a Wallac Arnold holiday voucher for £400. The Enter tainer of the Year was awarded a £1,50 holiday voucher, the 1995 winner bein Wigan's New Zealand ace **Henry Paul.**

Entertainer of the Month

Oct.	Alan Hunte (St. Helens)
Nov.	John Schuster (Halifax)
Dec.	Ellery Hanley (Leeds)
Jan.	Nick Pinkney (Keighley C.)
Feb.	Henry Paul (Wigan)
Mar.	Nigel Wright (Wakefield T.)
Apr./May	Bobby Goulding (St. Helens)

Entertainer of the Year

1987:	Ellery Hanley (Wigan)
1988:	Martin Offiah (Widnes)
1989:	Martin Offiah (Widnes)
1990:	Deryck Fox (Featherstone R.)
1991:	Garry Schofield (Leeds)
1992:	Shaun Edwards (Wigan)
1993:	Frano Botica (Wigan)
1994:	Jonathan Davies (Warrington)
1995:	Henry Paul (Wigan)

REFEREES

REFEREES' HONOURS 1994-95

Silk Cut Challenge Cup final:
Russell Smith

Regal Trophy final:
Stuart Cummings

Stones Bitter Premiership final:
Stuart Cummings

Second Division Premiership final:
Russell Smith

Wales v England:
Russell Smith

France v Wales:
John Connolly

Wales v Australia:
John Connolly

Great Britain Under-21s v Australia:
Steve Presley

France v Great Britain Under-21s:
Alan Bates

Cumbria v Australia:
John Connolly

SENIOR REFEREES 1995-96

● A two tier grading system was introduced at the start of 1995-96, Premier status referees taking charge of the Super League matches, Grade One the First and Second Division fixtures.

Premier Division

ALAN BATES
Date of birth: 18.4.58
Grade One: 1993-94
France v Great Britain Under-21s 1994-95

DAVID CAMPBELL (St. Helens)
Date of birth: 9.10.54
Grade One: 1989-90
Challenge Cup 1993-94
Regal Trophy 1993-94
Lancashire Cup 1991-92
Wales v France 1993-94

JOHN CONNOLLY (Wigan)
Date of birth: 30.9.59
Grade One: 1990-91
Second Division Premiership 1992-93, 1993-94
France v Great Britain 1993-94
Wales v New Zealand 1993-94
Wales v Australia 1994-95
France v Wales 1994-95
Cumbria v Australia 1994-95

ROBERT CONNOLLY (Wigan)
Date of birth: 30.9.59
Grade One: 1990-91

STUART CUMMINGS (Widnes)
Date of birth: 17.11.60
Grade One: 1991-92
Regal Trophy 1994-95
Premiership Trophy 1993-94, 1994-95
Divisional Premiership 1991-92
Lancashire Cup 1992-93
Charity Shield 1992-93

JOHN HOLDSWORTH (Kippax)
Date of birth: 25.1.47
Grade Two: 1979-80
Grade One: 1980-81
Challenge Cup 1986-87, 1989-90
Regal Trophy 1985-86, 1986-87, 1988-89, 1992-93
Premiership Trophy 1980-81, 1987-88, 1988-89,
    1990-91, 1991-92, 1992-93
Lancashire Cup 1982-83, 1985-86
Yorkshire Cup 1991-92
World Club Challenge 1987-88
Australia v New Zealand (3) 1991
France v Australia (2) 1990-91
France v New Zealand 1993-94
Wales v England 1980-81
Great Britain v Rest of World 1988-89
RL Chairman's XIII v Papua New Guinea 1987-88
Cumbria v Yorkshire 1981-82
France v Great Britain Under-24s 1982-83
War of the Roses 1987-88
Charity Shield 1987-88, 1989-90

KARL KIRKPATRICK (Warrington)
Date of birth: 3.12.64
Grade One: 1994-95

COLIN MORRIS (Huddersfield)
Date of birth: 11.3.57
Grade One: 1989-90
Premiership Trophy 1989-90
Papua New Guinea v France 1991
France v Papua New Guinea 1991-92
Wales v France 1991-92
Russia v France 1992
France v Great Britain Under-21s 1989-90
Charity Shield 1990-91
Cumbria v Papua New Guinea 1991-92
Cumbria v Australia 1992-93
War of the Roses 1991-92

RUSSELL SMITH (Castleford)
Date of birth: 24.1.64
Grade One: 1991-92
Challenge Cup 1992-93, 1994-95
Second Division Premiership Final 1994-95
Yorkshire Cup 1992-93
New Zealand v Australia (3) 1993
Wales v England 1994-95
France v Great Britain Under-21s 1991-92

RAY TENNANT (Castleford)
Date of birth: 7.4.49
Grade One: 1985-86
Challenge Cup 1988-89
New Zealand v Australia (3) 1989
European Club Championship 1988-89
Lancashire Cup 1989-90
Charity Shield 1988-89
Cumbria v Papua New Guinea 1987-88

Grade One

DAVID ASQUITH (York)
Date of birth: 20.6.53
Grade One: 1989-90

DAVID ATKIN (Hull)
Date of birth: 19.12.64
Grade One: 1992-93

ALAN BURKE (Oldham)
Date of birth: 21.1.57
Grade One: 1987-88
Lancashire Cup 1990-91

DAVE CARTER (Widnes)
Date of birth: 29.11.55
Grade One: 1984-85
France v Great Britain Under-21s 1988-89

STEVE CROSS (Hull)
Date of birth: 23.3.50
Grade One: 1986-87

BRIAN GALTRESS (Bradford)
Date of birth: 8.10.51
Grade One: 1988-89
Regal Trophy 1991-92
Second Division Premiership 1990-91
France v Great Britain Under-21s 1990-91

STEVE GANSON (St. Helens)
Date of birth: 4.1.70
Grade One: 1995-96

PETER GILMOUR (Workington)
Date of birth: 11.9.58
Grade One: 1990-91

PAUL GRIMSHAW (Atherton)
Date of birth: 28.8.65
Grade One: 1995-96

PAUL LEE (Leigh)
Date of birth: 28.7.57
Grade One: 1994-95

Russell Smith, Stones Bitter Referee of the Year 1994-95.

IAN McGREGOR (Huddersfield)
Date of birth: 27.12.53
Grade One: 1993-94

STEVE NICHOLSON (Whitehaven)
Date of birth: 5.4.61
Grade One: 1992-93

NICK ODDY (Halifax)
Date of birth: 16.4.62
Grade One: 1994-95

GARRY OWRAM (Bradford)
Date of birth: 15.7.55
Grade One: 1995-96

STEVE PRESLEY (Castleford)
Date of birth: 4.4.57
Grade One: 1993-94
Great Britain Under-21s v Australia 1994-95

DAVE REDFEARN (Huddersfield)
Date of birth: 15.12.52
Grade One: 1990-91

GRAHAM SHAW (Dewsbury)
Date of birth: 11.9.70
Grade One: 1995-96

COLIN STEELE (Askam-in-Furness)
Date of birth: 11.9.60
Grade One: 1987-88
Cumbria v France 1988-89

PETER TABERNER (Wigan)
Date of birth: 24.6.60
Grade One: 1995-96

THE ALLIANCE

FIRST DIVISION

	P.	W.	D.	L.	Dg.	FOR Gls.	Trs.	Pts.	Dg.	AGAINST Gls.	Trs.	Pts.	Pts.
Leeds	26	19	0	7	5	109	129	739	3	54	74	407	38
St. Helens	26	18	1	7	2	105	153	824	2	72	106	570	37
Wigan	26	18	0	8	1	113	180	947	5	72	96	533	36
Oldham	26	18	0	8	6	107	129	736	7	77	92	529	36
Warrington	26	17	0	9	5	125	152	863	2	66	84	470	34
Bradford N.	26	14	0	12	4	98	119	676	0	80	112	608	28
Dewsbury	26	13	0	13	3	71	105	565	2	76	104	570	26
Castleford	26	12	0	14	0	72	92	512	4	83	112	618	24
Salford	26	11	0	15	1	82	118	637	8	83	102	582	22
Hull	26	11	0	15	3	89	94	557	3	95	122	681	22
Wakefield T.	26	9	1	16	2	72	102	554	8	89	120	666	19
Featherstone R.	26	9	0	17	8	64	95	516	2	105	144	788	18
Halifax	26	8	0	18	2	49	71	384	6	117	151	844	16
Ryedale-York	26	4	0	22	11	64	65	399	1	151	185	1043	8

SECOND DIVISION

	P.	W.	D.	L.	Dg.	FOR Gls.	Trs.	Pts.	Dg.	AGAINST Gls.	Trs.	Pts.	Pts.
Sheffield E.	22	19	0	3	8	102	127	720	0	53	75	406	38
Hull K.R.	22	17	0	5	1	78	111	601	3	50	58	335	34
Keighley C.	22	16	1	5	1	98	143	769	3	40	55	303	33
Widnes	22	16	0	6	2	97	144	772	1	36	55	293	32
Workington T.	22	14	2	6	1	71	92	511	4	54	78	424	30
Leigh	22	13	1	8	2	75	109	588	1	61	76	427	27
Batley	22	13	0	9	2	66	86	478	1	56	70	393	26
Doncaster	22	12	0	10	2	82	113	618	6	63	104	548	24
Rochdale H.	22	12	0	10	0	73	95	526	3	69	86	485	24
Huddersfield	22	11	1	10	4	65	94	510	2	74	89	506	23
London B.	22	10	0	12	1	65	92	499	2	74	95	530	20
Swinton	22	8	0	14	0	52	83	436	2	93	127	696	16
Whitehaven	22	6	0	16	2	52	76	410	2	79	119	636	12
Hunslet	22	2	1	19	7	52	69	387	5	82	116	633	5
Carlisle	22	2	0	20	2	34	48	262	1	99	153	811	4
Barrow	22	2	0	20	2	30	50	262	1	109	176	923	4

ALLIANCE CHALLENGE CUP 1995
First Round

Barrow	4	Hull	54	Salford	54	Wakefield T.	26
Castleford	20	Dewsbury	14	Sheffield E.	16	Keighley C.	4
Featherstone R.	42	Hunslet	22	Swinton	29	Halifax	36
Huddersfield	29	London B.	32	Warrington	50	Rochdale H.	6
Leeds	34	Doncaster	18	Widnes	60	Whitehaven	4
Ryedale-York	17	Bradford N.	57	Wigan	8	Oldham	31
St. Helens	22	Hull K.R.	20	Workington T.	16	Carlisle	6

Byes: Batley, Leigh

Second Round

Batley	14	Salford	12
Castleford	26	Sheffield E.	5
Featherstone R.	40	Widnes	30
Halifax	22	Oldham	38
Hull	45	Workington T.	18
Leeds	10	Warrington	25
Leigh	14	Bradford N.	34
London B.	20	St. Helens	45

Third Round

Batley	19	Hull	16
Bradford N.	26	Castleford	12
Featherstone R.	22	St. Helens	42
Warrington	38	Oldham	25

Semi-Finals

Batley	6	St. Helens	38
Warrington	22	Bradford N.	36

Final

St. Helens	36	Bradford N.	10

LANCASHIRE COUNTY CHALLENGE SHIELD 1994-95

First Round

Barrow	14	Thatto Heath	16
Leigh	22	Simms Cross	14
Oldham	46	St. Helens	22
Salford	70	London B.	4
Swinton	30	Carlisle	7
Warrington	36	Rochdale H.	16
Widnes	36	Workington T.	24
Wigan	90	Whitehaven	0

Second Round

Salford	14	Wigan	48
Swinton	20	Leigh	12
Thatto Heath	12	Oldham	61
Widnes	27	Warrington	24

Semi-Finals

Swinton	6	Wigan	34
Widnes	10	Oldham	30

Final

Wigan	24	Oldham	10

YORKSHIRE SENIOR COMPETITION CHALLENGE CUP 1994-95

Preliminary Round

Batley	26	Featherstone R.	20

First Round

Batley	16	Halifax	19
Castleford	56	Huddersfield	8
Dewsbury	30	Hull	24
Hull K.R.	42	Hunslet	0
Ryedale-York	13	Bradford N.	38
Sheffield E.	31	Leeds	28
Wakefield T.	18	Keighley C.	19
Bye: Doncaster (Bramley withdrew)			

Second Round

Castleford	8	Sheffield E.	6
Dewsbury	21	Bradford N.	28
Doncaster	47	Halifax	6
Keighley C.	15	Hull K.R.	24

Semi-Finals

Bradford N.	22	Doncaster	19
Castleford	40	Hull K.R.	6

Final

Bradford N.	27	Castleford	10

ALLIANCE PLAYER OF THE YEAR

1995 Michael Shaw (Leeds)

POT POURRI

DIARY OF LANDMARKS

1895 August 29... the beginning. The Northern Rugby Football Union formed at The George Hotel, Huddersfield, following the breakaway from the English RU by 21 clubs who wanted to pay players for taking time off work to play.
September 7... season opens with 22 clubs.
Joseph Platt appointed Rugby League Secretary.

1897 April 24... Batley won the first Northern Union — later Rugby League — Challenge Cup final.
Line-out abolished and replaced by punt from touch.
All goals to be worth two points.

1898 Professionalism allowed but players must be in full-time employment.

1899 Scrum if player cannot release the ball after a tackle.

1901 Punt from touch replaced by 10-yard scrum when ball is carried into touch.

1902 Two divisions introduced.
Punt from touch abolished completely.
Touch-finding rule introduced with the ball having to bounce before entering touch.

1905 Two divisions scrapped.
Lancashire and Yorkshire County Cup competitions inaugurated.

1906 Thirteen-a-side introduced, from traditional 15.
Play-the-ball introduced.

1907 First tour — New Zealand to England. The tour party were RU "rebels".
First Top Four play-off for championship.

1908 Australia and New Zealand launch Rugby League.
First Australian tour of England.

1910 First British tour of Australia and New Zealand.

1915 Competitive rugby suspended for duration of First World War.

1919 Competitive rugby resumed in January.

1920 John Wilson appointed Rugby League Secretary.

1922 Title of Northern Rugby Football Union changed to Rugby Football League.
Goal from a mark abolished.

1927 First radio broadcast of Challenge Cup final — Oldham v. Swinton at Wigan.

1929 Wembley staged its first RL Challenge Cup final — Wigan v. Dewsbury.

1932 London exhibition match under floodlights at White City — Leeds v. Wigan.

1933 France staged its first Rugby League match — an exhibition between England and Australia in Paris.
London Highfield, formerly Wigan Highfield, became capital's first Rugby League team, also first to play regularly under floodlights.

1934 A French squad made a short tour of England before Rugby League was officially launched in France.

1935 European Championship introduced, contested by England, France and Wales.

1939 Second World War. Emergency war-time competitions introduced.

1945 War-time emergencies over.
Bill Fallowfield appointed Rugby League Secretary.

1946 First all-ticket match — Hull v. Hull K.R.

1948 King George VI became first reigning monarch to attend Rugby League match — Wigan v. Bradford Northern Cup final at Wembley.
First televised match — at Wembley — but shown only in London area.
Wembley's first all-ticket final.
International Board formed.

1949 Welsh League formed.

1950 Italian squad made brief tour of England.

1951 First televised match in the North — Britain v. New Zealand at Swinton.
First floodlights installation by Northern club, Bradford Northern.

1952 First nationally televised Challenge Cup final — Workington Town v. Featherstone Rovers.

1954 First World Cup, staged in France.

1955	London staged series of televised floodlit matches for the Independent Television Association Trophy.	**1977**	County Championship not held for first time since 1895, excluding war years.
	Welsh League disbanded.		Anglo-Australian transfer ban agreed.
1956	Sunday rugby for amateurs permitted by the Rugby Football League.	**1978**	Papua New Guinea admitted as full members of International Board.

1955 London staged series of televised floodlit matches for the Independent Television Association Trophy.
Welsh League disbanded.

1956 Sunday rugby for amateurs permitted by the Rugby Football League.

1962 Two divisions reintroduced, with Eastern and Western Divisions also formed.

1964 Substitutes allowed for injuries, but only up to half-time.
Two divisions and regional leagues scrapped.
One league system with Top 16 play-off for championship.

1965 BBC-2 Floodlit Trophy competition began with regular Tuesday night series.
Substitutes allowed for any reason up to and including half-time.
English Schools Rugby League formed.

1966 Four-tackle rule introduced for Floodlit Trophy competition in October, then for all games from December.

1967 First Sunday fixtures played, two matches on December 17.

1969 Substitutes allowed at any time.
Universities and Colleges Rugby League Association formed.

1971 John Player Trophy competition launched.

1972 Six-tackle rule introduced.
Timekeepers with hooter system to signal end of match introduced.
Colts League formed.

1973 Two divisions reintroduced.
March 4... British Amateur Rugby League Association formed.

1974 Drop goal value halved to one point. Had been reduced earlier in international matches.
David Oxley appointed Rugby League Secretary.
David Howes appointed first full-time Public Relations Officer to the Rugby Football League.
National Coaching Scheme launched.

1975 Premiership Trophy competition launched.

1976 Differential penalty introduced for technical scrum offences.

1977 County Championship not held for first time since 1895, excluding war years.
Anglo-Australian transfer ban agreed.

1978 Papua New Guinea admitted as full members of International Board.

1981 Rugby League Professional Players' Association formed.

1982 County Championship scrapped.

1983 Sin bin introduced.
Try value increased to four points.
Handover after sixth tackle introduced, among several other new or amended laws following meeting of International Board.
Anglo-Australian transfer ban lifted.

1984 Alliance League introduced in reserve grade reorganisation.

1985 First Charity Shield match played in Isle of Man.
War of the Roses launched on Lancashire v. Yorkshire county of origin basis.
Relegation-promotion reduced to three down, three up.

1986 Relegation-promotion altered for one year only to four down, two up to provide a 14-strong First Division for the 1987-88 season.

1987 Premiership doubleheader at Manchester United's Old Trafford launched with introduction of a Second Division Final.

1988 Colts scrapped for new youth scheme.
Six-man League Board of Directors appointed.
Fred Lindop appointed first-ever Controller of Referees.

1990 Russia introduced Rugby League and sent 90-man squad on three-match tour to Britain.

1991 Russian eight-club league launched.
Three divisions introduced for 1991-92 season.
Academy Under-18 league formed.
Blood bin introduced.

1992 Maurice Lindsay appointed Rugby League Chief Executive on retirement of David Oxley.
Ten-metre play-the-ball rule introduced.

1993   Controller of Referees Fred Lindop included in League HQ redundancy programme.

Two divisions reintroduced with three bottom clubs demoted to non-League status. National pro-am Conference League launched. County Cups scrapped.

1994   Broadcaster Harry Gration appointed Rugby League Public Affairs Executive on resignation of David Howes.

Top Australian referee Greg McCallum appointed Rugby League Referees' Coaching Director.

1995   Journalist Paul Harrison appointed Rugby League Media Manager on resignation of Harry Gration.

Disciplinary procedure of referees putting players on report introduced.

In-goal judges introduced.

Super League and summer rugby proposed for introduction in 1996.

Top Australian referee Greg McCallum, appointed Rugby League's Referees' Coaching Director in 1994, forcing his early retirement as a man-in-the-middle.

DISCIPLINARY RECORDS

This sub-section is a compilation of sendings off and disciplinary verdicts for first team players.

The following information is based on the workings of the League's Disciplinary Committee which meets weekly during a season.

– club not in existence	1994-95	1993-94	1992-93	1991-92	1990-91	1989-90
Barrow	4	2	3	6	5	5
Batley	5	3	4	7	4	1
Blackpool G.	—	—	0	6	2	9
Bradford N.	2	2	0	4	3	5
Bramley	8	3	4	2	5	4
Carlisle	1	9	6	2	4	0
Castleford	3	1	3	3	4	6
Chorley B.	—	—	0	5	7	3
Dewsbury	4	4	1	1	5	3
Doncaster	5	3	2	3	4	2
Featherstone R.	6	3	3	7	1	4
Halifax	1	1	1	2	3	8
Highfield	5	3	7	7	3	3
Huddersfield	1	3	6	2	1	7
Hull	3	1	3	2	1	3
Hull K.R.	3	0	0	1	3	3
Hunslet	7	5	3	2	6	6
Keighley C.	3	3	2	4	5	10
Leeds	1	2	1	2	5	3
Leigh	3	3	1	3	1	7
London B.	2	1	5	2	1	4
Nottingham C.	—	—	2	2	2	5
Oldham	6	2	6	5	3	6
Rochdale H.	5	1	2	4	5	3
Ryedale-York	4	4	2	1	3	7
St. Helens	4	3	1	6	1	6
Salford	1	1	0	0	5	4
Scarborough P.	—	—	—	1	—	—
Sheffield E.	2	1	4	7	2	3
Swinton	6	2	3	4	1	4
Wakefield T.	1	3	1	3	2	6
Warrington	3	0	2	6	2	4
Whitehaven	7	4	1	5	3	6
Widnes	5	0	5	2	2	6
Wigan	3	1	2	2	7	8
Workington T.	2	2	4	6	4	8
Totals	**116**	**76**	**90**	**127**	**115**	**172**

DISCIPLINARY ANALYSIS 1994-95

The following is a club-by-club disciplinary record for 1994-95, showing the players sent off in first team matches and the findings of the League's Disciplinary Committee.

The committee's verdict is featured in the brackets after the player's name, each number indicating the match ban imposed. SOS stands for sending off sufficient and NG for not guilty. A suspension reduced or increased on appeal is shown as follows, 6 to 4.

During 1988-89 the totting-up system for sin-bin suspensions was abandoned. Previously two points were issued for a 10-minute temporary dismissal, a one-match ban being imposed when the total reached six. Instead, the sin bins were recorded and taken into account when considering a full dismissal.

The 1984-85 season was the first time video action other than official BBC or ITV tapes could be offered in evidence.

Towards the end of the 1994-95 season, new referee supremo Greg McCallum introduced on-field reporting, with alleged offenders being reported to the league's Board of Directors for them to decide whether there was a charge to answer.

Club	Total sent off	Dismissed Player	Number of sin bins
Barrow	4	Paul Crarey (2), Shaun Morrow (1), Peers Bent (2), Stewart Quayle (2)	14
Batley	5	Wayne Heron (3, SOS), Andrew Parkinson (3,1), Glen Tomlinson (4)	17
Bradford N.	2	Karl Fairbank (2), Eugene Bourneville (2)	16
Bramley	8	Dean Hall (6, NG), Andrew Marson (3,2), Ray Ashton (NG), Julian Fisher (3), Gordon Long (2), Paul Garrett (NG)	18
Carlisle	1	Barry Quayle (SOS)	16
Castleford	3	Dean Sampson (4), Tony Kemp (2), Tawera Nikau (£100)	16
Dewsbury	4	Phil Cornforth (SOS), Andy Fisher (2), Ian Bates (1), Glenn Bell (2)	17
Doncaster	5	Simon Tuffs (2), Colin Maskill (SOS), Sonny Whakarau (2), Vila Matautia (SOS), Jamie Bloem (3)	23
Featherstone R.	6	Matt Calland (5,2), Leo Casey (4), Mark Aston (4), Gary H. Price (SOS), Andy Currier (NG)	23
Halifax	1	John Fieldhouse (NG)	15
Highfield	5	Andy Crehan (3,3), Carl Partington (NG), Norman Barrow (3), Glyn Owen (SOS)	9
Huddersfield	1	Stephen Barnett (NG)	15
Hull	3	Tim Street (4, NG), Steve McNamara (NG)	30
Hull K.R.	3	Paul Speckman (1), Andy Thompson (2), Nick Halafihi (SOS)	17
Hunslet	7	Richard Pell (3,1,NG), Michael Coyle (2,SOS), Richard Darkes (1), Chris Watson (3)	12
Keighley C.	3	Brendan Hill (NG), Darren Fleary (SOS), Ian Gately (SOS)	12
Leeds	1	Garry Schofield (2)	23
Leigh	3	Ken Jones (2), Russell Bridge (NG), Harmon Tuavao (NG)	12

London B.	2	Dixon McIvor (1), Peter Liddell (4)	11
Oldham	6	Craig Richards (2), Mike Kuiti (NG), Darren Abram (SOS), David Bradbury (seven-month ban), John Clarke (2), Jason Temu (2)	28
Rochdale H.	5	Wayne Reid (4 to 3), Steve Maudsley (SOS), Brian McCarthy (2), David Anderson (3, NG)	10
Ryedale-York	4	Leigh Deakin (NG), Neville Ramsey (SOS), Andy Precious (2), Bradley Davis (2)	8
St. Helens	4	Sonny Nickle (3, NG), Apollo Perelini (NG), Andy Northey (2)	19
Salford	1	Bob Marsden (£100)	20
Sheffield E.	2	Richard Price (2), Mark Gamson (2)	16
Swinton	6	Gavin Price-Jones (NG, mistaken identity), Paul Kay (4), Tony Humphries (2), Ian Skeech (SOS), Andy Purcell (2)	24
Wakefield T.	1	Ian Bowie (SOS)	16
Warrington	3	Bruce McGuire (2, NG), Paul Cullen (1)	17
Whitehaven	7	Les Quirk (4), Ged Blaney (2), Gary Hetherington (2), Mark Ryan (2), Kurt Sorensen (2), Nigel White (4), Mike Pechey (SOS)	13
Widnes	5	Mike O'Neill (4,2), Paul Hulme (2), David Smith (3), Andy Ireland (2)	16
Wigan	3	Kelvin Skerrett (3), Denis Betts (SOS), Henry Paul (NG)	22
Workington T.	2	Kyle White (3), Vincent Banet (2)	23

In addition, the following players were dealt with by the Disciplinary Committee after either being referred by the League's Board of Directors or placed on report by the match referee.

Referrals
Bradford N.: David Myers (three-month ban)
Dewsbury: Eddie Rombo(1), Shane Williams (1)
Huddersfield: Andy Pucill (4), Gary Senior (8)
St. Helens: Shane Cooper (5)
Swinton: Glenn Prince (3), Dave Harthill (1), Tony Humphries (5)
Whitehaven: Lee Anderson (2)

On report
Doncaster: Gordon Lynch (£50), Andy Rothwell (2)
Featherstone R.: Steve Molloy (1)
Huddersfield: Joe Naidole (3)
Leeds: Gary Mercer (1)
Oldham: David Stephenson (2)
Sheffield E.: Paul Broadbent (1), David Mycoe (2 to 1)
Wigan: Kelvin Skerrett (3)

● In addition to the League's Disciplinary findings, two players were dealt with by the International Disciplinary Committee during the 1994 John Smith's Tour by Australia. Great Britain skipper Shaun Edwards was sent off in the first John Smith's Test at Wembley and suspended for three matches and fined £1,000. Wigan prop Barrie McDermott was cited after their Kangaroo tour fixture and banned for two matches and fined £1,000.

SPONSORSHIP
This updated sub-section is a record of the sponsorship programme under the control of the Rugby Football League.

1994-95 COMPETITIONS:

Silk Cut Challenge Cup	£400,000
Regal Trophy	£410,000
Stones Bitter Championship and Premiership	£365,000
John Smith's Tests	£450,000
GRAND TOTAL	£1,625,000

QUEEN'S HONOURS
Ten Rugby League players have been awarded the MBE and two others the OBE by Her Majesty the Queen for their services to the game. Former Castleford player-coach Malcolm Reilly was awarded the OBE in June 1991, while Great Britain's full-time coach.

Player	Awarded MBE	GB Caps	Career	Clubs
Eric Ashton	June 1966	26	1955-69	Wigan
Geoff Gunney	June 1970	11	1951-73	Hunslet
Clive Sullivan	January 1974	17	1961-85	Hull, Hull K.R., Oldham, Doncaster
Chris Hesketh	January 1976	21+2	1963-79	Wigan, Salford
Roger Millward	January 1983	28+1	1963-80	Castleford, Hull K.R.
Neil Fox	June 1983	29	1956-79	Wakefield T., Bradford N., Hull K.R., York, Bramley, Huddersfield
David Watkins	January 1986	2+4	1967-82	Salford, Swinton, Cardiff C.
Ellery Hanley	January 1990	33+1	1978-	Bradford N., Wigan, Leeds
Jeff Grayshon	June 1992	13	1970-	Dewsbury, Bradford N., Leeds, Featherstone R., Batley
Jonathan Davies	January 1995	12+1	1989-	Widnes, Warrington
	Awarded OBE			
Malcolm Reilly	June 1991	9	1967-87	Castleford
Garry Schofield	June 1994	44+2	1983-	Hull, Leeds

ATTENDANCES

CLUB ATTENDANCE REVIEW

The following is a review of clubs' home attendances for League matches from 1986-87.

The main figure is the individual club's average gate for League games during that season. The figure in brackets indicates an upward or downward trend compared with the previous season.

Also indicated is the division the club competed in that season, i.e.,
1 — First Division, 2 — Second Division, 3 — Third Division.

Club	86-87	87-88	88-89	89-90	90-91	91-92	92-93	93-94	94-95
Barrow	1 2664 (+738)	2 1624 (−1040)	2 1594 (−30)	1 1997 (+403)	2 962 (−1035)	3 1003 (+41)	3 786 (−217)	2 1318 (+532)	2 957 (−361)
Batley	2 744 (−186)	2 859 (+115)	2 924 (+65)	2 1506 (+582)	2 1188 (−318)	3 1145 (−43)	3 925 (−220)	2 1227 (+302)	2 1509 (+282)
Blackpool G.	2 475 (−59)	2 922 (+447)	2 512 (−410)	2 780 (+258)	2 638 (−142)	3 309 (−329)	3 475 (+166)	−	−
Bradford N.	1 4312 (+377)	1 4723 (+411)	1 4969 (+246)	1 5584 (+615)	1 5274 (−310)	1 4725 (−549)	1 5082 (+357)	1 6513 (+1431)	1 5654 (−859)
Bramley	2 737 (−94)	2 858 (+121)	2 1004 (+146)	2 982 (−22)	2 805 (−177)	3 870 (+65)	2 980 (+110)	2 729 (−251)	2 758 (+29)
Carlisle	2 789 (+171)	2 763 (−26)	2 678 (−85)	2 574 (−104)	2 781 (+207)	2 800 (+19)	2 648 (−152)	2 603 (−45)	2 375 (−228)
Castleford	1 4758 (+1057)	1 4520 (−238)	1 6580 (+2060)	1 6428 (−152)	1 6019 (−409)	1 6465 (+446)	1 5658 (−807)	1 5555 (−103)	1 5090 (−465)
Chorley B.	−	−	−	2 806 (−)	2 690 (−116)	3 394 (−296)	3 434 (+40)	−	−
Dewsbury	2 669 (−1150)	2 658 (−11)	2 772 (+114)	2 1227 (+455)	2 955 (−272)	3 1140 (+185)	3 1108 (−32)	2 1366 (+258)	2 1859 (+493)
Doncaster	2 1543 (+854)	2 1450 (−93)	2 1906 (+456)	2 1965 (+59)	2 1458 (−507)	3 1158 (−300)	3 997 (−161)	2 1648 (+651)	1 3495 (+1847)
Featherstone R.	1 2606 (+286)	2 1879 (−727)	1 4379 (+2500)	1 4269 (−110)	1 4722 (+453)	1 4001 (−721)	2 2670 (−1331)	1 4030 (+1360)	1 3683 (−347)
Halifax	1 4891 (−53)	1 6521 (+1630)	1 8022 (+1501)	2 5921 (−2101)	2 4458 (−1463)	1 7181 (+2723)	1 6452 (−729)	1 6608 (+156)	1 5600 (−1008)
Highfield	2 331 (−32)	2 515 (+184)	2 298 (−217)	2 453 (+155)	2 632 (+179)	3 319 (−313)	3 378 (+59)	2 403 (+25)	2 550 (+147)
Huddersfield	2 524 (−154)	2 601 (+77)	2 1114 (+513)	2 1634 (+520)	2 1306 (−328)	3 2271 (+965)	2 1985 (−286)	2 2227 (+242)	2 2904 (+677)
Hull	1 5538 (−707)	1 5111 (−427)	1 6804 (+1693)	1 6218 (−586)	1 6699 (+481)	1 5892 (−807)	1 4860 (−1032)	1 4314 (−546)	1 4165 (−149)
Hull K.R.	1 4651 (−204)	1 4186 (−465)	1 5298 (+1112)	2 4851 (−447)	1 4952 (+101)	1 4752 (−200)	1 3609 (−1143)	1 3403 (−206)	2 1900 (−1503)
Hunslet	1 1050 (+328)	1 2678 (+1628)	2 947 (−1731)	2 1046 (+99)	2 767 (−279)	3 770 (+3)	3 724 (−46)	2 740 (+16)	2 852 (+112)

(continued)

469

Club	86-87	87-88	88-89	89-90	90-91	91-92	92-93	93-94	94-95
Keighley C.	2 445 (−240)	2 958 (+513)	2 961 (+3)	2 936 (−25)	2 985 (+49)	3 1196 (+211)	3 2060 (+864)	2 3032 (+972)	2 3723 (+691)
Leeds	1 6393 (−535)	1 9911 (+3518)	1 12060 (+2149)	1 12251 (+191)	1 11102 (−1149)	1 12164 (+1062)	1 11527 (−637)	1 9545 (−1982)	1 12516 (+2971)
Leigh	1 4232 (+1522)	1 4516 (+284)	2 2346 (−2170)	1 4568 (+2222)	2 1719 (−2849)	2 3014 (+1295)	1 3967 (+953)	1 3385 (−582)	2 1550 (−1855)
London C.	2 684 (−133)	2 615 (−69)	2 588 (−27)	2 841 (+253)	2 557 (−284)	2 724 (+167)	2 554 (−170)	2 734 (+180)	2 814 (+80)
Nottingham C.	2 368 (−119)	2 368 (−)	2 560 (+192)	2 577 (+17)	2 255 (−322)	3 270 (+15)	3 270 (−)	—	—
Oldham	1 3915 (−418)	2 3790 (−125)	1 5759 (+1969)	2 4401 (−1358)	1 5094 (+693)	2 3149 (−1945)	2 2809 (−340)	1 4062 (+1253)	1 3889 (−173)
Rochdale H.	2 877 (−390)	2 1106 (+229)	2 1027 (−79)	2 2510 (+1483)	1 2542 (+32)	2 1415 (−1127)	2 1308 (−107)	2 1063 (−245)	2 1089 (+26)
Ryedale-York	2 1520 (−1308)	2 1406 (−114)	2 2021 (+615)	2 2495 (+474)	2 1857 (−638)	2 1181 (−676)	3 1701 (+520)	2 1311 (−390)	2 1120 (−191)
St. Helens	1 7341 (+1319)	1 8417 (+1076)	1 9514 (+1097)	1 8555 (−959)	1 7391 (−1164)	1 8456 (+1065)	1 8908 (+452)	1 7264 (−1644)	1 7467 (+203)
Salford	1 2826 (+306)	1 3747 (+921)	1 5470 (+1723)	1 3720 (−1750)	2 2314 (−1406)	1 3785 (+1471)	1 4098 (+313)	1 4106 (+8)	1 3600 (−506)
Scarborough P.	—	—	—	—	—	3 777 (−)	—	—	—
Sheffield E.	2 708 (+10)	2 847 (+139)	2 838 (−9)	1 4038 (+3200)	1 4031 (−7)	2 2435 (−1596)	1 3069 (+634)	1 3050 (−19)	1 2661 (−389)
Swinton	2 1622 (−1084)	1 2987 (+1365)	2 1435 (−1552)	2 1678 (+243)	2 1737 (+59)	1 2702 (+965)	2 1051 (−1651)	2 788 (−263)	2 776 (−12)
Wakefield T.	1 2637 (+923)	2 2416 (−221)	1 5151 (+2735)	1 5428 (+277)	1 4848 (−580)	1 5022 (+174)	1 4505 (−517)	1 3822 (−683)	1 3438 (−384)
Warrington	1 4172 (+554)	1 4974 (+802)	1 4893 (−81)	1 5412 (+519)	1 5915 (+503)	1 5204 (−711)	1 4550 (−754)	1 6188 (+1638)	1 5380 (−808)
Whitehaven	2 1800 (−78)	2 1772 (−28)	2 1310 (−462)	2 961 (−349)	2 1035 (+74)	3 632 (−403)	3 1462 (+830)	2 1257 (−205)	2 1149 (−108)
Widnes	1 3840 (−179)	1 6262 (+2422)	1 8648 (+2386)	1 7858 (−790)	1 6793 (−1065)	1 6291 (−502)	1 5540 (−751)	1 4525 (−1015)	1 4086 (−439)
Wigan	1 12732 (+217)	1 13021 (+289)	1 14543 (+1522)	1 13973 (−570)	1 14493 (+520)	1 14040 (−453)	1 14553 (+513)	1 14561 (+8)	1 14195 (−366)
Workington T.	2 653 (−49)	2 737 (+84)	2 774 (+37)	2 691 (−83)	2 1426 (+735)	2 1884 (+458)	3 2040 (+156)	2 2603 (+563)	1 3776 (+1173)

COMPETITION ATTENDANCE REVIEW

		86-87	87-88	88-89	89-90	90-91	91-92	92-93	93-94	94-95
FIRST	Total	1,162,666	1,060,296	1,327,192	1,173,815	1,168,407	1,185,117	1,122,955	1,364,056	1,330,538
DIVISION	Av.	4,844	5,826	7,292	6,450	6,420	6,511	6,170	5,683	5,543
SECOND	Total	217,552	381,825	298,776	515,687	371,398	204,304	168,069	315,841	328,377
DIVISION	Av.	863	1,364	1,067	1,754	1,263	1,824	1,501	1,316	1,368
THIRD	Total	–	–	–	–	–	159,209	160,348	–	–
DIVISION	Av.						875	1,027		
LEAGUE TOTALS (1st & 2nd) *plus 3rd	Total	1,380,218	1,442,121	1,625,968	1,689,502	1,539,805	1,548,630*	1,451,372*	1,679,897	1,658,915
	Av.	2,805	3,121	3,519	3,549	3,235	3,253*	3,225*	3,499	3,456
CHALL-ENGE CUP	Av.	6,965	8,764	8,666	7,339	6,748	6,899	7,771	5,907	5,821
REGAL	Av.	4,122	3,570	4,987	4,876	3,515	4,007	3,624	2,690	3,627
PREMIER	Av.	15,154	13,462	15,856	16,796	12,483	13,513	12,788	13,165	11,425
10,000+ (No. of)		43	46	59	54	43	49	38	41	51

20,000-plus crowds . . . . A 10-year review

All matches except the Rugby League Challenge Cup final at Wembley

22,209	Britain v. New Zealand	Third Test	Elland Rd, Leeds	9 Nov. 1985
21,813	Wigan v. St. Helens	Division One	Wigan	26 Dec. 1985
23,866	Hull K.R. v. Leeds	RL Cup semi-final	Elland Rd, Leeds	29 Mar. 1986
32,485	Hull K.R. v. Leeds	RL Cup semi-final replay	Elland Rd, Leeds	3 Apr. 1986
28,252	Wigan v. St. Helens	Lancs Cup semi-final	Wigan	1 Oct. 1986
30,622	Wigan v. Australia	Tour	Wigan	12 Oct. 1986
20,180	Oldham v. Wigan	Lancs Cup final	St. Helens	19 Oct. 1986
50,583	Britain v. Australia	First Test	Manchester U. FC	25 Oct. 1986
30,808	Britain v. Australia	Second Test	Elland Rd, Leeds	8 Nov. 1986
20,169	Britain v. Australia	Third Test	Wigan	22 Nov. 1986
21,214	St. Helens v. Wigan	Division One	St. Helens	26 Dec. 1986
21,144	Warrington v. Wigan	John Player final	Bolton W. FC	10 Jan. 1987
20,355	Wigan v. St. Helens	Division One	Wigan	17 Apr. 1987
22,457	Wigan v. Halifax	Premiership semi-final	Wigan	10 May 1987
38,756	Warrington v. Wigan	Premiership final	Manchester U. FC	17 May 1987
36,895	Wigan v. Manly	World Club Challenge	Wigan	7 Oct. 1987
20,234	Wigan v. Warrington	Lancs Cup final	St. Helens	11 Oct. 1987
23,809	Wigan v. St. Helens	Division One	Wigan	27 Dec. 1987
25,110	Wigan v. Leeds	RL Cup round 2	Wigan	14 Feb. 1988
20,783	Salford v. Wigan	RL Cup semi-final	Bolton W. FC	12 Mar. 1988

(continued)

20,534	Halifax v. Hull	RL Cup semi-final	Leeds	26 Mar. 1988
25,117	Halifax v. Hull	RL Cup semi-final replay	Elland Rd, Leeds	30 Mar. 1988
21,812	St. Helens v. Wigan	Division One	St. Helens	1 Apr. 1988
35,252	St. Helens v. Widnes	Premiership final	Manchester U. FC	15 May 1988
22,968	Castleford v. Leeds	Yorks Cup final	Elland Rd, Leeds	16 Oct. 1988
20,709	Widnes v. Wigan	John Player final	Bolton W. FC	7 Jan. 1989
26,080	Leeds v. Widnes	RL Cup round 2	Leeds	26 Feb. 1989
26,529	Warrington v. Wigan	RL Cup semi-final	Manchester C. FC	25 Mar. 1989
21,076	Wigan v. St. Helens	Division One	Wigan	12 Apr. 1989
40,194	Hull v. Widnes	Premiership final	Manchester U. FC	14 May 1989
30,786	Widnes v. Canberra	World Club Challenge	Manchester U. FC	4 Oct. 1989
20,346	Britain v. New Zealand	Third Test	Wigan	11 Nov. 1989
27,075	Wigan v. St. Helens	Division One	Wigan	26 Dec. 1989
23,570	Leeds v. Wigan	Division One	Leeds	4 Mar. 1990
26,489	St. Helens v. Wigan	RL Cup semi-final	Manchester U. FC	10 Mar. 1990
24,462	Wigan v. Leeds	Division One	Wigan	10 Apr. 1990
40,796	Bradford N. v. Widnes	Premiership final	Manchester U. FC	13 May 1990
24,814	Wigan v. Australia	Tour	Wigan	14 Oct. 1990
54,569	Britain v. Australia	First Test	Wembley	27 Oct. 1990
46,615	Britain v. Australia	Second Test	Manchester U. FC	10 Nov. 1990
32,500	Britain v. Australia	Third Test	Elland Rd, Leeds	24 Nov. 1990
29,763	Wigan v. Widnes	Division One	Wigan	9 Apr. 1991
42,043	Hull v. Widnes	Premiership final	Manchester U. FC	12 May 1991
20,152	Wigan v. Penrith	World Club Challenge	Liverpool FC	2 Oct. 1991
26,307	Wigan v. St. Helens	Division One	Wigan	26 Dec. 1991
21,736	Wigan v. Warrington	RL Cup round 2	Wigan	16 Feb. 1992
20,821	Leeds v. Wigan	Division One	Leeds	15 Mar. 1992
33,157	St. Helens v. Wigan	Premiership final	Manchester U. FC	17 May 1992
20,534	St. Helens v. Wigan	Lancs Cup final	St. Helens	18 Oct. 1992
73,631	Britain v. Australia	World Cup final	Wembley	24 Oct. 1992
20,258	Leeds v. Castleford	Division One	Leeds	26 Dec. 1992
21,191	Wigan v. St. Helens	RL Cup round 2	Wigan	13 Feb. 1993
20,057	Leeds v. Wigan	Division One	Leeds	3 Mar. 1993
20,085	Bradford N. v. Wigan	RL Cup semi-final	Elland Rd, Leeds	27 Mar. 1993
29,839	Wigan v. St. Helens	Division One	Wigan	9 Apr. 1993
36,598	St. Helens v. Wigan	Premiership final	Manchester U. FC	16 May 1993
36,131	Britain v. New Zealand	First Test	Wembley	16 Oct. 1993
29,100	Wigan v. St. Helens	Division One	Wigan	26 Dec. 1993
22,615	Leeds v. Bradford N.	RL Cup quarter-final	Leeds	27 Feb. 1994
20,771	St. Helens v. Leeds	RL Cup semi-final	Wigan	26 Mar. 1994
35,644	Castleford v. Wigan	Premiership final	Manchester U. FC	22 May 1994
20,057	Wigan v. Australia	Tour	Wigan	8 Oct. 1994
57,034	Britain v. Australia	First Test	Wembley	22 Oct. 1994
43,930	Britain v. Australia	Second Test	Manchester U. FC	5 Nov. 1994
39,468	Britain v. Australia	Third Test	Elland Rd, Leeds	20 Nov. 1994
20,053	Leeds v. Wigan	Division One	Leeds	11 Dec. 1994
23,278	Wigan v. St. Helens	Regal Trophy	Wigan	8 Jan. 1995
21,485	Featherstone R. v. Leeds	RL Cup semi-final	Elland Rd, Leeds	1 Apr. 1995
26,314	Wigan v. St. Helens	Division One	Wigan	14 Apr. 1995
30,160	Leeds v. Wigan	Premiership Final	Manchester U. FC	21 May 1995

1994-95 ATTENDANCE ANALYSIS
FIRST DIVISION

Total 1,330,538
Average 5,543

Wigan topped the attendance chart for the 11th successive season, although they suffered an annual decrease of 366 spectators per League match. Leeds, who were runners-up to Wigan in three of the four Grand Slam events, attracted nearly 3,000 extra fans per League fixture to register their biggest average gate for more than a decade. Leeds were one of only four clubs to record an annual increase in support, newly-promoted Doncaster and Workington, plus third-placed St. Helens, being the others. The First Division average gate for the 240 fixtures was 5,543, an annual drop of 2.5 per cent from the 1993-94 figure of 5,683.

SECOND DIVISION

Total 328,377
Average 1,368

Second Division Champions Keighley Cougars topped the gates chart for the second successive season, adding 691 fans per league match for a 1994-95 average turnout of 3,723. A total of nine clubs registered an annual increase in support, including Highfield who moved off the bottom spot to be replaced by Carlisle. Compared with the 1993-94 average gate of 1,316, there was an annual increase of four per cent.

LEAGUE CHAMPIONSHIP

Aggregate 1,658,915
Average 3,456

The 480 First and Second Division fixtures staged in 1994-95 attracted an average gate of 3,456, an annual decrease of 1.2 per cent on the previous campaign's average of 3,499.

SILK CUT CHALLENGE CUP

The second successive season of the new-style Silk Cut Challenge Cup format suffered a 1.5 per cent drop in attendances. The 1994-95 average gate for the 49 involving professional clubs, including two replays, was 5,821, compared with the previous season's 5,907.

REGAL TROPHY

Support for the early season knockout trophy rose by 35 per cent, the 48 ties, including a replay, attracting an average gate of 3,627 compared with the previous season's figure of 2,690. The new Alfred MacAlpine Stadium at Huddersfield staged the Regal Trophy final in its debut season, attracting a capacity 19,636 crowd.

STONES BITTER PREMIERSHIP

A total of 79,976 spectators watched the 1995 seven-tie end-of-season tournaments, the average gate of 11,425 being a 13.2 per cent decrease on the 1993-94 average turnout of 13,165. A contributory factor was the rebuilding of one side of the Old Trafford ground, the attendance for the final being restricted to a sell-out 30,160.

SECOND DIVISION PREMIERSHIP

Excluding the Old Trafford final, the six Second Division Premiership ties attracted a total of 14,838 spectators. The 1994-95 average gate of 2,473 was an annual decrease 4.9 per cent compared with the previous season's figure of 2,600.

FIVE-FIGURE CROWDS

There was a total of 51 five-figure crowds, the best tally for five years, being boosted by the visit of the 1994 Australian tourists. The John Smith's Tour attracted eight five-figure attendances from 14 fixtures. As per tradition, the biggest gate was at Wembley for the 1995 Silk Cut Challenge Cup final which attracted a capacity 78,550. Of the 51 five-figure crowds, 20 were housed by Leeds and 18 by Wigan. There were 10 crowds of 20,000-plus, including all three Anglo-Aussie John Smith's Tests.

The 10,000-plus gates were divided into the following categories:

League 30
Australian Tour............................ 8
Challenge Cup 7
Regal Trophy 4
Premiership Trophy 2

STONES BITTER CHAMPIONSHIP	1994-95 Average	Annual Difference
Wigan	14195	(−366)
Leeds	12516	(+2971)
St. Helens	7467	(+203)
Bradford N.	5654	(−859)
Halifax	5600	(−1008)
Warrington	5380	(−808)
Castleford	5090	(−465)
Hull	4165	(−149)
Widnes	4086	(−439)
Oldham	3889	(−173)
★Workington T.	3776	(+1173)
Featherstone R.	3683	(−347)
Salford	3600	(−506)
★Doncaster	3495	(+1847)
Wakefield T.	3438	(−384)
Sheffield E.	2661	(−389)

Promoted 1993-94

SECOND DIVISION	1994-95 Average	Annual Difference
Keighley C.	3723	(+691)
Huddersfield	2904	(+677)
★Hull K.R.	1900	(−1503)
Dewsbury	1859	(+493)
★Leigh	1550	(−1835)
Batley	1509	(+282)
Whitehaven	1149	(−108)
Ryedale-York	1120	(−191)
Rochdale H.	1089	(+26)
Barrow	957	(−361)
Hunslet	852	(+112)
London B.	814	(+80)
Swinton	776	(−12)
Bramley	758	(+29)
Highfield	550	(+147)
Carlisle	375	(−228)

Relegated 1993-94

New Zealand Test loose forward Brendon Tuuta takes on the Leeds defence. Rovers will play in the re-shaped First Division.

FIXTURES

STONES BITTER CHAMPIONSHIP 1995-96

FRIDAY, 18 AUGUST 1995
Workington T.	v.	Wigan	7.30

SUNDAY, 20 AUGUST 1995
Castleford	v.	Oldham	3.30
Sheffield E.	v.	Leeds	3.15
St. Helens	v.	Bradford B.	3.00
Warrington	v.	London B.	3.00

WEDNESDAY, 23 AUGUST 1995
Bradford B.	v.	Warrington	7.30
London B.	v.	Halifax	7.30
Oldham	v.	St. Helens	7.30
Wigan	v.	Sheffield E.	7.30

FRIDAY, 25 AUGUST 1995
Castleford	v.	Leeds	7.30

SUNDAY, 27 AUGUST 1995
Halifax	v.	Bradford B.	3.00
Warrington	v.	Oldham	3.00
Workington T.	v.	Sheffield E.	3.00

MONDAY, 28 AUGUST 1995
St. Helens	v.	Wigan	2.00

WEDNESDAY, 30 AUGUST 1995
Leeds	v.	Warrington	7.30

FRIDAY, 1 SEPTEMBER 1995
Oldham	v.	Halifax	7.30

SUNDAY, 3 SEPTEMBER 1995
Bradford B.	v.	London B.	3.00
Leeds	v.	St. Helens	3.00
Sheffield E.	v.	Castleford	3.15
Wigan	v.	Warrington	3.00

WEDNESDAY, 6 SEPTEMBER 1995
Castleford	v.	Workington T.	7.30
Halifax	v.	Wigan	7.30
London B.	v.	Oldham	7.30

FRIDAY, 8 SEPTEMBER 1995
Sheffield E.	v.	Warrington	7.30

SUNDAY, 10 SEPTEMBER 1995
Leeds	v.	Halifax	3.00
Oldham	v.	Bradford B.	3.00
Wigan	v.	London B.	3.00
Workington T.	v.	St. Helens	3.00

WEDNESDAY, 13 SEPTEMBER 1995
St. Helens	v.	Sheffield E.	7.30
Wigan	v.	Castleford	7.30

FRIDAY, 15 SEPTEMBER 1995
London B.	v.	Leeds	7.30

SUNDAY, 17 SEPTEMBER 1995
Bradford B.	v.	Wigan	3.00
Halifax	v.	Sheffield E.	3.00
St. Helens	v.	Castleford	3.00
Warrington	v.	Workington T.	3.00

WEDNESDAY, 20 SEPTEMBER 1995
Oldham	v.	London B.	7.30
Warrington	v.	St. Helens	7.30

FRIDAY, 22 SEPTEMBER 1995
Leeds	v.	Bradford B.	7.30

SUNDAY, 24 SEPTEMBER 1995
Castleford	v.	Warrington	3.30
Sheffield E.	v.	London B.	3.15
Wigan	v.	Oldham	3.00
Workington T.	v.	Halifax	3.00

WEDNESDAY, 27 SEPTEMBER 1995
Leeds	v.	Workington T.	7.30

FRIDAY, 29 SEPTEMBER 1995
Halifax	v.	Castleford	7.30

SUNDAY, 1 OCTOBER 1995
Bradford B.	v.	Sheffield E.	3.00
London B.	v.	Workington T.	3.00
Oldham	v.	Leeds	3.00

WEDNESDAY, 1 NOVEMBER 1995
Bradford B.	v.	Castleford	7.30
London B.	v.	St. Helens	7.30
Oldham	v.	Workington T.	7.30
Warrington	v.	Halifax	7.30

FRIDAY, 3 NOVEMBER 1995
Leeds	v.	Wigan	7.30

SUNDAY, 5 NOVEMBER 1995
Castleford	v.	London B.	3.30
Sheffield E.	v.	Oldham	3.15
St. Helens	v.	Halifax	3.00
Workington T.	v.	Bradford B.	3.00

WEDNESDAY, 15 NOVEMBER 1995
Castleford	v.	Wigan	7.30
Halifax	v.	London B.	7.30
Workington T.	v.	Leeds	7.30

FRIDAY, 17 NOVEMBER 1995
Bradford B.	v.	St. Helens	7.30

SUNDAY, 19 NOVEMBER 1995
Leeds	v.	Sheffield E.	3.00
London B.	v.	Warrington	3.00
Oldham	v.	Castleford	3.00
Wigan	v.	Workington T.	3.00

WEDNESDAY, 29 NOVEMBER 1995
Sheffield E.	v.	St. Helens	7.30
Warrington	v.	Leeds	7.30
Workington T.	v.	Castleford	7.30

FRIDAY, 1 DECEMBER 1995
London B.	v.	Wigan	7.30

SUNDAY, 3 DECEMBER 1995
Bradford B.	v.	Oldham	3.00
Halifax	v.	Leeds	3.00
St. Helens	v.	Workington T.	3.00
Warrington	v.	Sheffield E.	3.00

WEDNESDAY, 6 DECEMBER 1995
Warrington	v.	Bradford B.	7.30

FRIDAY, 8 DECEMBER 1995
Sheffield E.	v.	Halifax	7.30

SUNDAY, 10 DECEMBER 1995
Castleford	v.	St. Helens	3.30
Leeds	v.	London B.	3.00
Wigan	v.	Bradford B.	3.00
Workington T.	v.	Warrington	3.00

WEDNESDAY, 13 DECEMBER 1995

St. Helens	v.	Oldham	7.30
Wigan	v.	Halifax	7.30

FRIDAY, 15 DECEMBER 1995

Warrington	v.	Castleford	7.30

SUNDAY, 17 DECEMBER 1995

Bradford B.	v.	Leeds	3.00
Halifax	v.	Workington T.	3.00
London B.	v.	Sheffield E.	3.00
Oldham	v.	Wigan	3.00

TUESDAY, 26 DECEMBER 1995

Bradford B.	v.	Halifax	3.00
Leeds	v.	Castleford	11.30
Oldham	v.	Warrington	3.00
Sheffield E.	v.	Workington T.	3.15
Wigan	v.	St. Helens	3.00

MONDAY, 1 JANUARY 1996

Castleford	v.	Sheffield E.	3.30
Halifax	v.	Oldham	3.00
London B.	v.	Bradford B.	3.00
St. Helens	v.	Leeds	3.00
Warrington	v.	Wigan	3.00

SUNDAY, 7 JANUARY 1996

Castleford	v.	Halifax	3.30
Leeds	v.	Oldham	3.00
Sheffield E.	v.	Bradford B.	3.15
St. Helens	v.	Warrington	3.00
Workington T.	v.	London B.	3.00

SUNDAY, 14 JANUARY 1996

Castleford	v.	Bradford B.	3.30
Halifax	v.	Warrington	3.00
Sheffield E.	v.	Wigan	3.15
St. Helens	v.	London B.	3.00
Workington T.	v.	Oldham	3.00

SUNDAY, 21 JANUARY 1996

Bradford B.	v.	Workington T.	3.00
Halifax	v.	St. Helens	3.00
London B.	v.	Castleford	3.00
Oldham	v.	Sheffield E.	3.00
Wigan	v.	Leeds	3.00

FIRST DIVISION

SUNDAY, 20 AUGUST 1995

Huddersfield	v.	Keighley C.	5.30
Hull	v.	Featherstone R.	3.15
Rochdale H.	v.	Batley	3.00
Wakefield T.	v.	Whitehaven	3.30
Widnes	v.	Dewsbury	3.00

WEDNESDAY, 23 AUGUST 1995

Batley	v.	Hull	7.30
Featherstone R.	v.	Dewsbury	7.30
Huddersfield	v.	Rochdale	7.30
Whitehaven	v.	Salford	7.30
Widnes	v.	Wakefield T.	7.30

SUNDAY, 27 AUGUST 1995

Dewsbury	v.	Batley	3.00
Hull	v.	Huddersfield	3.15
Rochdale H.	v.	Keighley C.	3.00
Salford	v.	Widnes	3.00
Wakefield T.	v.	Featherstone R.	3.30

SUNDAY, 3 SEPTEMBER 1995

Batley	v.	Wakefield T.	3.15
Featherstone R.	v.	Salford	3.30
Huddersfield	v.	Dewsbury	3.30
Keighley C.	v.	Hull	3.15
Widnes	v.	Whitehaven	3.00

WEDNESDAY, 6 SEPTEMBER 1995

Whitehaven	v.	Featherstone R.	7.30

SUNDAY, 10 SEPTEMBER 1995

Hull	v.	Rochdale	3.15
Keighley C.	v.	Dewsbury	3.15
Salford	v.	Batley	3.00
Wakefield T.	v.	Huddersfield	3.30

SUNDAY, 17 SEPTEMBER 1995

Batley	v.	Whitehaven	3.15
Featherstone R.	v.	Widnes	3.30
Huddersfield	v.	Salford	3.30
Keighley C.	v.	Wakefield T.	3.15
Rochdale H.	v.	Dewsbury	3.00

WEDNESDAY, 20 SEPTEMBER 1995

Dewsbury	v.	Hull	7.30
Salford	v.	Keighley C.	7.30
Wakefield T.	v.	Rochdale H.	7.30
Whitehaven	v.	Huddersfield	7.30
Widnes	v.	Batley	7.30

SUNDAY, 24 SEPTEMBER 1995

Batley	v.	Featherstone R.	3.15
Huddersfield	v.	Widnes	3.30
Hull	v.	Wakefield T.	3.15
Keighley C.	v.	Whitehaven	3.15
Rochdale H.	v.	Salford	3.00

SUNDAY, 1 OCTOBER 1995

Featherstone R.	v.	Huddersfield	3.30
Salford	v.	Hull	3.00
Wakefield T.	v.	Dewsbury	3.30
Whitehaven	v.	Rochdale H.	3.30
Widnes	v.	Keighley C.	3.00

WEDNESDAY, 1 NOVEMBER 1995

Batley	v.	Keighley C.	7.30
Featherstone R.	v.	Rochdale H.	7.30
Salford	v.	Wakefield T.	7.30
Whitehaven	v.	Dewsbury	7.30
Widnes	v.	Hull	7.30

SUNDAY, 5 NOVEMBER 1995

Dewsbury	v.	Salford	3.00
Huddersfield	v.	Batley	3.30
Hull	v.	Whitehaven	3.15
Keighley C.	v.	Featherstone R.	3.15
Rochdale H.	v.	Widnes	3.00

WEDNESDAY, 15 NOVEMBER 1995

Dewsbury	v.	Featherstone R.	7.30
Hull	v.	Batley	7.30
Rochdale H.	v.	Huddersfield	7.30
Salford	v.	Whitehaven	7.30
Wakefield T.	v.	Widnes	7.30

SUNDAY, 19 NOVEMBER 1995

Batley	v.	Rochdale H.	3.15
Dewsbury	v.	Widnes	3.00
Featherstone R.	v.	Hull	3.30
Keighley C.	v.	Huddersfield	3.15
Whitehaven	v.	Wakefield T.	3.30

WEDNESDAY, 29 NOVEMBER 1995

Batley	v.	Salford	7.30
Dewsbury	v.	Keighley C.	7.30
Featherstone R.	v.	Whitehaven	7.30
Huddersfield	v.	Wakefield T.	7.30
Rochdale H.	v.	Hull	7.30

SUNDAY, 3 DECEMBER 1995

Dewsbury	v.	Rochdale H.	3.00
Salford	v.	Huddersfield	3.00
Wakefield T.	v.	Keighley C.	3.30
Whitehaven	v.	Batley	3.30
Widnes	v.	Featherstone R.	3.00

SUNDAY, 10 DECEMBER 1995

Batley	v.	Widnes	3.15
Huddersfield	v.	Whitehaven	3.30
Hull	v.	Dewsbury	3.15
Keighley C.	v.	Salford	3.15
Rochdale H.	v.	Wakefield T.	3.00

SUNDAY, 17 DECEMBER 1995

Featherstone R.	v.	Batley	3.30
Salford	v.	Rochdale H.	3.00
Wakefield T.	v.	Hull	3.30
Whitehaven	v.	Keighley C.	3.30
Widnes	v.	Huddersfield	3.00

SUNDAY, 24 DECEMBER 1995

Huddersfield	v.	Hull	3.30

TUESDAY, 26 DECEMBER 1995

Batley	v.	Dewsbury	3.15
Featherstone R.	v.	Wakefield T.	3.30
Keighley C.	v.	Rochdale H.	3.15
Widnes	v.	Salford	3.00

MONDAY, 1 JANUARY 1996

Dewsbury	v.	Huddersfield	3.00
Hull	v.	Keighley C.	3.15
Salford	v.	Featherstone R.	3.00
Wakefield T.	v.	Batley	3.30
Whitehaven	v.	Widnes	3.30

SUNDAY, 7 JANUARY 1996

Dewsbury	v.	Wakefield T.	3.00
Huddersfield	v.	Featherstone R.	3.30
Hull	v.	Salford	3.15
Keighley C.	v.	Widnes	3.15
Rochdale H.	v.	Whitehaven	3.00

SUNDAY, 14 JANUARY 1996

Dewsbury	v.	Whitehaven	3.00
Hull	v.	Widnes	3.15
Keighley C.	v.	Batley	3.15
Rochdale H.	v.	Featherstone R.	3.00
Wakefield T.	v.	Salford	3.30

SUNDAY, 21 JANUARY 1996

Batley	v.	Huddersfield	3.15
Featherstone R.	v.	Keighley C.	3.30
Salford	v.	Dewsbury	3.00
Whitehaven	v.	Hull	3.30
Widnes	v.	Rochdale H.	3.00

SECOND DIVISION

SUNDAY, 20 AUGUST 1995

Highfield	v.	Barrow	3.00
Hunslet	v.	Chorley	3.30
Leigh	v.	Bramley	3.00
Swinton	v.	Hull K.R.	3.00
York	v.	Carlisle	3.15

TUESDAY, 22 AUGUST 1995

Hull K.R.	v.	Leigh	7.30

WEDNESDAY, 23 AUGUST 1995

Barrow	v.	Hunslet	7.30
Bramley	v.	Highfield	7.30
Chorley	v.	York	7.30

SUNDAY, 27 AUGUST 1995

Barrow	v.	Carlisle	2.30
Highfield	v.	Chorley	3.00
Hunslet	v.	Bramley	3.30
Leigh	v.	Swinton	3.00
York	v.	Hull K.R.	3.15

WEDNESDAY, 30 AUGUST 1995

Carlisle	v.	Swinton	7.00

SUNDAY, 3 SEPTEMBER 1995

Carlisle	v.	Highfield	3.00
Chorley	v.	Leigh	3.00
Hull K.R.	v.	Hunslet	3.15
Swinton	v.	Barrow	3.00

WEDNESDAY, 6 SEPTEMBER 1995

Bramley	v.	York	7.30

SUNDAY, 10 SEPTEMBER 1995

Barrow	v.	Hull K.R.	2.30
Chorley	v.	Bramley	3.00
Highfield	v.	Leigh	3.00
Hunslet	v.	Carlisle	3.30
York	v.	Swinton	3.15

SUNDAY, 17 SEPTEMBER 1995

Bramley	v.	Barrow	3.00
Carlisle	v.	Chorley	3.00
Hull K.R.	v.	Highfield	3.15
Leigh	v.	York	3.00
Swinton	v.	Hunslet	3.00

WEDNESDAY, 20 SEPTEMBER 1995

Bramley	v.	Hull K.R.	7.30
Chorley	v.	Swinton	7.30
Hunslet	v.	Highfield	7.30
Leigh	v.	Carlisle	7.30
York	v.	Barrow	7.30

SUNDAY, 24 SEPTEMBER 1995

Barrow	v.	Chorley	2.30
Carlisle	v.	Hull K.R.	3.00
Highfield	v.	York	3.00
Hunslet	v.	Leigh	3.30
Swinton	v.	Bramley	3.00

SUNDAY, 5 NOVEMBER 1995

Bramley	v.	Carlisle	3.00
Highfield	v.	Swinton	3.00
Hull K.R.	v.	Chorley	3.15
Leigh	v.	Barrow	3.00
York	v.	Hunslet	3.15

SUNDAY, 19 NOVEMBER 1995

Barrow	v.	Highfield	2.30
Bramley	v.	Leigh	3.00
Carlisle	v.	York	2.00
Chorley	v.	Hunslet	3.00
Hull K.R.	v.	Swinton	3.15

SUNDAY, 26 NOVEMBER 1995

Highfield	v.	Bramley	3.00
Hunslet	v.	Barrow	3.30
Leigh	v.	Hull K.R.	3.00
Swinton	v.	Carlisle	3.00
York	v.	Chorley	3.15

SUNDAY, 3 DECEMBER 1995

Barrow	v.	York	2.30
Carlisle	v.	Leigh	2.00
Highfield	v.	Hunslet	3.00
Hull K.R.	v.	Bramley	3.15
Swinton	v.	Chorley	3.00

SUNDAY, 10 DECEMBER 1995

Barrow	v.	Bramley	2.30
Chorley	v.	Carlisle	3.00
Highfield	v.	Hull K.R.	3.00
Hunslet	v.	Swinton	3.30
York	v.	Leigh	3.15

SUNDAY, 17 DECEMBER 1995

Bramley	v.	Chorley	3.00
Carlisle	v.	Hunslet	2.00
Hull K.R.	v.	Barrow	3.15
Leigh	v.	Highfield	3.00
Swinton	v.	York	3.00

TUESDAY, 26 DECEMBER 1995

Bramley	v.	Hunslet	3.00
Carlisle	v.	Barrow	2.00
Chorley	v.	Highfield	3.00
Hull K.R.	v.	York	3.00
Swinton	v.	Leigh	3.00

SUNDAY, 31 DECEMBER 1995

York	v.	Bramley	1.00

MONDAY, 1 JANUARY 1996

Barrow	v.	Swinton	2.30
Highfield	v.	Carlisle	3.00
Hunslet	v.	Hull K.R.	3.30
Leigh	v.	Chorley	3.00

SUNDAY, 7 JANUARY 1996

Barrow	v.	Leigh	2.30
Carlisle	v.	Bramley	2.00
Chorley	v.	Hull K.R.	3.00
Hunslet	v.	York	3.30
Swinton	v.	Highfield	3.00

SUNDAY, 21 JANUARY 1996

Bramley	v.	Swinton	3.00
Chorley	v.	Barrow	3.00
Hull K.R.	v.	Carlisle	3.15
Leigh	v.	Hunslet	3.00
York	v.	Highfield	3.15

THE 1995 HALIFAX CENTENARY WORLD CUP

7 October	England v. Australia	Wembley	3.00
8 October	Fiji v. South Africa	Keighley	2.30
10 October	Australia v. South Africa	Gateshead	8.15
11 October	England v. Fiji	Wigan	7.30
14 October	Australia v. Fiji	Huddersfield	2.00
14 October	England v. South Africa	Leeds	7.00

Group Two

8 October	New Zealand v. Tonga	Warrington	6.00
10 October	Papua New Guinea v. Tonga	Hull	6.15
13 October	New Zealand v. Papua New Guinea	St. Helens	8.00

Group Three

9 October	Wales v. France	Cardiff	8.00
12 October	France v. Western Samoa	Cardiff	8.00
15 October	Wales v. Western Samoa	Swansea	6.00

Semi-Finals

21 October	First Semi-Final	Old Trafford, Manchester	3.00
22 October	Second Semi-Final	Huddersfield	3.00

Final

28 October	Centenary World Cup Final	Wembley	3.00

PRINCIPAL DATES 1995-96

1995

13 August	Charity Shield — Leeds v. Wigan — at Royal Dublin Showground
20 August	Stones Bitter Championship commences
11/12 November	Regal Trophy (Second Round)
25/26 November	Regal Trophy (Third Round)
9/10 December	Regal Trophy (Quarter-Finals)
30 December	Regal Trophy (First Semi-Final)

1996

6 January	Regal Trophy (Second Semi-Final)
13 January	Regal Trophy Final
27/28 January	Silk Cut Challenge Cup (Fourth Round)
10/11 February	Silk Cut Challenge Cup (Fifth Round)
24/25 February	Silk Cut Challenge Cup (Quarter-Finals)
9 March	Silk Cut Challenge Cup (First Semi-Final)
23 March	Silk Cut Challenge Cup (Second Semi-Final)
29/31 March	Super League commences
27 April	Silk Cut Challenge Cup Final at Wembley